BASIC Theology

1st Edition

DAG HEWARD-MILLS

Scripture quotations are taken from the KING JAMES VERSION of the Bible, unless otherwise stated.

Excerpts in Chapters 1, 2, 4 from: *Dake's Annotated Reference Bible*, by Finis Jennings Dake. Used by permission of Dake Bible Sales; *Evidence that Demands a Verdict,* by Josh McDowell. Used by permission of Here's Life Publishers, Inc.

Excerpts in Chapters 13-15 from: *John Wesley,* by Basil Miller. Used by permission of Bethany House Publishers; *John Wesley, Into All the World,* by John Telford. Used by permission of Ambassador Publications; *The Spirit-Controlled Woman,* by Beverly LaHaye. Used by permission of Harvest House Publishers; *Derek Prince, A Biography,* by Stephen Mansfield. Used by permission of Charisma House; *DSM-IV-TR Casebook,* by Spitzer, Gibbon, Skodol and Williams, eds. Used by permission of American Psychiatric Publishing, Inc.; *The Final Quest,* by Rick Joyner. Used by permission of MorningStar Publications.

Excerpts in Chapter 19 from: *Evidence that Demands a Verdict,* by Josh McDowell. Used by permission of Here's Life Publishers, Inc.; *The Power of Faith,* Article in October 1999 issue of Reader's Digest, author Phyllis McIntosh.

Excerpt in Chapter 21 from: *Evidence that Demands a Verdict,* by Josh McDowell. Used by permission of Here's Life Publishers, Inc.; Poem by Gordon Lindsay. Source Unknown.

Excerpt in Chapter 24 from: *Last Words of Saints and Sinners,* by Herbert Lockyer. Used by permission of Kregel Publications.

Excerpt in Chapter 25 from: *Dake's Annotated Reference Bible,* by Finis Jennings Dake. Used by permission of Dake Bible Sales.

Excerpt in Chapter 26 from: *Final Dawn over Jerusalem,* by John Haggee. Used by permission of Thomas Nelson Publishers, Inc.

Excerpt in Chapter 31 from: *Five Great Evangelists,* J.H. Armstrong. Used by permission of Christian Focus Publications.

Excerpts in Chapter 32 from: *Snakes in the Lobby,* by Scott McLeod. Used by permission of MorningStar Publications; *The Final Quest,* by Rick Joyner. Used by permission of MorningStar Publications.

This Edition Published 2012 by
Hosanna Christian Bookshop & Publishing House
27, Ekenwan Road, Benin City, Edo State, Nigeria.
Tel: +234 8037380254, 8025810359
Email: lcibenincity@yahoo.com
2nd Printing 2012

E mail Dag Heward-Mills : bishop@daghewardmills.org

Call or send texts to : +233 246 598 158
Find out more about Dag Heward-Mills at: www.daghewardmills.org; www.lighthousechapel.org; www.healingjesus.org

Write to: Dag Heward-Mills, P.O. Box 114, Korle-Bu, Accra, Ghana

ISBN 10: 9988-596-69-3
ISBN 13: 9789988-596-69-9

Contents

Section I – BIBLIOLOGY - DOCTRINE OF THE BIBLE

Section II – THE DOCTRINE OF REGENERATION

Section III – THE DOCTRINES OF PRAYER AND FAITH

Section IV – THE DOCTRINE OF HOLINESS

Section V – SUCCESSFUL CHRISTIAN LIVING

Section VI – THE DOCTRINE OF SUCCESS AND PROSPERITY

Section VII – DEMONOLOGY

SECTION I

Bibliology - Doctrine of the Bible

The Origin of the Bible

1

■ THE WORD OF GOD

The Bible is the written Word of God: "Knowing this first, that no prophecy of the Scripture is of any private interpretation. For the prophecy came not in old time by the will of man: but holy men of God spake as they were moved by the Holy Ghost" (2 Peter 1:20,21).

SIX THINGS THAT THE WORD OF GOD IS

1. It is a specific revelation to man.

It reveals the nature of God to man. It explains the origin of man. It gives meaning to man's existence on earth. It reveals the future destiny of all creation.

Above all, it reveals God's merciful plan of redemption to us. "God, who at sundry times and in divers manners spake in time past unto the fathers by the prophets, Hath in these last days spoken unto us by his Son, whom he hath appointed heir of all things, by whom also he made the worlds" (Hebrews 1:1,2).

2. It is the gospel of salvation for mankind.

The gospel is the good news of Christ's saving power for us. The Bible is the only book that shows how man can be saved. "For I am not ashamed of the gospel of Christ: for it is the power of God unto salvation to every one that believeth; to the Jew first, and also to the Greek" (Romans 1:16).

3. It is authoritative and final.

The Bible is not a discussion of ideas and theories. It is an authoritative declaration of the facts. The truths that are expounded are awesome and non-negotiable.

The aura surrounding the Bible is partly due to its authoritative and irrevocable truths. "Therefore we ought to give the more earnest heed to the things which we have heard, lest at any time we should let them slip. For if the word spoken by angels was stedfast, and every transgression and disobedience received a just recompense of reward; How shall we escape, if we neglect so great salvation; which at the first began to be spoken by the Lord, and was confirmed unto us by them that heard him; God also bearing them witness, both with signs and wonders, and with divers miracles, and gifts of the Holy Ghost, according to his own will?" (Hebrews 2:1-4).

4. The Word of God is inspired divinely.

This is what differentiates the Bible from every other book. The Bible claims to have inspiration and motivation from God. In other words, it was virtually written by God through the hands of mortal men. "All scripture is given by inspiration of God, and is profitable for doctrine, for reproof, for correction, for instruction in righteousness:" (2 Timothy 3:16).

5. The Word of God is powerful and searching.

How true this is! Thousands of people are converted when the simple truths of the Bible are shared. I was changed by the Word of God when I encountered it. "For the word of God is quick, and powerful, and sharper than any twoedged sword, piercing even to the dividing asunder of soul and spirit, and of the joints and marrow, and is a discerner of the thoughts and intents of the heart" (Hebrews 4:12).

6. The Word of God is God's method for man's prosperity and abundant life.

God's method for prosperity is not by clever ideas and human tricks. It is through His Word. "This book of the law shall not depart out of thy mouth; but thou shalt meditate therein day and night, that thou mayest observe to do according to all that is written therein: for then thou shalt make thy way prosperous, and then thou shalt have good success" (Joshua 1:8). "My son, attend to my words; incline thine ear unto my sayings. Let them not depart from thine eyes; keep them in the midst of thine heart. For they are life unto those that find them, and health to all their flesh" (Proverbs 4:20-22).

INTRODUCING THE BIBLE

1. Six things that the Bible is

a. The Bible is God's inspired revelation of the original destiny of all things.

Here Heaven is opened, and the gates of Hell disclosed. It is the traveller's map, the pilgrim's staff, the pilot's compass, the soldier's sword, and the Christian's charter.

b. The Bible is the power of God unto eternal salvation and the source of present help, for body, soul, and spirit.

Christ is its grand subject, man's good its design, and the glory of God its end. It is a mine of wealth, the source of health, and a world of pleasure. (Romans 1:16; John 15:7).

c. The Bible is God's will or testament to men in all ages, revealing the plan of God for man here and now, and in the next life.

It will be opened at the judgement; and it will last forever. It involves the highest responsibility; will reward for the least to the greatest of labour; and will condemn all who trifle with its sacred contents.

d. The Bible is the record of God's dealings with man in the past, present and future.

It contains His message of eternal salvation for all who believe in Christ, and eternal damnation for all who rebel against the gospel.

e. As a literary composition, the Bible is the most remarkable book ever written.

It is a divine library of 66 books some of considerable size, and others no larger than a tract. These books include various forms of literature - history, biography, poetry, proverbial sayings, hymns, letters, directions for elaborate ritualistic worship, laws, parables, riddles, allegories, prophecy, and all other forms of human expression.

f. The Bible is the only book that reveals the mind of God, the state of man, the way of salvation, the doom of sinners, and the happiness of believers.

Its doctrines are holy, its precepts binding, its histories true and its decisions immutable. It contains light to direct, spiritual food to sustain, and comfort to cheer. Man should read it to be wise, believe it to be safe, and practice it to be holy; he should read it that it might fill his memory, rule his heart, and guide his feet in righteous and true holiness. He should read it slowly, frequently, prayerfully, meditatively, searchingly, devotionally; and study it constantly, perseveringly and industriously through and through - until it becomes a part of his being, generating faith that will move mountains.[1]

2. Eight things that the Bible is not

a. **The Bible is not an amulet, a charm, a fetish, or anything to work wonders by its very presence alone.**

It does not claim to be such; it does claim that if one will study and practice its teachings he will see wonders worked in his life both now and in the hereafter.

b. **The Bible is not a book of chronological events or an unbroken series of divine utterances.**

It was given, here a little and there a little, to many men through eighteen centuries (Isaiah 28:9-11); but regardless of this it, forms a perfect unity.

c. **The Bible is not a book of heavenly utterances in supernatural languages.**

It is God's revelation in the simplest human language possible.

d. **The Bible is not a book of mysteries.**

It explains its so-called mysteries, and is so self-interpreting that no mystery remains.

e. **The Bible is not a book that says one thing and means another.**

Generally, the passages have one simple meaning. In the few, which have a double meaning this fact, is quite clear, either from the verses themselves or from parallel passages. One cannot, as is sometimes said get a thousand different meanings from the Scriptures.

f. **The Bible is not a specimen of God's skill as a writer or logician.**

It is a book written by men who He used to record His revelation. The method was by giving them ways of expressing truth, and freedom in the use of their own language. What inspiration guarantees is unity of truth, not sameness of words and expressions.

g. **The Bible is not a book of systematic discourses on any one subject; but it does give divine information on practically every subject.**

One must collect together from here and there, all God's information through various writers, in order to know the whole truth. When this is done there is perfect harmony, and everything, which a man really needs to know about a subject, is clear.

h. **The Bible is not a book adapted to the tastes, customs and habits of any one nation or people; it is not for any one age or period of time.**

It is a book for which all people in all ages can conform and yet retain their own lawful customs and habits, which are not contrary to the will of God.[2]

■ THE INSPIRED WORD OF GOD

"Ye shall not add unto the word which I command you, neither shall ye diminish ought from it, that ye may keep the commandments of the Lord your God which I command you" (Deuteronomy 4:2).

THE CANON

Many so-called inspired writers claimed to be inspired of God. There were many letters and books that were available to God's people. There was therefore the need to define the officially accepted writings of inspired men. These officially accepted books and writings are what are known as the Canon of Scripture.

The Canon means "the body of sacred writings that are accepted as genuine and inspired." The Old Testament Canon is the list of Old Testament books and the New Testament Canon is the final accepted list of New Testament books and writings. An important truth you must not overlook is that the Church did not create the Canon or the books that we call scripture. The Church simply recognized the books that were inspired by God and publicly approved of them.

Notice what F.F. Bruce said:

When at last a church council - the Synod of Hippo in AD 393 listed the twenty-seven books of the New Testament, it did not confer upon them any authority which they did not already possess, but simply recorded their previously established canonicity. (The ruling of the Synod of Hippo was re-promulgated four years later by the Third Synod of Carthage.)

Since that time, there has been no serious questioning of the twenty-seven accepted books of the New Testament by Roman Catholics or Protestants.[3] As far as the Old Testament is concerned, the Christian Church and the Jews share the same Canon of Scripture. Although the Christian Church has the same Old Testament Canon, the number of books differs because:

- The Christian Church divides the books of Samuel, Kings and Chronicles into two books each.
- The Jews consider the minor Prophets as one book whereas the Christians consider them separately.
- The order of the books in the Christian Bible is different from the order in the Jewish law.

Here is a breakdown of the Jewish Old Testament Canon which is divided into the Law (Torah), The Prophets (Nebhim) and The Writings (Kethubhim).

Section 1: The Law (Torah)

Genesis

Exodus

Leviticus

Numbers

Deuteronomy

Section 2: The Prophets (Nebhim)

A. Former Prophets

Joshua

Judges

Samuel

Kings

B. Latter Prophets

Isaiah

Jeremiah

Ezekiel

The Twelve

Section 3: The Writings (Kethubim)

A. Poetical Books

Psalms

Proverbs

Job

B. Five Rolls

Song of Songs

Ruth

Lamentations

Esther

Ecclesiastes

C. Historical Books

Daniel

Ezra - Nehemiah

Chronicles [4]

THE SACRED WRITINGS

1. Five reasons why the canon of Scripture was defined

a. The Jewish people established their Canon of Scripture, which we call the Old Testament. Christians accept this Old Testament Canon primarily because Jesus accepted it.

The Jewish sacrificial system was ended by the destruction of Jerusalem and the temple in 70 AD. Even though the Old Testament Canon was settled in the Jewish mind long before 70 AD, there was a need for something more definitive. The Jews were scattered and they needed to determine which books were the authoritative Word of God because of the many extra scriptural writings and the decentralization. The Jews became a people of one book and it was this book that kept them together.

b. Christianity started to blossom and many writings of the Christians were beginning to be circulated. The Jews needed to expose these Christian writings vividly and exclude them from their writings and their use inthe synagogues.[5]

c. The New Testament Canon became necessary because of the emergence of heretics. Heretics were people who held opinions and practiced things which were contrary to accepted beliefs. For instance, Marcion 140 AD developed his own Canon and began to propagate it. The church needed to offset his influence by determining what the real Canon of New Testament Scripture was.

d. Many eastern churches were using books in services that were definitely incorrect. It called for a decision concerning the Canon.

e. The Edict of Diocletian 303 AD, declared the destruction of the sacred books of the Christians. Who wanted to die for just a religious book? They needed to know![6]

2. Twenty reasons why some writings were included or excluded from the Bible

When a writing is not part of the Bible it is called a non-canonical writing. The more well known rejected writings are the books of the Apocrypha as well as other writings. They are not accepted as canonical and therefore have been excluded from the Bible. What was the basis for their inclusion or exclusion from the Bible? Were they just haphazardly thrown in or were there very sound reasons for their inclusion in the Bible?

Below are several reasons why some of the writings were accepted or rejected for inclusion in the Bible.

a. **Many books and writings were accepted because Jesus Christ accepted them and quoted from them.**

Our Lord's endorsement of these books is more than enough to justify their inclusion of these writings as holy Scripture.

In the upper room Jesus told the disciples, "that all things must be fulfilled, which were written in the law of Moses, and the Prophets, and the Psalms concerning me" (Luke 24:44). With these words "he indicated the three sections into which the Hebrew Bible was divided - the Law, the Prophets, and the 'Writings' (here called 'the Psalms' probably because the Book of Psalms is the first and longest book in this third section)."[7]

Jesus disagreed with the oral traditions of the Pharisees (Mark 7, Matthew 15), not with their concept of the Hebrew Canon. "Then the Jews took up stones again to stone him. Jesus answered them, Many good works have I showed you from my Father; for which of those works do ye stone me? The Jews answered him, saying, For a good work we stone thee not; but for blasphemy; and because that thou, being a man, makest thyself God. Jesus answered them, Is it not written in your law, I said, Ye are gods? If he called them gods, unto whom the word of God came, and the scripture cannot be broken; Say ye of him, whom the Father hath sanctified, and sent into the world, Thou blasphemest; because I said, I am the Son of God?" (John 10:31-36). "There is no evidence whatever of any dispute between him and the Jews as to the canonicity of any Old Testament book." [8]

Jesus stated in Luke 11:51: "From the blood of Abel unto the blood of Zacharias, which perished between the altar and the temple: verily I say unto you, It shall be required of this generation." Again, in Matthew 23:35, he said, "That upon you may come all the righteous blood shed upon the earth, from the blood of righteous Abel unto the blood of Zacharias son of Barachias, whom ye slew between the temple and the altar."

Jesus here confirms His witness to the extent of the Old Testament canon. Abel, as everyone knows, was the first martyr (Genesis 4:8). Zechariah is the last martyr to be named in the Hebrew Old Testament order, having been stoned while prophesying to the people "in the court of the house of the Lord" (2 Chronicles 24:21). Genesis was the first book in the Hebrew canon and Chronicles the last book. Jesus basically said "from Genesis to Chronicles," or, according to our order, "from Genesis to Malachi." [9]

b. Some of the books were accepted because they were authoritative.

Some books were not authoritative and were believed not to have come from the hand of God.

c. When a book was not written by a holy man of God or a prophet, it was rejected.

The Scripture says that holy men of God spoke the words of prophecy as they were moved by the Holy Spirit. We cannot accept books and writings that do not come from holy men of God who were moved by the Holy Spirit.

d. Writings were accepted because they were authentic, genuine and original.

The Church Fathers had the policy of "if in doubt, throw it out!" This enhanced the validity of their discernment of canonical books.

e. Some writings were accepted because they were powerful and dynamic.

Writings that did not come with the life transforming power of God were not included.

f. Books that were received, collected, read and used by the people of God were accepted.

The Apostle Peter recognized, received and used the writings of Paul as Scripture. (2 Peter 3:16). The fact that Peter recognized the writings of Paul gave credence to the letters of Paul.[10]

g. Books that were excluded from the Jewish Canonical Scripture were rejected.

Such books were therefore excluded from the Christian Old Testament. You will notice that the Christian Old Testament is the same as the Jewish Torah (The Law), Nebhim (The Prophets) and Kethubhim (The Writings).

h. Jesus and the New Testament writers never once quoted from the Apocrypha and other unacceptable writings.

However, there are hundreds of quotes and references to almost all of the canonical books of the Old Testament. This is a fact that is even more striking when we realize that Paul, who even quoted twice from heathen poets, did not quote from the Apocrypha.[11]

i. The last Old Testament prophet predicted that the next messenger coming to Israel from God would be the forerunner of Christ (Malachi 3:1).

Most of the apocryphal books were written during the period of Malachi and Christ. These apocryphal writers were not the forerunners of Christ and therefore were not considered as significant enough for inclusion.

j. **Divine authority is not claimed by the apocryphal authors; and by others it is virtually disowned.**[12]

Consider the following statements in the Apocrypha:

"These five books of Jason I shall try to summarize in a single work; for I was struck by the mass of statistics and the difficulty which the bulk of the material causes to those wishing to grasp the narratives of this history" (2 Maccabees 2:23,24 The New English Bible).

"At this point I will bring my work to an end. If it is found well written and aptly composed, that is what I myself hoped for; if cheap and mediocre, I could only do my best" (2 Maccabees 15:38 The New English Bible).

k. **Some of the writings were rejected because they were at variance with Bible history.**

Such inaccuracies were not acceptable in the Bible.

l. **Some unacceptable writings, as well as the Apocrypha, are self-contradictory and in some cases opposed to doctrines of Scripture.**

m. **The Apocryphal books were not a part of the ancient versions of the Scripture.**

They were first added after 300 AD. The Laodicean Council in 363 AD rejected them as being uninspired, thus proving that by that time some were claiming inspiration for them.

n. **The Apocrypha is unacceptable because even the Roman Catholic Church did not accept it as canonical for 1,546 years.**

One wonders why they included the Apocrypha after so many years.

o. **Jewish historians did not regard the Apocrypha as Scripture.**

Josephus (AD 30-100), a Jewish historian, explicitly excludes the Apocrypha, numbering the books of the Old Testament as 22.

p. **Jewish philosophers did not regard the Apocrypha as Scripture.**

Philo (20 BC - AD 40), an Alexandrian Jewish Philosopher, quoted the Old Testament prolifically and even recognized the threefold division, but he never quoted from the Apocrypha as inspired.

q. **For the first four centuries after the death of Christ, no canon or council of the Christian church recognized the Apocrypha as inspired.**

r. **Many of the fathers of the early church spoke out against the Apocrypha; for example Origen, Cyril of Jerusalem, Athanasius.**

s. **Jerome (340-420 AD), the great scholar and translator of the Vulgate (4th Century Latin Version of the Bible), rejected the Apocrypha as part of the canon.**

He disputed across the Mediterranean with Augustine on this point. He at first refused even to translate the Apocryphal books into Latin, but later he made a hurried translation of a few of them.

After his death, and literally "over his dead body," the Apocryphal books were brought into his Latin Vulgate directly from the Old Latin Version.

t. **Many of the Reformers and even Roman Catholic scholars through the Reformation period rejected the Apocrypha.**

Martin Luther and the reformers rejected the canonicity of the Apocrypha.[13]

THE BIBLE IS SUPERIOR TO THE APOCRYPHA

Apocrypha comes from the Greek word "apokruphos" meaning 'hidden or concealed'. The Apocrypha consists of the books added to the Old Testament that are not considered canonical by Protestants. Listed below are four reasons why the Apocrypha is not canonical:

1. The Apocrypha abounds in historical and geographical inaccuracies and anachronisms.
2. The Apocrypha teaches doctrines which are false and fosters practices which are at variance with inspired scripture.
3. The Apocrypha resorts to literary types and displays artificiality of subject matter and styling which is out of keeping with inspired scripture.
4. The Apocrypha lacks distinctive elements which give genuine scripture their divine character, such as prophetic power and poetic and religious feeling.[14]

Most Christians do not know what the Apocrypha is and what it contains so I have decided to include a short summary of its individual books.

A SUMMARY OF THE APOCRYPHA

1. 1 Esdras (150 BC)

This book tells about the restoration of the Jews to Palestine after the Babylonian exile. It draws considerably from Chronicles, Ezra and Nehemiah, but the author has added much legendary material. The most interesting item is the story of the three guardsmen. They were debating what was the strongest thing in the world. One said, "Wine." Another, "The king." The third, "Woman and truth." They put these three answers under the king's pillow. When he awoke he required the three men to defend their answers. The unanimous decision was: truth is greatly and supremely strong. Because Zerubabel had given this answer he was allowed to rebuild the temple at Jerusalem.

2. 2 Esdras (AD 100)

Is an apocalyptic work, containing seven visions. Martin Luther was so confused by these visions that he is said to have thrown the book into the Elbe River.

3. Tobit (Early 2nd century BC)

Is a short novel. Strongly Pharisaic in tone, it emphasizes the Law, clean foods, ceremonial washings, charity, fasting and prayer. It is clearly unscriptural in its statement that almsgiving atones for sin.

4. Judith (About the middle of 2nd century BC)

Is also fictitious and Pharisaic. The heroine of this novel is Judith, a beautiful Jewish widow. When her city was besieged she took her maid, together with Jewish clean food, and went out to the tent of the attacking general. He was enamored of her beauty and gave her a place in his tent. Fortunately, he had imbibed too freely and sank into a drunken stupor. Judith took his sword and cut off his head. Then she and her maid left the camp, taking his head in their provision bag. It was hung on the wall of a nearby city and the leaderless Assyrian army was defeated.

5. Additions to Esther (About 100 BC)

Esther stands alone among the books of the Old Testament in having no mention of God. We are told that Esther and Mordecai fasted but not specifically that they prayed. To compensate for this lack, the additions have long prayers attributed to these two, together with a couple of letters supposedly written by Artaxerxes.

6. The Wisdom of Solomon (About AD 40)

Was written to keep the Jews from falling into scepticism, materialism, and idolatry. As in Proverbs, Wisdom is personified. There are many noble sentiments expressed in this book.

7. Ecclesiasticus, or Wisdom of Sirach (about 180 BC)

Shows a high level of religious wisdom, somewhat like the canonical Book of Proverbs. It also contains much practical advice.

For instance, on the subject of after-dinner speeches it says (32:8):

"Speak concisely; say much in few words..."

"Act like a man who knows more than he says."

And again (33:4):

"Prepare what you have to say, and then you will be listened to."

In his sermons John Wesley quotes several times from the Book of Ecclesiasticus. It is still widely used in Anglican circles.

8. Baruch (About AD 100)

Represents itself as being written by Baruch, the scribe of Jeremiah, in 582 BC. Actually, it is probably trying to interpret the destruction of Jerusalem in AD 70. The book urges the Jews not to revolt again, but to be in submission to the emperor. In spite of this the Bar-Cochba revolution against Roman rule took place soon after, in AD 132-135. The sixth chapter of Baruch contains the so-called "Letter of Jeremiah," with its strong warning against idolatry - probably addressed to Jews in Alexandria, Egypt.

Our Book of Daniel contains 12 chapters. In the first century before Christ a thirteenth chapter was added, the story of Susanna. She was the beautiful wife of a leading Jew in Babylon, to whose house the Jewish elders and judges frequently came. Two of these became enamored of her and tried to seduce her. When she cried out, the two elders said they had found her in the arms of a young man. She was brought to trial. Since there were two witnesses who agreed in their testimony, she was convicted and sentenced to death. But a young man named Daniel interrupted the proceedings and began to cross-examine the witnesses. He asked each one separately under which tree in the garden they had found Susanna with a lover. When they gave different answers they were put to death and Susanna was saved.

Bel and the Dragon was added at about the same time and called chapter 14 of Daniel. Its main purpose was to show the folly of idolatry. It really contains two stories.

In the first, King Cyrus asked Daniel why he did not worship Bel, since that deity showed his greatness by daily consuming many sheep, together with much flour and oil. So Daniel scattered ashes on the floor of the Temple where the food had been placed that evening. In the morning the king took Daniel in to show him that Bel had eaten all the food during the night. But Daniel showed the king in the ashes on the floor the footprints of the priests and their families who had entered secretly under the table. The priests were slain and the temple destroyed.

The story of the Dragon is just as obviously legendary in character. Along with Tobit, Judith, and Susanna, these stories may be classified as purely Jewish fiction. They have little if any religious value.

The Song of the Three Hebrew Children follows Daniel 3:23 in the Septuagint and the Vulgate. Borrowing heavily from Psalms 148, it is antiphonal like Psalms 136, having 32 times the refrain: "Sing praise to him and greatly exalt him forever."

9. The Prayer of Manasseh was composed in Maccabean times (2nd century BC)

As the supposed prayer of Manasseh, the wicked king of Judah. It was obviously suggested by the statement in 2 Chronicles 33:19 - "His prayer also, and how God was entreated of him... behold, they are written among the sayings of the seers." Since this prayer is not found in the Bible, some scribe had to make up the deficiency!

10. 1 Maccabees (1st century BC)

Is perhaps the most valuable book in the Apocrypha. It describes the exploits of the three Maccabean brothers - Judas, Jonathan, and Simon. Along with Josephus it is our most important source for the history of this crucial and exciting period in Jewish history.

11. 2 Maccabees (same time)

Is not a sequel to 1 Maccabees, but a parallel account, treating only the victories of Judas Maccabeus. It is generally thought to be more legendary than 1 Maccabees.[15]

The Superiority of the Bible 2

■ THE TRUSTWORTHY BIBLE

Let me share with you four reasons why the Bible can be trusted.

1. **The Bible can be trusted because promises made generations earlier have been kept.**

"Blessed be the Lord, that hath given rest unto his people Israel, according to all that he promised: there hath not failed one word of all his good promise, which he promised by the hand of Moses his servant" (1 Kings 8:56).

2. **The Bible can be trusted because God stands by His Word until it comes to pass.**

"For I am the Lord: I will speak, and the word that I shall speak shall come to pass; it shall be no more prolonged: for in your days, O rebellious house, will I say the word, and will perform it, saith the Lord God" (Ezekiel 12:25).

The Word of God also states, "For verily I say unto you, Till heaven and earth pass, one jot or one tittle shall in no wise pass from the law, till all be fulfilled" (Matthew 5:18); and further, "Then said the LORD unto me, Thou hast well seen: for I will hasten my word to perform it" (Jeremiah 1:12).

3. **The Bible can be trusted because it is unchanging in a changing world.**

"But the word of the Lord endureth for ever. And this is the word which by the gospel is preached unto you" (1 Peter 1:25).

4. **Heaven and earth will pass away but the Word of God will remain forever.**

"Heaven and earth shall pass away, but my words shall not pass away" (Matthew 24:35).

THE BIBLE IS SUPERIOR TO EVERY OTHER BOOK

Most people do not understand the uniqueness and superiority of this great book. It is a book like no other book. If someone asks you for the meaning of the word unique, you might as well say it means "Bible". Unique in the dictionary is defined as: the one and only. It also means: to be different from all others, having no like or equal. Consider these twenty-nine reasons why the Bible is superior to every other book on earth.

1. **The Bible is superior in the fact that it is the most reliable historic document of all time.**

When we do not have the original historical document, we must establish how reliable the copies are. This is done in two ways:

- The more identical manuscript copies of the original we have, the more sure we are that the copies reflect what is in the original document.
- The shorter the time interval between the copy and the original, the more sure we are that the copy reflects what is in the original.

"There are more than 5,300 known Greek manuscripts of the New Testament. Add over 10,000 Latin Vulgate and at least 9,300 other early versions (MSS) and we have more than 24,000 manuscripts copies of portions of the New Testament in existence today."

"No other document of antiquity even begins to approach such numbers and attestation. In comparison, the book Iliad by Homer is second with only 643 manuscripts that still survive. The first complete preserved text of Homer dates from the 13th century."[1]

John Warwick Montgomery says that "to be sceptical of the resultant text of the New Testament books is to allow all of classical antiquity to slip into obscurity, for no documents of the ancient period are as well attested bibliographically as the New Testament."[2]

Sir Frederic G. Kenyon, who was the director and principal librarian of the British Museum and second to none in authority for issuing statements about MSS, says, "...besides number, the manuscripts of the New Testament differ from those of the classical authors, and this time the difference is clear gain. In no other case is the interval of time between the composition of the book and the date of the earliest extant manuscripts so short as in that of the New Testament. The books of the New Testament were written in the latter part of the first century;the earliest extant manuscripts (trifling scraps excepted) are of the fourth century - say from 250 to 300 years later."

"This may sound a considerable interval, but it is nothing to that which parts most of the great classical authors from their earliest manuscripts. We believe that we have in all essentials an accurate text of the seven extant plays of Sophocles; yet the earliest substantial manuscript upon which it is based was written more than 1400 years after the poet's death."

Kenyon continues in *The Bible and Archaeology:* "The interval then between the dates of original composition and the earliest extant evidence becomes so small as to be in fact negligible, and the last foundation for any doubt that the scriptures have come down to us substantially as they were written has now been removed. Both the authenticity and the general integrity of the books of the New Testament may be regarded as finally established."[3]

2. **The Bible is superior to other books because archaeology has constantly confirmed its historical accuracy and validity.**

Nelson Glueck, the renowned Jewish archaeologist, wrote: "It may be stated categorically that no archaeological discovery has ever controverted a biblical reference." He continued his assertion of "the almost incredibly accurate historical memory of the Bible, and particularly so when it is fortified by archaeological fact."

William F. Albright, known for his reputation as one of the great archaeologists, states: "There can be no doubt that archaeology has confirmed the substantial historicity of Old Testament tradition."

Albright adds: "The excessive scepticism shown toward the Bible by important historical schools of the eighteenth and nineteenth centuries, certain phases of which still appear periodically, has been progressively discredited. Discovery after discovery has established the accuracy of innumerable details, and has brought increased recognition to the value of the Bible as a source of history."[4]

3. **The Bible is superior in its unity and continuity.**

Over forty authors wrote sixty-six books over a period of 1,500 years. Many never saw the writings of the others and yet there is no contradiction between any two of them. Collect any group of books of any other forty men on any subject and see if they agree.

Nine Facts about the Unity and Continuity of the Bible

a. The Bible was written over a 1,500 years span.

b. The Bible was written over 40 generations.

c. The Bible was written by over 40 authors from every walk of life:

- Moses, a political leader, trained in the universities of Egypt
- Peter, a fisherman
- Amos, a herdsman
- Joshua, a military general
- Nehemiah, a cupbearer
- Daniel, a prime minister
- Luke, a doctor
- Solomon, a king
- Matthew, a tax collector
- Paul, a rabbi

d. The Bible was written in different places:

- Moses in the wilderness
- Jeremiah in a dungeon
- Daniel on a hillside and in a palace
- Paul, inside prison walls
- Luke, while travelling
- John, on the isle of Patmos
- Others in the rigors of a military campaign

e. The Bible was written at different times:

- David in times of war
- Solomon in times of peace

f. The Bible was written during different moods:

- Some writing from the heights of joy and others writing from depths of sorrow and despair.

g. The Bible was written on three continents:

- Asia, Africa and Europe

h. The Bible was written in three languages:

- Hebrew: The language of the Old Testament. It was called "the language of Judah" in 2 Kings 18:26-28 and in Isaiah 19:18, "the language of Canaan".
- Aramaic: This was the "common language" of the Near East until the time of Alexander the Great (6th century BC - 4th century BC)
- Greek: The New Testament language. This was theinternational language at the time of Christ.

i. The Bible includes in its subject matter hundreds of controversial subjects. A controversial subject is one, which creates opposing opinions when mentioned or discussed.

Biblical authors spoke on hundreds of controversial subjects with harmony and continuity from Genesis to Revelation. The result is one unfolding story: "God's redemption of man!"

What F.F. Bruce Said about the Bible

"Any part of the human body can only be properly explained in reference to the whole body. And any part of the Bible can only be properly explained in reference to the whole Bible."

"The Bible, at first sight, appears to be a collection of literature - mainly Jewish. If we inquire into the circumstance under which the various Biblical documents were written, we find that they were written at intervals over a space of nearly 1400 years."

"The writers wrote in various lands, from Italy in the west to Mesopotamia and possibly Persia in the east."

"The writers themselves were a heterogeneous number of people, not only separated from each other by hundreds of years and hundreds of miles, but also belonging to the most diverse walks of life. In their ranks we have kings, herdsmen, soldiers, legislators, fishermen, statesmen, courtiers, priests and prophets, a tent-making Rabbi and a Gentile physician, not to speak of others of whom we know nothing apart from the writings they have left us."

"The writings themselves belong to a great variety of literary types. They include history, law (civil, criminal, ethical, ritual, and sanitary), religious poetry, didactic treatises, lyric poetry, parable and allegory, biography, personal correspondence, personal memoirs and diaries."[5]

4. The Bible is more distinctive than every other book ever published.

The Bible is superior to other books in its origin, formation, doctrines, principles, claims, moral tone, histories, prophecies, revelation, literature, present redemption and eternal benefits.

5. Unlike other books published, the Bible has a vast influence in this world.

The Bible has blessed millions of people of every generation. The Bible has contributed to the creation of the greatest civilizations on earth. It has given man the highest hope and destiny.

6. The wisest, most godly and honest men in this world acknowledge the Bible as the Word of God.

Only infidels and ungodly people reject the Bible.

7. Unlike many other books, the Bible was written by honest and godly men.

This is because it condemns all sin and records the sins and faults of its writers as well as others. This is something evil men would not do. Even good men would not do this unless they were inspired to do so to help others.

8. The Bible meets all the needs of mankind.

All man's present and eternal needs are met by the Bible.

9. The Bible has been preserved through the ages.

Written over 1,500 years

Whole kingdoms and religions have sought in vain to destroy it. God has made the Bible indestructible and victorious.

10. The Bible is superior to other books because the heavenly and eternal character of its contents prove it to be of God.

11. The preaching of the Bible changes the lives of people.

The response of humanity to this great book shows that it is of a supernatural and superior nature.

12. The Bible is superior in its infinite depths and lofty ideals.

13. The Bible stands out in supremacy by the unbelievable number of prophecies that it contains.

About three thousand three hundred prophecies have been fulfilled. Predictions made hundreds and even thousands of years earlier have been fulfilled. Not one detail has failed yet. About 2,908 verses are being fulfilled or will be fulfilled.

14. The Bible is superior in its miraculous nature.

Hundreds of miracles are recorded in the Scriptures. Miracles happen daily among those who pray and claim Bible promises.

15. The Bible is alone in its flawlessness.

The Bible is scientifically and historically correct. No one man has found the Bible at fault in any of its many hundreds of statements of history, astronomy, botany, geology, geography or any other branch of learning.

16. The Bible is superior in its adaptability.

The Bible is always up to date on every subject. It oan be applied to the lives of people who live in Africa, Asia, Europe or America. It was useful to people who lived a thousand years ago and it is still relevant to the people who live in the twenty-first century.

17. The Bible is superior in its moral and spiritual power.

It meets perfectly every spiritual and moral need of man.

18. The Bible is superior in its doctrines.

The doctrines of the Bible surpass all human ideas or principles of relationships, religion and culture.

19. The Bible is superior because it claims to be the Word of God.

Over three thousand eight hundred times, Bible writers claimed that God spoke what they wrote. In other words, the Bible itself claims to be the Word of God.

20. The Bible is superior in secular history.

Many pagan, Jewish and Christian writers confirm the facts of the Bible. They actually quote the Bible as being genuine, authentic and inspired of God.

21. The Bible is superior in its worldwide circulation.

Most authors have their books circulated within communities. You will be surprised to find that many authors who are very popular are not known at all in other parts of the world. Not so with the Bible![6]

"The Bible has been read by more people and published in more languages than any other book. There have been more copies produced of its entirety and more portions and selections than any other book in history.

Some will argue that in a designated month or year more of a certain book was sold. However, over all there is absolutely no book that reaches or even begins to compare to the circulation of the Scriptures."

What Hy Pickering Said about the Bible

Hy Pickering said that about 30 years ago, for the British and Foreign Bible Society to meet its demands, it had to publish:

One copy every three seconds day and night,

22 copies every minute day and night,

1,369 copies every hour day and night,

32,876 copies every day in the year.

It is deeply interesting to know that this amazing number of Bibles was dispatched to various parts of the world in 4,583 cases weighing 490 tons![7]

22. The Bible is superior in its worldwide translations.

The Bible was one of the first major books translated (Septuagint: Greek translation of the Hebrew Old Testament, ca 250 BC). It has been translated and retranslated and paraphrased more than any other book in existence.

Encyclopaedia Britannica says "by 1966 the whole Bible had appeared... in 240 languages and dialects... one or more whole books of the Bible in 739 additional ones, a total publication of 1,280 languages."

Three thousand Bible translators between 1950-1960 were at work translating the Scriptures.

The Bible factually stands unique ("one of a kind; alone in its class") in its translation.[8]

23. The Bible is superior in its continued existence through the years.

Being written on material that perishes, having to be copied and recopied for hundreds of years before the invention of the printing press, did not diminish its style, correctness or existence. The Bible, compared with other ancient writings, has more manuscript evidence than any 10 pieces of classical literature combined.

What John Warwick Montgomery Said about the Bible

"To be sceptical of the resultant text of the New Testament books is to allow all of classical antiquity to slip into obscurity, for no documents of the ancient period are as well attested bibliographically as the New Testament."

What John Lea Said about the Bible

John Lea in The Greatest Book in the World compared the Bible with Shakespeare's writings. He had this to say:

"It seems strange that the text of Shakespeare, which has been in existence less than two hundred and eight years, should be far more uncertain and corrupt than that of the New Testament, now over eighteen centuries old, during nearly fifteen of which it existed only in manuscript.

...With perhaps a dozen or twenty exceptions, the text of every verse in the New Testament may be said to be so far settled by general consent of scholars, that any dispute as to its readings must relate rather to the interpretation of the words than to any doubts respecting the words themselves. But in everyone of Shakespeare's thirty seven plays there are probably a hundred readings still in dispute, a large portion of which materially affects the meaning of the passages in which they occur."[9]

24. The Bible is superior in its ability to survive persecution.

What Sidney Collett Said about the Bible

Voltaire, the noted French infidel who died in 1778, said that in one hundred years from his time Christianity would be swept from existence and passed into history. But what has happened? Voltaire has passed into history, while the circulation of the Bible continues to increase in almost all parts of the world, carrying blessing wherever it goes.

Concerning the boast of Voltaire on the extinction of Christianity and the Bible in 100 years, Geisler and Nix point out that "only fifty years after his death the Geneva Bible Society used his press and house to produce stacks of Bibles." What An irony of history!

In AD 303, Diocletian issued an edict (Cambridge History of the Bible, Cambridge University Press, 1963) to stop Christians from worshipping and to destroy their Scriptures.

"...An imperial letter was everywhere promulgated, ordering the razing of the churches to the ground and the destruction by fire of the Scriptures, and proclaiming that those who held high positions would lose all civil rights while those in households, if they persisted in the profession of Christianity, would be deprived of their liberty."

The historic irony of the above edict to destroy the Bible is that Eusebius records the edict given 25 years later by Constantine, the emperor of Diocletian, that 50 copies of the Scriptures should be prepared at the expense of the government.[10]

25. The Bible is superior in its ability to endure criticism.

What H.L. Hastings Said About the Bible

H.L. Hastings has forcibly illustrated the unique way the Bible has withstood the attacks of infidels and sceptics.

"Infidels for eighteen hundred years have been refuting and overthrowing this book, and yet it stands today as solid as a rock. Its circulation increases, and it is more loved and cherished and read today than ever before. Infidels, with all their assaults, make about as much impression on this book as a man with a tack hammer would on the Pyramids of Egypt.

When the French monarch proposed the persecution of the Christians in his dominion, an old statesman and warrior said to him, "Sire, the church of God is an anvil that has worn out many hammers." So the hammers of infidels have been pecking away at this book for ages, but the hammers are worn out, and the anvil still endures.

If this book had not been the book of God, men would have destroyed it long ago. Emperors and popes, kings and priests, princes and rulers have all tried their hand at it; they die and the book still lives."

What Bernard Ramm Said About the Bible

"A thousand times over, the death knell of the Bible has been sounded, the funeral procession formed, the inscription cut on the tombstone, and committal read. But somehow the corpse never stays put.

No other book has been so chopped, knifed, sifted, scrutinized, and vilified. What book on philosophy or religion or psychology or belles letters of classical or modern times has been the subject to such a mass attack as the Bible? With such venom and scepticism? With such thoroughness and erudition? Upon every chapter, line and tenet?

The Bible is still loved by millions, read by millions, and studied by millions."[11]

26. The Bible is superior in the nature of its prophecies.

Wilbur Smith who compiled a personal library of 25,000 volumes writes:

"It is the only volume ever produced by man, or a group of men in which is to be found a large body of prophecies relating to individual nations, to Israel, to all the peoples of the earth, to certain cities, and to the coming of One who was to be the Messiah;

The ancient world had many different devices for determining the future, known as divination, but not in the entire gamut of Greek and Latin literature, even though they use the words prophet and prophecy, can we find any real specific prophecy of a great historic event to come in the distant future, nor any prophecy of a Saviour to arise in the human race.

"Mohammedanism cannot point to any prophecies of the coming of Mohammed uttered hundreds of years before his birth. Neither can the founders of any cult in this country rightly identify any ancient text specifically foretelling their appearance."[12]

27. The Bible is superior in its honesty.

The Bible deals very frankly with the sins of its characters. Read the biographies today, and see how they try to cover up, overlook or ignore the shady side of people. Take the great literary geniuses; most are painted as saints. The Bible does not do it that way. It simply tells it like it is.

28. The Bible is superior in its influence on surrounding literature.

What Cleland B. McAfee Said About the Bible

Cleland B. McAfee writes in The Greatest English Classic:

"If every Bible in any considerable city were destroyed, the Book could be restored in all its essential parts from the quotations on the shelves of the city public library. There are works, covering almost all the great literary writers, devoted especially to showing how much the Bible has influenced them."

What Kenneth Scott Latourette Said About Jesus

Kenneth Scott Latourette, former Yale historian, says:

"It is evidence of His importance, of the effect that He has had upon history and presumably, of the baffling mystery of His being that no other life ever lived on this planet has evoked so huge a volume of literature among so many peoples and languages, and that, far from ebbing, the flood continues to mount."

A professor once remarked: "If you are an intelligent person, you will read the one book that has drawn more attention than any other, if you are searching for the truth!"[13]

29. The Bible is superior because it has set unusual records.

i. The Bible is the first religious book to be taken into outer space.

ii. It is also one of the (if not the) most expensive books.

Gutenberg's Latin Vulgate Bible sold for over $100,000.The Russians sold the Codex Sinaiticus (an early copy of the Bible) to England for $510,000.

iii. The longest telegram in the world was the Revised Standard Version of the New Testament sent from New York to Chicago.

The Complete Message of the Bible 3

■ WRITTEN MESSAGES FROM GOD

God's messages for mankind can be gleaned from the Bible. There are eight major themes that run through the entire Bible.

THE NATURE OF GOD

1. God is a Creator

God created the heaven and the earth; he created all living creatures and he created man. "And God said, Let us make man in our image, after our likeness: and let them have dominion over the fish of the sea, and over the fowl of the air, and over the cattle, and over all the earth, and over every creeping thing that creepeth upon the earth. So God created man in his own image, in the image of God created he him; male and female created he them. And God blessed them, and God said unto them, Be fruitful, and multiply, and replenish the earth, and subdue it: and have dominion over the fish of the sea, and over the fowl of the air, and over every living thing that moveth upon the earth. And God said, Behold, I have given you every herb bearing seed, which is upon the face of all the earth, and every tree, in the which is the fruit of a tree yielding seed; to you it shall be for meat. And to every beast of the earth, and to every fowl of the air, and to every thing that creepeth upon the earth, wherein there is life, I have given every green herb for meat: and it was so" (Genesis 1:26-30).

2. God is a Provider

He is faithful in supplying our needs. "But my God shall supply all your need according to his riches in glory by Christ Jesus" (Philippians 4:19); "He that spared not his own Son, but delivered him up for us all, how shall he not with him also freely give us all things?" (Romans 8:32).

3. God is holy

There is no darkness, sin or fault in God. "In the year that king Uzziah died I saw also the Lord sitting upon a throne, high and lifted up, and his train filled the temple. Above it stood the seraphims: each one had six wings; with twain he covered his face, and with twain he covered his feet, and with twain he did fly. And one cried unto another, and said, Holy, holy, holy, is the Lord of hosts: the whole earth is full of his glory. And the posts of the door moved at the voice of him that cried, and the house was filled with smoke. Then said I, Woe is me! for I am undone; because I am a man of unclean lips, and I dwell in the midst of a people of unclean lips: for mine eyes have seen the King, the Lord of hosts. Then flew one of the seraphims unto me, having a live coal in his hand, which he had taken with the tongs from off the altar: And he laid it upon my mouth, and said, Lo, this hath touched thy lips; and thine iniquity is taken away, and thy sin purged" (Isaiah 6:1-7).

"But as he which hath called you is holy, so be ye holy in all manner of conversation; Because it is written, Be ye holy; for I am holy" (1 Peter 1:15,16).

4. God is Loving

God loves us with a sacrificial, unconditional love. "He that loveth not knoweth not God; for God is love. In this was manifested the love of God toward us, because that God sent his only begotten Son into the world, that we might live through him. Herein is love, not that we loved God, but that he loved us, and sent his Son to be the propitiation for our sins" (1 John 4:8-10).

5. God is Just

God has two sides: His goodness and His severity. He is fair and does not overlook sin, but will punish those guilty of sin. "Behold therefore the GOODNESS AND SEVERITY OF GOD: on them which fell, severity; but toward thee, goodness, if thou continue in his goodness: otherwise thou also shalt be cut off" (Romans 11:22).

2 THE CREATION AND THE ORIGIN OF MAN

1. God is the Creator of Heaven and Earth.

"In the beginning God created the heaven and the earth. And the earth was without form, and void; and darkness was upon the face of the deep. And the Spirit of God moved upon the face of the waters (Genesis 1:1,2). "For by him were all things created, that are in heaven, and that are in earth, visible and invisible, whether they be thrones, or dominions, or principalities, or powers: all things were created by him, and for him: And he is before all things, and by him all things consist" (Colossians 1:16,17).

2. God created the universe by speaking it into existence.

"Through faith we understand that the worlds were framed by the word of God, so that things which are seen were not made of things which do appear" (Hebrews 11:3).

3. God is the giver of life.

"The thief cometh not, but for to steal, and to kill, and to destroy: I am come that they might have life, and that they might have it more abundantly" (John 10:10).

4. Man is created in God's image.

"And God said, Let us make man in our image, after our likeness..." (Genesis 1:26).

5. Man was given dominion over earth.

"... and let them have dominion over the fish of the sea, and over the fowl of the air, and over the cattle, and over all the earth..." (Genesis 1:26).

3 THE FALL OF MAN AND THE CONSEQUENCES OF THE FALL

1. Man was tempted and fell into sin.

"And the Lord God said unto the woman, What is this that thou hast done? And the woman said, The serpent beguiled me, and I did eat. And the Lord God said unto the serpent, Because thou hast done this, thou art cursed above all cattle, and above every beast of the field; upon thy belly shalt thou go, and dust shalt thou eat all the days of thy life: And I will put enmity between thee and the woman, and between thy seed and her seed; it shall bruise thy head, and thou shalt bruise his heel. Unto the woman he said, I will greatly multiply thy sorrow and thy conception; in sorrow thou shalt bring forth children; and thy desire shall be to thy husband, and he shall rule over thee. And unto Adam he said, Because thou hast hearkened unto the voice of thy wife, and hast eaten of the tree, of which I commanded thee, saying, Thou shalt not eat of it: cursed is the ground for thy sake; in sorrow shalt thou eat of it all the days of thy life; Thorns also and thistles shall it bring forth to thee; and thou shalt eat the herb of the field; In the sweat of thy face shalt thou eat bread, till thou return unto the ground; for out of it wast thou taken: for dust thou art, and unto dust shalt thou return" (Genesis 3:13-19).

2. Sin entered into the world and through sin death came.

"For if by one man's offence death reigned by one; much more they which receive abundance of grace and of the gift of righteousness shall reign in life by one, Jesus Christ.) Therefore as by the offence of one judgment came upon all men to condemnation; even so by the righteousness of one the free gift came upon all men unto justification of life" (Romans 5:17,18).

3. The life of men became shorter and shorter as sin increased.

"For the wages of sin is death; but the gift of God is eternal life through Jesus Christ our Lord" (Romans 6:23).

GOD'S CHOICE AND DEALINGS WITH THE NATION OF ISRAEL: A TYPE OF THE CHURCH

1. God chose Abraham, Isaac and Jacob.

"Now the Lord had said unto ABRAM, Get thee out of thy country, and from thy kindred, and from thy father's house, unto a land that I will show thee: And I will make of thee a great nation, and I will bless thee, and make thy name great; and thou shalt be a blessing: And I will bless them that bless thee, and curse him that curseth thee: and in thee shall all families of the earth be blessed" (Genesis 12:1-3).

"And God said, Sarah thy wife shall bear thee a son indeed; and thou shalt call his name Isaac: and I will establish my covenant with him for an everlasting covenant, and with his seed after him. And as for Ishmael, I have heard thee: Behold, I have blessed him, and will make him fruitful, and will multiply him exceedingly; twelve princes shall he beget, and I will make him a great nation. But my covenant will I establish with ISAAC, which Sarah shall bear unto thee at this set time in the next year" (Genesis 17:19-21).

"And JACOB went out from Beersheba, and went toward Haran. And he lighted upon a certain place, and tarried there all night, because the sun was set; and he took of the stones of that place, and put them for his pillows, and lay down in that place to sleep. And he dreamed, and behold a ladder set up on the earth, and the top of it reached to heaven: and behold the angels of God ascending and descending on it. And, behold, the Lord stood above it, and said, I am the Lord God of Abraham thy father, and the God of Isaac: the land whereon thou liest, to thee will I give it, and to thy seed; And thy seed shall be as the dust of the earth, and thou shalt spread abroad to the west, and to the east, and to the north, and to the south: and in thee and in thy seed shall all the families of the earth be blessed. And, behold, I am with thee, and will keep thee in all places whither thou goest, and will bring thee again into this land; for I will not leave thee, until I have done that which I have spoken to thee of" (Genesis 28:10-15).

2. **God used Joseph to deliver Israel from starvation and famine.**

3. **God used Moses to deliver his people from bondage and teach them his laws.**

4. **God's people Israel, like the church, kept going astray to serve other gods.**

"Now will I sing to my wellbeloved a song of my beloved touching his vineyard. My wellbeloved hath a vineyard in a very fruitful hill: And he fenced it, and gathered out the stones thereof, and planted it with the choicest vine, and built a tower in the midst of it, and also made a winepress therein: and he looked that it should bring forth grapes, and it brought forth wild grapes. And now, O inhabitants of Jerusalem, and men of Judah, judge, I pray you, betwixt me and my vineyard. What could have been done more to my vineyard, that I have not done in it? wherefore, when I looked that it should bring forth grapes, brought it forth wild grapes? And now go to; I will tell you what I will do to my vineyard: I will take away the hedge thereof, and it shall be eaten up; and break down the wall thereof, and it shall be trodden down: And I will lay it waste: it shall not be pruned, nor digged; but there shall come up briers and thorns: I will also command the clouds that they rain no rain upon it. For the vineyard of the Lord of hosts is the house of Israel, and the men of Judah his pleasant plant: and he looked for judgment, but behold oppression; for righteousness, but behold a cry" (Isaiah 5:1-7).

3 GOD'S MASTER PLAN OF SALVATION THROUGH JESUS CHRIST.

1. **God's great, selfless love for humanity led him to devise a plan to save man from the consequences of sin.**

"...There is none righteous, no, not one" (Romans 3:10).

"For all have sinned: and come short of the glory of God" (Romans 3:23).

"For the wages of sin is death..." (Romans 6:23).

"For God so loved the world, that he gave his only begotten Son, that whosoever believeth in him should not perish, but have everlasting life. For God sent not his Son into the world to condemn the world; but that the world through him might be saved" (John 3:16,17).

"He came unto his own, and his own received him not. But as many as received him, to them gave he power to become the sons of God..." (John 1:11, 12).

2. **Christians are released into a new life of blessings in Christ Jesus.**

"Blessed be the God and Father of our Lord Jesus Christ, who hath blessed us with all spiritual blessings in heavenly places in Christ: According as he hath chosen us in him before the foundation of the world, that we should be holy and without blame before him in love: Having predestinated us unto the adoption of children by Jesus Christ to himself, according to the good pleasure of his will, To the praise of the glory of his grace, wherein he hath made us accepted in the beloved. In whom we have redemption through his blood, the forgiveness of sins, according to the riches of his grace; Wherein he hath abounded toward us in all wisdom and prudence; Having made known unto us the mystery of his will, according to his good pleasure which he hath purposed in himself: That in the dispensation of the fulness of times he might gather together in one all things in Christ, both which are in heaven, and which are on earth; even in him: In whom also we have obtained an inheritance, being predestinated according to the purpose of him who worketh all things after the counsel of his own will: That we should be to the praise of his glory, who first trusted in Christ. In whom ye also trusted, after that ye heard the word of truth, the gospel of your salvation: in whom also after that ye believed, ye were sealed with that holy Spirit of promise, Which is the earnest of our inheritance until the redemption of the purchased possession, unto the praise of his glory" (Ephesians 1:3-14).

"According as his divine power hath given unto us all things that pertain unto life and godliness, through the knowledge of him that hath called us to glory and virtue: Whereby are given unto us exceeding great and precious promises: that by these ye might be partakers of the divine nature, having escaped the corruption that is in the world through lust" (2 Peter 1:3,4).

THE RELEASE OF GOD'S ARMY: THE BUILDING OF THE CHURCH.

1. Christ will build a church, an army of believers who will win the lost at any cost.

"And I say also unto thee, That thou art Peter, and upon this rock I will build my church; and the gates of hell shall not prevail against it" (Matthew 16:18).

2. Christ gives all believers a duty to go into the whole world and preach the gospel.

"Go ye therefore, and teach all nations, baptizing them in the name of the Father, and of the Son, and of the Holy Ghost: Teaching them to observe all things whatsoever I have commanded you: and, lo, I am with you alway, even unto the end of the world. Amen" (Matthew 28:19,20). "But ye shall receive power, after that the Holy Ghost is come upon you: and ye shall be witnesses unto me both in Jerusalem, and in all Judaea, and in Samaria, and unto the uttermost part of the earth" (Acts 1:8).

3. Every single believer is a member of the army and is created specially to do good works for the Lord.

"For we are his workmanship, created in Christ Jesus unto good works, which God hath before ordained that we should walk in them" (Ephesians 2:10).

4. The Church is fearless, powerful, anointed and full of God's authority.

"Verily, verily, I say unto you, He that believeth on me, the works that I do shall he do also; and greater works than these shall he do; because I go unto my Father" (John 14:12).

THE ETERNAL JUDGEMENT OF NATIONS, SINNERS AND CHRISTIANS.

1. God will judge all nations.

Jesus spoke of the judgement of the nations. "And before him shall be gathered all nations: and he shall separate them one from another, as a shepherd divideth his sheep from the goats: And he shall set the sheep on his right hand, but the goats on the left. Then shall the King say unto them on his right hand, Come, ye blessed of my Father, inherit the kingdom prepared for you from the foundation of the world:" (Matthew 25:32).

2. God will judge all Christians.

"For we must all appear before the judgment seat of Christ; that every one may receive the things done in his body, according to that he hath done, whether it be good or bad" (2 Corinthians 5:10).

3. God will judge all sinners.

"And I saw a great white throne, and him that sat on it, from whose face the earth and the heaven fled away; and there was found no place for them" (Revelation 20:11).

THE ETERNAL FUTURE: A NEW HEAVEN AND EARTH.

God promises to create a new heaven and a new earth. "And I saw a new heaven and a new earth: for the first heaven and the first earth were passed away; and there was no more sea" (Revelation 21:1).

Bible Study Methods 4

■ BIBLE STUDY

"Study to show thyself approved unto God, a workman that needeth not to be ashamed, rightly dividing the word of truth" (2 Timothy 2:15). "These were more noble than those in Thessalonica, in that they received the word with all readiness of mind, and searched the scriptures daily, whether those things were so" (Acts 17:11). "For whatsoever things were written aforetime were written for our learning, that we through patience and comfort of the scriptures might have hope" (Romans 15:4).

Oh, the lost art of Bible study! It is sad to see that many Christians do not even read the Bible. Since many people do not read the Bible, they obviously do not study it. There are ways by which we can study the Bible effectively. Let us consider three types of Bible study.

- Microscopic Bible Study - reading very short passages, meditating on single verses and words, and examining the meanings of these verses and words using the English, Greek and Hebrew dictionaries and concordances.
- Topical Bible Study - this is done by studying individual topics like faith, love, patience and loyalty.
- Telescopic Bible Study - this involves studying the Bible from a broader perspective.

HOW TO HAVE A MICROSCOPIC BIBLE STUDY

1. Analyse each single word in the verse you are studying.
2. Find out the meaning of every single word in the verse with a dictionary.
3. Check your Bible for any related verses. Analyse these verses also.
4. Look for any corresponding Greek or Hebrew words and find their deep meanings.
5. Ask yourself the following questions:

i. What does this verse mean?

ii. What does this verse mean to me in my specific circumstances?

iii. What is God telling me personally?

iv. What is the verse saying?

v. What is the verse not saying?

vi. How can I apply it to my life?

vii. Is there a command for me to obey?

viii. Is there a warning in the verse for me to heed?

ix. Is there a good example to follow and a bad example to avoid?

x. Is there an allegory (story, parable) for me to interpret?

xi. Is there a promise for me to believe?

xii. Is there anything for me to pray about?

xiii. Who can I share this with?

6. Take note of all punctuation and quotation marks.

7. Never take a verse out of context.

HOW TO HAVE A TOPICAL BIBLE STUDY

1. Define the topic using a very good dictionary, e.g., Oxford's or Webster. Any topic can be chosen, for example; patience, zeal or love.

2. Look for all the verses that refer to the topic and read them aloud.

3. Study all these verses microscopically.

4. Find the following:

i. The Why and Why not of the topic. For example, "Why have patience?" or "Why not have patience?"

ii. The How and How not of the topic. For example, "How do you have patience?"

iii. The Where and Where not of the topic. For example, "Where do you practice love?" or "Where don't you practice love?".

iv. The When and When not of the topic. For example, "When should you be zealous?" or "When should you not be zealous?"

v. The What and What not of the topic. For example, "What is love?" or "What are the things that are not love?" e.g., love is not sex, sex is not love.

vi. The Who and Who not of the topic. For example, "Who should you be patient with?" or "Who should you not be patient with?"

5. Look for types of the topic. For example, the types of love: phileo, agape and eros.

6. Look for examples of the topic. Look for examples of patience in the Bible. Look for examples of zeal, e.g. Jesus.

7. Look for problems/mistakes related to the topic. What are the problems that come when you don't walk in love? What problems do people have when they don't have patience?

HOW TO HAVE A TELESCOPIC BIBLE STUDY

1. Read a whole book at a time, preferably in one sitting. Because you are reading large sections it would be easier to read more modern versions of the Bible.

2. Build up a complete picture.

3. Locate the central theme, key verses or passages.

4. Do a microscopic Bible study on key words that you come across.

TOOLS FOR AN EFFECTIVE BIBLE STUDY

1. BIBLES

You will need several Bibles to have an effective quiet time. Good Bibles to have are: Dake's Annotated Reference Bible (King James Version), Thompson's Chain Reference Bible (King James Version), New International Version, The Amplified Bible and the New American Standard Bible.

The Bible is God's book for us today. As you read it you will hear the voice of God speaking to you. As you study the Word of God, you will discover new revelations which will affect your life.

2. A NOTEBOOK

A Christian should have a book in which he writes down the things that God says to him or reveals to him. It is important to record teh dreams, visions and the words that God gives. "And the Lord said unto Moses, Hew thee two tables of stone like unto the first: and I will write upon these tables the words that were in the first tables, which thou brakest" (Exodus 34:1).

3. A DICTIONARY

Both Oxford and Webster's dictionaries are good dictionaries to have. You will always be surprised to learn the meanings of words which we often assume we know.

4. A CONCORDANCE

Every Christian should have a Strong's Concordance since it is exhaustive.

5. A GOOD ATTITUDE

Recognize God as the author. "God who at sundry times and in divers manners spake in time past unto the fathers by the prophets, Hath in these last days spoken unto us by his son, whom he hath appointed heir of all things, by whom also he made the worlds" (Hebrews 1:1,2).

Focus on Jesus as a central figure in the Bible. "Ought not Christ to have suffered these things, and to enter into his glory? And beginning at Moses and all the prophets, he expounded unto them in all the scriptures the things concerning himself" (Luke 24:26,27).

Be willing to receive instructions from the Lord. "All scripture is given by inspiration of God, and is profitable for doctrine, for reproof, for correction, for instruction in righteousness" (2 Timothy 3:16).

Allow God to change you. "But we all, with open face beholding as in a glass the glory of the Lord, are changed into the same image from glory to glory, even as by the Spirit of the Lord" (2 Corinthians 3:18).

HOW TO INTERPRET THE BIBLE

It is very important to interpret the Bible correctly whilst you are having your quiet time. The Holy Spirit is the author of the Word of God therefore He is the one who can lead us into the correct understanding. "Knowing this first, that no prophecy of the scripture is of any private interpretation. For the prophecy came not in old time by the will of man: but holy men of God spake as they were moved by the Holy Ghost" (2 Peter 1:20,21). Here are nine keys to interpreting the Bible correctly.

1. READ THE TEXT IN ITS CONTEXT.

a. Each word must be read in the context of other words in the verse.

b. Each verse must be read in the context of the chapter.

c. Each chapter in the Bible must be read in the context of the whole book.

d. You can make the Bible say almost anything you want it to. Anything that is taken out of its context becomes an oddity.

For instance, you can make the Bible say, "There is no God." You may ask, "How do you make the Bible say that there is no God?" Just take four words of Psalm 14:1 out of the context of the other words and you will have a false message. Psalm 14:1 says, "The fool hath said in his heart, There is no God." When you put the phrase, "There is no God," back in context, you get a different message. In other words, it is not a case of "there is no God", but a case of the fool saying in his heart that "there is no God".

If you take some Scriptures from the book of Song of Solomon out of context you may even think the Bible is discussing pornography. However, within its context you will discover a beautiful message of the love that God has created.

2. Do not spiritualise meanings of words.

If you take the language at its face value, you will save yourself from deception. When the Bible says in Matthew 8:17, "By his stripes we are healed," there is no need to spiritualise the meaning of the word "heal".

The word "heal" is easily defined in the dictionary. I have reproduced below the meaning of the word "heal" from a dictionary.

heal v. 1 (often foll. by up) become sound or healthy again. 2 .cause to heal. 3. put right (differences etc.). 4 .alleviate (sorrow etc.). healer n. [Old English: related to whole]

There is no reason to spiritualise or allegorise the meaning of any word. As you can see, the word "heal" can also mean to alleviate sorrow. For example, in the context of Matthew 8:17 you will notice that Jesus was not trying to alleviate sorrow but he was healing the sicknesses of the multitudes: "When the even was come, they brought unto him many that were possessed with devils: and he cast out the spirits with his word, and healed all that were sick: That it might be fulfilled which was spoken by Esaias the prophet, saying, Himself took our infirmities, and bare our sicknesses."

3. Believe what you read.

When the Bible says that Moses stretched out his rod over the Red Sea and the sea parted, you must believe that that is what happened: " And Moses stretched out his hand over the sea; and the Lord caused the sea to go back by a strong east wind all that night, and made the sea dry land, and the waters were divided. And the children of Israel went into the midst of the sea upon the dry ground: and the waters were a wall unto them on their right hand, and on their left" (Exodus 14:21,22). If you spiritualise the Scriptures, you will immediately stray into deceptive waters.

4. Find out the meaning of Hebrew and Greek words from which the English version was translated.

Whenever text is being translated from one language to another, there are difficulties in getting the correct words to fit. We encountered such difficulties when we were translating my books from English to French. I cannot imagine the difficulties the Bible translators encountered when they were translating the Bible from Hebrew and Greek to English.

Interpretation of what God is saying will be clearer when you have the privilege of understanding the language from which the Bible was translated. Going into the Hebrew and Greek is just an attempt to clarify the meaning of what is being transmitted.

5. Interpret punctuation marks properly.

Punctuation marks like full stops, commas, colons and semi-colons have important meanings. When you leave them out you will be subject to error. For instance, a colon means that text ahead explains further what has been said.

6. Understand the background (person, place and time).

It is important to understand the background of the writer. It is even more revelatory to know the time and place of the writing of that letter.

For instance, Paul instructed the Romans to be subject to authorities: "Let every soul be subject unto the higher powers. For there is no power but of God: the powers that be are ordained of God. Whosoever therefore resisteth the power, resisteth the ordinance of God: and they that resist shall receive to themselves damnation. For rulers are not a terror to good works, but to the evil. Wilt thou then not be afraid of the power? do that which is good, and thou shalt have praise of the same" (Romans 13:1-3). The Romans were under the rule of a very oppressive dictator, the emperor Nero.

This instruction is interesting when you understand the circumstances under which believers were operating. God was showing that it was wisdom to be subject to authorities. It is interesting to note that Christianity flourishes more under tyrannical rulers than under democracy. Perhaps this was part of God's wisdom to make people believe in Him.

Consider also that Paul was writing from prison when he said, "Finally, my brethren, rejoice in the Lord. To write the same things to you, to me indeed is not grievous, but for you it is safe" (Philippians 3:1).

Paul mentions joy fourteen times in the epistle of Philippians. And the key word is "rejoice". He taught that Christians were to rejoice in fellowship with one another (Philippians 1:3-11), in afflictions of the gospel (Philippians 1 :12-30), and in ministry for saints (Philippians 2 :1-18). He also taught that Christians should rejoice about the faithfulness of ministers (Philippians 2:19-30), in the Lord and not in Judaism (Philippians 3:1-21), in unity (Philippians 4:1-4) and always, in all things (Philippians 4:4-23).

However, we can misuse this concept of background and get into error. For instance, some would flout God's law and justify their disobedience by asserting that the instruction against a particular sin was given to a specific society in a past era. God's Word is timeless.

Knowing the background, that is, the place, time and writer is not to throw out Scriptures, which should not be violated, but rather to throw more light on them.

7. Consider secular material that throws more light on Scripture.

For instance, historical, archaeological, geographical and cultural materials can give more insight into what the Word of God is saying.

8. Interpret the Scripture by Scripture.

Interpret each passage in the light of the Bible teaching as a whole. Scripture cannot contradict itself; God cannot contradict himself. Parts of the Bible, which seem difficult to understand must be interpreted in the context of other parts of the Scriptures. It is not wise to struggle with isolated Scriptures.

For instance, some portions of the Old Testament, if read in isolation, may give one the wrong impression that God is interested in slaughtering large numbers of people. When examined in the context of other parts of Scripture, it would reveal that God loves all men and wants all men to be saved (2 Peter 3:8,9).

We also discover that God hates the sin of murder: "These six things doth the Lord hate: yea, seven are an abomination unto him: A proud look, a lying tongue, and hands that shed innocent blood" (Proverbs 6:16,17).

9. Ask the Holy Spirit to teach you His Word.

Ultimately God is the one who can teach you His Word. He has given us the Holy Spirit for that purpose. Ask the Holy Spirit to teach you His Word, "Howbeit when he, the Spirit of truth, is come, he will guide you into all truth: for he shall not speak of himself; but whatsoever he shall hear, that shall he speak: and he will show you things to come." (John 16:13).

WHAT GREAT MEN SAID ABOUT THE BIBLE

1. George Washington (1st President of the USA)

"It is impossible to rightly govern the world without God and the Bible."

2. Thomas Jefferson (3rd President of the USA)

"A studious perusal of the sacred volume will make better citizens, better fathers, and better husbands."

3. Andrew Jackson (7th President of the USA)

"That Book, Sir, is the rock on which our republic rests."

4. Woodrow Wilson (28th President of the USA)

"You will know the Bible is the Word of God when you read it: for in it you will find the key to your own heart, your own happiness, and your success. I beg of you that you read it, and find this out for yourselves... A man has deprived himself of the best there is in the world who has deprived himself of this (the knowledge of the Bible)."

5. Herbert Hoover (31st President of the USA)

"There is no other book so various as the Bible, nor one so full of concentrated wisdom."

6. Ulysses S. Grant (18th President of the USA)

"To the influence of this book we are indebted to the progress made in civilization, and to this we must look as our guide in the future."

7. Napoleon Bonaparte (Famous French General)

"The Bible is more than a book; it is a living being with an action; a power which invades everything that opposes its extension."

8. Alexander Cruden (Compiled the Cruden's Concordance)

"All other books are of little importance in comparison with the Holy Scriptures."

9. 800 Scientists of Great Britain, recorded in the Bodelian Library, Oxford

"We, the undersigned, students of the natural sciences, desire to express our sincere regret that researches into scientific truth are perverted by some in our own times into occasion for casting doubt into the truth and authenticity of the holy scriptures. We conceive that it is impossible for the Word of God written in the book of nature, and God's Word written in holy scripture, to contradict one another... Physical science is not complete, but is only in a condition of progress. Signed by all 800 scientists."

10. Daniel Webster (US statesman and orator)

"The Bible is the book of faith, and a book of doctrine, and a book of morals, and a book of religion, of special revelation from God; but it is also a book which teaches man his responsibility, his own dignity, and his equality with his fellow man."

"...If we abide by the principles taught in the Bible, our country will go on prospering and to prosper; but if we and our posterity neglect its instructions and authority, no man can bury our glory in profound obscurity."[1]

11. Abraham Lincoln (16th President of the USA)

"In regard to this great book, I have but to say, I believe the Bible is the best gift God has given to man. All the good Saviour gave to the world was communicated through this book. But for this book we could not know right from wrong. All things most desirable for man's welfare, here and hereafter, are to be found portrayed in it."

12. Winston Churchill (British Prime Minister during World War II)

"We rest with assurance upon the impregnable rock of Holy Scripture."

13. General Douglas MacArthur (A US military genius, and general commander of allied forces in SW Pacific during World War II)

" Believe me Sir, never a night goes by, be I ever so tired, but I read the Word of God before I go to bed."

14. John Quincy Adams (6th President of the USA)

"I speak as a man of the world to men of the world; and I say to you, search the scriptures! The Bible is the book of all others, to be read at all ages, and in all conditions of human life; not to be read once or twice or thrice through, and then laid aside but to be read in small portions of one or two chapters everyday, and never to be intermitted, unless by some overruling necessity."

15. Sir Isaac Newton (English philosopher and mathematician; formulator of the law of gravitation)

"We account the scriptures of God to be the most sublime philosophy. I find more sure marks of authority in the Bible than in any profane history whatever."[2]

Let me conclude with the words of Charles Dickens, the great English novelist and author of "David Copperfield", "Great Expectations" and "Oliver Twist":

"It is the best book that ever was or ever will be in the world!"

SECTION II
The Doctrine of Regeneration

The Concept of the New Birth

5

■ A UNIQUE FEATURE OF CHRISTIANITY

Being born again is one of the distinctive features of the Christian faith: "There was a man of the Pharisees, named Nicodemus, a ruler of the Jews: The same came to Jesus by night, and said unto him, Rabbi, we know that thou art a teacher come from God: for no man can do these miracles that thou doest, except God be with him. Jesus answered and said unto him, Verily, verily, I say unto thee, Except a man be born again, he cannot see the kingdom of God. Marvel not that I said unto thee, Ye must be born again" (John 3:1-3,7).

In this passage, Jesus had a discussion with a man called Nicodemus. Jesus was at home one night when Nicodemus came to Him. Nicodemus was a very important person in town. He could have been a Member of Parliament or the Chairman of the Metropolitan Assembly. Perhaps, he was a patron of the Methodist Church, the Catholic Church or the Lighthouse Church. He was a very important person. The Bible says he was a ruler of the Jews, a master of Israel, a leader in the synagogues.

Nicodemus would not come to see Jesus during the day. He came at night, so that all the people who respected him would not see him. This prominent Jewish leader said something to Jesus, which prompted Him to give an interesting reply.

When you look at the passage, you wonder why Jesus said all He said to the man. After all, Nicodemus did not ask Him, "How can I go to Heaven?"

He said to Jesus, "Rabbi, we know that thou art a teacher come from God: for no man can do these miracles that thou doest, except God be with him."

In other words, this man told Jesus that he recognized Him as a great man of God.

Jesus saw right through him and replied, "You must be born again."

Jesus saw right through him and replied; "You are a good person. I know you pay tithes and fast often. You are a Pharisee, and a ruler of the Jews, but you still need to be born again!"

Now, the questions we have to ask ourselves are these: Why did Jesus tell this man that he had to be born again? Why did He launch out into this sermon?

There are lots of people doing all sorts of religious things. These things look "Christian", but they are not. Such people are not born again. There is no religion that requires a person to be born again. All the major religions of this world give instructions for following certain rules of conduct. There is, however, no religion that claims an inner new birth. Christianity stands alone in this claim!

The word "born" means "to be produced or created". Therefore, to be "born again" means "to be produced or created again".

HOW TO BE BORN AGAIN

In order to become born again, a person must do two important things. First, he must believe in Jesus Christ as the Son of God: "Whosoever believeth that Jesus is the Christ is born of God..." (1John 5:1). Secondly, he must invite Jesus through prayer, to come into his heart or his life. He must say a prayer like this and mean it from the bottom of your heart:

"Lord Jesus, I come to You as a sinner, lost and condemned to Hell. I repent of my sins and ask for Your forgiveness. I believe with all my heart that You died on the cross and rose up again for my sins. I open my heart to You and receive You as my Lord and personal Saviour. Please take control of my life and make me what You want me to be. From today, I am Yours and You are mine. Thank You, Father for this wonderful gift of salvation, Amen."

The Spirit of God will then come upon him, and into his heart. Thus, his inner being will be born or produced again. God gives him a new heart and spirit altogether. "A new heart also will I give you, and a new spirit will I put within you: and I will take away the stony heart out of your flesh, and I will give you an heart of flesh. And I will put my spirit within you, and cause you to walk in my statutes, and ye shall keep my judgments, and do them (Ezekiel 36:26-27).

With that new spirit, he becomes a "new man" or a "new creature", and is ready to live a "new life". This new life is possible because a born-again Christian is actually a new person with a new heart. To be born again is as simple as that. Believe in Jesus. Ask Him into your heart. Confess Him as Lord. And you will be born again.

Who then is a born-again Christian? A born-again Christian is someone who has personally received Jesus Christ into his life and is determined to live a life controlled by the Word of God and under the guidance of the Spirit of God.

BIBLICAL PROOFS OF THE NEW BIRTH

1. Born of the Spirit: "...that which is born of the Spirit is spirit..." (John 3:6).
2. Regeneration: "...he saved us, by the washing of regeneration..." (Titus 3:5).
3. Born of God: "Whosoever is born of God doth not commit sin..." (1John 3:9).
4. A child of God: "...to them gave he power to become the sons of God..." (John 1:12).
5. Salvation: "For by grace are ye saved through faith..." (Ephesians 2:8).
6. A Christian: "...And the disciples were called Christians first in Antioch" (Acts 11:26).
7. A Saint: "...called to be saints..." (1Corinthians 1:2).
8. A Believer: "And believers were the more added to the Lord..." (Acts 5:14).
9. A Disciple: "...And the disciples were called Christians first in Antioch" (Acts 11:26).

■ AN ANALYTICAL STUDY OF THE NEW BIRTH

To understand the concept of being born again, we can consider the opposite; things that are not the same as being born again. This can be very revealing. For example: "...Seek ye first the Kingdom of God, and his righteousness; and all these things shall be added unto you" (Matthew 6:33). The opposite of this is: "...Seek ye not first the Kingdom of God, and all these things shall not be added unto you."

It is as simple as that. If you do not seek first the kingdom of God, you cannot expect God to give you the things you need. So, to understand the concept of being born again, we are going to look at twenty things that are NOT the same as being born again.

TWENTY THINGS WHICH ARE NOT THE SAME AS BEING BORN AGAIN

1. Admiring miracles

Whenever there is a miracle worker, large crowds gather. These crowds are often not stable crowds; they only gather for a reason and for a season. When Jesus himself organized miracle crusades, large crowds gathered but when he began teaching certain hard truths, he was deserted by all, except the twelve disciples (John 6). Both good and bad people admire miracles.

My wife once told me of some friends in America. Though they were not born again, they really enjoyed watching TV programmes which featured miracle working tele-evangelists. In Ghana today, there are crowds of miracle-seeking people flocking the churches. But I am sad to say that many of them are not born again. A deep admiration for miracles is not the same as being born again.

2. Befriending "men of God"

Nicodemus got acquainted with Jesus and became His friend. In the same way, there are many who have become friends of pastors and men of God. Befriending a man of God does not guarantee you a place in God's Kingdom: "...except a man be born again he cannot see the Kingdom of God" (John 3:3).

3. Sending money to church

Sending money to church is not the same as being born again. Some people have given money to churches for many years, but that is not a substitute for being born again. Other people also donate heavily towards special church projects such as harvests, (a type of fund-raising practised in some churches in Ghana) in order to become "Harvest Kings" and "Queens".

No matter how much money you contribute to the church, you still need to be born again. It is good to give to God. However, that will not result in the giver receiving special treatment at the gates of Heaven.

God is not a corrupt customs officer you can tip to let you into Heaven. Your money cannot buy you a ticket to Heaven. You must be born again!

The Bible gives an account of those who thought their good works could save them on the Judgement Day. They were certain that they were known by God but on that day, they had the shock of their lives when God told them, "...I never knew you..." (Matthew 7:23).

4. Joining a church

A person may join a church by registering as a member of that church and still not be born again. I have been in church all my life but I did not get born again until I got to form three in Achimota Secondary School in Accra, Ghana.

Everybody in Ghana, has at one time or the other, associated himself with a church—especially as they get older and know they are about to die. In a "religious" country such as Ghana, only a few people would say they do not want to belong to a church.

So you could easily be a member of a church, (because you want to be buried by that church) and not be born again.

5. Playing a role in church

There are several people who play various roles in a church. One such role is to sing as a chorister, preparing the hearts of the congregation for the sermon. However, a chorister can dutifully play this role without being born again. Once, during an altar call in our church, some choristers responded to the call to give their lives to Christ. This means they were members of the choir, but were not born again. It is possible to play a prominent role in church without being born again. A person who is not born again may join a church, get involved in church activities and even become a priest. There are priests standing behind the "sacred desks" in many churches who are not even born again!

Playing a role in church is not the same as being born again.

6. Praying everyday

Daily prayer, however regularly and diligently carried out, is not the way to salvation.

When I was a child, I once approached a priest and asked him, "Sir, how can I go to Heaven?"

Do you know what he told me? "My son, pray 'Hail Mary' three times a day, and 'Our Father' once a day, and you will go to Heaven."

I thanked him, and began to pray everyday, reciting The Lord's Prayer and Hail Mary. Oh, how I prayed! But, that was not the way to salvation! I diligently followed my priest's instructions but I was still not born again.

A minister of God shared an experience he had when he was a teenager. He said he had been a religious person, but at a point in his life he became seriously sick and died on his bed. When he died, he saw himself going down.

As he went deeper and deeper, he started protesting, "But I pray everyday, I go to church every Sunday."

But then he heard a voice telling him, "YOU ARE NOT BORN AGAIN!"

Meanwhile his mother, a born again Christian, was interceding for him.

Finally, when he got to a part of Hell, he saw a horrible-looking creature that lifted its hand to receive him. However, God delivered him, and he came back to life. Then, at another time, he fell sick and died again, but by then he had gotten born again. This time round, when he died he went up. Then a voice told him to go back because he had not finished his work on Earth. He came back to life, and is now a man of God.

You may be as religious as this man was, but if you are not born again, you will die and go to Hell. Simply praying to God everyday is not a substitute for being born again.

7. Reading the Bible

Reading the Bible and quoting the Scriptures is not a guarantee of salvation.

Some of us can easily be deceived into thinking that a person is a born again Christian just because he quotes the Scriptures.

You may be able to quote the Bible from Genesis to Revelation. This does not mean that you are born again. I notice that during election year in Ghana, some politicians mount political platforms and quote Scriptures to us. Why do they do this? They are trying to give us an impression that they are born again. They want the votes of the born-again Christians. But you see, we know them by their fruits. We know that their quoting of Bible passages is no guarantee to us that they are born again.

There are even theologians who have doctorate degrees, but are not born again.

8. Being baptized

Baptism is not the same as being born again. Jesus Himself commanded us to be baptized, but He said baptism should follow salvation.

In Jesus' instruction on baptism, it is clear that baptism follows believing. "Go ye into all the world, and preach the gospel to every creature. He that believeth and is baptized shall be saved..." (Mark 16:15,16).

Now notice that baptism follows believing. You have to believe before you are baptized. It has become the tradition to baptize children when they are eight days old. How can you believe when you are eight days old?

Baptism is immersion in water: a sign to the person being baptized and to all witnesses, that he is now born again. The "old man" of sin goes down into the water and the "new man" recreated in Christ emerges. This is a sign of what has happened inside. That is why baptism is supposed to be done in public, after you are born again.

We say baptism is a sign, because when you are born again, nothing actually happens physically for those around you to see.

So being baptized becomes a physical sign of what happened inside.

Sometimes you meet people who think baptism is the same as being born again. They think it is done in order to enable one to join a church. I once asked someone, "Are you born again?" His reply was, "No, I have not yet been baptized."

He had it all wrong. He needed to be born again first.

I was baptized after I got born again but I was also baptized when I was an eight-day-old baby. My baptism as a baby did not do anything for me. I just became a wet baby.

9. Being confirmed

In some churches, a person is baptized by the sprinkling of water on him when he is an eight-day-old baby. It is expected that when he grows up he will come back to the church to confirm his Christianity. This is what is known as confirmation.

I think that what really happened is this: At some point in the development of Christianity, people felt that they were "big-shots"—too big to be immersed publicly in water. It was humiliating for them to be put into water publicly.

I believe it was arranged for people to be baptized as children. Then, when they grew up, they were confirmed.

The result of all this is a lot of confirmed unbelievers on their way to Hell.

Being confirmed is not the same as being born again.

10. Taking Holy Communion

Taking Holy Communion is not the same as being born again.

It does not matter how much of the communion wine you drink, or the bread you eat. IT IS NOT THE SAME AS BEING BORN AGAIN.

Taking Holy Communion or the Lord's Supper is actually meant for born-again Christians, who eat the bread and drink the wine in remembrance of Christ's death. However, it is now common to find Reverend Ministers serving communion to die-hard sinners who are on their deathbeds, approaching the gates of Hell.

What is communion going to do to a dying sinner? He needs to know that he should be born again!

A whole crate of wine and a big loaf of bread which has been left in the Cathedral until it becomes "holy" may be served to a sinner but it will not take him to Heaven.

11. Being in a Christian family

Being in a Christian family is not the same as being born again.

I was brought up in a "Christian" family. So when I was an eight-day-old baby, I was baptized, then confirmed later. I was also given a Bible and a hymn book by my godmother in England, but it just gathered dust on the shelf.

Now, by this, you realize that I was in the church with my family for years until I became born again. I was not brought up in a Muslim home, where they do not believe in Jesus, but there was still a definite point in my life when I got born again.

I realize that for many people in the younger generation, the first genuine interaction they had with Christianity was one that challenged them to be born again.

However, I find that those who are a bit older or more orthodox are surprised (like Nicodemus), when they are told they must be born again.

They have been devoted "Christians" all their lives, probably singing all the hymns, songs and doxologies they know.

If after serving the Lord sincerely over the years, some young man comes along to tell them that they need to be born again, I can understand their surprise.

A "Christian" upbringing may have included reading the Bible, regular church attendance, singing of hymns and doxologies. However, that is no substitute for being born again.

12. Using Christian jargon

Using Christian jargon is not the same as being born again. What do we mean by Christian jargon? There are some words and phrases noticeable amongst Christians, such as: "Praise the Lord", "Hallelujah", "Glory", "Be blessed", and "Amen, Brother!"

I have worked with people in various Christian groups, sometimes with musicians. There are times I have felt that some of these people were not really born again.

I doubted if they were really Christians, yet they were so rich in Christian jargon. When they met you, they knew exactly what they were supposed to say.

I remember once there was a Christian wedding. This wedding was being held on the university campus. Now, during the ceremony some vandals began screaming from their windows, "GLORY! GLORY! AMEN, BROTHER!" They virtually disrupted the wedding with their shouts of Christian jargon. This obviously cannot mean that they were born again.

13. Denominationalism

Denominationalism, or "Churchianity", is not the same as being born again. Being a member of one of the great denominations of our day does not make you a born- again Christian.

You may be in the Lighthouse Church, but be an unbeliever. In the same way, you may be in the Methodist Church, but simply be a Methodist unbeliever.

The Catholic Church is a very powerful denomination whose members are very devoted. In my estimation, other churches are not as devoted and as charitable as the Catholic Church. In the north of Ghana, you will see some of the great things the Catholic Church has done for the world.

When I was in the medical school, I had the opportunity to learn first-hand about the Catholic Relief Services. This great denomination has wonderful social, medical, and relief services.

The Catholic Church is a denomination I really respect. It is very true that no Charismatic church has done one-half or a tenth of what the Catholic church has done (in terms of material, education, and social helps). God bless their hearts for all their efforts. However, it is my duty to inform all Catholics that they must be born again. Being part of your great denomination does not mean that you are born again. Sorry!

Being a member of a denomination, a branch of the Christian Church, does not make one a born-again Christian.

14. Being a moralist

Being a moralist is not the same as being born again. There are some people who are very moral but having good morals is not the same as being born again.

There are some people who would for instance, never break their marriage vows. I once spoke to an unbeliever, who belonged to an occult group.

This man told me, "I have been married for 17 years but I have never been unfaithful to my wife. I have been up and down. People have put pressure on me because I married somebody from another country." He went on to say, "Even though my wife cannot have a child, I will not be unfaithful to her."

This is a test many born-again Christians may not be able to pass. You would find that men would commonly divorce their barren wives in order to have a child.

But listen, being such a moralist does not mean you are born again. I congratulate you for your morality. I respect you for the fact that you never commit adultery or fornication. I am glad that you do not read pornography or chase prostitutes but I must still inform you that you must be born again!

Nicodemus was a moralist, that is why he was so surprised when Jesus told him that he needed to be born again. Jesus says to the moralist, "Marvel not that I say unto thee, Ye must be born again."

15. Being principled

Being principled is not the same as being born again. Some people are very principled and will not cheat you, even if they have the opportunity to do so. Some people are very principled. They will not cheat you, even if they have the opportunity to do so. Sometimes in examination situations, people cheat; but such principled people will not have anything to do with it!

In school, there were some students who did not belong to the Scripture Union (SU). Yet, they lived such principled lives. They would not even say anything negative about SU members, but they just would not be born again.

I had a friend like that. A very principled guy, but whenever I talked to him about Christ, he would just look at me with an expressionless face.

I have found it more difficult to bring to Christ, someone who is principled, has good morals, but is not born again!

Hard-core sinners are more aware that they need God. I was once walking with a young man who told me, "Pastor, I can't live without prostitutes! I must visit the prostitutes at least twice a day." Such a person is more likely to think that he needs to be born again.

On the other hand, a very principled person sees no reason why he must be saved. His excuse is often, "Why? I am a good person, why should I change?"

There are many doctors who will never involve themselves in the practice of illegal abortion. These are principled doctors who are not even born again. They simply refuse to do it. To them, abortion is murder. Yet, even such principled doctors need to be born again.

The principled person must also be born again.

16. Being respectable

Being respectable is not the same as being born again.

Indeed, you may have appeared respectable for years. All your life you may have been singled out and given leadership responsibilities, such as being the school prefect.

Perhaps, you are a person in authority now. You could be the President of a country, a parliamentarian, a Minister of State, a King, a

Chief, a headmaster or headmistress. Such positions are held in high esteem. Do not be deceived. That respect accorded you does not mean you are born again. Jesus says to the President, "Marvel not that I say unto thee, Ye must be born again."

17. Being popular

Being popular or famous is not the same as being born again.

I remember in Achimota Secondary School, there was this particular boy who was extremely short. Whenever he walked in or out of any school gathering, there was a great uproar, as everybody cheered him on. He was a very popular guy but he still needed to be born again!

You may be popular. People may hail you every where you go, but you still need to be born again! There are some popular politicians. In spite of their popularity they must still be born again! People may like you. Everybody may be pleased with you. Yet, being liked is not the same as being born again.

18. Obeying a new set of rules

Being born-again is not the same as obeying a new set of rules.

When you join a club, you may be presented with a new set of rules. An example of such a group is a Keep Fit Club or an Old Boys' Association. Such associations often have mottos, or what is perceived as their guiding principle. My wife's school, Wesley Girls' High School, has as its motto: "Live pure, Speak true, Right wrong and Follow the King".

This set of rules may be your guiding principle. Throughout your entire life you may be guided by these nice sounding phrases. Dear "old boy" and "old girl", you still have to be born again.

There are also lots of people with wise sayings. In Ghana, one of our popular wise sayings can be translated as, "The animal without a tail is protected by God". The deeper meaning of this is, "God takes care of the fatherless". How wise and impressive this sounds!

19. Being a good spouse

Being a good wife or a good husband does not mean that person is born again.

You may love your husband, look after him, submit to him, support him and pray for him but it does not mean you are born again. You may be living happily together, but it does not mean you will go to Heaven.

Such people are often surprised when you tell them to be born again. They will say, "Look at me! What is wrong with me? I am a good person, and this is my happy wife. We are living happily ever after."

I must say that there are some good non-Christian husbands, but whether you are a good spouse or not, you have to be born again!

20. Being rich or poor

Being rich or poor is not the same as being born again. If you are very rich and everything is going well, you may think you don't need to add anything to your life. In Luke 16:19-31, we read about the rich man. He was a fool, not because he was rich, but because in his rich state he did not acknowledge God. Often, rich people forget about God. Do not be a rich man be a wise and rich person.

Riches do not make one a fool. Indeed, it is better to be rich than to be poor. However, you still need to be born again, otherwise you will perish with your riches! The last that may be seen of you will be your grand funeral.

Your body may be left in the mortuary for a long time (as is the custom for Chiefs in Ghana). Your relatives may even insist on changing your funeral clothes several times during the funeral ceremony, as though you were a contestant in a beauty contest. Read about what the rich man said when he suddenly found himself in Hell—he became an evangelist, longing to send a message to his brothers so they would not come to Hell!

Being poor in this life is all the more reason why you must be born again. Your poverty and suffering in this life should not deceive you into thinking that there will be peace after death. Jesus says to the rich and the poor alike, "Marvel not that I say unto thee, Ye must be born again."

FOUNDATIONAL TEACHINGS FOR THE NEW BELIEVER

It is important for a person who becomes born again to fully understand his new life in Christ and to build up on what God has begun in his life.

SALVATION

1. Essential facts about salvation

a. The Bible indicates that human beings are sinners by birth and by lifestyle. "For all have sinned, and come short of the glory of God" (Romans 3:23).

b. The Bible teaches that the good things man does are seen as filthy rags that cannot please God. "But we are all as an unclean thing, and all our righteousnesses are as filthy rags" (Isaiah 64:6).

c. We can never be holy enough because we were conceived in sin. "Behold, I was shapen in iniquity; and in sin did my mother conceive me" (Psalm 51:5).

d. The Bible tells us that none can receive salvation by doing anything in particular. "For by grace are ye saved through faith; and that not of yourselves..." (Ephesians 2:8).

e. We are not saved by our good works but by our faith in Christ. "That if thou shalt confess with thy mouth the Lord Jesus, and shalt believe in thine heart that God hath raised him from the dead, thou shalt be saved" (Romans 10:9).

f. God will definitely punish the sins of men with curses, sicknesses and separation from God both in this life and in eternity. "But the fearful, and unbelieving, and the abominable, and murderers, and whoremongers, and sorcerers, and idolaters, and all liars, shall have their part in the lake which burneth with fire and brimstone which is the second death" (Revelation 21:8).

g. There are two reasons why God decided to save mankind:

  i The first reason is God's great love for His creation. John 3:16 says: "For God so loved the world, that he gave his only begotten Son, that whosoever believeth in him should not perish, but have everlasting life."

  ii. The second reason is that we could not save ourselves through good deeds like church membership, religion and our own righteousness. Isaiah 64:6 says: "But we are all as an unclean thing, and all our righteousnesses are as filthy rags...."

h. Jesus Christ had to die on the cross for us because the Bible teaches that without the shedding of blood, there is no forgiveness of sins. "And almost all things are by the law purged with blood; and without shedding of blood is no remission" (Hebrews 9:22).

2. Six powerful results of your salvation

Now that you have given your life to Jesus Christ, you have become born again. You have now received these blessings from the Lord:

a. **All your sins—past and present ones are forgiven by Jesus' sacrifice.**

Your future sins will also be forgiven if you confess them.

"If we confess our sins, he is faithful and just to forgive us our sins, and to cleanse us from all unrighteousness" (1 John 1:9).

b. **You have received eternal life.**

"Verily, verily, I say unto you, He that heareth my word, and believeth on him that sent me, hath everlasting life,..." (John 5:24).

c. **You are now a child of God.**

"But as many as received him, to them gave he power to become the sons of God,..." (John 1:12).

d. **You are now a new creation in Christ.**

"Therefore if any man be in Christ, he is a new creature: old things are passed away; behold, all things are become new" (2 Corinthians 5:17).

e. **Your name is written in Heaven in the Lamb's Book of Life.**

"And there shall in no wise enter into it any thing that defileth, neither whatsoever worketh abomination, or maketh a lie: but they which are written in the Lamb's book of life" (Revelation 21:27).

f. **You will go to Heaven, the New Jerusalem.**

"And the city had no need of the sun, neither of the moon, to shine in it: for the glory of God did lighten it, and the Lamb is the light thereof. And the nations of them which are saved shall walk in the light of it: and the kings of the earth do bring their glory and honour into it" (Revelation 21:23-24).

BAPTISMS

1. WHAT YOU MUST KNOW ABOUT WATER BAPTISM

a. **Baptism comes from the Greek word "baptiso" which means "immersion". Water baptism is therefore the immersion of a person totally into water. It is not sprinkling or pouring of water.**

"And Jesus, when he was baptized, went up straightway out of the water:..." (Matthew 3:16). "And John also was baptizing in Aenon near to Salim, because there was much water there: and they came, and were baptized" (John 3:23).

A lot of water is needed for baptism by immersion.

b. **Water baptism is a command to anyone who becomes born again.**

"And he said unto them, Go ye into all the world, and preach the gospel to every creature. He that believeth and is baptized shall be saved; but he that believeth not shall be damned" (Mark 16:15-16).

c. **Water baptism is a direct act of obedience to Christ's instruction.**

"He that believeth and is baptized shall be saved; but he that believeth not shall be damned" (Mark 16:16).

d. **Baptism is not for church membership, but an open declaration of our new stand in Christ.**

"For as many of you as have been baptized into Christ have put on Christ" (Galatians 3:27). When you are baptized you are openly declaring that you have by faith "put on Christ" so that men may see Christ in you.

e. **We identify with the death, burial and resurrection of our Lord Jesus Christ in baptism.**

"Therefore we are buried with him by baptism into death: that like as Christ was raised up from the dead by the glory of the Father, even so we also should walk in newness of life" (Romans 6:4). The lowering of the convert completely under the water pictures Christ's death; the submersion of the convert speaks of His burial and the raising of the convert from the water signifies His resurrection.

2. The baptism of the Holy Ghost

What is the baptism of the Holy Ghost? The baptism of the Holy Ghost is an experience the believer receives after being born again. It is a promise from God to all those who believe in Jesus Christ.

John the Baptist gave witness of Christ before His baptism that: "I indeed baptize you with water unto repentance: but he that cometh after me is mightier than I, whose shoes I am not worthy to bear: he shall baptize you with the Holy Ghost, and with fire" (Matthew 3:11).

a. What happens when a person receives the baptism of the Holy Ghost?

The initial sign that you are baptized with the Holy Ghost is that you speak in tongues.

"And when the day of Pentecost was fully come, they were all with one accord in one place.... And they were all filled with the Holy Ghost, and began to speak with other tongues, as the Spirit gave them utterance" (Acts 2:1-4).

"And when Paul had laid his hands upon them, the Holy Ghost came on them; and they spake with tongues, and prophesied" (Acts 19:6).

b. Who can receive the baptism of the Holy Ghost?

Anyone who is born again can receive the baptism of the Holy Ghost with the evidence of speaking in tongues.

"And these signs shall follow them that believe; In my name shall they cast out devils; They shall speak with new tongues..." (Mark 16:17).

3. How to receive the baptism of the Holy Ghost

a. Firstly, you must be born again.

This is the most important qualification.

"And these signs shall follow them that believe;...they shall speak with new tongues" (Mark 16:17).

b. Secondly, you must desire the Holy Spirit.

Then Peter said unto them, Repent, and be baptized every one of you in the name of Jesus Christ for the remission of sins, and ye shall receive the gift of the Holy Ghost.

"For the promise is unto you, and to your children, and to all that are afar off, even as many as the Lord our God shall call" (Acts 2:38-39).

Although it is a promise for every believer, God expects you to desire the gift so that when He pours out this blessing on you, it will not go waste or unused.

"But covet earnestly the best gifts..." (1 Corinthians 12:31). "...desire spiritual gifts..." (1 Corinthians 14:1).

c. Pray and ask God to baptize you with the Holy Ghost.

"If ye then, being evil, know how to give good gifts unto your children: how much more shall your heavenly Father give the Holy Spirit to them that ask him?" (Luke 11:13).

d. Exercise your faith by speaking out in tongues.

God is not going to put a radio box in your stomach and switch it on and off. He expects you to speak out! You must step out in faith and God will honour that faith. "And they were all filled with the Holy Ghost, and began to speak with other tongues, as the Spirit gave them utterance" (Acts 2:4).

Sometimes it is helpful to get a senior Christian to assist you by laying hands on you and praying along with you. This can greatly facilitate the process and eliminate doubt and fear. "And when Paul had laid his hands upon them, the Holy Ghost came on them; and they spake with tongues, and prophesied" (Acts 19:6).

When you start speaking in tongues for the first time, it may sound like a baby learning to speak—gibberish—but the Holy Ghost will enable you.

e. Once you start speaking in tongues, don't stop it. Keep on praying!

The Bible describes the speaking of tongues in two ways. First it as a:

i. River that flows out of your belly—"In the last day, that great day of the feast, Jesus stood and cried, saying, If any man thirst, let him come unto me, and drink. He that believeth on me, as the scripture hath said, out of his belly shall flow rivers of living water. (But this spake he of the Spirit, which they that believe on him should receive: for the Holy Ghost was not yet given; because that Jesus was not yet glorified.)" (John 7:37-39). So let the river flow!!

It is also a:

ii. Stammering tongue—"For with stammering lips and another tongue will he speak to this people" (Isaiah 28:11).

Tongues often sound like the voice of a stammerer—"ba ba ba ba" or "ma ma ma ma". This is a unique characteristic of the heavenly language.

4. Ten reasons why every believer must develop himself by speaking in tongues

a. Speaking in tongues is a promise to every believer.

"He that believeth and is baptized shall be saved; but he that believeth not shall be damned. And these signs shall follow them that believe; In my name shall they cast out devils; they shall speak with new tongues;" (Mark 16:16,17)

b. Speaking in tongues helps you to pray according to the will of God.

"Likewise the Spirit also helpeth our infirmities: for we know not what we should pray for as we ought: but the Spirit itself maketh intercession for us with groanings which cannot be uttered"(Romans 8:26,27).

c. Speaking in tongues builds you up to become a strong and powerful Christian.

"But ye, beloved, building up yourselves on your most holy faith, praying in the Holy Ghost" (Jude 1:20).

d. Speaking in tongues is talking to God directly in a language only He understands.

"For he that speaketh in an unknown tongue speaketh not unto men, but unto God: for no man understandeth him; howbeit in the spirit he speaketh mysteries" (1 Corinthians 14:2).

e. Speaking in tongues gives your spirit the opportunity to pray.

"For if I pray in an unknown tongue, my spirit prayeth, but my understanding is unfruitful" (1 Corinthians 14:14).

f. Speaking in tongues makes your spirit pray best about things concerning you.

Your spirit knows deeper things about yourself than any other part of you.

"For what man knoweth the things of a man, save the spirit of man which is in him? even so the things of God knoweth no man, but the Spirit of God" (1 Corinthians 2:11).

Sometimes you may not understand what you are going through in order to pray meaningfully in your normal language. However, you can still pray very effectively in tongues because your spirit knows many things that your mind hasn't yet grasped. Therefore allow your spirit to pray!

g. **Speaking in tongues makes you pray for a long time.**

You are not limited by language, vocabulary and how to express yourself and so you can pray for a long time. "For if I pray in an unknown tongue, my spirit prayeth, but my understanding is unfruitful" (1 Corinthians 14:14).

h. **Speaking in tongues is a better way to express thanks and appreciation to God.**

"Else when thou shalt bless with the spirit, how shall he that occupieth the room of the unlearned say Amen at thy giving of thanks, seeing he understandeth not what thou sayest? For thou verily givest thanks well" (1 Corinthians 14:16,17).

i. **Speaking in tongues makes you more aware of the power of Christ.**

You will become bold as you become more and more aware of the power that is at work in the believer. You can stand boldly as a true witness for Jesus. You are fearless in the face of demonic activity and your faith to deal with them is firm. "But ye shall receive power, after that the Holy Ghost is come upon you: and ye shall be witnesses unto me both in Jerusalem, and in all Judaea, and in Samaria, and unto the uttermost part of the earth" (Acts 1:8).

j. **Speaking in tongues makes you become more conscious of the presence of the Holy Spirit in you as you continue to communicate with God in tongues.**

The Holy Spirit is in us to help us. Being more aware of His presence helps you to develop a personal relationship with Him and engage His participation, contribution and influence in our lives. "And I will pray the Father, and he shall give you another Comforter, that he may abide with you for ever; Even the Spirit of truth; whom the world cannot receive, because it seeth him not, neither knoweth him: but ye know him; for he dwelleth with you, and shall be in you" (John 14:16-17).

The Journey on the Ship

Why should you go to heaven without experiencing all the blessings promised to believers to help our Christian lives here on earth? It will be like a man who saved all he could and bought a ticket to go to New York on a ship. He managed to use the rest of his savings to buy a box of cabin biscuits and drink. Throughout the journey he never mingled with the other passengers nor visited the restaurants, cinema halls, etc. He never used any of the facilities like the swimming pools, gyms and saloons.

He thought to himself, "I'm not rich. I can't afford all that! Some people are really blessed!" He would then retreat to his cabin to enjoy his cabin biscuits and drink.

A few days to the end of the journey the captain spotted the lonely traveller and asked why he had never seen him the whole time and whether he had any problems with the services they offered. He replied that from what he saw the services were excellent only he couldn't participate because he couldn't afford any. The captain's jaw dropped in utter amazement and shock – the reason? Everything on board was already paid for! The price of the ticket covered every facility on the ship! The man did not know! He had suffered needless pain and hardship throughout the journey. How sad!!

Unfortunately, many Christians are just like this lonely traveller. There are many things included in our "salvation ticket" but we are not enjoying them either because of ignorance or we refuse to accept them for ourselves. Speaking in tongues is part of the salvation ticket! Rise up and flow in it!!!

READING THE BIBLE REGULARLY AND SPIRITUAL GROWTH

1. Four important facts about the Bible

a. The Bible is God's Word to mankind.

"All scripture is given by inspiration of God, and is profitable for doctrine, for reproof, for correction, for instruction in righteousness: That the man of God may be perfect, throughly furnished unto all good works" (2 Timothy. 3:16,17).

b. God's Word gives us direction for our lives.

The Word of God guides us in what to say, what to do and where to go. All our decisions and actions must be based on this all-important book. "Thy word is a lamp unto my feet, and a light unto my path" (Psalm 119:105).

c. The Word of God helps to change our thinking and keeps us from the bad habits of our past like drinking, smoking, premarital and extra-marital sex, the practice of boyfriends/girlfriends, and other sins in our lives.

"Wherewithal shall a young man cleanse his way? by taking heed thereto according to thy word" (Psalm 119:9).

d. God's Word will make you a strong believer.

As you feed on the Word you grow in the Lord. Your spirit will grow and you will understand spiritual things. "And now, brethren, I commend you to God, and to the word of his grace, which is able to build you up, and to give you an inheritance among all them which are sanctified" (Acts 20:32).

"But the natural man receiveth not the things of the Spirt of God: for they are foolishness unto him: neither can he know them, because they are spiritually discerned" (1 Corinthians 2:14).

2. Things you must do with the Word of God

a. Desire the Word.

Just as babies survive and grow as they feed on milk daily, born-again Christians must survive and grow by daily feeding on the Word of God. "As newborn babes, desire the sincere milk of the word, that ye may grow thereby:" (1 Peter 2:2).

c. You must have a daily quiet time to read the Bible.

"This book of the law shall not depart out of thy mouth; but thou shalt meditate therein day and night, that thou mayest observe to do according to all that is written therein: for then thou shalt make thy way prosperous, and then thou shalt have good success" (Joshua 1:8).

Quiet time is a regular daily time you keep with the Lord. It is a personal, unhurried time in Bible reading and praying. Quiet time is a time that God communicates with you through His word and prayer.

d. Be determined to be a doer of the Word.

As a born-again Chrisitan, you must fully obey every aspect of the Word of God. You must change your life in accordance to whatever the Bible says.

"But be ye doers of the word, and not hearers only, deceiving your own selves. For if any be a hearer of the word, and not a doer, he is like unto a man beholding his natural face in a glass: For he beholdeth himself, and goeth his way, and straightway forgetteth what manner of man he was. But whoso looketh into the perfect law of liberty, and continueth therein, he being not a forgetful hearer, but a doer of the work, this man shall be blessed in his deed" (James 1:22-25).

PRAYING REGULARLY AND SPIRITUAL GROWTH

Prayer means talking to God. If you pray and develop a prayer life, you will grow in your relationship with God. You naturally develop a relationship with anyone you talk to often.

If for instance I preach to you, you will know what I am trying to say. But if you talk back to me, I get the chance to talk to you and you talk back to me. As this continues, the relationship becomes a little more intimate. You will begin to know me.

It is the same thing with God. God has preached to us, we read out His preaching from the Bible. But if you begin to talk to Him and He talks back to you, you will develop a relationship with Him and you will know Him and He will know you.

1. Six principles of prayer

a. It is important to spend some time with God in prayer every day.

"Pray without ceasing" (1 Thessalonians 5:17).

b. Prayer builds you up in your faith.

"But ye, beloved, building up yourselves on your most holy faith, praying in the Holy Ghost..." (Jude 1:20).

c. Every Christian should pray at least 30 minutes daily when he begins the habit of prayer.

You should move up to praying for an hour as you grow in your daily prayer habit. "And he cometh unto the disciples, and findeth them asleep, and saith unto Peter, What, could ye not watch with me one hour?" (Matthew 26:40).

d. Prayer helps you to overcome temptations.

"Watch and pray, that ye enter not into temptation: the spirit indeed is willing, but the flesh is weak" (Matthew 26:41).

e. You can pray about everything.

"Therefore I say unto you, What things soever ye desire, when ye pray, believe that ye receive them, and ye shall have them" (Mark 11:24).

f. You can accompany your prayer with fasting sometimes.

"But thou, when thou fastest, anoint thine head, and wash thy face; That thou appear not unto men to fast, but unto thy Father which is in secret: and thy Father, which seeth in secret, shall reward thee openly" (Matthew 6:17,18).

2. The four aspects of prayer: A.C.T.S.

a. Adoration

Praise and worship God for who He is and for what He means to you. You can sing a few songs of praise and worship. "After this manner therefore pray ye: Our Father which art in heaven, Hallowed be thy name" (Matthew 6:9).

"Bless the Lord, O my soul: and all that is within me, bless his holy name. Bless the Lord, O my soul, and forget not all his benefits: Who forgiveth all thine iniquities; who healeth all thy diseases" (Psalm 103:1-3).

b. Confession

i. Confess your sins

We must confess our sins to obtain God's forgiveness and healing for sins we commit or for things we failed to do and even for things in our hearts that we cannot see, for example pride. "If we confess our sins, he is faithful and just to forgive us our sins, and to cleanse us from all unrighteousness" (1 John 1:8,9).

ii. Confess your faith

We must also confess (declare, speak out) our faith in God's Word. What you believe in your heart and say with your mouth will come to pass: "For with the heart man believeth unto righteousness; and with the mouth confession is made unto salvation" (Romans 10:10).

"For verily I say unto you, That whosoever shall say unto this mountain, Be thou removed, and be thou cast into the sea; and shall not doubt in his heart, but shall believe that those things which he saith shall come to pass; he shall have whatsoever he saith" (Mark 11:23).

As you read the Bible you would come across things God has said about His children: Who they are! What they can do! What they have! You can confess them and believe God to bring them to pass in your life. You must constantly affirm that:

I am who God says I am!

I can do what He says I can do!

I have what He says I have!

"That the communication of thy faith may become effectual by the acknowledging of every good thing which is in you in Christ Jesus" (Philemon 1:6).

c. **Thanksgiving**

i. **Thank God in all circumstances.**

"In every thing give thanks: for this is the will of God in Christ Jesus concerning you" (1 Thessalonians 5:18).

ii. **Thank God for the things He does in your life.**

"Praise ye the Lord. O give thanks unto the Lord; for he is good: for his mercy endureth for ever" (Psalm 106:1).

iii. **Thank God in advance for what you have asked from Him but haven't yet seen.**

"Be careful for nothing; but in every thing by prayer and supplication with thanksgiving let your requests be made known unto God." (Philippians 4:6).

d. **Supplication (Asking God for your needs)**

i. **Ask Him for everything you need.**

"Ask, and it shall be given you; seek, and ye shall find; knock, and it shall be opened unto you" (Matthew 7:7).

ii. **Ask for things concerning other people.**

"I exhort therefore, that, first of all, supplications, prayers, intercessions, and giving of thanks, be made for all men; For kings, and for all that are in authority; that we may lead a quiet and peaceable life in all godliness and honesty" (1 Timothy 2:1,2).

REGULAR FELLOWSHIP AND SPIRITUAL GROWTH

To grow in your new life it is important that you do not stay at home without fellowshipping. You must find a Bible-believing church and attend the services regularly.

1. What is a Bible-believing church?

A Bible-believing church is a church where people are taught to be born again, trained to be effective Christians and the Bible is the only source of truth. When a coal of fire is separated from the coal pot, and other burning charcoal, it dies out. Like a coal of fire you cannot survive on your own. You must fellowship with other believers to keep the Gospel fire burning in you.

"Iron sharpeneth iron; so a man sharpeneth the countenance of his friend" (Proverbs 27:17).

2. How to Develop by Fellowshipping

a. **You must go to church regularly.**

Every Christian must fellowship regularly in a church, which is alive, born again, and Spirit-filled. It is very dangerous not to fellowship regularly.

"Not forsaking the assembling of ourselves together, as the manner of some is; but exhorting one another: and so much the more, as ye see the day approaching" (Hebrews 10:25).

Our Saviour, Jesus Christ, had the habit of going to the church of His day regularly.

"And he came to Nazareth, where he had been brought up: and, as his custom was, he went into the synagogue on the sabbath day..." (Luke 4:16).

What happened to Judas when he kept avoiding fellowship for "legitimate" reasons? Judas probably betrayed Christ because he often had to leave their fellowship to "sort out certain financial issues". Outside fellowship we are exposed to all sorts of temptations.

b. **You must make friends and move closely with other Christians.**

You must change your friends and walk with born again Christians. You cannot do well as a Christian if you remain close to unbeliever friends.

"Be not deceived: evil communications corrupt good manners" (1 Corinthians 15:33).

"I am a companion of all them that fear thee, and of them that keep thy precepts" (Psalm 119:63).

"And they continued stedfastly in the apostles' doctrine and fellowship, and in breaking of bread, and in prayers" (Acts 2:42).

DEVELOPING THE ART OF WITNESSING AND SOULWINNING

1. We must tell our friends about what has happened to us in Christ.

Your friends may come to know Christ because of your testimony. The woman of Samaria became a soul-winner when she met Christ.

"The woman then left her waterpot, and went her way into the city, and saith to the men, Come, see a man, which told me all things that ever I did: is not this the Christ? Then they went out of the city, and came unto him... And many of the Samaritans of that city believed on him for the saying of the woman, which testified, He told me all that ever I did" (John 4:28-30,39).

2. It is an important public declaration that shows that you are not ashamed of Christ before men.

"Whosoever therefore shall be ashamed of me and of my words in this adulterous and sinful generation; of him also shall the Son of man be ashamed, when he cometh in the glory of his Father with the holy angels" (Mark 8:38).

"For I am not ashamed of the gospel of Christ: for it is the power of God unto salvation to every one that believeth; to the Jew first, and also to the Greek" (Romans 1:16).

3. It is our responsibility as Christians to tell others about the truth.

"When I say unto the wicked, O wicked man, thou shalt surely die; if thou dost not speak to warn the wicked from his way, that wicked man shall die in his iniquity; but his blood will I require at thine hand. Nevertheless, if thou warn the wicked of his way to turn from it; if he do not turn from his way, he shall die in his iniquity; but thou hast delivered thy soul" (Ezekiel 33:8,9).

"And he said unto them, Go ye into all the world, and preach the gospel to every creature" (Mark 16:15).

"And Jesus came and spake unto them, saying, All power is given unto me in heaven and in earth. Go ye therefore, and teach all nations, baptizing them in the name of the Father, and of the Son, and of the Holy Ghost: Teaching them to observe all things whatsoever I have commanded you: and, lo, I am with you alway, even unto the end of the world. Amen" (Matthew 28:18-20).

"But ye shall receive power, after that the Holy Ghost is come upon you: and ye shall be witnesses unto me both in Jerusalem, and in all Judaea, and in Samaria, and unto the uttermost part of the earth" (Acts 1:8).

4. YOU MUST BEAR FRUIT.

"Ye have not chosen me, but I have chosen you, and ordained you, that ye should go and bring forth fruit, and that your fruit should remain: that whatsoever ye shall ask of the Father in my name, he may give it you" (John 15:16).

YOUR ROLE AS A CHURCH MEMBER

1. YOUR FIRST ROLE IN THE CHURCH IS THAT OF A FAITHFUL ATTENDEE.

Decide to attend all services, meetings and special programmes organized by the church. Just as you cannot eat once a month and say that you have enough food, you can also not come to church once a while and think that you have enough fellowship.

"Moreover it is required in stewards, that a man be found faithful" (1 Corinthians 4:2).

Faithful means constant, regular, reliable, dedicated and committed.

2. YOUR SECOND ROLE IN THE CHURCH IS THAT OF A STABLE CHRISTIAN.

You must be planted in a local church and be established there. Do not form the habit of roaming from one church to the other seeking signs and wonders or other solutions.

For example, a student on campus does not study medicine today, law tomorrow, and geography the next day. He will gain nothing and achieve nothing in the end.

It is important to be stable in one place. "The righteous shall flourish like the palm tree: he shall grow like a cedar in Lebanon. Those that be planted in the house of the Lord shall flourish in the courts of our God" (Psalm 92:12,13).

3. YOUR THIRD ROLE IS TO SUPPORT THE CHURCH FINANCIALLY.

You must support the church financially to help carry the Gospel to others who have not heard and to keep the church work running. God will bless and prosper you as you support His work. Allow Jesus to be Lord over your finances as well. You support the church financially by:

a. Giving offerings at services.

"Give, and it shall be given unto you; good measure, pressed down, and shaken together, and running over, shall men give into your bosom. For with the same measure that ye mete withal it shall be measured to you again" (Luke 6:38).

b. Giving your tithes or First & Best Fruits (ten per cent of your income) regularly every month or whenever you receive income.

(Honour the Lord with thy substance, and with the firstfruits of all thine increase: So shall thy barns be filled with plenty, and thy presses shall burst out with new wine" (Proverbs 3:9,10).

4. YOUR FOURTH ROLE IS TO MAKE YOUR TALENTS AND GIFTS AVAILABLE TO THE CHURCH.

Put your God-given abilities to full use in His house. God has given everyone an ability or talent that is beneficial to His church. Do not hide your abilities! Be ready to perform any special duties assigned to you by the leadership.

5. YOUR FIFTH ROLE IS TO KNOW YOUR PASTORS, LOVE AND RESPECT THEM.

a. Know them.

"And we beseech you, brethren, to know them which labour among you, and are over you in the Lord, and admonish you" (1 Thessalonians 5:12).

b. Respect them.

"And to esteem them very highly in love for their work's sake. And be at peace among yourselves" (1 Thessalonians 5:13).

c. Believe in them.

"...Hear me, O Judah, and ye inhabitants of Jerusalem; Believe in the Lord your God, so shall ye be established; believe his prophets, so shall ye prosper" (2 Chronicles 20:20).

d. Pray for them.

"Brethren, pray for us" (1 Thessalonians 5:25).

"Finally, brethren, pray for us, that the word of the Lord may have free course, and be glorified, even as it is with you" (2 Thessalonians 3:1).

"Pray for us: for we trust we have a good conscience, in all things willing to live honestly" (Hebrews 13:18).

May you be rooted and grounded in Christ until He comes again!

The Significance of the New Birth 6

■ UNDERSTANDING SALVATION

The concept of the new birth or salvation in Christ should be clearly understood by the believer, who should gain an understanding of what exactly has happened to him through Jesus Christ. A lack of understanding often leads to confusion and sometimes backsliding. In this chapter, the process of salvation is explained in seven "easy to understand" principles.

THE PRINCIPLES

1. Man is a spirit, has a soul and lives in a body.
2. The spirit of an unsaved man is dead and desperately wicked.
3. The spirit of a saved man is righteous and truly holy.
4. After salvation, the spirit of man is a newborn baby and it must grow.
5. After salvation, the mind is still the same; it must be renewed.
6. After salvation, the body is still the same; it must be kept under control.
7. After salvation, the mind is still open to all kinds of thoughts; it must be focused on the right things.

When we understand these principles, we will know why there is no religion that offers what Christianity offers. Christianity offers a change and a recreation of the wicked heart of man. Christianity is not a new set of rules. You do not get to heaven by obeying the "Do's" and "Don'ts" of human beings. Christ changes the heart of a person and gives him the power to control his body and to renew his mind.

MAN IS A SPIRIT, HAS A SOUL AND LIVES IN A BODY

The fact that a human being is actually a spirit living inside a physical body is one of the lesser known truths. When Paul wrote to the Thessalonians, he stated that God should affect them in all three areas: spirit, soul and body. "And the very God of peace sanctify you wholly; and I pray God your whole Spirit and Soul and Body be preserved blameless unto the coming of our Lord Jesus Christ" (1 Thessalonians 5:23).

A human being is not just a piece of meat. When Princess Diana died, many people in this world reflected on the reality of spiritual issues.

One day, I had a chat with a man in the lobby of a hotel. He asked me what I do and I told him that I was a pastor.

"Oh, I see," he said.

"Do you believe in God?" I asked him.

"Actually, I had just been thinking about this."

He continued, "When Princess Diana died, I wondered whether I was just a piece of meat."

I told him, "You are not just a piece of meat. There is more to you than a piece of meat."

When people speak in a very proud and arrogant fashion it is because they are not aware how real eternal things are. I will never forget my first day as a medical student in the dissection laboratory of the University of Ghana Medical School. It was about 2 o'clock in the afternoon when we were ushered into a large air-conditioned room containing twelve white marble tables. On each of these tables was a dead human being lying stark naked.

The dead bodies were those of ten men and two women. My friends and I gathered around one of the tables. There were stools around each table and I sat down staring at the dead body that lay before me. On the chest of this human being was a plaster with a name inscribed. The name of our cadaver was Cornelius.

I wondered to myself, "Who was Cornelius during his lifetime? What did he do for a living? How did he come to lie before us, ready for eighteen months of intensive dissection?"

As we sat there, our Anatomy lecturer came in. He happened to be a Christian. He said to us, "Go ahead and touch them, don't be afraid!" But in spite of his encouragement, many of us were scared by the whole scene.

This Anatomy lecturer said something that has stayed with me since then. He said, "This scene should make everyone of you seriously consider what life is all about."

He added, "If life just consists of the physical, then even goats are better. Because when goats die, they can be eaten, but human beings cannot be eaten."

I thought about that statement and I realized that life must consist of more than what we see physically.

Man is a spirit. The Bible says that God is the Father of spirits: "...shall we not much rather be in subjection unto the father of spirits, and live?" (Hebrews 12:9).

Man Is a Spirit

1. The Inner Man, Inward Man, or Hidden Man

The Bible describes the spirit of a man as the inner man, the inward man or the hidden man. The human body is actually the outward man, and the spirit is the inner man. Notice the terms "inner man", "inward man", or "hidden man" in the Scriptures. "For I delight in the law of God after the inward man" (Romans 7:22); "... strengthened with might by his Spirit in the inner man..." (Ephesians 3:16); "But let it be the hidden man of the heart..." (1 Peter 3:4).

If God is the Father of spirits, then we his children are spirits. That means that our bodies are just containers of the spirit. The Bible also describes the body as a house. "For we know that if our earthly house of this tabernacle were dissolved, we have a building of God, an house not made with hands, eternal in the heavens" (2 Corinthians 5:1).

"And it came to pass, that the beggar died, and was carried by the angels into Abraham's bosom..." (Luke 16:22).

Nothing was said about Lazarus' funeral. He was a poor man. Probably, no one even noticed that he had died. His body was probably thrown into a mass grave. I once passed by an unmarked grave. I saw three men throwing dead bodies from the back of a pick-up truck into a mass grave. I went up to the car and asked, "What are you doing?" They were hospital officials who had been sent to bury unclaimed bodies. I immediately remembered Lazarus and said to myself, "These are modern day Lazaruses."

But that is not the end of the story. After the body of Lazarus died, his spirit lived on!

Lazarus himself—the real man, was carried into Abraham's bosom. Remember also the testimony of the rich man. He had everything in life. He had better health care so he lived longer than Lazarus. Notice that the begger died before the rich man did. However, it came to pass that he also died. He probably had a grand funeral.

Years ago, I attended a funeral of someone whose funeral was very grand indeed. Dignitaries traveled from all over the country to attend the funeral. Special invitation cards were issued for the funeral. The corpse had several changes of clothing during the night. The most amazing part of the funeral was that a new road was actually constructed in the town to enable everybody to attend the funeral in comfort. I don't know if you are aware of the cost of constructing a road— it is very expensive!

No expenses were spared for the funeral of this great rich man. This funeral also reminded me of the rich man in Luke 16. But the story does not end there. The Bible says in Hell, he lifted up his eyes. The man still had eyes even though he was in Hell. He cried to Father Abraham that he should allow Lazarus to dip the tip of his finger in water to cool his tongue. "And in hell he lift up his eyes, being in torments, and seeth Abraham afar off, and Lazarus in his bosom. And he cried [mouth/voice] and said, Father Abraham, have mercy on me, and send Lazarus, that he may dip the tip of his finger in water, and cool my tongue; for I am tormented in this flame" (Luke 16:23,24).

Notice that different parts of the body have been mentioned. The picture of a man is being painted in this Scripture.

2. The Inner Man: The Real Man

The soul and spirit of Lazarus was in Abraham's bosom, and it was the soul and the spirit of the rich man that was experiencing the fires of Hell. The mortal remains of human beings remain on earth long after the spirit has departed to eternal life or damnation.

Dear friend, the Lazarus who was in Abraham's bosom was the real Lazarus. That was the soul and spirit of Lazarus. The rich man who was languishing in Hell was not the rich man who had been buried at that lavish funeral. It was the soul and the spirit of the rich man that was experiencing the fires of Hell. You can verify for yourself, whether the body stays in the grave or not! The mortal remains of human beings remain on earth long after the spirit has departed to eternal life or damnation.

I know that many Christians are not aware of this great reality that they are spirits, souls and bodies. Many Christians wake up in the morning and spend a long time bathing, brushing their teeth and getting ready. Many ladies spend over one hour getting ready to go out. After that they may have a good breakfast or lunch. Then these born-again Christians walk out of the door without even saying a prayer. They do this because they are not aware that they are more than a body. It is because they are not conscious that they are spirits living in a body that they spend all their time on the body only.

Many governments are not aware that a human being is made up of more than just a body and mind. They stress on education and physical fitness but they leave out the real person. Man is a spiritual being first of all! The body is just a mortal container of the human spirit.

It is time for Christians to be aware of the spirit that dwells in them. It is time for us to develop the human spirit. You can develop your human spirit by praying. "He that speaketh in an unknown tongue edifieth [builds up, charges] himself; but he that prophesieth edifieth the church" (1 Corinthians 14:4).

This Scripture speaks about buiding up yourself spiritually. The Bible says that when you speak in tongues you build up, charge and edify yourself spiritually. It is good to do bodily exercises. We are not against that! But what about spiritual exercises? Be conscious of your spirit within. You are a spirit, you have a soul and you live in a body.

2. Developing the human spirit

Christians who are not conscious that they are spirits living in a body, spend all their time on the body. When a person becomes aware of his spirit and soul, he spends time building up and developing the spirit. Man is a spiritual being first of all. The body is just a mortal container of the human spirit.

A Christians develops the human spirit by praying. "He that speaketh in an unknown tongue edifieth [builds up, charges] himself; but he that prophesieth edifieth the church" (1 Corinthians 14:4). This Scripture speaks about buiding up oneself spiritually by praying in tongues; to build up, charge and edify the human spirit.

The Soul of Man

1. What is a soul?

The Bible makes it clear that the soul is different from the spirit. "For the word of God is quick, and powerful, and sharper than any twoedged sword, piercing even to the dividing asunder of soul and spirit..." (Hebrews 4:12).

There is a dividing asunder (demarcation) between the spirit and the soul of a man. There are no clear definitions of the soul in the Bible. What we have are descriptions of the soul's activities. These help us to define what the soul of man is.

There are so many words in the Bible that are used to describe the activities of the soul. A soul can be said to be rejoicing (Psalm 31:7). The soul can magnify and bless the Lord (Psalm 103:2). The soul can be downcast (Psalm 42:5). The soul can be grieved (Judges 10:16). The soul can be discouraged (Numbers 21:4). The soul can be joyful (Psalm 35:9). These are just a few of the emotions that the soul expresses. We can therefore conclude that the soul is a part of man that experiences thoughts and emotions.

You will realize that the soul of the rich man was alive in Hell. The rich man had thoughts, feelings and emotions even though he was dead and in Hell. That is why he could remember Lazarus. The rich man thought things were still the same as when he was alive on earth.

2. What did Jesus say about the soul?

"For what shall it profit a man, if he shall gain the whole world, and lose his own soul?" (Mark 8:36). The spirit and the soul of man pass on into eternity after his death.

Man is a spirit (the inner man). He has a soul (feelings, thoughts and emotions). He lives in a body (the house of flesh). This is the first great principle I am sharing with you. When you know who and what you are, you will live your life in the right way and with the right attitude.

THE SPIRIT OF AN UNSAVED MAN IS DEAD AND DESPERATELY WICKED

When a person is not born again he has an "unsaved" spirit. There are many different ways the Bible describes a non-Christian: an unbeliever, a sinner and an unregenerate person. This is the condition of the human spirit before salvation: "The heart [unsaved spirit] is deceitful above all things, and desperately wicked: who can know it?" (Jeremiah 17:9).

There are some people who distinguish between unbelievers. They say, "This is a good unbeliever and this is a bad one." It is true that there are differences between people. The Word of God makes it abundantly clear that anyone who is not a believer has an unregenerate spirit and is capable of many evil things.

The Need for Regeneration

1. The spiritual state of man makes it necessary.

The fact that an unsaved man is in a terrible spiritual condition is revealed in Romans chapter one. The Bible says that God's wrath is being released against the wickedness of men. "For the wrath of God is revealed from heaven against all ungodliness and unrighteousness of men..." (Romans 1:18).

The human race has forsaken the living God and therefore God has given them up to become dead and darkened in their spirits. "...when they knew God, they glorified him not as God, neither were thankful; but became vain in their imaginations, and their foolish heart was darkened" (Romans 1:21).

The heart of the unsaved person is darkened and degenerate. God has gone a step further and given up mankind so that they may follow their own desires and perverted feelings. "Wherefore God also gave them up to uncleanness through the lusts of their own hearts, to dishonour their own bodies between themselves..." (Romans 1:24).

2. The mind of unsaved man is depraved

Not only is the spirit of the unsaved man darkened with death but the mind of the unsaved human race has also degenerated into a depraved condition. "And even as they did not like to retain God in their knowledge, God gave them over to a reprobate mind, to do those things which are not convenient..." (Romans 1:28).

The sinful human race is filled with every conceivable evil. The long list of evil characteristics are there for your reading. "Being filled with all unrighteousness, fornication, wickedness, covetousness, maliciousness; full of envy, murder, debate, deceit, malignity; whisperers, Backbiters, haters of God, despiteful, proud, boasters, inventors of evil things, disobedient to parents, Without understanding, covenantbreakers, without natural affection, implacable, unmerciful" (Romans 1:29-31).

3. This principle that an unsaved spirit is desperately wicked is manifest all around us.

God has warned against marrying non-Christians because a non-Christian has an unregenerate spirit and is capable of many evil things. One of the things that an unbeliever is filled with is covenant breaking (Romans 1:31).

Most unbelievers do not stick to their word. It is very rare to find an unbeliever who is faithful to his marriage covenant. One man told me, "I have never seen a faithful unbeliever husband before."

As I grew up in life, I came to discover that covenant breaking was a part and parcel of unbelievers' lifestyle. They say, "I will" and "I do", but they won't and they don't. This is the reason why God says Christians should not marry unbelievers. Many young ladies think that the pastors are trying to punish them by telling them not to marry unbelievers. God is trying to prevent your heart from being broken by a covenant breaker!

Do not be deceived by the dignified appearance of the unbeliever. The nature of an unsaved person is described in detail for you in Romans 1:29-31. Believe the Bible more than you believe your eyes. The Bible is the Word of God and is profitable for our instruction.

4. The wicked nature of an unbeliever will manifest sooner or later.

Shakespeare wrote in Macbeth, "There is no art to find the mind's construction in the face."

No one teaches a child to be wicked. Wickedness comes naturally to many little children. Why do children lie, cheat and steal without being taught to do so? It is because the unsaved spirit is at work again. Everyone is born into sin.

5. Man is born into sin.

That explains why man sins so naturally and effortlessly even as children. Our spirits are born in sin and wickedness. "Every one of them is gone back: they are altogether become filthy; there is none that doeth good, no, not one" (Psalm 53:3); " Who can say, I have made my heart clean, I am pure from my sin?" (Proverbs 20:9); "All we like sheep have gone astray; we have turned every one to his own way..." (Isaiah 53:6); "But we are all as an unclean thing, and all our righteousnesses are as filthy rags..." (Isaiah 64:6).

a. The youth also manifest the sinful, wicked nature of man.

When I was in secondary school, I couldn't understand the manifestation of wickedness in some of the students. They devised all sorts of unbelievable punishments. When I was in form one, I experienced torture at the hands of senior students. These senior students were not KGB torture specialists. They were just seniors with an unsaved nature. They could mash chloroquine tablets (a bitter anti-malarial drug) in gari (processed cassava) and give it to people to eat. They had punishments called "tower of liberty" and "monkey dance" which would make all your muscles go into spasms. I was once forced to do a "monkey dance" until I was virtually paralyzed. I couldn't walk for some hours.

Punishments were devised in which you would be sent to collect twenty buckets of manure from a farm two kilometers away. After doing this twenty times, you would have walked eighty kilometers with a heavy load. Where did all these ideas come from? They originated from the depraved and wicked heart of the unsaved man. "For all have sinned, and come short of the glory of God..." (Romans 3:23). I ask myself, "If such people were to come into political power what would they do to their enemies?"

b. All over the world, the depraved and perverted nature of the human race is manifest.

When I hear of the atrocities committed during wars I wonder, "What is happening to the human race?" Wickedness abounds in the heart of man because the heart of the unsaved man is dead and desperately wicked. This is not something that affects just White people or Black people—it is the nature of all mankind. "The heart is deceitful above all things, and desperately wicked: who can know it?" (Jeremiah 17:9).

During the Liberian Civil War, we heard of people being fed to the lions. One Liberian refugee told me how the rebel soldiers would throw children into a well. When the well was full of children, they would pour kerosene on top of the screaming children and light a fire. The soldiers would burn a whole well of little children. These are real things that actually happened!

Why are human beings so wicked and evil at heart? Why is it that when the opportunity presents itself, we see incredible acts of savagery? "The good man is perished out of the earth: and there is none upright among men..." (Micah 7:2).

A Lebanese man described something that he experienced during the war in Lebanon. He said, "One group would capture some prisoners that belonged to another faction. Then they would amputate the legs and arms of the captives and put the trunk (head, chest and abdomen, without legs and arms) of the people in a car and dispatch them to their homes." He told me how a friend's brother's arms and legs were amputated and how terrible an experience it was. He continued, "The limbless man was in such a pitiful condition that my friend had to shoot his own brother to end the torture."

These acts of barbarism are manifestations of a depraved and reprobate human race. Why is the world filled with homosexuals? Why do millions of people commit fornication and adultery on a daily basis? Why does stealing, killing and injustice abound everywhere? The world has got over five billion greedy, corrupt, degenerate and selfish people. God has given up the human race to its perverted way of life.

c. **It is this unsaved and degenerate people that Jesus came to the earth to save.**

"But God commendeth his love toward us, in that, while we were yet sinners, Christ died for us" (Romans 5:8).

This is why Jesus said a man has to be born again because the first time round, we were born in sin and we were conceived in evil. "Behold, I was shapen in iniquity; and in sin did my mother conceive me" (Psalm 51:5).

A New Creation

1. A PERSON'S ESSENTIAL NATURE IS CHANGED WITH THE SPIRITUAL BIRTH.

Another term for born again is regeneration. When you are born again, your essential nature is changed. That is why the Bible says when a man is in Christ, he is a new creature. God makes a new creation out of the old corrupt man.

When a man dies, there is no way you can keep him at home. No matter how much you love your brother, when the condition called death lays its icy hands on him you have to part company. The dead person must go to the mortuary and then to the grave. Husbands and wives who love each other have to part when death comes to lay hold on one of them. Why is this? The body of your loved one is dead. It begins to decay and degenerate. There is no way by which you can stay together.

God told Adam and Eve, "...in the day that thou eatest thereof thou shalt surely die" (Genesis 2:17). When Adam and Eve sinned, they died. The condition of spiritual death entered their spirits and it became impossible for God tofellowship with them anymore. He had to expel them from the garden and separate them from himself. The whole human race is separated from God because of sin.

Before a man is regenerated, he is estranged from God. His nature is essentially evil, corrupt and wicked: "The good man is perished out of the earth: and there is none upright among men..." (Micah 7:2).

2. SALVATION BREAKS THE WALL THAT SEPARATES MANKIND FROM GOD AS A RESULT OF SPIRITUAL DEATH.

"...and hath broken down the middle wall of partition between us...that he might reconcile both unto God..." (Ephesians 2:14,16).

That is why democracy and the rule of law are important. When one man with such a nature has unlimited power, he does many evil things.

In every nation where there is a military dictator, inconceivable atrocities take place. People are arrested and disappear into "thin air", whilst hard-earned properties are arbitrarily confiscated. Stories of torture, brutality and murder abound. Viciousness in secret and in the open, has always been the order of the day with tyrannical rulers.

A tyrant is simply an unsaved man who has unlimited power. That is why governments are supposed to have three different independent arms: the executive, the legislature and the judiciary. There is supposed to be a separation of powers. This is to prevent one group of "unsaved men" from having too much power over other human beings.

The law is supposed to protect the average citizen from the political powers that be. However, it is unfortunate that in many cases the executive controls the legislature and the judiciary, thereby giving absolute power to a few people. As Lord Acton (1834-1902) said in a letter to Bishop Mandell Creighton, "Power tends to corrupt and absolute power corrupts absolutely." When Judges are afraid for their lives and their jobs, they often cannot make unbiased decisions.

The difference betweem Christianity and every other religion is simple.

3. Christianity claims to change the essential nature of a man

Man is converted into a brand new creature with a brand new heart. In the Old Testament, the prophets predicted that the day would come when God would take out the stony heart and replace it with a heart of flesh. "A new heart also will I give you, and a new spirit will I put within you: and I will take away the stony heart out of your flesh, and I will give you an heart of flesh" (Ezekiel 36:26)

When a man is in Christ, he is a new person. He is regenerated. His spirit, the inner nature, is born again. There is a rebirth of the human spirit: "...that which is born of the Spirit is spirit" (John 3:6).

4. Outward changes are not the answer.

Obeying a set of rules does not change our hearts. Being born again is what affords every man the opportunity to have a new heart.

If you take a pig and wash it, bathe it and dress it up in a wedding suit, all you have is a dressed up pig. This same pig will return to the filth which it is used to because that is its essential nature.

I believe with all my heart that it is only a change in the unsaved nature of a man that can bring about a change in this world. New Year's resolutions and obeying rules do not change anything because the spirit of the unsaved man is dead and desperately wicked. No one toys with a dead thing. Dead things must be separated from living things. The only hope for a dead and wicked human spirit is the miracle of rebirth in Jesus Christ.

THE SPIRIT OF A SAVED MAN IS RIGHTEOUS AND TRULY HOLY

The new creation is righteous and truly holy. In other words, a man who is saved has undergone a radical transformation of the heart. Being born again is a spiritual operation in which God recreates your spirit. He takes out the old hardened and depraved heart and puts in a new righteous spirit.

His spirit is now a new creation in Christ. He is not a renovated and repainted version of an old thing. He is brand new. He is indeed newly created by God: "Therefore if any man be in Christ, he is a new creature: old things are passed away; behold, all things are become new" (2 Corinthians 5:17).

The New Life in Christ

1. Putting on the new man

So what happens next? What are we supposed to do when we are born or created again? "And that ye put on the new man, which after God is created in righteousness and true holiness" (Ephesians 4:24). This Scripture informs us that we are actually righteous when we are born again. God expects us to must put on (act like) the new spirit which is created in righteousness and true holiness.

The believer is God's workmanship created in Christ Jesus unto good works (Ephesians 2:10). Many times we come to God and say things that are not true. In an attempt to sound humble, we tell the Lord that we are sinners and we are not worthy to approach His throne. But that is not the case anymore. You are not a sinner anymore! You were a sinner. You are not unworthy anymore. You were unworthy some time ago. But now that you are born again, you are the righteousness of God. You are God's workmanship created in Christ Jesus unto good works (Ephesians 2:10).

Please do not insult God's new creation. Do not think you can impress God with self-demeaning prayers. It is time for you to acknowledge what God has done to your heart. The Bible says we are the righteousness of God in Christ Jesus. "For he hath made him to be sin for us, who knew no sin; that we might be made the righteousness of God in him" (2 Corinthians 5:21). If we are the righteousness of God, that means that we cannot be more righteous than we are today. The righteousness of God is the highest form of purity and "sinlessness". God is describing the status of the recreated human spirit.

Somebody once said, "I don't feel any different now that I'm born again!" This is not about feelings but about realities that have taken place. Can you feel your liver? Or your small intestines? Obviously not! But they exist within you!

If surgery was performed and your appendix was taken out, the doctors would inform you that they had removed a part of your intestine. Although you cannot feel that a part of your large intestines has been removed, you are supposed to accept the fact of what took place in your abdomen during the surgery. After the surgery, you are supposed to listen to the doctors' advice on how to live after such an operation. Sometimes the doctors will tell you not to eat certain types of food anymore, because that part of the intestines which digests such food has been taken out. You are told how to live after the surgery.

In the same way, God tells you how to live after being born again or recreated. Being born again is a spiritual operation in which God recreates your spirit. He takes out the old hardened and depraved heart and puts in a new righteous spirit. You don't feel it, but it is real. You are supposed to be aware of what has taken place and acknowledge it.

2. Acknowledging the New Man

We are to acknowledge our new nature. "That the communication of thy faith may become effectual by the acknowledging of every good thing which is in you in Christ Jesus" (Philemon 6). The Bible teaches us to acknowledge the good things that are in us because we are Christians.

We are not supposed to go around saying negative things about ourselves. If you say, "I am a badperson," you are hurting yourself. If you say, "I'm stupid!" or "I am a sinner" you are saying something that is contrary to the Word of God. It's time to acknowledge good things about yourself.

Any born-again Christian who lives in sin is living contrary to his new nature. If he continues in sin, it is by his own choice because the power of sin is broken and God has given him a new nature. It is no longer natural to do evil, it is against his very nature as a new creation.

Before you get born again, there are evil things you do without even noticing. After you're saved, something within tells you, 'This is wrong! Don't do it!" That is the new man crying from within. The Bible says, "Put on the new man." Act like a new person because you are new.

I became a medical doctor on the 10th of March 1989. On the 11th of March I didn't feel any different, in fact, I still felt like a student. I had to tell myself, "Hey, you are now a doctor. Act like one! Stop acting like a student and act like who you really are!" This is what God is saying to His "new creation" children, "You are new, righteous and truly holy. Act like it and walk in the newness of life." "Lie not one to another, seeing that you have put off the old man with his deeds; And have put on the new man, which is renewed..." (Colossians 3:9,10).

Acknowledging good things will make our faith come alive. Say to yourself, "I am the righteousness of God," "I'm a new person!," "I can make it!","I am holy", These confessions will take you out of sin into a life of practical holiness. There is always something on the inside that must work on the outside. Righteousness on the inside is working on the outside.

The Gift of Righteousness

1. Righteousness cannot be earned through any human effort or work.

The Bible says, "...much more they which receive abundance of grace and of the gift of righteousness shall reign in life..." (Romans 5:17). It is impossible to attain God's standards by your own efforts. "...all our righteousnesses are as filthy rags..." (Isaiah 64:6).

A born-again Christian has been instantaneously transformed into a righteous, new man. He can only increase his faith in his inherited righteousness, by practising more of his true nature.

2. Righteousness has an effect on the believer.

The believer who is conscious of his righteousness in Christ, will become as bold as a lion (Proverbs 28:1).

Through righteousness, he will rule and dominate in this life. I see you dominating the enemy through righteousness! I see you overcoming your adversaries through the gift of righteousness in Christ Jesus! Your right standing with God is truly a gift from your Heavenly Father. It is something you can never earn through human effort. Stand up now and become a world overcomer! You are no longer under condemnation!

AFTER SALVATION, THE SPIRIT OF MAN IS A NEWBORN BABY AND IT MUST GROW

The Bible calls new converts spiritual babies. When a person gets saved, a spiritual baby is birthed into the world. In much the same way that a baby matures into adulthood, it is important that the spiritual baby matures into an adult Christian. "As newborn babes, desire the sincere milk of the word, that ye may grow thereby" (1 Peter 2:2).

There are times when people have the wrong impression about what Christianity offers. The evangelist preaches and says, "Tonight is your night! Your life will never be the same again after today." He goes on, "After tonight, every yoke shall be broken in your life." He declares, "All you who are heavy laden must come to Jesus and He will give you rest!" This gives a feeling of an instantaneous breakthrough. But Christianity is not an instantaneous cure to all the ills of man!

The Christian's Process of Growth

Being born again is just the beginning of a long process. The spiritual baby must go through all the stages of growth and development. Without growth, the effect of Christ on his life is often not seen. There is very little difference between an unbeliever and a baby "born-again" Christian who has not bothered to grow. That is why we ask all converts to go to church and receive the Word so they can grow in the faith. If Jesus had not grown out of the baby stage to an adult man of 30 years, we would not have been saved by Him! Growth is important to bring out the true nature of the body.

Every Christian must go through three important stages of development: the baby stage, the childhood stage and then the stage of mature adulthood.

1. THE SPIRITUAL BABY

"As newborn babes, desire the sincere milk of the word, that ye may grow thereby:" (1 Peter 2:2). When a Christian is at the baby stage of his development, he has all the characteristics of a natural baby. All babies cry a lot. If you want to know if there is a baby in the house, just stand outside the gate and sooner or later you will hear some cries.

A spiritual baby is easily offended. Anyone who is easily offended is an immature spiritual baby. Little things offend him and he is always upset about one thing or the other. All churches have a lot of babies who are offended when the pastor does not say "hello" or visit them. Life is full of offenses. Those who offend you are often those close to you. Ask yourself: Am I easily offended? Do I always have something to complain about?

Perhaps you are a spiritual baby! Baby Christians, just like natural babies, are unable to help or control themselves. A baby defecates anytime, anywhere and in front of anyone. There are no controls whatsoever. A spiritual baby is unable to control his fleshly appetites. He continues to live in sin. He lives according to the dictates of his flesh and does whatever he feels like doing.

As you mature, you still have certain feelings but you don't yield to them unless it is appropriate. If you are living in immorality and have no control over your flesh, then you are probably a spiritual baby. A spiritual baby cannot help himself. He needs someone to counsel him and pray for him. Do you always need someone to pray for you? Can you not pray for yourself? Can you not read the Bible and seek for understanding yourself? If you cannot, then perhaps you are a baby in Christ!

2. THE CHILDHOOD STAGE

A child is unsteady and unstable; it is difficult to hold the attention of a child for more than a few minutes. "That we henceforth be no more children, tossed to and fro, and carried about..." (Ephesians 4:14). As attention span of children is very short, they are often unstable and unreliable. Any Christian who is carried about by every new "a la mode" pastor is a child. If you move around from church to church every few months, you are immature.

The pastor in each church cannot keep the attention of that childlike Christian for more than a few months or years. A man who constantly changes his mind about who he wants to marry is a child at heart. He is unsteady, tossed to and fro by every wind of doctrine and prophecy. Any Christian who can be made to leave his church because of a prophecy delivered to him by the new prophet is simply a child.

There are many childlike Christians in the Church today. Nothing satisfies them for more than a few minutes. Initially they are excited by the good Word. After this, they feel they need special prayers and anointing. After that, they are convinced that a holy bath is what will solve their problems. Nothing seems to satisfy them and they are always sniffing for something new. They come into the church full of praises for the church and its pastor. After a few months, they have changed their minds about what they said initially.

Another sign of a childlike Christian is that he engages in fruitless playful activity. He does not contribute to the home in any way. My children contribute nothing to the upkeep of the home. They eat food everyday without knowing where the food comes from. In fact, my children have never asked where the food on the table comes from. They are just happy to enjoy the provision!

A Christian who is in the childhood stage does not contribute to the growth of the church. He witnesses to no one and he invites no one. He does not support financially and does not pay his first and best fruits (tithes).

Ask yourself this question, "How much money does your child contribute to the upkeep of your home?" Nothing! Is he a part of your home? Certainly! He just plays and makes the house dirty, but contributes nothing. If you are part of a church but contribute nothing to make the church grow and prosper, you are a playful child who is enjoying good sermons free of charge. You are certainly a part of the church but you contribute nothing! You win no souls! You invite no one to church! You only come to church when you feel like it. Indeed you are a spiritual child!

3. Spiritual adulthood

When you reach the stage of maturity, you begin to love the meat of the Word. "But strong meat belongeth to them that are of full age..." (Hebrews 5:14). Bible study and the teaching of the Word are what enchant your spirit. Because the church is comprised of many babies and children, you will discover that a large number of Christians are not interested in the teaching of the Word. They want something dramatic and spectacular. Crowds of people gather when there is a sensational minister in the house.

A mature person understands the deep things of the Word of God. A mature person knows that he cannot live on signs, wonders and miracles. He knows that it is the Word that matters.

Another important feature of a mature person is that he is skilful in the Word of God. "...everyone that useth milk is unskilful in the word of righteousness: for he is a babe" (Hebrews 5:13).

To be skilful in the Word means to be able to share the Word of God effectively with others, through teaching and preaching. Do not make a mistake; every Christian is supposed to develop until he is able to preach and teach. It is not only pastors who are supposed to preach the Word of God. Preaching and teaching is characteristic of the mature stage of Christian development: "For when for the time ye ought to be teachers, ye have need that one teach you..." (Hebrews 5:12).

There is a time when every Christian must be a teacher of God's Word. Let this be your goal from today. Decide to be someone who is involved in teaching and preaching the Word of God. Keep on growing spiritually until you are able to preach and teach the Word of God. Move on from there to the higher realms of ministry that God has for You!

How to Develop the Human Spirit

"Developing your spirit" is another way to describe growing in spirit.

The mind of the human race is developed in schools and colleges. Consequently, we have made significant strides in science and medicine. Money and time are also spent to develop the body. There are keep fit clubs and gyms everywhere. The body is being developed into grotesque muscular giants. But dear friend, you are more than a body. You are more than a mind! You are a spirit living in a body and you have a mind. You must also develop your spirit. The question is, "How do you develop your spirit into maturity?"

1. The Word of God

The first key to developing the human spirit is the Word of God (1 Peter 2:2). Allow the Word of God to enter your spirit through your quiet time, Bible study and Bible reading. Every Christian must have a quiet time everyday.

Moses was a man who had a quiet time with the Lord; he went up to the mountain early in the morning to meet with the Lord. He took two tables of stone to write down the revelations that God would give him. "...Hew thee two tables of stone... And be ready in the morning, and come up in the morning... and present thyself there... And no man shall come up with thee..." (Exodus 34:1-3).

A quiet time of Bible study and prayer is the most consistent way to feed your spirit. Your spirit does not grow unless it is fed on the Word of God.

Another good way of taking in the Word is by listening to tapes. The second best way by which I have fed my spirit over the years is through listening to preaching tapes. "So then faith cometh by hearing, and hearing by the word of God" (Romans 10:17). God has given pastors and teachers to perfect the saints. You can receive the Word through these anointed men of God.

2. Praying in tongues

Another way that you can develop your spirit is by praying in tongues. Every Christian must develop the art of spending hours praying in the spirit.

The Bible says you build up yourself in the faith when you pray in the Holy Ghost. Praying in the Holy Ghost is the same as praying in tongues. "But ye, beloved, building up yourselves on your most holy faith, praying in the Holy Ghost..." (Jude 20).

Pray in tongues for an hour everyday and see what will happen in your spiritual life over the next three months. I guarantee you a change in your spiritual life if you will do this simple exercise. The Bible teaches us that you are spiritually charged and built up when you speak in tongues. "He that speaketh in an unknown tongue edifieth himself..." (1 Corinthians 14:4).

The Word and prayer will cause you to develop in the spirit and to become a giant for the Lord. Walk in these two keys of spiritual growth and nothing will be held back from you. I see God taking you out of your hiding place! I see him placing you before kings and prominent men as you develop your spirit!

AFTER SALVATION, THE MIND IS STILL THE SAME; IT MUST BE RENEWED

"And be not conformed to this world: but be ye transformed by the renewing of your mind, that ye may prove what is that good, and acceptable, and perfect, will of God" (Romans 12:2).

Salvation and the Mind

1. The mind is not recreated.

At the new birth, a Christian receives a new heart from God and not a new mind. It is therefore the duty of every Christian to renew his mind. There are many Christians who are genuine new creations but still have unrenewed minds.

A good church which constantly preaches and teaches the Word of God, will help in the renewing of the mind. There are many people who think that they know all there is to know in the Word of God. No one knows everything! The unconscious, incompetent person is pitiful because he does not know that he does not know!

Every Christian must decide to be a constant learner of the Word of God. He must never stop learning. You will always discover things that you do not know. Years ago I heard a pastor giving a testimony of his life. He spoke about how he got born again. Before he was saved, he was a pornographer by profession. That means he was someone who acted in pornographic films and posed for pornographic photographs. Sex was his work and he didn't see anything wrong with it.

He told us one day, "After I got born-again, I continued to live in fornication. I slept with one girl after the other and I never thought twice about it. It never occurred to me that there was something wrong with sleeping with someone you're not married to."

He continued, "I thought I was being a loving person to many girls. After all, love is a commandment from God."

One night, he was in bed with one of the girls when suddenly, a huge black figure appeared at the foot of his bed and he woke up in great fright. He was terrified and thought to himself, "Something is not right!"

The next day he decided to read the Bible and discovered where the Word of God says fornication is wrong. " But fornication, and all uncleaness...let it not be once named among you, as becometh saints..." (Ephesians 5:3). Believe it or not, this man was born again but because of his background, he did not even know that fornication was a sin. It could be that because of your background you are not even aware that certain things are sin.

2. The Mind Must Be Renewed

A person's background prior to salvation contributes to what he knows and believes; it therefore forms his character and directs the way he behaves. For instance, there are Christians who are prejudiced or even racist; and there are pastors who are racist in their thoughts and decisions.

Without even realizing it, we carry on doing wrong things although we are genuinely born again in our hearts. That is why we need the Word of God to renew our minds: "...be ye transformed by the renewing of your mind..." (Romans 12:2).

It is actually the renewing of our minds that brings about a visible transformation. When I became a Christian, I thought God wanted us to be poor. Somehow, my background taught me that poverty was more righteous than being prosperous. If you read the Bible, your mind will be renewed and your attitude will change. Transformation comes when the mind is renewed. The real change we look for in Christians comes through a renewal of the mind in the Word of God. Transformation comes when the mind is renewed. See your mind as a computer which has to be programmed. Whatever you feed into the mind is what will come out.

How to Renew the Mind

1. Read the Bible

Reading the Bible and receiving the Word of God causes a renewing of the mind and as result, a change in attitude. The old thoughts and ideas will be cleared out as you receive the Word. Jesus himself said, "Now ye are clean through the word which I have spoken unto you" (John 15:3).

2. Join a good church

The mind is also renewed by joining the right church and learning the right things. As a Christian receives the Word through his pastor, he will gradually experience a change in his mind, his way of thinking. "That he might sanctify and cleanse it with the washing of water by the word..." (Ephesians 5:26). That is why it is so important that you choose the right church to attend.

It is true that you are a new creation, but you also need a renewed mind. It is the renewed mind that will make you live out the new life. When people see the new life, they will know that something real has happened to you!

AFTER SALVATION, THE BODY IS STILL THE SAME; IT MUST BE KEPT UNDER CONTROL

There is no change in man's physical body following the spiritual birth. This important fact of the body being the same, will help the new Christian to understand why he still experiences the old feelings of jealousy, hatred, anger and lust, for example.

"But I keep under my body, and bring it into subjection..." (1 Corinthians 9:27). When you get saved, you must know that your body is the same old body. When you come forward to the altar and give your life to Christ, you do not change physically. If you were tall and skinny before salvation, you will still be tall and skinny after salvation. If you had long hair before you got born again, you'll still have long hair after salvation. What does this mean? Does it mean that nothing has happened to you? Not at all! Your spirit is recreated in God.

The body is still the same and you must realize this all important fact. Sometimes people give their lives to Christ and they believe that everything is going to be different from then. However, when they get home, they begin to feel the old feelings they felt before salvation. They experience lust within their bodies. They feel the old feelings of jealousy, hatred and anger. Now because they do not know this truth (that the body is unchanged), the devil begins to tell them, "You are not a real Christian", You are not saved", "You cannot be born again!"

Satan continues to harass you and says, "If you were really born again, such a thought or feeling would never occur to you."

The devil tells you, "None of the Christians sitting in this church has the kind of thoughts you have."

But that is a lie! We all have thoughts and feelings that we don't want to have even though we are born again.

The Need to Contend with the Flesh

1. The body must be brought under control.

Everyone who is born again still has the flesh to contend with. The apostle Paul was concerned about his flesh. He knew that his body was still the same and that it could disgrace him one day. "...I keep UNDER [control] my BODY, and bring it into subjection: lest that by any means, when I have preached to others, I myself should be a castaway" (1 Corinthians 9:27). Apostle Paul is the one who had personal revelations of Jesus Christ; he wrote half of the New Testament. He had so many visions and revelations of Jesus Christ. Very few people have had such spiritual experiences. Paul was one of the greatest apostles with signs and wonders following him. He raised the dead and the bites of snakes had no effect on him.

Yet, this great man was worried about his flesh. He felt his flesh could disgrace him at any time. That is why he kept his flesh under constant control. Notice what he said in the book of Romans. He declared that there was nothing good in his flesh. Even though he was born again, his flesh (body) was still the same. "For I know that in me (that is, in my flesh,) dwelleth no good thing..." (Romans 7:18).

No matter who you are, you still have a body to keep under control. Have you ever seen a spirit smoking or drinking alcohol? Certainly not! Spirits don't smoke. It is the flesh that drinks and smokes. Have you ever seen a spirit committing fornication? Surely not! It is the flesh that does all these evil things! That is why the Bible teaches us to present our bodies as a living sacrifice.

2. Identifying the works of the flesh

The works of the flesh are listed in Galatians chapter five: "Now the works of the flesh are manifest, which are these; Adultery, fornication, uncleanness, lasciviousness, Idolatry, witchcraft, hatred, variance, emulations, wrath, strife, seditions, heresies, Envyings, murders, drunkenness, revellings, and such like: of the which I tell you before, as I have..." (Galatians 5:19-21).

These works are not the works of Satan or evil spirits. They are the works of the flesh. The flesh is a real burden that we are saddled with through this life. That is why we have no confidence in the flesh (Philippians 3:3).

You are capable of everything you see listed in Galatians 5:19-21. That is why we must be merciful to Christians who fall into sin, because when we consider our own selves, we realize that we experience similar temptations and feelings in our flesh. "Brethren, if a man be overtaken in a fault, ye which are spiritual, restore such an one in the spirit of meekness; considering thyself, lest thou also be tempted" (Galatians 6:1).

Christians and Sin

One day I went to visit a friend of mine. He was a hardened sinner who was not interested in being born again. I sat with him in his bedroom and we chatted for many hours. At a point, the Holy Spirit made a way for me to witness to him about Christ. That was his day of salvation. For the first time, he listened to me as I preached to him. When I finished, he asked me, "What must I do?"

I said, "Let us pray and I will lead you to the Lord."

After I led him in the sinner's prayer, he looked at me and said, "Dag, thank you very much. I feel I am a changed person."

Then I thought, "If I have been able to lead my friend to the Lord, why don't I lead him to receive the baptism of the Holy Spirit?" I decided to do just that. I laid hands on him and to my surprise he received the Holy Spirit and began to speak in tongues fluently. Suddenly, something else happened.

When I touched him, he was "slain in the Spirit" and fell on his bed. He continued to bubble in tongues for some time. After about an hour, I decided to leave and come back to see him later. About five hours later, I returned to his house to visit him. When I got to the gate his sister told me that she didn't think he was home, but I went to his apartment anyway. When I got there, something told me to pause at the door before going in. I stood at the door and what did I hear? My new convert was fornicating in the bedroom with his girlfriend. Oh dear! So soon after a wonderful salvation experience and the Holy Ghost baptism! I was aghast!

Less than five hours ago this man had received Christ and was gloriously filled with the Holy Spirit. I personally ministered to him and heard him speak in tongues, and saw him "slain in the Spirit". How could he return so quickly into fornication? I asked myself, "Was this man really born again?" Does being born again have any effect on a person? The answer is: Yes, it does!

If anyone was ever born again and filled with the Holy Spirit, this friend of mine was. But the reality was that his body was still the same and was capable of committing all the sins of the flesh. As a baby Christian, my new convert had yielded his flesh to all the old sins. His flesh had once more engaged itself in sin, because it had not been affected by the "born again" experience. His flesh was still the same!

Never forget this! Even though you are born again, your flesh is still the same, you must keep it under control otherwise it will lead you into sin.

Practical ways to Control the Flesh

1. Be conscious of possible danger.

The Christian must be aware of the potential evil that is in his flesh. He should not give opportunities to his flesh: "...only use not liberty for an occasion to the flesh..." (Galatians 5:13). The reason why boarding schools have separate houses for boys and girls is because the school authorities do not want to give occasion and opportunity to the flesh. Fasting on a regular weekly basis is helpful in controlling the flesh.

2. Escape from temptations.

God warns clearly, "Flee youthful lusts" (2 Timothy 2:22). If God knew we could have won the fight for fleshly control, he would have told us to fight. On the contrary he urges us to run. When God says run, then you must run! Don't stand and fight. Flee for your life! Your body is still the same. Don't trust yourself to your flesh; there is no good thing in your body.

Give no place to the devil and give no opportunity to your flesh! "Neither give place to the devil" (Ephesians 4:27). If a Christian exposes himself to certain temptations, he will fall. What he needs is wisdom to help him stay far away from dangerous enticements of the flesh.

At the second coming of Jesus Christ, our human bodies shall be changed; transformed into immortal and incorruptible bodies.

There will be a permanent escape from sin; we will no longer be capable of sin. "...We shall not all sleep, but we shall all be changed... for the trumpet shall sound, and the dead shall be raised incorruptible, and we shall be changed. For this corruptible must put on incorruption, and this mortal must put on immortality" (1 Corinthians 15:51-53).

AFTER YOU ARE BORN AGAIN, YOUR MIND IS STILL OPEN TO ALL KINDS OF THOUGHTS; YOU MUST LEARN TO THINK ON THE RIGHT THINGS

"Finally, brethren, whatsoever things are true, whatsoever things are honest, whatsoever things are just, whatsoever things are pure, whatsoever things are lovely, whatsoever things are of good report; if there be any virtue, and if there be any praise, think on these things" (Philippians 4:8).

You may be a born-again Christian. You may keep your body under subjection. You may renew your mind on the Word of God regularly. But this does not close your mind to the attacks of the devil. Your mind is still open to all kinds of thoughts from the devil.

1. SATAN APPEALS TO THE MIND.

A born-again Christian has his mind is still open to all kinds of thoughts from the devil (Matthew 4:1; Mark 1:12; Luke 4:1). His mind is subject to the attacks of the devil.

When Satan attacked Jesus, he attacked His mind by appealing to His mind. The devil will always appeal to our minds.

The Bible teaches the believer to fight against these appeals from the devil and to cast down imaginations. "Casting down imaginations, and every high thing that exalteth itself against the knowledge of God, and bringing into captivity every thought to the obedience of Christ" (2 Corinthians 10:5). He must learn to capture his thoughts and make them obedient to the Word of God.

2. SATAN'S MOST POWERFUL TOOL IS "SUGGESTION".

The mind is the battleground. Jesus was tempted through the avenue of his thoughts. The fact that you are a Christian does not mean that you will only have good thoughts. A thought is like a bird that flies over a person's head. It may land on his head, but it must not be allowed to make a nest on his head. When ungodly thoughts come to the Christian, he must resist them immediately. That is the fight of every born-again Christian: to keep his mind pure at all times.

Some Christians are plagued with fear and worry. Fear is one of the terrible thoughts of the devil. Whilst working on the hospital ward as a medical student, I remember seeing many young patients die. I began to think about their plight and a spirit of fear oppressed me. The thoughts were so overwhelming that I had to sleep in order to forget what I was thinking about. Many times I saw myself sick and dying of the same diseases. I imagined my funeral and I imagined what I would look like in the coffin. I thought about all those who would attend my funeral and I worked out every detail in my mind. Fear is an oppressive spirit that works through the mind.

3. Resist the devil.

Whether it is worry, fear, or lust, the Christian must learn to cast down wrong imaginations. Thus he resists the devil. When the Word of God says the Christian must resist the devil, it means that he must resist the thoughts and suggestions that come from the pit of Hell.

The Bible tells us exactly what to think about. It tells us to think of things that are pure, holy and peaceful. "Finally, brethren, whatsoever things are true, whatsoever things are honest, whatsoever things are just, whatsoever things are pure, whatsoever things are lovely, whatsoever things are of good report; if there be any virtue, and if there be any praise, think on these things" (Philippians 4:8).

Gaining Control of the Mind

1. One of the best ways to control our thoughts is to listen to preaching tapes.
2. Christian music and videos are good tools to help in controlling the thoughts.
3. We must not give place to the devil. We give place to the devil when we allow evil thoughts to settle in our minds. Then, they will oppress and obsess a person until he becomes possessed.

A NEW UNDERSTANDING OF SALVATION

A new understanding of the concept of salvation through these seven great principles will enable the child of God to grow in grace. "Wisdom is the principal thing; therefore get wisdom, and with all thy getting get understanding. Exalt her, and she shall promote thee...a crown of glory shall she deliver to thee" (Proverbs 4:7-9).

In all your getting, get understanding. Wisdom is the principal thing. People who understand what is happening are the people who will experience God's victory. I see you blessed as you understand these seven great principles!

Eternal Destinations

7

■ A BIBLICAL LOOK AT LIFE AFTER DEATH

One sight which is common in every city, every town, and every village, is the funeral procession or burial service.

In my home city of Accra, Ghana, cemeteries get very busy at weekends. And though we would rather not think about it, funerals are a constant reminder that in the midst of life, death is ever present with us.

During memorial services, glowing tribute is paid to the dead (even if they were bad people)! We sob and show our grief with mournful church music in the background. While attending a funeral at Mankessim (a small town on the south coast of Ghana), I had the opportunity to learn about some of the elaborate rituals performed for the dead. The corpse had several changes of clothing (more like a fashion show)! First, it was wrapped in Kente—a rich, colourful, hand-woven cloth. Then it was dressed in a suit. Afterwards, in a Freemason's uniform, etc. In fact, there was a superfluous show of belated affection as friends and relations fussed over the corpse, stumbling over each other to pay their last respects. A new road leading to the funeral grounds had even been constructed. As you can see, funerals in Africa are BIG events!

Now like this man, many people known to us have died. Expired! Passed away! But...wait a minute! Where did all these departed souls go? I mean our friends, relations and loved ones who died, "Where did they go?" Think about it. Did they just slip into their graves to "rest in peace"? Or did they vanish mysteriously elsewhere? What happened to the victims of war in Bosnia, Rwanda and all the other war-torn parts of the world? And what happened to the many AIDS victims who died?

Can anyone tell me where our ancestors are right now? One thing we know for sure is, they are no longer with us. So where did they go? As a medical doctor, I have probably seen more people dying than the average man. With our high mortality rate in Africa, death is not a rare sight in some Ghanaian hospitals.

I remember my horror when, as a new medical student, I first entered the mortuary. The place was filled with the stench of death, and all around me were naked bodies of men, women and children. Some were young, others were old. Most had been struck down in the prime of life. Rich and poor lay side by side, all pride and dignity forgotten in this helpless state.

Really, I think everybody should at one stage in life, visit a mortuary. Then maybe we would realize the uselessness of this temporary life. As the Bible says, "All is vanity". As medical students working at the Accident Centre, we could encounter up to ten fatalities from one road accident alone. It was very distressing, and made one wonder where all these souls were going.

When a man dies, his spirit leaves his body. Without the spirit the body is dead. When Jesus died on the cross, the Bible makes us to know that He yielded up the ghost. This means that He gave up the spirit. His spirit came out of His body.

Likewise, we learn in the seventh chapter of Acts that when Stephen was being stoned to death, he said, "Lord Jesus, receive my spirit."

We can see here that when a man dies, his spirt moves from one point to another. The spirit cannot be affected by physical death. Although the body itself decomposes and returns to dust, the spirit lives on eternally. But where do their spirits go?

BEYOND THE GRAVE

1. Judgement

I have seen people die on the wards very often. You can almost see their spirits coming out of them as they gasp for their last breath. One minute they are alive, the next minute...they "pop off". Gone!

But where do their spirits go? Let's go beyond the grave and find out where they went. You see, according to God's Word, there is an appointment we must all keep after death. "...it is appointed unto men once to die, but after this the judgement" (Hebrews 9:27).

Basically, this judgement is a time for separation: when Christ (our Judge) takes His own (those who have yielded their lives to Him), and casts the rebellious sinners into Hell. "...and HE SHALL SEPARATE THEM one from another, as a shepherd divideth his sheep from the goats" (Matthew 25:32).

Talking about unrepentant sinners, Jesus said: "And these shall go away into everlasting punishment: but the righteous into life eternal" (Matthew 25:46).

2. Destinations

There are only two destinations beyond the grave: Heaven and Hell. The spirits of those who were righteous in Christ go to be with the Father in Heaven, while the spirits of those who rejected Jesus will be cast down to Hell.

Dear friend, there is more to life than marriage, money and your retirement home. I know a man who has a special bank account for his burial. He has everything planned out carefully to the last detail. Others have given elaborate instructions concerning their coffins and their graves. But that is where their plans end. Little do they realize that they are going beyond the grave!

If there are only two destinations beyond the grave after death, then there cannot be a third place —"Purgatory". Here, a soul is supposed to be kept for a while, until he is purged from his sins and carried to Heaven. That is just another lie of the devil!

HELL: A PLACE OF TORMENT

Hell is not a reform school. According to Mark 9:44, it is a place: "Where their worm dieth not, and the fire is not quenched."

Our Judge himself warns us about Hell and its unimaginable horrors, and offers us a wonderful and better alternative-Heaven. He said: "...I go and prepare a place for you...that where I am, there ye may be also" (John14:3).

One reason why we can believe in the existence of Hell is that Jesus himself preached more about Hell than many other subjects! For example, in the book of Luke, Chapter 16, Jesus recounts the story of the rich man and Lazarus in graphic detail.

Notice that this is no parable. In fact, Jesus began by saying, "There was a certain rich man..." In other words, there existed a particular person, not a figment of His own imagination. It goes on to say that the rich man died, and was buried. "And in hell he lift up his eyes, being in torments..." (Luke 16:23). Note that though his body had been buried, he could still see, hear and feel tormented. All this was happening in a particular place—a "place of torment" (verse 28). These events actually occurred somewhere. And that place is real.

Location of Hell

1. According to God's Word, Hell is beneath us.

Its specific geographical location is underground. Isaiah says: "Hell from BENEATH is moved...to meet thee..." (Isaiah 14:9).

In a book I read, a man of God gives a very vivid testimony about dying and going to Hell. He had been stricken with an incurable heart disease which kept him bedfast most of the time. The illness got worse till it came to a point where he knew he was dying. He had been baptized and had been going to church all his life, but was not saved.

When he died, he felt his spirit (his real self, the inner man) coming out of his body. He could see his lifeless body on the bed. Then he began to go down. As he went down into the pitch darkness, it became hotter and hotter. When he could go no further, a fearsome, beastly creature emerged from the darkness. The foul, demonic monster grabbed his hand to receive him. Then it begun to pull him through the thick darkness towards the unbearable heat.

Suddenly, a voice boomed from above. He did not understand the language. But the hand released him immediately, and his spirit sort of floated back up to the earth and into his body. This happened two more times, and each time his spirit was released to go back to the surface and into his body. Some months later his heart failed again, and he died. But this time he was born again. When his spirit came out of his body, he began to go up instead of down. This was sheer bliss; a totally different experience from his descent to Hell. Just then, he heard a voice saying, "Go back to Earth! Your work is not done!"

I believe this testimony by this man, because it lines up with Scripture. In Isaiah 14:15, the Bible talks about being "cast down to hell." So does Psalm 55:15. And while Ezekiel 32:27 talks about going down to Hell, Paul is even more specific in the fourth chapter of the book of Ephesians: "Wherefore he saith, When he ascended up on high, he led captivity captive, and gave gifts unto men. (Now that he ascended, what is it but that he also descended first into the lower parts of the earth?" (Ephesians 4:8-9).

2. Hell is in the lower parts of the earth.

Just think about it. So all this "descending" and "going down" leads somewhere after all. It leads to the lower parts of the earth!

Hell is not (as some have foolishly supposed), a gathering of all departed Rock and Reggae stars for an endless "jam". Mind you, there is no electricity in Hell, though there are many "wailers". In fact, the only thing that is close to singing in Hell is groaning, weeping and gnashing of teeth!

Hell cannot be just a state of mind. To dismiss it as an empty threat would be very risky indeed. Hell actually exists. It is a tangible, physical place and its location is down under; in the lower parts of the earth. Even as you read this, some people that you know are crying for help that will never, ever come.

THE DESCRIPTION OF HELL

The souls of men who die without Christ are not just flung into Hell indiscriminately. Hell is divided into different areas, prepared for different classifications of people. In the midst of the darkness, torment, pain, screaming, and all the horrors in the furnace, there is some order.

Different Departments in Hell

1. The entrance

First, there is a sort of "reception" area. "Hell from beneath is moved...to MEET thee at thy coming..." (Isaiah 14:9).

When the perished soul arrives in Hell, he is probably met by the most repulsive, foul-smelling, reptilian beasts at the gates of Hell. Then he is assigned to the part of Hell where the punishment most fits the crime.

2. The levels

"For a fire is kindled in mine anger, and shall burn unto the LOWEST hell, and shall consume the earth with her increase, and set on fire the foundations of the mountains" (Deuteronomy 32:22).

Notice the expression "lowest hell", is the superlative of the word "low" as in:

Low

Lower

LOWEST

The levels are not the same. There is a progression here. One level differs from the other. Now let us look at it again this way:

Low Hell

Lower Hell

LOWEST HELL.

So you see, there are different levels in Hell and the lower the level, the greater the torment.

God is a just God, with a fairer sense of justice than all of us put together. Therefore, the severity of the punishment will be proportional to the sins committed. For example, those who have caused the death of so many people through wars, murder and witchcraft, may get a more severe punishment than perhaps, pickpockets or petty thieves.

Even in our earthly legal system there is a sense of fairness in the administration of justice. We pronounce different judgements for different crimes. Even our prisons have different areas, solitary confinement and so on.

That is probably the way it is in Hell. There are various departments reserved for different groups of people. Now, let us discover what classes of people are predominant in Hell.

Hell: A "Big Shot" Society

Observe from Scripture that Hell has become the permanent address of many chief ones and kings of the nations: "Hell from beneath is moved for thee to meet thee at thy coming: it stirreth up the dead for thee, even ALL THE CHIEF ONES OF THE EARTH; it hath raised up from their thrones ALL THE KINGS OF THE NATIONS" (Isaiah 14:9).

This refers to kings, emperors, presidents, statesmen, film stars, business tycoons-the high and mighty in the society. The wealthy and the influential. The great leaders in history. The chief ones of the earth! Basically, Hell is a 'big-shot' society, full of high class and noble people.

This is not to say, of course, that there are no poor people there. However, the well-known disregard for the things of God by many rich people, has over the centuries populated Hell with them. While the Bible makes it clear that the poor are generally rich in faith, not many noble people have chosen the way to salvation. With all the comforts of affluence, the rich and powerful see no need for God. No wonder Jesus said the rich would find it hard to get to Heaven; because of the deceitfulness of riches.

So where are all the heads of state, pop stars, great philosophers, business magnates and other famous world figures who have died? Well, according to the Bible most of them are in Hell. And, while we hold state funerals for them and erect monuments in their honour, the old-timers of Hell will be saying to the newcomers: "...Art THOU ALSO become weak as we? art thou become like unto us? THY POMP IS BROUGHT DOWN to the grave, and the noise of thy viols: the worm is spread under thee, and the worms cover thee" (Isaiah 14:10,11).

Those who are far from God in this life, will still be far from God after death. Unfortunately, our glowing tributes will not change their destination. Neither can their wealth or their achievements buy them a place in Heaven. It should not be surprising then, that Hell's roll call will sound like a "Who's Who" of the rich and famous.

Expansion in Hell

1. To accomodate the multitudes

I remember that during my years as a medical student, housing for new doctors was woefully inadequate. So the authorities began the construction of new blocks of flats, to accommodate the increasing number of newly-qualified doctors. Thus, with the inflow of many more doctors, the doctors' flats began to expand.

In a similar way, Hell is currently undergoing some major rehabilitation and extension works. What for? In order to cater for the multitudes who, alas, are streaming in. "Therefore HELL HATH ENLARGED HERSELF, and OPENED HER MOUTH WITHOUT MEASURE: and their glory, and their multitude, and their pomp, and he that rejoiceth, shall descend into it" (Isaiah 5:14).

2. To accomodate the unsaved

The mouth of Hell is probably the main gate of Hell. It is being enlarged! It is being worked upon. How alarming! This means Hell is expecting much more human traffic!

Preparations are being made for those who are not Christians. This should make you sit up! This should also make the church of God sit up. It should shake us out of our slumber. It should make everybody sit up, especially those living in sin.

AUTOMATIC CANDIDATE FOR HELL: UNREGENERATED MAN

1. Inherited sin is a distinctive trait of the human race.

My wife Adelaide and I have tried to set a godly example in our home, doing our best to bring up our children in the nurture and admonition of the Lord.

But right from their infancy, we observe to our amazement a naughtiness which could not have come out of a godly atmosphere of love and peace. Who taught them to be so stubborn and disobedient? Who taught them to lie? Where did they pick it up from?

The Bible explains that sin came into the world through Adam, who was the father of the entire human race. When he sinned, he passed on that sinful nature to all his descendants like a hereditary disease-a family trait. "Wherefore, as by one man sin entered into the world, and death by sin; and so death passed upon all men, for that all have sinned..." (Romans 5:12).

This is why you don't have to teach a child how to lie. He just lies naturally. It comes automatically. Children steal and cheat automatically. They're self-willed and disobedient by nature. It just happens. And you did the same thing when you were a child, because we are all born in sin. We take after our forefather Adam.

In fact, sin is a family trait of the entire human race. That is why the Bible says: "For ALL have sinned, and come short of the glory of God..." (Romans 3:23).

Adam's sin turned men into natural born sinners, which resulted in a death sentence being passed on all men. This makes us all automatic candidates for Hell. In other words, every unsaved soul is bound to end up in Hell, from the President to the poorest man in the village. So you see, it's very easy to arrive at this fearful destination. Even if we just sit down, doing nothing (just minding our own business), we will still end up there. It's automatic. Our "Adamic" nature ensures that.

2. Spiritual death is the result of man's sin.

Now, we know from God's Word that the wages of sin is death-everlasting separation from God (Romans 6:23). Another word for "wages"is payment or salary. Your salary is your entitlement--what you are entitled to. Which means what you get for what you've done.

What we get for being sinners is eternal separation from a righteous God. That is why man in his natural condition is considered spiritually dead, instead of being spiritually alive to the things of God.

Have you noticed that all over the world the dead are separated from the living? Even cemeteries are usually located out of town to separate the living from the dead.

Think about all your loved ones who have died in the past. In spite of all the love you had for them, you could no longer share your home with them because they had developed a condition called "death".

They were buried in the graveyard, out of sight. And you left them there, because their condition made it impossible for you to have fellowship with them.

That's exactly how it is with God. Spiritually dead man is separated from a Holy God. Unless he is born again spiritually, and reconciled to God through Christ, man is headed for Hell. God's Word explains it simply: "Therefore as sin came into the world through one man, and death as the result of sin, SO DEATH SPREAD TO ALL MEN [no one being able to stop it or to escape its power] because ALL MEN SINNED" (Romans 5:12, Amplified Bible).

3. Unbelief will send man to hell.

Jesus, in His compassion for mankind, urged men to believe on Him and to flee from sin so that we would not perish but have everlasting life. Unfortunately, most people have not accepted this invitation, and have died in their sins, passing away into Hell. Alas, multitudes have literally poured into Hell over the years.

Multitudes? You mean masses of people? Yes, I'm afraid so. Jesus said: "Enter ye in the strait gate: for wide is the gate, and broad is the way, that leadeth to destruction, and MANY THERE BE WHICH GO IN THERE AT" (Matthew 7:13).

REASONS WHY MEN GO TO HELL

1. Ignorance

As a teenager, I regularly attended church and gave offerings, but I never heard anything about being born again. Never! Instead, I was made to understand that if I recited three "Hail Marys" and The Lord's Prayer once a day, I would make it to Heaven. However, if I had died, I would have perished in Hell, in spite of all my good intentions. What a shame!

Ignorance is sending more people to Hell than we imagine. I mean, people are simply not in the know! No wonder Isaiah says: "Therefore my people are gone into captivity, BECAUSE THEY HAVE NO KNOWLEDGE: and their honourable men are famished, and their multitude dried up with thirst. Therefore hell hath enlarged herself, and opened her mouth without measure..." (Isaiah 5:13,14a).

Nobody in their right minds would go to Hell if they really knew what it was all about. After all, most people want to serve God. That is why they practise religion. Actually, religion is man's search for God. But Jesus is the only way to God. Anyone who desires to do business with God can only do so through Jesus (John 14:6; 1Timothy 2:5).

2. Lack of biblical teaching

Many churches are full of sincere people seeking God. But without the proper teaching from the pulpit about God's plan of salvation, many churchgoers will be disappointed at the last trumpet.

Speaking of the Jews, Paul testified that they indeed had a zeal for God, but not according to knowledge. "For BEING IGNORANT of the righteousness that God ascribes (which makes one acceptable to Him in word, thought and deed), and seeking to establish a righteousness (a means of salvation) of their own, they did not obey or submit themselves to God's righteousness" (Romans 10:3, Amplified Bible).

What is God's prescription for finding Heaven and avoiding Hell? Jesus said: "...Except a man be born again, he cannot see the Kingdom of God" (John 3:3).

There is no other option. You must receive Christ as your personal Saviour. Being born again is not a new idea being propagated by some young churches. It is a fundamental, biblical instruction given by Christ to everyone! I know of course, that many people are sincere-but mistaken. However, I am sad to say that sincerity alone will not save anybody.

I also believe that every single Christian (especially pastors) will also give account to God, for withholding vital information about the reality of Hell from others. If souls are perishing because of ignorance, then those with knowledge will definitely be held accountable.

IS A TRANSFER POSSIBLE?

One big-shot found himself in Hell (Luke 16:23). From a distance he saw a former hustler relaxing in Heaven. This man was undoubtedly surprised to find himself in Hell and conscious, even after death. In his desperation, he sent a telex to Abraham asking for a possible transfer! But Abraham explained to him that transfer out of Hell was not going to be possible! Hell is a permanent situation! As the anguish of this man worsened, he sent another telex asking for a drop of water, not even a glass.

Abraham's response is stated clearly in the Bible: "And beside all this, between us and you there is a great gulf fixed: so that they which would pass from hence to you cannot; neither can they pass to us, that would come from thence" (Luke 16:26).

Dear friend, make sure you do not get into Hell, because once you are there, there is no way out!

ESCAPE FROM HELL

Dear Friend, as you read this, ask yourself—am I headed for Hell? Or am I headed for Heaven? Are you going to burn in the fires, flames, and fumes of Hell? You have a chance now to escape from Hell! Take this chance and give your life to Christ. Simply and sincerely accept Christ as your Saviour now.

If you want to be born again, please pray this prayer with me:

"Dear Lord, I don't want to go to hell. I realize I am a sinner. Please forgive me. Please come into my heart and be my Saviour. I accept and receive you NOW as my Master. I will obey your Word from today. Please help me to serve you from now on. Thank you Jesus.

Amen!"

USE ME, LORD!

Dear reader, it's time for you to prevent someone from going to Hell. God will not send any angels to evangelize the world whilst we are here.

We've played enough Christian games. Today I challenge you to become a roadblock to Hell.

What I am sharing with you is coming from my heart to yours. The harvest is truly great and the labourers are truly few. Let us arise and warn the world that there is a Heaven to gain and a Hell to avoid.

Let us prayerfully say:

"Father use me. Lord may my life, my words and my actions prevent others from going to Hell. If You can use anything Lord, please use me.

Amen."

SECTION III

The Doctrines of Prayer and Faith

How to Receive Answered Prayer 8

■ THE BASIS FOR ANSWERED PRAYER

Prayer is a privilege that God has given to His children. We can talk to our heavenly father directly and receive answers. I realize from the attitudes of many Christians that they do not believe that God really answers prayer. But why pray if you will not get results? I believe that you can have one hundred per cent results every time you pray.

1. God hears prayer: He is a living God.

Why pray if you will not receive an answer? Many people take prayer to be some kind of religious routine they must perform. God's Word guarantees us a hundred per cent results every time we pray. If you look closely at the Scriptures which speak about prayer, you will discover that Jesus did not say that we might possibly (perhaps, maybe, in the sweet by and by, all things being equal) get an answer to our prayers. He said that we would get an answer.

I want you to receive one hundred per cent results every time you pray. If it is real, it is real! If it is not real, it is not real! If God exists, then he can answer your prayer.

Is God alive? Is He real? Can He hear? Is He deaf? I am sure you know the answers to these questions. God is alive and well and He wants to bless you. If my God were a piece of wood or a stone, I would not serve Him. We do not worship the sun, the moon or the rivers. We worship a living God who has power to save and to deliver.

Elijah once challenged the false prophets of Baal. He told them that there was no use in serving a god who is not available. He was either alive or dead: "...Elijah mocked them, and said, Cry aloud: for he is a god; either he is talking or he is pursuing [using the bathroom!], or he is in a journey, or peradventure he sleepeth, and must be awaked" (1 Kings 18:27).

2. Inanimate gods do not respond to prayer.

Some years ago, a friend of mine went to a small town about a hundred kilometers outside of Accra in my country Ghana. He was visiting his hometown. Whilst in the town he had the urge to urinate. Unfortunately, he found no appropriate toilet immediately, so he went into an open space to relieve himself.

Suddenly, he heard screams and shouts from behind, and he turned round to face the anger of some local residents. They accused him of urinating on a stone, which happened to be their god! Their god could not protest!

This young man apologized profusely but there was nothing he could do about it. He had already bathed their god in his urine! When I heard this story I thought to myself, "If you are a god, can you not say anything when people urinate on you? Can you not protest at the first sprinkle of urine?" If you are a god, at least say something when someone urinates on you!

What am I trying to say? If God is alive, then He must be able to respond to you. He has given us His Word and He has promised to answer our prayers every time. "He shall call upon me, and I will answer him" (Psalm 91:15).

The Bible promises: "Then shalt thou call, and the Lord shall answer..." (Isaiah 58:9). These Scriptures tell us that God will answer us. God shall answer! How much more definite can it be? Either the Bible is true or it is not true. Either you believe it or you do not! Jesus said, "And I say unto you, Ask, and it shall be given you; seek, and ye shall find; knock, and it shall be opened unto you" (Luke 11:9).

There is no word that expresses a stronger assertion than the word shall. Believe that you will experience one hundred per cent answers to all your prayers.

You must know the rules of operation for every gadget you acquire. For instance, a car runs on fuel and not Coca-Cola. If you put Coca-Cola into your fuel tank, you will discover that your car will not work. If you put the right liquid into your fuel tank you will get one hundred per cent results every time you drive your car.

God wants us to have one hundred per cent results when we pray. Discover these important steps which will help you to achieve one hundred per cent results every time you pray.

VITAL STEPS TO ANSWERED PRAYER

1. THE FIRST STEP TO ONE HUNDRED PER CENT ANSWERED PRAYER IS TO LEARN TO PRAY YOURSELF.

Jesus taught us to pray to our heavenly Father: "And in that day ye shall ask me nothing. Verily, verily, I say unto you, Whatsoever ye shall ask the Father in my name he will give it you. Hitherto have ye asked nothing in my name: ask, and ye shall receive, that your joy may be full" (John 16:23,24).

Many people do not know how to pray themselves. They want somebody else to pray for them. They ask the pastor to pray for them. They kneel down before prophets and request special prayers. There is nothing wrong with being prayed for. But God wants you to learn how to pray for yourself!

There are some pastors who entrust themselves to prayer warriors. They depend on other people to pray for them. I cannot entrust something as important as prayer to other people. I pray for myself. I consider the prayer support of friends and prayer warriors as an extra bonus. I am not depending on it anyway.

Your Christian life should not depend on another person's prayers. Jesus said, "You ask the Father." You are supposed to be able to pray yourself. Remember that the prayers of a righteous man avail much (James 5:16). You are the righteousness of God in Christ (2 Corinthians 5:21). You are righteous enough to get results for your prayers. Start praying for yourself now. Do not depend on your pastor.

2. THE NEXT VITAL STEP TO ONE HUNDRED PER CENT ANSWERED PRAYER IS TO PRAY TO THE FATHER.

Jesus said that in "that day" we will not ask Him for anything. "And in that day ye shall ask me nothing..." (John 16:23).

What day is that day? Jesus was talking about the period when He would no longer be with the disciples. In that day, Jesus would not expect anyone to pray to Him directly. Jesus was directing us to pray to the heavenly Father himself. Is there any difference between praying to Jesus and praying to the heavenly Father? There must be, otherwise Jesus would not have told us what He did!

If you want one hundred per cent results, do what Jesus said you should do. Begin your prayer by saying, "Our Father," "Heavenly Father," "Dear Father," or "Father which art in heaven," etc. You will begin to experience better results.

Some people pray to Mary. That is unfortunate! Mary herself said that she was a mere servant of the Lord. "And Mary said, Behold the handmaid of the Lord; be it unto me according to thy word" (Luke 1:38). Why would you pray to a handmaid? Jesus did not teach us to pray to His mother. He taught us to pray to His Father. There is a big difference! I can understand how our holy mother Mary is respected for the role she played in bringing Jesus to this world. She was a great woman and a very special vessel. I truly respect and admire her. But I cannot pray to her. I will pray to my heavenly Father and I will receive a hundred per cent results, in the name of Jesus.

3. The third vital step to receiving one hundred per cent answered prayer is to use the name of Jesus.

Unfortunately, many people use the name of Jesus as an exclamation or a swear word. This has caused Christians to lose respect for the power in the name of Jesus. I announce to you that there is power in the name of Jesus! Your heavenly Father will respond when He hears the name of Jesus (John 16:23).

In my church, there are people who try to use my name to get certain things done. They know that the mention of my name in our setup will lead to rapid results. I have often heard it said, "Bishop said, so-and-so." Why do people engage in name dropping? It is because names have power.

The use of a name leads to rapid results. At the name of Jesus, every knee shall bow. Demons respond to the name of Jesus. Sickness responds to the name of Jesus. Satan will bow to the name of Jesus. There is power in that name. In the book of Acts, we see how the name of Jesus healed a man. "Be it known unto you all, and to all the people of Israel, that by the name of Jesus... doth this man stand here before you whole" (Acts 4:10).

But it is not only bad things which respond to the name of Jesus. Our Heavenly Father Himself responds to the name of Jesus. Jesus told us to use his name to get responses from the Father, to get results in prayer; not as a ritual, but as a vital key to receiving your blessings from Heaven.

4. The fourth step to receiving one hundred per cent answered prayer is to Abide in Christ.

Abiding in Christ is an important key to receiving any type of response from the Lord. "If ye abide in me and my words abide in you, ye shall ask what ye will, and it shall be done unto you" (John 15:7).

If you do not stay in the house, do not expect God to answer any of your prayers. A hundred per cent answered prayer is for people who stay in Christ and in His church. When you wander away from God, you become like the prodigal son. You are far from your Father. The prodigal son did not stay in the house.

He moved out and lived in a far country. He fellowshipped with harlots and ate with pigs. The only help he could get was from pigs! So he "asked the pigs" for some of their food. The "pigs" had compassion on the prodigal son so they gave him some of their food. Even if his father had wanted to give him food, there was no way he could have. He was simply out of the reach of his father. The prodigal son ended up in the custody of a man who put him to work with swine.

When you do not stay in the house, you will end up with the pigs. It is time to come back home. Staying in fellowship is an important key to receiving the blessings of the Lord. "But if we walk in the light, as he is in the light, we have fellowship one with another..." (1 John1:7). There are some people who think they can be good Christians without going to church. You are deceiving yourself! If you are walking in the light, you will have fellowship with others who are in the light. That is what this Scripture is telling you. Are you in the darkness or in the light? If you are in the light you will go to church and fellowship with other Christians.

5. The fifth vital step to one hundred per cent answered prayer is to let the Word of God abide in you.

It is important for God's Word to be in you. God does not do anything outside His Word. God's Word will direct you in your relationship with Him. "Order my steps in thy word: and let not any iniquity have dominion over me" (Psalm 119:133). God's Word directs you in prayer. God does not answer foolish prayers, neither does He do things against His Word. If you want to get hundred per cent answers to your prayers, stay in the Word.

6. The sixth step to one hundred per cent answered prayer is to obey the Lord.

The Scripture is very clear, which states, " And whatsoever we ask, we receive of him, because we keep his commandments, and do those things that are pleasing in his sight" (1 John 3:22).

God answers the prayers of people who obey him. If you are living a life of disobedience, God will not honor your prayers. If you had a disobedient son who did not please you, would you just give him anything he asked for? Certainly not! Neither does your heavenly Father answer the prayers of disobedient children. If God has called you to the ministry, just obey! Your obedience opens the door for answers to your prayers.

7. The seventh step to receiving answers to your prayer is to be a fruit bearing Christian.

Many Christians do not know why they are alive. If you are a born again Christian, the only reason why you are being kept alive is so that you can bear fruit. After all, Heaven is guaranteed.

You have a place in Heaven after you are born again. What else do you need? Earthly treasures are transient and useless. We are being kept alive on this earth so that we can win souls for Him. God wants every Christian to bear fruit.

One thing that many Christians do not know is that God has linked bearing fruit to answering prayer. "Ye have not chosen me but I have chosen you, and ordained you, that ye should go and bring forth fruit, and that your fruit should remain: that whatsoever ye shall ask of the Father in my name, he may give it you" (John 15:16).

The Scripture above is very clear. God will be happy to answer the prayer of someone who bears fruit. What do you do for God? What fruit are you bearing? If you sit in spiritual barrenness just wanting God to answer prayers, you may wait forever. Some people just know how to say, "Give me! Give me! Give me!" But what are you contributing to God's kingdom? There is a link between answered prayer and bearing fruit.

Receive this revelation into your spirit and begin to bear fruit from today. Do something in your church. Do not just sit there and watch. Stop being an observer. There is no blessing in being a spectator or a commentator. The blessings of one hundred percent answered prayer are for Christians who bear fruit.

There are two keys that will guarantee you answered prayer every time you pray. I will like to describe these steps as the "failure-proof" keys.

■ THE KEYS OF FAITH AND PERSISTENCE

Let us now consider these steps to answered prayer by the use of faith and persistence.

FAITH

1. THE EIGHTH STEP TO ONE HUNDRED PER CENT ANSWERED PRAYER IS TO USE FAITH EVERY TIME YOU PRAY.

Jesus taught great lessons on faith throughout His ministry. He often emphasized that people were getting blessed because they were using faith. "Therefore I say unto you, What things soever ye desire, when ye pray, believe that ye receive them, and ye shall have them" (Mark 11:24).

God says that if you draw away from faith, he will not be pleased with you: "Now the just shall live by faith: but if any man draw back, my soul shall have no pleasure in him" (Hebrews 10:38).

There are those who think that faith is not so important. They tend to draw away from the faith message and faith people. They feel that there must rather be an emphasis on patience, gentleness, holiness and on the other qualities of the fruit of the Spirit. I strongly believe that these qualities are important and play a special role in the Christian life. However, the importance of the fruit of the Spirit to the Christian experience should not make us play down on the importance of faith. The fact that the heart is important does not make the kidneys any less important. Both are necessary, and play special, unique roles.

2. FAITH IS A VERY SPECIAL VIRTUE WHICH HAS A ROLE IN EVERY CHRISTIAN'S LIFE.

The Bible says that without faith it is impossible to please God (Hebrews 11:6). It is interesting to note that the Word of God does not say: "Without love it is impossible to please God." The Bible does not say: "Without peace it is impossible to please God." The Bible is very clear on this fact: Without faith it is impossible to please God!

Abraham's faith in God was considered to be an act of righteousness. Abraham believed that El' Shaddai was able to give him a child at an old age. Abraham had his faults. He lied about his wife and surrendered her twice to unbeliever kings for their pleasure. In spite of his lying and cowardly behaviour, God was very pleased with Abraham because he had faith in God.

Maybe by your standards, Abraham would have been disqualified. But he was a great man in God's sight. His greatness was a result of his faith: "And being fully persuaded that, what he had promised, he was able also to perform. And therefore it was imputed to him for righteousness" (Romans 4:21,22).

God is happy, impressed and pleased when you believe in Him. When you believe that God will heal you, you make Him happy. When you believe that God will prosper you, you make Him excited. When you believe that your breakthrough is on the way, God is so pleased with you. When you have faith that you will live long, God is provoked to extend your life. When you believe that God will give you increase and abundance, you excite the deep parts of El' Shaddai. You make Him pour out the milk of His blessings into your life.

I see you walking in the great blessings of Jehovah! I see you enjoying an abundant life in God! I see you free from sickness and disease! I see the power of curses broken in your life! I see that God is pleased with you because you believe in Him!

From today, never doubt any part of God's Word. Accept that you are the champion He is speaking about.. Flow with the message of prosperity, healing and abundance. Always remember that God is happy when you believe in Him.

God is not a God of poverty. Since I came to know the Lord I have not decreased. I do not read about decrease, failure, setbacks and limitations in the Bible. I see only abundance, promotion and deliverance from my enemies. I see God lifting me up everyday! God did not bring you to Christ in order to demote and disgrace you. He brought you to Christ to lift and establish you in an abundant life. Jesus came that we might have life and have it more abundantly (John 10:10).

3. Jesus blessed the faith people.

Under the ministry of Jesus, several people experienced personal breakthroughs. Who were they? And why did they receive these miracles?

a. You will remember what Jesus said about the woman with the issue of blood. This was a woman who had suffered for twelve years without any breakthrough. She came up to Jesus and received an extraordinary miracle. What was the secret of her breakthrough? Jesus gave the answer in Mark 5:34: "...Daughter, thy faith hath made thee whole...."

b. Blind Bartimaeus received his sight miraculously. He was a noisy fellow who disturbed the service. But Jesus took notice of him and healed him. What was his secret? His secret was faith in God: "...thy faith hath made thee whole" (Mark 10:52).

c. The sinful woman who poured an alabaster box of ointment on Jesus' feet also received a miracle of forgiveness. Jesus said to the woman: "...Thy faith hath saved thee; go in peace" (Luke 7:50).

d. Ten lepers were healed and only one came back to say thank you. Jesus said these same words to him: "...Arise, go thy way: thy faith hath made thee whole" (Luke 17:19).

e. Two blind men came to Jesus and asked for the mercy of God. Jesus touched them and healed them. What were His words to these two men? "...According to your faith be it unto you" (Matthew 9:29).

Have you noticed that Jesus never said, "Thy love hath made thee whole" or "Thy holiness hath saved you." He never said, "According to your patience, be it unto you" or "Thy good character hath made thee whole?"

Please do not misunderstand me! I am not saying that these things are not important! I am saying that it is the people's faith that impressed Jesus. I am showing you that Jesus pointed out over and over that it was their faith that had brought the breakthrough. That is why the Bible says that without faith it is impossible to please God.

Have you ever thought of those men who broke through the roof of somebody's house in order to bring their paralyzed friend to Christ? Perhaps they were experienced thieves who were used to breaking into people's homes. Perhaps they were men who were used to jumping the queue and cheating others out of their rightful places. But the Bible tells us that Jesus noticed their faith and immediately responded to their needs (Luke 5:20).

Jesus did not dwell on the wrong they did by jumping the queue or removing the tiles from somebody's roof. He saw their faith. Jesus sees your faith. God sees your faith. It is time for you to rise up and believe things in the Word of God. According to your faith, it shall be done unto you! When you exercise faith in prayer, God responds in the same way that Jesus responded to these men. He is so impressed with your prayer. When you believe that you have received, you please God.

In order to exercise faith, you must believe that you have received what you are praying for. This means you will not have to pray over and over for the same thing. Begging and crying is not the same as praying with faith. Many Christians just cry and cry in a spirit of hopelessness. God is not against crying. But He is against faithless weeping. Trust God, He wants to give you the desires of your heart. From today, I want you to believe that you have received what you are asking for.

PERSISTENCE

Persisting in prayer is a guaranteed way to get one hundred per cent answered prayer. Jesus gave two vivid examples of how persistence gives one hundred per cent answered prayer.

"And he said unto them, Which of you shall have a friend, and shall go unto him at midnight, and say unto him, Friend, lend me three loaves; For a friend of mine in his journey is come to me, and I have nothing to set before him? And he from within shall answer and say, Trouble me not: the door is now shut, and my children are with me in bed; I cannot rise and give thee. I say unto you, Though he will not rise and give him, because he is his friend, yet because of his importunity he will rise and give him as many as he needeth" (Luke 11:5-8).

The second example of persistence in prayer: "And he spake a parable unto them to this end, that men ought always to pray, and not to faint; Saying, There was in a city a judge, which feared not God, neither regarded man: And there was a widow in that city; and she came unto him, saying, Avenge me of mine adversary. And he would not for a while: but afterward he said within himself, Though I fear not God, nor regard man; Yet because this widow troubleth me, I will avenge her, lest by her continual coming she weary me. And the Lord said, Hear what the unjust judge saith. And shall not God avenge his own elect, which cry day and night unto him, though he bear long with them? I tell you that he will avenge them speedily. Nevertheless when the Son of man cometh, shall he find faith on the earth?" (Luke 18:1-8).

Persisting means repeating. It means you will tirelessly go to the Lord in prayer. It means you will shamelessly cry to the Lord until He responds.

Persistence brings results even in the natural. Sometimes I receive a phone call, but I am unable to answer because I am too far from the phone. As I approach the phone, I have often thought to myself, "If only this caller would persist, I will answer the phone." Sometimes by the time I get to the phone, the person has given up. There are some who phone again. There are some who keep on phoning until I answer.

This principle of persistence brings results in many spheres of life. This principle of persistence works in prayer as well. Jesus said very clearly that the reason why you will get results is because you keep praying.

PERSISTENCE AND FAITH

Does the principle of persistence contradict the principle of faith? It is believed by some that when using the key of faith you wouldn't have to pray more than once.

What you must understand here is that there are different ways of expressing faith. Praying once and thereafter no more is one expression of faith. Praying over and over about the same issue, with a determination never to stop until you get an answer is also another expression of faith.

Each of these two expressions of faith are valid. Each of these two expressions of faith bring results. Each of these two expressions of faith were recommended by Jesus. Each of these two expressions of faith can make God answer your prayer.

There are many Christians who can testify about how they prayed persistently until God answered! There are also many others who have great testimonies about praying once and receiving answers. Jesus did not teach on only one of these styles of prayer. He taught both methods and guaranteed one hundred per cent results in each case. So what does this mean for you? It means you can use either one of the two methods and get positive results. This is somewhat like using your computer. You can access a file by entering your word processor. You can also access the same file by a hot key or by going through your file managing program. Both methods will get you the same results.

For those of you who do not understand computer programming, you can liken faith and persistence to killing a cat in different ways. You can drown it, poison it, shoot it or decapitate it. All of these methods will lead to a hundred per cent result - a dead cat!

"Faith" prayers work all the time. Persistence works all the time. Decide today to use any of these two keys. Both of these keys are failure proof. God has given you two assured methods for receiving one hundred per cent answered prayer.

PRAYING AMISS

Unfortunately, many Christians ask God for things He cannot give them: "Ye ask, and receive not, because ye ask amiss..." (James 4:3). God does not answer prayers that have gone amiss. Praying amiss means that you pray unacceptable, unsuitable, inappropriate, inadmissible, unallowable, unsatisfactory and impossible prayers. God will not do things which are against His principles.

HOW TO AVOID VIOLATING GOD'S PRINCIPLES

1. DO NOT PRAY FOOLISH PRAYERS.

Faith is very different from foolishness. There are many Christians who exhibit silliness when they pray. Some people ask the Lord for ill-considered things. God is not a fool. Please do not try to make Him one. The fact that you are allowed to exercise faith does not mean that you should be irrational. When God takes no notice of foolish prayers, do not say that prayer does not work. It is foolish prayers that do not work God does not respond to foolishness.

a. If you ask God for somebody's husband, you are praying a foolish prayer.

b. Some young men, starting out in life, ask the Lord for huge mansions and fantastically expensive cars. It is true that God wants to bless you, but do not expect God to promote you overnight. Look at your Bible carefully. All thepeople who were blessed experienced it over a period of several years.

c. If you are a married person and you do not use contraceptives to prevent pregnancy, please do not bind the babies in your wife's womb.

d. If you have a job to do and you do not do it, do not pray that your boss will be struck with blindness so that he will not see the lapses in your work. That is an imbecilic prayer request!

e. As you grow older do not bother to pray for your youth to return. It is goneforever. You cannot retrace your steps. There is a natural aging process whichyou cannot bind or revoke by absurd prayers!

f. Why do you bother to ask God to give you an airplane when you don't even own a bicycle? You might as well ask Him to make you the Queen of England. I do not want the angels in Heaven to think that you are suffering from feeblemindedness!

2. DO NOT PRAY UNSCRIPTURAL PRAYERS.

This is yet another step to gaining one hundred per cent answers to your prayers. God has given us His Word and He will not violate His own Word. "He hath shewed thee O man, what is good; and what doth the Lord require of thee..." (Micah 6:8).

If you do not know the Scriptures, you will not know if you are praying unscriptural prayers. This is why you must study your Bible everyday. Do not just trust what your pastor says because he is a pastor. Read it for yourself and grow up!

That is why God wants you to abide in the Word. If you are praying to God to help you to divorce, you are praying an unscriptural prayer. God does not want you to divorce. How can He help you to divorce? "What therefore God hath joined together, let not man put asunder" (Mark 10:9). This is an unscriptural request and God will not answer you! You may divorce by your own choice, but not with the help of God. God does not break up marriages; He brings people together.

3. Do not pray illegal prayers.

You must realize that there are divine laws operating in the universe. There is no use praying about things which cannot be done legally. I am not talking about the laws of your country. I am talking about the laws of God.

a. I hear some women praying that they will not experience any pain at all when they deliver their babies. Some do not even want to experience labour! If you read the Bible, you will discover that Eve and all women were cursed with having to suffer in bringing forth children. "Unto the woman he said, I will greatly multiply thy sorrow and thy conception; in sorrow thou shalt bring forth children; and thy desire shall be to thy husband, and he shall rule over thee" (Genesis 3:16).

b. Coming to Christ does not revoke that curse in any way. We are redeemed from the curse of the law and not from the curse of Adam and Eve. That curse came about as a legal punishment for disobeying the Word of God. It is the legal recompense for Adam and Eve's wrong doing and it has a legal right to remain. It is not your "feeble" prayer that is going to revoke a six thousand-year-old legal pronouncement.

c. In the same way, there is no man on this earth who can escape the curse declared over Adam. "In the sweat of thy face shalt thou eat bread till thou return unto the ground; for out of it was thou taken: for dust thou art, and unto dust shall thou return" (Genesis 3:19).

d. All men are experiencing the sweat on their faces. All men are returning todust. All men will go to the grave one day. It is just a matter of time. No matter who they are, all men have to sweat to prosper. No matter how rich they are they will return to the ground. There is no use praying against it. You cannot pray that you will prosper without working hard. You cannot pray that you will not die. That is illegal! Until Jesus returns, you and I have to go the way of all men. Great men like David knew that there was no escape from death. "Now the days of David drew nigh that he should die; and he charged Solomon his son, saying, I go the way of all the earth..." (I Kings 2:1,2).

e. What is the way of all the earth? It is the inescapable experience of death that all human beings must go through. There is no use in binding or cancelling it!

If you pray about things that cannot be answered, you will only erode your confidence in prayer. You will keep getting disappointed in God. Do not pray that you will not have to work hard. Working hard and sweating your way to prosperity is the legal way for us all to prosper. What you must rather do is to pray for wisdom to alleviate the effects of these curses.

It is the wisdom of medical science that alleviates the trauma of childbirth. Get medical science and things will be a little better. Through the wisdom of medical science, many women have experienced little pain in childbirth. Many women have had less sorrow in childbirth through the use of wisdom. I am not saying that God cannot alleviate the pain and trauma of childbirth. What I am saying is this: It is both difficult and illegal to remove a tenant who is legally occupying his place.

It is the wisdom that comes through education that lightens the load on the sons of Adam. All the sons of Adam will labour, but some labor is easier than others. I would prefer to be a doctor than a cleaner. In both cases, I would go through the sweating process to eat bread. But I assure you that the labour of a doctor is easier than that of a cleaner. Think carefully about what I am saying and the Lord will give you wisdom.

4. Avoid Difficult prayers.

Once Jesus visited a hospital. There were multitudes of sick people there. However, He prayed for only one person. "After this there was a feast of the Jews; and Jesus went up to Jerusalem. Now there is at Jerusalem by the sheep market a pool, which is called in the Hebrew tongue Bethesda, having five porches. In these lay a great multitude of impotent folk, of blind, halt, withered, waiting for the moving of the water. For an angel went down at a certain season into the pool, and troubled the water: whosoever then first after the troubling of the water stepped in was made whole of whatsoever disease he had. And a certain man was there, which had an infirmity thirty and eight years. When Jesus saw him lie, and knew that he had been now a long time in that case, he saith unto him, Wilt thou be made whole? The impotent man answered him, Sir, I have no man, when the water is troubled, to put me into the pool: but while I am coming, another steppeth down before me. Jesus saith unto him, Rise, take up thy bed, and walk" (John 5:1-8).

Why did He not pray for the other hundreds of people who needed help? Jesus operated in these very steps to getting one hundred percent results. He only dealt with cases, which He knew would yield positive results!

It may be God's will to heal everybody. Perhaps the circumstances under which everyone became ill were different. Perhaps in God's plan, it was not yet time for certain healings to manifest. Jesus knew that it was difficult to get involved in things that God was not doing. Jesus explained why He prayed for only one sick person when there were hundreds who needed a miracle. He said, "I do what I see my Father doing." In other words, if it is not something that God is actively and presently involved in, I will not even bother to pray about it (John 5:19). It may be legally right to do something, but it is very difficult to succeed in something if God is not presently involved with it. If Jesus did not pray difficult prayers, why should you bother? "Then answered Jesus and said unto them, Verily, verily, I say unto you, The Son can do nothing of himself, but what he seeth the Father do: for what things soever he doeth, these also doeth the Son likewise" (John 5:19).

PRAYING ARIGHT

If you do not use these principles, you will come up with a theory that God has three answers to prayer: "Yes", "No" and "Wait". Dear friend, it is very possible to get only a "Yes" answer from God for all your requests, if you can diligently practise the steps outlined in this book. Obviously, God will have to say "No" when you ask Him for things which are impossible for Him to do. Look at a few biblical examples.

1. Joab

Take for example Joab, the army commander of King David. He killed an innocent man and David cursed him. King David cursed Joab's family forever. He said, "Let it rest on the head of Joab, and on all his father's house; and let there not fail from the house of Joab one that hath an issue, or that is a leper, or that leaneth on a staff, or that falleth on the sword, or that lacketh bread" (2 Samuel 3:29).

If you study the details of this curse you will find out that sickness was to be a permanent part of Joab's family. Anyone who found himself praying for Joab's family would find himself praying a difficult prayer. It would be difficult, though not impossible, for the Lord to revoke the curse on Joab's family. This curse is different from God's curse on Adam and Eve, in that it was pronounced by a man. Adam's curse was pronounced by God himself and obviously carries more weight.

Perhaps some of Joab's relatives were at the hospital that Jesus visited. Perhaps that is why God directed Jesus to pray for only one person. Jesus explained that God had led Him to pray for only one person. Perhaps God was not ready to undo the curse on some people's lives. Perhaps God does not have sufficient reason to undo a legal curse that is on certain people and their families.

2. Jesus

Jesus emphatically stated that he could only do what he saw his Father doing: "...Verily, verily, I say unto you, The Son can do nothing of himself, but what he seeth the Father do..." (John 5:19).

Allow yourself to be led whenever you are praying. Do not pray amiss (unacceptable, unsuitable, inappropriate, inadmissible, unallowable, unsatisfactory and impossible prayers)! Be like Jesus and have one hundred per cent answers to your prayers.

TYPES OF PRAYER

There are different kinds of prayer; different strokes for different folks, as they say. There are different types of prayers that must be used for different types of situations: "Praying always with all [kinds of] prayer and supplication in the Spirit, and watching thereunto with all perseverance and supplication for all saints" (Ephesians 6:18).

In this life, you will experience a wide variety of situations. Thankfully, God has provided us with a wide variety of prayer types. Let us consider a few of these.

1. The Prayer of Consecration

In this type of prayer you offer yourself to the Lord for His perfect will to be done. God loves children who want His will to be done.

If you pray this prayer of consecration, God will be more likely to listen to your other prayers. Some people know only "Give me, give me, give me" prayers. There are times God is not interested in answering such prayers. He wants to hear a prayer of consecration.

Learn to spend hours asking the Lord for His will to be done. Jesus prayed in the garden of Gethsemane for three hours: "...and prayed, saying, O my Father, if it be possible, let this cup pass from me: nevertheless, not as I will, but as thou wilt" (Matthew 26:39). He had only one prayer topic. He did not pray about seventeen different things

Every Christian must have the prayer of consecration as one of His prayer topics. Pray that God will perform His will in your life. This prayer topic puts all other prayer topics in their right perspective. That is why I mentioned it as the first type of prayer that you need to pray.

2. Praying in the Spirit

"But ye, beloved, building up yourselves on your most holy faith, praying in the Holy Ghost" (Jude 20). What is praying in the Spirit? The answer is in the Bible: "For he that speaketh in an unknown tongue speaketh not unto men, but unto God: for no man understandeth him; howbeit in the spirit he speaketh mysteries" (1 Corinthians 14:2).

Every Christian can speak to God in mysteries. Praying in tongues is praying in the Spirit. God wants you to pray in tongues. A large percentage of my prayer is prayer "in the Spirit". I can give you many reasons why you should pray in tongues. One reason is that when you pray in the Spirit, God directs your prayer himself. He leads you to ask Him for what is necessary.

In Acts 2, the Bible says that the Spirit gave them utterance when they spake in tongues. When the Spirit gives you utterance, it means the Spirit is giving you the words to say. What better deal could you have?

Another important reason why you should pray in the Spirit is that it builds you up. 1 Corinthians 14:4 tells us that he who speaks in an unknown tongue edifies himself. The word edify speaks of charging up in the way a car battery is charged. We all need that regular spiritual charge up.

3. The Prayer of Faith

The prayer of faith is a prayer which has a great expression of faith: "...And the prayer of faith shall save the sick..." (James 5:15).

In Mark 11:24, the Bible teaches us to believe that we have already received what we prayed for. Believing that you have already received is different from believing that you will receive it one day.

Prayers of faith are especially effective against sickness and disease. As I said earlier, different types of prayer can be used to solve different problems.

4. The Prayer of Confession of Sins

It is important for us to confess our sins on a regular basis. Prayer which does not include prayer for forgiveness is insufficient.

We must always ask for mercy. We must pray for it! If we say that we are perfect, we are foolishly deceived. "If we say that we have no sin, we deceive ourselves, and the truth is not in us" (1 John 1:8).

5. The Short and Powerful Prayer

In Mark 4:36-39, Jesus found himself in a crisis situation. "And when they had sent away the multitude, they took him even as he was in the ship. And there were also with him other little ships. And there arose a great storm of wind, and the waves beat into the ship, so that it was now full. And he was in the hinder part of the ship, asleep on a pillow: and they awake him and say unto him, Master, carest thou not that we perish? And he arose, and rebuked the wind, and said unto the sea, Peace, be still. And the wind ceased, and there was a great calm."

He and His disciples were caught up in the middle of a very dangerous storm, and their very lives were being threatened. There was no time to find a quiet place to pray for the hand of God to move on their behalf. He just prayed a short but powerful prayer and the storm ceased!

Also in John 11:41,42, Jesus encountered another situation that demanded an immediate response. He needed a miracle for his family friends. His old pal Lazarus had been dead for four days. Everyone was looking up to Him. Could He go away and pray for three hours? The answer is no! He had to pray a short prayer and He needed results immediately. Listen to His prayer, "...And Jesus lifted up his eyes, and said, Father, I thank thee that thou hast heard me. And I knew that thou hearest me always: but because of the people which stand by I said it, that they may believe that thou hast sent me" (John 11:41,42).

These types of prayers come in handy when you are faced with a crisis situation. There is no time to retreat and pray. Pray a short and powerful prayer when you need to and believe that God has heard you. After the short and powerful prayer, act boldly just like Jesus did! You will have one hundred per cent results.

6. The Long Prayer

There are times that it is important to spend a long time in prayer. Jesus did this very often. "And it came to pass in those days, that he went out into a mountain to pray, and continued all night in prayer to God" (Luke 6:12). And also in Mark 1:35, we read: "And in the morning, rising up a great while before day, he went out and departed into a solitary place, and there prayed." You will notice that in both cases Jesus spent long hours praying. A great while is a long time. All night is also a long time. Develop the art of praying for several hours. Start with one hour and graduate to three hours. Then progress to five and seven hours!

Learn to pray all day and all night long. You will experience one hundred percent answers to your prayers. There are times you need to spend many hours in prayer. If Jesus had to, then you will also have to. There are times you do not have to change the prayer topic. You can pray on the same topic for hours. Jesus did it! It is not useless repetition, it is praying like Jesus did.

7. Loud prayers

Jesus prayed with strong cries and so can you. "Who in the days of his flesh, when he had offered up prayers and supplications with strong crying and tears unto him that was able to save him from death, and was heard that in he feared" (Hebrews 5:7). There is a difference between meditation and prayer. Some people claim to pray in their minds. What is the difference between praying in your mind and meditation? I think there is no difference!

I am not saying that you must always shout when you pray. Ninety per cent of the time you cannot hear me when I am praying. I usually pray very quietly. But there are times I pray with strong cries and tears. It is a dimension you must get into. There are some things that will only happen in your life when you pray like Jesus did.

8. Prayer of thanksgiving

God wants us to give thanks. "In every thing give thanks: for this is the will of God in Christ Jesus concerning you" (1 Thessalonians 5:18). Apart from the usual "Give me, give me, give me" prayers, God would love to hear some other types of prayers. He would love to hear you say "thank you". Discover the power of thanking the Lord. As you thank Him you will experience many breakthroughs.

Paul and Silas were in jail but they prayed and sang praises at midnight. They gave thanks to God at midnight. Suddenly, there was an earthquake and their chains were broken. This is the power of the prayer of thanksgiving. Even in the midnight of your life, a prayer of thanksgiving is appropriate. There are times in which it will be the most powerful type of prayer you can offer. It is the prayer that leads to earthquakes and broken bands. Move into this type of prayer and experience God's breakthrough for your life.

There is no darkness that can keep you down. There is no "midnight" that can keep you bound. I see God setting you free! I see you experiencing one hundred per cent answers to all your prayers! There shall be a performance of all that the Lord has said!

It is my prayer that your prayer life will rise into the realm of one hundred per cent answered prayer. God is your Father in Heaven. He has to answer your prayers. In fact, He loves to answer your prayers. This is your hour for answers to all your prayers. Indeed, there shall be a performance of all that God has said.

How to Pray Effectively 9

■ DANIEL'S PRINCIPLES OF PRAYER

"Now when Daniel knew that the writing was signed, he went into his house; and his windows being open in his chamber toward Jerusalem, he kneeled upon his knees three times a day, and prayed, and gave thanks before his God, as he did aforetime" (Daniel 6:10). You will notice from this Scripture that Daniel prayed three times a day. An important phrase used in this verse is "as he did aforetime". That means that Daniel had been praying these prayers on a regular basis. Daniel was not just praying because he was in trouble; he had a habit of praying.

Many times when people become prosperous they stop going for prayer meetings and eventually backslide. Not so with Daniel! He was the Prime Minister of his country, second in authority only to the king. He was a successful man who had risen from slavery to the high office of Prime Minister. He was one of the most respected and feared men in the nation. He was a major politician of the day. He was a civil servant. Yet, he prayed three times a day, everyday! We can learn several principles for successful prayer from Daniel's example.

1. PRINCIPLE NO. 1: PRAYER IS VERY IMPORTANT.

Someone once said that it is more important to know how to pray than to have a degree from the university. There are many things that are important in this life. A good education is important. Money is important. A good marriage is important. But, a good prayer life is most important!

Let this enter your spirit. In all your getting, get prayer! In all your activities, make room for prayer!

2. PRINCIPLE NO. 2: NO ONE IS EVER TOO BUSY, TOO BLESSED OR TOO SUCCESSFUL TO PRAY.

You may have a busy life style and you may be a very important person, however; I do not think that you are busier than Daniel was. Daniel was a Prime Minister, a leader in the nation. Many people think that Heads of State and Ministers of government have a relaxed and enjoyable life, flying all over the world. That is not true!

I am the head of a large organization myself, and I know that people in high positions do not have an easy life. The higher you go, the greater the responsibility you have.

There is so much hard work involved in staying on the cutting edge of life and ministry. Did you know that successful executives like Daniel are so stressed out that they are prone to diseases like stomach ulcers and heart attacks? These conditions are more common with very busy people because of the hard work that they do.

Daniel was one such person. He was a Prime Minister, yet he felt that he was not too busy to pray three times a day. If you think you are too busy to pray, then you are deceiving yourself. If you do not pray, it is because you do not want to pray. It is because you do not think that prayer is important now! Daniel was successful, yet he prayed. Why was he able to pray three times a day?

I have watched people in the church rise out of poverty into mega blessings. When they were poor, they had a lot of time to attend prayer meetings. But when they became blessed, they felt everything was all right. No! Everything is not all right! Your state of blessing is not the signal to stop praying.

3. Principle No. 3: Prayer is the source of our power and protection.

You must realize that it is prayer which releases the power of God on our behalf. Jesus knew the power of prayer. That is why he spent long hours in prayer.

Maybe you are a successful businessman, and you do not think that you need any of this spiritual "stuff". Perhaps you are a politician and you think your protection must come from fetish or occult powers. Let me tell you right now, there is power in prayer.

We do not need any other power when we have the power of prayer. There is protection for us when we pray. The last part of the armour of God is prayer (Ephesians 6:18). In other words, prayer is an important part of your spiritual defence.

In Ghana, many people become afraid when they prosper. They feel that somebody may use supernatural powers to try to kill them. You have nothing to fear when you are a prayerful person like Daniel. Many people wanted to kill Daniel. These people did not just think about killing Daniel, they actually plotted to eliminate him. Through the power of prayer, Daniel was protected from the lions. I see all the lions in your life scattering away in fear! I see your prayer power rising! I see you going forward because of a new found prayer life!

I see the heavens opening over your life! "...that Jesus also being baptized, and praying, the heaven was opened" (Luke 3:2). Never forget this! The heavens opened when Jesus prayed. Both physical and spiritual blessings rain upon you when you are a prayerful person.

4. Principle No. 4: Prayer is important in acquiring and sustaining the blessings of God.

Do you have anything that you are proud of? Have you achieved anything in this life? Let me tell you that it is by the grace of God. By the power of prayer, you will achieve many greater things. It is by prayer that you will sustain what God has placed in your hands.

I know of people who were given thousands of dollars as gifts. Today, that money has disappeared into thin air. God may give you something but it also takes His grace to sustain that blessing. Are you the pastor of a great ministry? Let me tell you, it takes prayer to sustain you in the ministry. Why do you think Jesus kept running away to pray?

There is a law of degeneration at work in the world. Everything is decaying. Your business is decaying. Your church is decaying. Your very life is decaying. It takes the power of God, through prayer, to preserve everything that God has given to you.

5. Principle No. 5: For prayer to be effective it must be habitual.

A man called Dostoyevsky said, "The second half of a man's life is made up of the habits he acquired in the first half."

Pascal said, "The strength of a man's virtues is made up of his habitual acts."

If you are going to be a great person in this life, you need to have good habits. An action becomes a habit when it is repeated many times; sometimes consciously, other times unconsciously. It becomes your custom!

Habits can be either good or bad. Remember that good habits are repeated as easily as bad habits. A good habit will lead to consistent breakthroughs even without intending to. Bad habits will also lead to consistent failure. If you decide to develop a habit of prayer, you are developing a habit for success.

Jesus went to church on the Sabbath because it was his habit. The Bible tells us that Jesus had customs or habits. "...as his custom [habit] was, he went into the synagogue on the sabbath day..." (Luke 4:16).

Daniel had a custom of praying three times a day. "...he [Daniel] kneeled upon his knees three times a day, and prayed..." (Daniel 6:10).

Life in the secular world is not designed to include a prayer time. Work starts early in the morning and continues late into the night. Weeks may pass before you even think of prayer. For many people, it is only an impossible situation that reminds them of the need for prayer. Dear friend, it is important for you to include prayer in your life.

God is not a spare tyre! A spare tyre is something that is never used except in emergencies. God is no fool. Whatsoever a man sows, he will reap. If you have time for God on a regular basis, He will have time to bless you on a regular basis. Only the mercy of God makes Him listen to some of our prayers.

Develop your prayer life until it happens spontaneously. Develop your prayer life until you pray habitually without even thinking of what you are doing.

I Made Time to Pray

When I was a medical student, I was very busy with my coursework. There was no time to pray at all. But because I had made prayer a part of my Christian life, there was no way I could do without it! I had to somehow include it in my schedule. I decided to pray late at night. I was usually so sleepy that I had to walk about just to stay awake. Prayer was so important to me that I could not leave it out of my life.

One night, as I headed for my room after one of such prayer times, I actually fell asleep whilst walking! It was only when I walked into the Spanish Department building of the university that I woke up from my sleep! I believe that God saw my earnest desire to keep praying in spite of an impossible medical school schedule.

6. PRINCIPLE NO. 6: PRAYER MUST CONTINUE BOTH IN TROUBLED TIMES AND IN TIMES OF PEACE.

Why do we wait for trouble before we pray? Would you take someone as a serious friend if he only called you when he was in serious trouble? In times of peace, he had no time for you. God is looking for someone who will fellowship with him in both good and bad times.

The more I preach, the better I become at preaching. The more you pray, the better you will become at prayer. In times of crises, you will find yourself rising up to the occasion and delivering powerful prayers that bring results.

7. PRINCIPLE NO. 7: EVERY NATION NEEDS LOTS OF PRAYER AND PRAYERFUL LEADERS.

There is no doubt that the world is ruled by wicked spirits in high places. The earth is covered with human beings at war with each other on a daily basis. Famine, war, epidemics and disasters abound! You just have to keep your eyes on the international news and you will hear about another major disaster.

Dictators of all kinds abound in many nations. Like snakes, which shed their skin, many dictators of yesteryears have a new "Democratic look" but are still tyrants and despots at heart.

Many national leaders are actually under the influence of evil spirits, and that makes them do the things they do. They cling to power instead of honourably allowing others to have a chance at leadership. Like vampires, they drink the blood of the nation's wealth and stack it away in secret places.

Charismatic leaders like Hitler lead entire nations into initial prosperity, and then eventual destruction through war. I always remember how things changed in South Africa after President DeKlerk replaced President Botha. A new leader led to the release of Nelson Mandela and the end of apartheid. It is important for us to pray for these leaders so that our nation will prosper. The right person at the helm of affairs will make a lot of difference to our nation. I believe that the presence of a prayerful person like Daniel made a lot of difference to that nation.

8. Principle no. 8: It is important to pray for long periods of time.

Years ago, the only prayers I knew about were those that the priests read out to us in church. The longest I could pray was thirty to forty seconds and that was when I recited the Lord's prayer. There were three prayers I knew how to pray: The Lord's Prayer, Hail Mary and a Prayer to the Angel of God!

However, as I grew in the Lord I learnt how to pray for myself. I can now pray for several hours at a time. I always remember the first time I prayed for three hours. I was a student in Achimota School (Prince of Wales College). I was in the midst of a crisis and I needed the intervention of the Lord. I can also remember the first time I prayed for seven hours. I was a sixth-former in the same Achimota School. I prayed from 10 a.m. to 5 p.m.

I enjoy praying for long hours. Praying for thirty minutes is almost like no prayer to me. Do not misunderstand me; I am not saying that God does not hear short prayers. I am saying that I have developed the art of praying for long hours like Jesus did. Jesus prayed for three hours in the garden of Gethsemane (Matthew 26:39,40,42-44). In this Scripture, Jesus was surprised that the disciples could not pray for one hour. "And he cometh unto the disciples, and findeth them asleep, and saith unto Peter, What, could ye not watch with me one hour?" (Matthew 26:40).

Jesus prayed all night before he chose his disciples: "And it came to pass in those days, that he went out into a mountain to pray, and continued all night in prayer to God. And when it was day, he called unto him his disciples: and of them he chose twelve, whom also he named apostles" (Luke 6:12,13).

Long prayer may not be an explicit instruction in the Bible, but it is implicit throughout the Word. Later in this chapter, I will teach you what to pray about when you decide to pray for long hours.

9. Principle no. 9: It is important to enter your closet for effective prayer.

Many Christians can only pray when they are in a group. They cannot stay in a room on their own and pray for one hour. That is a great handicap. There is a difference between praying alone and praying with a group of people. Both types of prayer are important.

If you can pray for three hours on your own then you can pray for six hours with other people. It is easier to pray in a group. Each time, you expand your ability to pray alone, you are expanding your ability to chalk great achievements in prayer.

10. Principle no. 10: Everyone must develop the ability and the formulae for praying four times a day.

There are four important times to pray:

morning, afternoon, evening and all-the -time. Jesus prayed in the morning and so do I. "And in the morning, rising up a great while before day, he went out, and departed into a solitary place, and there prayed" (Mark 1:35).

What is so important about morning prayer? Prayer in the morning is very good because you meet God before you meet the devil. You meet God before you meet the circumstances of life. God anoints you to overcome every mountain that you will encounter in your life.

Prayer in the afternoon signifies prayer in the midst of activities. When you pray in the afternoon, it signifies that in the heat of the day and in the thick of the battle, you recognize God as the most important force in your life. God will bless you for afternoon prayer. "And when he had sent them away, he departed into a mountain to pray" (Mark 6:46). You can take a little time off your lunch break and pray. That prayer will do you more good than a plate of rice will!

It is also important to pray in the evenings. When the Bible says "watch and pray", it does not mean keep your eyes open when you pray. What it actually means is, stay awake and pray. "And it came to pass in those days, that he went out into a mountain to pray, and continued all night in prayer to God" (Luke 6:12). There is something about praying in the night that is different from praying during the day. It is a very different experience. I have heard stories that witches are very active around 2 a.m. in the night. Perhaps when you pray in the night you are tackling the forces of darkness in a different way. After all, they are called the forces of darkness (night).

The fourth important time to pray is "all-the-time". "Pray without ceasing" (1 Thessalonians 5:17). Prayer is intended to be a never-ending stream of communication with your heavenly Father. He has given us the baptism of the Holy Spirit and the gift of speaking in tongues. I pray all the time. My wife tells me that sometimes I pray in my sleep! You can pray on the bus and on your way to work. You can pray softly to yourself when you are in the office. You can pray when you are in the shower. God is happy when His children are constantly in touch with Him.

I have a friend whose wife calls him on his mobile phone at least seven times a day. I have been in meetings with him when he had received not less that four calls from his wife. Nothing important, she was just keeping in touch! I think it is a nice thing. She phones without ceasing!

I see you praying without ceasing! I see you praying in the morning and in the evening! God is changing your life because of your newly found prayer life! Your marriage, business and ministry will never be the same by the time you finish reading this textbook! When, like Daniel, you decide to pray for long hours, you will discover that you will need to have a pattern or a formula for prayer. You need something that will guide you in your prayer life. In these next chapters, we will study the formulae for prayer.

Summary of Daniel's Principles of Prayer

- Prayer is very important.
- No one is ever too busy, too blessed or too successful to pray.
- Prayer is the source of our power and protection.
- Prayer is important in acquiring and sustaining the blessings of God.
- For prayer to be effective, it must be habitual.
- Prayer must continue both in troubled times and in times of peace.
- Every nation needs lots of prayer and prayerful leaders.
- It is important to pray for long periods of time.

- It is important to enter your closet for effective prayer.
- Everyone must develop the ability and the formulae for praying four times a day.

■ THE TIMOTHY PRAYER FORMULA

Someone may ask, "What do I pray about for one whole hour? I do not have anything to say after five minutes!" I have had that experience before. Many Christians begin to look at their watches after one and a half minutes of prayer. Somehow, it seems there is nothing left to say. That is why you need a prayer formula.

What is a prayer formula? A prayer formula is something that gives you guidelines for prayer. When you read through the Bible, you will discover exactly what to pray about. I call these prayer formulae. I want to share with you a few of these to help you develop a powerful prayer life.

1. Prayer for leaders

The Timothy prayer is a prayer that I have used many times. Here it goes: "I exhort therefore, that, first of all, supplications, prayers, intercessions, and giving of thanks, be made for all men; For kings, and for all that are in authority; that we may lead a quiet and peaceable life in all godliness and honesty. For this is good and acceptable in the sight of God our Saviour" (1 Timothy 2:1-3).

This Scripture tells us the types of prayers we must pray, and whom we must pray for. It tells us to pray for all men and specifically for leaders: Heads of State and anyone who has some form of authority over our lives. This prayer formula does not teach us to curse our leaders or to wish them evil.

There are four types of prayers we are to offer for each person who is in authority: supplications, prayers, intercessions and giving of thanks. We are to take each leader and pray that God would supply their needs. We are to thank God for their lives. We are to pray generally for them. Finally, we are to intercede for them.

Anyone who prays this "Timothian" prayer will experience four blessings from the Lord. You will experience a quiet life, a peaceful life, a godly life and an honest life. Whoever you are, this prayer formula can apply to you. There is someone, who has some form of authority over your life.

In my country, we have a President and a parliament who rule in the affairs of our nation. One way or the other, the decisions they take affect everyone. Recently, the entire country experienced a major power crisis which led to severe power rationing. Our church activities were greatly affected. Whether we liked it or not, the decisions taken by those in charge of electricity generation were affecting us.

The Word of God says that prayer for our leaders is important if we want to continue living a godly life.

Political Instability

Years ago, I was going to a broadcasting station to do a recording with a Christian group. When I got to a place called Danquah Circle, I realized that there was not a single car or human being in sight even though this is normally a very busy area. When I heard the sound of heavy artillery, I decided to retreat to my home for my dear life's sake.

I later found out that there had been a military takeover in the capital city of Accra. Some soldiers had decided to overthrow the military government of the day. Because of this coup d'etat, our Christian recording for television could not take place. Once again, we could not lead our godly lives because of instability in our nation's leadership.

Where we do not have peace and stability the work of God will not go on. Some time ago, I had a pastor and a church in Freetown, Sierra Leone during a war. I kept watching the news to see what was going on there. I heard a new war was starting there. If there is war over there, I cannot keep a pastor stationed there. How will I explain to the pastor's wife if something happens to him?

2. Kings and Princes

There are certain parts of Africa which are no-go zones. Missionary work and church work have grounded to a halt because it is not safe to be there. This is why God tells us to pray for kings and people in authority.

If you study Ezekiel, you will find out that although there was a King of Tyrus in the natural, there was also a King of Tyrus in the spiritual.

1. "Son of man, say unto the prince of Tyrus... Son of man, take up a lamentation upon the king of Tyrus..." (Ezekiel 28:2,12). It is clear that this prince of Tyrus is a human being because the Bible says, "...thou art a man and not God, though thou set thine heart as the heart of God..." (Ezekiel 28:2).
2. However, in verse twelve of the same chapter, the Bible says, "Son of man take up a lamentation upon the king of Tyrus..." (Ezekiel 28:12). This time the Bible says, "Thou hast been in Eden the garden of God..." (Ezekiel 28:13).
3. It continues in verse 14, "Thou art the anointed cherub [angelic being]..." (Ezekiel 28:14). This king of Tyrus was not a man; he was an angelic being. I am convinced that there are evil spirits that rule the nations. Tyrus had a supernatural being that ruled its affairs. This fellow was also called the king of Tyrus. Why was he called the king of Tyrus? Because he actually governed and ruled in Tyrus!

When Jesus was tempted in the wilderness, one of the offers that Satan made to him was to give him all of the kingdoms of the world. If Satan could not have given the kingdoms of the world to Jesus, it would not have been a temptation. It was a real temptation to Jesus because Satan was actually the one in control of the kingdoms of the world. You cannot give something that you do not have!

You and I can see that the world is headed towards eventual annihilation. There will probably be a nuclear war one-day. Some people sing, "He's got the whole world in His hands." I do not believe that is true. If the Lord had the whole world in His hands, the world would not be in the mess that it is in. If Jesus was ruling this world, there would not be wars in Rwanda, Burundi, Angola, Ethiopia, Eritrea, Central African Republic, Liberia, Sierra Leone, Democratic Republic of Congo, Congo Brazzaville, Bosnia, Afghanistan, Israel, Palestine and the list goes on!

If Jesus were in control of this world there would not be such injustice and wickedness throughout the world. The Bible tells us clearly that Satan is the god of this world: "In whom the god of this world hath blinded the minds of them which believe not, lest the light of the glorious gospel of Christ, who is the image of God, should shine on them" (2 Corinthians 4:4).

3. Divine Intervention

For some reason, Satan seems to have legal control over the nations of this earth. Before God can intervene in the affairs of men, He has to be invited by a legitimate citizen of this world. You and I are legitimate members of the world community. If the Lord gets involved without a legal invitation, Satan can accuse Him of the crime of illegal takeovers, such as happened with Iraq and Kuwait.

God is waiting for our invitation through prayer. When we invite Him to build our nations in freedom, justice and peace, he will do just that. Whenever Christians pray for leaders, there is a change.

Once, Abraham's wife was illegally taken by the King of the day. God appeared to the king called Abimelech, and said, "You are a dead man. You have taken somebody's wife to be your own." The king was scared; he thought he was going to die (Genesis 20:7). But God told him: "Tell Abraham to pray for you."

Why did God not deliver Abimelech right away? After all, He knew about the prayer that Abraham was going to pray. But no, God has to wait for the invitation of men before getting involved in the affairs of this world.

There are three main reasons why we need to pray for those in authority. First, we have to pray that the decisions of the nation will not be based on selfish and political desires only. The second reason is that the nature of all men is to grab and take as much as they can. We have to pray against corruption. Thirdly, we must pray for peace and freedom so that we may go about our Christian duties without any hindrance.

We need to pray that our leaders will truly love the nation. How can you know when a leader loves the nation? "For he loveth our nation and hath built us a synagogue" (Luke 7:5). When a leader loves the nation, he will build the nation and not his personal wealth.

AUTHORITIES AND INFLUENCE

1. Pray to avert frustration.

If you do not pray for those who have authority over you, your life may become frustrated. The Bible tells us that the heart of the king is in the hand of the Lord, and He turns it whichever way he wants. "The king's heart is in the hand of The Lord, as the rivers of water: he turneth it whithersoever he will" (Proverbs 21:1).

In Genesis chapter 40, you will find a very interesting story. There was a king who had a butler and a baker. The butler was in charge of everything in the home. The baker made biscuits, cakes and pies that the king enjoyed eating. Something happened in the workplace that made the king angry with both the butler and the baker. In his wrath, he had them thrown into prison. Whilst there, each of them had a dream which Joseph (who had been wrongfully imprisoned) interpreted. He predicted that the butler would be re-instated and the baker would lose his life.

Now, understand that both the butler and the baker were in trouble. Their very lives depended on the one they had displeased. Everything depended on how Pharaoh thought. Depending on his decision, someone would live or die. In this particular case, the baker died, just as Joseph predicted.

2. Pray to have favour with authorities.

There are times when your life depends on what someone thinks about you. The more you pray Timothy's prayer, the more favourable the thoughts of your boss will be towards you. I see you having favour in all that you do! I see the heart of the king having mercy on you!

Many young people must pray for their fathers in order to have the favour of God. I remember when I was in the university, I asked my father for a car. I realized that my father was spending a lot of money on horse racing. You see, my father had one of the largest horseracing stables in the country. He employed many people and bought horses from all over West Africa. I thought to myself, "If my father wants to, he can buy a brand new car for me."

One day, my father decided to buy a car for me; my prayers for him made the Lord turn his heart in my favour. I received a brand new car when I was in fifth year medical school. I rejoiced and used that car for the glory of God. I was the first church member of Lighthouse Chapel International to own a car. My car became the church bus and the church taxi. And I was happy to do it, because I knew that the Lord had provided.

God can bless you through those who are in authority over you. As you pray for them, God will give you favour! Things are changing in your favour! I see God turning the heart of every king in your life! They will not decide to kill you anymore. They will decide that you must live! I see many blessings rising up to embrace you! As you pray for fathers, bosses and presidents, you will experience only godliness, peace and quietness.

From today, every wife that prays for her husband will experience quietness in her house! From now on, your "unbeliever" husband will allow you to go to church! He will not stop you from going for all-night prayer meetings. He will not oppose your Christian life anymore because you are praying for him!

■ THE EPHESIANS PRAYER FORMULA

"Wherefore I also, after I heard of your faith in the Lord Jesus, and love unto all the saints, Cease not to give thanks for you, making mention of you in my prayers; That the God of our Lord Jesus Christ, the Father of glory, may give unto you the spirit of wisdom and revelation in the knowledge of him: The eyes of your understanding being enlightened; that ye may know what is the hope of his calling, and what the riches of the glory of his inheritance in the saints, And what is the exceeding greatness of his power to us-ward who believe, according to the working of his mighty power, Which he wrought in Christ, when he raised him from the dead, and set him at his own right hand in the heavenly places, Far above all principality, and power, and might, and dominion, and every name that is named, not only in this world, but also in that which is to come: And hath put all things under his feet, and gave him to be the head over all things to the church, Which is his body, the fulness of him that filleth all in all" (Ephesians 1:15-23).

Many people just gloss over Ephesians chapter one. They think it is too complicated to understand. However, God reveals to us a major formula for prayer in this chapter. I call it the Ephesians Prayer formula. Here are the six important steps in this formula.

1. GIVE THANKS

First of all, you must give thanks (Ephesians 1:16). Many people have become hardened and ungrateful. It is nice when you meet a few grateful people among the masses of ungrateful people in the world!

The first thing to do therefore, under this prayer formula, is to spend quality time thanking the Lord in prayer.

Thank Him for His goodness and mercies, thank Him for His protection, thank Him for His provision; the list is endless!

2. CRY TO THE LORD FOR REVELATION

The second important step is to cry out to the Lord for revelation. "That the God of our Lord Jesus Christ, the Father of glory, may give unto you the spirit of wisdom and revelation in the knowledge of him:" (Ephesians 1:17). This is one of my favourite prayer topics. You may know something, but until it is revealed to you in a deeper way, you do not really know it!

There is a difference between "head" knowledge and "revelation" knowledge.

Revelation Knowledge

I have always known that it is dangerous to drive very fast. I have seen large billboards that declare, "The speed that thrills is the speed that kills." One day I travelled to Tamale in the northern region of Ghana. I was driving at over 120 kilometers per hour when suddenly a cyclist crossed my path. I soon found myself somersaulting in the air. After that experience, I had revelation knowledge about driving too fast!

I remember one night, I was on a highway driving at about eighty kilometers per hour, when suddenly three cars overtook me with the speed of a bullet. Such was their speed that it looked as though my car was stationary. I smiled and thought to myself, "There was a time no car ever overtook me on a highway. These people do not have revelation knowledge." What I had experienced had given me a deeper understanding of the knowledge about over-speeding. We call this type of knowledge-Revelation Knowledge.

There is a difference between knowing something and having a revelation about it. The more I pray for revelation, the more I understand the Word of God. The cardinal thing that has taken me forward in my walk with God has been the revelation I have had in His Word. When you have had a revelation, you change. The cardinal sign of revelation is a change in your life.

Every year I have a deeper and progressive revelation of God and His Word. If you are a pastor, spend hours praying for wisdom and revelation. God anoints people who know Him. When I say know Him, I am talking about having a revelation of God through His Word. The things I am sharing with you in this book are things I know by revelation. They are more real to me than facts from a history book.

I often tell my lay pastors that this life is short and that the only thing worth doing is the work of the ministry. Jesus himself said to "lay up for yourself treasures in heaven". The revelation of this scripture is deep in my heart. But most people do not have a revelation of it. Although many people know this scripture, it has not been revealed to them. That is why I could give up a lucrative medical career for the ministry. I believe I will one day reap great heavenly rewards which are more valuable than any amount of money.

That is why I could give up a quiet life of wealth and privacy in exchange for a public, often criticized role of being a spiritual leader. I have a revelation of the truth, that, "Vanity of vanity... all is vanity" (Ecclesiastes 1:2).

The Lawyer Received Revelation

I once visited a dying man in the hospital. He was a young and successful lawyer struck down in the midst of his years with a deadly disease. I will never forget something he said to us; "If God would raise me up from this bed I will serve Him. Even if it means becoming a full-time preacher."

As this man lay dying, he realized how futile everything in this world really was. He suddenly had revelation knowledge about many things that are written in the Bible. Somehow we read the Bible but we do not get the revelation of it. When you pray for the Spirit of revelation, things which you have read over and over will come alive to you in a different way.

3. Pray for Understanding

The next step in the Ephesians Prayer Formula is to pray for understanding. "The eyes of your understanding being enlightened; that ye may know what is the hope of his calling, and what the riches of the glory of his inheritance in the saints..." (Ephesians 1:18). When you have understanding, you know why you should obey the Word of God. I often pray for the Spirit of understanding. When you have understanding, it helps you to obey God's instructions. Because I ask for understanding, God often shows me many deep things in His Word.

That is why I can preach "Twenty-five Reasons Why We Should Have a Mega Church". I teach "Twenty Reasons why Poverty is a Curse". I once taught, "Fifty-five Reasons why we Should Win Souls". Believe it or not, each of those reasons were different. "Ten Reasons Why We Should Not Commit Fornication", "Ten Reasons Why You Should Love Your Husband". When you have the Spirit of understanding you will know why God is speaking to you the way He is.

There are many Christian wives who are unwilling to do their duties in their marriage. The reason is, they do not have an understanding about the duties of a wife. I notice how the revelation of the importance of the duties of a wife comes alive when a woman is struck with the reality of an adulterous husband.

4. Pray about your calling

The 4th step in the Ephesian Prayer formula is to pray about your calling. "The eyes of your understanding being enlightened; that ye may know what is the hope of his calling, and what the riches of the glory of his inheritance in the saints..." (Ephesians 1:18).

Every Christian is called to a ministry. "For we are his workmanship, created in Christ Jesus unto good works, which God hath before ordained that we should walk in them" (Ephesians 2:10).

Christians were not recreated for nothing. God intends for every one of us to fulfil our divine call. We are called to do good works. We are called to be unmovable, steadfast, always abounding in the work of the Lord. I watch modern day Christians attend service after service. Christianity has become a kind of ritual for many people. They just attend church, sing songs and listen to a thirty-minute sermon. But there is more to the calling of God than that.

When I became a Christian, I joined a vibrant ministry that went around preaching the Word. To me, Christianity has always been an experience of soul-winning and establishing other Christians in the Lord.

The Reason for our Calling

I was once chatting with a taxi driver in London. He asked me where I was coming from. I told him, "I've just flown in from Amsterdam."

He said, "Oh, there are a lot of prostitutes there; did you have a good time?"

I answered, "Oh no! I'm a Christian. We don't live like that!"

He exclaimed, "Are you sure Christians don't do that? Do you really believe that stuff? Do you actually believe in Heaven?"

He went on, "If Heaven is really so nice then why don't we all commit suicide and go there right now."

Unfortunately I had got to the end of my journey and could not explain the hope (the reason) of my calling as a Christian. This taxi driver brought up a very valid point. If we are all just waiting to enter Heaven, why not just go there right away?

The answer is simple: Christians are not expected to kill themselves! Christians have an important calling to save souls and to establish people in the Lord. We cannot just rush to Heaven now! The hope (reason) for our calling is to bear fruit and win souls in this life.

That is why we are still here and have not left for heaven yet. According to Revelations 14:13, your works will follow you into Heaven. "...Blessed are the dead which die in the Lord from henceforth: Yea, saith the Spirit, that they may rest from their labours; and their works do follow them" (Revelations 14:13).

What you do on earth will determine how your stay in Heaven will be like. If you know why Christ has saved you, you will have a lot to do for him here on earth.

5. To know the riches of your inheritance in Christ

The next step is to know the riches of our inheritance in Christ "The eyes of your understanding being enlightened; that ye may know what is the hope of his calling, and what the riches of the glory of his inheritance in the saints..." (Ephesians 1:18).

This means we need to know what we have inherited as Christians.

When my father died, he left properties for his children. A few months after he died, we assembled in Court to listen to the reading of his will. We all wanted to know what the riches of our inheritance were. We took the time to find out what we had inherited. I did not know what my father had given to me. I had to go to the Court to find out for myself.

It is sad to say that many Christians do not bother to find out what God has in store for them. When you begin to discover what God has in store for you, you will be amazed. We need to pray to know what God has given to us.

Many people think that Christians are supposed to be poor. They think that pastors, in particular, are supposed to be impoverished. There are people who want ministers to come crawling to their doorsteps to beg for a tin of sardines and a loaf of bread. Is this what we have inherited from our heavenly Father? No, certainly not!

I do not intend to be poor just because I am a minister! I am sorry if that offends you, but I cannot see it in my Bible. Apostle Peter wanted to find out how he would benefit from following Christ, so he asked, "Lo, we have left all, and followed thee..." (Mark 10:28).

In other words, how do we benefit from serving you? Jesus answered him clearly. That answer applies to all of us, "...There is no man that hath left house, or brethren, or sisters, or father, or mother, or wife, or children, or lands, for my sake, and the gospel's. But he shall receive an hundredfold now in this time, houses, and brethren, and sisters, and mothers, and children, and lands, with persecutions; and in the world to come eternal life" (Mark 10:29,30).

The heritage of Christians and ministers is not lack and poverty. But if you do not find out or pray about it you will live in the darkness of that deception all the days of your life.

6. To know the greatness of God's power

The last step of the Ephesians Prayer Formula is to pray to know the greatness of God's power: "And what is the exceeding greatness of his power to us-ward who believe, according to the working of his mighty power..." (Ephesians 1:19).

There are certain Christians who do not want anything to do with the power of God. In the last days, the Bible teaches that some people will have a form of godliness but will deny the reality of the power of the gospel (2 Timothy 3:5).

One of the things you need to pray about is to know the power of the Holy Spirit. There are two types of churches in the world: teaching churches and power churches. Some churches emphasize the teaching and have nothing to do with the power of God. That is a mistake! You cannot take away miracles from the Bible. Without the miracles of the Bible all we are left with is philosophical literature.

It is because people do not believe in the power, that they are frightened by weird looking witches and fetish priests. We need to pray for the power until we experience it. You will not taste of God's power unless you pray for it! Thank God for nice teachings on Sunday. Thank God for good administration. However, there is a power dimension to Christianity and God wants you to experience it too.

Summary of the Ephesians Prayer Formula

- The 1st step is to give thanks with a grateful heart.
- The 2nd step is to pray for wisdom and revelation in the knowledge of him.
- The 3rd step is to pray for the eyes of your understanding to be enlightened.

- The 4th step is to pray to know your calling and the hope of your calling.
- The 5th step is to pray to know the riches of the inheritance of the saints.
- The 6th step is to pray to know the power of God.

THE LORD'S PRAYER FORMULA

"After this manner therefore pray ye: Our Father which art in heaven, Hallowed be thy name. Thy kingdom come. Thy will be done in earth, as it is in heaven. Give us this day our daily bread. And forgive us our debts, as we forgive our debtors. And lead us not into temptation, but deliver us from evil: For thine is the kingdom, and the power, and the glory, for ever. Amen" (Matthew 6:9-13).

One of the things that struck the disciples about the Lord Jesus was His ability to pray for long hours. They wanted to know what strategy, formula or trick He used in order to stay in prayer for such long hours. That is why they approached Him and said, "Lord, teach us how to pray." They needed to have a sort of guideline for their prayer lives. Jesus sat them down and gave them these eight steps to enhance their personal prayer lives.

1. GIVE THANKS AND WORSHIP THE LORD.

Jesus taught us that the first step is to say thank you and to worship the Lord. "Our Father which art in heaven, Hallowed be thy name" (Matthew 6:9). The first thing to do in this prayer formula is to spend time giving thanks to the Lord. For most people thanksgiving lasts for approximately forty-five seconds. However, we need to be grateful to the Lord for all that He has done for us. Thank Him for allowing you to see that day. Many people die everyday, it could have been you. The fact that you are alive is a miracle. Thank Him for your pastor and your church.

Thank Him that you can read this textbook. I have members in my Bible school who cannot write. During the classes, they have to record what is said on tape. They simply do not have the ability to read or write. I thank God for the fact that I am in the ministry. The fact that you are reading my book is a miracle of God. Some people can only see problems. God is touching your eyes right now! He is opening your eyes to see His blessings all around. In this first step of prayer, you must thank the Lord for what He has done for you.

A Sad Visit

Some time ago, I visited a friend of mine. He lived virtually on the street. He had become a drug addict, and he had no food or money. As I took some money out of my pocket to give to him, tears welled up in my eyes. I thought of how pathetic this young man's condition was. I realized that it could have been me. Somehow, by the grace of God I had come to know the Lord. I could have been smoking marijuana. After all, I saw many people doing it when I was younger. I could have been dead and buried long ago.

I have been in near-fatal car crashes. I have been in planes that almost collided with other planes on the runway. On two different occasions, I have been in aircrafts that landed and had to do an emergency takeoff in order to avoid a collision on the runway. But I am still here and I know I have something to thank God for.

My friends, if you cannot find something to thank God for, for at least ten minutes, then you have an ungrateful spirit. This first step of the Lord's Prayer Formula should last about ten minutes.

2. PRAY FOR THE KINGDOM OF GOD TO COME.

The second important step is to pray for the kingdom of God to come. "Thy kingdom come..." (Matthew 6:10). This step is my favourite step. I can spend three hours here. But if you do not have much time, you can spend just ten minutes on this. Please note here that the order is very important. The first thing is to pray for the church and the kingdom. Ask God to bless the church.

I teach my children to pray for church growth all the time. When the church is growing, it is an indication that more people are being saved everyday. Everybody is developing his personal kingdom. People are developing their financial strength. Most people do not really care about the church. Every Christian must first pray for the church to develop and grow.

Pray for your pastors instead of criticizing them. Men of God are human beings just like you. Pastors make so many mistakes everyday. Unfortunately, our mistakes are often publicized. Pray that God will protect His leaders from attacks of all sorts.

3. Pray that God's will be done.

The third step is to pray for the will of God to be done: "...Thy will be done in earth as it is in heaven" (Matthew 6:10). This can also take another ten minutes. Anyone who prays that God's will should be done in his life, cares for himself. If you love yourself, pray that the will of God be done in your life. I have come to believe that God's will is better than my will or anybody else's will.

Nobody knows the future, but God knows what He has in store for you. Jesus prayed for three hours in the garden of Gethsemane that the will of God be done. After you have prayed this prayer you can relax and allow events to unfold. When Judas and the Pharisees came to arrest Christ, he did not resist them. He believed and accepted that the events that were happening were the will of God, and indeed they were. Those events were leading him to his greatest victory over Satan.

If you want to have peace and confidence in this life, spend time praying that the will of God comes to pass in your life.

My Evening Prayer

Many years ago, I was a young medical student. I had no idea that I would be where I am today. In 1985, during the first term of my third year, I spent many hours praying that the will of God be done. Our school campus was near the Atlantic Ocean. Every night at 10 p.m. I went along with four other friends to the beach. I clearly remember standing on the rocks and the sand praying, "O Lord, let thy will be done."

As I stood on the dark shores of Ghana, I remembered how missionaries came to our nation and sacrificed their lives. I lifted up my hands on the beach and said, "Use me Lord. Let your will be done." I cried to the Lord and said, "You brought me here. I do not know the future. Whatever you want to be done, let it come to pass." I believe that today I am walking in the answers of those prayers. For several weeks, I prayed those same prayers.

Begin to spend time praying to God for his will to be done. Do you think the will of God will happen naturally? Certainly not! If it was going to happen naturally why would you have to spend time praying about it? The very fact that Jesus taught us to pray about it means that it is not automatic that the will of God will happen.

I see your future unfolding in a positive way! I see God lifting you up as you pray about His will! I see you marrying the right person as you spend time praying for the will of God to be done!

4. Pray for your daily bread.

The next step is to pray for our daily bread. "Give us this day our daily bread" (Matthew 6:11). Jesus taught us to pray for our daily needs. That means we are to pray about our jobs, marriages and everything that concerns us.

Some years ago I felt I was too spiritual to marry. But no one can be more spiritual than God. Do not be too spiritual to ask God for your physical needs. Ask him for a house. Ask him for bread. Do you want a husband? God is granting him to you right now as you read this book. Pray to the Lord for yourself. Spend some minutes mentioning your needs to the Lord. If you spend another ten minutes asking the Lord for your daily needs, your life will change dramatically.

When it comes to prayer do not depend on anyone, depend on yourself. Do not expect somebody to pray for you. Many times, people who you think are praying for you are actually sleeping. God is giving you a formula for prayer. Operate in it and walk in your blessings.

5. Pray for forgiveness.

The next step is to pray for forgiveness. "And forgive us our debts, as we forgive our debtors" (Matthew 6:12).

We all need forgiveness for our sins. There are two types of sins: sins of commission and sins of omission. We must be aware of our sinful nature as we approach the throne of grace. Appropriate the blood of Jesus for yourself. Ask the Lord to see you only through the eyes of the blood.

One of the first sins of commission is the sin of the mouth: lying, flattery, backbiting, gossip, etc. Another arena for sin is the mind. Many of us have committed murder, adultery and stealing in our minds. Our minds are often polluted with sin. We must come before the Lord and pray for mercy. As we ask the Lord for mercy, we must search our hearts to see whether we have forgiven the people around us.

Sometimes I listen to the way people condemn those who have made mistakes. It makes me sad! Are we not all human? Are we not all subject to the same temptations? Is it not by the grace of God that we survive?

When we come to this part of the prayer, we must correct any judgmental or arrogant attitudes.

One of the important sins to confess is the sin of omission. There are people who go to hell because a neighbor did not witness to them. There are friends who die and go to hell because we never told them about Christ. As we come before the throne, God sees all our mistakes. If we act as though we are perfect, we deceive ourselves and the truth is not in us. Spend another ten minutes asking the Lord to have mercy on your life.

6. Pray against temptation

The next important step in The Lord's Prayer Formula is to pray against temptation. "And lead us not into temptation..." (Matthew 6:13).

We are all human beings. When I hear of great men of God falling, I become so frightened. I wonder about myself. Many times I just pray that I will just make it safely to heaven. It is important for you to pray against temptations in your life. You may not know, but prayer strengthens you against temptations. On the night of betrayal, Jesus gave the disciples an eternal command, admonishing them to pray in case they fall into temptation (Mark 14:38).

Fasting Without Prayer is Dieting

Many years ago, I remember fasting for three days. By the third day, I was so weak that I could not rise out of the bed. This was the first time I had fasted for three days without any food at all. Because we had not prayed, I was almost unconscious.

Some months later I decided to try this fast again. This time I decided to wake up at 4 a.m. and spend a couple of hours in prayer before the day began. By the third day of the fast, I felt as though I had had something to eat. There was a great difference between the two fasts. I had such strength because I had been more prayerful. My Christian friend, prayer is a supernatural act and provides strength even when your flesh is weak. Spend about twenty minutes praying against temptations in your life.

7. Pray that God delivers you from evil.

The seventh step is to pray that God should deliver you from evil: "... deliver us from evil..." (Matthew 6:13).

It is important for you to pray against the evils in this world. Cover yourself with the blood of Jesus. In the days of Israel, they would sprinkle the blood of lambs over the lintels and doorposts. This was to prevent any evil from coming into the home. We are to do the same thing now but in a spiritual way. "And they shall take of the blood, and strike it on the two side posts and on the upper door post... and when I see the blood, I will pass over you..." (Exodus 12:7,13).

How do you sprinkle the blood? You sprinkle the blood of Jesus with your words. Apply the blood of Jesus over every part of your home and family. Place an injunction over every flying witch. Declare that your household is a no-fly-zone for every witch, wizard or evil presence.

Cancel every enchantment, spell, charm or lamentation that has been taken up against you. Declare that you will live and not die. Bind Satan and his agents. Have faith in God. Command angelic beings and the forces of heaven to be on guard around you. God will keep you as you pray against evil in your life.

8. Thank Him and give Him glory.

The final thing to do in the Lord's Prayer formula is to thank Him and to give Him glory: "... For thine is the kingdom, and the power, and the glory, for ever. Amen" (Matthew 6:13). Thank Him over and over. Declare that He is more powerful than the walls of opposition in your life. Declare that every mountain of impossibility is possible because of His power and His glory.

Lift up your hands and speak about His glorious power in your life. Declare that every serpentine agenda for your life cannot happen because of the power, kingdom and the glory of God. Thank Jehovah that He has time for you, to listen to your prayer. Thank Him that it is well with your soul. Thank Him that it is well with you.

If you follow these steps, you will have at least an hour and half of effective and fruitful prayer everyday. It is my prayer that these strategies for prayer will revolutionalize your spiritual life. May you move into greater heights in God's kingdom, as you apply these principles of prayer.

Summary of the Lord's PrayerFormula

- The 1st step is to give thanks and worship the Lord.
- The 2nd step is to pray for the kingdom of God to come.
- The 3rd step is to pray that God's will be done.
- The 4th step is to pray for your daily bread.
- The 5th step is to pray for forgiveness.
- The 6th step is to pray against temptation.
- The 7th step is to pray that God delivers you from evil.

Saving Faith

10

■ FAITH: THE MASTER KEY TO BREAKTHROUGH

"Now the just shall live by faith: but if any man draw back, my soul shall have no pleasure in him" (Hebrews 10:38). God is saying here, that if you draw away from faith, He will not be pleased with you.

There are those who think that faith is not so important. They tend to draw away from the faith message and faith people. They feel that there must rather be an emphasis on patience, gentleness, and holiness, for example. I believe these are important, and they all play special roles in the Christian life.

This, however, does not mean we should play down on the importance of faith to the Christian life. The fact that the heart is important to the body does not mean that the kidneys are not equally important. Both are important, and both have special roles to play.

Faith people also experience disappointments, sickness and other shortcomings. However, very generally speaking, I notice a trend of blessings, abundance and long life among those who believe for them.

WHAT IT MEANS TO LIVE BY FAITH

1. Every Christian must have faith and must exercise it.

Faith is the reason for breakthroughs and miracles in our lives. Faith is the reason for answers to prayer. Generally speaking, people who have faith are more prosperous than those who do not. I have noticed a difference between Christians who walk by faith and those who do not.

The Bible says: "But without faith it is impossible to please him: for he that cometh to God must believe that he is, and that he is a rewarder of them that diligently seek him" (Hebrews 11:6). The Bible states with emphasis and clarity: Without faith it is impossible to please God!

2. Every Christian must develop real faith.

When I was a younger Christian, the concept of having faith looked farfetched to me. After all, it seems unrealistic to command a mountain to move into the sea. Who could imagine such a thing? Even Jesus never transferred the mountains around Jerusalem to another location.

Faith has always seemed like something that emotionally strung people got involved with. It had looked like something that people who were not practical and down-to-earth got involved in. Faith people sometimes have the image of lazy Christians who are unwilling to work and just wish for good things to happen magically. But faith is none of these!

Faith is the assurance of things you are hoping for. "Now faith is the substance of things hoped for, the evidence of things not seen" (Hebrews 11:1).

Depending on your background, faith may seem more or less substantive. If you grew up in a critical and godless society, you will have less faith in the supernatural. In spite of this, when you are born again, you are given a measure of faith from God.

3. Every Christian has a measure of faith.

The Bible says: "...God hath dealt to every man the measure of faith" (Romans 12:3). This means that everyone has some amount of faith.

You may say, "I don't believe in anything!" But that is not true! Every time you sit on a chair you are exercising faith in the chair. You believe it will not collapse, that is why you sit on it without thinking twice. Every time you sit in a car or an airplane , you are exercising faith in technology. You are also putting your faith in the driver or the pilot in the cockpit.

Whether you know it or not, you have a measure of faith. It is important to develop that faith.

The subject of faith is a mysterious one and we have a lot to learn about it. I know of people who have exercised a lot of faith and this faith has resulted in many breakthroughs.

There are also people who have seemingly exercised faith, without getting the same results. I do not have all the answers and neither does anyone. The Bible describes faith as a mystery: "Holding the mystery of the faith in a pure conscience" (1 Timothy 3:9). It is our duty to seek after the Lord and learn all we can from him.

4. Every Christian is at a different level of faith.

It is important to know that your faith can be at a higher or lower level depending on several factors. You must know what level of faith you are at.

It is unreasonable to expect a three-year old boy to drive a real car. All he may be allowed to ride is a little tricycle, because he is just not capable of driving an adult's car. This, however, does not make him inferior. All it means is that the boy is not mature enough to handle a real car. When he is older and mature enough, then he will be capable of handling bigger things.

There are many Christians who are believing God for things well beyond their level of faith. You must know the level of your faith. There are many things I do not pray for. There are things I have not exercised my faith about. I know I am not ready to move into certain levels of faith yet. One day when I am ready, I will. When I do exercise faith at that level, I believe I will get one hundred per cent results.

TYPES OF FAITH

The Bible speaks of different levels of faith. The Word of God teaches us that you can have little faith, great faith, growing faith, dead faith, weak and strong faith and even shipwrecked faith. All these descriptive terms tell us that the status of your faith can vary.

1. Little Faith

"...O thou of little faith, wherefore didst thou doubt?" (Matthew 14:31).

2. Great Faith

"...I have not found so great faith, no, not in Israel" (Matthew 8:5-10).

3. Weak Faith

"And being not weak in faith..." (Romans 4:17-19).

4. Strong Faith

"He staggered not at the promise of God; but was strong in faith..." (Romans 4:20).

5. Exceedingly Growing Faith

"We are bound to thank God always for you, brethren, as it is meet, because that your faith groweth exceedingly..." (2 Thessalonians 1:3).

6. Increasing Faith

"And the apostles said unto the Lord, Increase our faith" (Luke 17:5).

7. Full of Faith

"...and they chose Stephen, a man full of faith and of the Holy Ghost..." (Acts 6:5).

8. Faith Unfeigned or Genuine Faith

"Now the end of the commandment is charity out of a pure heart, and of a good conscience, and of faith unfeigned" (1 Timothy 1:5).

9. Unwavering Faith

"But let him ask in faith, nothing wavering..." (James 1:6).

10. Rich Faith

"...Hath not God chosen the poor of this world rich in faith..." (James 2:5).

11. Perfect or Mature Faith (Fully Developed)

"Seest thou how faith wrought with his works, and by works was faith made perfect?" (James 2:22).

12. World Overcoming Faith

"For whatsoever is born of God overcometh the world: and this is the victory that overcometh the world, even our faith" (1 John 5:4).

13. Failing Faith

"But I have prayed for thee, that thy faith fail not..." (Luke 22:32).

14. Dead Faith

"Even so faith, if it hath not works, is dead, being alone" (James 2:17).

15. Shipwrecked Faith

"Holding faith, and a good conscience; which some having put away concerning faith have made shipwreck" (1 Timothy 1:19).

When you look at all these types of faith, you realize that faith is a very variable condition. Do you have strong or weak faith? Are you full of faith? Is your faith dead or alive? These are important questions that you must ask yourself.

HOW TO IMPROVE YOUR FAITH

You will notice that there are some types of faith that you should try not to have. Your faith must not be weak, little, dead or shipwrecked. Just as a weak or dead dog cannot guard your house, weak and dead faith can do you little good. If you are going to have a dog, get a strong one! If you are going to have faith, make sure you get living, strong and rich faith.

But how does one go from little faith to great faith? How does one acquire exceedingly growing faith? What is the secret to acquiring the faith that brings breakthrough? The answer is in the Bible. I am going to share with you biblical methods for improving your faith. There are three simple ways to improve your faith: hearing the right things, seeing the right things, and using it (your faith).

FAITH COMES BY HEARING

What we hear determines our beliefs. The Word of God teaches us that faith comes by hearing. "So then faith cometh by hearing, and hearing by the word of God" (Romans 10:17).

Whether you like it or not, what you believe in is determined by the things you hear. There are two ways by which every human being hears or listens to things: intentionally or unintentionally. Which ever way it is, your faith ends up being affected.

1. Prejudices come by hearing

In my country Ghana, certain tribes are believed to have certain characteristics. Many people believe in these characteristics, even though sometimes they have no basis for doing so. There is a tribe in Ghana which is believed to be steeped in witchcraft and juju power. One person told me that when Satan was cast out of Heaven, he fell into that region of Ghana and left his slippers there!

I know of people who refuse to rent their houses to people from that tribe, no matter how much they are willing to pay. Sometimes they have not even met anyone from that particular tribe, but because these sayings have been repeated over and over, people believe that they are true. Faith comes by hearing! I find it very interesting that although there are other regions and tribes which are equally or maybe even more involved with witchcraft and occult activities, they do not receive as much attention!

My impression of people from this tribe I referred to is that they are easy-going and very pleasant people. If I was to accept the things that have been said, perhaps I could not even flow with such people.

I know of pastors who are even afraid to have crusades in such regions because they have heard so much about the black magic power of the region. You see, if such pastors had heard more about the power of God, they would probably have believed that the power of God is greater and better than any other power. No power of the enemy can stand up to the power and the blood of Jesus.

I also know young women who are desperate for husbands, but who would prefer to remain unmarried rather than marry men from certain tribes. Why is this? They have heard over and over, that certain groups of people have certain negative characteristics.

I once asked a Nigerian man, "What do you Nigerians think about Ghanaians?"

He immediately responded, "O we see you as people who are poor and proud!"

I thought to myself, "Perhaps this message that Ghanaians are "poor and proud" is in the minds of many Nigerians." Maybe some have never even met any Ghanaian, yet they believe in their hearts that we are poor and very proud.

Where does this notion come from? It comes from what they hear all the time. I decided to ask several other Nigerians the same question. To my amazement, they all had the same impressions. Where did they get these ideas from? How come they believe these things about Ghanaians? Faith comes by hearing!

2. Fear comes by hearing

When I was going to get married, my wife was very hesitant to get involved with me. She had heard so many negative things from her mother and aunts who had told her that people from the tribe which I came from were disagreeable. They told her stories of women who had married from my tribe and were beaten up by their husbands. They went on to prove their theory by showing her that all the world-famous boxers of Ghana were from that tribe! My wife-to-be probably believed this because she had heard this from childhood.

Whether you like it or not, faith comes by hearing! Even when you hear a lie, it has the power to make you believe. That is why some politicians are afraid of churches. They know that our people believe what we tell them. This is the reason why politicians try to control the media. They know that people believe what they hear, whether it is true or not.

Have you ever asked yourself why one of the first places to be captured in a military coup d'état is the broadcasting station? It is important for the new rebels to make everyone, especially the army, believe that there is a new government. The army has instructions to defend the government in power. The armed forces can only switch allegiance when they have been informed that there is a newly established government.

What am I trying to say? All that I'm saying is that faith comes by hearing.

3. What you keep hearing is what you believe.

If you are in a church that believes in prosperity, you will believe that prosperity is a good thing and will gravitate towards it. If you are in a church which preaches that sickness and disease are sent from God to teach us humility, that is what you will believe. This is why Jesus said you must be careful about what you hear. "And he said unto them, Take heed what ye hear..." (Mark 4:24).

When I first became a doctor, many people said, "Now that you are a doctor you will be able to minister to people both spiritually and physically." What people don't realize is that for seven years, I heard all about the causes, progression and the outcome of every disease under the sun. Medical science teaches us that many conditions are hopeless. It teaches us how many situations are truly impossible and how the prognosis is often bleak.

After hearing such things for years, it is an uphill task to believe that God can and will undo the sicknesses that ravage the human race. I find it far easier to have faith when I don't know the medical implications of a thing. It is important to protect your ears.

4. Improve your faith by guarding your ears.

Faith comes by hearing. You must be careful about what you hear. If you hear that the economy is going down and therefore everyone is going down, you will believe and act accordingly.

Money, which is a piece of paper, depends on the faith of the masses. As soon as the faith of people in money or in the banking system drops, the whole financial world can collapse. Whenever there is bad news in some major financial centre, it sends ripples of fear into the minds of the millionaires of this world. They begin to scramble for their money. This is what causes stock markets and banks to go crashing down.

We must learn how important it is to guard our ears. You must not allow yourself to hear bad news and discouraging stories. Fear is a type of faith and it also comes by hearing. You must select your friends and walk with people who speak encouraging and positive words. I once had some friends who didn't believe in me. They criticized me all the time. They saw no good thing in my ministry. I got rid of all those people and now I am surrounded by friends who say positive things.

It is also important for you to speak positively over your children. If you tell them, "You are daft", "You are stupid" and "You are bad", they will soon believe that they are daft, stupid and bad. I know of children who have been called "devil" by relatives until they eventually turned out to be human "devils".

This is why listening to tapes is such an important spiritual exercise. You must intentionally acquire preaching tapes and soak them in.

You must not listen to worldly music. You must surround yourself with Christian music. Music has a message and you will soon believe what you are hearing.

FAITH IS AFFECTED BY WHAT YOU SEE

1. This principle is implied in Scripture.

Although the statement that faith is affected by what you see is not in the Bible, it is also true. What is not explicit in Scripture is often implicit in the Word.

When Peter walked on the water, he did very well and his faith worked perfectly until he saw certain things. "But when he saw the wind boisterous, he was afraid; and beginning to sink, he cried, saying, Lord, save me" (Matthew 14:30).

He saw the wind and the waves and this had a terrible effect on his faith. What you see affects your faith! Peter's faith dropped drastically and he began to sink. Peter did not hear a message of doubt to disturb his faith level. He was not told anything to fill his heart with doubt. He just saw the wrong things! He saw the wind and the waves in action and that is what struck at his faith.

2. Believe in spite of what you see.

It is sometimes better to pray and believe God about things without seeing certain things. When you begin to observe the wind, waves and the water, your faith can fly out of the window!

FAITH COMES BY USING IT

Faith increases with use. Everyone has a level of faith. The more you use it, the more it increases. If you believe God for a bicycle and it happens, your faith will rise and you will have faith to believe God for a car. It is like lifting weights; you start from a lighter object and graduate upwards.

Jesus told the parable of the nobleman who gave a pound each to his ten servants. On his return from a long journey, he inquired from each one how much he had gained by trading (using). You will discover from this parable that using of the one pound led to a natural increase in the number of pounds.

"He said therefore, A certain nobleman went into a far country to receive for himself a kingdom, and to return. And he called his ten servants, and delivered them ten pounds, and said unto them, Occupy till I come. But his citizens hated him, and sent a message after him, saying, We will not have this man to reign over us. And it came to pass, that when he was returned, having received the kingdom, then he commanded these servants to be called unto him, to whom he had given the money, that he might know how much every man had gained by trading. Then came the first, saying, Lord thy pound hath gained ten pounds. And he said unto him, Well done, thou good servant: because thou hast been faithful in very little, have thou authority over ten cities" (Luke 19:12-17).

I find it easier to pray for the sick now. Sometime ago it was difficult to exercise my faith in that area of ministry. After doing it for some time, it takes less effort to believe God for miracles of healing in miracle services. Faith definitely increases as you use it. God has given us the principle of gaining by trading. You gain as you trade! You increase as you use it!

As you use these three principles, your faith will gradually move from weak to strong and from little to great! You will no longer have dead or shipwrecked faith. As you hear testimonies of great things that God has done, your faith for the same will rise. Your faith will become exceedingly growing faith.

■ EXPRESSING FAITH IN WORDS

What do you want from God? Just name it! I have discovered that God is our greatest friend. Begin to name all the things that you desire from your heavenly Father. He is standing by to respond to your faith. Don't forget that God is impressed with people who believe in Him. Believe in a Good God.

1. GOD'S MANIFEST GOODNESS TO MANKIND

Traditionally, people have blamed the Lord for every bad thing that happened. Even in legal jargon, events like earthquakes, floods and tornadoes are called "Acts of God". What does this mean? They are blaming God for the bad things which occur! What about the devil? If God does all these evil things, what does the devil spend his time doing?

Whenever something bad happens, people would say, "God is moving in a mysterious way, his wonders to perform." In a certain sense, it is true that God is mysterious to us but, His real nature is revealed in the Word.

In Genesis Chapter One, God is known as "Elohim", the Creator of the universe and the Creator of nature. In the life of Abraham, God reveals Himself as "El'Shaddai". "El'Shaddai" is the God who goes against nature and blesses Abraham with a child in his old age. We see Him as the one who blesses His children giving them long life and prosperity.

How then do we blame him for every bad thing that happens? The devil wants you to believe that God is fighting against you. The opposite is true! God is the best friend you have. The God you serve is the God of promotion and blessing. If God did not hold back Jesus Christ, what good thing will He withhold from us? "He that spared not his own Son, but delivered him up for us all, how shall he not with him also freely give us all things?" (Romans 8:32).

The Bible describes God as the sun and the shield who gives grace and glory. God is giving you beauty for ashes right now! He's making your life glorious as you name it and claim it! "For the Lord God is a sun and shield: the Lord will give grace and glory: no good thing will he withhold from them that walk uprightly" (Psalm 84:11).

2. JESUS REVEALS THE NATURE OF GOD

I want you to remember an experience that the disciples had with the Lord. They were in a boat trying to cross the Sea of Galilee when a storm struck. What did Jesus do? Did He stand up and declare, "God moves in a mysterious way his wonders to perform"? Did He say, "I don't know why God has sent this storm to kill me, but He is working His perfect plan"?

No, He did not! He rebuked the storm: "...Then he arose, and rebuked the wind and the raging of the water: and they ceased, and there was a great calm" (Luke 8:24).

If God is the one who sent the storm to kill Jesus and the disciples, then Jesus actually rebuked God. By rebuking the storm, Jesus was disapproving of it. He was stopping the agents of destruction from shortening His life and ministry. Did Jesus rebuke God? Certainly not! The storm was not an "Act of God" sent to destroy them!

The Bible teaches us that it is the thief or the devil who comes to steal, to kill and to destroy. "The thief cometh not, but for to steal, and to kill, and to destroy: I am come that they might have life, and that they might have it more abundantly" (John 10:10).

God does not come into your life to destroy you! El'Shaddai does not come into your life to kill you. He is here right now to prolong your life and to extend your days. Your duty is to know and to believe that God is your friend who is trying to help you. In actual fact, God is your very best friend: "...and there is a friend that sticketh closer than a brother" (Proverbs 18:24).

The devil is the one who is trying to disgrace and destroy you! Satan is the one who has set limitations and barriers all around you. But today, as you rise up in faith to name it, claim it and take it, I see your enemies perish!

NAMING YOUR BLESSINGS

1. Ask and Receive

Because God is such a good God, He wants you to name your blessings. Traditionally, we have thought that having nice things is sinful. To be a holy Christian means to be nothing and to have nothing. But God has a bountiful store of blessings waiting for those that believe.

That is why His Word says you can ask for whatsoever you desire and you can receive it. "Therefore I say unto you, What things soever ye desire, when ye pray, believe that ye receive them, and ye shall have them" (Mark 11:24). This Scripture does not say, "Whatsoever things you need." It does not say, "Whatsoever things God desires for you." It says, "Whatsoever YOU desire." Please read it loud and clear! God is saying that you can have your desires. What do you desire? What is your wish? God wants you to name it! God wants you to ask for it! The reason why many Christians do not have answers to their prayers is because they do not ask.

Often we think we are carnal if we ask for nice things. But the Bible is very clear on this: "... ye have not, because ye ask not" (James 4:2).

If God did not withhold Jesus Christ from us, what good thing is He going to keep back from your life? (Romans 8:32).

One of the Scriptures I love is John 15:7. "If ye abide in me, and my words abide in you, ye shall ask what ye will, and it shall be done unto you" (John 15:7).

Jesus was teaching us that God is prepared to give us what we want. He said that you shall ask what you will and not what God wills for you. God knows that you have a will. You can choose to serve Him or not! God wants to work with people who have chosen to and are willing to serve Him.

The fact that you are a Christian does not mean that you no longer have a will or a desire for certain things. God knows that and He encourages you to come to Him and ask for what you wish. This is the Word of God.

2. Conditions to Answrered Prayer

Of course, there are some conditions. John 15:7 says that if you abide in Him and His Word abides in you, you can ask for what you want! When you abide in Christ your desires will line up with the Word of God. I came to know the Lord years ago. My desire now is to win more people to Christ. I desire to experience church growth and the blessings of the Holy Spirit.

Somebody may ask, "Don't you desire more money or cars?" The answer is no. If it was money I desired, I would simply practice medicine in America. That would be a simpler way of satisfying a desire for money. The problem many people have is that they think it is impossible to have more spiritual desires than carnal ones. It is not! There is a certain level of spiritual maturity where carnal things do not mean so much to you.

As you abide in Christ and His Word abides in you, you will desire things that are consistent with the Word of God. When you name them and claim them, you will receive them.

When you have the right heart, wealth and riches cannot destroy you. All the patriarchs who served the Lord were blessed with abundance and wealth. The prosperity of Abraham, Isaac and Jacob often intimidated their neighbors and incited jealousy. The Bible says that Abraham was very rich. God had made him rich.

In fact, at one time, Abraham wanted people around to know that it was not them who had contributed to his riches. Because of this he refused a large gift from the King of Sodom. "And Abram said to the king of Sodom, I have lift up mine hand unto the Lord, the most high God, the possessor of heaven and earth. That I will not take from a thread even to a shoe latchet, and that I will not take anything that is thine, lest thou shouldest say, I have made Abram rich:" (Genesis 14:22,23).

God was obviously prospering Abraham. Abraham knew that his prosperity was coming from one source: El' Shaddai. Remember that every good and perfect gift comes from above. Abraham's faith in God was not destroyed by his riches.

The Bible makes it clear that it is the love of money and not money itself that corrupts. "For the love of money is the root of all evil..." (1 Timothy 6:10).

From today, begin to name all the things that you desire from your heavenly Father. He is standing by to respond to your faith. Don't forget that God is impressed with people who believe in Him.

■ CONFESSIONS OF FAITH

The power of life and death is found in the tongue. Did you know that there is power in your tongue? And no ordinary power at that! "Death and life are in the power of the tongue: and they that love it shall eat the fruit thereof" (Proverbs 18:21). The power to live on is in your tongue.

You must tap into this great power of the tongue by naming your requests from God and by claiming them in faith. Claim your victory over darkness. Pronounce your deliverance from the spirits of inferiority and self-pity! You can do all things through Christ who strengthens you! Declare that you have overcome the demons of worry and anxiety! You are free from nervousness and headaches! Depression and madness have no power over your life!

I see you having favour in all that you do! The power for abundance and wealth rests in your ability to claim it! It is time to rise up and pronounce yourself free from cancer and disease. Claim a healthy and long life, in the name of Jesus. You are free from genetic and demonic curses.

Confess your faith about what you desire from the Lord. Traditionally, confession has always revolved around the subject of sin. However, it is important for us to know that there are four types of biblical confessions and not just one.

FOUR TYPES OF CONFESSIONS

1. Confessing your sins to the Father

The first type of confession is a confession of sin to the Father. This is the well-known type of biblical confession. It is important for Christians to confess their sins to God on a regular basis. The Bible tells us that if we think we have no sin we deceive ourselves and the truth is not in us.

None of us is without sin. No matter how hard you try, sin is part of our flesh and our minds.

That is why the scripture says if we say we have no sins we are actually deceiving ourselves. "If we say that we have no sin, we deceive ourselves, and the truth is not in us. If we confess our sins, he is faithful and just to forgive us our sins, and to cleanse us from all unrighteousness" (1 John 1:8,9).

It is a dangerous thing to think that you are sinless by your own strength.

There are three types of sins: the sins of commission, the sins of omission and the sins of the heart.

a. Sins of commission are the things you actually do. Those sins are easy to recognize and therefore easy to confess. When you have a negative thought, you definitely know that you have had a negative thought. It is easy to recognize and to confess this to God.

b. Sins of omission are the things we don't do. They are things we are supposed to do that we don't do. "Therefore for him that knoweth to do good, and doeth it not, to him it is sin" (James 4:17).

   Maybe God wants you to win somebody to Christ and you fail to speak out. That is a sin of omission. Perhaps God wanted you to pray and you failed to pray. Perhaps God wanted you to support His work financially and you didn't do it. You may not even be aware of the fact that you are sinning. That is why you need to confess your sins on a regular basis.

c. Sins of the heart are even more difficult to recognize. What we often do not recognize is that the heart of man is a very deep thing. There are times when your heart is full of evil and you are not even aware of it.

   That is why the psalmist cried out, "Search me, O God, and know my heart..." David wanted God to take evil things away from his heart. Sometimes our hearts are full of pride and rebellion and we do not even know it. But God looks at the heart (1 Samuel 16:7).

   The cry of the psalmist is an important prayer for us all: "Search me, O God, and know my heart: try me, and know my thoughts: And see if there be any wicked way in me, and lead me in the way everlasting" (Psalm 139:23,24).

   Why did King David want God to look into his heart? Couldn't David see whether there was something wicked in his heart? Perhaps not! We sometimes do not even know ourselves. No one knows a Toyota like the people who make Toyota cars. No one knows a Ford like the people who make Ford cars. No one knows you like the God who made you. The creator knows the creature better than anyone else!

2. Confessing your faults one to another

The second type of confession is the confession of faults one to another. Although confession of sins to the Father results in forgiveness, there are times it is necessary to speak to someone else about the problem you have. Confessing your faults to someone else is not done in order to receive forgiveness. Forgiveness is received from the Father when you confess your sins.

There are times when we need healing and restoration within our spirit. Talking about these things and confessing them out loud helps to heal and eventually overcome the psychological wounds that are acquired through sin.

The King James Version of James 5:16 says, "Confess your faults one to another... that ye may be healed..." The Amplified Bible throws more light on this same Scripture: "Confess to one another therefore your faults (your slips, your false steps, your offenses, your sins) and pray also for one another, that you may be healed and restored (to a spiritual tone of mind and heart)..." (James 5:16 Amplified Translation).

We all need to be restored to a spiritual tone of heart and mind. When you have made a mistake, you need restoration. Restoration comes through confessing to one another. Of course telling your problem to the wrong person will only lead to complications. However, I have noticed that people experience permanent healing and restoration through this second type of confession.

3. Confessing Christ for salvation

The third important type of confession is the confession of our faith in Jesus in order to receive salvation. "If thou shalt confess with thy mouth the Lord Jesus, and shalt believe in thine heart that God hath raised him from the dead, thou shalt be saved" (Romans 10:9).

Contrary to traditional opinion, it is not the confession of sins that leads to salvation, but a confession of Christ as your Lord and Saviour. It is important to confess your sins and repent genuinely, but the Bible makes it clear that it is the confession of Jesus Christ as Lord and Saviour that leads to the salvation of the soul.

Whenever you lead someone to Christ, in addition to whatever you say, ensure that the person is led to confess Jesus Christ as Lord and Saviour.

4. Confession of our faith

The word translated profession in the King James Bible version of Hebrews 10:23 comes from the Greek word, homologia. "Let us hold fast the profession [confession] of our faith without wavering..." (Hebrews 10:23). This word means "to agree". It is sometimes translated "profession" or "confession".

As a Christian body, there are things that constitute the essentials of our faith. Our Christian faith can be confessed or professed. We can speak out and declare what our essential beliefs are. What we call the Apostles' Creed is a good example of the confession of our faith. It is a good thing to say because it constitutes the essentials of what Christians believe. Virtually every line of this creed has a deep meaning.

The Apostles' Creed

I believe in God the Father Almighty, Maker of Heaven and Earth;

And in Jesus Christ His only Son our Lord, who was conceived by the Holy Ghost; born of the Virgin Mary; suffered under Pontius Pilate, was crucified, dead, and buried; He descended into hell; the third day He rose again from the dead; He ascended into Heaven, and sitteth at the right hand of God, the Father Almighty; from there He shall come to judge the quick and the dead.

I believe in the Holy Spirit; the Holy Catholic (universal) Church; the Communion of saints; the forgiveness of sins; the resurrection of the body, and life everlasting.

Amen.

You will notice that we believe that Jesus was born of a virgin and not just of a "young woman" as some are claiming today. There is a difference between a virgin and a "young woman"!

This confession also states that Jesus suffered under Pontius Pilate. Pontius Pilate is the only other person whose name is mentioned in this statement. He tried to wash the murder of Jesus off his hands but the church did not allow him to do so. That is why his name is mentioned here. We will never forget how he had Jesus killed!

This reminds me of some authorities today. They behave just like Pontius Pilate and refuse to do the right thing. They also cannot wash their hands! One day when the history books are being written, it will be stated that the church suffered under the hands of such people. Dear friend, beware, you cannot easily wash your hands!

This confession also speaks of Jesus rising from the dead. Our faith rests on this great fact of history. It is this and only this fact of His resurrection that separates Christ from every other religious leader. The tomb is empty! There is no place which is as revered as the tomb of Christ. His followers knew that He rose from that place!

Another interesting part of this confession is that Jesus will return to judge the living and the dead. When we say this confession, we remind ourselves of the coming judgement. We remind ourselves of the day of accountability. We declare that Jesus will return from the skies to judge people. Such a thing sounds crazy! Only mad people would believe something like that, some may say. But that is the Christian's faith! And when we say these things, we affirm our faith.

Finally, we declare that we believe in the church and in the communion (fellowship) of saints. We believe in spending our time in fellowship with other Christians. We confess that we are glad to go to church. We enjoy the company of other Christians. This is the confession of our faith. We must say it to remind ourselves of what we really believe. When we declare our faith, it becomes real to us. God wants us to say things that agree with our faith. Our words must confirm specific things we believe in our heart.

Claiming what you believe shows that you have the spirit of faith at work in your life! When a person has a spirit of drunkenness, he drinks a lot and is often drunk. When a person has a spirit of immorality, he gets involved in immoral acts.

When a person has a spirit of faith, he confesses positive things that he believes in. "We having the same spirit of faith, according as it is written, I believed and therefore have I spoken; we also believe and therefore speak" (2 Corinthians 4:13).

Confession of Specific Faith

Remember that you take your place in Christ and in Heaven by making a confession. You will also take your place in this life by confessing boldly the things that you desire from the Lord. It is time to rise up and claim them. It is time to rise up and speak them out. Declare that you will live long. Declare that you are unbeatable and unquenchable by the devil. Declare that you are undefeatable, "undiminishable", "unmolestable" and "undieable" before the age of seventy!

What do you lose by speaking out boldly? Instead of allowing thoughts of fear and panic to ravage your mind, declare that Satan cannot disgrace or limit you in this life. Declare that you are healthy, blessed, prosperous and rich! What do you have to lose? Open your mouth and declare that your enemies are disgraced and disappointed! Proclaim that God has given you beauty for ashes. Your life is beautiful from today! Your marriage and business are beautiful from today! Declare that beauty characterizes everything you do!

Take no notice of the frightening events all around you. If a thousand seem to be falling on your left and ten thousand on your right, declare that it will not happen to you. You have nothing to lose by declaring your faith. Speak it out for that is the spirit of faith at work!

CONFESSIONS AND HOW THEY WORK

1. Conversational confessions (claims)

You must be careful with what you say, even in casual conversation. Often it is in casual conversation that you declare the things that you really believe. At other times you can make deliberate commanding confessions. During these commanding claims, you lay hold on victories and breakthroughs by conscious and deliberate confessions.

Both of these types of confessions (conversational and commanding) have power.

A trap is a trap! Whether you put your foot in the trap intentionally or unintentionally does not matter. The trap will still function and grip your leg. You must know from today that your words will trap (snare) you whether you spoke intentionally or unintentionally. "Thou art snared with the words of thy mouth, thou art taken with the words of thy mouth" (Proverbs 6:2).

I remember how a distant relation would jokingly speak about a pimple on his face. He would point to the pimple and say, "This is my cancer". Obviously, he had no intention of acquiring cancer on his face. A few years later this same man developed a cancer on his face and eventually died of it. You are trapped by the words that you speak. Don't say things you don't mean. "Out of the same mouth proceedeth blessing and cursing. My brethren, these things ought not so to be" (James 3:10).

I know that most people think that the tongue is a small and insignificant member of the body. However, you must realize that it is like the power of a small rudder that controls huge ships.

I have ridden strong African racehorses. These horses often had the power and strength to run for miles at very high speeds. Yet, I was able to control these mighty horses by means of small bits in their mouths.

Your life is an important and complex thing, but it can be controlled by your tongue. Declare that your blessings are permanent! Claim your promotion in this life, in the name of Jesus! Openly thank the Lord that no weapon formed against you will prosper! Declare that you are marching on! I see you marching on and the gates of Hell cannot stop you! I see you free from the power of sin, shame and disgrace!

2. Commanding confessions (claims)

Some people wonder how this world came into existence. Stop searching and read the Bible. "Through faith we understand that the worlds were framed by the word of God, so that things which are seen were not made of things which do appear" (Hebrews 11:3).

God made the world through the power of the spoken Word. He simply said, "Let there be..." and there was! He spoke the world into existence by simple and powerful pronouncements. "Let there be light..." and there was light! When God spoke to the waters to be fruitful, the waters had no choice but to be fruitful (Genesis 1:20).

God wants us to imitate Him. Ephesians 5:1 tells us to be imitators of God. That means that we must be holy, because God is holy. That means we must be righteous, because we are imitating a righteous God. It also means that we are to frame our world by making declarations.

Some examples of declarations are: Let there be happiness in my home! Let there be abundance of all things in my life! Let my cup run over! Let my children live long and prosper! Let my body be healthy and live long! Let my enemies be blown away like the chaff of the wind! Let those that hate me wither and fade away! Let the crooked paths in my life be straightened! Let poverty run away from my home! Let righteousness characterize my life! Let holiness be part of my life from today! Let me be fruitful! Let me be pleasing to God in all that I do!

Be an imitator of God in this aspect of commanding, claiming, announcing and insisting on your blessings! Begin to imitate your Heavenly Father by affirming, declaring, demanding, maintaining, asserting and pronouncing your breakthrough. That is the God-kind of faith.

Did you know that you can speak to things that do not have physical ears and they will respond? Jesus did that all the time. He once spoke to a fig tree and said, "No man eat fruit of thee hereafter for ever" (Mark 11:14).

Jesus spoke to the wind and the sea. The sea has no ears, but it can respond to your commands of faith! "And he arose, and rebuked the wind, and said unto the sea, Peace, be still. And the wind ceased, and there was a great calm" (Mark 4:39).

One time Jesus even spoke to a dead body. He commanded the dead person to listen. Jesus interrupted the funeral procession and raised a young man back to life in the city of Nain. "And he came and touched the bier [coffin]; and they that bare him stood still. And he said, Young man, I say unto thee, Arise. And he that was dead sat up..." (Luke 7:14,15).

I see you commanding your dead business to resurrect! Declare over your shop the victory of Jehovah! Speak to your bank account and tell it to come alive! Announce to every mountain facing you that it will have to move! Affirm the fact that every impossible situation will be made possible! Insist that you have the victory everyday, in spite of what you see or feel! "For we walk by faith, not by sight" (2 Corinthians 5:7).

3. Confessions and Feelings

Confessions of faith are not the same as seeing and feeling things. We do not live by our feelings. Feelings are real, but God has not asked us to live by them. We are to live by our faith. The father of faith, Abraham, believed that he would have a child. In spite of how he felt, he called those things that were not, as though they were: "(As it is written, I have made thee a father of many nations,) before him whom he believed, even God, who quickeneth the dead, and calleth those things which be not as though they were" (Romans 4:17).

I know that there are many things that do not seem realistic. God is not asking you to be realistic; He is asking you to walk by your faith. God is telling you to believe in His Word. You will never be the same after you apply these laws to your life.

HOW TO MONITOR YOUR FAITH LEVEL

1. Your level of faith is assessed by the claims you make.

The Bible says that because you believe you speak. That means that your claims are a direct result of your faith level. If you want to assess yourself, listen to your proclamations and declarations.

The bigger your claims the bigger your faith. Great faith brings forth great declarations! It is time to speak about living long! It is time to speak about healing power! It is time to declare how God has prospered you by faith! It is time to declare that you are fruitful in the vineyard of the Lord! Claim your place among God's generals! Claim your place in God's glorious army! Declare that you are one of the righteous trees planted by the Lord! Do not be afraid of falling. Declare that you will stand and not fall!

2. You can have what you say.

Can you really have what you say? The answer is yes! You are actually experiencing what you have said with your mouth. Mark 11:23-24 tells us that mountains will respond to what you say. Begin to say big things, because you have a big God. Say them consistently! That is how you make your claim. It is time to name it, claim it and take it! Take no notice of the doubters. There will always be an opposition party. There will always be a commentator.

Notice how many times the word "say" appears in Mark 11:23, 24: "For verily I say unto you, That whosoever shall say unto this mountain, Be thou removed, and be thou cast into the sea; and shall not doubt in his heart, but shall believe that those things which he saith shall come to pass, he shall have whatsoever he saith. Therefore I say unto you, What things soever ye desire, when ye pray, believe that ye receive them, and ye shall have them."

It appears five times. God is telling you that you will have what you say. The promise is not that you will have what you think! This verse is not promising that you will have what you hope for, it is promising that you will have what you say!

Enter in like a little child right now and receive great breakthroughs by claiming your blessings. You are what you say you are! And you can do what you say you can do! You are beautiful because God has made you so! You are successful because you say so! You are intelligent and wise because that is what you are claiming to be!

"Oh pastor, is it that simple?" It is as simple as you make it to be!

You cannot experience any of the blessings of the kingdom of God unless you enter in like a little child. If you live in Africa, you will find yourself surrounded by many unsolvable problems. There are many hopeless situations in this great continent.

Today, I am offering you an answer which is not found through governments or politicians. The master key to your blessing is to name it, claim it and take it!

Paul said that he could do all things through Christ. I also believe that I can do all things through Christ who strengthens me.

Never say, "I cannot do it!" You will have what you say. You will experience the things that you say. I am not telling you to be unrealistic, I am telling you to exercise faith. I am a very realistic person, but I am continually exercising my faith. It is important to balance the handling of certain realities with the exercising of faith.

You may have to take medicine in order to stay alive. That does not mean you do not have faith. You can exercise your faith as you take that medication, by constantly declaring your faith and victory over disease and sickness. Remember, you will have what you say.

Apostle Paul was the greatest teacher of faith, yet he was also a practical man. He advised Timothy not to drink water but to use a little wine for his stomach and other diseases. "Drink no longer water, but use a little wine for thy stomach's sake and thine often infirmities" (1 Timothy 5:23).

AVOIDING ERROR WHEN EXPRESSING FAITH

1. Stay with the Word of God.

When it comes to naming and claiming, the most important thing for you to do is to stay with the Word of God. God will not back foolish and childish claims. Your earthly father would take no notice of you if you claimed certain unrealistic and impractical things.

If you spend time confessing foolish imaginations, even the devil will take no notice of you! You are NOT the Queen of England so there is no use for you to spend time confessing that! I am NOT the Prince of Wales and there is no need for me to claim that! Do not confess unrealistic things that will not happen.

Once you stay with the Word of God you are on safe ground. "...I say unto you, The Son can do nothing of himself, but what he seeth the Father do: for what things soever he doeth, these also doeth the Son likewise" (John 5:19).

2. Affirm the Word of God.

There are three things that you can confess with safety. You can confess what you are in Christ, what you have in Christ and what you can do in Christ.

Let us run through a few of the things that are clearly stated in the Word of God. I want you to affirm and attest to the fact that you are what the Bible says you are. I want you to declare that you can do what the Bible says you can do. I want you to insist to all and sundry that you have what you say the Bible says you have.

BIBLICAL CONFESSIONS

1. I Am

a. I am born again.

"That if thou shalt confess with thy mouth the Lord Jesus, and shalt believe in thine heart that God hath raised him from the dead, thou shalt be saved [born again]" (Romans 10:9).

b. I am a new creature.

"Therefore if any man be in Christ, he is a new creature: old things are passed away; behold, all things are become new" (2 Corinthians 5:17).

c. I am complete.

"For in him dwelleth all the fulness of the Godhead bodily. And ye are complete in him, which is the head of all principality and power" (Colossians 2:9,10).

d. I am delivered.

"Who hath delivered us from the power of darkness, and hath translated us into the kingdom of his dear son" (Colossians 1:13).

e. I am free.

"Stand fast therefore in the liberty wherewith Christ hath made us free..." (Galatians 5:1).

f. I am blessed.

"Blessed be the God and Father of our Lord Jesus Christ, who hath blessed us with all spiritual blessings in heavenly places in Christ" (Ephesians 1:3). "According as his divine power hath given unto us all things that pertain unto life and godliness, through the knowledge of him that hath called us to glory and virtue" (2 Peter 1:3).

g. I am an heir.

"...Wherefore thou art no more a servant, but a son; and if a son, then an heir of God through Christ" (Galatians 4:6,7).

h. I am a king.

"And hath made us kings and priests unto God and his Father..." (Revelations 1:6).

i. I am the righteousness of God.

"For he hath made him to be sin for us, who knew no sin; that we might be made the righteousness of God in him" (2 Corinthians 5:21).

Based on these Scriptures you have a right to make these claims. I tell you, your faith will become effective and powerful as you confess these things which are in line with the Word of God.

Many Christians want to know how to have faith that works. Faith that works is the faith that makes confessions. The faith that is effective is the faith that vocalizes its claims. It is not enough to think or dream, you must speak out! This is an eternal principle of the Word of God.

Notice this amazing Scripture in the Book of Philemon: "That the communication of thy faith may become effectual by the acknowledging of every good thing which is in you in Christ Jesus" (Philemon 6). Faith becomes effective when you acknowledge and affirm the good things that are in you because of Christ.

2. I Have

a. I have all things.

"According as his divine power hath given unto us all things that pertain unto life and godliness, through the knowledge of him that hath called us to glory and virtue" (2 Peter 1:3).

b. I have dominion.

"And God said, Let us make man in our image, after our likeness: and let them have dominion..." (Genesis 1:26).

c. I have the desires of my heart.

"Delight thyself also in the Lord; and he shall give thee the desires of thine heart" (Psalm 37:4).

d. I have the spirit of power, love and a sound mind.

"For God hath not given us the spirit of fear; but of power, and of love, and of a sound mind" (2 Timothy 1:7).

e. I have the blessings of Abraham.

"Christ hath redeemed us from the curse of the law, being made a curse for us: for it is written, Cursed is every one that hangeth on a tree: That the blessing of Abraham might come on the Gentiles, through Jesus Christ; that we might receive the promise of the Spirit through faith" (Galatians 3:13,14).

f. I have the Greater One in me.

"...greater is he that is in you, than he that is in the world" (1 John 4:4).

g. I have the power of God working through me.

"But unto them which are called, both Jews and Greeks, Christ the power of God, and the wisdom of God" (1 Corinthians 1:24).

h. I have the wisdom of Christ operating through me.

"But unto them which are called, both Jews and Greeks, Christ the power of God, and the wisdom of God. But of him are ye in Christ Jesus, who of God is made unto us wisdom..." (1 Corinthians 1:24,30).

The Scriptures you are reading are the legal and scriptural basis for making these confessions. You can declare these things over and over because they are Bible-based. These are not the words of an irresponsible dreamer. These are the words of a faith-filled Christian.

In Luke 7, when Jesus encountered the centurion whose servant was ill, He marvelled at the great faith of this centurion. The centurion said, "Do not come to my house. Just stand where you are and say something"! He said to Jesus, "Speak in a word and my servant will be healed." The man had confidence in the spoken Word of God. Thank God for things that are written but it's time now to speak. It's time now to name it and claim it!

3. I Can

a. I can do all things!

"I can do all things through Christ which strengtheneth me" (Philippians 4:13).

b. I can reign in life!

"...they which receive abundance of grace and of the gift of righteousness shall reign in life by one, Jesus Christ" (Romans 5:17).

c. I can do greater works than Jesus did!

"Verily, verily, I say unto you, He that believeth on me, the works that I do shall he do also; and greater works than these shall he do; because I go unto my Father" (John 14:12).

d. I can cast out devils!

"And these signs shall follow them that believe; In my name shall they cast out devils..." (Mark 16:17).

e. I can heal the sick!

"And these signs shall follow them that believe... they shall lay hands on the sick, and they shall recover" (Mark 16:17).

f. I can overcome this mountain!

"For whatsoever is born of God overcometh the world: and this is the victory that overcometh the world, even our faith" (1 John 5:4).

g. I can make it!

"For whatsoever is born of God overcometh the world: and this is the victory that overcometh the world, even our faith" (1 John 5:4).

Paul prayed for the Ephesian Christians, that the Lord would open their eyes to see the riches of their inheritance. (Ephesians 1:18). In other words, God wants His children to see how rich an inheritance He has given to them. From today, I want you to see your rich inheritance! I want you to accept that all these things are real! Say them over and over again. There are some people who think the faith message is past. You are making a big mistake if you try to leave out faith. Jesus said, "These things ought you to do, not neglecting the others."(Matthew 23:23)

Is the Faith Message Outmoded?

Whenever Christians find a new message, they often neglect the earlier message. If you leave out faith, you will find yourself coming back to pick it up. There can be no victorious Christian life without faith. I speak positive confessions about my life everyday. I confess boldly about how fruitful I am in the kingdom. That is what I am believing God for and that is what I am seeing.

I see you rising up into your blessing now! I see you becoming more Christ-like and more glorious! You are what God says you are! You are not a failure! You are not a disgrace! There is no shame in your life!

God has lifted you up and promoted you! Your enemies shall be blown away like the chaff of the wind! I see God increasing you! Everything you touch is blessed! I see your business flourishing! I see your family flourishing! Your prosperity has become like the dust of the earth! Your blessings have become like the stars in the sky! Your great increase has become like the sand on the sea shore!

You are no ordinary person! You are a champion! You are a true champion! You can win! God is strengthening your right hand to conquer the enemy! Do not be afraid from today, the devil is the one who is frightened! Rise up and speak over the church you are pastoring! Speak to the empty chairs and tell them to be filled! You are anointed! You are full and not empty!

Command your intelligence to respond to your confessions! Command your decisions to line up to the positive claims you are making! You can win! You are indeed a successful person!

I see you with Solomonic and Davidic success! Enjoy the blessings of El' Shaddai! The blessings of the breast are your portion! You will have no need from today because the Lord has heard your cry!

Declare that you have one hundred per cent answers to your prayers. Declare that you are a good husband or wife. Maintain your confession that quarrels are not part of your marriage.

Speak over your children. Call them blessed. Call them angels. Call them anointed! Declare over your old car: you are new and a blessing to me!

■ HOW TO TAKE IT

"Be strong and of a good courage: for unto this people shalt thou divide for an inheritance the land, which I sware unto their fathers to give them. This book of the law shall not depart out of thy mouth; but thou shalt meditate therein day and night, that thou mayest observe to do according to all that is written therein: for then thou shalt make thy way prosperous, and then thou shalt have good success" (Joshua 1:6,8).

1. IT TAKES COURAGE TO ACT ON YOUR FAITH.

Joshua was the army general who took the Promised Land. If you want to walk into your possession, study the life of Joshua and follow his example. Joshua was told to be strong and very courageous. He was also told to meditate on the Word of God. All these were to enable him to obey the Word of God. To 'take your claims', means to act on the Word of God. It means to act on your faith and thereby possess your possession.

It takes courage to act on your faith. That is why God told Joshua to be strong and very courageous. It takes courage to do an altar call.

It takes courage to pray for the sick. What about if no one is healed? That is where courage comes in.

If you want financial prosperity, you must obey the Word of God, which tells us to work hard. Galatians 6:7 teaches us that we reap whatever we sow. Whatever you put in, you will reap either a thirty fold, a sixty fold, or a hundred fold.

Proverbs 6:6-8 tells us that ants are prosperous. "Go to the ant, thou sluggard; consider her ways, and be wise: which having no guide, overseer, or ruler, provideth her meat in the summer, and gathereth her food in the harvest" (Proverbs 6:6-8).

They mind their own business and work without supervision. If you really want the financial prosperity that you are confessing, then you must decide to work without supervision - like the ant. Do you want to experience a financial breakthrough? It is not enough just to confess great things.

2. You must obey the Word of God.

You must obey the Word of God which instructs you to give your tithes and offerings regularly. "Upon the first day of the week let every one of you lay by him in store, as God hath prospered him, that there be no gatherings when I come" (1 Corinthians 16:2).

Without tithing and giving offerings, your confessions about prosperity will have no effect. "Bring ye all the tithes into the storehouse, that there may be meat in mine house, and prove me now herewith, saith the Lord of hosts, if I will not open you the windows of heaven, and pour you out a blessing, that there shall not be room enough to receive it" (Malachi 3:10). You might just as well say, "Twinkle, twinkle little star, how I wonder what you are; up above the world so high, like a diamond in the sky"!

When God decides to honour your confessions and comes to the earth with your blessings, He will be looking for your seed. God will be looking for the seed that you have planted so that He can bless you supernaturally. But if there is no seed, what can God bless? He has nothing to work with.

It is not enough to just name it and claim it. You must go a step further and obey the Word of God. That is how you take it! You must act on your faith. Every time you give money to God, it is an act of faith. We believe that your money is not a stone, it is a seed. It is going to germinate and bring forth much fruit.

Generosity is honoured by the Lord. When God sees your acts of generosity which confirm your claim to prosperity, He will supernaturally pour out His blessings upon you. "There is that scattereth, and yet increaseth; and there is that withholdeth more than is meet, but it tendeth to poverty. The liberal soul shall be made fat: and he that watereth shall be watered also himself" (Proverbs 11:24,25).

Are you confessing for a happy marriage? Then be courageous and obey the biblical instructions of marriage. If the Bible says submit to your husband, be strong and submit! You will receive many blessings because of your submission.

Husbands, decide to love your wives practically. It is not enough to confess that you have a happy marriage. It is time to take a happy marriage by obeying the Word of God courageously.

Take your miracle healing by acting on the Word of God! Believe that you have the healing and act as though you have it. If you need to take medicine in order to stay alive, then take it.

But keep confessing the Word. There are times that the confessions in themselves, amount to an act of faith. God will honour your faith and prolong your life.

Are you believing God for an anointed ministry? Confess it! In 1983, I made important confessions about my future ministry. I confessed that I was fruitful. I pronounced over my life the blessing of fruitfulness. I believe that those confessions are working out after almost fifteen years. But it is not enough to just speak. You must pray and study your Bible.

3. Gain a personal knowledge of God.

A personal knowledge of God is the greatest key for anointing. Knowing God personally is something that many ministers lack. Do you listen to tapes? If you do, you are doing something right!

But you need to go a step further and know God personally for yourself. You can have what you say, but you must act on it. Faith without works is dead faith. "What doth it profit, my brethren, though a man say he hath faith, and have not works? Can faith save him?" (James 2:14).

When Abraham stretched his hand to sacrifice Isaac, God saw one of the greatest acts of faith in human history. That act gave life to the promises and confessions of Abraham. Abraham had a name which meant that he would be the father of many nations. He believed that his descendants would be like the stars in the sky, the dust of the earth and the sand on the sea shore. How could such incredible things happen? Only through living faith! Abraham's faith came alive when he courageously obeyed the Lord. Decide to obey God. Fear is what will make you disobey. If you have faith in the Lord, you will obey what He tells you to do.

In the account of the last judgement, the sheep are moved to the right and the goats to the left. It is a similar thing with your faith. The real ones are separated by the fake ones by the acts of faith that accompany them. When a confession has no confirming actions, it is actually a dead and useless claim. If you make a claim to prosperity, you must courageously go to work. You must work very hard.

The Tightrope Walker

You may have heard of the story of the man who walked across a tight rope that was tied over a waterfall. The tourists around cheered and clapped as the man performed this amazing feat. Next, the man pushed a wheelbarrow across the same tight rope. Below him was a fall of several hundred feet. This man amazingly pushed the wheelbarrow successfully to the other side. He was met with cheers and declarations of support.

He then asked the crowd, "Which of you believe that I could put a human being in the wheelbarrow and push him across this tightrope?"

The whole crowd shouted in approval saying, "We believe and know that you can do it!"

The tightrope walker then asked for one volunteer from the supportive crowd to sit in the wheelbarrow which he would push across the waterfall. There was a hush among the crowd and no one came forward. You see, the crowd claimed that they believed the man could do it, but no one was prepared to act on his claims. This meant that their faith was actually dead and useless.

If you do not back your confessions with positive actions, your faith will be a dead and useless item, worthy of the rubbish dump.

Christian friend, it is time to act on your faith. You have named it. You have claimed it. Now take it, in Jesus name!

SECTION IV
The Doctrine of Holiness

The Sin of Immorality

11

1 John 2:2
1 John 1:9

■ THE SIN OF FORNICATION

"But fornication, and all uncleanness, or covetousness, let it not be once named among you, as becometh saints" (Ephesians 5:3). Fornication is sexual intercourse before marriage. The equivalent of fornication in marriage is adultery, that is, when you have sex with anyone who is not your marriage partner.

God's standard for the Christian life is that no believer should ever be involved in fornication. Christians should not have a history of regularly committing fornication. Neither should they ever be involved in it. Not even once! But unfortunately, even in Christian circles, fornication is commonly found amongst born-again Christians.

This "cancer" of fornication is rapidly affecting the Body of Christ, because many Christians who get involved in fornication do not know its spiritual and physical implications. They do not know its complications.

FIFTEEN REASONS WHY YOU MUST NOT COMMIT FORNICATION

1. FORNICATION IS DISOBEDIENCE.

The first reason why you should not commit fornication is that it is disobedience to God. "...Behold, to obey is better than sacrifice, and to hearken than the fat of rams" (1 Samuel 15:22). We are all subject to the temptation to fornicate. But the priority of every Christian must be to obey the Lord. If you do not obey God you stand to lose. Obedience means more to God than any great sacrifice that you can make to Him. Some of you come to church, put your offering in the basket, pay your tithes, lift up your hands and worship his Majesty. You give sacrifices of praise to God. But God prefers your simple obedience to your many offerings and your lifted hands.

I once met a lady who told me that the commandment not to commit fornication is an old-fashioned law, meant for the olden days. She argued that it was no longer a realistic instruction. Even if it does not make sense to you, your duty is still to obey God.

Christianity has to do with your relationship with the Lord. As a Christian, you are dependent on God, and it is only the Lord who can bless you. If you choose to disobey and disregard God, I do not know what kind of relationship you want to have with Him. When you disobey God, you incur God's curses upon your life.

Some people complain that it is difficult to obey God. "It costs so much," they say. Dear friend, the truth is that it pays to obey God but it costs to disobey Him. You will realize that when God gives us a commandment, it is for our own good. It pays to obey God but it is very expensive to disobey Him.

2. FORNICATION WILL DESTROY YOUR SOUL.

When you commit fornication, the Bible says you will destroy your soul: "But whoso committeth adultery with a woman lacketh understanding: he that doeth it DESTROYETH his own SOUL" (Proverbs 6:32). This means that fornication will have an effect on you spiritually. Anybody who is involved in fornication gets affected spiritually. You may not know exactly how it affects you. But it does affect you, and will lead you to backslide.

On Sunday mornings, there are people sitting in church knowing very well what they did the night before. Some Christians even come to church straight from their boyfriends' beds. Your pastor may not know what you have done. He may have shaken hands with you, but did not have any word of knowledge about you! So you continue in sin. Know that it is gradually destroying your soul; your inner self is affected! With experience I have come to see that when somebody commits fornication, his spiritual life takes a nose-dive. When a Christian falls into immorality his lifestyle changes. The destruction of the soul has begun.

3. FORNICATION WILL DESTROY YOUR BODY.

When you commit fornication you commit sin directly against your own body. "Flee fornication. Every sin that a man doeth is without the body; but he that committeth fornication sinneth against his own body" (1 Corinthians 6:18).

When you commit fornication you commit a crime against your body. You are destroying your body. If you commit a crime against the State, you are said to be destroying the State. That is why the State will arrest and prosecute you. In the same way when you commit fornication, you commit a crime against your body, and God will prosecute you for that. "...know ye not that your body is the temple of the Holy Ghost...?" (1 Corinthians 6:19).

4. YOU MAKE COVENANTS WITH ALL SORTS OF PEOPLE.

Sex is intended to be a binding experience between two people. Know that when you commit fornication, you make a covenant with whoever you had sex with. God's plan is that when a woman has sex for the first time, her hymen is broken and blood is shed. Whenever blood is shed some sort of agreement or covenant is created. That means when you have sex with different people, you may actually be entering into union with them.

Agreements are made because blood is shed. That is one of the reasons why Paul asked, "...shall I then take the members of Christ, and make them the members of an harlot? God forbid" (1 Corinthians 6:15).

Such covenants are for real. They can affect you for the rest of your life. I have seen people who have been crippled all their Christian lives because of fornication. Some Christians never rise out of the covenant of fornication.

The son of a fetish priest came to our church some years ago. He told us how he got involved in witchcraft. He said he once slept in the cemetery with his father. After seven days his father cut his hand, drew his blood and mixed it with his own. Then they both drank the blood and made a permanent agreement. A covenant of witchcraft! This brother was under that covenant. A time came when he had to decide between his father, (that is following the fetish) and following Christ. This young man could not break away from this blood covenant. Friend, I am talking about blood covenants! He left the church after some months and went back to his father's shrine. Although he was born again, and knew the Lord, he could not easily break away from his covenant.

Blood and covenants are real things so do not sleep with just anybody. You may be sleeping with a witch and that witch will be in your home all the days of your life.

5. Fornication brings evil spirits into your life.

The Bible says: "...Babylon the great...is become the habitation of devils, and the hold of every foul spirit, and a cage of every unclean and hateful bird" (Revelation 18:2).

A stronghold of evil spirits is a refuge, a sanctuary or a hiding place for demons. Why did so many evil spirits come to live in Babylon? Why has Babylon become a hold of demons?

According to Revelations 18:3, "For all nations have drunk of the wine of the wrath of her fornication, and the kings of the earth have committed fornication with her." The kings, the ministers of state, the rich and the famous have committed fornication with her. That is why evil spirits have come into her life.

Fornication attracts evil spirits into your life. This is so true of many Christians' lives. Evil spirits have aggregated and congregated in them because of their fornication.

When God says do not do something He knows why! Some of the evil spirits that come into you can prevent you from ever getting married. Some evil spirits can cause you to backslide. Some of them will cause you to marry the wrong person. Some of them can cause you to have a bad marriage. Some of these evil spirits can also lead you into unfaithfulness in your marriage. The list is endless. Do you want to become a hiding place for demons?

6. Fornication brings sickness.

There are a host of diseases that only come about through sexual intercourse. We call these STDs (sexually transmitted diseases). The germs that cause these diseases will have access into you when you commit fornication.

Let me mention only ten of them. Please notice how big the names of these "animals" are!

- Neisseria Gonococcus - this causes Gonorrhoea.
- Treponema Pallidum - this causes Syphilis.
- Chlamydia Trachomatis - this causes Non-Specific Urethritis.
- Hepatitis "B" virus - this causes Liver diseases.
- Herpes Simplex type II virus - this causes Herpes Genitalis.
- Trichomonas Vaginalis - this causes Vaginitis.
- Lymphogranuloma Venereum
- Haemophilus Ducreyii - causes Soft Sore (Chancroid).
- Urinary tract infection
- Cancer of the cervix - frequent sex at an early age predisposes you to cancer of the cervix.

If you wait till you marry before having sex, you may save yourself from all these diseases. But if you continue to commit fornication, then remember that all these "animals" will enter your body and make you sick!

7. Fornication brings death.

Fornication will kill you if you acquire the Human Immuno Virus (HIV). Unless God works a miracle, you may die of AIDS. HIV is now a death sentence.

It is sad to say that in the charismatic churches there are many Christians who are HIV positive. A laboratory technician once gave me some alarming statistics. A team of lab technicians organized a blood donation event in a charismatic church and out of about a hundred people who donated blood, a large percentage tested positive for HIV. In other words, our churches have significant numbers of people with the HIV virus. Fornicating with your fellow church member may mean your death! Those who are HIV positive can develop AIDS. And when you have AIDS, it means you have just a few more years to live.

8. Fornication brings unwanted pregnancies.

Do you want to attend school with your child? When I was in secondary school, there was a man in the sixth form who was said to have a child in form one. How could this be? Probably due to an unwanted pregnancy earlier on in his life.

9. Fornication brings unwanted abortions.

If you commit fornication and become pregnant, it is most likely that you will want to hide it; by committing abortion. You are falling into the same trap that David fell into when he committed adultery. Murder is the commonest evil that follows the sin of fornication. Abortion is the sin of murder. Many fornicators are murderers. Multiple abortionists are multiple murderers.

Dear friend, you may not know that abortion is murder. Medically speaking, abortion is the termination of human life. The human life may be just a few cells, but it is human life! Are you a murderer?

10. Fornication brings infertility.

Let me explain how fornication brings infertility. During an abortion, various instruments similar to knives and forks are introduced into the womb. This often leads to infection. And this infection often leads to blocking of the fallopian tubes. Young lady, if your fallopian tubes are blocked you will not be able to become pregnant. Then you may find yourself in every deliverance centre-looking for healing. Receive your deliverance now by obeying the Word.

11. Fornication brings unwanted children.

Unwanted children are usually products of fornication. Why should you be pregnant when you are a 16-year-old student? Your child is supposed to be your daughter or son and not your younger sister or brother!

12. The unwanted children become social deviants.

Whenever a child is not wanted, he becomes a reject in society: a "pikin na bollo" as we say in my country, Ghana. Many deviants in society have a background of having been unwanted.

I remember a young boy who beat up his mother and left home. No one knows where he is. I asked why a young sixth-former should behave in this unbecoming manner. The answer can be traced to his mother's history. This young lad was a product of his mother's fornication when she was only 15 years old.

The boy had been made to stay with different aunties and other relatives. You see, his mother had to continue schooling. When his mother eventually got married, she was ashamed of her unwanted child. So he continued staying with other sympathetic relatives. Naturally, the young lad grew up doing very poorly in school.

He was suspended several times and became what we call a social deviant, a very bitter boy. Now whose fault is it? Do not blame any child who is born out of fornication if he becomes a social deviant!

13. Fornication brings disgrace.

Although fornication is an international and cross-cultural sin committed by many people-it is still a disgraceful act. "A wound and dishonour shall he get; and his reproach shall not be wiped away" (Proverbs 6:33). Save yourself from this disgrace!

14. Fornication brings hurts and wounds.

Read the story of Tamar and Amnon in the second book of Samuel, Chapter 13. Fornication leads to many hurts. Tamar was hurt. Absalom her brother was hurt. King David was hurt. The relationship between Tamar and Amnon was broken forever.

What you must realize is that fornication is essentially wrong and evil. It only leads to many terrible and devastating complications in life.

15. Fornication breaks marriages.

Fornication is often the last straw that breaks the camel's back in unhappy marriages. Remember, it is only in the case of adultery that God allows divorce. God knows that this is the sin which has the ability to destroy marriages.

PHYSICAL STEPS TO AVOIDING FORNICATION

How can we save ourselves from this disgraceful sin? We are all men of like passions subject to the same temptations as everyone else. I believe the Lord has shown me some important steps that will keep us all from sin. Four of these steps are spiritual and eight are physical. Let us start with the physical steps.

1. No untimely relationships

Very young people should not enter into relationships for courtship. "To every thing there is a season, and a time to every purpose under the heaven" (Ecclesiastes 3:1).

There is a time for entering into a relationship. Why do you want to enter into a relationship when you are still in school? You do not even have a job in sight! In my church, I do not recognize relationships of teenagers. I will advise you to break it in the name of Jesus! You worry yourself for nothing when you play with relationships at the wrong time.

2. Relationships only unto marriage

You must only enter into relationships that lead to marriage. The only intimate relationship between men and women that God approves of is marriage. A Christian man and woman must move towards God's plan, which is marriage.

When I proposed to my wife many years before I actually married her, I asked her two questions: "Can you marry a doctor? Can you marry a pastor?" Marriage was what I had in mind.

She was in love with me so she said yes! I had decided that I was going to marry her. She was not just a friend or girlfriend. She had passed on to become someone special-the person who was going to be my wife and the bearer of my children.

I remember asking a young man who had been in a relationship with a sister in church for two years, "Are you getting married?" His response was "I don't think we will. We are just in a relationship."

I think a lady must be foolish to be in such a relationship. The man is just using you, and will throw you away one day. The relationships that God approves of are relationships that are headed towards his will; and his will is marriage! If you know that your relationship is not going towards marriage, then it is just going towards fornication. Stop right there!

3. Holy relationships

The Bible says there is a time to "refrain from embracing" (Ecclesiastes 3:5). If you are in a relationship, there is a time to refrain from embracing. I can hold my wife, I can hug her and I will not be doing anything wrong. But those of you who are not married are not expected to do so.

Even when you touch your fiancée's hand, "osmosis" begins to occur! In my church we have a few rules for counselling young people in relationships. We do not just tell you to live a holy and a pure life, but you are specifically told what living holy entails. You must only have holy relationships!

4. Early marriage

I encourage people to marry young. The more Christians delay the marriage ceremony, the more likely they are to end up living in sin. What are you waiting for? In certain churches there are road blocks to marriage. Couples are presented with so many obstacles to delay marriage. But that should not be the case.

The Bible encourages you to have a wife when you are young; wife of your youth. "Let thy fountain be blessed: and rejoice with the wife of thy youth" (Proverbs 5:18). Do not use the lack of money as an excuse, because you can marry if you really want to. Marry whilst you are still young. Do not wait until you have all the comfortable things in life before venturing into marriage.

When I decided to get married, somebody whispered to my wife to marry someone who had everything in life. I certainly did not qualify because I had nothing! I have been through some really hard times with my wife, where we did not have any money. We had to warn our visitors to sit in a particular way because our chairs were weak and broken. She even had to go abroad to work to buy us some furniture. I have truly struggled with my wife, so I love her. I did not have to wait until I was an old man to get married.

I love the people with whom I have been through struggles and difficulties. They are different from those who have come in a time of total blessing. When you are already established in life, you will have people interested in you because you are already blessed. But the wife of your youth will marry you not because of what you have, but because of who you are. It is a blessing to marry young.

5. Non-polygamous marriage

The only person you must be naked with is your wife. "And they were both naked, the man and his wife, and were not ashamed" (Genesis 2:25). Not your girlfriend, fiancee, nurse or secretary.

You are not supposed to have any other wife. God does not endorse polygamy. A polygamous lifestyle encourages fornication.

In Ghana, we have "official" polygamy, where a man maintains two or three wives. But there is an "unofficial" version of polygamy which is practised by most successful people in Ghana. They have an official wife whom they take to official functions and appear in public with. There are also the unofficial women in the lives of these men. And this is common practice by most of the "big shots" in our society.

Such men have no intention of divorcing their wives. They will spend the weekends at special places with these "side" girls. They travel with them to Paris, and generally have a good time with them. But they still maintain the official marriage. We must keep this culture of unofficial polygamy far from us, if we want to avoid fornication.

6. Sexually active marriages

We need to have sexually active marriages. There are many marriages which are not sexually active. It is amazing that before people get married they want to hold and touch each other, but when they get married they can lie by each other like logs. Why commit fornication when you can commit love. "Drink waters out of thine own cistern, and running waters out of thine own well" (Proverbs 5:15). Sex can be likened to drinking water. And we drink water several times in a day. So the Bible admonishes you to have sex several times, so you will not thirst for any other woman.

There is more symbolic language in Proverbs 5. "Let thy fountains be dispersed abroad..." (Proverbs 5:16). What in sex looks like a fountain? God's rule for healthy marriages is that the fountains should be allowed to disperse abroad. You must allow the fountains to flow. Some fountains have been closed two weeks or six months. Such fountains are not blessed!

"...and rivers of waters in the streets" (Proverbs 5:16). What could these streets be? If the fountains are going to flow into the streets, then God says: "Let them be only thine OWN, and not strangers'..." (Proverbs 5:17). If you are married, your wife's breasts must satisfy you at all times Proverbs 5:19). (Why should you be playing with somebody's breast, when you have your own wife's.

One of the ways to prevent fornication if you are married is to have sex regularly. When you eat and are satisfied, you do not feel like eating any more. Women especially should know that when they have sex regularly with their husbands, they prevent them from having extra-marital affairs.

A man of God fell into sin. I was sitting with him after he admitted he had impregnated one of his church members, and he was crying. I was so sad, I wanted to know how it happened. He described the difficulties of sex he had with his wife. She did not want to have sex with him. She kept complaining that she was tired, or cold. As soon as her husband committed adultery, she became active. She realized her husband's adultery was a product of what was going on at home. Some wives are just waiting for their husbands to commit adultery and then they will wake up!

SPIRITUAL STEPS TO AVOIDING FORNICATION

1. Honesty

You need honesty to save yourself from fornication. If you have a problem and need help, you have to be open about it. The doctor cannot help you unless you open up and tell him your problem. No one can help you if you do not ask for help. Everybody needs help. But not everybody wants help. You need to open up and share your problems with honesty. Without the belt of truth and sincerity you can never receive help from God.

There is a story about a Christian brother who always thought the messages preached in church were directed at others. The pastor would minister under the power of the Holy Ghost, and this Christian brother would sit in the church assuming the message was for somebody else.

After the service, he would thank the pastor and say, "Pastor, bless you for this message. I believe you really ministered to THEM. You really touched THEIR hearts. It's a message THEY really needed."

The pastor tried to modify his sermon so that the man would realize that he was actually talking to him but it was to no avail. Then one day, it rained and there was a flood. No one but this brother came to church. As he sat there alone, the Pastor said to himself, that at last this young man would know that the message was for him.

The pastor preached his heart out. After that the brother came up and said, "Pastor, that was a very powerful message. If only THEY had come to church today, in fact, THEIR lives would have been touched!" And that's how it is. We preach the Word, and people always assume it's for somebody else! We are simply not honest enough to accept that we have a problem.

2. Prayer

We need prayer to be able to deal with sin. "And said unto them, Why sleep ye? rise and pray, lest ye enter into temptation" (Luke 22:46). Prayer is very important to prevent you from falling into temptation. Prayer strengthens you for whatever is coming your way.

Next time you fast, get up early and pray before the day. You will find supernatural strength to go on. This strength comes from prayer. When you pray you build up your spirit and become spiritually strong. The Bible says the body without the spirit is dead. That means the day your spirit goes out of your body, you will die. It also means that whatever is happening in your body is affected by your spirit.

Prayer helps you to fight off certain temptations. That is why Jesus said pray, in case you fall into temptation. That is why Jesus prayed all the time. Once, Jesus prayed for forty days and nights. Soon after praying and fasting, the devil came to tempt him, but he was too strong for the devil. The devil had chosen the wrong time to attack Christ.

Many years ago, the devil tried to bring a temptation my way. But that day, the Lord led me to pray for hours. I did not even know why the "tongues" seemed to be rolling out of me. That prayer delivered me!

The Bible says we do not know what to pray for as we ought. Nobody knows what is going to happen tomorrow. But God knows!

That is why he said we should watch and pray in case anything happens. The disciples slept on that fateful night. All of them were tempted, and all of them fell. It is not only Judas who forsook Christ on that night. All the disciples deserted their master in the day of his greatest need.

3. Deliverance

Some cases of fornication need deliverance. Other cases do not. If you are always being unfaithful to your husband or wife, you need to be delivered. Some people need to see a pastor and undergo deliverance from evil spirits, especially the chronic fornicators.

If you have a chronic problem, then you need deliverance. If something drives you to fornicate, certainly it cannot be God who drives you. "...For oftentimes it had caught him: and he was kept bound with chains and in fetters; and he brake the bands, and was DRIVEN OF THE DEVIL into the wilderness" (Luke 8:29).

When something drives you to sin over and over, you probably need deliverance. It is only the devil who drives people. God does not drive people! God does not drive us. Even when you need to be saved, God will not force you to be saved.

I believe that what we need to do is to be humble enough to admit that we need deliverance and to ask our pastors to help us. God does not force us to do anything. I have come to see that if YOU want to go to Hell, YOU will go to Hell and God WILL NOT stop you. I learnt years ago not to force people into Heaven.

God will not force you to get your deliverance, you must seek God yourself.

4. Seek grace and mercy

I think the grace of God is the most important factor. Because you may use all the other steps but you will still fall.

You can use every "mathematical" or logical step under the sun: deliverance, followed by honesty, plus sexually-active marriage and non-polygamous marriage, right through to early marriage, divided by a holy relationship, multiplied by a relationship unto marriage, to the square of no relationship! It is by grace and grace alone!

The song writer said, "Through many dangers, toils and snares, I have already come. T'was grace that brought me safe thus far, and grace will lead me home." Friends, it is grace that will see us through!

The Sins of the Tongue

12

■ THE IMPORTANCE OF DIRECTING THE TONGUE

The tongue is very vital to our lives as human beings. As a physical organ, it gives us the ability to taste and speak. In the spiritual sense, the tongue controls our destiny, regardless of our status as Christians or unbelievers.

According to Proverbs 18:21, "Death and life are in the power of the tongue..." This means that the power of cancer, leukaemia, paralysis, long life, health and wealth are all embedded in the tongue. The tongue controls death and life!

The Tongue's Creative Power

1. God made man in His own image with creative ability.

When God was in the process of creating the earth, He spoke with his mouth. He said, "Let there be...", and there was! These were creative words. They were spoken out of faith. These words created the world and brought life into being.

The land and the host of animals were created. The sea, the fish, the mountains, the green grass, the waterfalls and the rivers that we see were all created by faith-filled words.

2. The creative ability of man is in the tongue.

It can be argued that if human beings were made in God's image, then he has also made it possible that his image will possess this creative power. What we should not forget is that he did not put this creative power in our feet, hands, hearts or kidneys. The creative power lies in our tongue.

The Tongue's Destructive Power

1. The tongue has power to give life and to kill.

The tongue is a very powerful instrument. But unfortunately, we are often unaware of the power it possesses. It is dangerous to handle dynamite when you do not know what you are dealing with - it can kill you. Many Christians have been killed by their own tongues. We almost always take our words for granted. Many Christians pass negative comments on their own lives, without knowing the far reaching effects.

Whoever you are and whatever you do, your language must not be poisonous: "...the tongue... is an unruly evil, full of deadly poison" (James 3:8). The first thing to note about this Scripture is that it was not written to unbelievers, but to Christians. According to the Bible, no man can tame his tongue. It takes the Holy Spirit to help the believer control his tongue.

The tongue is full of poison; poison that can kill. It is this very poison that we will be learning about in the next few pages.

2. The tongue's venom has a similar effect to that of a poisonous snake.

When a snake strikes you, it poisons your blood stream. Some types of snake poison affect the nervous system. Other types affect the cardiovascular system. When the poison hits the nervous system, many of the nerves become paralysed and you may stop breathing and die. When the other type of poison hits the cardiovascular system, you may begin to bleed internally and externally. Whichever type of poison it is, you better deal with it as fast as you can - or else you will be in big trouble. Poison kills!

I remember in 1982, my class was in a laboratory at the university's zoology department for a lesson on snakes. (We had to learn about different snakes and their poisons, since we were medical students.) A visiting lecturer brought out a huge viper from a glass container. He opened the mouth to expose the fangs of the snake. There were these two frightening and deadly fangs within the mouth.

The lecturer put his hand inside the mouth, near the fangs and squeezed some of the poison from the snake. (This is sometimes done to produce anti-snake serum to treat snakebites.) But something went wrong during the demonstration and the viper wriggled itself loose and struck the hand of the lecturer. He had a little cut. We were so scared, because we knew this man could easily die. Luckily, he was treated and he survived. Why were we so worried? Because we knew that the poison had the power to end the man's life.

Let's say a snake poisons someone you love - for instance your father. Your father is probably the one who pays your school fees. It means that within the mouth of a poisonous snake is the ability to stop you from going to school. Within the mouth of the snake is the ability to take away the father of a child or the husband of a wife! If a poisonous snake bites a pastor, it will take away the shepherd and scatter the flock.

These are the realities of poison. Just as we took the poison out of that snake's mouth, we can also take the poison out of your tongue. It may be difficult, but it can be done. But the question is "How do you remove this poison?"

First of all, you have to know what this poison is and how it works. Then you can find an antidote for it. Let's now begin to examine several important types of poison that are found in the tongue. Understanding these different types will help you to know how to deal with them.

■ THE DEADLY POISONS OF THE TONGUE

One thing I'm sure about is that many Christians do not know the effect that lies have on their lives. This is because lying is probably the commonest sin of all. Big lies, small lies, spoken lies, unspoken lies and half-truths are all lies. I once asked a congregation, "How many of you have been involved in the sin of lying?" Almost all the people present raised their hands. People simply do not know the damaging effect of lies on their souls.

THE POISON OF LIES

1. Lies destroy the conscience of man.

The first damaging effect of lies is that it sears your conscience. You see, your conscience is the measuring rod that keeps you in line with God. Your conscience is the still small voice that tells you when you are wrong. When your conscience is damaged, you no longer have that correcting and refining influence to keep you on the right track. People with seared conscience are known to have committed terrible crimes against humanity. They are callous, and no longer care whom they hurt or offend. A Christian without a good conscience is like a nation without a police force. That Christian will commit greater and greater sins. He will start from "white" lies to "small" lies and then graduate to "bigger" lies. From there he may actually begin to indulge in criminal acts.

A Christian Liar

I once had an encounter with a classic Christian liar who had little or no conscience. Some years ago, our church, the Lighthouse Chapel International used to rent the medical school canteen in the city for church services. We needed some wooden chairs, and this gentleman was introduced to me as a good Christian carpenter who could do the job.

At the time, I was not experienced in dealing with these artisans. I trusted everybody, especially if they told me they were Christians. We paid this gentleman a large sum of money in advance, and received his assurances that he would do a great job.

Weeks later, when it was time for delivery of the chairs, he demanded extra money to complete the job. He failed to deliver on schedule and when we confronted him, he told us a lie about having sent the chairs to a workshop on the outskirts of the city where he could produce the best quality. Our visit to that workshop revealed that we were dealing with a diabolical liar. He had been deceiving us all along, and we were not aware of it.

The church abounds with such Christian liars. Some unbelievers even have a better conscience than some Christians. "Speaking LIES in hypocrisy; HAVING THEIR conscience seared with a hot iron" (1 Timothy 4:2).

2. Lying hardens the heart.

Lying is a dangerous folly, because you gradually believe your own lies. This is self-deception. This leads us to the next damaging effect of a lying tongue: a hardened heart. The Bible calls it "deceiving your own self" (James 1:22).

From the stage of self-deception, liars graduate into the deadly condition known as hardness of heart. "Harden not your hearts..." (Hebrews 3:8).

Many people are invited to church. They sit under the anointing and hear the Word of God, but do not respond or change their lives. Although some people are not born again, they convince themselves that they are Christians. Gradually, they develop the deadly condition known as 'hardness of heart'. This is a stage where God can no longer reach you.

God tried to reach Pharaoh. Indeed, God tried harder than he had tried with any human being I have known under the sun. He tried every method. He sent Moses, and Aaron. These were preachers, pastors, prophets and men of God. They were also miracle workers who performed miracles of healing, miracles of supernatural lice, flies and frogs. All this, just to convince one man. God had to kill every first born Egyptian before Pharaoh would listen to reason.

By the time God finished trying to convince one man, he had destroyed a whole nation. In other words, the condition of a man's heart destroyed a whole nation. And even after God had destroyed the whole nation, Pharaoh was still not fully converted.

It is dangerous to hear the truth and lie to yourself that what you are hearing is not true. You may need some "Pharaohic" treatment to change your mind. Haven't you heard the testimonies of so many people who got converted after all their chickens died, or after armed robbers attacked them?

When you are deceiving yourself, simple methods of communication no longer work with you. Counselling doesn't work, preaching doesn't work, teaching doesn't work, and advice doesn't work. What may now work are the "frogs and flies" of Pharaoh.

3. Lies are tools of Satan.

Lies are the instruments the devil uses to work great evil. "The instruments also of the churl [wretch] are evil: he deviseth wicked devices to destroy the poor with lying words..." (Isaiah 32:7). Lies form an integral part of most wicked and bad things. There is a saying that, 'All thieves are liars, all liars are thieves'.

Most wicked activities cannot go on without a lie being told here or there. Dictators for example, cannot suppress entire nations without the propaganda of lies and deception, which they continually perpetrate. Have you not noticed that wicked and undemocratic dictators do not allow a free and an independent press to operate? They desperately need the assistance of diabolical lies to stay in power and oppress the masses.

Whenever you speak a lie, what you are actually doing is grasping one of Satan's favourite tools. You are joining hands with the devil and you are playing his game. Jesus calls him the father of liars (John 8:44).

The Church Is Attacked

Some time ago, I experienced an attack against my church and ministry by some members in the community. We had entered into an agreement with the local government to develop a car park by the church in exchange for building a community facility. As time went on, these people who felt they had a cause to fight, attacked our property and broke into the contractor's storage shed. This led to their arrest by the police. However, whilst on bail they began a campaign of lies against me, the pastors and the church.

Although the entire project was intended to be a kind gesture to the community, it turned out to be one of the nastiest experiences for our church. As I said earlier, evil does not work without the power of lies and deception. The problem with these individuals in the community escalated to the point where all sorts of high-ranking government officials got involved. These boys went 'behind our backs' and said several things to them, many of which were untrue.

As the situation got out of control, we had to go and see these government officials ourselves. I remember one office in particular, where these boys had already been with their version of the story. Their version, of course, was tainted with lies. When we arrived at the office, we asked to see the minister. We had to wait for some hours, after which we were welcomed in politely and asked to narrate our story. One of my associates was the spokesman for that day. He gave the background to our problems with our brothers from the community. The minister listened quietly, giving an occasional nod here and there.

At the end of the narration, the minister said, "Well, I understand your problems, and I can appreciate your difficulties, but there is something I also want to point out."

He continued, "I hear there is one of your pastors who claims that he does not respect me because he says I am an uneducated person who has accidentally become a minister of state."

We were dumbfounded! He was clearly referring to one of my pastors. "What on earth is this man talking about? I thought to myself."

He went on, "I hear this pastor also said in the church, that I was seen distributing machine guns at the market to quell a recent demonstration."

By this time we were totally confused. We wondered, "What are these lies?"

I gasped, "This is not true! It is a complete lie and a fabrication." I went on, "Everyone knows that we wouldn't say anything like that!"

"How can this man believe such a lie?" I thought. But these liars had already influenced him.

I insisted that there was no truth in what he had been told. However, the minister went on to outline his background as a professional and spoke at length, describing some of his achievements. He also pointed out to us he had been at home during those demonstrations in question, and could not have distributed any machine guns. Unfortunately, this man had been influenced by a lie. And this lie had a damaging effect on the church's image and our integrity.

Later on, another witness disproved these lies, but much damage and hurt had already been done. We were told later by a district authority officer about the identity of the individual who had spread these lies. The liar is reported to have said, "I was only saying this to add some spice to our story." You see, their goal could not have been achieved without the help of lies.

This is the point I am trying to make. Evil cannot succeed without the help of lies. Lies are tools in the hands of the enemy. Lies are the weapons of Satan. Do not join hands with diabolos - the devil.

Through experience I have come to realise that about 90 per cent or more of Christians are involved in lying. The Bible is saying that other people's lives are destroyed because of your lies. There are believers who lie as easily as they breathe.

I trust people who speak the truth. No matter what you have done, or the sin you have committed, if you tell the truth you are on your way to receiving help.

In Isaiah 1:18, God says that, "come and let us reason together, though your sins be as scarlet, they shall be white as wool. Though they may be red as crimson, they shall be white as snow". He wipes the slate clean. When you are wrong and you admit it, it changes your situation. "He that covereth his sin shall not prosper..." (Proverbs 28:13).

4. Lies generates God's hatred.

There are six things the Lord hates, and lying is one of them (Proverbs 6:16,17). He hates lies. Be honest when you discern that you have a problem. Get help while you can. I have done it before. When I was a young Christian I went to see my leaders and pastors to help me when I had a problem.

Be honest with yourself. Correct any lies you may have told. I have had people come back to me to recant their lies. On some occasions I have had some church members tell me, "Pastor, when I came to your office for counselling, I lied to you, but now I want to tell you the truth." God will bless such people. That is the beginning of something new. By God's standards it is always better to speak the truth and face the consequences. What is it that you have to say? Say it. Be bold, and be strong. That is the beginning of your redemption and your spiritual breakthrough.

God hates liars so much that He has decided to put them all together in one place - Hell. Liars are lined up together with sorcerers, murderers, and abominable people, and sent into Hell. "...the abominable, and murderers... and sorcerers... and All liars, shall have their part in the lake which burneth with fire and brimstone..." (Revelation 21:8). Most Christians will not have anything to do with sorcery and witchcraft, but I know many Christians who would very easily tell lies.

THE POISON OF FLATTERY

1. A flattering tongue is destructive.

"To flatter" means "to excessively praise someone insincerely in order to gain favour for yourself." Many leaders are surrounded by people who flatter them. They speak words which are not true in order to feed their ego. They make the leader feel that he is the greatest and the best. "There is no one like you," they say. The Bible warns against flattery: "For neither at any time used we flattering words..." (1 Thessalonians 2:5). "...A FLATTERING mouth worketh ruin" (Proverbs 26:28).

It is not only secular leaders who fall prey to flattering hypocrites. Christian leaders are also subject to the insincerity of such people. What then is the effect of flattery? The answer is destruction and ruin.

In Ghana, where I live there are traditional chiefs and rulers who do not wield 'real' political power. During traditional gatherings such as festivals, there are official flatterers who double as linguists to hail the chiefs and say many great things about them. Some of the accolades are so fantastic that it just makes you wonder! Many of these chiefs are even made to feel like God himself.

I want to show you some of the amazing words of praise that are showered on some of these chiefs.

1. The first one is (and I'm using the Ashanti language here): Konini, wo na wo twere ebo ma ebopae. This means, "Great warrior, you are the one who leans on a rock and make it break." Let's ask ourselves now, who can lean on a rock and make it break?

2. Another flattering phrase is: Hene kese, wo na wo tia nsuo mu ma nsuo we. This also means, "Great king, you are the one who steps in water and make it dry up." Let's ask ourselves again, who on earth can step in water and cause it to immediately dry up. Once again, human beings are made to feel "super human".

3. Another amazing flattery is: Wo na wode kenten ko nsuo trenee ano ede nsuo ba fie. This means, "You are the one who goes to fetch water from the river with a basket." Imagine that! Fetching water with a basket! Who on earth can do that?

4. Another incredible utterance of flattery is: Wo na wode wo nsapan ekum gyata. This means, "You are the one who kills the lion with your bare hands." Think about that! Killing a lion with your bare hands! Only people like Samson could do that, and that by the anointing!

2. Flattery is a negative infusion of pride.

What is the effect of all this flattery? You see, flattery is one of the deadly poisons of the tongue. It makes you think that you are what you are not. Flattery is an injection of pride. Therefore, flattery is a trap leading to a 'fall'. Because "pride goeth before a fall".

It makes ordinary men think they are God. But no man is a god. All men are mortal. That is why great kings and princesses are here today and gone tomorrow. Mighty billionaires who have everything are also here today and gone tomorrow. "Your fathers, where are they?... do they live for ever?" (Zechariah 1:5).

Remember the story of Herod in the New Testament. He was a good speaker and a powerful orator. "And upon a set day Herod, arrayed in royal apparel, sat upon his throne, and made an oration unto them. And the people gave a shout, saying, it is the voice of a God, and not of A man. And immediately the angel of the Lord smote him, because he gave not God the glory: and he was eaten of worms..." (Acts 12:21-23).

This man attended a ceremony and was the main speaker. After his speech, people crowded around him and shouted his praises.

They told him, "We've never heard anyone speak the way you spoke today. It was just supernatural."

They continued, "You know, if God Himself were to have spoken, He couldn't have done any better than you did, O great Herod."

They injected pride into him. Herod believed he was becoming God. The Lord had to prove immediately that he was a mere man. He died that very day.

I remember years ago, I asked one of my fathers in the ministry, "How are you able to overcome pride, when you preach so powerfully?"

He remarked, "I've noticed that when I finish ministering there are many people who give me all sorts of praises. After analyzing it for a while I realized that pride was being served to me on a silver platter."

He continued, "Because of this, whenever I finish preaching and the Lord has moved powerfully, I quickly slip out to avoid being served with pride."

You see, this man of God had learned that flattery was a deadly poison, which would eventually kill him. Remember, pride comes before a fall. Remember also that it was flattery that led to the execution of Herod.

When I preach, I do not look out for anybody to praise me. When I first started out preaching, I was very interested in people's comments after my sermons. The post-preaching comments had two effects on me. Most of the time they encouraged me. I realised that after some time however, that when nobody made a comment after the service, I was discouraged.

Then the Lord spoke to me, "Do not look out for what anybody has to say. Just preach what I ask you to preach, whether they like it or not. You are doing your job!"

With that attitude I was suddenly liberated, and have continued to preach successfully without looking for the praises of men. After all, people will tell you what they know you want to hear.

3. FLATTERY RESULTS IN DELUSIONS.

When people notice that you love their sweet words, they increasingly shower you with half-truths and lies. The flattery has begun and the fall is imminent! "...with flattering lips and with a double heart do they speak. The Lord shall cut off all flattering lips..." (Psalm 12:2,3).

The Deluded Politician

I know of an aspiring presidential candidate who thought he was very popular. This man had people around him who told him he was the people's choice in several sections of the nation.

They told him, "The whole of the North and the whole of the West is for you."

"Really?" He marvelled.

"Oh yes. You have no challenger in these regions," his aides replied.

Then they asked, "If only we could have some more money to go campaigning in another region, that whole area would fall to you." So he dished out some more money to these political activists until they had 'milked' him of all his money. They flattered this poor aspirant into thinking that the whole country was in support of him.

This deluded and impoverished presidential aspirant eventually received very few votes. How disillusioned and shocked he must have been! Such are the rewards of flattery. And I know it is the same story for many such politicians. They are sweet-talked into spending all of their money, and they believe the lies that are told them. Flattery is indeed one of the deadly poisons of the tongue.

You must not only be wary of being flattered. You must also take care not to become a flatterer yourself. Do not say things that you do not believe in your heart. There is a punishment reserved for flatterers. God says that he will cut off your lips (Psalm 12;3). Do you want your lips to be cut off? If not, then stop lying to your leaders, and telling them things that are not true. Let us pray for our leaders, that they may be delivered from the host of flatterers, sycophants, liars, hypocrites and men-pleasers. These people are only seeking recognition and special favours.

Many pastors flatter their congregations. They tell them things that are not true. That is dangerous. There are times when the pastor will have to speak some hard truths, and not pamper the congregation with soft sermons. In some cases, you may have a very dear church member living in sin, but in order not to lose him you alter and sugarcoat your messages. This is common, but very dangerous because it angers God and wears him out. "...Wherein have we wearied him? When ye say, Every one that doeth evil is good..." (Malachi 2:17).

Sometimes when I preach, people wonder what my political inclinations are. Do I believe in the opposition party or do I support the ruling government? It would be dishonest of me to declare I am neutral. Nobody is. I do have a stand. I believe that some political groupings may do a better - though not perfect - job than some others. (And I am entitled to my opinion under the Constitution!) However, there are many people who wonder where I really stand because of some of the things I say. You see, you cannot expect me to say your evil is good, just because I voted for you. The Bible says, "Woe unto them that call evil good, and good evil..." (Isaiah 5:20).

I intend to preach the truth. I intend to call black, black, and white, white. You cannot expect me to say that lawlessness and injustice are right when they are not. The Word of God says, "Woe unto them... that put bitter for sweet, and sweet for bitter!" (Isaiah 5:20). "He that saith unto the wicked, Thou art righteous; him shall the people curse, nations shall abhor him" (Proverbs 24:24). You see, with time people see through your hypocrisy. People secretly admire leaders who are bold and truthful. The 'nation' in the above verse could also symbolize the church. "...with flattering lips and with a double heart do they speak" (Psalm 12:2).

THE POISON OF PROFANE LANGUAGE

1. PROFANE LANGUAGE IS IMMORAL, DIRTY, INDECENT, FILTHY, LEWD, OR UNWHOLESOME TALK.

The Bible instructs the Christian to reject profane, vain or godless chatter. "But shun profane and vain babblings: for they will increase unto more ungodliness" (2 Timothy 2:16). As a believer, profane words must never be part of your language.

Some years ago when I was working at the hospital, there was a nurse who was loaded with profane jokes. She would speak obscenities and make lewd suggestions all day long. When we arrived on the ward, it wouldn't take her long to produce some off-colour story with sexual innuendoes. There are many workplaces like that with indecent people who try to involve you in their godless chatter. But the Bible says that this godless chatter will only lead to more ungodliness.

Profane language defiles the person speaking, and defiles the hearers as well. The Word of God says, "And there shall in no wise enter into it any thing that defileth..." (Revelation 21:27).

2. PROFANITY LEADS TO MORE CARNALITY.

Understand one thing: death and life are in the power of the tongue. Spirituality and carnality are therefore under the control of the tongue. You become more carnal and godless as you allow your tongue to keep speaking indecent things. Remember that singing is almost the same as speaking. Songs are basically words with a melody.

When I was in the university, there was a hall of residence which had a profane choir. They modified holy and beautiful hymns written by great men of God, replacing the original words with detailed descriptions of the sexual organs and the sexual act. Many Christians who lived in the hall of residence which had this profane choir, have complained in later years that they found it difficult to sing some of these songs and hymns in church. They had heard the profane version for so long that during worship times, these obscene lyrics would immediately come to mind.

These students also had their own version of our national anthem. Some of you may just laugh it off. But this is no joke - this is one of the deadly poisons of the tongue. "...neither shalt thou profane the name of thy God..." (Leviticus 18:21).

I know that there are some Christians who need a "spiritual" mouthwash. They are Christians all right, but their tongues need a bit of cleansing.

THE POISON OF TALEBEARING

1. TALE-BEARING CAUSES DIVISIONS.

Tale-bearing is another of the deadly poisons of the tongue. The Bible teaches us that it has the ability to separate best friends. When I look back on my life I remember some wonderful friendships I enjoyed. Today, some of these close friendships no longer exist - because of tale-bearing.

Tale-bearing is a principal cause of division in churches. "Thou shalt not go up and down as a talebearer among thy people...". (Leviticus 19:16). The tale-bearer is the agent who brings about Satan's purpose for destroying God's people (Proverbs 26:20).

A tale-bearer can be likened to someone who goes from house to house to deliver his goods. "...wandering about from house to house... tattlers also and busybodies, speaking things which they ought not" (1 Timothy 5:13).

The Bible makes it clear that when a tale-bearer is in your midst there is always trouble. A gossip within a group can easily destroy it, whether it has a spiritual purpose or not.

Sometimes a tale-bearer will create division between two pastors in the church. He will also create division between pastors and members of the congregation. This is very common. Indeed, he can even separate husbands and wives: "...mark them which cause divisions and offences... and avoid them" (Romans 16:17).

2. TALE-BEARING CAUSES WOUNDS.

I have had very close friends who are no longer that close to me because of tale-bearing. Some newsmongers came in between us and attributed things to me that I never said. When a tale-bearer becomes close to your friend, separation will gradually set in between the two of you. "The words of a talebearer are as wounds, and they go down into the innermost parts of the belly" (Proverbs 18:8).

Every Christian must be wary of such people. It is also important to examine your own life so that the Holy Ghost can deal with any tendency of tale-bearing. The Bible says in clear terms that the tale-bearer will be cut off from the inheritance of God's children.

I would describe one city in Europe, as a city of tale-bearers. I know you will be wondering which city this is, but I will leave you to guess here. Where there are many tale-bearers there is a lot of talk, gossip, hearsay, and rumour mongering (Proverbs 11:13). Divisions are caused in churches in this city because of the existence of tale-bearers who have nothing better to do with their time. They have one story after another, which they peddle over the phone in the evenings. No wonder the work of God is stifled in this city.

THE POISON OF BLASPHEMY

1. BLASPHEMY SHOWS CONTEMPT OR IRREVERENCE FOR GOD.

"To blaspheme" is "to speak in an irreverent way about God or sacred things."

Jesus was an anointed preacher in town. He ministered under the power and the unction of the Holy Ghost. He raised the dead, He cleansed the lepers and He cast out devils. Then a group of people accused him of being a false prophet using the power of demons. "And the scribes which came down from Jerusalem said, He hath Beelzebub, and by the prince of the devils casteth he out devils" (Mark 3:22). In other words, they were saying that Jesus was an occultist, or wizard. They claimed that Jesus was anointed of the devil to deceive people. They ascribed the power behind Jesus' powerful healing crusades to the devil, when it was really the Holy Spirit at work.

They unknowingly criticised the Holy Spirit and all that he stood for. This prompted Jesus to give a teaching on blasphemy, especially blasphemy against the Holy Spirit. "Verily, I say unto you, All sins shall be forgiven unto the sons of men, and blasphemies wherewith soever... But he that shall blaspheme against the Holy Ghost hath never forgiveness, but is in danger of eternal damnation: Because they said, He hath an unclean spirit" (Mark 3:28-30).

2. Some Christians show irreverence towards sacred things.

Through experience I have found out that it is not only unbelievers who make this mistake. Born-again Christians also make the mistake of blaspheming with their tongues. Can a Christian blaspheme? Yes. Look at the definition of blasphemy again. Blasphemy is not only speaking irreverently against God. But, blasphemy is also speaking irreverently about sacred things. Ministers of the gospel are in a certain sense, sacred. This is because they have been set apart to minister the holy things of the Lord.

It is a very common thing for Christians to speak irreverently against preachers they do not even know, when all they have just heard is a rumour or a publication filled with half-truths. Whenever you accuse a minister or a healer of being a false prophet, deceiver, anointed of the devil, drug pusher, occultist or fornicator, you could be blaspheming.

I have noticed some journalists and broadcasters who very confidently bunch up all men of God, and speak and write irreverently about them. If ordinary men would sue you in court for slander, do you not think that Jehovah Nissi will also take you to the High Court of the universe for defaming his church?

Every Christian must be very careful about the comments he makes about God's servants. You didn't appoint them, God did. You have no right to interfere with God's church. I want to say here that some people are interfering with things that do not concern them. I liken this interference to meddling in someone's marriage, when you have not been asked to.

When I wanted to marry, I chose a young lady from among all the others I could see. I preferred her to them, and that was my choice. Nobody has the right to discipline or correct my wife for me. If I think that there is anything wrong with her, I will deal with it myself, because I chose her. She is my responsibility, not yours. Do not interfere with things that do not concern you. If I think my wife is so bad (and she is definitely not bad) that I need to get rid of her, it is entirely up to me to take that decision and implement it. Once again I say, it is not your responsibility.

3. Blasphemy is unauthorised interference with God-ordained authority.

Do not interfere where you have no jurisdiction. God has called that man of God. If God thinks that man of God is a charlatan and a hypocrite, then God who appointed him, will, in his own way dismiss him. You cannot dismiss another man's employee. Why should you try to dismiss and destroy God's appointed servants through publications, broadcasts and poisonous words? You are making a grievous mistake! This mistake is called blasphemy - speaking irreverently about sacred things.

Perhaps you might think you are just passing judgement on a man. But it may cost you your life, your business, your marriage, your future and even your children and the generations after you. Jesus said blasphemy against the

Holy Spirit would not be forgiven. "...but the blasphemy against the Holy Ghost shall not be forgiven... neither in this world, neither in the world to come" (Matthew 12:31,32). This also means blaspheming against things that are being done under the inspiration of the Holy Spirit will not be forgiven.

4. The blasphemer sins against God himself.

Do not be in a hurry to pass judgement on things you do not fully understand. How mistaken we are when we think we are dealing with mere men, only to find out we are actually dealing with God! You may think that you are dealing with man, but you will find out to your surprise and embarrassment that you are actually dealing with God.

What did Paul discover when he was struck down on the road to Damascus? "...I am Jesus whom thou persecutest..." (Acts 9:5). He discovered that it was actually the Lord he had been persecuting all along! Paul was a zealous and a moral person who thought he was fighting for a good cause. But when he had an accident on the way to Damascus and developed blindness in his eyes, he began to think again. "...it is hard for thee to kick against the pricks [thorns]" (Acts 9:5).

Some people may need some of this "Pauline" treatment in order to be cured of their interfering and blaspheming spirit. I can understand how people can mistakenly treat ministers as mere men.

Apostle Peter experienced this same treatment. Peter did some fundraising in his church, and received pledges and money in support of the ministry. However, two of his church members, Ananias and Sapphira came along with a lie about the amount of money they had pledged. They discussed it at home and fabricated a story they were going to tell the pastor.

Listen carefully to Apostle Peter's response, "...why hath Satan filled thine heart to lie to the Holy Ghost..." (Acts 5:3). You see, they thought they were dealing with an ordinary human being, but they found out that in dealing with the man of God they were actually dealing with God Himself. This mistake cost them their lives. We all know Ananias and Sapphira died that same day. The cause of their death was not tuberculosis, heart failure, systemic lupus erythematosus, buruli ulcer, ventricular fibrillation or polycythaemia rubra vera. The cause of death was simply lying to a man representing the Holy Spirit.

God Confirms His Servant

A man of God told the story of what happened to a critic who visited his church. He said this skeptic sat in the congregation and kept thinking to himself that the preacher was a con man and a liar. Then the Lord opened his eyes, and he saw a huge and a tall angel standing behind the man of God.

Whenever the man of God walked to the side, the angel would also move in the same direction. At times as he was ministering, the angel would whisper into his ear. The preacher at those points would smile and continue ministering. (The preacher himself was unaware of the presence of the angel.) This sceptic was very surprised to discover such heavenly involvement and support for this pastor he thought was a charlatan.

This vision was an eye-opener for a potential blasphemer. Listen to me, friends. Be careful what you say about men of God. You have no idea of the spiritual approval they may have from Heaven.

5. The blasphemer may shorten his own life.

Some Christians may even die before their time because of blasphemy. With their own mouths, they cut their lives short. You may think that because someone is a controversial figure he must be doing something wrong. But I have discovered that the higher you go in ministry or public life, the more controversial you appear to outsiders. People have all sorts of amazing impressions and ideas about public figures.

Although I have always believed in miracles and healing, there was a time I was not actively ministering to the sick. When the Holy Spirit started to work miracles and amazing healings through my ministry, I was very surprised to hear a rumour that I had been to India, to acquire some 'powers'. I laughed in amazement. I have never been to India and I am not aware of any powers that can be acquired there. The only power that I know of is the power of the Holy Ghost. But once again, I realised that each time the Holy Spirit is at work there are people who will allow themselves to be used to blaspheme.

I know many ministers who have become known as controversial figures because of the gospel. The more they did God's work, the more controversial they became.

Everywhere Paul went, he was considered a controversial person. The crowds did not like him in most of the cities he ministered. At one point, soldiers had to escort him away because the crowds were so angry with him. People were filled with so much hatred for him (Acts 16:19,20).

Paul, also experienced much blasphemy in his ministry. "And when they opposed... and BLASPHEMED, he shook his raiment, and said... Your blood be upon your own heads..." (Acts 18:6). Perhaps, if Paul had lived in our time, he would have hit the headlines in the tabloids time and time again. Many Christians would have said, "If you were really doing the right thing you would not have so much trouble all the time."

As a minister or Christian, do not be too concerned about having people think and speak well of you all the time. Jesus said, "Woe unto you, when all men shall speak well of you..." (Luke 6:26).

Jesus is our example-setter. Jesus is our Commander-in-Chief. We take instructions from him. If anyone speaks against us, he will have the Holy Spirit and Jehovah El'Shaddai to reckon with.

THE POISON OF FOOLISH TALKING

1. INDISCRIMINATE TALK

Foolish talking is simply the talk of a fool: Neither filthiness, nor foolish talking..." (Ephesians 5:4). A fool says all that he is thinking, but wise people learn to say what is appropriate in every situation. Foolish speaking can cost you your life.

Remember the story of Joseph when he had a dream. He dreamt that his father and his brothers were bowing down to him. Obviously, he didn't create his own dream. It was a dream in which the Spirit of God was showing him the future. "And Joseph dreamed a dream, and he told it his brethren: and they hated him yet the more" (Genesis 37:5). Joseph made the mistake of blurting out all of the vision and plan of God at the wrong time. And more especially, to the wrong people. That was foolish talking. This foolish talk led eventually to his being kidnapped and taken hostage.

There are things God reveals that you must not tell anyone. Keep them in your heart. At the right time they will come to pass. I have many things in my heart that I have not yet spoken about - it would be too dangerous.

2. ENDLESS CHATTER

There are many other forms of foolish talking. One common type is the endless chitchat of some ladies. You must realise that in the multitude of chatting you are likely to say something wrong. You are likely to speak a wrong word and sin: "For in the multitude of...many words there are also divers vanities..." (Ecclesiastes 5:7). The women who God commends have what we call a "quiet spirit" (1Peter 3:4).

I believe that much speaking, especially about godless things, drains the anointing. Jesus said, "...the words that I speak unto you, they are spirit [anointing], and they are life" (John 6:63).

What this means is that the words Jesus spoke actually contained the anointing. This also means that the more he ministered and spoke, the more the anointing was being imparted. That is why anyone serious about ministry, will conserve the anointing instead of dissipating it through godless chatter.

3. Failure to give God glory

The last form of foolish speaking I want to consider is speaking without giving glory to God. We must be careful to give glory to God and acknowledge him in all that we say.

I remember the story of a man who escaped from an earthquake in San Francisco. He was interviewed on television. The interviewer asked him how he managed to escape with his life after being buried for three days in the rubble. This man foolishly said, "I was able to survive under the rubble of this earthquake because of my strong will power." How foolish! A week later, this same man who claimed he had strong will power had a heart attack and died suddenly. Tell me, where was his will power during the heart attack?

Instead of giving glory to God for saving his life, he was talking about his will power. How foolish! The Bible says, "There is no man that hath power over the spirit to retain the spirit; neither hath he power in the day of death..." (Ecclesiastes 8:8).

Let us be careful to give God the glory for the things He does for us. Foolish and empty talk only reveals our emptiness and ignorance.

THE POISON OF EXPRESSING DOUBT

1. Unbelief

The expression of doubt through our words is one of the things God hates. If you study the Bible carefully, you will find out that the Lord becomes very angry with doubting children. He wants us to trust and believe in Him. He wants us to follow Him, and know that it is well with us because he is Jehovah: the one who keeps covenants and promises.

In the book of Hebrews, there is a question: "But with whom was he grieved forty years..." (Hebrews 3:17). Was it the adulterers? Was it the idolaters? Was it the thieves? No. It was those who did not believe. You may be surprised, but God may be angry with you because of your lack of faith in his ability to bless you.

Remember the story of the twelve spies. Ten of them said, "We cannot do it. It is not possible!" I call them the "Cannot-Do" people. "...the men that went up with him said, we be not able to go up against the people... And they brought up an evil report..." (Numbers 13:31,32).

Notice here, that the words we be not able, are described by the Bible as evil. Observe that the ten spies poisoned the minds of multitudes of people with their "impossibility attitude".

2. The "impossibility" attitude

There are some people who are filled with phrases like this:

We can't make it!

It's too late!

It's not possible!

It hasn't been done before!

It will be controversial!

What will people say?

It's too expensive!

We don't have enough money!

We don't have enough time!

We have never done this before!

We don't do things like this here!

I know this thing will end in a disaster!

I'm pulling out!

I'm scared!

Let's be reasonable!

We've always done it this way!

Words of doubt are one of the deadly poisons of the tongue.

3. The possibility attitude

However, there is another group of people who will say:

Go for it brother!

It's a great idea!

Nothing is impossible!

It can be done!

It's not too late!

I'll make time for it!

We can make an extra sacrifice!

We will go the extra mile!

We can work overtime!

The lack of money cannot stop us!

Let's try it anyway!

I can do all things through Christ who strengthens me! These are the types of words that Jesus wants to hear us say. We are a "Can-Do" people. We can make it. God is on our side! "I can do all things through Christ which strengtheneth me" (Philippians 4:13).

THE POISON OF SLANDER

1. To slander is to lie.

To "slander" is "to utter maliciously untrue statements about someone." It also means "to defame, vilify, misrepresent, and denigrate another." In other words, to slander is to lie.

Bitterness: Root of Slander

Once upon a time, there was a young lady who was in a relationship with a good friend of mine. When her relationship with my good friend was disintegrating, she came along and began to narrate a long story about how evil her fiancé was. She said incredible things about this brother, making him out to be unfaithful and treacherous. However, I knew this brother and I knew that her story was calculated to discredit him.

I remember very clearly in my office, telling this young lady, "Listen, you better forgive this brother. You are simply too bitter. Secondly, these stories you have just told me about him are very damaging."

I pleaded with her, "Please, do not repeat these stories anywhere else! You will be destroying my friend's image and credibility. Do you understand what I'm saying?"

"Yes." she nodded tearfully. "I will not repeat this anywhere."

A few days later I came across somebody who had talked to this young lady. I realised that this young lady had spread her story as far and as wide as she possibly could. She even went to the extent of going to the lecturers of this young man to tell them how my friend had mistreated her. Obviously, my friend suffered a lot from this girl's slanderous stories.

After some weeks, this lady recovered from her bitterness. She came to see me in my office and said something that I have never forgotten.

She said, "Do you remember all the things I told you about Brother X? They were not true."

I was startled, "You mean it?"

She said, "Yes. They were not true."

So I asked, "Did you tell anyone else?"

She admitted, "I told many people in church. But Pastor, I want you to do me a favour. Could you please announce in church that all the things I said were not true?"

She was actually asking me to announce that her slanderous stories were not true! But it was too late. The damage had already been done. And she would have to sort that out with God.

2. Slander is destructive, and usually irreversible.

It paints a picture that cannot be unpainted. It is difficult to erase from the minds of people the impressions and feelings that are conveyed by slanderous publications and stories. There are many ministers who go around this life wearing the images that are created for them by the secular press. The slanderous rumours of wicked people contribute to an unfortunate image of many well-meaning pastors.

There are many people who will not go to Heaven because they can no longer receive from certain men of God. They cannot even stand the sight of some pastors because of all the negative stories and slander that is spread about God's people.

Do you remember that Peter the apostle began his ministry with a slanderous story surrounding him? It was rumoured that he had stolen the body of Christ from the tomb, and was claiming that Jesus had actually risen from the dead. Do you realise that this story alone could keep many people from believing in Peter's message of the risen Christ? Do you know that in his time, many people saw Peter as a grave looter and a liar? The Bible actually tells us that people were paid to propagate this slanderous lie. They regarded him as an unemployed fisherman and a charlatan who was capitalising on other people's insecurities and making a business out of the church. Such is the effect of slanderous poison, even today.

There are some places that I have found difficult to minister, because of the slanderous stories spread by a renegade pastor. In fact, I have discovered to my surprise that pastors are best at slandering other pastors and helping to destroy other ministers.

THE POISON OF BACKBITING

1. Backbiting is a surprise attack.

"Backbiting" means to be "bitten in the back." That is, to slander someone in his absence. Being bitten in the back is different from being bitten in the front. This is because of the surprise element and the absence of protection for one's back parts. The Bible teaches us in Ephesians chapter 6 about the protective armour of God. However, you will notice that there is no armour for the back parts of the Christian. That is why backbiting is so painful.

Backbiting, one of the poisons of the tongue is very common in divided, strife-filled churches.

Many people cannot develop trusting relationships because they are not sure about what is said about them behind their backs. And where there is no trust there is no relationship and no unity. I don't want to have any friends I'm not sure about. A true friend is someone who says the same positive things about you, whether you are present or absent.

2. Backbiting destroys relationships.

Wherever there is backbiting there is no trust, and strong relationships cannot be built. Once, someone asked me why a certain group of ministers did not seem to be united. Then, I didn't really know why. But with time I came to discover it was the poison of backbiting that kept everyone apart.

Ministers

I remember being at a meeting with some senior pastors. We had a cordial discussion and I thought to myself, We are such good friends.

I mused, "There is such love and unity amongst this group of ministers."

A few days later, I met one of the ministers who was present at the meeting, in his home.

He said to me, "How do you find Pastor X?" (Referring to another minister who was also at the meeting.) Then he continued to say some awful things about Pastor X. Meanwhile, a few days earlier we had been happily chatting together with him. I began to feel terrible. Initially, out of respect I didn't say anything.

But as the cynical and sarcastic comments flowed from this man, I interrupted and said, "Why are you saying what you are saying? How can you say this about Rev. X when we just had a meeting with him?"

I went on, "With all due respect, I don't think it is right to say this about someone who thinks you are his friend." "The north wind driveth away rain: so doth an angry countenance a backbiting tongue" (Proverbs 25:23).

You see, people get to know the things you have said about them with time. Because very few things are secret. In the process of time everybody loses confidence in meetings and relationships.

If I have something to say I will tell you to your face. I don't believe in pretending to be your good friend, smiling at you, then turning around in your absence to stab you in the back. That is backbiting! A painful bite in the back!

Church Workers

Pastors need the operation of the gifts of the Spirit to identify backbiters. I remember some years ago there was a young lady who would minister beautifully before I preached. I trusted her as one of my loyal and dedicated church members.

One day, as I slept, the Spirit of the Lord gave me a dream. In the dream, I was fighting with her. We were trading punches like common street fighters. Our arms were flailing in the air. Then I suddenly woke up and couldn't believe what I had just dreamt about.

The Spirit of the Lord told me, "This seemingly loyal lady whom you think is one of your trusted people is a slanderous backbiter. She joins others to speak much evil against you. But when she sees you she is full of smiles and encouraging words."

Within the next few days, what I had seen in the dream came to light. The Lord had revealed this to me to protect me from the poison of this person's tongue.

Associates

One minister friend recounted how the Lord gave him a revelation about his associate pastor.

He said to me, "My associate sounds very humble and loyal. For many years this man has been by my side, apparently supporting and helping to build. I could hardly believe that the Lord was revealing something negative about this particular pastor."

He went on, "I had a dream. In this dream somebody attacked me in my house. I rose up to defend myself. This attacker had a dagger with which he was trying to stab me. As I struggled with my assailant, I reached out to grasp a black hood he had over his face. Up to this point I didn't know who my assailant was. Finally I was able to lift the hood. Lo and behold, it was my associate. I shouted 'Hey! Pastor X. Is it you? Are you trying to kill me?'

Then he woke up. From that point, further revelations came out concerning this associate. He had been secretly spreading dissension and dissatisfaction amongst the congregation and other leaders. This was affecting church growth, he told me. And it was this discovery that led to the eventual removal of this backbiting associate. My friend's church was thus saved from decline.

You see, backbiting poisons relationships and churches with mistrust and suspicion. "...God gave them over to a reprobate mind... backbiters, haters of God, despiteful..." (Romans 1:28,30).

THE POISON OF MURMURING

1. Murmuring distracts God's army.

I believe the church is an army. We have a mission and a vision. The church is not just an institution to organize weddings and funerals for people. The church is a powerful tool in the hands of the Lord for the harvesting of souls in this lost and dying world. "And the Lord shall utter his voice before his army..." (Joel 2:11).

How can we save the lost when we are not disciplined? How can we save the lost when we cannot take instructions without murmuring? What sort of army goes to battle with complaining and disputing ranks? An army officer in my church told me, "There is a saying in the army, 'Obey before you complain'."

Murmuring is the undertone disagreement and protest over an issue or situation by discontented people. It is something that every Christian must avoid at all costs: "Do all things without murmurings and disputings" (Philippians 2:14).

Christian leaders must keep murmuring to a minimum. Identify murmuring as one of the enemies of progress in the work of the Lord. From experience, I would prefer not to have any murmurers in my church, even if they are wealthy or influential. I submit that the only good murmurer is an absent murmurer!

Remember that the children of Israel were rapidly streaming out of Egypt and into the Promised Land. God was blessing them, and things were getting better. But when they encountered some difficulties they began to complain, and this murmuring led to the termination of their progress.

A Vivid Example

I recall being invited to minister in a large church. This church had once been a leading ministry in that city. However, at the time I spoke there, it was no longer at the forefront.

I told them, as the Spirit directed me, "It is because of your continuous murmuring that the progress of your church has halted. The Lord had great plans for you. But murmuring destroyed it all." I continued, "It is very common to hear of leaders and members from this congregation making all sorts of unsavoury remarks about their church and senior pastor."

I revealed that it was this very well-known characteristic that was responsible for their decline. Controversial though it may sound, I told them to leave the church if they could not remain in it without murmuring.

2. Murmuring destroys Christian leaders.

The poison of murmuring destroys many a potential Christian leader: "Neither murmur ye, as some of them also murmured, and were destroyed..." (1 Corinthians 10:10).

Many years ago, I attended a meeting of a church group to which I belonged. At the close of the service the pastor decided to take a second offering. When he announced it, I immediately turned to the person sitting by me and murmured, "Why take a second offering? It's not necessary." She said nothing but gave me a look I will never forget.

Suddenly my heart smote me and I realised I had done something wrong. I felt so bad that I had complained, even though it was unknown to the pastor. After the service I went up to the pastor and said, "I have something to tell you. Can I please speak with you privately?"

He said, "Okay, what's the matter?"

Then I confessed that I had murmured against him when he had decided to take an extra offering. The pastor was very surprised, but touched. He put his hand on my shoulder and said these words which I will never forget, "God is going to use you!"

I felt better after this and I believe that the words of this man of God were a blessing to me. They have come to pass after many years!

CONCLUSIONS ON DEATH AND LIFE

The Tongue and Life

When we talk about death we are thinking of funerals, mortuaries, buying of coffins and death certificates. We imagine standing by graves weeping and sobbing our hearts out. But the tongue apparently controls this terrible thing called death. "Death and life are in the power of the tongue..." (Proverbs 18:21). Can you believe that? Well, the law of gravity works, whether you believe in it or not. Our personal beliefs do not affect these laws at all.

You can speak either "death" or "life" into your life. You can also speak death into your marriage, or speak life into it. If your marriage is dying, decide to speak life into it. Say positive things about your husband. Think about all his good sides, and find something positive to say. You are speaking life into your marriage.

Complaints and Death

There are some pastors who speak death into their ministries and churches. They are always complaining about one thing or the other. I do not complain about the ministry. I consider it a privilege to be a minister.

A pastor's wife once said mournfully to her husband, "Now that we are in the ministry, we have no privacy. The church members think that everything comes directly from the offering. We have lost our self-respect."

But he said to her, "Do not complain about the ministry. Be glad and see the many positive aspects of it. People's lives are being changed. You are involved in the most worthwhile job of all."

He told her, "Apart from everything on this earth, when you get to Heaven you will have an extra reward."

He went on, "Say to yourself, 'I'm glad I'm in the ministry. I'm glad I have an opportunity to serve the Lord. I'm in the best job of all." Then she brightened up. You see, you can speak happiness and joy into every aspect of your life.

Decisions for Life

You may think that this is just a theory, but I tell you, these are the words of Almighty God. This is the Word of the living God. Death and life are under the control of the tongue. Let us decide not to destroy our lives with any of the "poisons" we have discussed above. "Let the words of my mouth...be acceptable in thy sight, O Lord..." (Psalm 19:14).

Life is precious. Our churches are precious. Our pastors are precious. Our husbands and wives are precious. Our nation is also precious. Let us not kill and destroy what God has given us with our tongues. May we like Isaiah say, "The Lord God hath given me the tongue of the learned, that I should know how to speak..." (Isaiah 50:4).

The Sin of Accusation 13

■ WHAT IS AN ACCUSATION?

An accusation is a charge or an allegation made against someone. It puts blame and points fingers at a person. An accusation is a statement saying that you think someone is guilty of doing something wrong, especially of committing a crime. These statements, which are directed at a person, constantly minister a withering and weakening guilt. Only very strong-hearted people can live with persistent accusations for a long time.

Even though accusations come out of human mouths, they are anointed by the accuser of the brethren himself. Satan is the accuser in the midst of the brethren. "And I heard a loud voice saying in heaven, Now is come salvation, and strength, and the kingdom of our God, and the power of his Christ: for the ACCUSER of our brethren is cast down, which ACCUSED them before our God day and night" (Revelation 12:10).

Although the devil is commonly known as the accuser of the brethren, he is actually the accuser in the midst of the brethren. In your leadership experience, you will meet different kinds of people. Perhaps one of the most daunting enemies you will ever encounter is "the accuser in the midst of the brethren". Problems come in different levels but one of the highest problems is to encounter an accuser in the midst of the brethren.

At the highest point of your ministry, you will struggle with the accuser. Accusation is Satan's topmost strategy for dealing with an unconquerable enemy.

SATAN'S BEST WEAPON

1. Satan has different formats by which he operates.

He may come to you in the form of a tempter, a liar, a murderer or a deceiver. However, if he takes you on as an accuser, the battle has been lifted to the highest possible level. This principle is played out in the life of Jesus Christ.

2. In the beginning of Jesus' ministry, the devil came to Him as a tempter.

Initially, the devil came to him in the form of a tempter. Jesus Christ was tempted in the wilderness for forty days. Satan lied to Him in the wilderness and desperately tried to deceive Him.

3. Later in His ministry, the devil attacked Jesus in the form of a murderer.

Throughout His ministry, the Lord was attacked by the devil in the form of a murderer. "...He was a murderer from the beginning..." (John 8:44). On several occasions Satan tried to kill

Jesus through mob action but He would escape. "And they got up and drove Him out of the city, and led Him to the brow of the hill on which their city had been built, in order to throw Him down the cliff. But passing through their midst, He went His way" (Luke 4:29-30 NASB).

On another occasion, the devil tried to drown Jesus in the Sea of Galilee but he was not successful because Jesus rebuked the storm. It was not God who brought the storm; otherwise, Jesus rebuked God's wisdom by rebuking the storm. "But as they sailed he fell asleep: and there came down a storm of wind on the lake; and they were filled with water, and were in jeopardy. And they came to him, and awoke him, saying, Master, master, we perish. Then he arose, and rebuked the wind and the raging of the water: and they ceased, and there was a calm" (Luke 8:23-24).

4. Jesus' ministry came to an end when the devil put on the garb of an accuser against Him.

Jesus' ministry was finally brought to an end when Satan put on the garb of an accuser. Jesus endured one week of intense accusations, which brought His ministry to an end. This week of intensive accusations, started from Palm Sunday until He was crucified. In Matthew 21:1-17, you will see how He entered Jerusalem triumphantly and cleansed the temple. You will notice how the questions and accusations started from the day after He arrived in Jerusalem (Matthew 21:23).

a. Accusation was the devil's deadliest weapon against the Lord.

Satan pulled out his deadliest weapon of accusation and unleashed it against the Lord. The weapon of accusation was finally deployed. For a whole week before the Passover, the Lord was in the temple being questioned and examined (accused) by the Pharisees. "Then went the Pharisees, and took counsel how they might ENTANGLE HIM in his talk. And they sent out unto him their disciples with the Herodians, saying, Master, we know that thou art true, and teachest the way of God in truth, neither carest thou for any man: for thou regardest not the person of men. Tell us therefore, What thinkest thou? Is it lawful to give tribute unto Caesar, or not? But Jesus perceived their WICKEDNESS, and said, Why TEMPT ye me, ye hypocrites?" (Matthew 22:15-18). The Lord was questioned about every aspect of His life and ministry.

For several days, the Lord endured the wickedness and hypocrisy of those who questioned him in the temple. In the last twenty-four hours of His life, He was also accused in the palace of the high priest, in Pilate's court and also in Herod's palace.

Jesus met this series of high-level accusations with a variety of responses. He answered the temple questions succinctly and made fools out of His accusers. "When they had heard these words, they marveled, and left him, and went their way" (Matthew 22:22). They had never heard anything like that before. "The officers answered, Never man spake like this man" (John 7:46). However, when in the court of Pilate and other heathen rulers, he answered nothing to the questions that were levelled at Him. "And he answered him to never a word; insomuch that the governor marvelled greatly" (Matthew 27:14).

As you can see, Satan has different guises under which he attacks. In this section of the textbook, we will be dealing with the accusers who are used by the devil to intimidate you. Perhaps you suffer from a plague of accusations in the ministry. Often you do not understand what is happening to you. By the time you finish this textbook, God will give you wisdom to fight the enemy.

PEOPLE COMMONLY EMPLOYED AS ACCUSERS

In my country, some people are commonly employed as security guards. There are also people who are commonly employed as butchers and khebab sellers. Similarly, there are some people whom Satan commonly employs as accusers. These people fall into the category I call "familiar friends" of the accused. "Yea, mine own familiar friend, in whom I trusted, which did eat of my bread, hath lifted up his heel against me" (Psalm 41:9). Familiar friends are the familiar people of your life like:

i. Friends

ii. Husbands

iii. Wives

iv. Sons

v. Daughters

vi. Beloveds

vii. Associate Pastors

viii. Church Members

ix. Journalists

x. Classmates etc.

For accusations to have any impact, they must be channelled through someone close.

Brushing off Accusations

Are accusations not statements that are true or false? If they are not true, why don't you just ignore them? But it is never as easy as that.

- Accusations are anointed from Hell.
- Accusations are spiritual things.

They are tiny arrows loaded with satanic poison. As soon as the poison enters your blood, it spreads through your whole being attacking your heart. Like some fast-spreading natural poison, you are greatly affected by a seemingly little dart. I have seen mighty giants of God totally ruffled by unfounded accusations, which looked insignificant to the bystander. Such is the power of accusation. It is a puzzling weapon and its effects are mysterious. Truly, accusations are spiritual weapons.

THE POINTING OF THE FINGER

"Then YOUR LIGHT WILL BREAK OUT LIKE THE DAWN, And your recovery will speedily spring forth; And your righteousness will go before you; The glory of the LORD will be your rear guard. Then you will call, and the LORD will answer; You will cry, and He will say, "Here I am.' IF YOU REMOVE the yoke from your midst, THE POINTING OF THE FINGER and speaking wickedness" (Isaiah 58:8-9 NASB).

1. Accusations are also called "the pointing of the finger".

Such is the evil released by the pointing of the finger, that the light in your life and ministry will actually grow dim from it. Your light will break forth like the dawn and there will be recovery if you put away the pointing of the finger!

2. Ministries cannot prosper once a finger-pointing person is allowed to flourish nearby.

Much of the darkness in the body of Christ is as a result of the incessant accusations made by brother against brother, sister against sister, husband against wife, and so on.

3. A pastor must know the people around him who are used to accuse him.

Every good leader must understand the principles of accusation. You can wither and weaken in ministry through diverse accusations!

4. YOUR MINISTRY CAN ACTUALLY BE MISDIRECTED BY ACCUSATIONS.

I have experienced that myself. Perhaps this is the most important section of this textbook and I pray you will study it seriously.

The book of Revelation shows how God dealt decisively with the accuser of the brethren. It reveals four amazing benefits of silencing accusations. In these four benefits, we see everything that we desire from God - strength, salvation, power and the kingdom of God. O how much power and strength will be released into your life if the pointing of the finger was not there.

5. THE VOICE OF THE ACCUSER DISCOURAGES YOU FROM ENTERING THE MINISTRY.

Most ordinary people do not feel that they are qualified to serve God. Most of the people I have trained in the ministry were discouraged and accused by the devil. But I simply encouraged them constantly to serve God and become priests in spite of their shortcomings.

This encouragement was completely contrary to the voice of the accuser in their lives. That voice told them they were not good enough! But my constant encouragement to serve God and to trust Him silenced the voice of the accuser. Suddenly, weak and incapable people received salvation, power and strength to do God's work.

THE BENEFITS OF DEALING WITH THE ACCUSER

"And I heard a loud voice saying in heaven, Now is come SALVATION, and STRENGTH, and the KINGDOM OF OUR GOD, and the POWER OF HIS CHRIST: for the accuser of our brethren is cast down, which ACCUSED them before our God day and night" (Revelation 12:10).

This Scripture shows four clear blessings of dealing with accusers.

1. Salvation is the first benefit of silencing accusers in your midst.
2. Strength is the next important benefit for eliminating accusers from your little fellowship.
3. The kingdom of our God will come when the accuser of the brethren is cast down.
4. Finally, the power of Christ is released when the accuser is dealt with.

All these benefits are clearly outlined in the Scripture as being things that happen when the accuser is silenced. If you allow an associate minister to point fingers at you, you will be weakened and the power of God in your life will be reduced. The salvation and the coming of God's kingdom are dependent on you dealing with the accuser.

■ THE LAWS AND PURPOSES OF ACCUSATION

Most people do not understand what is happening to them when they are being accused. Because they do not realize what is happening, they play into the hands of the accuser. In this chapter, I want to share some of these hidden laws, which govern the "hows" and "whys" of accusation. Understanding these laws will help you to fight your enemy and gain the upper hand.

THE LAWS

LAW NO. 1 YOUR RELATIONSHIPS WILL BE POLLUTED BY ACCUSATIONS.

Accusations can be likened to the pouring of Satan's faeces or urine on relationships. Accusations can be likened to Satan vomiting on precious relationships. Somehow, these accusations have the effect of dirtying everything. Pure relationships are poisoned by even the slightest accusations! Nothing is ever the same once you have been accused.

A brother who is accused of having an interest in a particular sister never has a normal relationship with that person anymore. Somehow, that relationship is polluted. He may actually have an interest in someone else. Nevertheless, tension develops in the particular direction of the accusation and everything that was pure looks and feels evil even though it is not! Such is the defiling and polluting power of an accusation.

One pastor described how his pure and undefiled relationship with his church members had been spoiled by his wife accusing him about specific women. He explained, "My wife claims I am interested in certain people. Since then, every time I speak to these people I am supposed to be interested in, I feel sinful. I feel as though I am doing something wrong." "Nothing is the same anymore," he explained. "Everything has changed and I can no longer work effectively with many people."

"Also, my relationship with my wife has changed. I find myself keeping things from her which I never used to do. I have to avoid her seeing and knowing certain things so that she will not have missiles with which to fight and accuse me." He lamented, "I never thought my marriage would degenerate to such a state."

Many pastors poison the relationship between themselves and their associates by accusing them of evils that have not occurred to them. From that time, their relationship is marred and infected with the defilement of accusation. Do not be surprised if one day these people do exactly what they are accused of doing.

I remember a university student who worked in our tapes ministry. He was an honest, hardworking and sacrificial brother who did much to help the ministry. One day, some questions were asked about the finances of the tapes department. In the ensuing discussions, this brother felt he was being accused of stealing. He was shocked because he had sacrificed many things to help the tapes ministry.

From that time, our relationship was tainted and it deteriorated until he left the church. I felt very sad about this brother's departure. Since then, anytime there is stocktaking or auditing at the tapes department, I warn them to be very careful about what they say, lest they sound accusatory. Accusations will poison beautiful relationships and change them forever.

Rick Joyner, in his vision, described the accusations and condemnations of demons in exactly the same way.

A Terrible Vision of Accusers

"Above the prisoners, the sky was black with vultures named Depression. Occasionally, these would land on the shoulders of a prisoner and would vomit on him. THE VOMIT WAS CONDEMNATION. When the vomit hit a prisoner, he would stand up and march a little straighter for a while, and then slump over, even weaker than before. Again, I wondered why the prisoners did not simply kill these vultures with their swords, which they could have easily done.

As I watched I realized THESE PRISONERS THOUGHT THE VOMIT OF CONDEMNATION WAS TRUTH FROM GOD. Then I understood that these prisoners actually thought they were marching in the army of God! This is why they did not kill the little demons of fear or the vultures - they thought these were God's messengers! The darkness from the cloud of vultures made it so hard for these prisoners to see that THEY HAD NAIVELY ACCEPTED EVERYTHING THAT HAPPENED TO THEM AS BEING FROM THE LORD. They felt that those who stumbled were under God's judgment, which is why they attacked them the way they did - they thought they were helping God."[1]

This chapter is an attempt to kill the vultures which are vomiting slime upon God's servants. It is an attempt to rise up and reject the deception that the slime coming from these vultures is truth from God. This chapter is an attempt to reject the notion that many of the accusations we hear are actually true.

It is an open confrontation against accusing women who are destroying their husbands' ministries in the secret places! It is a rejection of the lies that are peddled about God's anointed through rebellious pastors! It is a strong stand against the condemnation, news and rumours, which look like truth from God! It is in defiance of the relentless accusations and condemnation meted out to honourable men who have taken up the mantle of service to the King.

LAW NO. 2 YOU WILL BE ACCUSED OF THE EXACT OPPOSITE OF WHAT YOU REALLY ARE.

Amazingly, Satan's strategy is to accuse you of the opposite of what you really are. Many times, ministers labour under the accusations of things they are far from. Men who are as far from being thieves as the sun is from the earth are accused of stealing. Men who will never commit adultery until they die are accused incessantly of being adulterous.

You would have thought that if you accused someone of something remote, it would have no effect on him. Surprisingly these accusations have a powerful effect on the accused.

a. Moses was accused of being a murderer.

Moses was accused of trying to kill the Israelites even though he was doing the opposite. God had sent him to deliver the Israelites but the people accused him of trying to kill them all. Notice these Scriptures: "And they said unto Moses, BECAUSE THERE WERE NO GRAVES IN EGYPT, HAST THOU TAKEN US AWAY TO DIE in the wilderness? wherefore hast thou dealt thus with us, to carry us forth out of Egypt? Is not this the word that we did tell thee in Egypt, saying, Let us alone, that we may serve the Egyptians? For it had been better for us to serve the Egyptians, than that we should die in the wilderness" (Exodus 14:11-12).

"And the children of Israel said unto them, Would to God we had died by the hand of the LORD in the land of Egypt, when we sat by the flesh pots, and when we did eat bread to the full; FOR YE HAVE BROUGHT US FORTH INTO THIS WILDERNESS, TO KILL THIS WHOLE ASSEMBLY WITH HUNGER. (Exodus 16:3). And the people thirsted there for water; and the people murmured against Moses, and said, WHEREFORE IS THIS THAT THOU HAST BROUGHT US UP OUT OF EGYPT, TO KILL US AND OUR CHILDREN AND OUR CATTLE WITH THIRST?" (Exodus 17:3).

b. Moses was accused of being proud.

Moses was accused of exalting himself and of being proud. But the Scriptures tell us that he was the meekest man on earth. "Now the man Moses was very meek, above all the men which were upon the face of the earth" (Numbers 12:3).

They assembled together against Moses and Aaron, and said to them, "You have gone far enough, for all the congregation are holy, every one of them, and the LORD is in their midst; so WHY DO YOU EXALT YOURSELVES above the assembly of the LORD?" (Numbers 16:3).

c. Jesus was accused of destroying God's house.

Who has done more to build God's house than the Lord Jesus? Who loved the temple so much that he cleansed it of thieves? Who came to earth and sacrificed his life for the house of God? No other person but Jesus Christ!

Yet He was accused of planning to attack and break down the temple. "WE HEARD HIM SAY, I WILL DESTROY THIS TEMPLE THAT IS MADE WITH HANDS, and within three days I will build another made without hands" (Mark 14:58).

The question I ask is, "Did this accusation have the desired effect?"

The answer is, "Yes, it did. It worked."

The accusations, even though fantastic and contrary to the known character of the preacher, had the desired effect. Jesus was condemned to death for this accusation.

Perhaps your ministry is ending because of baseless accusations. God will work it out by His power like He did for Jesus.

d. Jesus was accused of wanting political power.

Jesus was accused of being interested in the throne of Caesar. How far from the truth can we go? Jesus' eyes were on the throne of Heaven by the side of the heavenly Father. It is important to recognize that wicked accusations may actually point to the complete innocence of the accused. However, it takes a very seasoned and wise person to recognize what is happening.

"And the whole multitude of them arose, and led him unto Pilate. And they began to accuse him, saying, WE FOUND THIS FELLOW PERVERTING THE NATION, AND FORBIDDING TO GIVE TRIBUTE TO CAESAR, SAYING THAT HE HIMSELF IS CHRIST A KING" (Luke 23:1-2).

e. Jesus was accused of many different things.

"For MANY BARE FALSE WITNESS AGAINST HIM, but their witness agreed not together" (Mark 14:55-56). "And the chief priests ACCUSED HIM OF MANY THINGS: but he answered nothing" (Mark 15:3).

LAW NO. 3 THE MOST EFFECTIVE ACCUSERS ARE THOSE CLOSEST TO YOU.

Those whose accusations will have the greatest effect are those who are closest to you. The accusations of close people sound credible because of where they have worked. Let me attempt to grade accusations according to the closeness of the accuser.

The accusations of a church member will have more effect than the accusation of a non-church member. The accusations of a general pastor will have less effect than that of a close associate. But the accusations of a wife will carry much more weight than that of any associate. "Even my close friend in whom I trusted, Who ate my bread, Has lifted up his heel against me" (Psalm 41:9 NASB) The closer he is the more credible he sounds. The input of Judas was greater than the input of anyone else because he was a close disciple of Christ.

One day, somebody told me an interesting proverb. He said, "It is only when you go to the edge of the river that you will hear the crabs coughing."

"What does that mean?" I asked.

He explained, "When you stand afar off and watch crabs running around on the beach you will never know that they actually have a cough. It is only when you are near enough that you will hear them coughing." He continued, "In other words, it is those who are intimately involved who know what is really going on."

It is therefore such close people who hear the coughing crabs who are the best accusers. I also heard somebody say that if a crocodile comes from under the water in the pond and says, "There is a snake under the water then you must believe him." In other words, it is the crocodile who knows what is going on under the water.

What do all these mean to us? They are warnings for people who work closely with the leader. Every close person is a potential future accuser. Friends, close associates, personal assistants, husbands, wives, children are all at risk of becoming accusers. Actually, almost all accusers come from this list. If God has placed you in an honourable position and brought you near, beware lest the accuser uses you to do his work.

LAW NO. 4 YOUR ACCUSATIONS WILL NOT STOP UNTIL YOU UNTIL YOU REACT WRONGLY.

Moses eventually made a mistake in his ministry. He was under constant pressure from the accusations. Under persistent provocation he disobeyed God. This is the ultimate intention of the accuser. To push you until you change course and falter.

John Wesley came under intense pressure to alter his course of ministry. His wife did not want him to write letters to certain people. She did not want him to carry out his ministry duties of travelling to the churches. But the strong founder refused to alter his ministry. "Married or no, he saw no reason why he should change the course or tenor of his life. He entered in his journal, 'I cannot understand how a Methodist preacher can answer to it to go to preach one sermon or travel one day less in the married than in the single state.'"[2]

Notice how Moses buckled under the persistent claims that he was a liar and a murderer. Instead of obeying the Lord, he reacted wrongly. He hit the rock with his rod instead of speaking to it. This cost him his ministry and he never saw the promised land.

"And there was no water for the congregation: and they gathered themselves together against Moses and against Aaron. And the people chode with Moses, and spake, saying, Would God that we had died when our brethren died before the LORD! And why have ye brought up the congregation of the LORD into this wilderness, that we and our cattle should die there? And wherefore have ye made us to come up out of Egypt, to bring us in unto this evil place? it is no place of seed, or of figs, or of vines, or of pomegranates; neither is there any water to drink. And Moses and Aaron went from the presence of the assembly unto the door of the tabernacle of the congregation, and they fell upon their faces: and the glory of the LORD appeared unto them. And the LORD spake unto Moses, saying, Take the rod, and gather thou the assembly together, thou, and Aaron thy brother, and SPEAK YE UNTO THE ROCK BEFORE THEIR EYES; and it shall give forth his water, and thou shalt bring forth to them water out of the rock: so thou shalt give the congregation and their beasts drink. And Moses took the rod from before the LORD, as he commanded him. And Moses and Aaron gathered the congregation together before the rock, and he said unto them, Hear now, ye rebels; must we fetch you water out of this rock? And MOSES LIFTED UP HIS HAND, AND WITH HIS ROD HE SMOTE THE ROCK TWICE: and the water came out abundantly, and the congregation drank, and their beasts also. And the LORD spake unto Moses and Aaron, Because ye believed me not, to sanctify me in the eyes of the children of Israel, therefore ye shall not bring this congregation into the land which I have given them" (Numbers 20:1-12).

LAW NO. 5 THE UNDERLYING CAUSES OF ACCUSATION ARE THE COMMON CAUSES OF MADNESS.

"And the scribes and Pharisees WATCHED him ...that they might FIND AN ACCUSATION against him ... And they were FILLED WITH MADNESS" (Luke 6:7, 11). Notice how they watched Christ to find something to accuse him of. Eventually, they were filled with madness. Fear and hatred are common causes of accusation.

Men and women full of fear and hatred become the outlet of satan's accusations. This is another reason why you must keep your heart pure. Keep fear and hatred far from your heart. Let me share with you a little bit of medical science so that you will understand the relationship between accusations and mental illness.

The Causes of Madness

Two cardinal symptoms of madness (schizophrenia) are paranoid delusions and auditory hallucinations. With auditory hallucinations, the patient hears voices accusing him, talking to him and discussing him. With paranoid delusions, the patient is fearful and believes in the existence of things that are not real; and cannot be convinced otherwise.

In mental illness, fears drive the patients down the road of lunacy. In spiritual illness, fears also drive the person down the road of accusations. In mental illness, the fearful state progresses until the patients hear voices and imagine things that are not real. Do not allow the raging fears of this life to be in your heart. They may drive you towards a mental illness which you never expected. In mental illness the patient believes in things that are not real. With spiritual problems, people are deceived and they cling to their deceptions. It is these deceptions that grow into delusions.

Actually, with the privilege of my medical eye, I have noticed that many apparently normal people are labouring under some form of mental illness. Because mental illness spans a range of behaviour and because there are long periods of lucidity, many of these cases are not picked up.

Many women have succumbed to raging fears and insecurities and have gradually walked the road of mild to moderate psychosis (mental illness). I have actually confirmed the diagnosis of mental illness in many Christians but cannot approach them because they have not sought medical help from me.

Have you noticed that many murderers are filled with passionate hatred for someone? It is this hatred that drives them to do the unthinkable. They knowingly sentence themselves to life imprisonment and hell. This is madness in full manifestation!

The Madness of the Priests

"And while he yet spake, lo, Judas, one of the twelve, came, and with him a great multitude with swords and staves, from the chief priests and elders of the people" (Matthew 26:47).

The behaviour of the Pharisees and the accusatory priests can best be described as madness. They were filled with such hatred for the Saviour that they did the unthinkable. They "killed" God on a cross. They were so full of fear that they employed Judas to betray someone who walked around openly.

The role of Judas, as a betrayer, is even more mystical when you consider how Jesus openly whipped the temple dwellers a few days earlier. Their fear of Christ was demonstrated by the kind of army that was sent to arrest one unarmed preacher in a garden. "Then Jesus said unto the chief priests, and captains of the temple, and the elders, which were come to him, Be ye come out, as against a thief, with swords and staves? When I was daily with you in the temple, ye stretched forth no hands against me: but this is your hour, and the power of darkness" (Luke 22:52-53).

Law No. 6 Your Accuser Thrives on Non-Biblical Quotations, Proverbs and Sayings but not on the Word of God.

Accusations thrive on non-biblical quotations and sayings. One day, I received a document from someone who wanted me to believe that my church was a cult-like organization. Initially, I was taken aback by the document, which seemed to be an authority in describing cults.

This document claimed that one characteristic of cults is an emphasis on loyalty. This fellow was therefore pointing out to me that because I have taught on loyalty and written books on loyalty, our church has strong characteristics of a cult. These cleverly composed arguments sound true, but can be very misleading. As I studied this paper, I realized that there was absolutely no scriptural backing for these authoritative statements.

Which Bible verse says that when a church teaches on loyalty it is cult-like? Is there not so much in the Bible that teaches us to be faithful? What was the fate of Judas? Did Jesus not say it would have been better that he was not born? About which other sin did Jesus ever say it would have been better that the sinner was never born? How can the teaching on loyalty and faithfulness to God and His servants be categorized as questionable? Even the suggestion of this is demonic!

The Quips of Women

In addition, other wisecracks have gained prominence and become the basis for wrong behaviour and accusations. In churches, there are unspiritual women living by fear and trumped up accusations against their husbands and men in general.

These women refuse to bend to the Word of God. They have answers to everything and rely on such statements as, "It's a woman's world." "I am a woman and I know what it feels like." "You are not a woman and you will never understand certain things." They say things like, "You are men, you are all the same." "That is how men think." "Women are made differently." "You are a man. You have knowledge but no experience of the pain of a woman, etc."

All these clever statements sound reasonable and legitimate. They may be clever but they are not biblical. They must not give strength and foundation to the practice of evil. We cannot allow the accuser into our midst no matter the garb or costume he wears. He may be all dressed up in pretty dresses and nice hair-dos but it is still the devil!

LAW NO. 7 WHEN YOUR ACCUSER IS PROVED WRONG, HE WILL FOLLOW UP WITH SEVERAL OTHER DESPERATE ACCUSATIONS.

Unfortunately, many accusations do not hold water. The accuser is now at risk of being disgraced for making false allegations. This makes him desperate and he resorts to multiple and diverse forms of accusations which become even more bizarre.

The madness builds up as the accuser prosecutes his case and calls in witnesses to confirm that for which he has no proof. Jesus was spat on and buffeted with slaps and scornful words. "Some began to spit at Him, and to blindfold Him, and to beat Him with their fists, and to say to Him, Prophesy! And the officers received Him with slaps in the face" (Mark 14:65). Why did they spit on him? To make him as dirty as they wanted him to be? But our Lord was clean and innocent of all allegations made against Him. Why cover His face and ask Him to prophesy? They wanted desperately to prove that He was a false prophet.

Do not be surprised if your accusers become desperate to find something to use against you. It is not easy to live with anyone who is searching for a flaw in your life. Since you are a human being, you are likely to slip up at one point or another.

John Wesley said to his wife, "I dislike the not being safe in my own house. My house is not my castle. I cannot call even my study, even my bureau, my own. They are liable to be plundered everyday. You say, 'I plunder you of nothing but papers'. I am not sure of that. How is it possible I should? I miss money too, and he that will steal a pin will steal a pound. But were it so, a scholar's papers are his treasure, my journal in particular. 'But I only took such papers as relate to Sarah Ryan and Sarah Crosby'. That is not true. What are Mr. Landey's letters to them? Besides, you have taken parts of my journal which relate to neither one nor the other."

It is a very uncomfortable feeling to have an accuser as a member of your cabinet or in your home! Jesus did not have it easy. He was under constant scrutiny from people who desperately wanted to find something wrong about Him. "And as he said these things unto them, the scribes and the Pharisees began to urge him vehemently, and to provoke him to speak of many things: Laying wait for him, and seeking to catch something out of his mouth, that they might accuse him" (Luke 11:53-54).

LAW NO. 8 ANYONE ASSOCIATED WITH YOU WILL BE ACCUSED AS WELL.

Accusations are quickly generalized to include people who associate with you. My assistant pastor is accused of many of the things that I am accused of. If you are not prepared to be collectively accused you cannot be part of the team. Don't expect to be the Mr. Clean of the team. You are not greater than Jesus. If He was accused then you will be too.

When similar accusations are leveled at you, it means you are closer to your leader. If Christ was accused of various things, so will you be. If He was accused of destroying the temple, do not be surprised when you are accused of destroying a church. It is an honour to be accused alongside your leader. It is a sign of your closeness. It shows that you have taken up His identity. Thank God for your loyalty.

Peter was accused of being part of Christ's little band. He was the closest and the one who had dared to stay around during the crisis. No wonder the accusations were falling on him as well. "And after a little while another saw him, and said, THOU ART ALSO OF THEM" (Luke 22:58) Another lesson is that it takes a lot to handle certain accusations. Peter's answer to the accusation was to deny it instantly. And Peter said, Man, I AM NOT" (Luke 22:58).

You must respect men of God who are able to live and minister normally, in spite of numerous allegations and accusations on their life. Peter wilted away at the accusation of a little maid. Perhaps you would not last a day if you were to experience the accusations of your father! You never know what somebody is going through on your behalf.

LAW NO. 9 THERE ARE PARTICULAR ACCUSATIONS THAT CAN PUSH YOU AROUND.

a. There are particular accusations that work best on you.

Satan will find out what really gets you upset. Then he will hammer on that until you freak out. Pilate refused to crucify the Lord until the worrying voice of the accuser rang above the din of the crowd. "And from thenceforth PILATE SOUGHT TO RELEASE HIM: but the Jews cried out, saying, IF THOU LET THIS MAN GO, THOU ART NOT CAESAR'S FRIEND: whosoever maketh himself a king speaketh against Caesar. WHEN PILATE THEREFORE HEARD THAT SAYING, HE BROUGHT JESUS FORTH, and sat down in the judgment seat in a place that is called the Pavement, but in the Hebrew, Gabbatha" (John 19:12-13). This voice accused him of not being loyal to Caesar. Pilate was a hard man, known for his brutish behaviour. He was not one to be pushed around by a crowd. But when the accusation came forth everything changed and he gave up the innocent Christ. Do you see how powerful accusations are?

b. Accusations can bend the unbendable and push the unyielding leader around.

Satan knows what can push you around! He knows what you hate to hear and he will find somebody to say it to you. Are you the one whose mouth is used to speak words of accusation?

Pastors do not like to be called thieves so when Satan wants to hinder the finances of a ministry, he uses the voice of the accuser to suggest that the pastor is a greedy money-lover. Through this accusation, his hands are weakened and he is unable to raise funds.

Pastors' wives know that their husbands loathe being called adulterers. They realize that their husbands do not even want to have that association. Like the Jews who manipulated Pilate to crucify Christ, many Christian wives manipulate their husbands to crucify (eliminate, sack, wipe out, reject, preclude, sweep away and remove) other ladies they dislike or fear! Ladies, sorry for this comparison but it was too appropriate to allow it to pass by. Please do not be angry with me!

LAW NO. 10 THE MOTIVE FOR ACCUSATION IS DEEPER THAN THE ISSUES PRESENTED.

a. Accusation is a spiritual thing. It is deeper than the issue over which you are being accused.

That is why when you modify your behaviour in response to the accusation, a new set of allegations arise. This is the cardinal sign that the accuser has located you. A minister was accused of being involved with drugs. He tried to overcome this cloud that hung over his ministry. He set up drug rehabilitation centres to help drug addicts. This was to prove that he was definitely not into drugs. He did many other good works but the accusations continued.

For as long as I knew this minister, he was constantly bombarded with one thing or another. Public interviews and public relations efforts yielded very little fruit. Why did the journalists never relent in their efforts to accuse this man of God? One day one of the journalists confessed, "My aim is to make anyone who goes to that church feel ashamed." What a motive! This man of God was experiencing the unrelenting attack of a journalist because the journalist hated the pastor and wanted to destroy his ministry! Therefore, every modification this minister made in response to the allegations registered as "no work done". No matter the change in behaviour, a new allegation always springs up. This is the cardinal sign that the accuser has located you.

b. Satan's intention is to stop you from doing the good works.

You will find out that accusations will persist whether or not certain physical things change. Christ, our Saviour was a perfect example. His ministry was associated with lunches, parties and breakfast meetings. John the Baptist's ministry was associated with fasting and a life in the wilderness. But in each case the barrage of accusations intended to stop the ministry continued, "But whereunto shall I liken this generation? It is like unto children sitting in the markets, and calling unto their fellows, And saying, We have piped unto you, and ye have not danced; we have mourned unto you, and ye have not lamented. For John came neither eating nor drinking, and they say, He hath a devil. The Son of man came eating and drinking, and they say, Behold a man gluttonous, and a winebibber, a friend of publicans and sinners. But wisdom is justified of her children" (Matthew 11:16-19).

c. Sometimes there is no need to even think about what you are being accused of.

Nothing you do will change anything. The problem is not what you are doing. The problem is with the accuser.

Notice this interesting testimony by Beverly LaHaye in her book "The Spirit-Controlled Woman", which demonstrates this same principle: "Another hang-up common to Martha Melancholy is jealousy. Not given to 'insincere flirtation' Martha often marries a man who is outgoing and friendly to everyone. It is not uncommon for her to ride home in icy silence after a party because her husband flirted with every woman there. Since her husband's male ego gets so little food at home, he unwisely seeks it as social gatherings and he may often think, 'Nothing I do ever satisfies that woman'."[3]

Seated opposite the beautiful wife of a wealthy and dynamic Christian businessman, I was startled to hear his melancholic wife asking, "Would you explain why I am so jealous of my husband even when I know I have no reason for it?" It seems that he had dismissed three successive secretaries and finally hired the homeliest gal he could find because of his wife's jealousy. But it still didn't solve her problem.

I responded, "The problem is not with your husband; you just don't like yourself." Tears ran down her cheeks as she admitted to strong feelings of rejection. Later, her husband commented on their love life: "When her groundless suspicions make her jealous, I can't touch her. But when she is sorry for her accusations, she can't get enough of me. I never know whether to expect feast or famine!"

There are mysterious purposes for accusing someone. These hidden intentions are not known to most Christians. If you understood what accusations do, you would be very hesitant to accuse anyone. Accusations destroy people. Accusations destroy relationships between people. The effects of these accusations are often permanent.

THE PURPOSES OF ACCUSATION

1. The first purpose of accusations: To degrade the accused person.

Accusations degrade you in your own eyes. Accusations make the accused person have a low estimation of himself. You therefore lose the zeal to do well. The zeal to be good or to remain a good person goes after you have heard certain accusations. You say to yourself, "after all they are not expecting anything good from me. I will just be myself. I do not care anymore.

Once you are degraded, you are good for nothing. You are not useful for any great mission. This is where fathers come in. Fathers believe in their children even when they are sacked from school. They love their children even if they are pregnant out of wedlock. They constantly say good things to their children. "I believe in you! You can make it!" It is these words which counteract the degradation that is imposed on the accused person, and give him power to rise up again.

I remember when I began our church I was accused of several things. I was told, "You have no business entering the ministry. You are not a pastor! You are a medical student and nothing more." My own associate pastor questioned my calling. My associates and church members would have discussions to analyze my preaching and my calling. Some said, "He is not called by God." Others said, "He is called." I became so frightened of the church that I would have a running stomach on Saturday nights. I asked my beloved (fiancée) whether I would have diarrhoea every Saturday for the rest of my life. I was so scared to preach on Sundays.

My critics and accusers would line up and sit on the second row to assess my calling. My hands would shake as I held the microphone. I experienced tremors as though I was suffering from Parkinson's disease.

Whilst I preached, one look at their faces was enough to dry up my mouth. There would be no more saliva in my mouth and I would need to drink water desperately to moisten my mouth, otherwise my tongue could no longer move within my mouth. Sometimes, someone would have to get water for me urgently during the sermon and I was also accused of being interested in the girl who would give me water!

One day, I had a vision and saw myself in a boxing ring, boxing away against an opponent. I suddenly realized who I was fighting with - a prominent lady and church member. The Lord revealed to me that this person and some others were fighting against me with their tongues. He said to me, "Cast out the scorner and strife and contention will go away." I did exactly that and dismissed the leader of my accusers. He went out of the church and most of the accusers left as well. After getting rid of the accusers I became stronger.

This is what the Bible teaches. Strength comes when you cast away accusers! I did not become a more anointed or experienced pastor immediately. But I did become stronger by not having them around me! Those accusations could have driven me out of the ministry as they were intended to. I would never have written this textbook and you would never have benefitted from this ministry.

2. The second purpose of accusations: To disgrace you.

Accusations also disgrace the accused in the sight of others. Satan wants to disgrace you through accusations. Have you not noticed that when someone is accused of a crime and has to defend himself he is usually disgraced? Defending yourself in court is usually a disgraceful experience. You are never the same after the accusations have come and gone. Somehow people believe that the accusations were true. They think you escaped on technicalities. Michael Jackson was accused of child molestation. He went to court for several weeks. Even though he was acquitted of all these charges, he is not the same person. The shine and the glimmer have dimmed.

As your reputation is blackened, people cannot receive from you. Your ministry is prevented from spreading. Fewer and fewer people want to listen to you. They believe you are an evil person. "...as many as received him, to them gave he power..." (John 1:12). In order to receive the power, you must receive the person. If the person is blackened, and made out to be evil, how can you receive him?

I remember a man of God who experienced unrelenting accusations from his own wife. She was obsessed with the possibility of him having affairs with several women in the church. One day, God gave him a vision in which he revealed that he was being attacked by a spirit of disgrace.

In this vision he found himself in the toilet like every other person, and attending to a call of nature. It happened that whilst still attending to this call of nature, he had a distinguished visitor whom he respected very much. Surprisingly, his wife brought the visitor to the toilet to see him. The whole room smelled terribly as it does for everyone else, and her husband was very embarrassed. He asked for the visitor to be made to wait elsewhere. But she insisted that the person stand just outside the toilet and speak to him from there. This poor husband had to speak from behind the door to the honourable guest who was made to stand in the terribly smelling area. In the vision, the husband was so embarrassed by this experience. When he woke up, he realized that he was encountering a spirit of disgrace in his life, which wanted to embarrass him for no evil done.

I also remember years ago, when a great evangelist had planned a crusade for Ghana. His forerunner was in the country and stayed in a hotel that my father owned. One of the pastors of our city came in to meet this crusade director. Unfortunately, this Ghanaian pastor spent a long time blackening the reputation of one of the seasoned ministers of the city. As we passed by, we heard snippets of their conversation.

For every second that went by, the reputation of this senior pastor was blackened with soot from this other pastor's mouth. From the kind of things that were said about him, he would only look like a spiritual golliwog!

The aim of accusations is to ensure that you will never be received. But God will ensure that you are received at the places where you must be received. Your ministry cannot be hindered by any human being. God is above everything and He will bring His will to pass in spite of all that is said about you.

3. The Third Purpose of Accusations: To Make You Fall into Sin.

After being accused and degraded, many develop a low esteem and actually begin to do the things people (the accusers) expect of them. "As a man thinketh in his heart, so is he" (Prov erbs 23:7). Satan's clever plan now begins to work. You find yourself doing the evil that was spoken about you. This is why experienced people do not even bother to listen to certain accusations. It is not that they are arrogant, but these things tend to push you towards an intended target.

I remember counselling a pastor who was married to an accusatory and insecure woman. This pastor told me tearfully how his wife constantly suspected him of having affairs with ladies in the church. He said to me, "I love my wife and I am not having an affair with anyone." For years, their marriage continued swinging through the highs and the lows created by one accusation after another. The Pastor narrated how one day, his wife was approached by someone who had had a vision that her husband had had an affair with someone in the church. With tears in his eyes, he told me that his wife believed the lady wholeheartedly and actually arranged a meeting with the visionary for him to discuss her vision of his adulterous affair. The pastor told me how he was totally embarrassed by this encounter. He lamented, "How could my wife believe this vision and actually arrange the meeting? She does not believe nor trust me."

One day I said to the wife, "If your husband ever has an affair with anyone I would blame you. You have done the work of Satan and accused him, suspected him and disgraced him for years." I also said to her, "If your husband does ever have an affair, my love and respect for him will not change. He has withstood your withering accusations for years and I do not even know how he has survived." She did not seem to understand what I was saying. I continued, "Because you have accused him for so long, it would be your greatest victory for him to actually sleep with someone. This would vindicate you and prove that you have been right all along." This is a common but amazing reality. The accuser actually wishes that the accusations come true so that she would be proved right in the eyes of the people she has made her claims to.

Eventually, after many years, this pastor did end up having a sexual encounter with a lady who was not even one of the suspected persons. The pastor explained to me: "I was so low. I felt my wife did not love me and that she actually hated me. This drove me into the arms of this lady who was so welcoming and kind to me." Naturally, this pastor was devastated and his ministry was greatly affected. I felt sorry for this minister because he had fallen prey to a clever, sustained, long-term strategy of the devil.

Dear friend, watch out for accusations. They are having an effect that you cannot imagine. The Scripture teaches that accusations weaken you and take away your power. It is time to silence the accuser. No one can flourish in the presence of accusers.

4. The Fourth Purpose of Accusations: To Generate Hatred and Bitterness in the Accused

Satan's aim is to induce a spirit of hatred in your heart. Once you are full of bitterness, many other evils will grow. It is natural to hate your accusers. It takes supernatural grace to love your accusers. Every minister experiences this temptation. Once there is hatred and unforgiveness in your heart, a door is opened through which Satan will bring disease, death and other difficulties.

Many ministers have hatred within them for someone. Usually they have not forgiven someone for things said against them. This person may be an associate, a church member or even a journalist. But this is just a trap to push you into unforgiveness. I have seen ministers trembling with hatred for church members who departed with a string of accusations. Don't forget that Satan wants to fill your heart with bitterness. It is a long-term strategy of the devil to finish you off.

5. The Fifth Purpose of Accusations: To Bring About Separation.

One of the purposes of accusations is to separate the accuser and the accused. Usually it is important for the accuser to be close to the accused. For instance, a senior pastor and his assistant can be separated through accusations. A husband and a wife easily move apart and become distant when one person constantly accuses the other of various things. Husbands and wives grow further and further apart as they accuse each other of various deficiencies through the years. Before they married, they praised each other and bestowed words of love on each other. Positive words bring people closer, negative accusations separate even the closest of friends!

Churches are divided into groups through accusation. The Ashanti tribe is separated from the Ewe tribe through various accusations that they fling at each other. The divide only gets deeper and wider as the accusations increase.

6. The Sixth Purpose of Accusations: To Discourage and Confuse You.

"So I will incite Egyptians against Egyptians; And they will each fight against his brother and each against his neighbor, City against city and kingdom against kingdom. Then the spirit of the Egyptians will be DEMORALIZED within them; And I will CONFOUND (CONFUSE) their strategy" (Isaiah 19:2-3 NASB).

The Scripture above shows how when a brother attacks another brother it demoralizes and confuses their front. The Egyptians would become confused because of the kinds of attacks they would get. When you are accused, you become discouraged and disillusioned. Accusations have the power to take the life and spirit out of you. When all your good deeds are seen in a negative light your zeal is dampened.

Years ago, one of my best friends and brothers was living with his auntie. One day something was stolen from their house and the auntie accused him of stealing the things. He had lived happily with this auntie and her family for many years. He was shocked that he was being accused of stealing. His few possessions were searched and he was threatened greatly by the auntie and the uncle. However, he had not stolen anything. It was actually someone else who had stolen the items.

Eventually it was proved that he did not steal the things. But he told me his relationship with the auntie and her entire household was never the same after that. It is not a nice feeling that someone should think of you as a thief. Discouragement and now separation had set in. Close, important relationships were destroyed by accusations.

7. The Seventh Purpose of Accusations: To Turn a Friend into an Enemy.

"So I will incite Egyptians against Egyptians; And they will each fight against his brother and each against his neighbor, City against city and kingdom against kingdom. Then the spirit of the Egyptians will be DEMORALIZED within them; And I will CONFOUND (CONFUSE) their strategy" (Isaiah 19:2-3 NASB).

When Satan wants to turn good brothers against each other, he uses his weapon of accusation. Accusation has the mysterious effect of turning best friends against each other. Husbands and wives who came together through deep love and affection can turn into enemies. It is an amazing thing to watch how relationships deteriorate into the opposite of what it was at the beginning.

Churches would have been a hundred times bigger if there were no accusations. Junior Pastors level accusations against the senior pastor and leave the church with a section of the membership. Many churches have a breakaway church situated somewhere nearby. These two churches are usually led by pastors who used to be friends, but now are enemies. This enmity was created by accusations. Satan is the author of all these things. God wants us to be one body. Let us recognize the accuser in our midst and refuse to be used to accuse on another.

Abner Turned against Ishbosheth

An example of how good friends are turned into enemies was when Abner turned against his own king. Abner had established and supported Ishbosheth to be the king of Israel. He did this faithfully and fought wars against King David. One day something happened that changed all this. Ishbosheth accused Abner of wrongfully relating with a lady. Abner was so upset about this accusation that it turned him against the king. He quickly undid all that he had done for Ishbosheth and became his enemy. It was an amazing turnaround. Read it for yourself.

"Now Saul had a concubine whose name was Rizpah, the daughter of Aiah; and Ish-bosheth said to Abner, "Why have you gone in to my father's concubine?" Then Abner was very angry over the words of Ish-bosheth and said, "Am I a dog's head that belongs to Judah? Today I show kindness to the house of Saul your father, to his brothers and to his friends, and have not delivered you into the hands of David; and yet today you charge me with a guilt concerning the woman. May God do so to Abner, and more also, if as the LORD has sworn to David, I do not accomplish this for him, to transfer the kingdom from the house of Saul and to establish the throne of David over Israel and over Judah, from Dan even to Beersheba. And he could no longer answer Abner a word, because he was afraid of him" (2 Samuel 3:7-11 NASB).

Do you want to turn your best friend into an enemy? Then go ahead and accuse him. Do you want your husband to hate you and become your enemy? Then I suggest that you begin to accuse him. Ask Ishbosheth what happened to him and you will receive wisdom. Do you want to lose your associate pastor? Then accuse him instead of encouraging him. This is why I encourage people even though I can see their faults. In the midst of much love and encouragement, it is easy to address faults and deal with them without the bitterness of accusation. I am able to correct and rebuke those that work with me on almost anything. I do this gently and very sparingly after making sure that the message of love is louder and clearer than anything else.

I spoke to a lady who was constantly accusing her husband of having an affair with someone. This brother had not done any of the things she was claiming. As the months went by, she maintained her unproved allegations. She would not budge or relent. "My husband is committing adultery," she insisted.

She could not see that she was turning her own husband into an enemy. In a desperate attempt to gain the love of her husband, she was pushing him further away and actually making him hate her. Her own husband turned into an enemy. I watched as that couple walked down the road of increasing separation and hatred for each other.

Countless women practice this form of accusatory love. "Accusatory love" sends out accusations that are intended to frighten the husband away from other women and to draw him to her. Unfortunately, this type of love has the opposite effect and actually makes the husbands hate their wives.

8. The Eighth Purpose of Accusations: To Turn You into an Accuser Yourself.

When you are accused, you often become an accuser yourself. You often rise in self-defence to protect yourself from the onslaught. This is a dangerous development. Every minister should watch out for this. Not only have you developed bitterness, hatred and enmity, but you are now putting on the garb of an accuser. You and Satan now join forces and work together as partners. Perhaps this is the most deadly development in the response to accusations.

To see this clearly you only have to observe human behaviour in politics. The opposition or minority groups come up with numerous accusations and allegations against the ruling party. The president and his ruling party respond vehemently with counter-accusations about unrelated issues. Parliament is basically a theatre for accusations and counter-accusations. It is an arena where hatred is generated and existing divisions are deepened. No one sees the good in the other; meanwhile, each is as bad as the other.

9. The ninth purpose of accusations: To stop you in your tracks.

Satan desires to stop you from doing the good works God has called you to. One of the most effective ways is to find something to accuse you of. After planting several churches in Europe, I was accused of so many different evils. Years of hearing negative things eventually took their toll on me. I lost interest in Europe and did not want to plant churches there anymore.

Hindrance to Church Planting

One time, I was in a particular city in Switzerland. A group of people who wanted us to start a church there had gathered to meet with me. As they spoke earnestly of their desire to have a church in the city, I looked at them suspiciously. I thought to myself, "These very people will turn against me and accuse me of coming here to hunt for money."

I mused, "They are the same as the other accusers in those European cities. It is just a matter of time before they point the finger at me. I decided not to start the church there. "They don't deserve it," I concluded. Later on, I realized that I had stopped church planting because of accusations.

When Satan wants to stop you, he has one weapon that works: accusation, accusation, accusation! It will stop you in your tracks!

Some time ago, I was the leader of a fellowship. I had many members who were scattered all over the city. When we were in school, I would see all my members and care for them. However, during the holidays I had to visit them to minister to them. One day, I was visiting a particular sister at a small shop where she worked for her auntie.

As I entered the shop, I heard someone whisper behind the counter, "Your boyfriend is here." I was taken aback because I was not her boyfriend, and I had no intention of becoming her boyfriend. After hearing that comment, it was difficult to minister to the girl. I lost interest in following her up and decided to stop visiting and ministering to her. You see, that comment was an accusation that led me to stop my ministry to this needy soul. The effect it had on me was to stop me from doing my good work. I left her to her fate! Evil spirits took over and eventually she became possessed with demons. The last time I heard of her, her life was destroyed and she had gone mad!

Satan wanted access to my sheep and he wanted me to stop being a shepherd. He simply used his weapon of accusation and it was good enough! I was stopped in my tracks by a simple accusation.

10. The tenth purpose of accusations: To control you.

Accusations can stop you but they can also control you. They become a basis for decisions you take. Eventually, you will find yourself on a course completely different from what God intended for you. Years ago the Lord led me to begin a fellowship of ministers in my city.

I was concerned about what some people would say and think about me. I heard people say, "Who does he think he is? He is a small boy! When did he come on the scene? Does he think he is gong to rule over us?" I felt very bad and ended up forming a democratic group to please them. Interestingly, none of the people whose comments and accusations I was responding to ever joined the fellowship, even though I had made it democratic for their sakes. Later on, I found myself unable to fulfil the commission God had given me. I realized that the comments and accusations of people had guided my decisions concerning that fellowship. I had been controlled by these insinuations and accusations until my ministry was stifled.

Some people are called to be pastors but do not want to be associated with the priestly profession. This is because they have heard numerous accusations against ministers and would not like to be one of them. This keeps many well-meaning people out of the ministry. Through effective accusations, Satan keeps the number of ministers as low as he can.

a. Witchcraft through accusations

This is how witchcraft develops. Witchcraft is the use of any power other than the power of God to control people. Sadly, the only biblical examples I have are examples of women moving their husbands against the will of God.

Eve moved the hand of Adam to pluck the fruit of the tree of good and evil. Since then we have been struggling on earth to make ends meet. To make things worse, we are all in danger of going to Hell! If it had not been for the mercies of God, we would all be condemned. Jezebel moved the hand of her husband, Ahab, to kill an innocent man. Through her influence, the king joined a long list of evil kings and murderers on their way to Hell. Herod's wife moved the hand of her husband to kill (eliminate, delete, preclude, reject, wipe out, remove, obliterate) the prophet, John the Baptist.

One way of establishing control is to accuse and pester someone with words. You control someone when you accuse them of what they would not want to be. People tend to recognize what you would not want to be and accuse you of being exactly that. Each accusation gets you heated and angry. Through persistent accusations, controlling people stop you from doing certain things, which they do not like.

As someone continues to accuse you, he achieves a level of control over your life and this is witchcraft. This kind of witchcraft is not easy to recognize. It is only after a long time that you may recognize that you are being controlled. Sometimes those accusing you do not know that they have moved into the realm of witchcraft! It takes a very strong spiritual person to maintain his course in spite of accusations. Lesser men are unable to hold their course. Sometimes they react by simply snuffing out the accuser.

b. Strong men withstand accusations

John Wesley is an example of a man whose wife tried to control his life. She accused him endlessly of having affairs with different women who were writing to him and serving him. She knew that John Wesley, being who he was, would utterly dislike and even fear to be so described. Although these accusations may seem natural, or even legitimate, it is important to diagnose witchcraft when it is manifesting.

One day, John Wesley, founder of the Methodist Church, wrote a letter to his wife. His very words reveal the passion with which he asked to be free from the controlling power of his wife through accusations. He begged his wife to allow him to be controlled by God and by his conscience.

John Wesley's Letter to His Wife

"I love you still, and am as clear from other women as the day I was born. At length know me and know yourself. Your enemy I cannot be. But let me be your friend; suspect me no more; asperse me no more; provoke me no more. Do not any longer contend for mastery; for power, money or praise. Be content to be a private insignificant person, known and loved by God and me. ATTEMPT NO MORE TO ABRIDGE ME OF THE LIBERTY, WHICH I CLAIM BY GOD AND MAN. LEAVE ME TO BE GOVERNED BY GOD AND MY OWN CONSCIENCE; then shall I govern you with gentle sway, and shew that I do indeed love you, even as Christ the church."[4]

Obviously, God and our consciences are better guides than the raging jealousy and hatred of a woman. John Wesley never left his marriage. He remained married to the same person in spite of the withering accusations he suffered. This is true Christian virtue played out to its fullest and I honour him for that.

d. Weaker men wither under accusations

Weaker men do not respond so well to this sort of treatment. I remember a brother who got married and lived happily with his wife for several years. After many years, this couple was not able to have a child. Later, several stormy situations arose and the brother decided to divorce his wife. It was an unfortunate turn of events.

One day, this brother released a bombshell. He said, "I did not leave my wife because we did not have a child. I left her because I could no longer take the accusations. She would constantly accuse me of having affairs with one person or another. She thought I was trying to have a child outside the marriage."

He described how there were times she would accuse him of having affairs with people he did not even know. She even accused him of having an affair with a bystander at a bus stop whom he had never spoken to in his life.

Accusations separate couples and this couple was separated by incessant accusations. The more she accused him, the more they separated. And the more they separated, the more she accused him. The day came when he broke away.

This is not a good reason for divorce. I am just giving this example to illustrate how different people respond to accusations. John Wesley weathered the accusations and understood what was happening to him. But lesser people do not weather the storm, they wither away from the onslaught that greets them on a daily basis.

11. The Eleventh Purpose of Accusations: To Induce Fear.

Satan wants you to be filled with fear. Fear is an evil spirit which is a forerunner spirit and the way maker spirit for other unclean devils. When your mind is filled with fear, it usually makes a way for other evils. That is why fear is a way maker and a forerunner spirit.

One day, a senior minister told me something his wife had said. He had had an argument with her about various things. She warned him to change his ways. She said, "You go on and have affairs with those girls. You will lose your ministry!" This was a pastor of a large church. Fear gripped his heart and he thought to himself, "Lose my ministry?" Mercy! The thought of all the possibilities raced through his mind and he became more fearful. Once the spirit of fear is in you, other spirits can have access to you. Perhaps one day you will say, what I feared greatly has come upon me. Do not allow fear to make a way for other stronger demons to enter your life.

12. The Twelfth Purpose of Accusations: To Weaken the Minister.

Accusations reduce self-confidence and self-esteem. This weakens the hand of the accused. One day, a pastor decided to have a three-day miracle convention. The power of God flowed and he ministered to the congregation with signs and wonders. When he got home after the second night of powerful ministrations, his wife summoned him for a meeting.

She said, "During the ministration time, I was not happy with the way you were laying hands on certain people. "It seemed that you were laying hands on some particular girls longer than others."

The brother was taken aback, "What?" he stuttered. "Which girls were these?" he asked. The brother explained, "There was no such intention and I do not understand what you are talking about."

Anyway, the next day, he had to continue his miracle service. When it was time for laying on of hands, he did not know what to do. When he felt the spirit leading him to pray for some people, he would think of his wife and how she was keeping a close eye on him. He was so intimidated that he was hardly able to minister to anyone. He mumbled a few words and closed thé service. Such is the power of accusation; to weaken and to remove self-confidence from strong men.

Another brother who had a very good reputation in the church had this sorrowful tale to tell. When he got married, his wife began to accuse him of being interested in other church members. She did not want him to relate with certain people. One time, as his custom was, he went dancing in front of the church with a group of other Christians. He had done this several times but now she claimed he was dancing closer to certain sisters. She was convinced about her evidence. She believed that he was interested in the dancing girls.

With weepy and tearful eyes, she spoke about the pain her husband was causing her due to his dancing. "My heart is in pain," she moaned, "I am a woman and I know what I see. I would not say such things unless there was a good reason!" This dear brother could no longer dance in church. Every dance and every move now had an evil connotation.

13. The thirteenth purpose of accusations: To deceive you.

Faith comes by hearing and hearing by the Word of God. After hearing something for a while, it is difficult to disbelieve it. People tend to believe what they hear, no matter how absurd it sounds. Accusations will make you believe that you are a bad person when you are actually a good person. The devil will tell you that bad people are not welcome at certain places. He will ask you to go away from the company of the saints and other good people. Satan will try to keep you away from the places God has called you to.

Persistent harassment with accusations can lead to a good person becoming convinced that he is bad. In medical science, there is something called folie a deux which means "the madness of two".

A good example of folie a deux is the story of this couple: the husband accused the wife until she believed that she was what she was being accused of. She actually believed that she was doing something that she was not doing. In a particular case, the husband complained that his wife had had many extramarital affairs, with many different men, all through their married life. He insisted that in one two-week period she had had as many as a hundred different sexual experiences with men outside the marriage. His wife herself agreed with his assessment of her behaviour, but would not speak of her experiences, saying that she "blocks" the memories of the adultery out. She denied any particular interest in sexuality, but said that apparently, she felt a compulsive drive to go out and seek sexual activity despite her lack of interest.

The patient had been married to her husband for about twenty years. He was clearly the dominant partner in the marriage. The patient was fearful of his frequent jealous rages, and apparently, it was he who suggested that she enter the hospital in order to receive hypnosis. The patient maintained that she could not explain why she sought out other men, that she really did not want to do this. Her husband stated that on occasion, he tracked her down, and when he had found her, she acted as if she did not know him. She confirmed this and believed that it was because the episodes of her sexual promiscuity were blotted out by "amnesia". When the physician indicated that he questioned the reality of the wife's sexual adventures, the husband became furious and accused the doctor and the ward attendant of having sexual relations with her.

Extensive counselling was not able to bring out the memory of periods of sexual activities. The patient did admit to a memory of having had two extra-marital relationships in the past: one twenty years before the time of admission and the other, just a year before the admission. She stated that the last one had actually been planned by her husband and that he was in the same house at the time. She continued to believe that she had actually had countless extramarital sexual experiences, though she remembered only two of them.

It was diagnosed by psychiatrists that the husband, the chief informant had delusional jealousy, believing that his wife was repeatedly unfaithful to him. Apparently, under his influence, his wife has accepted this delusional belief, explaining her lack of memory of the events, by believing that she had "amnesia". Because her delusional system developed as a result of her close relationship with another person who had an already established delusion (i.e. her husband) and because her delusions were similar in content with his delusions, the diagnosis was Shared Psychotic Disorder traditionally known as "folie à deux".[5]

As you can see, the madness is shared by both the accuser and the accused. This true story illustrates the concept of accusations leading to deception. Faith comes by hearing. There comes a time you must silence the accuser and not allow yourself to hear the rubbish talk of the enemy about you. Be careful lest you believe things that are not true. Pastor, do not believe the lies and accusations that are spoken about you. You are a good person. You are an honoured servant of the Lord. Even the fact that you have attempted to serve the Lord makes you an honourable person.

14. The Fourteenth Purpose of Accusations: To Stereotype You.

A stereotype is a fixed pattern or picture that occurs without variation. Through accusation, Satan creates a picture which he claims will not vary, even in your case.

For instance, there may be a stereotype that all artisans are liars. Therefore when you become an artisan, it is a natural inference that you must be a liar. Another example of a stereotype is that all pastors have affairs with their church members. Another stereotype is that all bosses have affairs with their secretaries. Another stereotype is that all politicians are thieves and liars. Yet another stereotype is that all stepmothers are wicked.

When you come along, Satan's goal is to stereotype you. All he has to say is that you are this kind of stereotype. As soon as that stereotype is associated with you, you find it difficult to shake off that picture. When you become a pastor, you will constantly battle with the stereotype that you must be a man who has affairs with his church members. If you become a secretary you will constantly battle with the stereotype that you must be a woman who has affairs with her bosses. If you ever become a stepmother you will battle the stereotype that you must be a wicked and heartless woman who has no love or pity for her stepchildren.

15. Fifteenth Purpose of Accusations: To Destroy Relationships.

Another name for the "accuser of the brethren" is the "accuser in the midst of the brethren". Satan loves to enter our sweet fellowship and get us to accuse one another. Suddenly, the cordial relationship is broken and everyone is against the other. Watch out for people who point out something bad in everyone! The spirit of the accuser is upon them. Accusations create mistrust between lovers. Suspicion sets in and everyone gets ready for battle.

A classic example is found when the relationship between King David and the Ammonites changed from friendship to enmity. David had an excellent relationship with the Ammonites and intended it to continue that way. He sent a message of condolence with a very good intention, to the new king of Ammon. Unfortunately, the new king interpreted this gesture wrongly and accused David of spying. This accusation brought about the end of all the good relations between the two nations.

Whenever a good intention is misinterpreted and accusations are exchanged, love turns into hatred. Millions of relationships have gone sour through this cycle of good intentions being rewarded with accusations. This is what is called the David-Hanun syndrome.

a. How best friends become enemies

"Now it happened afterwards that the king of the Ammonites died, and Hanun his son became king in his place. Then David said, 'I will show kindness to Hanun the son of Nahash, just as his father showed kindness to me'. So David sent some of his servants TO CONSOLE HIM concerning his father. But when David's servants came to the land of the Ammonites, the princes of the Ammonites said to Hanun their lord, 'DO YOU THINK THAT DAVID IS HONORING YOUR FATHER because he has sent consolers to you? Has David not sent his servants to you in order to search the city, to spy it out and overthrow IT?' So Hanun took David's servants and shaved off half of their beards, and cut off their garments in the middle as far as their hips, and sent them away. When they told it to David, he sent to meet them, for the men were greatly humiliated. And the king said, 'Stay at Jericho until your beards grow, and then return'. Now when the sons of Ammon saw that they had become odious to David, the sons of Ammon sent and hired the Arameans of Beth-rehob and the Arameans of Zobah, 20,000 foot soldiers, and the king of Maacah with 1,000 men, and the men of Tob with 12,000 men. When David heard of it, he sent Joab and all the army, the mighty men. The sons of Ammon came out and drew up in battle array at the entrance of the city, while the Arameans of Zobah and of Rehob and the men of Tob and Maacah were by themselves in the field. Now when Joab saw that the battle was set against him in front and in the rear, he selected from all the choice men of Israel, and arrayed them against the Arameans" (2 Samuel 10:1-9 NASB).

Pastors who have good intentions for their congregations are shattered when they hear wicked accusations about themselves. Senior pastors are shocked when they find out that their juniors, for whom they had such good intentions, suspect them of trying to harm them. Relationships quickly deteriorate and accusations are exchanged. This is how the David-Hanun syndrome is repeated.

b. Church divides into little pieces

I remember a denomination whose founder died tragically. There was much sorrow as all the junior pastors who had worked under their overseer mourned. The funeral was a big event and thousands of people attended it.

The pastors had worked together for years under their Bishop. As time went on the pastors decided to establish a foundation to support the family of the dead overseer. After thousands of dollars were raised for the founder's family, the records of the foundation were kept secret from another section of the pastors. It appears some felt that those pastors could not be trusted with the details. This is when the accusations began. One group accused the other of keeping the records secret so they could steal from them. Another group accused the other of deeming them too insignificant to be told what was going on. Yet another group said they had no right to keep the information secret in the first place.

Even though everyone started out with good intentions to provide support for the founder's family, the accuser in the midst of the brethren divided and scattered everyone. The pastors only had good intentions as they tried to set up this founder's trust. As people tried to protect the money and ensure its proper use, accusations only heightened and increased. Needless to say, this denomination began to break up into different groups. Today, the entire denomination is fragmented and scattered into little bits and pieces.

This is the work of the accuser in the midst of the brethren. Churches are divided, husbands are set against wives, and wives against their husbands; women's groups against men's groups. Church members are postured against their pastors and pastors are set against other pastors. The David-Hanun syndrome is working fully in churches, families, businesses and homes. Meanwhile, everybody has a good intention and everyone means well. No one understands why there is no "flow" and no unity.

c. Can the accuser break a threefold cord?

"And a threefold cord is not quickly broken" (Ecclesiastes 4:12). I remember a church, which was run by a strong leader with two equally strong and gifted assistants. The leadership of this church was a great example of a threefold cord. These three ministers held the fort in a spectacular fashion, preaching, teaching and leading worship in tandem and setting a wonderful example of partnership and teamwork. Many church leaders admired the success of this anointed trio. They seemed to have all the keys for fruitfulness, largeness and effectiveness in ministry.

They used the key of the two witnesses: "By the word of two or more witnesses a thing is established" (Matthew 18:16). When the leader would preach a controversial message, the other assistants would speak on the same theme but use a different Scripture and sermon title. This equally strong message resounded through the church and their words were established. Indeed, their sermons were like the oracles of God. Even those who were not a part of their church were affected by whatever they said. They used the key of common love: "They were together and had all things in common..." (Acts 2:44) This trio related as brothers and their families related closely. When one of them would have a baby the others would be at the hospital and get involved with all the goings-on.

One day, I was chatting with one of them and he said to me, "Some people think they can divide us, but we cannot be divided." He continued, "They don't know how close the three of us are. Do you know what we talk about? We share everything and we even talk about our private sex lives with one another." He laughed disparagingly at people who made any attempt to divide their powerful team. They used the key of unity: "...how pleasant it is for brethren to dwell together in unity..." (Psalm 133). This trio was united in all respects.

One day, a member of this powerful leadership trio visited me at home. As we chatted, he told me about how an enemy pastor of their church had tried to divide them.

He said, "This guy always wants to meet my senior pastor without the two of us. He is forever trying to meet him and to say things to him on the side. He is jealous of the unity we have."

"Really," I answered. "Why would he do something like that?"

He continued, "You won't believe what he said the other day." I remember exactly where he sat as he narrated his tale.

He said, "This fellow had the audacity to tell my senior pastor that God had given him a revelation."

"What was the revelation," I asked.

He answered, "He told my senior pastor that he had seen him in the spirit with two "Goliaths". One Goliath was standing on his right and one on his left.

"What were these Goliaths doing?" I asked.

"He said God had shown him that these two Goliaths would attack him one day and try to take over the church!"

"Amazing," I mused. "Two Goliaths trying to take over the church?"

"So who are these two Goliaths? I asked.

"We are the Goliaths! Myself and the other associate. Can you believe it? He is calling us Goliaths! And he is saying that we are going to take over the church."

This pastor found it preposterous that anyone could imagine them ever being divided. Who could separate this ideal partnership of two perfect assistants?

However, Satan watches every united team closely, hoping for a chance to become the accuser in the midst of the brethren. He does not think any team is impregnable! He does not consider any group untouchable! Just a few years after this incident, the perfect trio began to disintegrate right before our very eyes. They hurled railing accusations at one another. The accuser in the midst of the brethren had penetrated their ranks. After months of bitter allegations and counter accusations, the perfect trio parted company and went their separate ways.

Employees of the Accuser 14

■ POTENTIAL ACCUSERS

Satan would like to talk to us directly. He would like to say how bad we are and describe our sins to us as vividly as possible. Fortunately, he does not have that chance because we are operating in different realms. Satan is a spirit operating in the spirit realm and we are human beings operating in a physical realm.

Accusations are very effective, and Satan relies heavily on them. He, therefore, needs workers to carry his foul and degrading messages. Satan knows he can weaken, degrade, deceive and even control God's servants through accusations. Satan desperately needs workers he can employ as his mouthpiece. He will rain foul, slimy faeces on God's holy men through these workers. Do not become the mouthpiece of Satan. Satan wants to defecate and vomit on God's servants. Will you be the anus of Satan from where he will spray good people with his defiling accusations?

Never Accept Satan's Job Offer

Do not accept this job from the devil. Accusations are the trademark of the devil. I want you to learn a lesson from the angel Gabriel who refused to accuse even Satan. Why would Gabriel not want to accuse someone who is a confirmed, certified, evil being? Because that is not the way of God. As soon as you begin to accuse someone, you have taken over from Satan and you have done the work of a demon!

"Yet Michael the archangel, when contending with the devil he disputed about the body of Moses, durst not bring against him a railing accusation, but said, The Lord rebuke thee" (Jude 9).

If even an angel would not accuse satan why would you choose to accuse someone as good as your pastor? Why would you accuse your husband or your wife? Can the evil in your husband or your wife be compared to the evil that is in Satan? Then why do you accuse them? Pray for them and love them.

God is the only one who can change a human being! You will not bring about a positive change in someone by accusing him. He may be pushed around for a while by your accusations but one day he will rebel. "No more," he will say. "I will choose my own way from now on." That is what John Wesley said in a letter to his wife. "Attempt no more to abridge me of the liberty, which I claim by God and man. Leave me to be governed by God and my own conscience..."

Who will be the mouthpiece of Satan and do the work of demons? Not everyone can do this work of accusing people. Some people are more suitable than others are. Some people are actually predisposed to this finger-pointing ministry! Let me give you some examples of the type of people predisposed to becoming accusers.

THE LIST OF POTENTIAL ACCUSERS

1. EVIL MEN: IT IS SAID THAT IT TAKES A THIEF TO CATCH ANOTHER THIEF.

Usually, evil people know how the evil mind works. Innocent people do not have the slightest idea about many possible evils. It is when you are corrupted that certain ideas even occur to you. Sometimes, I hear people accusing others of things, which I find absurd. I ask, "How could they think of such a thing?" Yet, some of these accusations are proved to be realities. Many times these ideas come to people from experience.

You see, when you have used your office to steal millions of dollars before, you will know that large amounts of money can be stolen by politicians. You will not find it unusual to suggest that someone would steal such monies.

Is it not interesting that it was Judas, the thief, who pointed a finger at Christ for not caring for the poor? This is the way to know the evil men in your midst. They seem to spot evil and accuse quickly because they themselves are evil. "Then saith one of his disciples, Judas Iscariot, Simon's son, which should betray him, Why was not this ointment sold for three hundred pence, and given to the poor? This he said, not that he cared for the poor; but because he was a thief, and had the bag, and bare what was put therein" (John 12:4-6).

2. BITTER AND UNFORGIVING PEOPLE

These people have suffered many hurts and pain. They therefore trust no one and expect no good thing from anyone. Some people who come out of bad relationships become the wildest accusers of their future partners. They have no trust.

Because African leaders have looted the treasuries of their nations, Africans generally do not trust their leaders. The best of leaders are met with numerous accusations about their lives. It is difficult to lead an army of suspicious and accusing people. "Moreover David was greatly distressed because the people spoke of stoning him, for all the people were embittered, each one because of his sons and his daughters. But David strengthened himself in the LORD his God" (1 Samuel 30:6 NASB).

Notice how David's men thought of stoning (attacking) David. These men were hurting and grieving men. They were ripe and ready to become accusers.

3. INSECURE AND JEALOUS PEOPLE

People who are not secure in their positions tend to attack anything that comes around them. An insecure female dog, which has littered will attack anyone who comes near her puppies. She feels a threat to the lives of her children and herself.

Insecure senior pastors attack their associates and accuse them of disloyalty and unfaithfulness. Insecure husbands and wives constantly accuse their spouses of having an interest in other parties. Often, the husband or wife is jealous of how their partner seems happy in the company of others. This generates jealousy and insecurity. An insecure head of state constantly fears being overthrown. He is constantly spying on people and accusing those around him. He may execute some members of his government from time to time to discourage mutinous ideas from growing.

One pastor was transferred and for the first time had the job of heading the church and relating with all sorts of people. One day, his wife freaked out and accused him of being in love with the worship leader. This pastor was so shocked at the accusation that he almost had a fit. But his wife would not relent. Unexpectedly, she asked him, "Tell me, are you in love with her? She continued, "Come on, do you love her? I need an answer now!" Her husband was bewildered but she continued with her confrontation. She said, "You should see the way you look at her! She hammered on, "You should hear your voice on the phone when you are talking to her." One day, she said to him, "I know you are having an affair with a married woman and you know what I am talking about." She was convinced that he was in love with her. Sadly, this outburst marked a major downturn in this minister's marriage. All the negative effects of accusation played out in the marriage, which had hitherto been peaceful. This is how insecurity becomes a problem for marital couples. In the ministry, honourable men are sometimes accused in private by their insecure wives. I do not blame you if you do not understand these examples.

The Pharisees were insecure because Jesus had a huge following. They sought to destroy him because He threatened their very existence. The hypocrisies of the Pharisees were exposed by Christ. Even Pilate could see through their insecurities and jealous accusations. "But Pilate answered them, saying, Will ye that I release unto you the King of the Jews? For he knew that the chief priests had delivered him for envy" (Mark 15:9-10).

4. Fearful people

A good example of an accusatory person is the servant who was given one talent. He accused his master of being hard and of reaping what he did not sow. However, the root of these accusations were revealed when he said, "I WAS AFRAID and I hid the talent in the ground." His fearful spirit made him attack his master with accusations.

"Then he which had received the one talent came and said, Lord, I knew thee that thou art an hard man, reaping where thou hast not sown, and gathering where thou hast not strawed: And I WAS AFRAID, and went and hid thy talent in the earth: lo, there thou hast that is thine" (Matthew 25:24-25).

These are people who harbour the spirit of fear. Such people are fearful of many possible evils. They are constantly expecting the worst thing to happen. Such people tend to accuse those around them of something very bad. They may accuse their best and most honest workers of stealing. They may accuse their husbands or wives of having affairs. The great fears they have in their hearts are manifested through accusations.

5. Men of hatred

"But this cometh to pass, that the word might be fulfilled that is written in their law, they hated me without a cause" (John 15:25). Accusations are manifestations of hatred. Satan uses people who hate you to accuse you. Your accuser is the one who hates you most. The hatred that politicians have for one another is manifest through the accusations they hurl at each other. Please do not say you love someone whom you accuse! You do not love him! You hate him because you hate the one you accuse!

6. Witches

A person with a controlling spirit is a witch. Accusations harass and threaten God's servants. Accusations are perfect tools to control great people. A witch is someone who has realized that she has this power to twiddle people around her thumb. She controls people and makes them do things they would not have done. She wields this power through relentless accusations.

A minister complained that he no longer felt free in his home. Witchcraft had modified his domestic behaviour! He told me how he had to always hide his phone from his wife who would search through the phone for incriminating text messages and evidence of questionable phone calls. In the end, he became a fugitive in his own house, running to answer calls in private and rushing about to ensure that his phone was not available for inspection.

This controlling witchcraft had converted a normal husband into a strangely-behaving man who lived on tenter-hooks in his own home. One day, a friend living with him noticed the tension surrounding his handling of the phone and asked, "What is wrong with you?"

He said, "My wife charges me with various allegations. The other night she accused me of being interested in someone. She confronted me and said, 'Can't you leave that girl alone?' She continued her barrage, 'You speak to her first thing when you wake up and she is the last person you talk to before you go to bed.'" He lamented, "I have no such interest and God knows my heart. I have never had anything to do with any lady and God knows my heart."

This lady was trying to control her husband's life, relationships, and even his use of his phone. Through horrible-sounding accusations she tried to deter him from calling or speaking to people. It takes a strong person to see through these accusations and not be confused.

Jezebel sent a frightening message to Elijah about how she was going to kill him. This was a form of accusation. Elijah was under threat for the lives of the four hundred prophets of Baal who had perished under his ministry. Jezebel, the named witch in the Bible harassed the man of God in her day. "Then Jezebel sent a messenger unto Elijah, saying, so let the gods do to me, and more also, if I make not thy life as the life of one of them by to morrow about this time" (1 Kings 19:2).

She controlled her husband with her words and her actions. "Jezebel his wife said, 'IS THIS HOW YOU ACT AS KING OVER ISRAEL? Get up and eat! Cheer up. I'll get you the vineyard of Naboth the Jezreelite'" (1 Kings 21:7 NIV).

7. Ungrateful people

People who are not thankful for what they have received often have little restraint when attacking loved ones. "I don't owe you anything," they say. The Israelites accused Moses of trying to kill them. They were not grateful to him for delivering them from Egypt. If you were thankful for the privileges that have come to you through certain people, you would never want your mouth to be used to rain slime, vomitus and faeces on them.

In my experience, I find that accusers are often ungrateful people with short memories. They do not understand how God had been good to them through certain people. They wanted to stone Jesus (a physical form of accusation) without cause. Jesus answered them, "Many good works have I shewed you from my Father; for which of those works do ye stone me?" (John 10:32).

8. Forgetful people

The children of Israel forgot how they had suffered as slaves. They forgot the experience of passing through the Red Sea. They forgot how the armies of Pharaoh had drowned in the Red Sea. They forgot how bitter waters had been sweetened by Moses. They forgot the manna that came from Heaven. They forgot about the pillar of cloud by day and the pillar of fire by night. They forgot how much gold they had carried out of Egypt. And so they complained and accused Moses of numerous unbelievable crimes including, evil intentions, murder and genocide (killing entire groups of people).

"THEY FORGAT God their saviour, which had done great things in Egypt; Wondrous works in the land of Ham, and terrible things by the Red sea. Therefore he said that he would destroy them, had not Moses his chosen stood before him in the breach, to turn away his wrath, lest he should destroy them. Yea, they despised the pleasant land, they believed not his word: BUT MURMURED in their tents, and hearkened not unto the voice of the LORD" (Psalms 106:21-25).

9. Hard-hearted people

People with hardened hearts cannot believe in the grace of God. They do not trust in the love of God. They cannot forgive. They cannot believe there is any good thing in someone who has made a mistake. They cannot receive counsel. They cannot stop attacking fathers, pastors and authority figures. Their hearts are hardened. These are perfect vessels meet for the devil's use as accusers.

10. A person with a melancholic temperament

"If you remove the yoke from your midst, THE POINTING OF THE FINGER and speaking wickedness..." (Isaiah 58:9 NASB). Melancholics are perfectionists. It is easy for them to feel that people have stepped out of line. They have their own laws of life and expect people to measure up to their standards. With such a personality it is easy to see wrong in many things and to point them out. The pointing out of people's weaknesses often becomes full-blown accusations. Be careful that you do not become the finger-pointing member of the church.

11. A person with a phlegmatic temperament

Phlegmatic people are perceived as good, calm people who stay out of trouble. A phlegmatic person, not affected by the Word is usually a very lazy person. These phlegmatic Christians are therefore often self-righteous people, perfect in their own eyes. Such people quickly notice when others fall short. They can become judgmental and accusatory. The servant who accused the master of being harsh was actually a slow-moving and lazy person, perhaps a phlegmatic man.

"His lord answered and said unto him, Thou wicked and SLOTHFUL servant, thou knewest that I reap where I sowed not, and gather where I have not strawed..." (Matthew 25:26).

12. Disloyal people

Often, when someone turns against his father without justification, he becomes an accuser. He often needs to justify himself to others for the stand he has taken. Ministers who turned against me without a cause have often railed strings of accusations against me. I have a long list of different things I have been accused of. I have been accused of almost every evil under the sun. Watch out for disloyal men! They are top class accusers employed by Satan to poison the church. Absalom, the disloyal son who tried to kill his father, accused him to outsiders. He accused his father of neglecting the kingdom and mismanaging affairs.

"And Absalom rose up early, and stood beside the way of the gate: and it was so, that when any man that had a controversy came to the king for judgment, then Absalom called unto him, and said, Of what city art thou? And he said, Thy servant is of one of the tribes of Israel. And Absalom said unto him, See, thy matters are good and right; but there is no man deputed of the king to hear thee. Absalom said moreover, Oh that I were made judge in the land, that every man which hath any suit or cause might come unto me, and I would do him justice!" (2 Samuel 15:2-4).

13. Your enemies

Accusation is the language of your enemy. I detect the presence of an enemy by any hint of suspicion or accusation. In parliament, enemy parties accuse one another of different evils because they are political enemies. When husbands and wives are not lovers but enemies, they accuse one another of even imaginary things. Do not think that you love your wife if you accuse her! You do not love your husband if you accuse him of different things. Accusation is the language of an enemy and not a friend.

I am amazed that ministers love to be interviewed by journalists who accuse them of a variety of evils. They do not perceive that they are sitting with an enemy. You can never justify yourself to your enemy. He hates you and wants to see you destroyed.

Jesus did not bother to respond to interviews with evil men. He could speak for hours to his disciples, but when he was in the presence of accusers, clothed in the garb of justice, he clamped up and said nothing. "And while He was being accused by the chief priests and elders, He did not answer. Then Pilate said to Him, 'Do you not hear how many things they testify against you?' And he did not answer him with regard to even a single charge, so the governor was quite amazed" (Matthew 27:12-14 NASB).

14. People with something to cover up

Often people cover up their own sin by being the first to attack! They take the battle to the enemy's gate by being the first to strike. Watch the accusers very well. They are often evil men with many things to hide. The author of accusation is the devil. God does not accuse anyone. This means that he who is truly righteous and holy does not accuse.

Is it not ironical that Ahab would accuse Elijah of troubling Israel? Who was causing more trouble in Israel than Ahab? And yet this very person had the audacity to accuse Elijah of troubling Israel. "And it came to pass, when Ahab saw Elijah, that Ahab said unto him, Art thou he that troubleth Israel? And he answered, I HAVE NOT troubled Israel; BUT THOU, and thy father's house, in that ye have forsaken the commandments of the LORD, and thou hast followed Baalim" (1 Kings 18:17-18).

15. Mentally unwell people

Mentally unstable people suffer from delusions. One of the cardinal symptoms of madness is delusions. When a person has a delusion, he believes things that are not true in spite of contrary evidence. He often accuses the other party of various crimes, which are not real. Watch every accuser closely. He or she may be suffering from a mental problem that needs medical attention.

■ ACCUSING WOMEN

Every man of God has different devils and problems to contend with. Some men of God have to deal with powerful accusing women who have the capacity to stop them in their tracks.

Unfortunately, this topic is rarely spoken about because few men of God would ever reveal what they experience in the privacy of their homes. After all every pastor is supposed to have a happy marriage and a blissful existence with his beautiful, well-chosen spouse.

There are rare moments when a man of God speaks about his personal difficulties and experiences. Besides these rare glimpses, there is virtually no insight into the challenges that some ministers do encounter.

It is therefore necessary to read between the lines and receive instruction and encouragement from others who are experiencing similar temptations. God's servants must open their eyes to see and their ears to hear.

As Isaiah stated, many of God's servants are blind and deaf. They simply cannot interpret the veiled messages that are given by God's men. "Who is blind but My servant, or so deaf as My messenger whom I send? Who is so blind as he that is at peace with Me, Or so blind as the servant of the LORD? You have seen many things, but you do not observe them; Your ears are open, but none hears" (Isaiah 42:19-20 NASB).

CHALLENGING OUR FAVOURITE MEN

1. JOB

Many of our favourite people in the Bible were challenged by accusing women. We do have some glimpses, which reveal the challenges that some of our favourite men encountered. Most of these men reacted decisively against evil coming to them through women. Job, for instance, was pushed towards damnation by his wife. Listen to her: "Then said his wife unto him, Dost thou still retain thine integrity? curse God, and die" (Job 2:9). But Job reacted instantly and rebuked his wife. He would serve God and have none of her foolishness. He said to his wife, "You speak as one of the foolish women speaks. Shall we indeed accept good from God and not accept adversity? In all this Job did not sin with his lips" (Job 2:10 NASB).

2. MOSES

Another of our favourite men was Moses. You would have thought that Moses would enjoy a smooth ride as he led the people of God with many miracles. But Miriam, his sister, was not impressed. She rose up with an accusing tongue and charged him for marrying the wrong person. "And Miriam and Aaron spake against Moses because of the Ethiopian woman whom he had married: for he had married an Ethiopian woman" (Numbers 12:1).

She was not impressed by Moses' success at the Red Sea nor was she impressed by his achievements in the wilderness. She took him on squarely and challenged him about his private life. Moses trembled at the accusations of Miriam. But God intervened and struck her with leprosy. God did not seem to be bothered by what Miriam was complaining about. It is what God says that matters. No matter what issue your wife or any woman may bring up, never forget that she is not God and she is not a god! God is still God and it is His opinion that matters. "...wherefore then were ye not afraid to speak against my servant Moses? And the anger of the LORD was kindled against them; and he departed" (Numbers 12:8-9).

3. DAVID

King David had won great victories in various battles. But his wife, Michal was not impressed by what impressed outsiders. She knew David too well to be taken in by the crowds that sang his praises. She knew David had killed Goliath, but it did not matter. She knew David was anointed but she was not impressed. All she thought of was how David was undressed in front of the giggling girls in the congregation. "Then David returned to bless his household. And Michal the daughter of Saul came out to meet David, and said, How glorious was the king of Israel to day, who uncovered himself to day in the eyes of the handmaids of his servants, as one of the vain fellows shamelessly uncovereth himself!" (2 Samuel 6:20)

But David responded decisively. He disagreed with Michal. "I was not displaying in front of those church girls! I refuse to accept that comment! I cannot accept this kind of talk in my house! Do not re-describe my worship as undressing in front of little girls who are enamoured with me! My mind was on God and is still on God!" And that was the end of Michal! And that would also be the end of many wives of ministers of the gospel if they would respond that decisively to accusations. David was so angry that he said that he would continue dancing and playing before the Lord. "I will do more and I will go as far as I want to!" He said, "I have my freedom to serve God and I refuse to be controlled by you. You are not God and I will not obey you! I will obey God whom I love!"

Can you imagine if David had been restrained in his worship? What would have happened if he had followed the warped and narrow-minded prescriptions of Michal? "And David said unto Michal, It was before the LORD, which chose me before thy father, and before all his house, to appoint me ruler over the people of the LORD, over Israel: therefore will I play before the LORD. And I will yet be more vile than thus, and will be base in mine own sight: and of the maidservants which thou hast spoken of, of them shall I be had in honour. Therefore Michal the daughter of Saul had no child unto the day of her death" (2 Samuel 6:21-23).

4. Elijah and John the Baptist

Elijah had a long-standing conflict with King Ahab. After a while he found out that he was actually dealing with a woman called Jezebel. She was the witch who was fighting him from behind the scenes. Naboth also found out that he was fighting with Jezebel and not her husband, Ahab. Naboth actually lost his life because of Jezebel's involvement in the vineyard case. Jezebel his wife said to him, "Do you now reign over Israel? Arise, eat bread, and let your heart be joyful; I will give you the vineyard of Naboth the Jezreelite" (1 Kings 21:7 NASB). After manipulating Ahab from behind the scenes, she threatened Elijah openly and directly. "Then Jezebel sent a messenger unto Elijah, saying, So let the gods do to me, and more also, if I make not thy life as the life of one of them by to morrow about this time" (1 Kings 19:2).

STAGES TO BECOMING A JEZEBEL

Women do not become Jezebels overnight. They go through seven stages, which they must recognize if they are to deal with this tendency. A spiritual woman is able to detect, admit and confess these tendencies before they override all her Christian virtues.

Stage One

Involves women having what I call flashes of annoyance at the sight or presence of certain people. This is a kind of unexplained displeasure or even discomfort when the person comes around. When such a person enters the scene, you are no more at ease.

Stage Two

Is a state in which the woman does not want the presence of certain people. These people should not be close by. They should not be in any environment or place where they are; be it home, work, church, small group, etc. In stage two, the woman takes active measures to avoid being together with or near the other person. If she has any power she would use it to ensure the other person is kept out of sight.

Stage Three

This is when the lady has nothing positive to say about another woman. She sees nothing good or positive in the other person. For instance, someone may say, "The lady sang very well!" But the lady in stage three will say that the instrumentalists are the ones who made the song nice. Another instance is where someone may comment on the beauty of the newsreader but the person in stage three would chip in that it is the free costumes and the make-up artists that make the newsreader look nice! Someone may also say that, "That lady has been promoted because of her hard work." But the stage three lady would be sure to counteract, that the boss likes her and that is why she seems to be doing well. Somehow, no positive comment comes forth from a person in stage three about another woman.

Stage Four

This is when negative remarks are made about the undesirable person. Initially, there was nothing positive to say but now there are a lot of negative things to remark about. Complaints about the other person's behaviour and attitude are often given. The displeasure and dislike are now fully expressed!

STAGE FIVE

This is when there are clashes between the women; unexplained quarrels, confrontations and conflicts. There is no end to the discord between these ladies. Often there is not much explanation to the clashes and the continuation of conflict seems to be unavoidable.

Each blames the other for a bad attitude. They also blame each other for failing to speak or share openly about certain things because of the other party's evil mind. Usually, both ladies would claim that they have good relations with everybody else and that they are not the type that quarrels with anyone. Each lady uses this as proof that there is nothing wrong with her, but the main problem is the witch in the other lady. Sometimes the clashes take on the form of silence and extra reservedness.

STAGE SIX

This is the stage of hatred and elimination. One lady would like to get rid of the other and use all her powers to do so. If she has the power, she would eliminate, terminate and delete the undesirable person. In some cases murder even occurs. This stage of elimination explains the frequent turnover with domestic helpers, who work more directly with the women.

STAGE SEVEN

This is the stage of delusions. A woman who has progressed through these stages without any restraint from the Word of God moves dangerously towards delusions, madness and the arbitrary use of every power she has. Such people are full of accusations about the other party and cannot be convinced about anything different from her beliefs.

Fighting Him in Secret

Powerful women, suffering from delusions, are able to fight against the greatest anointings that have ever walked the earth. What greater anointing is there than the anointing of Elijah or John the Baptist? Yet Jezebel and her New Testament sister, Herod's wife fought against God's anointed servants. Jezebel and her spiritual sister, Herod's wife, are classic examples of fully deluded women who live out the evil within them. They followed their delusions to their logical conclusions. These powerful women have a secret which they deploy against God's servants. The secret is that they take on these anointed men in secret and when they are alone.

Elijah was informed that he was the only person in Israel who was to die within the next twenty-four hours. Can you imagine how he felt? The entire government machinery had been marshalled to eliminate one humble prophet who had a home in the desert. Elijah was terrified and he ran for his dear life! Jezebel was more powerful than all the four hundred false prophets put together. She put Elijah to flight. Elijah had to call on any cross-country or marathon experience that he had to save his life. Even his servant could not keep up with his speed and abandoned him in Beersheba.

This is exactly what happened to John the Baptist. He was alone in the prison cell when he heard the sound of marching feet. There appeared two men with a big tray and the sharpest knife in Israel. Underground and all alone he screamed and shouted: "What a contradiction this is. I have done no evil. I have only helped to restore morality and to reduce corruption in the city." But they would have none of that. After all they were alone with John the Baptist. There was nothing he could do and no one could help him in this secluded and secret place. They sawed off his head slowly cutting through the neck muscles, his trachea, the carotid arteries and finally separating the cervical vertebrae until John the Baptist was well and truly decapitated. What a messy scene was created as the blood of John the Baptist squirted out from his headless body unto his clothes and the Scriptures, which he had been reading in preparation for his next sermon; he had hoped to deliver that sermon in two weeks time!

This man of God was attacked alone where no one could be called upon to help! No one would understand what was happening to John the Baptist. Everyone in town was happy and there was a party going on upstairs in the castle. There was singing and dancing because it was the king's daughter's birthday. No one could understand or relate with John the Baptist's problems on such a festive occasion. That is how it is with men of God. No one really understands what happens to them underground and in the secret places where few ever venture. Jesus said there was no greater man born of women than John the Baptist. And yet a woman had taken him on in secret and destroyed him.

Dear minister, you are not greater than John the Baptist or Elijah. These stories are to encourage you to fight on and to understand that greater people than yourself have struggled in ministry against the power of accusing and threatening women. Unfortunately not all of them survived. But we console ourselves that the will of God always comes to pass. I love a Scripture, which gives me the assurance that God's will is what happens at the end of the day. "The LORD of hosts has sworn saying, Surely, just as I have intended so it has happened, and just as I have planned so it will stand" (Isaiah 14:24 NASB)

John Wesley in the Dungeon?

John Wesley was the great founder and leader of the Methodist church. His life and ministry was plagued by the problem of an accusatory and threatening woman. Of course, he would never say so because the problem was personal. He encountered his problem all alone in the privacy of his room. He suffered the confusion that besets a man of God who needs to love his belligerent wife and yet fulfil his ministry. He had no comment or book that we know of in which he spoke of his problems. However, a glimpse into the dungeon is given to us by a long letter that he wrote to his wife. It is revealing, and every sentence of this letter is a summary of the dungeon experience. His wife was called Molly and this is a letter he wrote to her.

"Coleford October 23rd, 1759

Dear Molly,

I will tell you simply and plainly the things which I dislike. If you remove them, well. If not, I am but where I was.

1. I dislike your showing any one of my letters and private papers without my leave. This never did any good yet, either to you or me or anyone. It only sharpens and embitters your own spirit. And the same effect it naturally has upon others. The same it would have upon me but that (by the grace of God) I do not think of it. It can do no good. It can never bring me nearer, though it may drive me further off. And should you do as you often threaten me, then the matter is over. I know what I have to do. In all this you are fighting against yourself. You are frustrating your own purpose if you want me to love you. You take just the wrong way. No one ever was forced to love another. It cannot be: love can only be won by softness; foul means avail nothing. But you say, 'I have tried fair means and they did not succeed'. If they do not, none will. Then you have only to say, 'this evil is of the Lord; I am clay in his hand'

2. I dislike not having the command of my own house, not being at liberty to invite even my nearest relation so much as to drink a dish of tea without disobliging you.

3. I dislike the being myself a prisoner in my own house, the having my chamber door watched continually, so that no person can go in or out but such as have your good leave.

4. I dislike the being but a prisoner at large even when I go abroad, inasmuch as you are highly disgusted if I do not give you an account of every place I go to and every person with whom I converse.

5. I dislike the not being safe in my own house. My house is not my castle. I cannot call even my study, even my bureau, my own. They are liable to be plundered everyday. You say, "I plunder you of nothing but papers". I am not sure of that. How is it possible I should? I miss money too, and he that will steal a pin will steal a pound. But were it so, a scholar's papers are his treasure, my journal in particular. 'But I only took such papers as relate to Sarah Ryan and Sarah Crosby'. That is not true. What are Mr. Landey's letters to them? Besides, you have taken parts of my journal which relate to neither one nor the other.

6. I dislike your treatment of my servants (though, indeed, they are not properly mine). You do all that in you lies to make their lives a burden to them. You browbeat, harass, rate them like dogs, make them afraid to speak to me. You treat them with such haughtiness, sternness, sourness, surliness, ill-nature, as never were known in any house of mine for near a dozen years. You forget even good breeding, and use such coarse language as befits none but a fish wife.

7. I Dislike your talking against me behind my back, and that everyday and almost every hour of the day; making my faults (real or supposed) the standing topic of your conversation.

8. I dislike your slandering me, laying to my charge things which you know are false. Such are (to go but a few days back) 'that I beat you,' which you told James Burges; that I rode to Kingswood with Sarah Ryan, which you told Sarah Rigby; and that I required you, when we were first married, never to sit in my presence without my leave, which you told Mrs. Lee, Mrs. Fry and several others, and stood to it before my face.

9. I dislike your common custom of saying things not true. To instance, only in two or three particulars. You told Mr. Ireland 'Mr Vazzilla learnt Spanish in a fortnight'. You told Mr. Fry 'Mrs. Ellison was the author as to my intrigue in Georgia'. You told Mrs. Ellison 'you never said any such thing; you never charged her with it'. You also told them 'that I had laid a plot to serve you as Susannah was served by the two elders'.

10. I dislike your extreme, immeasurable bitterness to all who endeavour to defend my character (as my brother, Joseph Jones, Clayton Carthy) breaking out even into foul, unmannerly language, such as ought not to defile a gentlewoman's lips, if she did not believe one word of the Bible.

And now Molly, what would anyone advise you to that has a real concern for your happiness? Certainly,

1. To show, read, touch those letters no more, if you did not restore them to their proper owner.

2. To allow me the command of my own house, with free leave to invite thither whom I please.

3. To allow me my liberty there, that anyone who will may come to me, without let or hindrance.

4. To let me go where I please and to whom I please without giving an account to any.

5. To assure me, you will take no more of my papers nor anything of mine without my consent.

6. To treat all the servants where you are (whether you like them or no) with courtesy and humanity and to speak (if you speak at all) to them, as well as others, with good-nature and good manners.

7. To speak no evil of me behind my back.

8. Never to accuse me falsely.

9. To be extremely cautious of saying anything that is not strictly true, both as to the matter and the manner; and

10. To avoid all bitterness of expression till you can avoid all bitterness of spirit.

These are the advises which I now give you in the fear of God, and in tender love to your soul.

Nor can I give you a stronger proof that I am your affectionate husband. John Wesley"[1]

Derek Prince in the Dungeon?

Derek Prince married two women and said only good things about his wives. What do you expect him to say? Bad things? Even if he had challenges with his wife I would not expect him to talk about them or share them with the public. Would you? However, there are glimpses into the lonely "John the Baptist-in-the-dungeon experiences".

As many second wives do experience, Derek Prince's second wife, Ruth was not liked much by Derek Prince's family and some of his minister friends. When Ruth, the second wife first arrived, Derek Prince's daughter, Johanne had a dream in which Ruth was pushing Derek in a wheelchair. They were in a building somewhere in New York when suddenly, Ruth pushed Derek violently down a great flight of stairs. All the while, Derek was screaming Johanne's name. When Johanne awoke, she was understandably horrified by the dream. This dream was apparently confirmed by Don Basham's daughter who had a similar dream. These dreams did not help much to welcome Derek Prince's second wife!

Ruth, the second wife saw it as her duty to drive Derek Prince to the greatness she believed he was called to. Many people, however, remember her as a controlling woman. She was said to have regimented Derek Prince's life and schedule to the last possible detail. This made things difficult for Derek Prince and those around him. When she and Derek visited the homes of family or friends, Ruth would announce exactly what Derek Prince would eat and when he would have his meals. Sometimes her instructions were sent in advance. Once, Derek Prince went shopping with his wife and some friends. Derek Prince put some things in the shopping basket, which his wife did not want him to have. Ruth did not like it and immediately took the things away from Derek. In the end she became angry and reprimanded him so loudly that everyone in the shop heard her rebuking him. Some described her as "pretty raging and harsh".

When people called the house and asked for the man of God, they would be told he was sleeping or praying. Derek Prince, unaware of this, would wonder why people never called his house. The over-protectiveness of Ruth Prince led to a form of isolation. His second wife was described by some people as "a frustrating combination of control and insecurity". Many of the people around Derek Prince believed that she actually hindered his ministry.

Someone's comment on Derek Prince's marriage was that the couple probably entered a vicious cycle with Ruth trying to control Derek Prince's life to earn his love and Derek resenting the domination and withholding his love from Ruth.[2]

Indeed, there were many good sides to Ruth and she did much to also help his ministry. The point I am trying to make is this, the picture of perfection presented by most ministers to the TV cameras is often not real. There are battles in the secret places which must be fought and won. Insecurity, accusations and control must be understood for what they really are. You must be bold to fight the enemy in the dungeon. Don't let them cut off your head before your time.

The Power of Accusations

15

■ VARIOUS TYPES OF ACCUSATIONS

1. Accusations by Direct Allegations

This is the easily recognized form of accusation. The voice of the accuser rings loud and clear through the statements that come forth. "You are proud and rude." "You are a drunkard." "You did not really want to marry me." "You prefer someone else," "You are in love with the pastor." "Can you not leave that young girl alone?" These are examples of direct allegations voiced out boldly by the confident accuser.

Notice this verse in which the servant directly accused his master. "Then he which had received the one talent came and said, Lord, I KNEW THEE THAT THOU ART AN HARD MAN, reaping where thou hast not sown, and gathering where thou hast not strawed" (Matthew 25:24).

2. Accusations by Criticism

Criticism is making an opinion about someone's faults or bad qualities. It is a statement showing disapproval. Criticism is simply another form of accusation. Do not criticize people. Learn to speak good things and not evil. Do not be a person who constantly notices faults in people. Do not look out for bad qualities and point them out. Pray for people, rather than accuse them!

Notice how Aaron and Miriam accused Moses of marrying the wrong person. "And Miriam and Aaron spake against Moses because of the Ethiopian woman whom he had married: for he had married an Ethiopian woman" (Numbers 12:1).

3. Accusations by Murmuring: Do All Things Without Murmuring.

Murmuring is when unfavourable comments and statements are made undertone. Murmurings are not intended to be heard by the accused but have the effect of poisoning anyone who hears them. Murmuring prevented the children of Israel from entering the Promised Land. God hears all our undertone comments and remarks! God is not deaf!

One day, a pastor was enjoying the music in the church as the choir ministered and his wife was by his side. As he flowed happily with the music, his wife made a comment. At first he thought he had not heard right. He asked "Pardon, what did you say?"

She whispered, "I said that I realize you cannot keep your eyes off her when she is singing."

Even though this remark was undertone it was powerful and loaded with venom. You can imagine the effect it had on someone who was just about to preach.

4. Accusations by Being Present

"Now there was a day when the sons of God came to present themselves before the Lord, and Satan came also among them" (Job 1:6).

The very presence of certain people sends a message to all. The presence of police at a crime scene is a message that something criminal may have happened. The very presence of a uniformed officer always means something. When Satan came for the meeting of the sons of God, his mind was full of accusations. His thoughts were classic accusations: "Does Job serve God for nothing?" In other words, Job was not a sincere servant of God. Satan was accusing Job of not really loving God. Certain people's minds are simply full of accusations. Their presence speaks volumes of suspicion.

5. Accusations by Being Absent

The absence of certain people at meetings sends a loud message. This is why people speak of boycotting meetings. By boycotting meetings, they send a message, which is louder and stronger than, if they had come in person.

"And it came to pass, when he was come to Jerusalem to meet the king, that the king said unto him, Wherefore wentest not thou with me, Mephibosheth?" (2 Samuel 19:25). The absence of Mephibosheth at the time when King David fled was a message! The absence of Mephibosheth indicated he was not really on David's side.

One day, a pastor told me how his wife's absence on a ministry trip broke his heart. He had asked his wife to please come along with him but she refused. Throughout the trip, the absence of his wife ministered an accusation to him! It weakened him and made it difficult for him to minister. His wife had refused to come with him claiming that he was happier with other people. She said to him, "You don't really want me around and I know it."

When he asked his wife again if she would come, her response was simple, "Are you going with your people? If you are going with those people of yours, I am not coming!" His heart was broken and he limped away to his programme.

6. Accusations by Writing

"And in the reign of Ahasuerus, in the beginning of his reign, WROTE THEY UNTO HIM AN ACCUSATION against the inhabitants of Judah and Jerusalem" (Ezra 4:6).

This is the main method of accusation employed by journalists. They write stories which misrepresent events and remarks of honourable men and accuse them of much evil. A government usually becomes the enemy of the press, as journalist's heap up one accusation after another.

Many journalists are in search of a sensational story that will make the headlines. They need something spectacular that will make their newspapers sell. Unfortunately, honourable people fall victim to this quest for headline stories. Often, apologies for mistaken stories are small and insignificant. The damage is done already.

7. Accusations by Suggestions and Insinuations:

An insinuation is an indirect suggestion that something unpleasant is true. The fact that you have not made a direct allegation does not mean that you are not accusing. Sometimes these insinuations are more painful than direct allegations.

Instead of saying Jesus did not deserve such treatment Judas suggested that they were being wasteful. "...To what purpose is this waste? For this ointment might have been sold for much, and given to the poor" (Matthew 26:8-9). Little comments can have far-reaching effects. One senior pastor sent a brother on a mission to help a nearby branch church become more established. This brother was excited about his new challenge. Unknown to him, the senior pastor's wife berated her husband for that move.

She had said to him, "You are sending away people's husbands so that you can have more time with their wives."

"What are you saying," the pastor exclaimed.

But his wife insisted, "You are sending out this man to get him out of the way."

The pastor retorted, "How can you even think that way? How does your mind work?"

But the damage was done. This pastor was affected by this comment and decided not to send out the person. His very motives had been challenged to the core. Naturally, it is the work of God which suffers. Many things are stopped through insinuations. That is the Jezebel spirit of controlling witchcraft.

8. Accusations by Sarcasm

Sarcasm is a way of using words that are the opposite of what you mean, in order to be unpleasant to somebody or to make fun of him. Sometimes, you may make a comment to someone but you mean the opposite. You may say, "thank you" but you mean "I hate you". You may say "God bless you" but you are actually wishing the person evil.

Naaman could see the greed in the eyes of Gehazi. "And Naaman said, Be content, take two talents. And he urged him..." (2 Kings 5:23).

One day, I sent a message to someone. My message was simple. I said, "Tell that guy that I said 'thank you'." However, the messenger refused to take the message. He knew that my thank you was loaded and did not really mean thank you. What it actually meant was, "I have taken note of the evil which you have done to me."

9. Accusations by Silence

Many times silence speaks louder than words. The very silence of someone at a meeting can send a message. Not a word may be spoken but the silence of the committee member speaks volumes and says, "I don't enjoy working with you. You are a dictator. You always want to have your own way." "And Absalom spake unto his brother Amnon neither good nor bad: for Absalom hated Amnon, because he had forced his sister Tamar" (2 Samuel 13:22).

10. Accusations by a Continuous Dropping

Continuous complaining that comes in little bits is a continuous dropping. "A continual dropping in a very rainy day and a contentious woman are alike" (Proverbs 27:15). Sometimes women feel that if they are too strong on an issue then they are being harsh.

Little hints about the same issue given as frequently as possible seems less confrontational. However, the greatest flood that I ever saw in my city did not come from a powerful tropical rainstorm but from a continuous dropping that lasted several hours. Watch out for the people who pester you with a continuous dropping.

11. Accusations by a Contentious Woman

A contentious woman is an ill-natured, cantankerous person. This kind of woman will never agree, never give up, never give in, never say die, never flow, never yield, never bend, never say sorry, never bow, never back down, never concede defeat, never stop talking, never stop quarrelling, never stop arguing, never stop disagreeing and never stop opposing everything.

Accusatory women are contentious women who drive you away from their presence. It is better to be away from the presence of Satan, the accuser. This Scripture shows that the accuser can inhabit beautiful women and use them to wear out God's servant. "It is better to dwell in the wilderness, than with a contentious and an angry woman" (Proverbs 21:19). Truly, the wilderness would be a better home for you than the house you built. "It is better to dwell in a corner of the housetop, than with a brawling woman in a wide house" (Proverbs 21:9). John Wesley wrote to his wife and said, "I dislike not being safe in my own house."[1]

12. Accusations by Re-describing Events

It is a clever trick to re-describe and re-present events in a way that make them look evil. It is easy to re-tell a story in a way that darkens the event and makes things look negative. All you have to do is to highlight some areas and leave out some. This is what was done to Jesus. They re-presented His statements until He looked like a suicide bomber and an anarchist. "We heard him say, I will destroy this temple that is made with hands, and within three days I will build another made without hands" (Mark 14:58). "And they began to accuse him, saying, We found this fellow perverting the nation, and forbidding to give tribute to Caesar, saying that he himself is Christ a King" (Luke 23:2). Watch out for people who re-tell events and make things look nasty, immoral and evil.

■ SOURCE OF ACCUSATORY POWER

I have often wondered why accusations have the effect they do. One day, I had the privilege of interacting with a great man of God. This man was a true spiritual giant. He had accomplished many things for the Lord. As he took us around his facilities, I was amazed at the things that God had accomplished through him. As we walked and drove round the various buildings, he made certain remarks, which made me sad. He seemed to be defending his reputation. He seemed to want to explain himself to us. But I thought to myself, "Why is this man even bothering to clear his name?" Then I remembered that a strange son of his had accused him of many evils. This disloyal pastor had maligned and defamed my honourable host. Much had been said in the media about the allegations against this man. I realized that even this giant in the Lord had trembled under the sting of the accuser. I tell you, nothing can bring a great man to his knees like accusations! They need not be true! They just have to be accusations!

I want us to understand what makes accusations so powerful. Let us get to the bottom of this mystery. Let us find the source of accusatory power. When you understand why accusations are powerful, you will be able to overcome their effects.

1. Accusations are powerful because they are all, basically, true.

"For I know that in me (that is, in my flesh,) dwelleth no good thing" (Romans 7:18). An accusation is a dirty trick that capitalizes on the existing sinfulness and weakness of men. It points the finger at our weak spots and weak points. Almost everything that we are accused of is true. The only thing I can liken accusations to is to a cripple being made fun of by a normal person. It is like pointing out to a paralyzed person that he is incapable and abnormal.

a. Accusing someone is like laughing at a deaf and dumb person and showing him how deficient he is in his hearing and his speech.

How do you think the deaf and dumb person would feel when his deficiency is being demonstrated to others? That is what it is like when a sinner is being told that he is sinful.

The Bible already shows us how far from God we are. If you can imagine it, we are millions of years away from God's nature. "For as the heavens are higher than the earth, so are my ways higher than your ways, and my thoughts than your thoughts" (Isaiah 55:9). We are so far from true holiness and righteousness. Sin has separated us so far from God. It is only His mercy that brings us close.

The Bible teaches us that we are essentially sinners. There are enough Scriptures that declare us hopelessly and helplessly sinful. There is deep-seated evil in the heart of every human being and we know it. We need no one to confirm this well-established truth.

Notice all these Scriptures that confirm all that I am sharing: "There is none righteous, no, not one" (Romans 3:10). "All have sinned and come short of the glory of God" (Romans 3:23). "The heart is deceitful above all things, and desperately wicked: who can know it?" (Jeremiah 17:9).

Also, great men of God confessed that they were woefully sinful and inadequate when they came into the presence of God. Isaiah said, "Woe is me! for I am undone; because I am a man of unclean lips, and I dwell in the midst of a people of unclean lips: for mine eyes have seen the King, the LORD of hosts" (Isaiah 6:5).

Job found out that he was a very bad person when he came to the presence of the Lord. He actually abhorred himself when he realized what he was. "I have heard of thee by the hearing of the ear: but now mine eye seeth thee. Wherefore I abhor myself, and repent in dust and ashes" (Job 42:5-6).

The great prophet, Daniel, also confesses how evil he was, "We have sinned, and have committed iniquity, and have done wickedly, and have rebelled, even by departing from thy precepts and from thy judgments" (Daniel 9:5).

Also, the apostle Paul, at the end of his life described himself as the chief of sinners. He said, "...that Christ Jesus came into the world to save sinners, of whom I am chief" (1 Timothy 1:15). He called himself the chief of sinners in his very last letter. Paul called himself a wretched man who could not get rid of his sinfulness. "O wretched man that I am! who shall deliver me from the body of this death?" (Romans 7:24).

John Wesley Wandered

Interestingly, great men of God feel no sense of worthiness at the end of their lives. Notice what John Wesley said about himself at the end of his life. He said, "I have been wandering up and down between fifty and sixty years, endeavoring, in my poor way, to do a little good to my fellow creatures; and now it is probable that there are but a few steps between me and death; and what have I to trust to for salvation? I can see nothing that I have done or suffered that will bear looking at. I have no other plea than this: I the chief of sinners am, but Jesus died for me."[2]

b. Jesus warned us to stay off judging others.

That is why Jesus warned us to stay off judging other people. Whatever judgment you pass is a judgment on yourself. "Therefore you have no excuse, everyone of you who passes judgment, for in that which you judge another, you condemn yourself; for you who judge practice the same things" (Romans 2:1 NASB).

Be careful when you accuse and judge someone. The Bible says that you are actually practising the same things for which you judge another. I believe that everything I have been accused about is true in principle. I actually feel that they are true and I endeavour to confess my sins everyday.

If someone accused me of stealing the church's money, I would believe it is true. Perhaps I have taken money that I was not aware of? Perhaps I have mismanaged some of God's money? Perhaps I have wasted the church's money? Perhaps I have overpaid myself? Perhaps I have enjoyed luxuries that were not right? How could I tell? In all honesty, my sinful nature is real and I cannot deny it even though I am a preacher.

That is why I confess my sins everyday. If someone accused me of adultery I would believe that it is true and I would confess my sins. I cannot deny much because Scripture says that if you look on a woman to lust after her you have already committed adultery (Matthew 5:28). I must have done this many times over and I always pray for mercy for my soul. If somebody accused me of witchcraft I would agree because rebellion is as the sin of witchcraft (1Samuel 15:23). I must have been rebellious against the Lord many times.

We must be like Daniel who confessed these terrible sins in the first person. He believed he had committed them. His thinking was not, "I am greatly loved by the Lord. I am a great prophet of God." His thoughts were more, "I am a sinner who needs the grace of God." Notice his prayer:

"And I prayed unto the LORD my God, and made my confession, and said, O Lord, the great and dreadful God, keeping the covenant and mercy to them that love him, and to them that keep his commandments; We have sinned, and have committed iniquity, and have done wickedly, and have rebelled, even by departing from thy precepts and from thy judgments: Neither have we hearkened unto thy servants the prophets, which spake in thy name to our kings, our princes, and our fathers, and to all the people of the land. O Lord, righteousness belongeth unto thee, but unto us confusion of faces" (Daniel 9:4-7).

c. **The power of accusation lies in the power of truth.**

It is the truth of this sinful nature that gives power to accusations. No matter how you deny an accusation it will have an effect on you. No matter how untrue an accusation is it will damage you. You will think about what was said and you will be disturbed. You will be uncertain about whether the allegations are really true or not. I know of no other weapon that can administer confusion to your life in such large doses.

2. Accusations are powerful because they stereotype you.

It is because these accusations match you so perfectly with a known stereotype that they have such power over you. Accusations tend to categorize or stereotype a person. These stereotypes are associated with a number of evils. These stereotypes have been proven guilty over and over. Statistics show that these stereotypes do the things they are accused of.

A woman who becomes a stepmother by virtue of her husband's past frolicking is matched perfectly with the stereotype of the wicked and selfish stepmother. No matter what she does and how much she cares for her stepchildren, she matches too well with the wicked stepmother stereotype. She will probably live her entire life under that shadow.

The stereotype of an unmarried, young, pretty lady in the church is that of a husband seeker. It is very easy to believe that every single young lady in the church is simply seeking a husband. No matter how spiritual she looks, it is believed that she is looking for a husband. She fits perfectly into the husband-seeking stereotype. Such a person may be accused of even hoping to snatch somebody's husband.

A stereotype of men is the adulterous husband who cannot stick to his wife. Therefore, when a married man with a grumpy, out-of-shape wife is accused of adultery, he fits perfectly into the adulterous husband stereotype. Matching a man to this stereotype is very powerful because such a man is a perfect match for that category.

I remember a single, unattached lady who was the worship leader in her church. She led the praises and she loved to worship God. She and many other sisters in the church had enjoyed a good relationship with their pastor.

One day, out of the blue, the pastor's wife came up to her and said, "You can never have my husband. No matter what you do, you will never have him! I want you to know that I have three children with him and he will never marry you!" "I just want you to know," she concluded. The worship leader was shocked, to say the least. She did not understand what was happening. The pastor found himself in a very uncomfortable situation, having to balance the relationship between his wife and his worship leader. To say the least, the relationships became awkward and permanently disrupted.

This sudden accusation by the pastor's wife had tremendous power because the worship leader fitted into the "single lady, husband-seeking" stereotype whilst the pastor also fitted the "adulterous husband with a grumpy wife" stereotype. It is because these accusations match you so perfectly with a known stereotype that they have such power over you.

3. Accusations have power because they thrive on the power of deception.

If what the accuser of the brethren says is the right thing, then judgment must be meted out to us. Somehow, God does not pass the judgments that correspond to all these accusations. If most accusations were followed up, many of the accused people would have to be put to death and sent to Hell.

Somehow, the accusations are not valid. We have been declared not guilty to all charges, allegations and accusations because of the blood of Jesus. The blood of Jesus and the mercy of God have changed the equation and rendered the accusations useless. Satan knows this but he still intimidates us and harasses us with accusations, guilt and fear until we are confused. He fights us with so much confusion that we do not know whether we are good or bad!

Because of the blood of Jesus we are forgiven and we are free. God actually loves us and really likes us though it is difficult to believe sometimes. He wants us to be with Him and he has a deep, passionate and warm feeling for us. Because of accusations, I sometimes find it difficult to believe that God loves me. I feel sinful and I know the reality of sin in me. Satan thrives on these feelings and condemns me constantly. But we shall overcome the accuser of the brethren in Jesus' name.

4. Accusations have an effect because Satan's spiritual power is behind every accusation.

Satan is a spirit and he works spiritually through the weapon of accusation. Satan intimidates and harasses God's servants. His aim is to remove you from the ministry and stop you from doing the good things God has called you to. I assure you, many of the bad thoughts that come to your mind are from the devil.

Resist the power behind the accusations and recognize that a spiritual force is working against you. You are a good person and God believes in you!

■ OTHER WORKS OF THE ACCUSER

The devil attacks a Christian in several forms. Moses and our Lord Jesus experienced the onslaught of the devil in the form of an accuser. They sustained relentless attacks in the form of complaints and accusations. The anointing upon Moses was of the highest order. God used Moses to build his people into a great nation.

Jesus was perfect and yet he was accused until his life was snuffed out. Everyone who takes up the call of God is truly an honourable person. In spite of what people say, very few people ever opt for the service of the Lord. Very few people have the faith to obey the call to ministry. In spite of this great effort, ministers are vilified and denigrated constantly. Every attempt to serve God in ministry is a great and honourable effort. Yet why are ministers constantly accused of various evils? Ask Moses and ask the Lord Jesus Christ.

Moses finally erred in ministry when he responded to the complaints of the people. He was perfect in obedience to the Lord, fulfilling every detailed command that God gave him. It was the incessant complaints of the children of Israel that pushed him to the brink. Accusations push people to do things that they would not otherwise have done.

1. The accuser opposes us.

When our first church was being built, Satan attacked us in the form of an antagonistic man. He opposed everything we did in the community. He fought against us and drew the government, the community and the media against me. I was amazed at how kind gestures had turned into the most complicated persecution of my ministry. "But the prince of the kingdom of Persia withstood me one and twenty days..." (Daniel 10:13).

2. The accuser tries to kill you.

This is another thing to expect from the accuser of the brethren. He will try to kill you. And I mean this literally. Satan would love to eliminate you through any possible means. He would love to drown you, poison you, strangulate you, kill you in an accident, inflict a disease on a part of your body.

Do not take this lightly. Every minister must take precautions to keep himself alive. Give no place to the devil. I have been in planes that almost crashed. I have been in cars that somersaulted. I have been inflicted with disease that almost killed me. In all these, I see the accuser trying his hand as a murderer. "The thief cometh not, but for to steal, and TO KILL, and to destroy..." (John 10:10).

3. The Accuser tempts us.

"Then was Jesus led up of the Spirit into the wilderness to be TEMPTED OF THE DEVIL" (Matthew 4:1). I have been tempted by the devil in many different ways. I am sure you would like to know what temptations I have had. Well, I cannot give the details here but I have been tempted in almost every thing you can imagine. One day, the Lord told me that I had overcome a season of temptation. I was surprised to hear this but He explained that I had experienced a season of temptation, which I had survived.

Three Temptations of Ministers

Every minister will experience three temptations. Jesus experienced them and so will you. You will experience temptations with the flesh. Jesus was tempted to turn stones into bread to satisfy His flesh.

You will experience temptations to misuse your authority and power. Jesus was tempted to use His power to jump off a cliff and to call for angels.

Finally, you will be tempted to use the shortcut of ministry. Satan offered Jesus a fast way to win the world. "Bow down and worship me," he said, "and the whole world will be given back to you." This shortcut says, go the quick way where there is no pain, no sacrifice and nothing hard. Fortunately, Jesus did not fall to any of these temptations.

4. The accuser wants us to be worldly.

Satan is the prince of this world. He is the spirit behind the worldly trends and fashions. As Christians become more worldly, they are playing into the hands of the prince of the world. Ministers are constantly under pressure to do and say things that the prince of the world desires. Ministers are pressurized into becoming worldly, motivational speakers rather than preachers of divine secrets. In addition, many ministers have become givers of good advice about the felt needs of their members. This is worldliness in the pulpit. This is a departure from the preaching of divine mysteries, which Christ has given to us. "Love not the world, neither the things that are in the world. If any man love the world, the love of the Father is not in him. For all that is in the world, the lust of the flesh, and the lust of the eyes, and the pride of life, is not of the Father, but is of the world" (1 John 2: 15,16).

5. THE ACCUSER WANTS TO MAKE US UNCLEAN.

The devil wants to make you dirty. His aim is to bring all manner of filthiness into your life. All kinds of lustful and immoral activities will make you dirty. Certain films, pornography, secular music and profanity are Satan's tools to dirty your life. The devil is often called an unclean spirit. (Mark 1:23).

6. THE ACCUSER WILL INFLUENCE YOU THROUGH THE AIR.

"... ye walked according to the course of this world, according to the PRINCE OF THE POWER OF THE AIR, the spirit that now worketh in the children of disobedience" (Ephesians 2:2). The accuser has possessed the airwaves of every nation. As the prince of the power of the air, he channels much evil through the radio, television and internet. This is why it is important for Christians to gain access and control of the airwaves of their countries. You must fight to go on air and join the battle in the atmosphere. Elections are won and lost in the air. The morality of a nation is destroyed in the air. But souls are also won through the airwaves.

7. THE ACCUSER WILL TRY TO MAKE YOU WORTHLESS

The name Belial means worthlessness. Satan is trying to make your ministry worthless. He wants to make you personally worthless! "By means of a whorish woman a man is brought to a piece of bread" (Proverbs 6:26). Satan wants to reduce you to the lowest possible level in this life. That is the spirit of poverty, uselessness and worthlessness. Be delivered in Jesus' name!

8. THE ACCUSER WILL TRY TO RULE YOU.

Satan is the ruler of darkness. When you walk in sin and darkness, you are walking into his hands. Stay away from sin, stay away from that realm and stay close to the light. "For we wrestle...against the RULERS OF THE DARKNESS of this world..." (Ephesians 6:12).

9. THE ACCUSER WILL DECEIVE YOU.

Satan's strength towards you is deception. Persistent lying and deceptive tricks have made him the master deceiver of all time. He will try to deceive you into believing many things that are not so. Most of our difficulties come from our delusions. Most of our sorrows are because of erroneous things that we have believed. If Satan is able to deceive the whole world, then you must constantly ask yourself what current delusion you may have. "...that old serpent, called the Devil, and Satan, WHICH DECEIVETH the whole world..." (Revelation 12:9).

10. THE ACCUSER WILL FIGHT WITH YOU.

"Be sober, be vigilant; because YOUR ADVERSARY THE DEVIL, as a roaring lion, walketh about, seeking whom he may devour" (1 Peter 5:8).

Expect the fight of your life as you step into ministry! You will be fighting until your very last day. Intelligent demons, wicked spirits and wrestling powers will engage you until you lie down in the grave. You need supernatural wisdom and closeness to God to survive. It is not about power. It is about fighting a liar and a clever deceiver. Adversary means a challenger, an opponent, an enemy and an antagonist. You can expect to be antagonized and challenged throughout your entire ministry. That is one of the key works of the accuser in the midst of the brethren.

Silencing the Accuser 16

■ THE STRATEGIES FOR DISARMING THE ACCUSER

There are many benefits of fighting the accuser in your life. There are also many different ways you must take on this vicious enemy.

1. Prayer

"Seeing he ever liveth to make intercession for them" (Hebrews 7:25). Prayer is the way to fight the spiritual power that is behind accusation. Jesus ever lives to make intercession for us. The intercession of Christ is directly countering the accusations of Satan. Prayer is the opposite of accusation. As Satan points out our weaknesses, Jesus is presenting his blood before the throne, explaining why we must not be condemned.

Join your prayer with the prayers of Christ and counteract the force of accusation against your ministry. Set up prayer warriors to intercede for you constantly so that the power of the accuser will be broken.

2. Open confrontation

"They say unto him, Master, this woman was taken in adultery, in the very act. Now Moses in the law commanded us, that such should be stoned: but what sayest thou? This they said, tempting him, that they might have to accuse him. But Jesus stooped down, and with his finger wrote on the ground, as though he heard them not. So when they continued asking him, he lifted up himself, and said unto them, He that is without sin among you, LET HIM FIRST CAST A STONE AT HER. And again he stooped down, and wrote on the ground. And they which heard it, being convicted by their own conscience, went out one by one, beginning at the eldest, even unto the last: and Jesus was left alone, and the woman standing in the midst. When Jesus had lifted up himself, and saw none but the woman, he said unto her, Woman, where are those thine accusers? hath no man condemned thee? She said, No man, Lord. And Jesus said unto her, Neither do I condemn thee: go, and sin no more" (John 8:1-11). Jesus introduced the accused to the accusers and asked the accusers to implement the judgment of their allegations. He wanted them to carry their accusation to its logical conclusion.

Many accusers love to hide behind the curtain and shoot their arrows. They do not want anybody to know what they think or say. Openly confronting accusers can be a good way to free yourself. Years ago, I confronted a brother who was accusing me of not being called to the ministry. I said to him, "If I am not called, why are you in this church? If I am not anointed, why do you come to this church every week?"

This fellow was shocked at the confrontation. You see, accusers love to hide and say things about you. When they see you, they phlegmatise and flow as though everything is normal. You would never know what is said behind your back by the smiles and jolly friendship they exhibit.

3. TEACHING

Teaching is a powerful tool that deals a deadly blow to ignorance and deception. Jesus responded to several of his accusations with teachings. Let me give you a few examples. You can hold a large team together when you teach them. Most leaders just warn their followers to desist from certain things. But teaching is more powerful than issuing warnings.

a. **Jesus was accused of not letting His pastors fast, so He taught on the new wineskins.**

"The disciples of John and of the Pharisees were fasting. Then they came and said to Him, 'WHY DO THE DISCIPLES OF JOHN AND OF THE PHARISEES FAST, but Your disciples do not fast?' And Jesus said to them, 'Can the friends of the bridegroom fast while the bridegroom is with them? As long as they have the bridegroom with them they cannot fast. But the days will come when the bridegroom will be taken away from them, and then they will fast in those days. No one sews a piece of unshrunk cloth on an old garment; or else the new piece pulls away from the old, and the tear is made worse. And no one puts new wine into old wineskins; or else the new wine bursts the wineskins, the wine is spilled, and the wineskins are ruined. But new wine must be put into new wineskins'" (Mark 2:18-22 NKJV).

b. **When Jesus was accused of not washing His hands, He gave a teaching that addressed the issue.**

"Then the Pharisees and scribes asked him, WHY WALK NOT THY DISCIPLES ACCORDING TO THE TRADITION OF THE ELDERS, but eat bread with unwashen hands? He answered and said unto them, Well hath Esaias prophesied of you hypocrites, as it is written, This people honoureth me with their lips, but their heart is far from me. Howbeit in vain do they worship me, teaching for doctines the commandments of men" (Mark 7:5-7).

c. **Jesus was also accused of being a mere carpenter posing as a man of God. In response to this, He gave a teaching on how a prophet is not accepted in his own home.**

"IS NOT THIS THE CARPENTER, the son of Mary, the brother of James, and Joses, and of Juda, and Simon? and are not his sisters here with us? And they were offended at him.But Jesus said unto them, A prophet is not without honour, but in his own country, and among his own kin, and in his own house" (Mark 6:3-4).

d. **Jesus was accused of eating with sinners, so He taught on evangelism.**

"And when the scribes and Pharisees saw him eat with publicans and sinners, they said unto his disciples, HOW IS IT THAT HE EATETH AND DRINKETH WITH PUBLICANS AND SINNERS? When Jesus heard it, he saith unto them, They that are whole have no need of the physician, but they that are sick: I came not to call the righteous, but sinners to repentance" (Mark 2:16-17).

4. COMMON SENSE LOGIC

One of the ways to counteract accusations is to use common sense to make nonsense of the accusations. You must learn to use logical arguments that destroy the foundation of the accusation. Jesus did this often.

When Jesus was accused of having political aspirations he answered with logical arguments. He said, "If my kingdom were of this world, my servants would fight." Is it not logical for a king to have his army fight for him? "Jesus answered, My kingdom is not of this world: if my kingdom were of this world, then would my servants fight, that I should not be delivered to the Jews: but now is my kingdom not from hence" (John 18:36). I use those arguments a lot. I ask questions like, "If I was after money, would I not practise medicine?" "If all I wanted were nice cars and a nice house why would I choose to be a priest? Could I not just practice medicine in America and earn lots of money for myself?" Common sense alone will dispel numerous baseless accusations from the mouths of hateful enemies of the cross.

5. Agreeing with your Accusers

"AGREE WITH THINE ADVERSARY QUICKLY, whiles thou art in the way with him; lest at any time the adversary deliver thee to the judge, and the judge deliver thee to the officer, and thou "be cast into prison" (Matthew 5:25).

The Bible teaches us to agree with our accusers. The truth is that we are guilty of almost everything we are accused of. Agreeing with your accuser can be a powerful strategy to silence the accuser. Jesus used this method when he was on trial. By saying, "I am" and "thou sayest" He agreed with His accusers. It was now up to them to follow their prosecution to its logical conclusion.

Jesus Agreed with His Accusers

"AND JESUS SAID, I AM: and ye shall see the Son of man sitting on the right hand of power, and coming in the clouds of heaven" (Mark 14:62). "And Pilate asked him, Art thou the King of the Jews? AND HE ANSWERING SAID UNTO HIM, THOU SAYEST IT" (Mark 15:2).

6. Silence

Not answering accusations that are levelled against you is yet another way to silence the accuser. Journalists hate to hear the wise words, "I have no comment to make at this time." Journalists love to interview controversial figures. Each time a public figure is interviewed, he says something they can hold on to and accuse him of. One of the best policies for the ministers is to make no comments and to give no interviews about anything for any reason! Jesus saw no reason why He should answer questions. All he had to say was what he had preached. They could get the tapes if they wanted to, and hear it for themselves. Pastors must learn from the Saviour.

People questioning you in a hostile environment is not going to give a true picture of who you are. People should listen to what you preach and make up their minds. Hopefully, they will be saved and convicted by the time they have heard your message.

"Jesus answered him, I spake openly to the world; I ever taught in the synagogue, and in the temple, whither the Jews always resort; and in secret have I said nothing. WHY ASKEST THOU ME? ASK THEM WHICH HEARD ME, what I have said unto them: behold, they know what I said" (John 18:20-21).

Jesus used this strategy when he met with Pilate. Pilate could not believe that Jesus would not speak to him. If Jesus did not want to speak to Pilate, how come pastors yearn to be interviewed by the secular world? Why are we so different from our Saviour? "And went again into the judgment hall, and saith unto Jesus, Whence art thou? But JESUS GAVE HIM NO ANSWER. Then saith Pilate unto him, SPEAKEST THOU NOT UNTO ME? knowest thou not that I have power to crucify thee, and have power to release thee? Jesus answered, Thou couldest have no power at all against me, except it were given thee from above: therefore he that delivered me unto thee hath the greater sin" (John 19:9-11).

You must not be ashamed of the accusations that are levelled against you. Our father has given us a cup to drink. Shall we not drink it? Allow the accusers to go ahead and paint you in whatever colours they wish. God is judge and he will vindicate you. There is nothing that anyone can do to prevent you from fulfilling God's call. Like Jesus told Pilate, no one can have power over your life and ministry except God gives it. God is in control and His hand is over all of us.

A WARNING TO ACCUSERS

Psalm 109 contains a prophetic prayer against accusers. In the twentieth verse, the Psalmist summarizes his desire that all he has said should be the reward of his accusers, "Let this be the reward of my accusers from the LORD, and of those who speak evil against my soul" (Psalm 109:20 NASB).

This is one of the most terrible and detailed curses you will find anywhere in the Bible. It ranges from the present life to the future of all descendants of the accuser. It is a sober warning to us all to leave God's servants alone. God will judge them. There is no point in you invoking Psalm 109 against your life. Read it for yourself and decide to stay away from the reward of accusations.

"O God of my praise, Do not be silent! For they have opened the wicked and deceitful mouth against me; They have spoken against me with a lying tongue. They have also surrounded me with words of hatred, And fought against me without cause. IN RETURN FOR MY LOVE THEY ACT AS MY ACCUSERS; But I am in prayer. Thus they have repaid me evil for good And hatred for my love. Appoint a wicked man over him, AND LET AN ACCUSER STAND AT HIS RIGHT HAND. When he is judged, let him come forth guilty, And let his prayer become sin. Let his days be few; Let another take his office. Let his children be fatherless And his wife a widow. Let his children wander about and beg; And let them seek sustenance far from their ruined homes. Let the creditor seize all that he has, And let strangers plunder the product of his labor.

Let there be none to extend lovingkindness to him, Nor any to be gracious to his fatherless children. Let his posterity be cut off; In a following generation let their name be blotted out. Let the iniquity of his fathers be remembered before the LORD, And do not let the sin of his mother be blotted out. Let them be before the LORD continually,

That He may cut off their memory from the earth; Because he did not remember to show lovingkindness, But persecuted the afflicted and needy man, And the despondent in heart, to put them to death. He also loved cursing, so it came to him. And he did not delight in blessing, so it was far from him. But he clothed himself with cursing as with his garment, And it entered into his body like water And like oil into his bones. Let it be to him as a garment with which he covers himself, And for a belt with which he constantly girds himself. LET THIS BE THE REWARD OF MY ACCUSERS FROM THE LORD, AND OF THOSE WHO SPEAK EVIL AGAINST MY SOUL" (Psalm 109:1-20 NASB).

The Sin of Hypocrisy

17

■ DECEPTION

Deception is a very dangerous condition, which comes about by repeated lying. When we knowingly and continuously lie, we begin to believe the lie. Self-deception occurs when we do something wrong, but repeatedly tell ourselves that what we are doing is right. In the end, we will believe when we commit sin, that we are actually doing the right thing. Having done a wrong thing so many times and for so long, a deceived person is convinced that it is the right thing.

During the dark years of Nazi Germany, the Nazis convinced themselves that killing Jews was right. At a point they believed that the Germans were really a special race which was superior to every other race. They also believed that all their problems were caused by the Jews. Then they came up with what they called the FINAL SOLUTION: How to solve the Jewish problem. They believed in it, preached it, taught it in schools and they gradually eliminated and annihilated as many Jews as possible. They must have believed it with all their hearts, because they killed the Jews consistently. They murdered thousands and thousands of them. The Germans used some of the crudest methods the human brain could possibly devise. In some cases, they made the Jews dig trenches, and then told them to line up by these pits. Then they shot all of them in cold blood.

If we continue to lie to ourselves about something, we will begin to believe that the wrong is right. On the other hand, we also know that right is right. So now we will have two acceptable standards-right is right, and wrong is also right. This is the foundation for double standards and double-dealing, which is the double life.

Unfortunately, there are so many Christians who are two people in one.

Some years ago, I used to be a musician and moved around with many other musicians. Many of them had two personalities.

When they stood on stage they would sing songs like, *Amazing Grace, I Love You Lord,* and many other beautiful songs. Yet, if you met them off stage, their lives were something else.

It got to a point when I was no longer impressed with any gospel singer on stage.

There are many singers and choristers who sing beautifully, but have horrible private lives. They have two lives! One life is when they sing and lift up their voices to the Lord. The other life is when they are off stage.

Indeed, some of these singers can even bring you to tears. But then when you get closer, you would wonder whether these people are even Christians.

Your life on stage should conform with the one in private. If someone comes to live with you, he should discover that the character on stage is the same as the one at home.

As a pastor, I know I could easily fall into a dual life. Therefore, I consciously check the things that are private, which nobody knows about.

I do my best to make my private life line up with the Bible.

What I say and what I do must tally.

One dangerous thing for a pastor to do is to have a double life. Some ministers would even admonish the congregation not to copy their lifestyles!

My father once said a priest told him to do what he said, but not what he did.

"Do what I say, but don't do what I do," he told his parish.

If you are in a church where the pastors stand and say one thing, but turn around to do another, then you must leave that church! It is a dangerous place because the pastor is practising duality!

DUALITY: LIFE OF DOUBLE STANDARDS

1. The tendency to have a hidden, secret life

People who are called Christians and yet live a different lifestyle in addition to the Christian one are guilty of hypocrisy, which is the art of living a double standard life. This usually happens when there are two personalities or two natures embodied in one person

There is one lifestyle displayed in public, and the other one shown in private. Such a pretentious person has one behaviour pattern he exhibits when he comes into public. This is usually to impress the people around. He has another type of behaviour when nobody can see him. For those who claim to be Christians, one lifestyle is displayed in church, and the other, outside of church.

2. Predisposition towards sinfulness

The reuslt of deception is a manifestation of the spirit of hypocrisy, the spirit of lies and the spirit of self-deception. One of the greatest forms of deception is self-deception. Often when I counsel people and can get them to understand the problem they are faced with, much of the work is already done. When doctors are able to diagnose the sicknesses of patients, often it means that fifty per cent of the work is done because the doctor now knows exactly what he is dealing with.

God's expectation is that as children of God, no form of sinful living should be found in us. Fornication, uncleanness and the like should never be associated with any Christian. "But fornication, and all uncleanness, or covetousness, let it not be once named among you, as becometh saints" (Ephesians 5:3).

Samson, a Biblical Model of the Dual Life

Samson was a perfect example of someone with a dual life. His dual behaviour was so classic that every Christian must learn something from him.

1. Separated and unequally yoked

Samson had a religious, separated side, which was shown by the fact that he never cut his hair. Yet, he was unequally yoked to the things of the world. There are Christians who appear separated from the world, but yet live in sin. Samson's life was one that was separated and yet was entangled in the world.

He was separated because he was a Nazarite, that is, someone who was not supposed to live like the rest of the people. He was unique, in the sense that he was not supposed to drink, or cut his hair. He didn't cut his hair, and it was a sign of his consecration to God. It was an open sign to everyone that Samson was a Nazarite, separated unto God.

At the same time, he was practising another kind of quiet evil, by linking himself with the devil and the world. These two things were going on in his life at the same time.

This was a man who would not cut his hair, who claimed to be charismatic, who was wearing the Nazarite hair; a sign that he was separated to God.

However, at the same time, He wanted to have an unbeliever wife (Judges 14: 2-3). He was a man anointed of God, yet he indulged in worldly pleasure. And there are many people doing that today, including pastors! There are many pastors who have two personalities and two lives. There are also many church members who have two personalities.

There is the personality that is displayed when they walk through the church gate: holier than everybody else. Once they get out of the church gates into their homes or offices, however, they move into their other lives. This is a different thing altogether.

Some of you reading this book are just like that. You are in the church and you claim to be born again. Your friends think that you are a believer, but on the side you are playing around with the world. Your best friends are unbelievers, which makes you just like Samson.

The amazing thing is, it is not that you are even in an ordinary youth or charity group. You are in a born-again church where you hear life-changing sermons over and over again, and yet your best friends are unbelievers. If your favourite friends at school and at work are openly declared non-Christians, you have a big problem!

2. Anointed and Worldly

Samson also played with God. He wore the long hair, which was a sign that he was a member of a Christian church, but he still dabbled in fornication with the world. Apparently separated, but also with the world.

There was a man who was talking about some of our charismatic churches. He boasted, "Every Sunday, I pick up a girl from these charismatic churches. I just have to pass by the junction after church on Sunday and give one of them a lift, and I'll have one of the so-called born-again sisters to sleep with."

Many years ago Rev. Sackey, one of my associate ministers, was the manager of a hotel. One day, a lady came there with a Lebanese man. They checked into a room together and were there for about an hour. My dear pastor was sitting at the reception when this lady came out of the hotel room shouting in tongues—she was a tongue-talking born-again Christian! Yet on the quiet, she was having affairs with men in hotels. She is likely to be seen on Sunday in a well-known charismatic church, lifting up her hands in worship. She is playing with God.

Spiritual Duality is a condition which predisposes to fornication and adultery. Do not play any double games with God! I can just see Samson with his long hair as he walked through town. Everybody knew that meant that he was an anointed man of God, separated unto God, walking in the things of God and a member of the church. Yet he wanted to marry an unbeliever.

When he told his father who he wanted to marry, he asked, "Is there no woman in Israel you can marry?"

Samson replied, "Oh no, this is the girl I want."

How can you even think of marrying a complete outsider when you are a believer separated unto God? It is dangerous to lie to yourself that the wrong things you do are right.

3. Spiritual and Carnal

Samson was a spiritual person and yet he was carnal. At certain times, he gave the impression that he was very spiritual. At other times, it was surprising how carnal he could be.

The contrast is such that you wonder if this carnality and spirituality could be in one person? "...the Spirit of the LORD began to move him at times..." (Judges 13:25). The Spirit was upon the man and yet he was carnal. He was so spiritual that he was the spiritual leader of Israel for twenty years. However, we realize that he had a woman problem: He was a playboy although he had the Spirit of God.

I remember a man of God whom I respected very much. He also used to play this kind of game. He was a powerful preacher, and I was really moved every time he ministered. Yet this man was also playing around with many of the women in his church.

It is said that one day, when he was fornicating with one of the women, she asked him, "So, after doing this how will you be able to preach tomorrow?"

He replied, "When I sin like this, then the anointing comes even more."

There are people who commit fornication just before going to church. Really, it does not make any difference to them. Some Christians go a step further to fornicate with people whose names they don't even know! Such people could even be the most expressive when they come to church. They are spiritual and at the same time carnal.

Look at Samson, he loved to go out for prostitutes. He slept with one woman after the other. He did all this, in spite of the fact that the Spirit of God was upon him. For twenty solid years he was in the ministry, and yet he played with these problems!

4. Mighty in Ministry and Weak in Private Life

It is dangerous to be both mighty and weak. If your pastor knows that you are weak, he can pray for you but if you pretend to be mighty, how can he know that you need help? If you are mighty, nobody will spend time to counsel or minister to you, but if you show that you are weak, attention will be given to you. If you are weak, but present yourself as strong, you are preventing your own deliverance. You are covering what needs help.

One day a lady went to see a doctor, a gynaecologist. When the lady rose to leave the consulting room, the doctor asked, "Is that really the reason why you came to see me?"

She had come for consultation without divulging the real problem. The doctor had a feeling that there was more to it than met the eye, and that there was something that she couldn't bring herself to say. This was actually the case.

When you appear strong even though you are weak, nobody can help you. When you confess, "I'm weak, I need help," the mighty people in ministry can come to your aid. As a pastor I have come to see that there are people I don't particularly need to visit, because they are strong! But then sometimes there is a weak one, and I have to rush there because he needs attention. When you look strong like Samson, you won't get any attention.

Samson was mighty in ministry, killing thousands. At the same time he was a weak man when it came to his private life. He was mighty publicly but the opposite in private. If you had the opportunity to visit him at home, you would see a different life altogether.

The book of Judges, in chapter 16, and verse 3, recounts that he carried the gates of the city on his shoulders. What a mighty man! In this sense he was not weak. He was so mighty that he killed one thousand people with a jaw bone.

Judges 16:14-17 portrays Samson as being morally weak. This allowed Delilah to take advantage of him. She overcame the mighty man because he was also a weak man. The Philistines recognized this weakness also, and capitalized on it to eventually conquer Samson.

Many public officers and officials in many nations are like that. In public life they look so dignified and respectful. When they are interviewed on television, they sound so powerful but in their private lives, they are morally and maritally weak.

5. Nasty and Nice

There are some people who are very nice when they are in public, but are extremely nasty when they are at home. Their spouses and children know them to be very impatient and abusive, but those outside the home see them as the sweetest people on earth.

I have met many husbands who complain that the way their wives speak to the pastors make them feel that their spouses respect and love their pastors more than their own husbands. The contrast is such that they cannot help but notice the humility and gentleness which their wives reserve for their pastors and outsiders. Such a wife or husband has a dual life. They have two different natures: the nasty nature which they display in private (usually those close to them have to endure it), and the nice nature which they display in the open. In fact, some of the nicest people are also the nastiest. Perhaps, it is a reflex to camouflage their nastiness at home. Such people take extra precautions to appear nice to outsiders, especially those they meet for the first time.

6. Mature and Yet Childish

Samson judged Israel for twenty years. It takes maturity to be a judge, and to be able to lead a nation for this number of years. Looking at Samson's life, you may get the impression that he was just lustful, chasing one prostitute after another. However, he was a judge for twenty years. That is maturity in ministry.

Most charismatic churches in my country Ghana, have not been in the ministry for twenty years. Yet Samson was. However, Samson had another side of his personality which made him behave like a child.

In Judges Chapter 15 and verse 1, he caught three hundred foxes and tied their tails in pairs. Then he set them on fire and sent them into the Philistines' farms. This was Samson's revenge on his father-in-law for giving his bride to his best man.

His behaviour was childish. It is a child who would think of running around to catch foxes, tie their tails and light them up with fire. There are simpler ways of burning a farm. The man was clearly childish in his thinking. Yet, at the same time, he was a very mature man who gave reasonable judgements for at least twenty years.

There are many Christians like that. Their level of understanding of God's Word is excellent, yet they are so childish. A child is very unsteady and unstable. A child cannot sit at one place for a long time.

There are many childish Christians who despite their knowledge of God's Word, cannot settle down in any church. Today, you will meet them in this church, the next time, you will find them in another church. They just cannot belong anywhere. They are unsteady and unstable, yet they have great knowledge. It takes maturity to belong to a church.

One Sunday evening, I "tuned-in" to a Christian talk show (on the radio) on my way home from church (I usually leave church very late). That night, the discussion was on churches and pastors. As I listened to the discussion I marvelled at how wise and mature the arguments sounded.

Then I suddenly recognised the voice of one of the contributors. He was one of the most unstable Christians I had ever known. He had once been a member of my church, but had since moved to at least two other churches. This fellow had such wise comments to make on the behaviour of pastors and churches, yet he was like a child—unable to belong to any church for a long period. Perhaps, he knows too much to belong anywhere. He is mature and yet childish.

Another feature of a child is that it cries a lot. Children are often easily hurt, and they need a lot of time and attention. In the church setting, anybody who behaves in this manner is considered a child. Childish Christians sometimes know a lot of Scriptures and have been Christians for a long time, yet they still get easily hurt and need much attention. A mature person doesn't seek attention, but rather gives it.

Maturity is needed in every facet of our lives. It takes maturity for a man to say, "This is the woman I am going to marry and no one else." It takes a mature man to settle down with one of the many beautiful ladies he sees around him. That is why people respect married men. A child cannot settle. That is why a man who does not want to settle may not be regarded as a man yet. He is still a boy.

7. Loyal and slanderous

There are people who claim to be loyal and yet are very slanderous and double-tongued. They have two tongues: one speaks good and the other evil. "Likewise must the deacons be grave, not doubletongued..." (Timothy 3:8). The Bible describes duality of the tongue as being double-tongued. There is only one animal that seems to have two tongues-the snake!

As I shared earlier, some years ago, I was in a fellowship meeting when the pastor took a second offering. I got angry and complained to a sister sitting by me, but the look she gave me shut me up. Immediately, my heart smote me. After the service, I went up to the pastor and confessed to him what I had said. He was very surprised. Stretching out his hands, he told me God was going to use me. I could have complained bitterly about the man of God as I sat there. Then after the service, I could have approached him with a big smile, telling him how much I enjoyed the sermon. To him, I would have sounded very loyal but I would have been "stabbing him in the back", pretending to have a loyal tongue.

A person with two tongues is a follower of the devil, who slanders the saints before God. The devil is described as: "...the accuser of our brethren...which accused them before our God day and night" (Revelation12:10).

8. Worshipping with your mouth, yet rebelling in your heart

God is sick of duality and of all forms of pretense. When the Israelites practised duality, God became so angry that He refused to accept their sacrifice. He queried, "To what purpose is the multitude of your sacrifices unto me?...Bring no more vain oblations; incense is an abomination unto me;...I cannot away with; it..." (Isaiah 1:11). God was tired of their hypocrisy, and told them that he would not heed their prayers because after praying they turned and did evil. God said, "Away with it! I cannot, and I do not want it."

Truly, there are so many Christians who sing, lift up their hands, and tell the Lord that they love him-but these are often empty words.

Many women feel dejected when they realize that the man who claimed to love them had been lying all along. Some women become so heartbroken that they cannot believe the words of any man for the rest of their lives.

If a woman finds out that the love of her life has other girlfriends, she will not take it lightly. When such a man returns to her with his sweet words, she may very well explode! This scenario can be likened to the way God feels about those who literally live in sin, but come to church with all those beautiful words and songs.

God does not take it lightly when your heart is far from Him but to those around, you appear to be serving Him in earnest.

9. Goodness and badness

The dual person exhibits both goodness and "badness": "...your goodness is as a morning cloud, and as the early dew it goeth away" (Hosea 6:4). The morning cloud and the early dew are things that appear for a short while and then vanish almost immediately.

Some people would know the dual person to be bad and wicked. Another group of people would know him to be a very good person.

If you went to the home of a person living a dual life, the members of his family would readily supply you with tales of his evil deeds. If you also went to talk to his colleagues at work or in the church, they would tell you of his goodness and kindness.

The goodness of such a person is temporary, and is only revealed to a selected few. Those living dual lives might appear to be good, but their goodness is short-lived.

10. Men pleaser and God pleaser

Is it possible to please God and men at the same time? Paul states, "...for if I yet pleased men, I should not be the servant of Christ" (Galatians 1:10).

According to Paul, if he pleases men, he cannot please Christ. It is as simple as that! There is no way you can please men and think or believe you are pleasing God.

Walking with the Lord on this long road of ministry, I have had to do many things that were often not pleasing to men. I simply could not please men. When I responded to the call of God on my life, I displeased my parents.

Think about it! You sent your child to school. He did well and qualified as a doctor. Would you be pleased if he told you he had decided to become a pastor instead? At the time I took this decision, my church was very small and unimpressive. I remember my father-in-law offered to speak to the Hospital Administrator to get me transferred to a new department because I had been posted to the mortuary. My family thought that perhaps I didn't want to work in such a place. But no! I was going into the ministry because I wanted to obey and please God. Thank God, they now admire the church.

If you want to please men, you will never be a servant of Christ.

To avoid living a dual life, you may sometimes have to go contrary to man's opinion, and just please God.

If your parents want you to marry an unbeliever just because he is wealthy, you will have to go contrary to their desire, because the Bible commands us not to marry unbelievers!

Your family may not be happy, but God will be pleased with you. Someone who is living a dual life will have to bend the rules to please his family. Are you pleasing men or pleasing God?

11. Impressive and unimpressive

I have realized that as human beings, most of us want people to be impressed with us. We wish the people around us would be impressed with what we have: our cars, our appearance etc.

The person living a dual life will do and say everything possible to impress his friends and those around him. Sometimes, people go to the extent of going for bank loans in order to live a certain kind of lifestyle to impress friends.

Many people live above their means because they want to present a certain image of themselves. The person living a dual life may be regarded as wealthy and living in luxury—when in reality, he is living on borrowed glory. Soon his creditors will catch up with him, and the image he has built around himself will come crumbling down! That is when the people he has deceived will be disappointed and unimpressed with him.

It is good to be liberated from that constant desire to impress others. If I had tried to impress people, my church, Lighthouse Chapel International would not have gotten to this stage. I would have spent our income on impressive cars, clothes and lifestyles, trying to impress those on the outside. There is no need to impress anyone. If you are a worthy person, people will get to know who you are, what you are, and what you are made up of. It is just a matter of time. Do not be impressive on the outside and unimpressive on the inside.

12. Good start, poor finish

In the book of Judges, Chapter 13, we observe the beginning of Samson's ministry and in the book of Judges we see his end. "And Samson said, Let me die with the Philistines..." (Judges 16:30). When Samson began his ministry, the Spirit anointed him for service. There are many people who started so well. They were anointed but because they lived dual lives, just like Samson, they died in the midst of demons and their enemies.

There was a man I knew about, who God raised up to perform spectacular miracles. Some of the miracles were just beyond human understanding. I watched this video clip, in which a man paralysed with cancer of the spine was healed by this minister. Being a medical doctor, I understand what cancer of the spine means, especially one that makes you unable to walk. It was amazing to see a totally paralysed man suffering from cancer, healed, walk, jump and run before our eyes.

However, at the end of his life, this man of God who was so used by God, divorced his wife and became a drunk. He died alone in a motel, apparently of some liver disease. He was just like Samson. He started well but ended badly.

What is the use of starting well but ending in the midst of demons? Samson died in the midst of unbelievers; he died in the midst of his enemies. He was killed by the enemy.

God Is Not Mocked

God is not blind! God is not a fool! God is not a man! God cannot be mocked. He sees what we are doing: "The eyes of the LORD are in every place, beholding the evil and the good" (Proverbs 15:3).

Your pastor is human, so he may not see you sinning. You can even lie to him. There are many Christians in church who have lied to their pastors and have gotten away with it, but God is not a man. He is the one you are dealing with. You cannot lie to God!

Duality is a cursed life and dual people never end well; they die in disgrace. It will never be well with us if we play a double game with God.

The Sin of Unforgiveness

18

■ CHRISTIAN FORGIVENESS

The Bible tells us that when we are born again, we become "new men", or "new creatures". "And that ye put on the NEW MAN...Let all bitterness, and wrath, and anger, and clamour, and evil speaking, be put away from you, with all malice: And be ye kind one to another, tenderhearted, forgiving one another, even as God for Christ's sake hath forgiven you" (Ephesians 4:24,31,32).

When a man becomes a doctor or an army officer, he is expected to behave in a certain way. In the same way, a certain pattern of behaviour is expected of anyone who claims to be a Christian or a "new man".

CARDINAL ATTRIBUTE OF THE CHRISTIAN

1. A NEW MAN MUST BE ABLE TO FORGIVE.

One of the primary qualities of a new man is that he forgives. The new man should not live in unforgiveness.

According to biblical principles, the new man must not live his life according to what goes on in this world. In the world, people hardly forgive; it is natural for a person not to forgive, but to seek revenge.

However, when you become a new man, God expects you to forgive.

Indeed, one cardinal difference between the Christian and the unbeliever is that the Christian has the ability to forgive and release the offender.

2. A NEW MAN MUST FORGIVE ACCORDING TO THE "LORD'S PRAYER" TEST.

Now, how can you be sure that you have forgiven somebody? Often we say, "I have forgiven. I have nothing in my heart against him." However, you will find that there is still a grudge you bear somewhere in your heart.

As a pastor, I have stood in the pulpit and said that I had nothing against anybody; but in reality, I had something against someone. I thought that I had forgiven the person. Unknowingly, I had not. Later into the year, I realized that I really hadn't forgiven this person.

Through my search of the Scriptures, the Lord showed me what I call the "Lord's Prayer test". This is a test to prove whether you have truly forgiven your offenders or not.

The test: pray the Lord's Prayer. Keep praying. When you get to the point where you refer to those who trespass against you, you should specifically mention the name of the person who offended you.

It is important to specifically mention the name of that person. So the prayer becomes for example, "...And forgive me for my trespasses, as I forgive Araba Lucy." In other words, "If I have not forgiven Araba Lucy for her sins against me, please do not forgive me!!"

If you are able to pray like that, asking God to forgive you specifically in relation to your forgiveness of certain people in your life, it is very likely that you have forgiven them. However, if you cannot mention the person by name in this prayer, then you have not forgiven.

Think of that man who promised to marry you. You waited for him for six years, but he deceived you and ruined your life. Remember you need to forgive even him. Insert his name into the Lord's Prayer, to see whether you have really forgiven him.

Apply the Lord's Prayer test to every ugly or unpleasant situation you have ever encountered. This will help you to determine whether you have truly forgiven the person, because you need to do so!

3. 493 Trillion versus 28 Thousand

Often, even as new people in Christ, Christians find it difficult to forgive, because they least expect that certain individuals would hurt them. The feeling is that if anybody would hurt them, it shouldn't be a particular person.

Sometimes best friends become worst enemies. Yes, even husbands and wives can become sworn enemies. The closest person who told you he loved and cared for you, can become your worst enemy.

As new people in Christ, we need to remember that God has forgiven us for lots of horrible things.

The Unforgiving Servant

To illustrate this point, Jesus told the parable of the unforgiving servant. He compared the Kingdom of God to a certain King who wanted to settle accounts with all his servants. One servant owed him 10,000 talents. When he was unable to pay, the King thought of selling him, his wife, children and all his property but the servant begged for mercy. "...:Lord, have patience with me...Then the lord...was moved with compassion, and...FORGAVE him the debt" (Matthew 18:26-27).

However, this same servant found a fellow servant who owed him just 100 pence and immediately hell broke loose. Despite his cry for mercy, the unforgiving servant threw his fellow servant into prison, till he settled all his debts. This was reported to the King. "Then his Lord... said...O thou wicked servant, I forgave thee all that debt...Shouldest not thou also have had compassion on thy fellow servant...? And his Lord was wroth, and delivered him to the tormentors...likewise shall my heavenly Father do also unto you, if ye from your hearts forgive not every one his brother their trespasses" (Matthew 18: 32-35).

Talents could be either gold or silver talents.

One golden talent is worth 29,085 US dollars. One talent of silver is equivalent to 1,920 US dollars.

10,000 gold talents is two hundred and ninety million, eight hundred and fifty thousand dollars ($290,850,000).

Current conversion of $290m into cedis (the currency of my country, Ghana) becomes four hundred and ninety-three trillion cedis-that is ¢493,000,000,000,000 (at today's exchange rate). That is the amount that this young servant owed his master.

The equivalent of 100 pence in cedis is twenty-eight thousand, nine hundred cedis (¢28,900).

God has forgiven us ¢493,000,000,000,000 and we are required to forgive our friends ¢28,900.

Perhaps you think that you were not a bad person, even as an unbeliever. Maybe you were not a diamond thief or a drug pusher, so you think this 490 trillion does not apply in your case. It applies to everyone who has been a sinner before. Without raising a finger or uttering a word, man's heart is already wicked (Jeremiah 17:9). Sometimes, in talking about what somebody has done to us, we forget that we have also wronged God and man before.

4. From God's point of view, a Christian who cannot forgive, is rather strange.

God will forgive you if you murder, lie, fornicate, commit adultery, and practise witchcraft. However, God will not forgive you if you bear someone a grudge: "...forgive...that your Father also...may forgive you your trespasses" (Mark 11:25). That is the point at which God stops forgiving you. If you have an unforgiving nature, the implications are far-reaching. It indicates that perhaps you are not a "new man", or that you are just a pretending Christian.

Over the years, I have come to see and believe that unforgiveness is one sin that God will not forgive. It may be for you the difference between life and death. Moreover, the sin of unforgiveness is to me, even more dangerous than the sin of fornication. Often, because unforgiveness is not seen physically, many Christians feel that they can get away with it, but it is deadly if it is left unchecked in your heart.

God will not hear your prayer, and He will not prosper or bless you if unforgiveness lingers in your life. God will be angry with you, because He forgave you, but you would not forgive others!

Remember, the Bible tells us the Lord was wroth with His servant for not forgiving. In addition, the Bible says the man who did not forgive his brother was handed over to the tormentors. Many Christians do not know why they are being tormented in this life. It could be because of unforgiveness.

Many times, we commit the same sins over and over again. Then we come to God expecting Him to forgive us. God looks at our numerous sins and says, "Okay, I have forgiven you." However, we come back with the same sin over and over and God has to forgive us. Now, if we refuse to forgive our brothers in the same way, do you not think that God will be angry with us?

Sometimes unforgiveness lingers on and on, even long after the offence has been committed. People even bear grudges against dead relatives and enemies. It is a dangerous condition!

THE SIGNS OF LINGERING UNFORGIVENESS

1. Malice

According to Ephesians 4: 31, one of the signs of unforgiveness is malice. "...and evil speaking, be put away from you with all malice".

"Malice" according to the dictionary means, "a desire to harm others".

When Brother "A" does something against you, and you have the desire to harm or hurt him, that is malice. The desire to harm others shows you that you haven't forgiven the offender. When you have truly forgiven, you won't desire to harm the offender. Do you think God desires to harm you? Can you imagine what would happen to you if ever God should decide to harm you?

If you are a wife and you have a secret desire to harm or punish your husband, then that is malice. Sometimes wives punish their husbands by denying them sex. Some women cannot "commit" love with their husbands because of something they did. I have heard some women complain, "I can't bring myself to take off my clothes and do this with him. I'll go crazy if I have to sleep with him again." Once you feel this way, you have not forgiven.

One way you can tell that you have not forgiven, is when you feel uncomfortable at the mention of the offender's name. At the point when you can say, "Lord, I let him go," or "God will take care of it," then malice is gone. When you curse the offender, wish him ill or plan how to hurt him, then malice is still lingering. You might complain and wonder why people hurt you so often. That is not the point! God expects us to forgive. Malice must go away.

2. Anger

The dictionary defines "anger" as "a strong feeling of hostility and displeasure".

I remember one lady came with her husband to the church office. The husband said something which was not exactly complimentary about his wife. She exploded. The hostility was so glaring, and her behaviour was so bad that her husband rebuked her. "Is this the way to talk? Don't you respect the pastor?" he asked her. Then I sensed that the strong feelings of hostility between the husband and the wife were because of unforgiveness.

If you have this strong feeling of hostility when- ever you see someone who once offended you, then there is some unforgiveness lingering in your heart.

3. Wrath

"Wrath" can also be defined as "extreme anger". One sign of the presence of extreme anger is that the person begins to act "wild".

Once, a man was so angry that he threw all the lunch that had been set before him on the wall. Afterwards, when tempers had cooled down, he had to struggle to clean the stained wall (anger really makes you do some foolish things)!

Extreme anger or wrath is a sign of lingering unforgiveness.

4. Clamour

The dictionary defines "clamour" as "loud abusive language, and loud demands or protests".

How can you come to church so nicely dressed, looking so sweet and holy, and then go home and quarrel everyday with everyone? If your next door neighbour decides to record the string of loud abuses that come from you, your pastors would be surprised at your behaviour.

I believe that a Christian should not be loud and abusive in any circumstance.

Clamour or loud abusive language is a sign of lingering unforgiveness. I know of a Christian church where there was so much disharmony that the pastors fought openly in church. They shouted at each other, and even used tear gas on each other. What a disgrace!

5. Evil speaking or slander

To "slander" is "to say bad things about someone, or to backbite".

When someone slanders another person, usually what is said about that person is false. Those who slander, often have the intention of destroying another person. People who slander their spouses must be watched very carefully. Slanderous people are often full of bitterness.

There may be genuine complaints, but when it is continuous, then such a spouse has a deep-seated problem of unforgiveness.

A husband once complained to me, "Pastor, my wife is very wicked. In fact, she is a witch! If you have ever seen a witch before, you'll know what I'm talking about." I told him, "Then you must have been a wizard to have married her!" I take particular notice of people who say negative things to bring others down.

I have heard pastors speak carelessly and negatively about other ministers. Sometimes these are people with whom they claim to have a good relationship. I take particular notice of such ministers. From my own experience I have come to know that, "He who talks to you about others will talk to others about you."

6. Bitterness

"Bitterness" can be defined as "degenerated unforgiveness". I define bitterness as a "long-standing degenerated unforgiveness".

The word "degenerate" is defined as "to pass into a worse state than one which is considered normal or desirable". Thus, when a situation passes from one stage to a worse state, it can be described as degeneration. Unforgiveness which stays in your heart for a long period of time, degenerates into bitterness.

The cardinal sign of bitterness is that it begins to poison other people. The Bible cautions that when bitterness is permitted, it will spill over and defile others. "...lest any root of bitterness springing up trouble you, and thereby many be defiled" (Hebrews 12:15).

I know some people who are so filled with hatred for their wives, husbands, mothers, fathers, or other relatives. A good example of a bitter person is a woman who has been hurt by a man.

The story line is often similar: The man approached you and told you, "I love you honey. You are the sweetest lady I've ever known, and I want to love you. When I saw you, my heart moved from the left to the right. I want you to know that if you were on the other side of the Mediterranean, I would swim across just to bring you some ice cream!" Perhaps he also said, "There is only one pebble I see whenever I walk on the beach and THAT IS YOU!"

You believed it when he told you he had seen many ladies, but that you were different. What you didn't know was that he had other pebbles on the beach, and that he had told other ladies these same stories.

You were a virgin and wanted to remain so until you got married, but he convinced you to give in to him, with the promise that he would marry you anyway. So he began sleeping with you. You did things you never dreamt of doing with your body. In fact, you also had to commit several abortions because you were not ready for babies. Then, one day he lets out the bomb, that he cannot marry you after all.

So many suitors wanted to marry you at the prime of your youth, but you refused them because of this "sweet talker". Then after you turned thirty-eight, most men shied away from you.

Now you bear this man a grudge. You begin to hate him. Then you begin to hate him with a passion. With time, you have come to hate all men.

You could not forgive that man, so you have lumped all men into this category. Your hurt has become a long-standing degenerated type of unforgiveness—bitterness.

Sometimes, such people begin to champion women's causes out of bitterness. They may remain unmarried for the rest of their lives. It can even develop and degenerate further into lesbianism. Lesbians are often bitter women. Bitter against men who perhaps hurt them sometime in their lives.

Men can also be bitter against women. I remember a London taxi driver told me of his experience. Because of this experience he has vowed never to marry. He had a live-in girlfriend whom he looked after. He took her to school, paid her fees, fed her and gave her everything she wanted for years. If she wanted anything, all she needed to do was to ask. She was almost like a wife.

Then at a point, he began to suspect her of infidelity. So one day, he told her that he was going on a business trip and would return after a week. To be certain that she would believe his story, he asked her to see him off.

He went to the Kings Cross Station with her, got on a train and waved goodbye to her. However, at the next stop he got down, took another train and came back into town.

He did not go straight back home, but went to a drinking pub to while away the time till two a.m. Then he went home. When he climbed upstairs and entered the bedroom, here was his "girlfriend-wife", in his bed with another man. Both of them were stark naked in his bed. So he threw her naked out of his flat and called the police.

After this experience he decided never to get married, or to trust any woman. He could not forgive that girl, and he has now extended it to all other women.

When such hurt degenerates into hatred, it is bitterness. Beware of becoming bitter after bad experiences. When a bitter person speaks, it affects, influences and poisons others.

HOW FORGIVENESS CAN BE MADE EASY

1. Recognise the reality of offences.

Trusted ones may offend. Often, hurting people find it difficult to forgive because they cannot believe that the offender was the same person they trusted so much. This could explain the unwillingness of some spouses to forgive when their husbands or wives cheat on them.

Sometimes the emotional pain one goes through is almost unbearable, and as human beings it is not easy to forget. Though we may find it difficult to forgive, what God is saying to us is that it is very important to forgive no matter how traumatic the pain may be.

2. Analyse the offender.

There is the need to analyse the offender very well-that is, the person who did whatever to hurt you. Luke 23:34 gives an example of Jesus analysing the offenders. He said, "Father, forgive them, for they know not what they do...." The Son of God explained why they needed to be forgiven: because "they know not what they do."

If you analyse the offender, you will realize that although he is doing evil, he may not be fully aware of the implications of his action. As soon as you analyse it this way, it will help you relate well with whoever offends you.

Let me share with you a personal experience. I remember when one of my junior pastors was extremely rude to me. This pastor spoke in a way he should never have spoken—least of all, to me.

He shouted and threatened me. I was then sitting with one of my senior associate pastors. As this was going on, I looked at him and I said to myself, "He does not know what he is doing." As he continued displaying and behaving in an unbecoming manner, I said to myself, "I am very sure he doesn't know what he is doing. Maybe he is confused or disturbed."

Later on, my associate said he thought I would dismiss him immediately, because the junior pastor's behaviour was appalling; but I made the excuse for him that he did not know what he was doing or he would not have behaved in this way and it helped me to relate with him.

Learn to make excuses for people. Jesus made excuses for His own murderers! Perhaps your offender is sick, ignorant or confused. If you are able to analyse those who offend you in this way, you will be able to forgive them. By analysing in this way, you will find that you have the capacity within you to forgive. It helps you to understand why a person behaves in a particular way. Otherwise, you can never forgive.

2. Analyse your past sins.

When you analyse your past sins, you will find out that you will not be so hasty to judge anybody. This is because you might have done the same thing (or something worse) before. Probably, you might have acted the same way if you had been confronted with the same issue.

Galatians 6:1 cautions: "...If a man be overtaken in a fault, ye which are spiritual, restore such an one in the spirit of meekness; considering thyself, lest thou also be tempted." When you consider yourself, you will be more willing to forgive. When you think about your past sins, you will realize that you are not any better.

In the time of Jesus, some people who felt they were "holier" brought a woman who had been caught in adultery. They wanted to punish her by stoning her. Jesus, who understood this principle of analysing people's past, asked for any man who had not sinned to throw the first stone. No one dared throw a stone because they all knew they had past sins.

When you consider your own self you will not be so hasty to judge other people. As a born-again believer, you should be forgiving, especially when unbelievers offend you. Just remember what you did as an unbeliever. If it had not been for Christ, perhaps you would have done worse things. So analyse your past when you find it difficult to forgive your neighbour.

3. ANALYSE THE OUTCOME.

Out of jealousy and hatred, Joseph's brothers sold him into slavery. After thirty years, God raised him from prison to become the Prime Minister of Egypt. Unaware of his new identity, his brothers came to him for help during a severe famine. Later, Joseph revealed himself to them. Out of remorse they fell down and begged him to be merciful to them. Joseph forgave them when he analysed the outcome of their misconduct. "...be not grieved, nor angry with yourselves, that ye sold me hither: for God did send me before you to preserve life...to preserve you a posterity in the earth, and to save your lives...it was not you that sent me hither, but God..." (Genesis 45:5,7,8).

Sometimes, when you analyse the way things have turned out, or the way things are going to turn out, you can easily forgive.

I remember that years ago, when I founded my church as a young medical student, I invited a pastor from one of the great charismatic churches in Ghana, to come to my church and minister. This man of God who had been preaching and encouraging us in my little fellowship at the university for many months, sent a message to me that, he would not "sow amongst thorns". Upon starting a church, I had suddenly been rejected by a man of God I highly respected.

So I asked myself, "When did we become 'thorns'?" He had been preaching in my fellowship of "thorns" for many months! I was very surprised, because I thought then, that he was my friend. Instead, he rather influenced my associate to leave me and the church. This almost broke up the baby church. He then told my associate to be careful not to associate with someone who was not "called".

This departure of my immediate assistant generated all sorts of problems among my own church members, who now began to analyse me, whether I was "called" or not.

That was not the only trial. I was also under fire everywhere. Some of my classmates in the medical school called me names, as I carried the church drums and musical instruments up and down to church.

"Why should you start a church? Who are you? Who do you think you are?" they asked me.

When I was going to get married, my parents-in-law went to see one pastor to ask to use his church facilities for our wedding. The Lighthouse Chapel International, did not have a church building then. He told them that he would allow us to use his church only on the condition that we close down our church. I had no friends anymore.

I remember inviting all the pastors I knew to my wedding. Believe it or not—no one showed up. When pastors were called to take photographs with the bridal train, there were none. I was completly rejected. It was as though I was evil. People just threw me away for starting a new church. At a point I felt like committing suicide. However, now I realize that the Lord wanted me to be independent of man's help and praise. The Lord wanted me to stand on my own, go through the pains that I had to go through, and rise up to bear a particular fruit in His Kingdom. Today, the "small, rejected" church has expanded not only in Ghana, but has branches all over the world. It worked!

Recently I saw some of these people who rejected me and I told them exactly what Joseph said to his brothers: "You meant it for evil but God turned it out for good." God knows that I don't bear them any grudge. These people are all my friends today, because God has helped me to forgive them. When you look at the outcome, you realize that you have the ability to forgive!!

4. See the disadvantages of unforgiveness.

Are there any disadvantages of unforgiveness? YES! God will not forgive you for any of your sins, and you are not going to have any prayer answered. Moreover, the devil will torment you. Powerful men of God may lay hands on you, but the tormentors will still be there.

I heard of a pastor's wife who was suffering from multiple sclerosis. She had suffered emotional hurts from within and without the church. She could not forgive those who had criticized her husband (sometimes it is the pastors' wives who endure a lot of ministerial hurts and pains). When her husband travelled, God ministered to her to forgive. When she forgave those people who hurt her, she received her healing miraculously. To her husband's utter surprise, here she was, standing at the airport waiting for him when he returned from a trip. This was a wheelchair-bound woman; and there she was, free from unforgiveness and therefore free from multiple sclerosis.

The tormentors can have access to torment us with sicknesses, diseases, poverty, and marital disharmony, when we do not release those who hurt us. Could that explain your lack of breakthroughs? This is the price you will pay for unforgiveness.

5. See the advantages of forgiveness.

One of the major advantages of forgiveness is that forgiveness makes you a great person! Not only will your prayers be answered but you become more powerful spiritually, physically and emotionally. Forgiveness makes you a great person.

The South African President, Nelson Mandela is considered one of the greatest men in the world —because of forgiveness. Mandela was sent into prison for 27 years, by the apartheid white government. He was separated from his home, his wife and children. He spent the better part of his life in prison. This is a man who under normal circumstances should not forgive, but he has been able to forgive his white oppressors and formed a reconciliatory government with them. This is what makes him great.

In forgiving, you become great. "But there is forgiveness with thee, that thou mayest be feared" (Psalm 130:4). Your ability to forgive will make people fear you! Forgiveness makes you a great person.

6. Decide to obey God.

It is better to obey God than to harbour unforgiveness. "...to obey is better than sacrifice, and to hearken than the fat of rams" (1 Samuel 15:22). God is not asking or begging the Christian to forgive. It is a command.

The advantages of forgiveness outweigh whatever "sweet revenge" we think we will get by bearing grudges. Just obey and forgive, and the Lord will bless your life.

SECTION V

Successful Christian Living

Developing a Personal Relationship with God

19

■ THE QUIET TIME

"Quiet Time" is time you spend with God alone. If anybody were to ask me what the greatest secret of my relationship with God is, I would say without any hesitation that it is the power of the quiet times I have with him everyday.

SEVEN THINGS THAT HAPPEN DURING QUIET TIME

1. DURING QUIET TIME YOU DEVELOP THE MOST IMPORTANT RELATIONSHIP OF YOUR LIFE.

A natural relationship develops between any two people who spend quality time together. Spend quality time with God. Many Christians do not know the importance of this time with God.

2. HAVING A QUIET TIME MAKES YOU DEVELOP THE MOST IMPORTANT PERSONAL HABIT OF ALL TIME: A REGULAR TIME WITH YOUR CREATOR.

I have a quiet time everyday and I spend quality time with the Lord.

3. DURING YOUR QUIET TIME YOU DRAW NEAR TO GOD AND HE DRAWS NEAR TO YOU.

"Draw nigh to God, and he will draw nigh to you. Cleanse your hands, ye sinners; and purify your hearts, ye double minded" (James 4:8).

4. A QUIET TIME MAKES YOU READ THE MOST IMPORTANT BOOK IN THE WORLD.

The Bible is the most important book in the world. It is the most outstanding volume known to the human race.

Professor M. Montiero-Williams, in comparing other religious books to the Bible said, "Pile them, if you will, on the left side of your study table; but place your own Holy Bible on the right side - all by itself, all alone - and with a wide gap between them. For, ...there is a gulf between it and the so-called sacred books of the East which severs the one from the other utterly, hopelessly, and forever ...a veritable gulf which cannot be bridged over by any science of religious thought."[1]

5. A QUIET TIME, IS YOUR PERSONAL SCHOOL OF THE WORD.

During your quiet time, you sit and learn at the feet of the Greatest Teacher Jesus left us: the Holy Spirit. He will teach you many things and show you many wonderful revelations in the Word. "I have many things to say unto you, but ye cannot bear them now. Howbeit when he, the Spirit of truth, is come, he will guide you into all truth... and he will shew you things to come" (John 16:12,13).

6. During your quiet time, you increase in your personal knowledge of the Scriptures.

Your personal quiet time gives you the opportunity to add knowledge to your faith. "...add to your faith virtue; and to virtue knowledge" (2 Peter 1:5).

A Christian is expected to grow in his knowledge of the Lord. "But grow in grace and in the knowledge of our Lord and Saviour Jesus Christ" (2 Peter 3:18).

7. During your quiet time, you experience the presence of God.

Adam experienced the presence of the Lord in the Garden of Eden until he backslid. "And they heard the voice of the Lord God walking in the garden in the cool of the day: and Adam and his wife hid themselves from the presence of the Lord God..." (Genesis 3:8).

There is a hunger in every man. There is a search in every human being for the presence of God. We all long for the presence of Jehovah. There is nothing like the presence of God. Every preacher longs to feel the presence of God as he ministers.

The church service is not the same without the presence of God. Your life will have fullness of joy as you experience the presence of God in your quiet time. "Thou wilt show me the path of life: in thy presence is fulness of joy; at thy right hand there are pleasures for evermore" (Psalm 16:11).

FOLLOW THE GREAT MEN WHO HAD QUIET TIMES

1. Moses had quiet times with God.

"And the Lord said unto Moses, Hew thee two tables of stone like unto the first: and I will write upon these tables the words that were in the first tables, which thou brakest. And be ready in the morning, and come up in the morning unto mount Sinai, and present thyself there to me in the top of the mount. And no man shall come up with thee, neither let any man be seen throughout all the mount; neither let the flocks nor herds feed before that mount. And he hewed two tables of stone like unto the first; and Moses rose up early in the morning, and went up unto mount Sinai, as the Lord had commanded him, and took in his hand the two tables of stone. And the Lord descended in the cloud, and stood with him there, and proclaimed the name of the Lord. And the Lord passed by before him, and proclaimed, The Lord, The Lord God, merciful and gracious, longsuffering, and abundant in goodness and truth, Keeping mercy for thousands, forgiving iniquity and transgression and sin, and that will by no means clear the guilty; visiting the iniquity of the fathers upon the children, and upon the children's children, unto the third and to the fourth generation. And Moses made haste, and bowed his head toward the earth, and worshipped. And he said, If now I have found grace in thy sight, O Lord, let my Lord, I pray thee, go among us; for it is a stiffnecked people; and pardon our iniquity and our sin, and take us for thine inheritance. And he said, Behold, I make a covenant: before all thy people I will do marvels, such as have not been done in all the earth, nor in any nation: and all the people among which thou art shall see the work of the Lord: for it is a terrible thing that I will do with thee" (Exodus 34:1-10).

2. God commanded Joshua to have a daily quiet time.

"This book of the law shall not depart out of thy mouth; but thou shalt meditate therein day and night, that thou mayest observe to do according to all that is written therein: for then thou shalt make thy way prosperous, and then thou shalt have good success" (Joshua 1:8).

3. Adam had quiet times until he backslid.

"And they heard the voice of the Lord God walking in the garden in the cool of the day: and Adam and his wife hid themselves from the presence of the Lord God amongst the trees of the garden. And the Lord God called unto Adam, and said unto him, Where art thou? And he said, I heard thy voice in the garden, and I was afraid, because I was naked; and I hid myself" (Genesis 3:8-10).

4. Prophet Micaiah knew the habit of quiet time.

"But Zedekiah the son of Chenaanah went near, and smote Micaiah on the cheek, and said, Which way went the Spirit of the Lord from me to speak unto thee? And Micaiah said, Behold, thou shalt see in that day, when thou shalt go into an inner chamber to hide thyself" (1 Kings 22:24-25).

5. Jesus had quiet times too.

Jesus had His personal quiet time "a great while before day". "And in the morning, rising up a great while before day, he went out, and departed into a solitary place, and there prayed" (Mark 1:35).

He also taught His disciples to separate themselves from everybody and spend time alone with God. "But thou, when thou prayest, enter into thy closet, and when thou hast shut the door, pray to thy Father which is in secret; and thy Father which seeth in secret shall reward thee openly" (Matthew 6:6).

6. David had quiet times with God.

"O God, thou art my God; early will I seek thee; my soul thirsteth for thee, my flesh longeth for thee... When I remember thee upon my bed, and meditate on thee in the night watches" (Psalm 63:1,6).

THREE STRATEGIES FOR A SUCCESSFUL QUIET TIME

1. Strategy # 1 - Set a practical, unchangeable and regular time for your quiet time.

Set a regular time when you meet God. It is very important that you set a regular time for your quiet time. Life is such that important things are often overlooked. If you do not schedule a constant period for a quiet time I assure you that you will leave it out.

The best time for a quiet time is first thing in the morning. Notice that Moses had his quiet time in the morning. "And be ready in the morning, and come up in the morning unto mount Sinai, and present thyself there to me in the top of the mount. And no man shall come up with thee, neither let any man be seen throughout all the mount; neither let the flocks nor herds feed before that mount" (Exodus 34:2,3).

2. Strategy # 2 - Withdraw from the presence of other people.

A quiet time is not a prayer meeting involving all the members of your household. A quiet time is not another church service or fellowship meeting. It is an intimate time between you and your God. It is a private moment that you must cherish. You will notice that Moses could not have his quiet time in the presence of others. "And no man shall come up with thee..." (Exodus 34:3).

A quiet time is a time when you are alone with God. You cannot develop a personal relationship with someone unless you are alone with the person. It must be possible to withdraw yourself from the company of others so that you can be alone with God. If you can afford it, you must create for yourself a private place in your home where you go to pray and meet with God.

3. Strategy # 3 - Create an atmosphere that is conducive for fellowship with God.

You can do this by playing good worship music in the background. If you do not have any such music you can worship the Lord yourself. As you worship the Lord, the presence of the Lord will fill your room. God inhabits praises. There is an atmosphere in which God's presence thrives. I find it easier to pray when I am playing worship music or preaching tapes. There is no need to struggle in an icy and hardened atmosphere. Put on some music and worship the Lord!

THE HIDDEN POWER OF A QUIET TIME

The reason why many people do not have a quiet time is because they do not know the effect it has on them. Let me share with you fifteen powerful effects of having a daily quiet time.

1. A daily quiet time prevents hurts and reduces pain in this life.

Much of the pain and hurts of this life would have been avoided if we had used the light of life. "Then spake Jesus again unto them, saying, I am the light of the world: he that followeth me shall not walk in darkness, but shall have the light of life" (John 8:12).

When a man gropes about in darkness he often hurts himself by bumping into unexpected or unforeseen objects. How painful it is to hit your shin against a table. The pains and hurts we experience in our lives are because we have not picked up the lamp of God. "Thy word is a lamp unto my feet, and a light unto my path" (Psalm 119:105). "There will I make the horn of David to bud: I have ordained a lamp for mine anointed" (Psalm 132:17). What is this lamp that God has specially prepared for His anointed ones? It is the Word of God!

The sorrows that some have experienced in marriage have come because they did not use the lamp of God to guide them into marriage. Many people pick up the lamp of God after they have been severely injured by the experiences of life. A lamp is not intended to soothe your pain but to prevent you from getting hurt. How much better a life we would have if we would pick up this lamp on a daily basis. The lamp will keep us from the pain and injuries.

It is only a quiet time that can provide you with constant illumination. If you live in darkness from Monday to Saturday and only receive a little light on Sunday, surely your life will not be the same as someone who lives in constant illumination. Do you want constant illumination for your life? Begin to have a regular quiet time!

You will reduce the sorrow of your life by using the true light that God has ordained for you. It is the only light which can light the way for every man on this earth. "That was the true Light, which lighteth every man that cometh into the world" (John 1:9).

2. A daily quite time guarantees a good harvest of nice things.

This is because a daily quiet time is the sowing of spiritual seeds into your spirit. The Word of God is the great seed that you plant in your heart when you have a quiet time. "Now the parable is this: The seed is the word of God" (Luke 8:11). "Being born again, not of corruptible seed, but of incorruptible, by the word of God, which liveth and abideth for ever" (1 Peter 1:23).

Every time you have a quiet time you are making an investment into your life. You sow the seed of the Word of God and it will yield the fruit of love, peace and joy in the Holy Spirit. Have you wondered why there is little or no love, peace and joy in your life? These fruits can only come as you sow a spiritual seed into your life. "For he that soweth to his flesh shall of the flesh reap corruption; but he that soweth to the Spirit shall of the Spirit reap life everlasting" (Galatians 6:8).

Most Christians sow into the flesh. They invest in their flesh. They invest time, money to the development of their flesh and their earthly existence. Others invest seeds of television, pleasure, sex, alcohol and drugs into their flesh. The harvests that come from such seeds are horrific. Most pastors are pastoring sheep who live under the devastating effects of a massive harvest from the flesh. It is our duty as pastors to lead the sheep to invest in their spirits on a daily basis.

3. A DAILY QUITE TIME BURNS AWAY UNWANTED THINGS.

When this fire is received on a daily basis, no evil can remain as part of your character. "Wherefore thus saith the Lord God of hosts, Because ye speak this word, behold, I will make my words in thy mouth fire, and this people wood, and it shall devour them" (Jeremiah 5:14).

Some things can only be removed by fire. The Word of God is like fire. A daily dose of that fire will take care of every unwanted element in your personality or character.

4. A DAILY QUITE TIME BREAKS DOWN EVIL STRONGHOLDS.

Because a quiet time leads to the breaking and the burning of evil things in our lives. Christians who do not have quiet times often have bad character. The strongholds in most Christians' lives cannot be broken away by one powerful sermon. Anyone who does not have a regular quiet time has a lot of things that need to be burnt and broken down. "Is not my word like as a fire? saith the Lord; and like a hammer that breaketh the rock in pieces?" (Jeremiah 23:29).

5. A DAILY QUITE TIME LEADS TO THE CUTTING AWAY OF UNVANTED ASPECTS OF OUR LIVES AND CHARACTER.

Once again you will see that Christians who just listen to sermons on Sundays but have no regular cutting away of evil tendencies are very different people from those who have a regular quiet time. "For the word of God is quick, and powerful, and sharper than any twoedged sword, piercing even to the dividing asunder of soul and spirit, and of the joints and marrow, and is a discerner of the thoughts and intents of the heart" (Hebrews 4:12).

6. A REGULAR QUIET TIME PUTS A WEAPON INTO THE HAND OF THE BELIEVER.

Satan has a good laugh at Christians who are unarmed and exposed. The daily act which Satan hates and fears is when you arm yourself daily with the sword of the Spirit. Prayer is good. Fasting is good. Going to church is good. But none of these can replace the daily arming of God's soldier.

The Word of God has a way of slipping out of our hands. This is because of the pressures of the world in which we live. The opinions of unbelievers, sinners, worldly Christians have a way of eroding the effect of the Word of God on our lives. This is why it is necessary to regularly place the sword into our hands so that we will be ready for every trick of the devil. "And take the helmet of salvation, and the sword of the Spirit, which is the word of God" (Ephesians 6:17).

7. Quiet times deliver Christians and pastors from delusions and deceptions about who they are.

It shows us what we are to do to please the Lord. "But be ye doers of the word, and not hearers only, deceiving your own selves" (James 1:22).

The prophet Isaiah thought he was good enough. His messages in the first five chapters of Isaiah were very strong against the people. He would often say, "Woe unto them."

"Woe unto them that rise up early in the morning, that they may follow strong drink; that continue until night, till wine inflame them!" (Isaiah 5:11).

"Woe unto them that draw iniquity with cords of vanity, and sin as it were with a cart rope" (Isaiah 5:18).

"Woe unto them that call evil good, and good evil; that put darkness for light, and light for darkness; that put bitter for sweet, and sweet for bitter!" (Isaiah 5:20).

"Woe unto them that are wise in their own eyes, and prudent in their own sight!" (Isaiah 5:21).

"Woe unto them that are mighty to drink wine, and men of strength to mingle strong drink" (Isaiah 5:22).

One day, God decided to reveal Himself to Isaiah. Isaiah was shocked when his real condition was revealed by God. All it took was one glimpse of God in His glory. Immediately, Isaiah was delivered from his delusions. He changed his message at once. He said, "Woe is unto me!" He no longer said, "Woe is unto them."

"Then said I, Woe is me! for I am undone; because I am a man of unclean lips, and I dwell in the midst of a people of unclean lips: for mine eyes have seen the King, the Lord of hosts" (Isaiah 6:5).

As we correct people and see other people's faults all the time, may God help us to see our own failings. May we see ourselves the way God sees us. Do not be impressed by what people say to you. Do not receive the flattery of human beings. What is highly esteemed in the sight of men is often an abomination in the sight of God.

"And he said unto them, Ye are they which justify yourselves before men; but God knoweth your hearts: for that which is highly esteemed among men is abomination in the sight of God" (Luke 16:15).

Once I thought I was doing well in the ministry. The Lord revealed Himself to me in a vision and showed me a picture of some greasy faeces. Then He told me that, that was what I looked like to Him. I was full of sorrow for my pathetic condition and I wept before the Lord. I wondered why the Lord had anything to do with me. You see, most people, including myself, thought I was doing well. Dear friend, a regular time with God will save you from delusions.

The Word of God is like that. God shows Himself to you. Every time you read the Word of God, you see God. When Isaiah saw the Lord, he had no deceptions about what he was. Pray that God will reveal Himself to you as you read the Bible everyday. Many church members would not be as proud, arrogant and presumptuous as they are if they knew what they looked like before God. Many Christians would not accuse their leaders if they had just a glimpse at what they were really like in the sight of God.

The Word of God is a mirror. It will show us the real picture. A quiet time will reveal the truth to you every time.

We are so subject to delusions and deceptions that we need a regular input of the Word of God in our lives. I cannot overemphasize the need for regularity for the ministration of the Word in our lives. Only a quiet time can give you the regular input that is needed for a constant deliverance from deception.

8. A DAILY QUIET TIME WILL GIVE GREAT SPIRITUAL GROWTH.

A daily quiet time exposes you regularly to spiritual food. The Word of God is milk for your soul (1 Peter 2:2). It is bread for the hungry (Matthew 4:4) and it is meat for the men (Hebrews 5:12) and it is sweeter than honey for dessert (Psalm 19:10).

Charismatic churches are full of thousands of undeveloped spiritual babies. The pastors of today's charismatic churches are seen by their members as superstars who have the answers to everything. This is not the case. Perhaps we pastors enjoy having people depend on us. They look to us as though we are semi-gods with a panacea for every problem.

When I was growing up as a Christian, I belonged to a Scripture Union fellowship. I did not belong to a large charismatic church. There was no superstar TV personality pastor in SU fellowship. We were directed to the Word of God as the source of everything. I am so grateful that the first thing I learnt in the Scripture Union was to have a daily quiet time. I remember the day I was taught to have a daily quiet time. Little did I know that I was being directed towards the most important thing in Christianity - the Word of God. I was being shown how to receive milk on a daily basis, meat and bread for all my needs and something sweeter than honey when I wanted something sweet.

A spiritual x-ray of a large charismatic church will reveal tiny undeveloped Christians who shout Christian slogans and clichés and hail their pastors as though they were pop stars or soccer heroes. Is it any wonder that Christianity today is a far cry from what it used to be? There is very little sacrifice. There is very little advancement of the kingdom. And there is so much carnality. Carnality is a sign of immaturity. Why is so much of the Body of Christ immature? Because most Christians do not have a daily quiet time.

Christians today depend on a quick microwave snack from their pastors' Bibles on Sunday morning. Is there any comparison between a child who has a balanced meal everyday and someone who has a quick microwave thirty-five minute sermon snack every other week? It's time to grow. It's time to benefit from the milk, bread, meat and honey that is in your Bible. Having a daily quiet time is the best habit I learned as a Christian.

9. A DAILY QUIET TIME BRINGS INNER HEALING.

"He sent his word, and healed them, and delivered them from their destructions" (Psalm 107:20).

The Word of God has a way of healing us of our pain and wounds. God will touch you where it hurts if you will allow Him. And He will heal you of every situation in your life.

Spiritual, emotional and psychological problems are the most difficult to solve. Doctors often struggle with these problems to no avail. The diagnosis and treatment of spiritual, emotional and psychological problems are one of the most difficult areas for medicine. But God has a solution. The solution is in His Word. A daily dose of God's powerful Word will bring healing to every inner wound. What did Jesus say? "The Spirit of the Lord is upon me because He has anointed me to preach the gospel to the poor; he hath sent me to heal the broken hearted. (Luke 4:18)" How was Jesus going to heal the broken hearted? Through the Word of God!

10. A DAILY QUIET TIME BRINGS HEALING TO THE BODY.

"My son, attend to my words; incline thine ear unto my sayings. Let them not depart from thine eyes; keep them in the midst of thine heart. For they are life unto those that find them, and health [medicine] to all their flesh" (Proverbs 4:20-22). The Hebrew word for health is, "marpe" which means "medicine".

It may sound difficult to believe but God's Word actually brings healing to our physical bodies. The Bible says that they are life and health to the flesh. The flesh means the physical body.

I will like to quote to you a very interesting article I read in Reader's Digest:

"The notion that religious faith can promote physical well-being is not new. Most of us have heard of cases in which someone, seemingly by sheer faith and will, has miraculously recovered from a terminal illness or survived far longer than doctors thought possible. What is new is that such rewards of religion are becoming the stuff of science.

"We cannot prove scientifically that God heals, but I believe we can prove that belief in God has a beneficial effect," declares Dale A. Matthew, M.D., Associate Professor of Medicine at Georgetown University Medical Center in Washington, D.C. "There's little doubt that healthy religious faith and practices can help people get better."

Compelling Evidence

Just how powerful is the evidence linking faith and health? More than 30 studies have found a connection between spiritual or religious commitment and longer life. Among the most compelling:

A survey of 5,286 Californians found that church members have lower death rates than non-members, regardless of risk factors such as smoking, drinking, obesity, and inactivity.

Those with a religious commitment had fewer symptoms or had better health outcomes in seven out of eight cancer studies, four out of five blood pressure studies, four out of six heart disease studies, and four out of five general health studies.

People with a strong religious commitment seem to be less prone to depression, suicide, alcoholism, and other addictions, according to one research analysis.

One of the most extensive reviews demonstrates that the connections between religion and health cut across age, sex, cultural, and geographic boundaries. It includes more than 200 studies in which religion was found to be a factor in the incidence of a disease, explains Jeffrey S. Levin, a former professor at Eastern Virginia Medical School in Norfolk.

Levin found an association between good health and religion in studies of children and older adults; of U.S. Protestants, European Catholics, Japanese Buddhists, and Israeli Jews; of people living in the 1930's and 1980's; of patients suffering from acute and chronic diseases.

How Prayer Heals

Why does faith appear to have such a powerful protective effect? Experts offer several possible explanations.

Going to religious services guarantees contact with people. Social support is a well-documented key to health and longevity.

Faith gives a sense of hope and control that counteracts stress. "Commitment to a system of beliefs enables people to better handle traumatic illness, suffering, and loss," says Harold G. Koenig, M.D., director of the center for the study of religion, spirituality, and health at Duke University Medical Center.

Praying evokes beneficial changes in the body. When people pray, they experience the same decreases in blood pressure, metabolism, heart and breathing rates as the famous "relaxation response" described by Herbert Benson, M.D. of the Harvard Medical School. Reciting the rosary, for example, involves the same steps as the relaxation response: repeating a word, prayer, phrase, or sound, and returning to the repetition when other thoughts intrude.

While the relaxation response works regardless of the words used, Benson says, those who choose a religious phrase are more likely to benefit if they believe in God.

Can Others' Prayers Heal?

Researchers are investigating whether the prayers of others can heal. Benson and his colleagues, studying coronary-bypass patients, and Matthews, studying people with rheumatoid arthritis, are trying to confirm findings of an oft-quoted 1988 study by cardiologist Randolph Byrd, M.D.

Dr. Byrd divided 393 heart patients in San Francisco General Hospital Medical Center into two groups. One was prayed for by Christians around the country; the other did not receive prayers from study participants.

Patients did not know to which group they belonged. The group that was prayed for experienced fewer complications, fewer cases of pneumonia, fewer cardiac arrests, less congestive heart failure, and needed fewer antibiotics.

Even more confounding are controversial studies suggesting prayer can influence everything from the growth of bacteria in a lab to healing wounds in mice. "These studies on lower organisms can be done with great scientific precision, and the findings can't be explained away by, say, the placebo effect," says Larry Dossey, M.D., author of Prayer Is Good Medicine.

Doctors as Believers

Dr. Dossey became so convinced of the power of prayer that he began to pray privately for his patients. Nevertheless, he and other experts tread cautiously in this area. "We certainly don't want to start selling religion in the name of science," he says. "People need to make their own choices."

And yet, health care institutions are beginning to pay attention to the faith-health connection. Conferences on spirituality and health have been sponsored by Harvard Medical School and the Mayo Clinic. Nearly half of U.S. medical schools now offer courses on the topic.

In a survey of 269 doctors at the 1996 meeting of the American Academy of Family Physicians, 99% said they thought religious beliefs could contribute to healing. When asked about their personal experiences, 63% of doctors said God intervened to improve their own medical conditions.

Clearly, their patients agree that prayer is a powerful tool in healing. Polls by Time/CNN and USA Weekend show that about 80% of Americans believe spiritual faith or prayer can help people recover from illness or injury, and more than 60% think doctors should talk to patients about faith and even pray with those who request it.

This yearning for a connection between religion and medicine is partly a reaction to a health care system that has become increasingly rushed and impersonal. "In medicine, the pendulum had swung so far toward the physical that it almost totally excluded anything spiritual," Dr. Dossey says. "This didn't feel right to patients or many physicians, and the pendulum has begun to swing back."

How Faith Fits in

So what does this mean for the average person? It does not mean adding worship to the list of healthy things you can do. You can't adopt faith as you would a low-fat diet.

What you can do is speak up if you're facing illness or surgery and would like your belief to be part of your health care. That doesn't mean you should expect your doctor to pray with or for you. But it's reasonable to expect him to listen to your needs, arrange a visit from the hospital chaplain, or allow time for prayer before you're wheeled into the operating room.

"Faith" Koenig maintains, "offers people some control over their lives as opposed to just depending on a medical profession that's becoming more distant and mechanized every day." [2]

11. A daily quiet time causes cleansing.

"Now ye are clean through the word which I have spoken unto you" (John 15:3). "Sanctify them through thy truth: thy word is truth" (John 17:17).

As Isaiah said, "We have unclean lips and we dwell in the midst of unclean people." Thank God that a daily quiet time provides cleansing. Have you ever wondered why there is very little of God's power in the Church today? It is because of the sin and the filth that is in the Church.

"For this ye know, that no whoremonger, nor unclean person, nor covetous man, who is an idolater, hath any inheritance in the kingdom of Christ and of God. Let no man deceive you with vain words: for because of these things cometh the wrath of God upon the children of disobedience" (Ephesians 5:5,6).

12. A daily quiet time produces faith in the average Christian.

"So then faith cometh by hearing, and hearing by the word of God" (Romans 10:17).

Faith comes by hearing and hearing by the Word of God. The more you read the Bible, the more you will believe in God's power to save. The Bible is littered with hundreds of stories of God's deliverance. You will see people at the brink of death who were saved by God. You will read about people in difficult and complex situations who were saved by the power of God. These testimonies inspire faith. Do not take it for granted. Do not think that you know everything about God. A daily dose of the Word of God will increase your faith.

13. A daily quiet time drives away weariness, dejection and depression.

"For as the rain cometh down, and the snow from heaven, and returneth not thither, but watereth the earth, and maketh it bring forth and bud, that it may give seed to the sower, and bread to the eater" (Isaiah 55:10).

The Word of God is like rain and snow that cools and refreshes. You will be blessed by the cooling and refreshing effect of a daily quiet time. As I go about I often become weary and unhappy if I have not been able to have time with the Lord. I cannot explain it. You have to experience it for yourself. The refreshing and calming effect that a time in the presence of God produces cannot be compared with anything.

14. A daily quiet time produces power for the ordinary Christians.

"For I am not ashamed of the gospel of Christ: for it is the power of God unto salvation to every one that believeth; to the Jew first, and also to the Greek" (Romans 1:16).

The gospel of Jesus Christ (which is the Word of God) is the power of God unto salvation. There is power in the Word of God. There is healing in the Word of God. When you expose yourself to the Word of God you are exposing yourself to a supernatural power. God is actually in His Word. He is the Word. "In the beginning was the Word and the Word was with God and the Word was God." God is the Word or the Word is God. Expose yourself to the Word and you are exposing yourself to God. The power of God will be real to you.

What power is able to change the lives of thousands of young people who would have been dancing, drinking, smoking and infecting each other with HIV? I am not talking about elderly men and women without any life or strength. I am talking about young men and women who are changed by the power of God's Word.

Someone once said of my church, "Your church is like a large youth group." You see, my church is made up of mostly young people. I have thousands of young people who serve the Lord with all their heart, might and strength. What has changed the course of their lives? Is it the laying on of hands? Is it fasting? No! It is the Word of God. The Word of God is the power of God with the ability to save and to change.

15. A DAILY QUIET TIME CAN MAKE YOU WISER THAN YOUR ENEMIES, YOUR TEACHERS AND THE ELDERS.

"Thou through thy commandments hast made me wiser than mine enemies: for they are ever with me. I have more understanding than all my teachers: for thy testimonies are my meditation. I understand more than the ancients, because I keep thy precepts" (Psalm 119:98-100).

A daily quiet time will give you the right perspective of life. You will be delivered from delusions about what life has to offer. It will guide you and convert your soul. You will see life from a different perspective. A daily quiet time will make you wiser than the average person around you.

Recently, I was walking on some huge golf courses that belonged to a single Japanese man. As I looked at the vast amount of land that belonged to this gentleman, I hoped that this man knew God. You see, one day he will have to leave this earth and leave the vast properties that he owns.

The Word of God makes you value what is truly valuable. The Word of God makes you see the wealth of this world in the right perspective. Jesus said, "Lay up for yourself treasures in heaven (Matthew 6:20)." When the Word of God is in you, you will say to yourself, "I will lay up for myself treasures in heaven," - that is true wisdom.

DON'T LOSE YOUR ONLY CHANCE FOR A PERSONAL RELATIONSHIP WITH GOD

"Not every one that saith unto me, Lord, Lord, shall enter into the kingdom of heaven; but he that doeth the will of my Father which is in heaven. Many will say to me in that day, Lord, Lord, have we not prophesied in thy name? and in thy name have cast out devils? and in thy name done many wonderful works? And then will I profess unto them, I never knew you: depart from me, ye that work iniquity" (Matthew 7:21-23).

One of the least understood statements of Jesus is, "I never knew you." These people were prophesying in His name. They were doing many wonderful works in His name but Jesus said, "I never knew you." I have always wondered how it is possible to do the work of God without knowing God. Dear friend, you had better believe what Jesus said.

It is possible to be a member of a church and to do great things for God but not know God. A daily quiet time will make you have a personal relationship with the Lord. Nothing else can make you have a personal relationship with the Lord. Coming to church a thousand times is different from having a personal one to one interaction with the Lord. It is this personal interaction with the Lord which most Christians lack.

It seems that God is more interested in the personal relationship than the great public works that we do in His name. A quiet time will make you have that personal knowledge of God. A daily quiet time will prevent you from going to hell. A quiet time will save you from the delusion that working for God is the same as knowing Him. There are people who work for me but don't know me personally. I have employees who hardly know me. They may recognize me when I come around, but they do not have a personal relationship with me. I have many shepherds and pastors who work in the church with me. But I do not have a personal relationship with all of them. Definitely, there is a difference between those who just work for me and those who have a personal relationship with me.

How come I have a personal relationship with some of my pastors and shepherds? The answer is simple.

Some of these pastors and shepherds make the effort to be close to me and to interact with me personally. Now I know them personally and can even call them friends. There are people in my church who do wonderful works in the name of the church or on my behalf. But the reality is that I don't know them personally.

Earlier on, when someone would ask me how they could do better in the ministry, I would give them twenty-five principles for church growth and then I would show them eighteen strategies for effective evangelism. I might show them seven steps to an excellent ministry. But now, if you ask me that same question I would say, "Just draw closer to God and know Him personally." You see, there is no point in running around on His behalf when you do not know Him personally.

It is time to know Him personally. It is said that pastors worldwide pray an average of seven minutes a day. If the pastors are spending less than ten minutes with their heavenly Father, then perhaps the ordinary members are spending a few seconds every week with their Lord. It is no wonder the Church is the way it is.

It is time to know Him personally. The only way is to have a regular daily quiet time. Do you expect God to come to you to develop a relationship with you? Certainly not! It is up to you and I to draw near to Him on a daily basis. "Draw nigh to God, and he will draw nigh to you…" (James 4:8). In this regard, a daily quiet time may actually be your passport to Heaven.

When you meet someone in public and shake his hand you can hardly say you know him. In my home, I have a picture which my mother-in-law took with President Clinton, former president of the USA. When she showed it to us, we said, "Wow, when did you meet him? How did you get to know him?"

She smiled and told us about how she had a brief interaction with him and managed to take a picture with him at a conference. The picture gives an impression that he knows her. But the reality is that he doesn't know her at all, and she doesn't know him either. Meeting someone in public does not mean that you know him at all.

Knowing about someone is different from knowing the person. There are many people who know about me but do not know me. Some people who see me from afar may have the impression that I am proud. Some people may hear me speak and think that I am a difficult person. May God forgive me for my sins. However, some people who know me personally may have a different impression.

Knowing God from afar is very different from knowing Him personally. Your impressions from afar will only change when you get closer to Him. The way you can develop that personal relationship with God is not in public at the church service. You do not develop a personal relationship with God by attending conventions and crusades. You cannot develop a personal relationship with anyone by interacting in public. There has to be communication at a personal level. There has to be a personal interaction! There has to be a quiet time. You can know God personally by spending time with Him during your quiet time.

AVOID SHALLOWNESS BY THE POWER OF QUIET TIME

"And these are they likewise which are sown on stony ground; who, when they have heard the word, immediately receive it with gladness; And have no root in themselves, and so endure but for a time: afterward, when affliction or persecution ariseth for the word's sake, immediately they are offended" (Mark 4:16,17). Shallowness is the disease of the Charismatic Christian. A lot of talk but no depth. Even our churches are shallow and without depth. A shallow end without depth.

I once visited a place near the Sahara Desert. I was amazed that there were only a few Charismatic or Pentecostal churches there. You see, for all our noise, we the Charismatic and Pentecostal churches have no real outreach to the places of greatest need. So it is with the Christians. We are loud, noisy, "praisey" people with lots of positive confessions. And yet, there is little depth in most of us. It is time to come out of shallowness.

Seven Symptoms of Shallowness in Christians

1. A lack of knowledge of the Scriptures.

Many charismatic Christians do not know what the Bible says about many things. We conducted an exam in one of our churches. Here came a gentleman who claimed to be a shepherd/leader. I gave him a Bible and said to him, "Show me where the Bible speaks about the resurrection." This gentleman could not find where the Bible talked about the resurrection. This is truly a symptom of shallowness. People are in churches shouting and singing but they have no depth. No wonder Charismatic Christians are easily swayed by the next wave of sensationalism.

2. Inability to quote Scripture.

Quoting Scriptures is different from knowing where things are in the Bible. Any Christian of depth will be able to quote Scriptures. Every Christian should have a version of the Bible from which he quotes accurately.

I was recently preaching in a very large Charismatic church and I began to ask questions. I said to one, "Please quote John 1:12." I said to another, "Please quote 2 Corinthians 5:17." I said to yet another, "What is Romans 6:23?"

Amazingly, most of the Christians who fill Charismatic churches cannot quote these Scriptures. Yet, these are some of the basic scriptures for every believer's foundation. There can be no progress with God unless we have depth. Scripture memorization is essential. Jesus Christ memorized scripture.

In Matthew 4 when the devil tempted Jesus, He accurately quoted Scriptures from Deuteronomy and paralysed the devil with them.

3. Inability to pray for at least one hour a day.

Shallowness is caused by failure to interact with the Lord. Anyone who has some depth with God spends at least an hour every day in the presence of the Lord. When you know God one hour will be too short for you. Conduct a survey in any large Charismatic church. Ask how many Christians have spent at least one hour inprayer and Bible reading on that day. You will find out that very few people spend more than a few seconds with God. No wonder most of them are shallow and don't know God.

4. Inability to lead and teach after being a Christian for two years.

"For when for the time ye ought to be teachers, ye have need that one teach you again which be the first principles of the oracles of God; and are become such as have need of milk, and not of strong meat" (Hebrews 5:12).

After someone has been a believer for some time he is expected to also share the things he has received. Paul clearly said that there is a time when a believer is expected to be a teacher. "For when for the time ye ought to be teachers, ye have need that one teach you again..." (Hebrews 5:12). The failure of the majority of believers to rise into Christian leadership is simply a sign of shallowness in the congregation.

5. A LACK OF INTEREST IN CHRISTIAN BOOKS AND TAPES.

Shallow Christians rarely read Christian books. A Christian book will take you deeper than you are. It will take you higher in the Lord. Show me someone who reads Christian books and listens to tapes and I will show you someone who is going deeper with the Lord.

6. INABILITY TO WORSHIP GOD.

I will give you an assignment. Next time you go to church, look around and see how many are singing the songs. Many of the Christians do not even know the songs. They mumble and stumble along as the worship leader leads the congregation.

The reality is that they do not know God and have no personal desire to worship Him. It's just a part of the service that has to run its course. They wait for the entertainment that will come from the pastor's jokes. Ask yourself, "Am I a worshipper?" Can you sing the song alone in your home?

7. INABILITY TO FELLOWSHIP REGULARLY.

The shallowness of many Christians is once again manifested in their inability to regularly fellowship with the Lord and with others. "But if we walk in the light, as he is in the light, we have fellowship one with another, and the blood of Jesus Christ his Son cleanseth us from all sin" (1 John 1:7).

They struggle to attend church every Sunday and often arrive late. It is almost as though they have a chore to do. Let me ask you a question. When a man is developing a personal relationship with a woman does he not enjoy interacting with her? Does he not long to see her again? The deeper the relationship the greater the interaction will be.

We will have a deep relationship with our God as we have a daily quiet time. Shallowness will be taken away from the church and Christianity will have more meaning for us all.

Obtain Wisdom Keys Through the Power of Quiet Time

1. QUIET TIME WILL SHOW YOU THAT THERE ARE TWO KINDS OF WISDOM: HUMAN CLEVERNESS AND THE WISDOM OF GOD.

"Who is a wise man and endued with knowledge among you? let him show out of a good conversation his works with meekness of wisdom. But if ye have bitter envying and strife in your hearts, glory not, and lie not against the truth. This wisdom descendeth not from above, but is earthly, sensual, devilish. For where envying and strife is, there is confusion and every evil work. But the wisdom that is from above is first pure, then peaceable, gentle, and easy to be entreated, full of mercy and good fruits, without partiality, and without hypocrisy" (James 3:13-17).

2. A QUIET TIME WILL SHOW YOU THAT HUMAN CLEVERNESS IS A POOR SUBSTITUTE FOR THE WISDOM OF GOD.

"Where is the wise? where is the scribe? where is the disputer of this world? hath not God made foolish the wisdom of this world? For after that in the wisdom of God the world by wisdom knew not God, it pleased God by the foolishness of preaching to save them that believe. For the Jews require a sign, and the Greeks seek after wisdom: But we preach Christ crucified, unto the Jews a stumblingblock, and unto the Greeks foolishness; But unto them which are called, both Jews and Greeks, Christ the power of God, and the wisdom of God. Because the foolishness of God is wiser than men; and the weakness of God is stronger than men" (1 Corinthians 1:20-25).

3. A QUIET TIME MAKES YOU MOVE PROGRESSIVELY AWAY FROM HUMAN CLEVERNESS AND TOWARDS THE WISDOM OF GOD.

"Let no man deceive himself. If any man among you seemeth to be wise in this world, let him become a fool, that he may be wise. For the wisdom of this world is foolishness with God. For it is written, He taketh the wise in their own craftiness" (1 Corinthians 3:18,19).

"And it came to pass in those days, that he went out into a mountain to pray, and continued all night in prayer to God. And when it was day, he called unto him his disciples: and of them he chose twelve, whom also he named apostles; Simon, (whom he also named Peter,) and Andrew his brother, James and John, Philip and Bartholomew, Matthew and Thomas, James the son of Alphaeus, and Simon called Zelotes, And Judas the brother of James, and Judas Iscariot, which also was the traitor" (Luke 6:12-16).

4. A QUIET TIME INTRODUCES YOU TO REAL WISDOM BECAUSE YOU BEGIN TO FEAR, RESPECT AND OBEY GOD.

"The fear of the Lord is the beginning of wisdom: and the knowledge of the holy is understanding" (Proverbs 9:10).

"The fear of the Lord is the beginning of wisdom: a good understanding have all they that do his commandments: his praise endureth for ever" (Psalm 111:10).

"And unto man he said, Behold, the fear of the Lord, that is wisdom; and to depart from evil is understanding" (Job 28:28).

5. THE QUIET TIME IS THE KEY TO GOD'S WISDOM AND THEREFORE TO YOUR PROMOTION.

"Wisdom is the principal thing; therefore get wisdom: and with all thy getting get understanding" (Proverbs 4:7).

6. BY HAVING A QUIET TIME YOU EXALT WISDOM IN YOUR LIFE AND THEREFORE BRING YOURSELF TO HONOUR.

"Exalt her, and she shall promote thee: she shall bring thee to honour, when thou dost embrace her" (Proverbs 4:8).

7. A QUIET TIME IS YOUR KEY TO WISDOM AND THEREFORE YOUR KEY TO VICTORY.

"Wisdom is better than weapons of war: but one sinner destroyeth much good" (Ecclesiastes 9:18).

"And they were not able to resist the wisdom and the spirit by which he spake" (Acts 6:10).

"Then shall the lame man leap as an hart, and the tongue of the dumb sing: for in the wilderness shall waters break out, and streams in the desert" (Isaiah 35:6).

"This book of the law shall not depart out of thy mouth; but thou shalt meditate therein day and night, that thou mayest observe to do according to all that is written therein: for then thou shalt make thy way prosperous, and then thou shalt have good success" (Joshua 1:8).

8. A QUIET TIME IS YOUR KEY TO BECOMING WEALTHY BECAUSE YOU HAVE ACCESS TO THE WISDOM OF GOD.

"Riches and honour are with me; yea, durable riches and righteousness. That I may cause those that love me to inherit substance; and I will fill their treasures" (Proverbs 8:18,21).

"Length of days is in her right hand; and in her left hand riches and honour" (Proverbs 3:16).

"The crown of the wise is their riches..." (Proverbs 14:24).

Key Priorities for the Christian

20

■ DEFINING "PROTON"

The priorities of Jesus are stated throughout the Gospels. When you are a sinner, you basically choose between two opinions: good and evil. As you grow in the Lord, your options increase and you begin to have more to choose from. This time your choices are not between good and evil but between good and good. In terms of what to do, there are often several good things to choose from. When you get to that point it is important that you understand the concept of priorities: "Which one do I do first?" Jesus gave us a great revelation on some things that should be done before others.

It is interesting to study how many things Jesus said should be done first. Whenever Jesus spoke of the first or the foremost issue, He used the Greek word "proton". In this chapter, we take a look at the proton issues; things that Jesus said should be done first.

"Proton" means "the first, first in time, order and number".

"Proton" also means "that which is first in rank and value."

"Proton" speaks of "the most important thing" and "that which precedes all others".

Finally, the "proton" issue is the "foremost issue."

1. ANYTHING THAT IS NOT DONE FIRST SEEMS TO LOSE ITS SIGNIFICANCE.

God is very patient with us. Many have disobeyed Him and seem to have gotten away with it. The importance of the Word of God seems to fade as we carry on in disobedience. Very soon that which is more important than anything else becomes despised and irrelevant. Today, I minister under the anointing and many respect me for the ministry. But if I had not obeyed God when I did, I may have lived out my life normally as a medical doctor. Discussions about the call of God would have seemed insignificant and irrelevant.

Sitting amongst my medical colleagues in various hospitals, the thought of being a pastor would have sounded ridiculous. I would have said to my friends, "Let me tell you about a silly idea I once had. Did you know that I once wanted to be a pastor? When we were younger, we were over-spiritual and impractical."

Have you never met grown-ups who said they were originally lined up for priesthood? In their old age they try to compensate for their disobedience through their children. I know a man who tried to force one of his children to become a priest. He said to his son, "God called me to be a priest but I didn't do it. You become that priest and I will give you property and money so that you lack nothing." At the end of their lives they desperately want to compensate for a life of non-compliance and non-cooperation with God.

Dear friend, I can assure you that the longer you walk in your own ways the more distant and unrealistic the commands of God will seem. There is a reason for proton. Proton, doing first things first, saves you from deception. God will take care of you and be with you as you flow in His will.

2. Anything that is not done first may never be done.

Delay often means cancellation. Anything that is not done first may never be done. I never knew that delaying something could actually lead to its cancellation.

There was a day I had to make a trip from London to New York to minister. I was actually scheduled to minister in Maryland that night. Unfortunately, I had a very early flight from Heathrow Airport in London, to Amsterdam and then I was to connect from Amsterdam to New York. Somehow I did not believe the time I saw on my ticket. I thought it was too early to be true. When I got to the airport, for the first time in my life, I was too late to check-in or to board the aircraft. I had missed the check in time by about twenty minutes. I was disappointed. I had to wait for the next flight to Amsterdam!

"You cannot make your first connection to New York but you can get a later flight," they told me. I realized from the time, that I would still make it to New York and just in time to drive to Maryland. So I called New York and told the pastor when I would be arriving and told him that we would need to drive rapidly to Maryland. I assured him that we were in good time and that the programme would surely come on in spite of the slight delay.

In Amsterdam, I confidently boarded my connecting flight to New York knowing that it would soon take-off and I would be on my way. After a while, I looked out of the window and I saw people spraying the wings of the plane.

Then came the announcement: "There is so much ice on the engine that it will not be safe to take-off. It will take us one hour to get rid of it. Please bear with us." I did another calculation and I still felt I could just make it to Maryland for the programme. The whole church would be waiting for me. They had been expecting me for weeks.

Unfortunately, it was not to be so. After the ice problem was solved, a new one arose, introducing even further delays. This time they said the toilets in the plane were not working and they had to fix them. I had never heard of toilets in a plane not working but it was happening live! It took another two hours before we were finally ready for take-off.

I sat in anguish as the minutes went by, imagining how many people would have gathered for the programme. Eventually, I had to accept that the programme would be cancelled because I would not make it in time. As I sat in my chair, I reflected over how the twenty-minute delay in London had cancelled my entire programme.

It was then that the Lord spoke to me, "Do you see that delay can mean cancellation?" The Lord showed me that the delay in obeying His Word could lead to my never doing His will! The Lord showed me that He had allowed me to have this experience so that I would learn how the delay in doing His will sometimes leads to my never doing it.

Many who intend to obey God will never end up obeying Him because they put the wrong things first. Their marriage, their PhDs, their MBAs, and their five-year trip abroad, all come before obedience to the Lord. Obedience to God, which they put in second place never materialized.

I have watched with sadness as people who should have been full-time in the ministry postpone it till after they accomplished certain things. Unfortunately that delay permanently closed the opportunity for them to be in full-time ministry. What people don't realize is that with time, circumstances change so much that the will of God does not seem realistic any more.

Delay often means cancellation but many do not know this fact. Has God spoken to you? What has He asked you to do? Maybe obeying God is not proton for you. Perhaps a thousand different things come before your obedience to the Lord.

3. It is an insult to give the second place to that which should be first.

Many do not realize that it is insulting to make God your second or third option. One day, while I was preaching, I identified several young ladies who did not have husbands. I suggested to them to get married to a nice young man in church. They all refused.

"Why don't you want to marry him, is he not a handsome man?"

"Yes he is," they answered.

"Is he a spiritual person?"

"Yes he is. He is even a pastor."

"Does he not have a car and a house?"

"Yes he does. Actually his car is very nice."

"Then why don't any of you want to marry him?"

"Because he has a wife already," they answered.

I continued, "But you can be his second wife?"

In chorus they all cried out, "No way, no sir, we will not be second wives, we want to be number one."

They felt insulted that I would offer them the second position. They wanted to be wives but not second wives. These young ladies wanted to be wives but only if they would be the first and only wives.

This is how God feels. He knows we will serve Him but He wants us to serve Him first. It is actually an insult to put God after anything! Unfortunately, God is constantly relegated to the second, third and sometimes tenth place of importance. It is time for God to take His proton (foremost) position in your life.

4. Problems abound when that which is to be first becomes second.

When something that is supposed to be done second is done first, many things go wrong. I was recently in one African country and my host took me to a cemetery. I was amazed at the fresh graves that were gradually filling every space.

At a dinner, with another pastor friend, he gave me an incredible account of the number of funerals that he was conducting in his city. He told us that they had so many funerals that pastors no longer conducted funeral services. The funerals were so numerous that cell leaders had to conduct burial services of church members. I listened in amazement. He went on to describe how they no longer buried people lying down because there was no space in the cemetery. He described how they buried them vertically, standing up! The coffins were actually placed vertically into the ground to save space. In other words, the dead bodies would stand, rather than lie down. I thought to myself, "In such a situation do you say, "stand in peace," or "rest in peace"?

What was the cause of this unprecedented wave of death in this country? Why were so many people dying? The answer was simple: the second thing had come before the first thing. Sex had come before marriage. Sex is supposed to be experienced only after marriage. In this country, sex was an experience occurring largely outside the context of marriage. A wave of death had swept through that nation because the first thing had become the second and the second thing first.

PROTON AND RELATIONSHIPS

"Therefore if thou bring thy gift to the altar, and there rememberest that thy brother hath ought against thee; Leave there thy gift before the altar, and go thy way; first (PROTON) be reconciled to thy brother, and then come and offer thy gift" (Mathew 5:23-24).

The word "first" was translated from the Greek word proton. As I said earlier, the word proton means "the first", "first in time, order and number". Proton, also means "that which is first in rank and value". Proton speaks of "the most important thing" and "that which precedes all others". Finally, the proton issue is the "foremost issue".

Jesus is teaching us that a good relationship with everyone should come before worshipping Him in church. It is easy for us to lift up our hands in worship. But the Lord has made it clear that we need to sort out our relationships before we come to Him. This is a priority for the Lord. He said we should do this before we worship. Why is it so important for us to leave our gifts at the altar before worshipping Him?

1. Having good relationships proves that you are not a liar.

"If a man say, I love God, and hateth his brother, he is a liar: for he that loveth not his brother whom he hath seen, how can he love God whom he hath not seen?" (1 John 4:20). This Scripture shows that if you cannot love the people you see, but claim to love God, you are actually a liar. God does not want a bunch of liars lifting their hands in prayer. Would you feel happy if a large group of liars came to your gate seeking for help? Would you not call the police?

2. Having good relationships proves that you are not a murderer.

"Whosoever hateth his brother is a murderer: and ye know that no murderer hath eternal life abiding in him" (1 John 3:15). The Bible teaches that when you hate your brother, you are a murderer. God does not want murderers knocking at His door. How would you feel if a large group of murderers assembled at your home seeking audience with you? Would you not be terrified?

3. Having good relationships proves that you are not abiding in death.

"We know that we have passed from death unto life, because we love the brethren. He that loveth not his brother abideth in death" (1 John 3:14). "To abide in death", means "to be separated and isolated from God". Who wants to live in a permanent state of separation from God? It is very important that we straighten out our relationship with the Lord. God wants us to come out of this state before we approach Him in prayer, praise and worship. How would you feel if a large group of dead bodies assembled at your home desiring to be with you? Would you not be terrified?

4. Having good relationships proves that you are no longer living in darkness.

"He that saith he is in the light, and hateth his brother, is in darkness even until now. He that loveth his brother abideth in the light, and there is none occasion of stumbling in him. But he that hateth his brother is in darkness, and walketh in darkness, and knoweth not whither he goeth, because that darkness hath blinded his eyes" (1 John 2:9-11). Read the Scripture above and you will realize that to love your brother is so important in your spiritual walk. Failing to do so will open you up to the danger of stumbling. You will live in darkness. Every time you approach the Lord, a cloud of darkness is seen approaching the throne. How would you feel if a cloud of darkness surrounded your home everyday? Would you not be terrified?

That is why God insists that we straighten out our relationships first.

5. Having good relationships proves that you have forgiven those that have wronged you

"And when ye stand praying, forgive, if ye have ought against any: that your Father also which is in heaven may forgive you your trespasses. But if ye do not forgive, neither will your Father which is in heaven forgive your trespasses" (Mark 11:25-26). Without forgiveness, God will not hear your prayer. He will not receive your worship. Without forgiveness, you are wasting your time at the altar.

PROTON IN RELATION TO THE KINGDOM

"But seek ye first (PROTON) the kingdom of God, and his righteousness; and all these things shall be added unto you" (Matthew 6:33). God wants the first part of everyone's life. The first part of our lives is the season of productivity. It is the period in which people abound in faith, hope, love and fertility. Seek the kingdom of God before you seek your personal kingdom of wealth, comfort and security. There are many reasons why the kingdom of God must be sought first and in the first part of your life.

1. The kingdom of God requires an early start.

The kingdom of Heaven also requires a lot of time and attention. The commonest characteristic of large churches is that the pastor has been there for many years. It takes a long time to grow a congregation from the fellowship stage to the mega church stage.

If you think that the work of God can be done in a few weeks, or months, you deceive yourself and the truth is not in you. It takes many years for something substantial to be accomplished in ministry. Let me give you an exercise. Take any well-known and large ministry and find out when the pastor really began his ministry.

Jesus Himself began His preparation for ministry as a child. Samuel the prophet was brought to the temple as a child. The preparation takes many years. This is why Levites became priests only by the age of thirty. From thirty years old and upward even until fifty years old, all that enter into the host, to do the work in the tabernacle of the congregation. Numbers 4:3. This is why Jesus started His ministry by the age of thirty. And Jesus himself began to be about thirty years of age, being (as was supposed) the son of Joseph, which was the son of Heli, Luke 3:23.

Because the work of God requires so much time both for preparation and actual ministry, it must be the first thing in your life. Many people put off the ministry because they actually despise it; they feel thats it is something that can be done within a short time.

2. The kingdom needs young people

There are many things that only young people can do. There are things I did when I was younger that I cannot do today. For instance, I remember when I was in secondary school, I fasted for almost one school term. I wonder if I could do something like that today. I used to hold "dawn-broadcasts" (open-air preaching at dawn) in many places.

As a student, I did many exciting things for the Lord. All night prayer meetings, dawn broadcasts, twelve-hour prayer meetings, seven-hour prayer meetings etc. Although I basically do the same things today, there are obvious changes in the intensity and style. I really cherish the more youthful years I spent in Christ.

In those years I memorized entire chapters of the Bible. It is the verses I learnt in those days that form the basis of my Scripture knowledge today.

Perhaps you do not know why God wants you to take Him as the first thing in the first part of your life. Perhaps you want to give God your years of weakness and trembling. The first part is the best part: when you are strong, energetic and zealous. That is the part that God wants!

3. The kingdom of God needs faith, hope, and love.

"Remember now thy Creator in the days of thy youth, while the evil days come not, nor the years draw nigh, when thou shalt say, I have no pleasure in them" (Ecclesiastics 12:1). The Kingdom of God needs energetic people for the ministry.

There is a lot of stress and strain in the ministry. Contrary to what people think, pastors are often very stressed and very tired. They rarely have time for themselves and their families.

In the first part of your life you are full of faith, hope and love. Watch the older people and you will notice that they have less "spring in their gait". Tiredness and weariness has set in. Bad experiences have made them weary and suspicious of everyone. They trust no one and are unwilling to try new things. The spirit of adventure is gone. They are hardened by their lives' experiences. Older people have seen pain, bitterness and death. Yes, they believe in God but it is a little different from a younger person's faith.

In the first part of your life, you are not yet broken-hearted. It is this part that God badly wants. God wants the first part of your life. The book of Ecclesiastes, Chapter 12, aptly describes this. "Keep your creator in mind while you are young! In years to come, you will be burdened down with troubles and say, "I don't enjoy life anymore." Your body will grow feeble, your teeth will decay, and your eyesight fail. The noisy grinding of grain will be shut out by your deaf ears, but even the song of a bird will keep you awake. You will be afraid to climb up a hill or walk down a road. Your hair will turn as white as almond blossoms. You will feel lifeless and drag along like an old grasshopper..." (Ecclesiastics 12:1,3-5 Contemporary English Version).

It is said that King Solomon wrote the book of Song of Solomon in his youth, the Proverbs in his middle age and the Book of Ecclesiastes in his older years. You will notice that the mood of each of these books is different. In the Song of Solomon, he is excited and in love. In the Book of Proverbs, he shares practical wisdom for regular life. But in the Book of Ecclesiastes, his mood is quite different. He describes many of life's experiences as inconsequential, vain and futile.

"Nothing makes sense. I have seen it all—nothing makes sense" (Ecclesiastics 12:8 Contemporary English Version). This drop in mood greatly affects the work of God. It takes faith and hope in Heaven to take up your cross and sacrifice for an unseen God.

I enjoy the company of the younger Christian leaders in my church. They seem to enjoy what I preach more than the older ones. Many times they crowd around me after church just wanting to chat with me. They seem to believe everything I say, no matter how hard it sounds.

I remember one day in particular, I was talking to a group of older pastors. The younger university folks gathered around me as usual. As I continued chatting with them, I noticed as the older ones slunk away one after the other until I was left with only the young people. I wasn't saying anything in particular that pertained to young people, but the older guys were just not interested.

In the first part of your life you are very responsive, zealous and teachable. God can reach out to you and turn you in almost any direction. As you get older you become uninterested and disillusioned. There seems to be a teachable and humble spirit in the first part of our lives.

4. The kingdom of God cannot be despised.

There are many jobs that require job-seekers to be below the age of thirty. Why do you think many companies recruit people below a certain age? Because they want to get the best out of them! Don't despise the church. There are people who say they will work for God when they retire.

Which occupation can be compared with the high calling of ministry? Medicine, law, engineering, architecture, carpentry, computing, banking, journalism, research, pharmacy, mining, management, acting, singing, dancing, plumbing, masonry or piloting cannot be compared with the ministry of the Lord Jesus Christ. "But what things were gain to me, those I counted loss for Christ. Yea doubtless, and I count all things but loss for the excellency of the knowledge of Christ Jesus my Lord: for whom I have suffered the loss of all things, and do count them but dung, that I may win Christ" (Philipians 3:7-8).

The priesthood is the high calling of God. And that is what I am involved with. On this earth, the priesthood is despised.

I once had a pastor who couldn't find a wife because he was a pastor. The mother of his would-be bride, refused to allow her daughter to be engaged to a pastor. She felt that a pastor was an aimless, jobless man without prospects. On one occasion, she even sent an emissary to find out if he really worked with the church as he claimed. She also wanted to find out what kind of work he could possibly be doing. The bride's mother's envoy could not hide her surprise when she found out that the church actually had offices and that there was a lot of work going on in these offices.

5. The kingdom cannot be delayed.

Some people think their marriages cannot be delayed, their schools cannot be delayed and their work cannot be delayed. But let me tell you what cannot be delayed: the Kingdom of God!

Jesus said we should not say that there are yet four months till the harvest. In other words don't say that there is more time. Don't introduce delays for the Kingdom of God. "Say not ye, There are yet four months, and then cometh harvest? behold, I say unto you, Lift up your eyes, and look on the fields; for they are white already to harvest" (John 4:35).

Unknown to many people, this earthly life is very time-related. Every instruction or opportunity is time-related. Hear this and hear it very well: every instruction that God has given to you has an invisible timer on it. A countdown begins from the moment God speaks to you. The available time to perform that duty reduces with every passing hour. Many think they are just biding their time and will take God seriously later. Do not be deceived! The expiry date of your grace period is fast approaching.

When Princess Diana was planning her wedding to her Egyptian boyfriend, she didn't know that she was not far from the night of her accident. She was oblivious to the fact that she was to be the subject of the largest funeral of all time. She didn't know the time. Do you know the time? Do we know the time?

If God has called you to the ministry a clock has begun to tick. A time will come when you will no longer be able to fulfil that instruction.

Sometimes God speaks to you, "Finance my Kingdom." Perhaps that comes along with a five-year period wherein you can obey Him.

Perhaps He tells you, "Go out as a missionary." Maybe that has a ten-year period wherein you could fulfil it. Some people spend seven years of that period doing other things and then in the last three years attempt to obey God. But their time is almost up. Nothing effective can be done in the remaining three years.

6. Jesus rejects all those who put their family, business or personal wealth before the kingdom of God.

"And sent his servant at supper time to say to them that were bidden, Come; for all things are now ready. And they all with one consent began to make excuse. The first said unto him, I have bought a piece of ground, and I must needs go and see it: I pray thee have me excused. And another said, I have bought five yoke of oxen, and I go to prove them: I pray thee have me excused. And another said, I have married a wife, and therefore I cannot come" (Luke 14:17-20). Many decent Christians hide behind their families or legitimate businesses to stay away from obeying God.

Unfortunately, Jesus specifically mentions these things as reasons that will not stand before Him. Nothing, and I mean nothing is more important than God and our service to Him. When God calls you, you have no right to use your wife, husband or children as a reason to stay away. When God calls for you, you have no right to use your business or personal wealth as a reason to stay away. Read it for yourself. Contrary to what many dignified and self-righteous people think, your service to God is more important than any of these things.

John Wesley, the founder of the Methodist church had major problems with his wife. She did not want him to continue corresponding with some of the congregants in his parish. John Wesley preached on Sunday, got married on Monday and preached the next day. In less than a month, he was on the road again. Neither wife nor family could stop him from doing what his heart loved most. Today, the Methodist Church stands as a veritable testimony to the unyielding commitment of John Wesley to the things of God.

Eventually, he was separated from his wife and spent the last twenty years of his life alone. When she died, he was only told about it some days after she had been buried. One writer commented on this marriage. He said the kindest assessment that could be made of John Wesley's wife was that she was mentally challenged. John Wesley knew his God and nothing was going to take him away from his call. His wife was either going to help him or step aside. Nothing was going to keep him from the Lord whom he loved.

Below is an excerpt from the book "Five Great Evangelists" by John H. Armstong, showing us some of the challenges John Wesley faced and his resilience to stay on track. He was determined to work for the Lord. I am not saying that it is right to be separated from your spouse or anything like that. Please do not misunderstand me! I am simply showing you what John Wesley went through in his determination to continue his ministry. I am illustrating a certain commitment to the work of God in spite of difficult marriage circumstances. I know it will help some people.

"John had known Mrs. Vazeille briefly when they were married in February 1751. He had preached on a Sunday, married her on a Monday, and preached again on the Tuesday following. Two weeks later, he set out for Bristol, leaving Mary behind. After four days away from her, John wrote, 'My body is stronger and stronger – and so is my love to you. God grant it may never go beyond His will! O that we may continue to love one another as Christ has loved us.' After a few days back in London, he headed north. He wrote in his journal a month after marriage, 'I cannot understand how a Methodist preacher can answer it to God, to preach one sermon or travel one day less, in a married state than in a single state.' He may have had an eye on Charles when he wrote this. He had left itinerant ministry and settled into a very happy marriage.

John and Mary began their relationship poorly and from this beginning it went downhill fast. When asked to explain why he had married without consulting the members of the Oxford Holy Club, who had all agreed to the idea of mutual approval, he sought to explain himself. He referred to his marriage as being undertaken to 'break down the prejudice about the world and him' and that until two weeks before, he had never thought about such a marriage. Is it surprising, then, that the trouble was not far away?

Just a few weeks after the wedding John wrote Mary telling her to open his personal mail during his long absence. When she began to read the letters that came to him from women all over Britain she became almost insanely jealous. She objected to correspondence from one woman in particular. Further, she refused to travel with him in his ministry, thus never becoming the model companion he thought he had married. Her open complaints against him only made things worse and she showed an amazing capacity for real meanness. She would steal her husband's letters, take portions that were of questionable matter, and then turn them over to the public press. On at least one occasion she physically attacked him. She repeatedly accused him of adultery. By 1753 Ned Perronet called her 'absolutely intractable.' John and Mary seemed to try, for awhile, but there was no way he felt that he could shirk his responsibilities at this point in his life. They were separated in 1755 and though they tried several reconciliations, off and on for nearly twenty years they had almost nothing to do with each other afterwards. It was a marriage that never should have happened.

Wesley cannot be completely exonerated of blame in this bad marriage. He chose poorly and he really had no business getting married under the circumstances. Yet it is also certain that Mary knew what she was entering into when she married John Wesley. She had a fairly full idea of what she would face as his wife. Professor Umphrey Lee has summed up the situation well:

Southey may be right that Mrs. Wesley deserves to be placed along with Xanthippe and Job's spouse as one of the three bad wives, but John Wesley deserves the place which someone has given him as one of the world's worst husbands.

Wesley resolved to not contend with Mary further and said by writing: 'you have wronged me much but not beyond forgiveness.' It is significant to observe his sentiments in several letters that he mailed to her in which he said:

I love you still, and am as clear from other women as the day I was born. At length know me and know yourself. Your enemy I cannot be. But let me be your friend; suspect me no more; asperse me no more; provoke me no more. Do not any longer contend for mastery; for power, money or praise. Be content to be a private insignificant person, known and loved by God and me. Attempt no more to abridge me of the liberty which I claim by God and man. Leave me to be governed by God and my own conscience; then shall I govern you with gentle sway, and shew that I do indeed love you, even as Christ the church.

In early 1771, Mary left John permanently. His journal entry written in Latin, says: ' I did not leave her; I did not send her away; I shall not call her back.' She died, October 8,1781, at the age of seventy-one, after having been for over thirty years a terrible burden to her husband. He was not informed of her death until two days after her burial."[1]

IMPORTANCE OF *PROTON* IN OUR WEAKNESSESS

PROTON AND OUR FAULTS

"And why beholdest thou the mote that is in thy brother's eye, but considerest not the beam that is in thine own eye?Or how wilt thou say to thy brother, Let me pull out the mote out of thine eye; and, behold, a beam is in thine own eye? Thou hypocrite, first (PROTON) cast out the beam out of thine own eye; and then shalt thou see clearly to cast out the mote out of thy brother's eye" (Matthew 7:3-5).

1. Jesus warned us to consider our own faults before commenting on the faults of others.

In order to help us further, He gave a blanket suggestion: "Judge not!" In other words, say nothing about anything! This is one of the commonest problems of Christians. How we love to criticize people, how we love to see the mistakes in our friends! I want to show you a frightening truth, which if understood, will help us shut our mouths until we get to Heaven.

2. The Scripture above, affirms the reality of a beam in your eye.

The Scripture is not suggesting the possibility of a beam being in your eye. It is affirming the reality of a beam in your eye. "Why do you look at the mote in your brother's eye without noticing the beam in your eye?" In other words there is a beam! It is there whether you know it or not.

This is the reality that most people can't appreciate. Every sin, mistake or fault you see in someone is already in you. When you see a brother or sister in fornication or adultery, just begin to see yourself. You are seeing another version of yourself.

You may ask, "Pastor, how is this possible?" The answer is in the Scripture: "but considerest not the beam that is in thine own eye?"

"To consider" means "to think deeply, analyze, to meditate, to ponder and to reflect". When you reflect deeply on the issue you will realize that you are also guilty. Do you remember the woman who was caught in the act of adultery? The people wanted to stone her but Jesus made them consider their own lives.

He told them, "After considering your own state carefully, you may go ahead and execute this lady." After a little reflection, the accusers slunk away one after another. Dear reader, when I understood this Scripture, my mind began to race. I thought of all the possible sins I knew of. After serious consideration, I realized that I was genuinely guilty of every sin, even the far-fetched ones.

One day, I had a vision of one of our churches. They were having a camp meeting. It was as though I was standing above them. As they lifted their hands and worshipped, the Lord said to me: "Murderers and fornicators." I said,

"Lord, how can this be? These are holy children of God who really love you." The Lord gave me just two Scriptures: "Whosoever hateth his brother is a murderer: and ye know that no murderer hath eternal life abiding in him" (1 John 3:15). "But I say unto you, That whosoever looketh on a woman to lust after her hath committed adultery with her already in his heart" (Matthew 5:28).

The Lord told me, "Most Christians hate somebody somewhere." By God's standards, that makes them murderers. He continued,

"Most men lust after women everyday." According to God's standards, this is the same as adultery. Suddenly, I could see how those in this group could be described as adulterers and murderers.

One day, I conducted an experiment. I addressed pastors in the presence of the congregation , "All pastors who have committed adultery should please stand up."

Most of the pastors felt uneasy. They looked at me wondering what I was up to. No one stood up.

Then I said, "All pastors who have ever lusted after a woman should please stand up!"

They all stood up smiling in agreement. They were thinking, "Lust is a lesser crime and for that we shall stand." When they were all standing, I announced to the church that these pastors were all adulterers. They were dumbfounded. But I explained the Scripture to them. In God's eyes, we are adulterers. Perhaps we have committed adultery a thousand times without even knowing it.

3. It makes no sense to point at and analyze the faults of another Christian.

It makes no sense to point at and analyze the faults of another Christian because there is an implanted beam in both of your eyes. How funny we must look in Heaven as we accuse one another of crimes that we are guilty of ourselves.

Even the September 11 tragedy teaches us this principle. It is easy to point a finger at an Islamic terrorist. It is even easier to blame the training camps of Al Qaeda and terrorist leader Osama Bin Laden.

However, a little consideration on the part of Christians will show us that our lack of missionary zeal and our disobedience to the Great Commission leaves these nations at the mercy of other religions. Today, false religions are taking root in poor African countries. Places that were traditionally Christian are changing into a mixture of Islam and Christianity. Regions that were Islamic are becoming radicalized, giving rise to such terrorists. Perhaps we are greater murderers because we refuse to go and preach. Perhaps the blood of all these people is on our hands because we failed to reach them with the Gospel of Jesus Christ. "When I say unto the wicked, Thou shalt surely die; and thou givest him not warning, nor speakest to warn the wicked from his wicked way, to save his life; the same wicked man shall die in his iniquity; but his blood will I require at thine hand" (Ezekiel 3:18).

The Scripture tells us that we will have to account for the blood of sinners we failed to warn. The church today is busy enjoying itself in "merry-go-round" activities which make no advances into enemy territories. Security, safety, more shelter and more personal well-being are the hallmarks of the church today. Where are the missionaries? Where are the radicalized Christians who are ready to stand up and be counted?

Mature Christians rarely have any comment to make about another brother's difficulties. When you hear of scandals and problems (motes), you bow your head in fear and trembling knowing that your (beam) is there. Our approach to God is only made possible by the blood of Jesus. If we say we have no sin we are living in the highest kind of deception. "If we say that we have no sin, we deceive ourselves, and the truth is not in us" (1 John 1:8).

PROTON AND OUR PROBLEMS

"Or else how can one enter into a strong man's house, and spoil his goods, except he first (PROTON) bind the strong man? and then he will spoil his house" (Matthew 12:29). Deal first with the spiritual roots of your problems otherwise you will never have the breakthrough you need. The strong man speaks of the devil and the spiritual factors that make things happen.

1. Except we address problems from the spiritual perspective, they often never get solved.

Whether God's blessing is needed or Satan has to be bound, it is important that the spiritual nature of issues is addressed.

Many problems have spiritual roots. Often we try to solve problems without dealing with the root cause. A carnally-minded person has his mind on natural causes thereby eliminating the spiritual factors. The fact that we are educated does not mean that spiritual causes must be left out of our thinking. The God of the "Gaps Theory" Education and science are not contrary to spiritual things. At the bottom of it all we believe that it is God who works things out. Some people have tried to explain religion and spiritual things with a theory known as the "Gaps Theory". In this theory, people claimed that whenever there was a lack (a gap) of human knowledge, the existence of God was used as an explanation. However when there were more scientific discoveries to explain the phenomenon, the concept of God was removed.

For instance, they claim that when men did not understand the principles of evaporation and conversion, the phenomenon of rain was ascribed to God's mercy. But when science discovered how rain was brought about, God was eliminated from that gap. These atheists believe that through science, almost all the gaps of knowledge have been filled and that is why many people do not need to believe in God any more. However, your education should not make you eliminate God. I am a medical doctor and a scientist in my own right. My education and my knowledge have made me believe in God even more.

Unfortunately, we make ourselves fools when we eliminate God from our thinking. "And even as they did not like to retain God in their knowledge, God gave them over to a reprobate mind, to do those things which are not convenient" (Romans 1:28). When you do not retain God in your knowledge, you develop a reprobate mind. Always include God.

2. You must know that God is the source of all blessings and the devil is the cause of all the evil around us.

Every good and every perfect gift comes from God. It is the highest kind of deception to think that the good things in your life came just by your hard work. It is the Lord who promotes, it is the Lord, who lifts up, and it is the Lord who blesses. "For promotion cometh neither from the east, nor from the west, nor from the south. But God is the judge: he putteth down one, and setteth up another" (Psalm 75:6-7).

PROTON AND OUR MISTAKES

"Command therefore that the sepulchre be made sure until the third day, lest his disciples come by night, and steal him away, and say unto the people, He is risen from the dead: so the last error shall be worse than the first (PROTON)" (Matthews 27:64). The first error speaks of the initial mistake that leads to all other mistakes. We must look out for this first error because it has a way of opening the door for a series of errors.

1. The errors of the Pharisees.

The first mistake of the Pharisees was to become religious and self-righteous. "Those by the way side are they that hear; then cometh the devil, and taketh away the word out of their hearts, lest they should believe and be saved" (Luke 8:12).

Their second mistake was to reject the ministry of grace and truth that came through Christ. "He came unto his own, and his own received him not" (John 1:11).

Their third mistake was to become jealous of the Lord Jesus. "For he knew that for envy they had delivered him" (Matthew 27:18).

Their fourth mistake was to murder Christ. "And they crucified him, and parted his garments, casting lots: that it might be fulfilled which was spoken by the prophet, They parted my garments among them, and upon my vesture did they cast lots" (Matthew 27:35).

Their fifth mistake was to disbelieve His resurrection. "And when they were assembled with the elders, and had taken counsel, they gave large money unto the soldiers, Saying, Say ye, His disciples came by night, and stole him away while we slept. And if this come to the governor's ears, we will persuade him, and secure you. So they took the money, and did as they were taught: and this saying is commonly reported among the Jews until this day" (Matthew 28:12-15).

The last error was to persecute those who proclaimed the good news of Jesus Christ and His resurrection. "And as they spake unto the people, the priests, and the captain of the temple, and the Sadducees, came upon them, Being GRIEVED THAT THEY TAUGHT THE PEOPLE, and preached through Jesus the resurrection from the dead. And THEY LAID HANDS ON THEM ..." (Acts 4:1-3).

As you can see, the first error opened the door to a series of more serious errors. "Command therefore that the sepulchre be made sure until the third day, lest his disciples come by night, and steal him away, and say unto the people, He is risen from the dead: so the last error shall be worse than the first" (Matthew 27:64).

2. THE ERRORS OF KING DAVID.

King David had murdered Uriah, one of his trusted soldiers. This was one of the low points in the life of David. But this was not the first error. The first error was when he stayed at home at a time when kings were supposed to be at war. "And it came to pass, after the year was expired, at the time when kings go forth to battle, that David sent Joab, and his servants with him, and all Israel; and they destroyed the children of Ammon, and besieged Rabbah. But David tarried still at Jerusalem" (2 Samuel 11:1).

The second error was adultery with Bath-sheba. "And David sent and enquired after the woman. And one said, Is not this Bath-sheba, the daughter of Eliam, the wife of Uriah the Hittite? And David sent messengers, and took her; and she came in unto him, and he lay with her; for she was purified from her uncleanness: and she returned unto her house" (2 Samuel 11:3-4). The third error was the murder of Uriah, Bath-sheba's husband. "And he wrote in the letter, saying, Set ye Uriah in the forefront of the hottest battle, and retire ye from him, that he may be smitten, and die" (2 Samuel 11:15).

These two examples clearly show that the first error is often a door to many more errors.

■ THE IMPORTANCE OF *PROTON* IN OUR WALK WITH THE LORD.

PROTON AND FRUITFULNESS

"For the earth bringeth forth fruit of herself; first (PROTON) the blade, then the ear, after that the full corn in the ear" (Mark 4:28). Even in bearing fruit, there is an order. The fruit you may bear at a certain stage of your life may just be a prelude to other fruit that God has in store for you. "First the blade, then the ear and after that, the full corn." That is the order in which it comes. Some people are going to be full-time pastors but God wants them to start out as lay pastors. Some people are going to be great evangelists but the first part of their ministry may be to pastor a church.

God has called some of you to have huge churches. Before this full corn will appear, the blade and the ear must appear first. There are pastors who stand in huge auditoriums every Sunday. But it didn't begin that way. For some of them the first ten years of ministry only produced "the blade". Keep going and "the ear" is going to come forth; finally the full corn is going to be manifested to all.

PROTON AND INHERITANCE

"But Jesus said unto her, Let the children first (PROTON) be filled: for it is not meet to take the children's bread, and to cast it unto the dogs" (Mark 7:27).

1. THE BLESSINGS OF A FATHER MUST FIRST BE DIRECTED TO HIS CHILDREN.

Thereafter others may benefit. There is a custom amongst certain Ghanaian tribes by which the nieces and the nephews of a man are the first to inherit their uncle's property. This tradition is not biblical and Christians must not practise it. I know many children who have been devastated by their father's decision to give his best inheritance to his sister's children, instead of to his own children. Their fathers do this because they claim that they can be certain that the children that came from their sisters' wombs are truly related to them. However, they can never really tell whether the child that came from their wife's womb is really their child. Such a tradition is based on the highest kind of fear and mistrust.

2. There are situations in which those who should receive the blessings first are not open to receive their father's blessings.

There are times I have wondered as those nearby wallowed in familiarity. Strangers and unfamiliar people come from afar and take the first blessing which belongs to the children. Since the servant is not greater than his master, if this is what happened to Christ, it will happen to us. "And I say unto you, That many shall come from the east and west, and shall sit down with Abraham, and Isaac, and Jacob, in the kingdom of heaven. But the children of the kingdom shall be cast out into outer darkness: there shall be weeping and gnashing of teeth" (Matthew 8:11-12).

It is significant that the Lord appeared first to Mary Magdalene. "Now when Jesus was risen early the first day of the week, he appeared first to Mary Magdalene, out of whom he had cast seven devils" (Mark 16:9).

PROTON AND MARY MAGDALENE

Women had a special place in the ministry of Jesus. They were not called to be apostles or pastors. Jesus did not have any woman in His team of twelve disciples. But why did He appear first to Mary Magdalene? This is a great lesson to all of us.

1. Your importance to the Lord Jesus is not determined by the magnitude of the task given to you.

Your personal faithfulness, dedication and commitment to the Lord Jesus is more important than anything else. Mary Magdalene was at the scene of the crucifixion. She was personally dedicated to the ministry of the Lord Jesus Christ even though she had no special position or function. The proton commandment of the Lord Jesus is to love God with all your heart.

2. One of the highest indicators of your maturity in Christ is your love for and intimacy with the Lord.

Could it be that Mary Magdalene is higher than the twelve apostles because she loved the Lord? Will people who love the Lord be higher than those who just work for Him? Do you love the Lord? Do you love Him personally? There are many that will come in Christ's name and say, "I did this great work, I healed the sick, I cast out demons, I accomplished this in Your Name." But Jesus will say, "I never knew you."

It seems that knowing God is far more important than the things we do for Him. In one of Paul's last letters, he prayed: "That I may know him". Mary Magdalene was not a high official in the church. After this incident, we never hear of her any more. One thing we do know however, is that she knew the Lord personally and loved Him dearly.

After the ordeal of the crucifixion and the resurrection, Jesus saw it fit to appear first to Mary Magdalene. Of all the people that Christ appeared to, she was found worthy to be the first. May you be found worthy of such visions and blessings! I pray for you that you will not just work for the Lord but know Him intimately!

PROTON AND YOUR JOURNEY

"And into whatsoever house ye enter, first say, Peace be to this house" (Luke 10:5).

1. THE FIRST THING TO BRING TO ANY HOME IS THE PEACE OF GOD.

The Scripture above teaches us to have our feet shod with the gospel of peace. How you start a visit determines the tone of your stay. Many people start their interaction with others on a carnal note. It then becomes more difficult to establish a spiritual relationship with someone you have known carnally.

2. HOW YOU START YOUR RELATIONSHIPS DETERMINES THE FUTURE OF THE FRIENDSHIP.

I remember the unfortunate story of a zealous brother who backslid in a new school. This friend of mine had to attend sixth form in this new boarding school. On the first day of school, some unbelievers hailed and befriended him. Upon their first interaction, they thought he was an unbeliever and really liked him. Unfortunately, this brother had no chance to tell them that he was a born-again Christian who spoke in tongues and prophesied. He had no chance to first say, "Peace be to this house."

Before long, they were offering him cigarettes, girls and booze. His opportunity to inform them of his Christian beliefs was gone. How could he tell them that he was a religious person when they had accepted him as one of their gang? This brother paid dearly for not saying first of all, "Peace be to this house." Proton speaks of the things you must do first. For the next two years, he experienced a horrible era of backsliding and sin.

I always like to first present the Gospel of peace. I want you to know where I stand. You must first know that I am a believer. I remember years ago, when I attended an interview for the medical school. Students had gathered from all over the country and I didn't know any of them. When I entered the hall where the students were waiting to be called in, everyone looked up to see who this lanky young man was. I looked around and saw their staring faces. I opened my mouth and began to speak boldly in tongues. Everyone heard those tongues. Immediately, they knew that I was some kind of born-again, charismatic zealot.

In that instance, I fulfilled this Scripture which says, "First say peace be to this house." I had indirectly informed them about the Gospel of peace which I stood for. From that moment unbelievers and Christians alike knew my stand.

One day, I visited a sister in Volta hall, the ladies' hall of the University of Ghana, in Accra, Ghana. As I knocked on her door, I noticed several invitation cards in her message box. Out of curiosity, I picked one of them and read it. It said:

You are invited by ...
Tall hunk of a toe-tapper
Love lapper and this is the gapper
...its me, Mr. Pee

I read this wondering what it meant. It was actually an invitation to a wild party. And this was not the only invitation she had. There were several similar invitations for this young lady. I thought to myself : "We are all in the first year of the university, how come she has been invited to so many parties and I have not received even one invitation?" This young lady had not made her stand clear and that is why unbelievers had the boldness to invite her for wild parties.

PROTON AND SUFFERING

"But first (PROTON) must he suffer many things, and be rejected of this generation" (Luke 17:25).

1. You must experience some suffering before enjoying the higher blessings of God.

I have noticed that there is no successful minister who does not have a story of suffering and difficulties. Recently, a visiting minister, whose ministry I knew little about, came to speak in our church. As he shared his life testimony, I marvelled at how this principle is played out consistently in everyone's life.

He had been through many things. He had been hungry on many occasions; he had encouraged his wife on several occasions. He had been without money and food many times. This man is now a very successful minister in the country where he lives. The story is always the same. The suffering comes before the glory.

2. Paying this price is nothing compared to the glory that will be revealed in your life.

On the day the temple was dedicated, Solomon made many sacrifices to the Lord. After the sacrifices had been offered, the glory filled the temple and no one could stand to minister. God was moved by the sacrifice. God is still moved by your sacrifice.

The glory of God will surely come after the sacrifice. "Also king Solomon, and all the congregation of Israel that were assembled unto him before the ark, SACRIFICED SHEEP AND OXEN, WHICH COULD NOT BE TOLD NOR NUMBERED FOR MULTITUDE. And the priests brought in the ark of the covenant of the LORD unto his place, to the oracle of the house, into the most holy place, even under the wings of the cherubim: For the cherubims spread forth their wings over the place of the ark, and the cherubim covered the ark and the staves thereof above. And they drew out the staves of the ark, that the ends of the staves were seen from the ark before the oracle; but they were not seen without. And there it is unto this day. There was nothing in the ark save the two tables which Moses put therein at Horeb, when the LORD made a covenant with the children of Israel, when they came out of Egypt. And it came to pass, when the priests were come out of the holy place: (for all the priests that were present were sanctified, and did not then wait by course: Also the Levites which were the singers, all of them of Asaph, of Heman, of Jeduthun, with their sons and their brethren, being arrayed in white linen, having cymbals and psalteries and harps, stood at the east end of the altar, and with them an hundred and twenty priests sounding with trumpets:)

It came even to pass, as the trumpeters and singers were as one, to make one sound to be heard in praising and thanking the LORD; and when they lifted up their voice with the trumpets and cymbals and instruments of musick, and praised the LORD, saying, For he is good; for his mercy endureth for ever: that then the house was filled with a cloud, even the house of the LORD; So that the priests could not stand to minister by reason of the cloud: FOR THE GLORY OF THE LORD HAD FILLED THE HOUSE OF GOD" (2 Chronicles 5:6-14).

The Power and Beauty of the Words of Jesus 21

■ SUPERIORITY TO ALL WORDS

It is enough to place the Words of Jesus above all human words. We only need to know for certain what Jesus believed in, to believe the same. Today, the Words of Jesus are separated from the rest of Scripture by red ink in many Bibles. Formerly, the beautiful words of Christ were indiscriminately mingled with the rest of Scripture. Modern Bibles assign the deserved honour to these timeless Words. They are placed in a class of their own. A class without equal.

At the Reformation, men focused on the work of Christ on Calvary. Later, the person of Christ was the focus of attention. In later years, the details of His earthly life from the manger to the cross became the focus of intense study. However, I believe that the hour has come when His Words will be the focus of attention. A study of the earthly life and the works of Christ are different from a study of the Words of Christ.

The church today has in them, more of the Pauline epistles than the Gospels. As the end approaches, His Words will take preeminence in the church. Saint Paul must be read in the light of Christ rather than Christ in the light of Saint Paul.

Fortunately, the unique value of the Words of Jesus is being recognized. At last, these Words have been assigned the distinction and the commanding authority they deserve. As someone said, Jesus is the best teacher of His own religion.

The brief commands that pronounced healing on numerous sick bodies leave the reader in awe of the Saviour.

The sentences from the Sermon on the Mount have been lodged in the memories of all Christians.

The parables of Jesus have never failed to charm their readers.

The farewell discourses recorded in the book of John have in every generation been the guidance and consolation of the Church.

The rambling stories of Jesus are unforgettable and unrivalled.

Truly, the power and beauty of the Words of Jesus are cherished by all and sundry.

WHAT JESUS SAID ABOUT HIS OWN WORDS

1. Jesus taught that words in general are not trivial things.

Jesus took a very high and unusual view of the value of words in general. There is nothing that appears more trivial to the ordinary man than a word. No, said Jesus, it does not end there, and it does not end ever. Words are not trivial. When they are called into existence they become living things which travel through time and space, doing good and evil; and they will confront us again at the last day. "But I say unto you, That every idle word that men shall speak, they shall give account thereof in the day of judgment" (Matthew 12:36).

2. Jesus taught that words would be used as a basis for judgement.

The influence of our words on our destiny will be extraordinary: "...for by thy words thou shalt be justified and by thy words, thou shall be condemned." (Matthew 12:37). There is nothing of which the average man is more surely convinced than that his tongue is his own, and that he can at will make it utter words, either good or evil.

3. Jesus taught that words were the unmistakable portrayal of a person.

If the speaker be good, then his words are good, but if the speaker be evil, then his words are inevitably evil. "O generation of vipers, how can ye, being evil, speak good things? for out of the abundance of the heart the mouth speaketh" (Matthew 12:34). A man cannot alter the character of his words unless he first alters his own nature. For out of the abundance of the heart, the mouth speaks. Such was Christ's concept of words, and such were His own Words. They were the overflowings of His very heart.

4. Jesus declared in sober earnest that His words would outlast the created heavens and earth.

"Heaven and earth shall pass away: but my words shall not pass away" (Luke 21:33). Poets and thinkers have sometimes boasted that their words would survive the most permanent works of man such as pyramids and monuments. But Jesus declared that His Words would outlast the most stable works of God.

5. Jesus spoke of the attachment to His words as the sign of attachment to Himself. Jesus considered devotion to His words to be the test of discipleship.

"...If you continue in my words then are you my disciples. You will know the truth and the truth will make you free" (John 8:31, 32).

"Jesus answered and said unto him, If a man love me, he will keep my words: and my Father will love him, and we will come unto him, and make our abode with him. He that loveth me not keepeth not my sayings: and the word which ye hear is not mine, but the Father's which sent me" (John 14:23-24).

6. When Mary was seated at His feet listening to His words, He declared that she was doing the one thing that was needful.

"But one thing is needful: and Mary hath chosen that good part, which shall not be taken away from her" (Luke 10:42).

7. Jesus attributed to His words the power of cleansing the heart.

"Now ye are clean through the word which I have spoken unto you" (John 15:3).

"Verily, verily, I say unto you, If a man keep my saying, he shall never see death" (John 8:51). "It is the spirit that quickeneth; the flesh profiteth nothing: the words that I speak unto you, they are spirit, and they are life" (John 6:63).

"Then Simon Peter answered him, Lord, to whom shall we go? Thou hast the words of eternal life" (John 6:68).

8. Jesus alleged that the eternal destiny of His hearers would depend on the attitude they assumed to His words.

"He that rejecteth me, and receiveth not my words, hath one that judgeth him: the word that I have spoken, the same shall judge him in the last day" (John 12:48).

"Therefore whosoever heareth these sayings of mine, and doeth them, I will liken him unto a wise man, which built his house upon a rock: And the rain descended, and the floods came, and the winds blew, and beat upon that house; and it fell not: for it was founded upon a rock. And every one that he areth these sayings of mine, and doeth them not, shall be likened unto a foolish man, which built his house upon the sand: And the rain descended, and the floods came, and the winds blew, and beat upon that house; and it fell: and great was the fall of it" (Matthew 7:24-27).

WHAT OTHERS SAID ABOUT THE WORDS OF JESUS

"...Never man spake like this man" (John 7:46).
"...What a Word is this!..." (Luke 4:36).

The Words of Jesus are the Words of the Son of God. No other man ever spoke like He did. His Words have outlasted any other words spoken by any other person. Even though Jesus was only thirty years old when He began to speak, it is obvious that His Words were not the words of a young zealot trying to impress people. They were the most profound sayings ever known to man. Down through the centuries, men from all walks of life have commented on the uniqueness of the Words of Jesus. I have produced a few of these quotations for your benefit.

Jesus Christ is the outstanding personality of all time...No other teacher - Jewish, Christian, Buddhist, Mohammedan - is still a teacher whose teaching is such a guidepost for the world we live in. Other teachers may have something basic for an Oriental, Arab, or an Occidental; but every act and word of Jesus has value for all of us. He became the light of the world. Why shouldn't I, a Jew be proud of that?

Sholem Ash

For when we consider what a large number of sayings are recorded of--or at least attributed to Him, it becomes most remarkable that in literal truth there is no reason why any of his words should ever pass away in the sense of becoming obsolete...contrast Jesus Christ with other thinkers of like antiquity. Even Plato, who though some four hundred years before Christ in point in time, was greatly in advance of him in respect of philosophic thought, is nowhere in this respect as compared with Christ. Read the dialogue and see how enormous is the contrast with the gospels in respect of errors of all kinds, reaching even into absurdity in respect of reason, and to sayings; shocking to the moral sense, yet this is confessedly the highest level of human reason on the lines of spirituality when unaided by alleged revelation.

G.J. Romanes

After reading the doctrines of Plato, Socrates or Aristotle, we feel the specific difference between their words and Christ's is the difference between an enquiry and a revelation.

Joseph Parker

For two thousand years, He [Jesus] has been the Light of the World and His words have not passed away.

Morris

His [Jesus] words were so completely parts and utterances of himself, that they had no meaning as abstract statements of truth uttered by him as a divine oracle of prophet. Take away himself as the primary (though not the ultimate) subject to every statement and they all fall to pieces.

F.J.A. Hort

But Jesus' words and acts are impressively integral and we trust those sayings we judge to be authentically his as revelatory of his person. When Jesus uses the personal pronoun 'I' ('but I say to you amen, I say to you') he stands and backs every word with personal fidelity and personal intentionality. If his words and acts are messianic in character, it is because he intends them to be, and if he intends them to be, then he is thinking of himself in messianic terms.

Gruenler

Christ' words are of permanent value because of his person; they endure because he endures.

Thomas

Statistically speaking, the gospels are the greatest literature ever written. They are read by more people, quoted by more authors, translated into more tongues, represented in more art, set to more music, than any other book or books written by any man in any century in any land.

But the words of Christ are not great based on the grounds that they have such a statistical edge over any others words. They are read more, quoted more, believed more and translated more because they are the greatest words ever spoken. And where is their greatness? Their greatness lies in their pure, lucid spirituality in dealing clearly, definitively, and authoritatively with the great problems that throb in the human breast; namely who is God? Does He love me? What should I do to please him? How does He look at my sin? How can I be forgiven? Where will I go when I die? How must I treat others?

No other man's words have the appeal of Jesus' words because no other man can answer those fundamental human questions as Jesus answered them. They are the kind of words and answers we would expect God to give, and we who believe in Jesus' deity have no problem as to why these words came from his mouth.

Bernard Ramm

Never did the speaker seek to stand more utterly alone than when He uttered His majestic utterance. Never did it seem more improbable that it should be fulfilled. But as we look across the centuries we see how it has been realized. His words have passed into law, they have passed into doctrines, they have passed into proverbs, they have passed into consolations, but they have never 'passed away'. What human teacher ever dared to claim an eternity for his words?

Maclean

Systems of human wisdom will come and go, kingdoms and empires will rise and fall, but for all time to come Christ will remain 'the Way, the Truth, and the Life.'

Schaff

No revolution that has ever taken place in society can be compared to that which has been produced by the words of Jesus.

Mark Hopkins

Christ's message is inexhaustible. Each generation finds it new and exciting.

Thomas

It is something said, "Everything that Jesus said has been said before him by others". Let us grant that this is true, what then? Originality may or may not be a merit. If the truth has already been uttered, the merit lies in repeating it, and giving it new and fuller application. But there are other considerations to be borne in mind. We have no other teacher who so completely eliminated the trivial, the temporal, and the false from his system. No one selected just the eternal and the universal, and combined them in a teaching, where all these great truths found their congenial home. These parallels from the teachings of others to that of Christ are brought together from this quarter and from that; how is it that none of these teachers furnishes us with any parallel to the teachings of Christ? As a whole, while each of them gives us such truths as he expresses mingled with a mass of what is trivial and absurd? How was it that a carpenter, of no special training, ignorant of the culture and learning of the Greeks, born of a people whose great teachers were narrow, sour, intolerant pedantic legalists, was the supreme religious teacher the world has known, whose supremacy here makes him the most important figure in the world's history?

W.S. Peake

Although without formal rabbinical training, he showed no timidity of self-consciousness, no hesitation as to what he felt to be truth. Without any thought of Himself or His audience, He spoke out fearlessly on every occasion, utterly heedless of the consequences to Himself, and only concerned for truth and the delivery of His father's message. The power of His teaching was also deeply felt. "His word was with power" (Luke 4:32). The spiritual force of His personality expressed itself in His utterances and held His hearers in its enthralling grasp. And so we are not surprised to read of the impression of uniqueness made by Him: "Never man spake like Him" (John 7:46).

The simplicity and charm and yet the depth, the directness, the universality, and the truth of His teachings made a deep mark on His hearers, and elicited the conviction that they were in the presence of a teacher such as man had never seen before. And thus the large proportion of teaching in the Gospel, and the impressions evidently created by the Teacher Himself, are such that we are not at all surprised that years afterwards the great Apostle of the Gentiles should recall these things and say, "Remember the words of the Lord Jesus" (Acts 20:35). The same impression has been made in every age since the days of Christ and His immediate followers, and in any full consideration of His person as the substance of Christianity great attention must necessarily be paid to His teaching.

Griffith Thomas[1]

If God became a man we would expect a superman with super sayings. These super sayings are what have been captured in red letters in some Bibles.

CHARACTERISTICS OF THE WORDS OF JESUS

1. The sayings of Jesus were often so absolute that many have found them difficult to believe.

Many of the Words of Jesus appear to be extreme and are therefore ignored by a large number of believers. "But I say unto you, That whosoever is angry with his brother without a cause shall be in danger of the judgment: and whosoever shall say to his brother, Raca, shall be in danger of the council: but whosoever shall say, Thou fool, shall be in danger of hell fire" (Matthew 5:22).

2. The Words of Jesus were not influenced by men.

Most speakers are influenced by their audience. Ex-presidents give speeches and are paid over a hundred thousand dollars per session. Obviously you would want to say things that impress and please your audiences. Not so with Jesus. He had no one to please except His father. Jesus did not even attempt to get the respect of men. "I receive not honour from men" (John 5:41). It seemed He did not crave the approval of men; neither did He crave a large following. What He seemed to desire was to please His Father.

3. The Words of Jesus were so simple that they are rarely forgotten, even by children.

Once you hear either the sayings or the parables of Jesus, you rarely forget them. There have been many backslidden people who came back to God because they remembered their Sunday school Bible stories and Bible verses.

4. The Words of Jesus were easily understood by common people.

"... And the common people heard him gladly" (Mark 12:37).

5. The Words of Jesus were so anointed that they changed the lives of those that heard them.

"It is the spirit that quickeneth; the flesh profiteth nothing: the words that I speak unto you, they are spirit, and they are life" (John 6:63).

6. The Words of Jesus contain great love and kindness.

"Then came Peter to him, and said, Lord, how oft shall my brother sin against me, and I forgive him? till seven times? Jesus saith unto him, I say not unto thee, Until seven times: but, Until seventy times seven" (Matthew 18:21-22).

7. The Words of Jesus are superior to the words of Peter, James, John and Paul.

Paul, Peter, James and John were the servants of Christ. Although the Words of Jesus are lumped together with the teachings of Paul and other prophets, they should be separated because they are truly the Words of God. It is only fitting that they be typed out in red. What Jesus said must be taken more seriously than what Paul or Peter said. Remember that Paul is not the second Son of God. Paul was a servant of Jesus Christ. The Lord has used the writings of Paul to bless the church but these cannot be substituted for the Words of the Son of God Himself.

All that Paul, Peter or James taught must be received in this context. They were apostles building on the foundation laid by Christ Jesus. The very fact that the Lord allowed other apostles to write should not become a snare to us. We must receive the writings of the other apostles but we must know the difference.

Christ set the greatest example of teamwork and fruitfulness. He did not prevent others from ministering. He encouraged them and did not care if people were greatly blessed by these apostles.

However, it is up to us not to fall or walk into deception, but to recognize the Words of Jesus as the ultimate and final statements of truth. The Words of Jesus must be the guiding post for all Christians and ministers. We must assess our ministries by the Words of Jesus.

8. The Words of Jesus define the standards of heaven.

Our depraved and corrupt world has its own fallen standards for everything. Our estimation of good and bad is often very different from the standards of Heaven. We are often surprised to see what Jesus called the greatest or the least. Our human opinion is often a far cry from the judgement of God.

"At the same time came the disciples unto Jesus, saying, Who is the greatest in the kingdom of heaven? Whosoever therefore shall humble himself as this little child, the same is greatest in the kingdom of heaven" (Matthew 18:1,4).

9. The Words of Jesus contain the marking scheme for our final judgement.

"And then will I profess unto them, I never knew you: depart from me, ye that work iniquity" (Matthew 7:23). What will we be judged about? What questions will we be asked on that great

Day of Judgement? Jesus clearly outlined the basis for each one of our judgements. I know of no one who spoke with such clarity about life after death.

I have studied anatomy, physiology, biochemistry, pharmacology, chemical pathology etc. None of these books even broach the subject of what will happen after death. None of these books comments on this terrifying question.

The research of all scientists ends at the grave. The physicians arrive at a frontier they cannot cross. The philosophers reach the limits of their knowledge. The pathologist dissects the remains of the dead but cannot find out where the soul went.

The professors stumble at the pertinent question of life after death. But not Jesus! He confidently describes the after-life with authority never seen before.

10. The Words of Jesus contain the mysteries of heaven.

These mysteries are reserved for those who would search and discover great truths for themselves. "It is the glory of God to conceal a thing: but the honour of kings is to search out a matter" (Proverbs 25:2).

WHAT JESUS SAID ABOUT GLORIFYING GOD

"Herein is my Father glorified, that ye bear much fruit; so shall ye be my disciples" (John 15:8). Jesus clearly shows us how the Father is glorified.

1. God is glorified through the fruit we bear.

The more fruit we bear, the more we bring glory to the Father. Sometimes, you wonder what people are after. It is time to take the Words of Jesus seriously. Some pastors are not content with bearing much fruit because they bear this fruit under the banner of another man's ministry. I have watched as ministers have left the place of fruitfulness and moved into the deserts of ministry. Perhaps, it is more important to them to be independent than to bear fruit. It should be the desire of every minister to bear much fruit. Unfortunately the desire for money, position and fame is not compatible with the desire for fruitfulness.

2. Fruitfulness must be on top of the agenda of every true man of God.

Always ask yourself: "What can I do to bear more fruit than I am already bearing?" This is the reason why I want to have more churches. This is the reason I constantly press for church growth. That is why I write more books and preach as much as I do. I am striving for fruitfulness. I know that "Herein is the Father glorified..."

God placed the desire for fruitfulness in my heart. I have prayed for years that I would be fruitful.

For a brief period, I lived in Cleadon Village, Sunderland, England. Often, I was home alone and had a lot of time to pray. I always remember one rainy night when I walked up and down the road praying for fruitfulness. There are times you particularly remember your prayers because in that moment, you connected to Heaven in a special way.

That night, I believe I connected to Heaven in a special way. I had one cry on my heart, "Lord make me fruitful." I was only twenty years old then but God heard my prayer and now, more than twenty years later, I see much fruit around me. But it is still not enough, I want to bring more glory to the Father by bearing even more fruit.

Unfortunately, we have replaced God's explanation of what glorifies Him with our definition of what glorifies Him.

One day, a brother came from the university campus with "good news". He said, "God is being glorified on campus, the Spirit is moving." I was very interested to know what was happening so I asked, "Really, what is happening?"

With a broad smile he answered, "Many students have passed their exams!" My brother had equated the passing of exams to the move of the Spirit of God. I explained to him that the passing of exams was a great thing but the indicator of the move of God was when people were saved and gifts of the Spirit manifested.

When our desires are met, we think God is being glorified. The hymn is sung "To God be the glory great things He has done." To us, a new car or a new house means God is glorified.

When weddings take place we like to sing to the glory of God. The parents of the bride and groom will say, "God has glorified Himself today." The bride will say, "God has brought glory to His name." Dear sister, I am sure there was glory at your wedding. But Jesus said He would be glorified when you bear much fruit.

"Herein is my Father glorified, that ye bear much fruit; so shall ye be my disciples" (John 15:8).

3. Staying connected to Jesus is the master key to bearing much fruit.

"I am the vine, ye are the branches: He that abideth in me, and I in him, the same bringeth forth much fruit: for without me ye can do nothing" (John 15:5). Human effort can never substitute the effect of being deeply connected to Jesus. The fruit you bear is a result of your connection to God.

Without walking in the ways and Words of Jesus, you cannot bear fruit. Without the connection to Jesus and the Father, there will be little fruit. The fruit of a man of God's ministry is therefore a sign of his connection to the vine.

A study of the vineyards of Palestine shows that some of the vines do not bear much fruit. They were vines alright but the connection to the roots was not deep and therefore they did not bear fruit. The fruit you bear is a reflection of the connection between you, the Father and Jesus.

By inference, we could say that people who have no fruit are not connected to Him. Without Him you can do nothing. Everybody knows that! That means that people who are doing nothing are probably without Him.

WHAT JESUS SAID ABOUT ACHIEVEMENT

"... for without me ye can do nothing" (John 15:5b). When Jesus was saying that we could not do anything without Him, He was saying that without being spiritual, you cannot succeed in this life and you can do nothing.

It may seem like some people achieve a lot without Him, but it is not so. "Except the Lord build the house, they labour in vain that build it" (Psalm 127:1).

1. Jesus said that we could do nothing without Him.

Comparing the men of Babel gives tremendous insight to the concept of achievement. The men of Babel desired a great name but it was Abraham who got the great name. The men of Babel wanted to get to Heaven but it was Abraham who got to Heaven. It seems that a portion of Heaven is even named after him: Abraham's bosom.

The story of the tower of Babel is a good example of men coming together to achieve something for themselves. They said, "Let us build something for ourselves. Let us make a name for ourselves. Let us prevent ourselves from being scattered." God was not in their thoughts. They depended on the power of unity rather than on the power of God. "And they said, Go to, let us build us a city and a tower, whose top may reach unto heaven; and let us make us a name, lest we be scattered abroad upon the face of the whole earth" (Genesis 11:4). However, without God, all their human efforts ended in confusion and fragmentation.

2. All the efforts we make without God will end in confusion and scattering.

Many attempts to be happily married have ended in confusion and scattering. Divorce is the separation of families. Many attempts to be rich have ended in confusion. Many attempts at higher education and higher achievement have not brought the happiness men expected. The result has often been confusion and despair. Who can do these things for us? Only the Lord can.

Just a few verses after the unfortunate story of the men of Babel is the story of Abraham. Abraham lived a life of obedience to God. He did not try to achieve anything for himself. God told him, " I will make you a great nation and I will bless you and make your name great." "And I will make of thee a great nation, and I will bless thee, and make thy name great; and thou shalt be a blessing" (Genesis 12:2).

Isn't it amazing that all the goals of the men of Babel were given freely to Abraham? Abraham accomplished all the goals of the men of Babel. His achievements were only because he trusted God. Today, Abraham's name is great. Everyone in the world has heard of Abraham, including those in the most remote corners of my country, Ghana. Six thousand years later, Abraham has a great nation in Israel and the men of Babel have nothing! We all know that Abraham is in Heaven because of the story of Lazarus and the Rich Man.

What a mighty God we serve! He is able to accomplish more than we can think or imagine! A life lived in obedience and faith towards God cannot be compared to a life of strenuous human efforts for self-establishment. That is why I am in the ministry, and that is why I am serving the Lord, obeying Him and living for Him. All I have is what He gives me. All I do is what I do with Him. Without Him I do not even want to live.

WHAT JESUS SAID ABOUT DECLINE

"If a man abide not in me, he is cast forth as a branch, and is withered; and men gather them, and cast them into the fire, and they are burned" (John 15:6).

1. Jesus told us that when we do not abide in Him, He will cast us off and we will wither.

"To wither" means "to decline, to shrink", and "to be lowered in rank". In your life and ministry you must look out for these trends.

"To wither" also means "to decrease, to be lowered in rank" and "to be downgraded". Sometimes a weakening and declining ministry is a result of disconnection from Jesus. Once the branch is disconnected from the vine, the withering begins.

2. It is your duty to press close to the vine.

Stay connected to God! Press hard to stay close and to be intimate with God. God is always doing a new thing. Perhaps the Lord moved on long ago and you have been left behind. This may be the explanation for the decline and the downgrading of your ministry.

3. Declining ministries may be disconnected from the current move of God.

I once saw an amazing picture. It was the picture of a bridge over dry ground. Believe it or not the river had moved from under the bridge to the side of it. Because of this, the bridge no longer passed over water but over dry land. This had happened because of a severe flood. After the floodwaters dropped, the river had amazingly shifted! "What would they do now that the river has shifted?" Would they still use the old bridge? I have outlined below a few of the possibilities.

- You could say that we invested a lot of money in this bridge and therefore we are not going to abandon it now.
- You could say, "This bridge has worked for us from the beginning and we don't see why it will not work now."
- "We have sentimental and emotional feelings for this bridge and cannot bring ourselves to abandoning it."
- You could also say, "This is the way we've done it all these years and we are going to be faithful to our original bridge."
- "We don't have enough money to build a new one."
- I am sure some would say, "It will take too much to start something new."

Dear pastor, wake up to the realities. Things have changed! If you don't accept the fact that the river has moved and decide to build a new bridge, the usefulness of your bridge will decline. There will be no one walking on your bridge any more. Your ministry is like that bridge. Many souls walked on it to salvation because then, it was relevant. Your bridge is connected to the right spots on the ground. But when your bridge is no longer connected to the right spot, people will not need it any more. The number of people who cross the bridge will decline. Oh, how many ministries and men of God wither because of this? Often it is not the presence of sin, but they are not connected, and abiding in Christ. They are not learning the new things that God is doing.

HOW JESUS WILL DECIDE WHO THE GREATEST IS

"Whosoever therefore shall humble himself as this little child, the same is greatest in the kingdom of heaven" (Matthew 18:4).

1. The divine measurement of greatness is completely different from the earthly.

I once attended an international gathering of pastors of large churches. These were pastors of the largest churches in their countries. All the pastors had airs of importance around them. Most of us were preoccupied with ourselves and how successful we had been in our respective nations. I wondered to myself, "Who is the most successful pastor here? Who is the greatest?"

I sat by one American pastor who asked me about the income of my church. I hesitated. He then told me the income of his church. I did a quick calculation in my head and I realized that this pastor takes in one month what I take in a year.. I became even more hesitant to declare the income of my church. It sounded too little to be true.

Then another American mentioned how much he spent on television per hour. I realized that he paid for one hour what I paid for one year of TV broadcast. As we moved around the room chatting and making friends I would ask, "What is your church like?"

One person would mention, "I have sixteen thousand members," "I have twenty thousand members," "I have eleven thousand members." I tell you, I couldn't find anybody with less than ten thousand members! I became intimidated as I walked among the "greats" in ministry.

Later on, I met these pastors at the Hilton Hotel of that city. Many of them were at ease in the environment of wealth. They had travelled first class and were very comfortable in a five-star environment. Of course I was also happy to be there and made myself comfortable. Later that night, I thanked God for putting me amongst the greatest pastors on earth. Surely, I thought, I must now be one of the greatest pastors too. "This is the company I want to be in," I mused. "And I am going to stay close to these wonderful and great men of God."

Later on, we attended the conference and when I arrived in the entrance lobby, the administrator walked up to me and stuck a badge with some little flowers on me. I looked at it and it said ,"V.I.P". I thought to myself, "I am going higher with every passing minute." I looked around to see whether other people had this same badge and I noticed that it was just a select few who had this badge. Those of us with the V.I.P. badges were escorted to the front rows of the hall. As I sat on the front row, I looked back and I knew that God had lifted me from the ranks and promoted me.

When I was finally leaving the conference, I was taken to the airport in a fantastic, black, executive car. I felt like a president. I knew for sure that God had elevated me in the ministry. As I sat in the backseat of my car, I noticed all kinds of modern gadgets in the car which included a television. I pressed a few of the buttons and began to enjoy them. I sat back, crossed my legs and enjoyed the ride to the airport. The car was like a large executive sitting room. Surely I had reached the heights of ministry and was rubbing shoulders with the greatest! I now had my confirmation that I was indeed one of the greatest.

It was years later that the Lord gave me a new understanding of who He considers to be great.

2. The greatest amongst us is the most humble.

Jesus never talked about the size of your church, the car you drive, or the money you have. Actually, the greatest pastor at that conference was the most humble amongst us. Unfortunately success and wealth are usually not bedfellows of humility. Most wealthy and successful people lose the humility they had. The greatest amongst us was not the one with the V.I.P. badge, but the most humble one at heart. Thank God that it is possible to be humanly great and also great in the eyes of God. We must strive for greatness in the sight of God.

One day, I sat with a group of my pastors. I told them, "You may be greater than me in Heaven." They laughed. "How could you say something like that?" They were so used to submitting to me and seeing me ahead of them.

I asked them, "Can you not imagine me serving you in Heaven?"

I told them, "Don't be deceived by what you see on earth. The greatest amongst us is the most humble at heart." The first shall be last and the last shall be first.

Mercy, Lord!

HOW JESUS DEFINED THE WORK OF GOD

"Jesus answered and said unto them, This is the work of God, that ye believe on him whom he hath sent" (John 6:29).

"Verily, verily, I say unto you, He that believeth on me, the works that I do shall he do also; and greater works than these shall he do; because I go unto my Father" (John 14:12). I have always used the verse in John 14:12 as a standard for my life, a mark I must attain. To be able to do the works of Jesus and possibly, greater works, is one of my goals. Most of the time, I forget about the greater works. At least, I want to be able to do the works that Jesus did.

1. Jesus' works were preaching, teaching and healing.

These Scriptures above explain why we do not see the works of Jesus in many churches. The only condition for doing these great works is believing. He did not say that any one who was anointed would do the greater works. He did not say anyone who had seen a vision would do the greater works. He said, "He that believeth, the works that I do shall he do also and greater works than these shall he do."

2. John 6:29 gives a direct key to doing the works of Jesus: to believe.

Many times, I have asked myself how I can do these works of God. But it is a question that Jesus answered. The simple answer from Jesus was "believe". Of course we all claim to believe but why are we not able to do these great works? I know that we would have expected Jesus to say something like "Pray more, be holy, seek the face of God." But all He said was "believe". A little analysis will reveal that most of us do not really believe the Words of Jesus. I say that we do not believe because our lives demonstrate the exact opposite of the Scriptures. Here are two Scriptures that we commonly disbelieve.

a. I go to prepare a place for you.

"In my Father's house are many mansions: if it were not so, I would have told you. I go to prepare a place for you." (John 14:2). If we believed that the Lord was preparing a place for us, our lives would be quite different.

However, by the attitude of the ordinary Christian, it is obvious that we have little regard for these Words of Jesus. If He is preparing a place for us, that is all well and good. But we need some mansions here and now. We couldn't care two hoots about any mansion in the sky. We need a mansion in town and we want it now! This very attitude keeps us from being eternity-minded. Because Christians do not consider eternity, they are unable to really work for God.

2. Don't lay up treasures on earth.

"Lay not up for yourselves treasures upon earth...But lay up for yourselves treasures in heaven..." (Matthew 6:19-20). There could be no clearer instruction than this. He said, " Prepare for Heaven. Lay up your treasure over there! Do not bother to pile up things on earth".

Yet, most of the church, led by its pastors, are busy laying up treasures on earth. Even when we are poor, we have a goal to lay up as much treasure as we can,on this earth. Our vision is to do the exact opposite of what Jesus asked us to do. As long as we do not picture treasures in Heaven, we will not be motivated to work for God.

The ordinary Christian is highly motivated to work for institutions like the Barclays Bank or other banks. They see it as a way to lay up treasures on earth. How difficult it is for us to leave prestigious secular jobs and work in the church. It is seen as the highest kind of folly. To work in the church is perceived as madness. But working for God makes you lay up treasures in Heaven.

A professor of the Medical School I attended, once asked his staff, "Where do you go to church?" When the professor found out that he came to my church, he laughed for several minutes. Then he asked, "This Dag Heward-Mills, is he normal?"

"Why do you ask whether he is normal?" asked the gentleman.

The professor answered, "Does a normal person behave that way? Does a normal medical student start a church in a classroom?" Then he continued laughing.

One lady was told that she needed to see a psychiatrist because she wanted to work in the ministry instead of elsewhere. These anti-work-for-God attitudes are also attitudes of born-again Christians. It was a born-again Christian who thought his sister needed to see a psychiatrist because she wanted to work in the church.

Such disbelief is not found only amongst unbelieving professors but also amongst born-again charismatic believers. This attitude which despises eternal work is found in my own church. It is found amongst lay pastors. It is even found amongst full-time pastors who pray that their children will never work for a church. Laying up treasures in Heaven, is the kind of truth we choose to ignore. Laying up treasures on earth (the exact opposite of what Jesus taught) is seen as the more sensible thing to do.

It is these amazing attitudes that show what we really believe. It is no wonder that we cannot do much of the work of God. Moslems often show a much higher faith in the life after this life. Their suicide-bombers are the greatest evidence of this. All over the world, these suicide-bombers die fearlessly for their faith. Meanwhile, Christians cower in fear, disbelief and weakness, unable even to change jobs for the gospel's sake.

Where are the missionaries of old who gave their lives in foreign nations that the Gospel may advance? Where are the martyrs of the early church who died for their faith? These heavenly-minded people laid down their lives for the Kingdom of God to advance. These men, conscious of eternity, have brought real advancement to the Church of God. They really demonstrated that they believed. That is how come they did the works of God.

WHAT JESUS SAID ABOUT SACRIFICE

"And when he had called the people unto him with his disciples also, he said unto them, Whosoever will come after me, let him deny himself, and take up his cross, and follow me" (Mark 8:34).

1. Jesus said we should take up our crosses and follow Him.

This speaks of sacrifice. Oh, how we sacrifice for other things! Our pastors and our churches are earthly-minded. Don't you see that a new Gospel that teaches us to grasp at earthly things has replaced the Words of Jesus?

Thousands of people followed Jesus until He told them to drink His blood and eat His body. As soon as Jesus preached about sacrifice, His church reduced in size. But that is how to do the works of Jesus. To believe in the cross and all that it stands for. I believe that the preaching of the cross will become popular again. The preaching of the cross is the preaching of the true Gospel. It is time to return to the cross. It is time to sing about the cross again.

Today, Christians believe more in their earthly existence than in their heavenly reward. If we were to pay the same price we pay for earthly things, perhaps the work of God would be done.

I once spoke to a doctor and asked how many years he had studied medicine. He answered, "About twenty-two years." I thought to myself, "Is it not marvellous?" Someone can spend twenty-two years of his life to acquire a profession he will use for another twenty years. But how many days of our lives do we sacrifice in order to follow Jesus?"

Unfortunately, we don't really believe the ministry is something worth dying for. I always ask myself, "What is the difference between my ministry and that of Christ?" Where are the healings? Where is the preaching and the teaching?"

If you want to follow Jesus you must believe in the reality of sacrifice. You must follow the example of Jesus and pay the high price God is asking of you. You must preach about the cross. You must take up your cross. You cannot sit in the bank and send people to the cross. It doesn't work that way. You have to take up your cross and follow Jesus who took up His cross!

HOW JESUS DEFINED THE KEY TO NEW DIMENSIONS IN MINISTRY

"And said, Verily I say unto you, Except ye be converted, and become as little children, ye shall not enter into the kingdom of heaven" (Matthew 18:3).

Pastors are often the opposite of children. They get to a point where they cannot be taught any longer. Most pastors do not listen to tapes. They do not say "Amen" when the preaching is going on. They do not lift up their hands when the worship is going on.

Most pastors would never respond to an altar call, no matter how much they needed the prayer. We are so conscious of ourselves and would not like to look foolish before anyone. Because we are so different from children, we are unable to enter the Kingdom. Salvation is not the only thing that requires a childlike attitude.

1. Childlikeness is required to enter every other department of the Kingdom of God.

You will not enter a higher dimension of preaching or church growth because you refuse to be childlike. A child is ready to learn something new. A child believes that he doesn't know everything. Children believe almost every fairy tale. But you believe almost nothing. I have had to be childlike to improve my preaching. I have constantly modified my style and approach to preaching. Initially my preaching was commonsensical because the person I understudied was a rational, common sense teacher. With time I realized that my people were more open to stirring, rousing and exciting preaching. I decided to learn how to do that as well. I had to learn this from those who were good at it.

I had to be childlike and open to a completely different kind of ministry. When you are a rational, common sense preacher it is easy to look down on inspirational, emotional and encouraging speakers. With pride, you disdain them because they don't seem to say much. There does not seem to be much substance in their many words. You think to yourself, "He does not have enough points or Scriptures."

2. Childlikeness in the ministry will enable you to learn from anyone.

This includes people below you and people you don't respect. You will never look down on another man of God and consider him to be irrelevant. You will know that there is something to learn from everyone.

I often learn something from every church I visit. Recently one of my branch churches had a special dress down outreach service and I thought it was an excellent idea. I decided to copy them immediately. I have no problem learning from my own sons in the ministry.

Most of us are kept out of new dimensions of ministry because of our pride and self-importance. How could I be superior to another minister? Why would I be overconfident and develop an air of self-importance? This attitude keeps us from entering newer and higher dimensions of ministry.

There was a time in my ministry; I didn't minister the Spirit much. However there was a pastor who flowed in all kinds of weird manifestations of the Spirit. I was curious, I was childlike, and I wanted to learn as much as I could. I began to attend programmes where he was ministering. I also invited him to our church. I would watch in amazement as this pastor ministered under a peculiar anointing. Every kind of manifestation of the Spirit would take place. I once saw a lady moving on the floor like a snake!

One day, this pastor was invited to another church and he ministered there for a few days. I later met the pastor who invited him. I was surprised at the derogatory remarks he made about this "minister of manifestations". He confidently intimated that , "These manifestations take us nowhere and there is nothing to them."

But I wondered to myself, "Why is this pastor cutting himself away from something new?" We often cut ourselves away from new and higher dimensions of God's Kingdom. No one knows it all. God has intentionally given bits of knowledge to different parts of His body. This is God's design. It is intended to humble us. It is intended to make us need each other and ask each other for help.

What can be more humbling than to have to ask someone for help? Because I had a childlike (learner's) attitude towards the manifestations of the Spirit, I now minister and flow comfortably in that area.

I remember when I wanted to go into the healing ministry. I prayed about it and asked the Lord what to do. The Lord pointed out a particular minister to me. He told me to follow him and I would receive the anointing to minister to the sick. As I began to listen to this minister's tapes, I found them difficult to understand.

My wife found them even more difficult to comprehend. Once, I said to myself, "What kind of preaching is this? No one could possibly understand it." But I kept on listening to his tapes and following his ministry. As I humbled myself and continued, a day came when things began to fall in place. I suddenly understood what was going on and could follow the message. I would watch him minister and I would get blessed. I began to know what to do in the healing ministry. Gradually, I climbed into a very difficult but worthwhile dimension of ministry. What a humbling journey it is to enter into new dimensions of God's Kingdom!

Dear pastor, you may be kept out of many wonderful aspects of God's Kingdom because you are not childlike. A child does not look at age, sex or background! A child simply receives! Humble yourself in the sight of the Lord and He will lift you into new dimensions of ministry!

WHAT JESUS SAID ABOUT THE MOTIVATION FOR PASTORS

"But I receive not testimony from man: but these things I say, that ye might be saved" (John 5:34).

"How can ye believe, which receive honour one of another, and seek not the honour that cometh from God only?" (John 5:44). The "honour of man" is the single greatest influence on ministers apart from the Holy Spirit. The honour of man is simply the respect and admiration that comes from other men in society. Jesus made it clear that He did not receive respect and admiration from men. This means that He did not do anything because men would honour Him. He explained, "How can you believe which receive honour one from another?" In other words how can you flow with God when it is important for you to have the respect and the honour of men?

I have discovered that the honour of men is the single most powerful determinant of what people do. Without knowing it, most of us have a group of human beings whose admiration and respect we crave. We long for them to approve of us and to admire our achievements. Our schooling, our spouses, our cars, houses, food, and our clothes are all designed to attract the credit of people around us. Just like the Holy Spirit, the honour of man is an invisible influence, but it is very real. Virtually every decision a ministry makes is a decision between following the Holy Spirit and following the honour of men. Let me give you seven examples:

1. THE HONOUR OF MAN WILL PREVENT YOU FROM BECOMING A PASTOR.

When I became a pastor initially, there were not many pastors in town. It was not an honourable thing to become a pastor. I heard people ridiculing me for calling myself a pastor. The thoughts of people's impressions of me could have kept me from obeying the call of God.

2. THE HONOUR OF MAN WILL PREVENT YOU FROM HAVING A CHURCH.

Having a church in the part of the city where our church is, was also challenging. It is situated at Korle Gonno, one of the deprived and difficult parts of Accra, Ghana. Who would want to come to church in such an area? The church building that we had acquired sat in the middle of a huge rubbish dump. Were we building a church to receive the admiration of men or were we building under the influence of the Holy Spirit?

Many years ago when I became a Christian, I would not have joined the church I did if the honour and admiration of men had been important to me. The church I joined was started by a former drug addict who had not gone beyond class three in school. I once took my little sisters to that church and they could not contain their laughter for one and a half hours as they listened to amazing grammatical blunders. The church service was held in the corridor of the pastor's father's house. My elitist family and friends could not easily relate with such a church and such a pastor.

Was I looking for the respect and admiration of the elitist community of Accra? Or was I looking to find the glory of God? I receive not honour from men.

3. The honour of man sometimes directs people to marry the wrong person.

Amazingly, we seem to need the approval and endorsement of people in our little world for even a marriage partner. There are people who marry doctors because the community will admire the marriage partnership. What do people say and what does God say? What people say seems to be so strong that it has virtually taken control of men of God. Don't forget what Jesus said: That which is highly esteemed in the sight of men is an abomination in the sight of God.

"And he said unto them, Ye are they which justify yourselves before men; but God knoweth your hearts: for that which is highly esteemed among men is abomination in the sight of God" (Luke 16:15).

Unfortunately, the honour of men which is so powerful in its influence, leads us to choose things which are an abomination to the Lord. Could it be that you put aside the will of God because you did not have the admiration of men? Perhaps you married an abomination because you sought the honour of men. Perhaps, in seeking for the admiration of men, you left the godly option and chose the wrong person. I receive not honour from men!

4. The honour of man will stop you from preaching the messages that God wants you to preach.

I would have changed the message I preached if I were looking for the honour of men. There are dignified messages that appeal to the intellect of the upper class and aristocratic community of my city. I could impress them with high-sounding words and secular teachings.

Someone once said my preaching was too simple. I thought to myself, "Who was simpler than Christ? Even little children understand His teachings." There are times people have even wondered whether I speak English properly because I don't speak with a certain polished diction.

I want to be like Paul who said: "And I, brethren, when I came to you, came not with excellency of speech or of wisdom, declaring unto you the testimony of God. For I determined not to know any thing among you, save Jesus Christ, and him crucified" (1 Corinthians 2:1-2).

I have stayed with the message of salvation and soul-winning. I know that I do not sound as impressive and dignified as some may want. But do I want to please God or do I want to please men? Paul said that if he pleased men, then he was not a servant of God. "For do I now persuade men, or God? or do I seek to please men? for if I yet pleased men, I should not be the servant of Christ" (Galatians 1:10).

Notice that pleasing men actually conflicts with our service to God. Why would Paul say that if he pleased men then he could not be a servant of God? It is because pleasing men is often diametrically opposed to pleasing God.

When I began to show my miracles services on TV, some of my church members appealed that I show only teaching services. They told me how some university lecturers were very impressed with my teaching services, and were worried that I would lose the respect and admiration of such noble people. "What will they think about you when they see you pouring oil on hundreds of people? What will they think when they see people falling down and screaming in the church service?" they asked me. Did people fall down and scream when Jesus ministered to them?

"And when the unclean spirit had torn him, and cried with a loud voice, he came out of him" (Mark 1:26).

Do I want to be like Jesus or do I want to be what the professor in the university wants me to be?

Ministering to the sick is not possible when you love the honour of men. You will stay as far away as possible from that if you want the respect and admiration of the upper class of society. You see, the noble have surgeons and doctors ready to treat them in European and American hospitals. They don't seek solutions in the church. When people stand to testify that they are healed of headaches and pain in the knees, the noble chuckle in disdain.

One night, a medical doctor watched me minister to the sick on TV. He sent a message to me through a doctor who was a member of my church. He said, "Tell Dag that if he wants to heal the sick he should come right here to the ward. We have sarcomas, chondroblastomas, cancers of the knee, and many other wild diseases on the ward. Tell him this is where the action is. He should come here to perform his wonders." This fellow made other condescending remarks about the ministry.

Having worked on the ward before, I know what is there. I do know that spiritual healing looks ridiculous in the eyes of surgeons, physicians, paediatricians and obstetricians. The question is: "Do I care about looking foolish before such people? Do I care about being despised by my medical colleagues and fellow doctors? Whose respect and admiration do I want? Jesus Christ's or Professor Big Stuff's?" I receive not honour from men.

5. The Honour of Man Will Prevent You From Being Full-Time in Ministry.

Being full-time in ministry would be impossible if I wanted the respect and admiration of men. My own father told me he could not imagine his son eating off the collection of church members.

Let me ask you a question, "In the eyes of men, which is more honourable: living off the collections of the poor masses or living from the income of a surgeon? Which of these would win more admiration: Being a pastor of a church in a slum of Accra or being a gynaecologist in Manhattan?" I want to be like Jesus and I want to be able to say, "I receive not honour from men."

Perhaps, there are more gifted people with higher callings than myself. However, many of these callings were never fulfilled because men loved the admiration of other men. I receive not honour from men! "But all their works they do for to be seen of men..." (Matthew 23:5).

6. The Honour of Man Will Lead You to Possess Things You Shouldn't Possess.

Perhaps you fear the scorn and disapproval of men. I tell you that if there is any one thing that guides us, it is this disease I call "seeking the honour of men".

The cars that we drive are often dictated by the honour of men. We have to drive cars with particular names. We sacrifice so much in order to have certain types of cars so that human beings would admire and endorse us.

There was a time that I was afflicted by this disease. Without knowing it, I wanted to drive certain cars to make men respect me. I realized that I was looking for men's admiration. Without knowing it,

I wanted them to be in awe of my wealth and power. Like many pastors do, I unconsciously thought people would respect my ministry because of my car.

As I grew up in the Lord, I didn't want people to notice me as I passed by, much less notice the car that I drove. I receive not honour from men!

7. THE HONOUR OF MAN WILL STOP YOU FROM RAISING THE FUNDS NECESSARY FOR MINISTRY WORK.

I once had a meeting with some pastors and told them about a need to take up some special offerings. I told them to lay aside their dignity and to seriously exhort the people to give. I explained to them, "If you guys do not receive the offering seriously, it will greatly affect the plans we have for the ministry."

Some weeks later, I found out that some of the pastors had ignored my instructions. So I met them again to find out why they had not taken the offerings the way I taught them. It was then that I realized that many of these pastors were under the influence of the honour of man.

Even though they were pastors, they were concerned about their reputation in the ministry. They did not want the congregation to think they were the kind who were into the ministry for money. They wanted to look good and dignified at all times.

Because I am a full-time minister, I had already lost that dignified stance where I could distance myself from money issues.

Pastors and the Approval of Man

Many times, without knowing it, the honour of man has been the strongest influence on ministers. Why wouldn't you want to stand on the corner of a street and preach? It is because you think you are a dignified pastor who is above the ranks of a zealous new convert. The church has shifted away from many practical things that yield tangible results. We don't care if the great commission is not fulfilled, once we can keep the good name we think we have in society.

Most pastors seem to want the approval and friendship of heads -of -state and government officials. Today friendship with presidents and politicians is used as a credential and stamp of approval. Have you noticed that Jesus never visited Herod or Pontius Pilate? He never sought to be friends with these secular authorities. How different we are today.

Pastors travel from nation to nation, meeting one president after another. When we tell our congregations that we met the President of Milagabostal City, for instance, there is a thundering applause of approval. However, if we inform them that 15 converts were won in Potomanto Village, there is a deafening silence, as the congregation doesn't seem to understand what it means! Meanwhile, there is great rejoicing in Heaven over one soul that is saved. Which Bible verse says, "There is great rejoicing in Heaven over one president that is visited?" It seems we are not looking for the applause of Heaven but the applause of men. "But all their works they do for to be seen of men..." (Matthew 23:5).

The big ministries which could reach the remote villages and towns of our nations rarely spend any time, effort or money on these places.

One day, I travelled to the north of Ghana for evangelism and church planting. I later discussed the trip with a pastor friend. When I mentioned that I had planted a church in that place, he sniggered and said, "You do well to plant churches in such places. As for me, I don't go to such places." I thought about his schedule. I realized that even though his ministry could afford to reach remote areas, it hardly did so. Perhaps God had not called him to such harvest fields. On the other hand, it is possible that God had called him, but he found it easier to work where men would recognize and endorse his ministry.

Dear friend, it is easier to work in the cities where men can endorse your ministry. After all, no one sees you when you are in that village. Don't forget that the honour of God is far more important than the approval and honour of men. I receive not honour from men!

Jesus Rebukes the Pastors

"And love the uppermost rooms at feasts, and the chief seats in the synagogues, And greetings in the markets, and to be called of men, Rabbi, Rabbi" (Matthew 23:6-7). Unfortunately, the church today has become very similar to the group of people Christ encountered when He ministered on earth. Pastors today have developed similar characteristics to Pharisees and Sadducees.

I never knew that where a pastor sat was so important. My first encounter with this phenomenon was when a great healing evangelist visited Ghana. I noticed the politics that surrounded "who sits where". It was very important for people to be seated in front and on stage. I myself really wanted to be on stage, where the action was. I witnessed a regrettable incident, in which a very senior pastor had taken his seat in the front row. Suddenly, the host pastor and one of the healing evangelist's associates came up and pointed to him and said, "You, move." This senior minister was shocked as he was moved to the second row, to sit by me. I felt very sad about this.

On another occasion, a great man of God visited us in Ghana. This was another huge event where thousands were in attendance. We had invited all the great pastors of our nation to be at the programme. No matter how I tried, it seemed I would offend somebody. One of the pastors was deeply offended that I would put him on the second row whilst others he felt were junior to him were on the first row. Because of this, he shunned the rest of the programme.

Nowadays, whenever I have such programmes, I am always scared that I will offend somebody. I try my best to treat everyone with the greatest dignity and respect. But there always seems to be some problem.

Can you believe that my greatest headache when organizing a crusade is not the counselling of the new converts but the seating arrangement of the bigwig pastors?

One day, whilst discussing how to organize another big event, I said to my fellow organizer, "I have a bright idea, why don't we have a stage without any seats so that everyone sits in the congregation?" We tried to implement this plan but it just wouldn't work. We ended up overcrowding our stage with so many chairs so that no one would be offended! Even then, our struggle wasn't over. Who was going to sit on the first row?

Dear friend, what is important is not where we sit. The greatest in Heaven is the servant and not the most impressive pastor.

"But he that is greatest among you shall be your servant. And whosoever shall exalt himself shall be abased; and he that shall humble himself shall be exalted" (Matthew 23:11-12).

Once, I met with a group of young men and ladies who wanted to be pastors. I asked them, "Why do you want to be pastors?" None of them gave a satisfactory answer. It seemed they just wanted to be appointed as pastors. So I asked them, "Have you become like the Pharisees? You love greetings in the public places. You love to be called "pastor, pastor".

Instead of loving God and loving His people, we love the acclamation which comes with the ministry. Mercy forever! I do not write this because I am any different. I am as guilty as any one else. May God help us all! Ministers are unknowingly prey to pride, insecurity, and the fear of man. Without knowing it, our greatest influence is not the Holy Spirit. Other spirits like the fear of man have become our guiding posts.

■ THE PRIORITIES OF JESUS

1. The priorities of Jesus are revealed in the Gospels.

Whenever Jesus used the word "first", He was teaching us that there were some things that had priority over others. You will notice from the Scriptures below how Jesus commanded us to do certain things first (before others).

"Therefore if thou bring thy gift to the altar, and there rememberest that thy brother hath ought against thee; Leave there thy gift before the altar, and go thy way; first be reconciled to thy brother, and then come and offer thy gift" (Matthew 5:23-24).

"But seek ye first the kingdom of God, and his righteousness; and all these things shall be added unto you" (Matthew 6:33).

"And why beholdest thou the mote that is in thy brother's eye, but considerest not the beam that is in thine own eye? Or how wilt thou say to thy brother, Let me pull out the mote out of thine eye; and, behold, a beam is in thine own eye? Thou hypocrite, first cast out the beam out of thine own eye; and then shalt thou see clearly to cast out the mote out of thy brother's eye" (Matthew 7:3-5).

"Or else how can one enter into a strong man's house, and spoil his goods, except he first bind the strong man? and then he will spoil his house" (Matthew 12:29).

"Jesus said unto him, Thou shalt love the Lord thy God with all thy heart, and with all thy soul, and with all thy mind. This is the first and great commandment" (Matthew 22:37-38).

"Thou blind Pharisee, cleanse first that which is within the cup and platter, that the outside of them may be clean also" (Matthew 23:26).

The priorities of Jesus are stated throughout the Gospels.

2. The concept of priorities has to do with which option should be given first place.

When you are a sinner you basically choose between good and evil. As you grow in the Lord you begin to have more options. Your choices are no longer just between good and evil, but sometimes between good and good. In terms of what to do there will be several good things to choose from. When you get to that point it is important that you understand the concept of priorities. Which one should I do first?

It is interesting to know the number of things Jesus said should be done first. The Scriptures above give examples of things that Jesus said should be done first. When something that is supposed to be done second is done first, many things go wrong.

Sex before Marriage or Marriage before Sex

I was recently in an African country where my host took me to a cemetery. I was amazed at the fresh graves that were gradually filling every space. At a dinner with another pastor friend, he gave me an incredible account of the number of funerals that he was conducting in his city. He told us that they had had so many funerals that pastors no longer conducted funeral services. Cell leaders had taken over this duty.

I listened in amazement. He went on and described how they no longer buried people lying down because there was no space in the cemetery. He described how they buried them vertically, standing up! I thought to myself, "In such a situation do you say, "Rest in peace," or "Stand in peace'?" What was the cause of this unprecedented wave of death? Why were so many people dying?

The answer was simple: the second thing had come before the first thing. Sex had come before marriage. When marriage comes before sex, these things ideally do not occur. Sex is supposed to be experienced only after marriage. In that country, sex is an experience occurring largely outside the context of marriage. This is just one example of how many complicated problems occur because priorities get mixed up.

JESUS, HOW MUCH TIME DO WE HAVE?

What is the time according to God's clock? There are three times that are running simultaneously. These are "my time", "your time" and "the time". "Then Jesus said unto them, My time is not yet come: but your time is alway ready" (John 7:6). Take a look at your watch right now. In the natural that is your time. Take a look at some one else's watch. That is his time. But what is the time? In real life, every watch has a slightly different time. My watch is usually set a few minutes fast to help me overcome the spirit of lateness. Other people have more accurate watches. This phenomenon gives rise to a multitude of different times for everyone.

1. In the spirit realm, we all have different times.

My time is different from your time. That is why Jesus said, "My time is not yet come but your time is always ready."

A few years ago, Princess Diana shocked the world by making a sudden and tragic exit. No one expected her to die when she did. No one expected her to die on the Sunday morning that she died. A week before she died, if you had asked me, "What is the time?" I would have said, "It is Sunday morning, and time for church".

If you had asked her the same question she would probably have answered, "It is another Sunday morning; and a few days before I go to be with my boyfriend in France." But the time was actually seven days to her death. Unfortunately she didn't know it.

On the Saturday before she died, she was having dinner with her Egyptian boyfriend in Paris. If someone had asked you, "What time is it?" you might have said, "It is eight o'clock."

If someone had asked her she may have said, "It is Saturday night, and a time of lovemaking and dreaming of a better future." But she was wrong; the real time for her was a couple of hours before the end. She was also one week closer to her funeral.

"My time" speaks of where I am in the timetable of my life. "Your time", speaks of where you are in the timetable of "your life", and "the time", speaks of where we are in God's overall timetable.

2. Unknown to many people, this earthly life is very time-related.

Every instruction or opportunity is time-related. Hear this and hear it very well: every instruction that God has given to you has an invisible timer. A countdown begins the moment God speaks to you. The available time to perform that duty reduces with every passing hour. Many think they are just biding time and will take God seriously later. Do not be deceived! The expiry date of your grace period is fast approaching.

Like I said, Princess Diana might have been planning for her wedding. What she didn't know was that she was not far from the night of her exitus. She was oblivious to the fact that she was to be the subject of the largest funeral of all time. She didn't know the time. Do you know the time? Do we know the time?

If God has told you to do some work, the clock has begun to tick. A time will come when you will no longer be able to fulfil that instruction. Sometimes God speaks to you: "Finance my Kingdom." Perhaps that comes along with a five-year period wherein you can obey Him. Perhaps He tells you: "Go out as a missionary." Maybe that instruction has a ten-year lease.

Some people spend eight years of that period doing other things and then in the last two years, attempt to obey God. But their time is almost up. Nothing effective can be done in the remaining two years. One day, God is going to remove the element of time from our lives. This has been prophesied in the book of Revelation where He swore that there would no longer be time. But until then, everything we have to do is very much related to a ticking clock.

Dear Christian, if you think you have forever to please Him you are living in the highest kind of deception.

"And sware by him that liveth for ever and ever, who created heaven, and the things that therein are, and the earth, and the things that therein are, and the sea, and the things which are therein, that there should be time no longer" (Revelation 10:6).

"To every thing there is a season, and a time to every purpose under the heaven" (Ecclesiastes 3:1).

I read a book in which the author said, "Write the books you intend to write and write them now." He continued, "At another stage of your life, you will not write the same things you would have written then." How true that is. Perhaps if I were to write the books I wrote some years ago now, I would not write them in the same way today.

Five More Lives

Once, my children were playing on their play station. There was this creature that was making its way through a jungle with all sorts of amazing traps and ambushes. Gigantic wheels would appear and roll over their player. Deep ridges would appear into which the player would fall. Eagles flew over trying to kill the player. As I watched, my son's player was suddenly destroyed by a huge animal, which came from nowhere. Then I said, "Oh, sorry, that is the end of the game. You've lost your player." But he answered "Oh, don't worry I have five more lives. The game is not over at all."

The computer games of our world have deceived us into thinking that we have multiple lives. We have nothing but one life and one death. The clock is ticking and opportunities are passing by.

There will even be a time when you will hear the Word of God but will not be able to repent. In the book of John, Jesus said, "Do not say that there are yet four months." In other words do not give yourself extra time.

3. There is no extra time.

This is the time of the harvest. It is time to respond now. "Say not ye, There are yet four months, and then cometh harvest? behold, I say unto you, Lift up your eyes, and look on the fields; for they are white already to harvest" (John 4:35).

Gordon Lindsay, a man of God, who built Bible schools and churches in the sixties, wrote this powerful poem. It depicts the life of a young man who was offered the opportunity to get involved in the harvest. He procrastinated until he was too old to obey God. He never intended to disregard the call of God. But before he realized, his life was over.

Read this poem by Gordon Lindsay. I believe it will bless your heart:

Sunrise and skies are fair
A day begins without a care
A day for joy, a day for leisure
A day for thrills, a day for pleasure
Youth is merry and young, youth is gay
The great reaper is far away

But there is a call, 'tis the master's voice
I need you today, may I be your choice
A harvest is waiting and the fields are white
Will you join the reapers in the morning bright
Awake oh youth to the heavenly vision

Because multitudes, multitudes are in the
Valley of Decision.
The morning sun high above the earth
A cry of distress in the midst of mirth
Heathen are born and heathen are dying
Is there none to hear them crying?
"Oh yes," said the youth, count me as one
To help in this harvest till the day is done
Yet he lingered on for a little more fun

High sun, high noon
You'll be hearing from me soon.
I've married a wife, I've property to see
Five yoke of oxen acquired by me
I'll soon heed the call, I'll join the band
Ready to give the reapers a hand
But he carried on he had a bargain in hand

Afternoon sun and afternoon light
The golden ore hastened its flight
Conscience still hard memories daunted
Wealth, he had acquired, yet more was wanted
Many were the possessions he proudly
flaunted

Houses and barns, lands and farms
Streams and ponds, stocks and bonds
Chickens and hogs, forest and logs
Crops and flack, meadows and haystacks
Orchards and berries, vineyards and cherries
Day was waxing, day was waning
Still the rich man was entertaining
For a sinister voice had spoken and said
On with the fun, on with the dance
Go ahead and make merry while you have the
chance

You're a man of the times, you're ten feet tall
He saw time yet for the call
So a little more jolly and a little more fun
And the hours slipped away until there were
none

Sunrise to sun fall
The day was wasting on the western wall
Hands still busy with a thousand things
As evening descends and curfew brings
The day had faded into twilight red
As multitudes hasten to join the dead
"I am ready", "I am ready" said the man at last
But shaking hands could not hold fast
His hair unnoticed had turned to gray
Still he thought it was yesterday
Alas, harvest past, it was too late
To save those who had gone to a Christless
grave

Where is the silver and where is the gold?
Where are the possessions to another soul?
Where are the sheep that grazed the hill?
And where are the cattle that drank from the
river?

Where are the barns that were filled with
plenty?
And where are the thoroughbreds one hundred
and twenty?
Where are the heirlooms? Where are the
treasures?
Where is the laughter? Where are the
pleasures?
Where are the porters? Where is the wine?
Where are the delicacies? And the dinners that
are so fine?
Sun sunk low. And night descended
The summer is gone, the harvest is ended
O for a chance for time extended!!
A wasted life was never intended!!
Sun fall and noon rise
What is left of the rich man's prize?

Go out to the valley to yonder hill
And see the marble standing still
Treasures were offered in heaven
But he took instead
The cold reward of the unsaved dead!

And what of us who live today?
This is our home let us not stay!!
A call to the harvest till it shall end
Work now, work fast, and reap my friend
New dawn and sunrise
Till the faithful the master will give the prize.[3]

■ JESUS' VARIATIONS FROM THE NORM

Jesus answered and said unto them, "Ye do err, not knowing the scriptures, nor the power of God" (Matthew 22:29).

You must have heard the saying: "There is an exception to every rule." Whether this is true or not, Jesus introduced numerous scriptural exceptions to well-accepted principles. A failure to understand these exceptions led the Pharisees to vehemently oppose Christ. A lack of knowledge of the whole Scripture made them so right that they became wrong.

For example, the saying: "Physician heal thyself", is a well-accepted saying. It is true and must be practised all the time. A physician's remedy, if worth anything, must first work on the physician himself. It could be that the physician's potion is poisonous and a good place to test it is on the physician himself. But Jesus introduced a biblical exception.

He responded to that demand by saying that a prophet is not without honour except in his own country. This means there are occasions when the physician's potion does not work. That is, in his home. In this case, "Physician, heal thyself", does not apply. Jesus used one Scripture to draw the bigger picture.

"But Jesus said unto them, A prophet is not without honour, but in his own country, and among his own kin, and in his own house" (Mark 6:4).

1. Exceptions to keeping bad company

On another occasion, Jesus was accused of spending a lot of time fellowshipping with sinners (Luke 5:29-35). The Pharisees were not comfortable with a religious leader who was so at ease in the midst of well-known criminals. They confronted Him with this well-accepted divine principle "Bad company ruins good morals". Jesus knew this principle but He knew a little more. He knew the biblical exception and He told them, "They that are whole need not a physician, but they that are sick. I came not to call the righteous but sinners to repentance."

2. Exceptions to fasting

Almost every biblical rule has biblical exceptions and variations. Jesus was criticized about His disciples not fasting. Fasting is a well-accepted biblical practice. Jesus Himself fasted and never spoke against fasting. Then why were His disciples not fasting? Why did it seem that He was going against a well-accepted scriptural norm? How could He violate something that was unquestionably a good spiritual activity?

This was because, He knew a biblical exception to the rule which the Pharisees and Sadducees did not know. He said to them "Can you make the children of the bride chamber fast when the bridegroom is with them?" By this saying, Jesus introduced a biblical exception to the rule based on divine timing. He explained that there was a time when it was not appropriate to fast even though fasting is a good thing. "And he said unto them, Can ye make the children of the bridechamber fast, while the s bridegroom is with them?" (Luke 5:34).

When you walk with God, you will need to know not only the biblical principles but the biblical exceptions and variations to the rules. Otherwise you will become a New Testament Pharisee. Error sets in when we know the Scripture without the power or the power without the Scriptures. Both are needed to keep us on the path of righteousness. Jesus answered and said unto them, "Ye do err, not knowing the scriptures, nor the power of God" (Matthew 22:29).

In my walk with God, I have found that many things that were right became wrong when the Lord was not leading me there.

3. Exceptions to prayer

Prayer is good but unbelievably there is a time when it is not a good thing to pray. It may be time to preach or time to rest and you may be in prayer. The well-accepted biblical rule that we should pray without ceasing has variations and exceptions sometimes based on timing.

In the Garden of Gethsemane, Jesus urged His disciples to pray. But at a point, He urged them to sleep. In other words, don't bother to pray any more, just sleep!

"And he cometh unto the disciples, and findeth them asleep, and saith unto Peter, What, could ye not watch with me one hour? Watch and pray, that ye enter not into temptation: the spirit indeed is willing, but the flesh is weak. Then cometh he to his disciples, and saith unto them, Sleep on now, and take your rest..." (Matthew 26: 40,41,45).

God is not a book. The Bible is not a god. The Bible is not God. The Bible contains the principles, the rules and the Scriptures. It takes a personal and intimate relationship with God to stay close to God. The Pharisees were sticklers for the rules and principles they had found.

Because they did not know God, they thought God was a principle or a rule. Jesus showed repeatedly that knowing God was more than knowing rules and principles. God is the author of these rules and laws.

4. Exceptions to preaching and teaching

There are times God has showed me principles from His Word. For instance, He has led me to focus on preaching, teaching and healing. As I carried on emphasizing church planting and evangelism based on the Scriptures that I understood, I found the Lord leading me to do things that I had formerly disregarded. The Lord warned me to follow Him and not to become a Pharisee who was so bent on the laws and principles he had learnt.

The same Jesus whose last words were, "Go into the world and preach the gospel," is the same Jesus who said, "When I was hungry, you did not feed me. When I was sick you did not visit. When I was in prison, you never thought of me. Then shall the righteous answer him, saying, Lord, when saw we thee an hungred, and fed thee? or thirsty, and gave thee drink? When saw we thee a stranger, and took thee in? or naked, and clothed thee? Or when saw we thee sick, or in prison, and came unto thee? And the King shall answer and say unto them, Verily I say unto you, Inasmuch as ye have done it unto one of the least of these my brethren, ye have done it unto me" (Matthew 25:37-40).

Visiting prisoners is not the same as planting a church. Caring for the sick is not evangelism. It is a biblical variation from my long-standing view of the work of God.

How quickly we become Pharisees filled with self-righteousness when we are so sure we are doing the right thing. A deeper understanding of Jesus' Words will reveal what it means to walk with God.

5. Exceptions to sabbath activities

When Jesus was criticized about His disciples plucking corn and eating it on the Sabbath day, He once again brought an exception and variation to the law. He pointed out how David had eaten the shew bread with his followers. He then gave another principle which the Pharisees did not know, "The Son of man is Lord also of the Sabbath."

"For the Son of man is Lord even of the sabbath day" (Matthew 12:8). This means that God is the creator of the rules and laws and He is higher than them.

6. Exceptions to poverty

Once, Jesus asked His disciples to go on evangelism without making financial provision. He told them not to bother about taking extra money or supplies. "And he said unto them, Take nothing for your journey, neither staves, nor scrip, neither bread, neither money; neither have two coats apiece" (Luke 9:3).

However, not so long after He sent them again and this time He told them to take enough money, clothes and supplies.

"Then said he unto them, But now, he that hath a purse, let him take it, and likewise his scrip: and he that hath no sword, let him sell his garment, and buy one" (Luke 22:36).

Once again, you learn the principle of not equating God to a rule that you have learnt. Following God is more than following a couple of learnt rules. If all we needed were rules, then we would no longer need God Himself. There is no particular rule that can replace our relationship with God.

This reality has made me conscious of my need to follow the Lord and to be close to Him personally. None of the things I have learned can replace a personal day to day walk with the Lord. What I perceive as being right today may be wrong for tomorrow.

JESUS IS THE TRUTH

No particular rule, doctrine or principle is truth; Jesus himself is the truth. He said, "I am the way the truth and the life." (John 14:6).

Following Jesus closely is our best chance of abiding in truth. Today, it is easy to see that the Pharisees were incredibly estranged from truth. They were far from the truth because they were far from God Himself.

What about us? How far are we from God? Perhaps we also have some old principles that we cherish. We think that by following these rules we will be following God.

Can you see how many movements and churches become distant from the Lord? Many churches have rejected the current commands of God in order to keep their traditions.

"And he said unto them, Full well ye reject the commandment of God, that ye may keep your own tradition" (Mark 7:9).

This is the number one cause of backsliding among religious people. May God help us all!

A Biblical Study on Backsliding

22

■ WHAT IS BACKSLIDING?

Many years ago I learnt through experience that backsliding can be likened to walking on a road with no signboards. In our Christian walk there are no signboards to warn you that you are backsliding. There is no sign that says, Hell and Destruction: 200 meters ahead. There's simply no such sign! Backsliding happens gradually, until you are drawn somewhere you never expected to be. Gradually but certainly, you slide there.

God raised up the Prophet Jeremiah at a time when Israel and Judah were about to be taken captive in Babylon. He used Jeremiah to show the people of Israel the backslidden state of their hearts.

1. The central theme of the book of Jeremiah is backsliding.

Jeremiah, also known as "the weeping prophet", had most of his messages centered on the theme backsliding. He was often at "war" with the people of Israel, constantly warning them to repent and change from their wicked ways.

The weeping prophet was concerned about the wayward attitude of his people. He repeatedly urged them, "Turn away from your wicked ways. Stop doing evil! Repent and come back to God." He attempted to show them in many different ways what it meant to backslide. Yet the people of Israel and Judah refused to change. Jeremiah gives several vivid descriptions of the backslidden state. Backsliding is real and can be analyzed by studying the different forms of backsliding described by Jeremiah. The prophet used real-life situations to describe this very common spiritual phenomenon. It is a common occurrence in the Christian world.

2. Other Scriptures affirm the warning against backsliding.

The Bible says, "...for many be called, but few chosen" (Matthew 20:16). In other words, many start out with Christ but many still fall away.

The Bible also says, "...he that endureth to the end shall be saved" (Matthew 10:22). Many who come to Christ, fall away later.

The Bible cautions in 1 Corinthians 10:12, "Wherefore let him that thinketh he standeth take heed lest he fall."

The Bible warns against the of Satan, which may cause a Christan to fall away. "Lest Satan should get an advantage of us: for we are not ignorant of his devices" (2 Corinthians 2:11).

The Christian must seek the help of God to prevent him from falling: "Now unto him that is able to keep you from falling, and to present you faultless before the presence of his glory with exceeding joy, To the only wise God our Saviour, be glory and majesty, dominion and power, both now and ever. Amen" (Jude 24, 25).

THE BOOK OF JEREMIAH AND DESCRIPTIONS OF BACKSLIDING

1. BACKSLIDING IS LIKE EXCHANGING FOUNTAINS FOR BROKEN CISTERNS.

"...they have forsaken me the fountain of living waters, and hewed them out cisterns, broken cisterns, that can hold no water" (Jeremiah 2:13). When I was a medical student, I was sent on a working visit to Danfa, a Ghanaian village, for two weeks. Once, during a field trip, we came across another remote village that had no running water. Since the village had no running water, they had dug a large hole in the ground where water gathered. Often, this water was dirty and brownish. The people in the village bathed, defecated and urinated in it. At the same time they drank from it and used it to cook. This water obviously gave them various diseases and sicknesses.

In the Bible, backsliding people are likened to people who have access to clear running water, but exchange it for dirty smelly water – just like what I saw in that village. I am sure you would wonder why someone would leave sweet, fresh, infection-free water, for sickness-infested and dirty water. There are believers who have had access to a life of holiness and godliness. However, they have rejected that to live a sinful and demon-controlled life. God has given you an alternative to the dirty brown water.

God is telling you that when you backslide you are going back to something terrible, which will eventually kill you. He is telling you not to do something as absurd as drinking that muddy water again.

God has given the Christian an alternative to the dirty brown water. The alternative is to choose God. The alternative is to stay close to God.

2. BACKSLIDING IS LIKE BECOMING A DEGENERATE WILD VINE.

"...art thou turned into the degenerate plant of a strange vine...?" (Jeremiah 2:21). The next Bible description of backsliding is that of a good plant which has degenerated into a thorny and strange vine.

Here, God shows us how a farmer's plantation from which he was expecting a good yield turned into a field of thorns and useless weeds.

The believer is that beautiful plant of the Lord, which can degenerate. Why on earth would you want to allow yourself to degenerate into a thorny and worthless shrub? This is how God sees you when you backslide.

God's problem with Israel was that He had invested so much love, care, tenderness and time into their lives. Yet they had turned into disobedient, hard-hearted and wicked people. Will you allow yourself to become a worthless creature before God? The answer should be a definite, "No!"

3. BACKSLIDING IS LIKE BECOMING A WILD CAMEL.

"...thou art a swift dromedary traversing her ways" (Jeremiah 2:23). A backsliding Christian is also described as a swift dromedary traversing her ways. A dromedary is another name for a camel. It is a wild and swift creature, which strays anywhere. The heart of a backsliding person is as unrestrained as a wild camel. It is not under the control of anything. It is loose and wild.

I remember some years ago I went to visit a backsliding Christian in London.

A Backslidden Friend

The best way I could describe this person was loose and wild. I was trying to bring him back to the Lord. It took me a long time to locate his house. I eventually got to his flat after midnight. He was surprised to see me, and welcomed me into his home. As we got to talking, he realized why I had come. Being a one-time mature Christian who had backslidden, he knew all the scriptures I intended to quote.

So at a point he interrupted me and said, "Listen, I know what you are going to say, and I know all the Bible verses you are armed with tonight. But I want you to know that I don't really care."

So he took out his cigarette and started smoking right in front of me.

He said, "I want you to see me smoking. Because I am not under any restrictions."

Then he took out an album and showed me some pictures he had taken with his girlfriend. Some of these pictures were quite suggestive and lewd.

He said, "I want you to see me as I really am. This is how I am now. This is what I do. And there is nothing anyone can do about it!"

Once again he was making the point that he could do anything he wanted to, and that no one could control him. You see, backsliders are like wild camels which have no restrictions and boundaries anymore. Your Christian life is supposed to be governed by God's Word.

When a person backslides he begins to do what he wants to do, and not what God wants him to do. He's like a wild animal with no checks and controls. God's Word gives us guidelines that are for our own good but a backslider chooses to live outside God's law. What a pity!

4. Backsliding is like becoming a wild ass.

"A wild ass used to the wilderness, that snuffeth up the wind at her pleasure; in her occasion who can turn her away..." (Jeremiah 2:24). I prefer the New Berkeley translation of this verse, which says: "Like a wild donkey accustomed to the wilderness, in the heat of her passion snuffing up the wind: in the time of her mating who can turn her lust away?" (Jeremiah 2:24 New Berkeley Version)

Many backsliders are like wild animals heated up with passion looking for a mate. The Amplified Bible puts it this way: "No males seeking her need weary themselves; in her month they will find her seeking them."

The Moffatt translation of the Bible elaborates further: "No male need trouble to search for her; all can find her at mating time."

I remember one time going on a visit to search out a backsliding sister. I went with a good friend of mine, with whom I was doing some pastoral work . When we got to this backsliding sister's house, I told her that we had come to find out how she was doing in the Lord. Her house was in a part of the city I didn't know very well and it had taken us about three hours to find the house.

When we got there she looked at me with a straight face and said, "I cannot talk to you now because I am cooking."

Then I said, "We have come a long way to see you, and won't you even offer us a seat?"

She insisted that she had no time for us. So after mumbling a hurried exhortation to stay with the Lord, we scurried off. This young girl, who had no time for us, found time for an unbeliever boy who was 'chasing' her. She had no time for the Christian brothers who wanted to help her in her spiritual life. But the unbeliever boyfriend had no problem gaining access to her.

A backsliding Christian becomes prey to unbelievers. Unbelievers can easily lead a backslider astray into sin. Show me a backsliding Christian, and I'll show you an easy prey for the devil and his cohorts.

Satan capitalizes on the fleshly passions of backsliders, and has little problem finishing them off.

5. A BACKSLIDER IS LIKE A LADY WHO FORGETS HER ORNAMENTS.

"Can a maid forget her ornaments... yet my people have forgotten me..." (Jeremiah 2:32). According to Jeremiah, the backslidden person is like a woman who forgets to put on her ornaments. Many women are attached to their earrings, necklaces and make-up. Some women will never appear in public without adorning themselves with these accessories. (Unfortunately, many ladies substitute outer beauty for inner beauty. They have no time to pray, or read their Bibles but they spend a lot of time putting on all sorts of ornaments everyday!)

I must say I have rarely seen a lady who is not attached to her trinkets. God compares the backslidden person to a young lady who has forgotten to beautify herself with her numerous dresses, shoes, necklaces, earrings, mascara and the rest. How unusual!

Jeremiah realized that these things were part and parcel of every normal woman, and that women were very attached to these trappings. He likened this bond between a woman and her ornamental accessories to the relationship that exists between a believer and God.

God describes the act of backsliding as a woman forgetting her ornaments. In other words, backsliding and going away from God is a very unusual thing. It may not look unusual in the natural, but in the sight of God and the angels it is a very strange phenomenon indeed.

Some people remind me of this very thing. Once upon a time they used to sing, praise, worship and even lead other Christians. Today, they are just nominal Christians. One thing I am sure of, is that some Christians do not even know that they are backslidden.

If a vibrant charismatic Christian leader becomes just a nominal, principled individual in society, he must understand that he has backslidden. Although people may consider him a good person, in the sight of God he has fallen from the high state that he used to be in - leading people to the Lord, exhorting them, sharing the Word, laying hands on people and so on.

One person comes to mind every time I think of this Scripture. She was a vibrant, witnessing and fruitful Christian.

"Oh Pastor, We Still Go to Church"

Now and again, when I see her I ask, "How is your christian life?"

She smiles and says, "Oh Pastor, we still go to church."

All I can say for her is that she is a good and moral person who does no harm to anything or anyone. But there used to be more to her Christianity than that! Can a person who was so attached to the active, fruit-bearing Christian experience be separated from this state so easily? I wonder how the heavenly cloud of witnesses feel when they see this happen. Jeremiah could only describe it in one way—a woman separated from her ornaments.

6. A BACKSLIDER IS LIKE A BRIDE WHO FORGETS HER WEDDING GOWN.

"Can a maid forget her ornaments, or a BRIDE her ATTIRE..." (Jeremiah 2:32). Many brides are in love with their wedding gowns. Before the wedding day, they hang them in their wardrobes to ensure that they don't get stained. Often, the gown is prepared in advance for the great day (and some gowns cost more than a year's salary!).

The bride's gown is worn for only a few hours, but the bride spares no expense when she is buying it. Many women are thrilled to be the bride - the star of the day, the most beautiful woman of the day, the princess of the moment. She walks down the aisle in splendor. No woman forgets her wedding gown!

God is saying that when you go away from Christ, you are like a bride who forgot to wear her wedding gown on her wedding day. This is why God is so horrified when Christians forget their God and backslide. It is simply implausible, inconceivable, and beyond belief. The Bible maintains that a bride cannot be divorced from her wedding dress. That is why God was horrified when you first showed signs of backsliding.

7. A backslider is like a lover playing the harlot.

"...thou hast played the harlot with many lovers..." (Jeremiah 3:1). God compares the backslider to a woman who is married to the man of her dreams, but then decides to go after other men. She jumps over the wall at night, leaves her dear, beloved, charming prince in bed and goes to hunt for "fresh blood". I know that many people find the profession of prostitution horrifying and repulsive. They cannot imagine how people can abuse their bodies for a living.

I remember a lovely woman who had a respectable husband. After some years of marriage, this lady began to have affairs with other men. She would climb over the wall and run away at night, when her noble husband was asleep. Can you imagine that? But let me ask you something else. If your wife not only left you, but went out into the streets to become a prostitute, would that not even be worse? How would it feel like to pass by the "red light" district and discover your wife busily trading her wares? You would be shattered!

This is exactly how God feels when He sees the children He so loves standing out there in the world and selling themselves to the works of Satan. How sad!

MORE BIBLICAL DESCRIPTIONS

1. A backslider is like a dog who eats its vomit.

"As a dog returneth to his vomit, so a fool returneth to his folly" (Proverbs 26:11).

When it comes to food I am very particular about what I eat. My mother always gave me piping hot food, so I am not used to eating food that is not very hot. I have decided not to eat anything I don't want to eat.

I remember once during a visit to the Far East, I sat at table with some dignitaries.

I must admit it was a very difficult experience for me having to swallow a few morsels of what looked like eels, snakes, clams and so on.

God knows how difficult it is for us to eat things we do not like. For most of us there are things we just wouldn't eat, even if we were starving. For example, your own vomit.

I recall one particular day when I saw a dog in my house vomiting some disgusting, pudding-like substance.

It was so smelly I just avoided that area of the house. About an hour later, I passed by and I was very shocked to find the dog eagerly lapping up the pudding of vomit. How utterly disgusting! I wondered why the dog was eating it. Was there no other food?

Some of you must have seen this phenomenon before. Well, that is exactly what you look like when you go back to your old ways, old boyfriends, old girlfriends and old habits you once vomited out. God is utterly surprised at you.

This reminds us of the prodigal son who ended up eating pig feed. The prodigal son is another description of the backslidden believer. He demanded his share of his father's property and walked out of his father's house. He journeyed to a far country and wasted all his substance on riotous living. In the end he had to feed with pigs. "And he would fain have filled his belly with the husks that the swine did eat..." (Luke 15:16).

And that is what it means to backslide. If you have the opportunity to eat at table with your Christian family, why must you end up eating with pigs?

2. A BACKSLIDER IS LIKE ONE WHO CHOOSES "LIFE" AND EXCHANGES IT FOR "DEATH".

Dear Christian friend, I have tried in these last few pages to describe the horrors of backsliding as graphically as I possibly can. What else can I say? If this message is not clear to you, you may either be deaf, blind or simply dishonest. God is telling us clearly that once we have come to know Him, we will do well to stay with Him. There is no turning back and no falling away.

"But we are not of them who draw back unto perdition..." (Hebrews 10:39).

"...No man, having put his hand to the plough, and looking back, is fit for the Kingdom of God" (Luke 9:62).

The Causes and Psychology of Backsliding

23

■ PRINCIPAL CAUSES OF BACKSLIDING

I know that there are many causes of backsliding, but in this chapter, I will try to give you the predominant causes, as the Lord has shown me.

SHALLOWNESS

1. THE SHALLOW CHRISTIAN HAS NO ROOTS AND MAY FALL AWAY IN THE TIME OF TESTING.

The parable of the sower gives various reasons why some of the seeds could not grow: "... and these have no root, which for a while believe..." (Luke 8:13).

Some seeds could not grow because they fell on rocky soil. Jesus explained that these are the ones who receive the Word of God with joy, and even believe for a while. But in the time of testing, they fall away because they have no root.

A time of testing will surely come for every Christian. If you are shallow, in the time of testing, you will fall.

Through experience I have noticed that many Christians do not have deep roots. They do not know God for themselves. They cannot even explain why they do the things they do. They don't know why they belong to a particular church. They do not know why they speak in tongues. They do not even know why they give offerings. When they face a little criticism, they get confused and have no defense.

Having no personal experience with God, these are the people who can never say, "God spoke to me." They have no convictions of their own.

My Personal Conviction

A close friend who brought me up in the Lord deviated from Christianity, and became a member of a cult. But I did not follow him into that cult because I had my own deep-rooted convictions.

I know why I am serving the Lord, and so my father, mother or closest friend cannot change my mind. Many Christians who are not rooted in sound biblical doctrine can easily be persuaded to follow fables. Some born-again believers fall away because they do not know the difference between the true gospel, and the beliefs of sects like the Jehovah Witnesses.

Witnessing to a Jehovah's Witness

Once, I was standing in an area within the city of Accra when a Jehovah's Witness came up to me to try to convert me to his faith.

He asked, "Do you believe in the Holy Spirit?"

I replied, "I certainly do!" Then I asked him, "Have you heard of 'speaking in tongues'?"

He said, "Yes. But I don't believe in it."

So I asked him, "What is this...?"

Then I released a string of tongues in the direction of this sincere (but sincerely wrong) gentleman. This ended our conversation. He fled! If I were not convinced that speaking in tongues is an ability which comes with the Holy Spirit, he could have confused me. But I knew my Bible, and I knew (as I still do today) that the Holy Spirit is from God, and speaking in tongues is one of his gifts.

Don't just speak in tongues because others are speaking in tongues. You must know why tongues sounds like a monotonous and repetitive language. It is because the Bible says, "with a stammering tongue will I speak to you". Tongues is described as a stammering tongue. It is not just an ordinary language. It is a heavenly language that comes out in a stammering fashion.

2. The shallow Christian falls away when there is a church crisis.

You may be in a church, but if you are not "deep" you will fall away at the next shaking and crisis. Next time there is a problem in the church, your membership and commitment will be shaken.

Only a "shallow" Christian would fall away when a great man of God gets into some scandalous sin. What have the sins of that man of God got to do with your own salvation? Why on earth would you think of leaving Christ because of your pastor's mistakes? Christians behave in this way because they themselves are shallow!

Don't Follow Me, If I Don't Follow Christ

I am the pastor of a very large church. I know many people would do anything I tell them to. But I always tell my church members not to follow me if I do not follow Christ. After all, I am also a man, and can make mistakes. I tell them, "If I tell you to do something that is not biblical, do not do it. Only do things which can be supported by the Bible."

If you are not sure about anything your pastor is saying, just ask him, "Please Sir, what is the scriptural basis for this new revelation?"

Not abiding by this principle is the reason why some so-called pastors can bathe their members in the nude (what they call "holy" baths). Some so-called ministers are also able to dupe people out of all their earthly possessions. This is because the pastors know that they are dealing with shallow people.

Paul said, "Follow me as long as I follow Christ." He was a man subject to like passions, so whatever he did had to be scrutinized by the book of books: The Bible!

3. The shallow Christian follows the crowd into danger.

Did you know that Aaron led the people of Israel to build a golden calf after God had delivered them from Egypt? These people were saved all right, but were shallow in their experience with God.

When Moses was held up on the mountain, the Israelites in their shallow faith, turned shortly to idols and declared, "These be thy gods, O Israel, which brought thee up out of the land of Egypt."

Don't be shallow and light, blown about by every wind of doctrine! Don't just follow the crowd! It is shallow people who just follow the crowd.

Many became calf worshippers in the days of Aaron because they followed the crowd. Many murmured and were destroyed in the days of Moses and the ten spies because they followed the crowd. Many got involved in the killing of Jesus, the Son of God because they followed the crowd.

Following the crowd can be dangerous. Don't be a shallow Christian. Be deep. Don't be a believer for just a while. Let your roots grow deep. As the songwriter says, "Draw me deeper, Lord!"

EMPTINESS

1. There are many Christians who are empty.

The word echo in 1 Corinthians 13:1 comes from the emptiness I am talking about here. "... I am no better than echoing bronze..." (1 Corinthians 13:1 Ronald Knox Translation).

Christians who are empty have nothing in them. I call them "airy Christians". They have little or none of the Word of God in them; neither are they full of the Holy Spirit or of love. They may speak in tongues, but the Bible says whenever they do so, they are just making a lot of noise.

I think the Ronald Knox Translation of 1 Corinthians 13:1, which I have quoted above, really brings out the concept of spiritual emptiness. If I have no love, "I am no better than echoing bronze or the clash of cymbals." I say once again, the echo and the clash are a result of the emptiness within.

2. Empty Christians are targets for the enemy.

Emptiness will attract other things to fill that empty space. A spiritual vacuum will be filled with spiritual things, either positively or negatively. Nature abhors a vacuum, and every space will be filled. "And when he [an evil spirit] cometh, he findeth it unoccupied..." (Luke 11:25 Goodspeed Translation)

Empty Christians are targets for the enemy. The devil will try to fill you with evil and backsliding tendencies because of the emptiness within you. There is the need for every Christian to be filled with the Spirit, with love and with the Word. Stephen was not empty; he was full of something positive: " ... and they chose Stephen, a man full of faith and of the Holy Ghost..." (Acts 6:5). That is why he did not backslide, but went on to become a great evangelist.

Fill your spirit with the Word of God, with faith, with good Christian music. (By the way don't mess around with non-Christian music; it will fill your mind with junk!) Fill your time with church activities. If you don't fill your life with these good things something else will fill it.

Empty Christians are loud and noticeable but not substantial. Drive away the emptiness from your spiritual life. This is a fundamental key to staying power for the Christian race.

LUST

1. Lust will lead a Christian to desert his faith.

To lust after something is to have a strong, excessive desire for something. Usually it is an uncontrollable, sometimes obsessive desire for a particular thing. One dictionary calls 'lust' an animal desire. Be wary of all forms of lust, whether it's financial lust, sexual lust or power lust.

Demas loved the world; that is why he deserted Paul. "For Demas hath forsaken me, having loved this present world..." (2 Timothy 4:10). If you love somebody, you will eventually gravitate towards that person. This explains why young ladies will leave their loving parents and marry virtual strangers. Love or lust is one of the reasons for that gravitational pull. If you love the world: its money, its women, its men, and its glitter, you will find yourself gravitating towards these things. It is therefore important that the Christian should not have any strange love in his heart.

I have one "love" for my Lord, and a second "love" for my wife. I cannot allow any other "love" to exist in my heart.

There are many Christian ladies who have such strong desires to marry that they will sacrifice all principles and all the rules in order to get married.

2. Lust corrupts.

Remember the Scripture, "... having escaped the corruption that is in the world through lust" (2 Peter 1:4).

The prodigal son had a strong desire for the world. He wanted to leave home so he could have the pleasures of the world. He was deceived and wanted something else. But there was nothing else! He soon found out that the situation out there was not as good as it was at home.

Often Christians feel they are missing out on something in the world. Sometimes they feel they are losing out on money, sex, glamour and so on. Apart from the love of Christ, if you have any other love in you, you need to be careful of it. If you have any strange lusts in you, you must kill them now, or they will grow up and take over your life.

I once saw a baby snake in my garden. It looked very much like an ordinary worm but it was definitely a snake. So I said to myself, "If I don't kill it now, one day it could kill me." I thought, "It is too dangerous to leave this thing alive. Let me kill it now," I decided.

That is how we must deal with some of those desires lurking within us. Deal with them like I dealt with that snake. Kill them now, when they are small and harmless. If you allow them to grow and to develop, they will destroy you one day.

BITTERNESS

1. Offences may result in bitterness if unchecked.

Many people who walk out of a church are offended Christians who became bitter. They were probably genuinely offended, but their wounds never healed. "...lest any root of bitterness springing up trouble you..." (Hebrews 12:15).

The Importance of Recovering from Offences

When my wife was pregnant with our second son, Joshua, I sometimes went with her to the antenatal clinic. To while away the time I engaged in conversation with one of the doctors. One morning as I chatted with this doctor, I noticed that one of his toes was missing.

So I asked, "What happened to your toe?"

He answered, "I am a diabetic patient, and I once had an injury to that toe. (You know, the wounds of some diabetic patients don't easily heal)." He continued, "I hit my toe on an object, but after some time the wound did not heal. This wound deteriorated until it affected my whole leg."

He lamented about how the doctors had even considered amputating his whole leg. However, in the end they decided to cut off only the toe in question."It was a very traumatic experience for me. That's how I ended up without a toe," he concluded.

As I mused over the story of this missing toe, the Spirit of God spoke to me and said, "This is what happens to Christians who get hurt and never fully recover from their hurts."

The Holy Spirit showed me how many Christians and pastors allow their hurts to degenerate into unhealed, gangrenous wounds of the heart. He continued, "They separate themselves from other Christians in the name of being cautious and not wanting to be hurt all over again. This separation eventually leads to total isolation from the body of Christ and backsliding."

Personal Testimony

Sometimes I think of all the hurts I've experienced in this ministry, and how they have tended to isolate me. I can remember when my former pastor offended me, and refused to support me when I started out in ministry!

I invited all the pastors I knew to my wedding. But none of them attended. When it was time to take group pictures, the Master of

Ceremonies called out for all pastors to come forward. But there was no one. I was totally rejected by the other ministers in the city.

A close family friend and neighbour once called me the leader of a cult! I have had trusted pastors betray me and turn against me. I have experienced mid-stream desertion in ministry by trusted people. I have had faithful church members I invested a lot in, fight against me!

I even decided at a point to stay away from interactions with many people. But, as I thought about the doctor's toe, I realized what was gradually happening to me. I was being cut off from the rest of the church in Ghana, just like this man's toe. And it was all because of unhealed wounds and hurts. I decided then to allow the wounds in me to heal.

I have noticed that there are many seniors in the ministry who have become disappointed, disillusioned, and unforgiving. I have watched as great ministers who once affected the whole nation, become isolated and cut off themselves from the rest of the body of Christ.

Wounded Church Members

One time I was in my office counselling, when a young man came to me.

He boldly stated, "I have decided to be in your church because I believe this is where God wants me to be."

I queried, "Why did you leave your former church?"

He replied, "I was led by the Spirit to come here."

I asked, "Apart from the Spirit's leading did anything else happen to make you decide to leave that church?"

He hesitated, "Well... there was a slight problem..." And he went on and on about problems that had arisen in his previous church.

I immediately knew that what I suspected was true. This man was hurt, and his unresolved hurts had caused him to be cut off from his church. This is one of the commonest reasons for people backsliding and leaving churches.

2. Satan causes isolation through offences.

If Satan can isolate you through hurts, he will have the opportunity to speak to you and make you backslide.

Backsliding Love

Married couples also backslide in their relationships towards each other. They start out with hot, strong and fiery love, which is often blind and unseeing. However, many couples, after several years of marriage, either just co-exist or even hate each other. How did they backslide from love to hatred? Often the hurts and offences of marriage were never fully resolved until they were virtually cut off from each other. This is one of the favourite tricks of the devil.

You are more vulnerable when you are isolated. Hebrews 12:15 warns us that bitterness can trouble us greatly.

SINFULNESS

1. Sin is a major cause of backsliding.

Many of the Christians who walk out of church and backslide have often been living in sin. Although they were in church, some of them used to commit fornication, adultery, stealing, and other sins. These are the church members who easily become annoyed with their pastors for preaching about their evil deeds. They do not want certain portions of the Scriptures to be referred to. They feel uncomfortable when certain subjects are preached in church. They also hate hard-hitting, Holy Ghost inspired messages that lay bare the realities of righteous living.

One morning, a friend of mine was chatting with her colleague in the office.

She asked him, "How was your week-end?"

"Oh, it was fine! I went to church on Sunday," he replied.

"How was church?" she asked.

He answered, "I'm not impressed with my church anymore. I don't think I'll go back there again."

She was surprised and wondered, "What's wrong with your church? You've been going there for sometime now."

He answered, "The pastor's sermons are not uplifting. I tell you, we are not blessed!"

He went on, "If he wants to preach, he should just preach. But all this going on about fornication, and people having girlfriends isn't necessary."

You see, this married man was having an affair with a young lady in the office and he didn't like his sin being exposed. I tell you, there was nothing wrong with that pastor's preaching. Fornication is a subject in the Bible which must be addressed. Backsliding Christians can easily leave a church to avoid the confrontations of God's Word, instead of admitting their sins and repenting.

2. When a believer sins and acknowledges his mistake, he is on his way to being healed.

Address the sin in your life. "My son, if sinners entice thee, consent thou not" (Proverbs 1:10). Correct the mistakes. Deal with every evil thought and habit. This will keep you in the Lord. Sin is definitely a primary cause of backsliding.

LYING

1. The Bible classifies liars with wicked poeple.

Liars are compared to wicked people who shed innocent blood. "These six things doth the Lord hate...a proud look, a lying tongue, and hands that shed innocent blood" (Proverbs 6:16,17).

There are born again Christians who habitually lie through their teeth. They lie to God and to man without batting an eyelid.

The Bible says: "Stand your ground then, with truth for your belt..." (Ephesians 6:14 Twentieth Century New Testament). This belt of truth holds the whole armour together. Truth, honesty and sincerity are things that hold your entire Christian life together. Without sincerity your Christian life will disintegrate, and you will backslide.

The Demon-Possessed Girl

I remember being in a service once with some other brethren. There was a young lady who had been prophesying and holding up the whole service for periods of time.

She would stand up whilst the leader was preaching, and interrupt the service with very long prophecies. She would command the priest to stop the administration of communion. This young girl would prophesy and make the entire congregation kneel down and stand up at will.

Many of the leaders were inexperienced, and didn't know what to do. So they would stand back as this young lady dominated the entire service. I had been told about this young lady who had been controlling the meetings, but had never seen her myself.

That day, I realized that I was seeing the manifestation of an evil spirit, 'live'. This young lady stood up and began to take over the service with her prophecies just as had been described to me. So I got out of my seat, took a couple of brothers with me, and escorted her into the basement of the building. I knew that an evil spirit was controlling this young lady. As soon as we got into the basement, this young lady's eyes widened and blazed.

She looked straight at me and said, "Do not quench the Spirit!"

I could virtually see the demons dancing in her eyes. This almost unsettled me as I wondered, "was I quenching the Holy Spirit?"

Then I said, "You foul spirit, in the name of Jesus. I command you to stop your activities and come out of this girl."

She immediately went into all sorts of writhing movements. The spirit began to manifest, spoke to us using the girl's voice and said many things. I cannot give all the details of this deliverance episode in this book. However, there was one thing that struck me, which I want to highlight here.

I asked the demon spirit, "How did you come into this lady?"

That spirit said, "The belt of truth was loose."

The demons had gained access to this young girl's life because the protective armor of truth, sincerity and honesty was deficient in one way or the other. I cannot tell you how exactly this girl's belt of truth was loosed. That is not important to you. What is important is your belt of truth.

2. Lying opens the gate to evil spirits.

Are you honest? Are you sincere? When you make a mistake do you admit it easily? Are you truthful to yourself and to God? I tell you, there are many people who lie to themselves continually and tell themselves, "I am okay", when they know they are not.

Do not deceive yourself! Be honest and sincere! Be straightforward! Jesus said, "You will know the truth and the truth will make you free." Don't be angry when you hear the truth. It is the truth that you need.

REBELLION

1. The Bible compares rebellion to witchcraft.

There is one sin which is compared to witchcraft in the Bible. That is the sin of rebellion. "For rebellion is as [like] the sin of witchcraft..." (1 Samuel 15:23).

Rebellion is the fight against all authority.Rebellion often camouflages itself as the fight for independence. Many so-called freedom and independence fighters are actually downright rebels. Africa, for instance, has had its fair share of rebels. There have been rebellions and uprisings against governments all over Africa.

There are also many rebellious elements in the church. There are rebellious pastors who break out of their rightful positions as branch pastors, assistant pastors and so on. There are rebellious church members who break out of their God-given places within churches. (I assure you that rebels usually have very spiritual reasons for the things they do!)

2. Rebellion stems from the heart.

Every rebellious child of God has rejected legitimate authority in his life. The result therefore is backsliding. I have known Christians who do not want anything, be it human or divine, to instruct them concerning their lives. Rebellion is a cardinal factor in the backsliding phenomenon.

It was rebellion against his father's authority that led the prodigal son to leave home. The rebellion in the prodigal son's heart led him to eat with pigs. I am sure you don't want to end up eating with pigs. Don't be a rebel.

All rebels are destined to end in one way. Ask the prodigal son, ask Judas, ask Absalom, ask Adonijah, ask Ahithophel, ask Shimei, and ask Lucifer to tell you what happened to them when they rebelled. All rebels are headed for one judgement: EXECUTION!

FOOLISHNESS

1. Foolishness leads to complications and eventual backsliding.

Many Christians do foolish things. "He that trusteth in his own heart is a fool..." (Proverbs 28:26). They venture into places only fools would dare. There are some situations, and some people who will lead you into trouble.

Some young unmarried Christian couples court disaster when they engage in certain things. Sometimes during courtship, some Christians can be found in "unhealthy" situations after midnight. Then when you become pregnant before your wedding, you get surprised that you fell into sin! Why should you be surprised?

There are some ladies whose specialty is to wine and dine with married men. And their excuse is that they work with these men. "Oh, It's just a business lunch," they say. But I tell you, they are playing with fire.

I have seen Christian brothers and sisters live in the same flat, and even in the same room, all in the name of saving money. The next thing that happened was they fell in "love". Then before you could say, "Jack Robinson" they had a baby. Foolishness has a price. "All things are lawful for me, but all things are not expedient..." (1 Corinthians 10:23).

2. Spiritual strength must never be overestimated.

God has continually drummed it into me that being a pastor does not make me immune or special. The Lord has made it clear that he will treat me as he treats everyone else. So no matter who you are, if you walk in foolishness and absurdity you will backslide. It is as simple as that. Some types of behaviour are straightforward foolishness. You should never overestimate your spiritual strength. "Fools make a mock at sin..." (Proverbs 14:9).

■ THE PSYCHOLOGY OF BACKSLIDING

The psychology of backsliding deals with the way backsliders think. It deals with the attitudes of a defecting Christian. You see, the Bible says we should guard our hearts with all diligence: "Keep thy heart with all diligence; for out of it are the issues of life" (Proverbs 4:23).

Backsliding is one of the issues of life. The issue of backsliding comes from the heart. A thought in the heart becomes an attitude. An attitude becomes an action. And these actions become behaviour patterns.

It is the attitudes in the heart of a backslider that give him the false confidence in his backslidden state.

ATTITUDES THAT FORM IN THE HEART OF A BACKSLIDER

1. Attitude #1 - "I'm not alone, others are backsliding too."

I have noticed that one of the things we do, is to find out who else is in a condition similar to ours. And when we get involved in something we also try to take others with us (like drowning men). But the Bible says, "... every man shall bear his own burden" (Galatians 6:5).

You may take confidence in the fact that others seem to be doing as badly as you are. But that is a false assurance.

I remember when I travelled to a city in Ghana and visited a brother whom I had known to be very zealous for the Lord. Unfortunately, this brother whom I even considered to be in the rank of a minister had backslidden, and had made a young lady pregnant. He no longer went to church regularly. When my wife and I got to his house, we chatted a bit, and asked, "How are you doing spiritually?"

He said, "Oh, God is good." Then he immediately changed the topic and asked whether we had heard about another good friend of ours who had backslidden terribly.

"Brother X's condition is very unfortunate," he lamented.

He added, "Have you heard? He's fallen into very bad company, and doesn't go to church at all."

He was trying to make us see that this brother's condition was even worse than his. As we were going home in the car, I asked my wife if she noticed that this brother seemed to have taken some reassurance in the fact that our other friend was in an even worse state.

You can tell when people are trying to reassure themselves. Just listen to the things they say. They say things like: "Nowadays a lot of people don't go to church... City life is too busy for regular church attendance... There are now many Christians who drink a little beer with their food..."

Dear friend, don't be deceived by the existence of a crowd. You may think that everybody is sinning just like you are. But when Christ comes you'll be very surprised to find people whom you thought would go to hell with you, passing you by on their way to heaven!

A friend once told me about an incident that jolted him into becoming a Christian. He told me, "I was a party-going, night-life person with lots of girlfriends. One day, I was going home in a friend's car after one of our usual parties when I noticed that the car was unusually quiet."

"So I decided to slot in some good old disco music to liven up the atmosphere. I picked up one of the tapes lying in the front of the car and inserted it. To my utmost surprise, instead of music, I heard the sound of preaching."

I exclaimed, "Hey, what's this? Since when did you start listening to such things? Are you also one of those born again people?"

And his friend replied, "Hey, I am securing myself."

My friend said to me "I began to think very fast; If our car was to have had an accident and we were both to die, he may have gone to heaven, and I would have gone to hell!!"

My friend suddenly realized that he had been deceived into thinking that everyone of his friends was a ruthless sinner like he was. People were secretly seeking God and securing their places in heaven.

You better make sure that you are doing the right thing. Do not look at the crowd. You are born alone, and you will die alone. Do not even look to your husband or your wife. It is unusual for husbands and wives to be born on the same day. It is even more unusual for them to die on the same day.

You will stand before God as an individual. Never forget that fact of life.

2. Attitude #2 - "I have a lot of time, Christ is not really coming soon."

The world is truly amused when we say that Christ is coming soon. They think it is a theory cooked up by some deranged people.

On the other hand, some Christians know that Christ's Second Coming is a reality. But they think that it won't happen very soon. At least, not in their lifetime. They suppose they can enjoy themselves and forget about the future. But what they forget is that Christ's coming will be a very unexpected event. "...The day of the Lord so cometh as a thief in the night. For when they shall say, Peace and safety; then sudden destruction cometh upon them, as travail upon a woman with child; and they shall not escape" (1 Thessalonians 5:2,3).

A pregnant woman who is due might be all right one moment,and the next moment, go into labor. Severe pain will strike her and a baby will be born. So will the coming of the Lord be. Everything will be all right one day and the next, total chaos in the world. Jesus compares His coming to the coming of a thief. No one expects a thief. I remember years ago when thieves broke into my father's house. We were not expecting anything of the sort, but it just happened. The whole world will be very surprised when Jesus comes again.

Many of you have taken God's grace period of repentance for granted. Indeed, this grace period means nothing to some of us. The grace period has rather become more time to play the 'fool'. This is how backsliders think. I have more time! I have much more time!! You may be planning to have your grand wedding. But it may never come on. Perhaps, those who are in school may never complete their courses. The trumpet will suddenly sound, and those of us who are washed in the blood of the Lamb, and ready for the Saviour would be caught up in the clouds to be with Him forever.

3. Attitude #3 - "There are short cuts to everything, including going to Heaven."

The world is under the delusion that there are short cuts to everything. Unfortunately, some Christians think in the same way. They assume that there must be some short cut to Heaven since there seems to be a short cut to almost everything.

You cannot escape the Christian rudiments and go to Heaven. You cannot escape the cross. Jesus said, "Take up thy cross and follow me." There is no short cut around the cross. You must take it up. In this day and age of instant coffee, instant tea and jet travel, everybody wants to have things fast, quick and short.

When I was in boarding school, I learnt the hard way that short cuts must be avoided.

An Experience with a Judas

Those of us in the junior forms were asked to do some general scrubbing in school. I obtained an excuse duty slip from the doctor. It exempted me from any assigned duties for the next four days.

I happened to discuss this excuse duty slip with a friend, and excitedly told him how I wouldn't have to do any hard work for the next four days. Then he came up with what I thought was a bright idea.

He suggested, "Why don't you write '1' before the '4' so it reads '14' days instead of '4'? You will then have fourteen whole days to relax."

As I mused over this suggestion, I thought, "What a good idea! No one will notice."

But this friend was the first Judas I was to meet in my life. After I had taken his suggestion and changed the '4' to '14', this same friend reported me to the seniors. He told them that I had forged my excuse duty slip.

Every one pounced on me, and I was charged. I tell you, I suffered greatly for that mistake. First of all, my four days of excuse were cancelled. I was given the most difficult jobs to do. And then I was given extra punishment. From that time I decided, No more short cuts in life. I realized long ago that there was no short cut to Heaven. I will have to go the hard way.

We may think that there is a shorter way to Heaven, but there is only one way to Heaven. It is not through Allah, Islam, fetish, chanting or meditation. It is only by accepting the Lord Jesus Christ as your personal Saviour and being born again. There is no short cut.

In the secular world, wise businessmen are wary of any "get-rich-quick" schemes. Many however, are not tired of trying one quick scheme after the other. So they take advantage of every opportunity to make some quick money.

Get-Rich-Quick Schemes

Someone once asked our church to join a new "get-rich-quick" bank.

He explained, "As a growing church you will need a lot of money to help complete your building project."

But I immediately said, "It sounds too good to be true, and too quick to be real."

So we didn't join it.

A few weeks later, I heard of how that new bank had collapsed. Many people lost their money. I also heard of how some churches had lost huge sums of money by saving there.

The Bible says the kingdom of Heaven is like a mustard seed, which needs time to grow to become a great tree. When you put the seed into the ground, it will need to go through the long process of dying and growing before yielding fruit. Unfortunately, some of us want to escape the processes of dying and growing up. You cannot expect to just put money in the offering and hope that everything will be all right. You cannot avoid the reality of fasting, praying, fellowshipping and witnessing. These are Biblical standards we just cannot avoid!

4. Attitude #4 - "God loves me too much to punish me."

I have heard Christians say that God will never punish them. They quote, "For God so loved the world..." They argue that since God loves the world so much He will not destroy them. They say, "I know God will forgive me." Because of this they add sin to sin without batting an eyelid. God's nature is like two sides of a coin. One side of the coin shows the head, and the other side shows the tail. One side of God's character shows His great love, and the other side shows His judgement.

A Christian sister spoke of a woman who was having an affair with her best friend's husband. Because the two ladies were good friends they would often speak on the phone. Every time this adulteress put the phone down, she would sigh and say, "O God, forgive me for what I'm doing." Strangely, she still didn't stop destroying her friend's marriage.

Some people feel that God will not punish them. That is why they continue in sin. When God shows you one side of his character you will see love, forgiveness and mercy of the highest order. God will forgive and forget your sins. But a time will come when God will show you the other side of His nature; which is judgment, justice, fairness, equity and jurisprudence. These are the two sides of God's nature. We are now in the dispensation of Grace. God is showing you mercy and love. Think about all the wicked sins you have committed, but still receive His forgiveness.

At a certain point, the Spirit of the Lord will not strive with man anymore. God has to judge you, otherwise there will be chaos in the Kingdom. "The king by judgment establisheth the land..." (Proverbs 29:4). God loves you so much that He will punish you when He has to.

5. Attitude #5 - "I have more time, I'm not going to die soon."

People think that because they are young they still have a lot of time. Also they think they have enough of their lives ahead of them to sort things out with God.

Some years ago, the whole world shook at the news of the death of Princess Diana and her millionaire companion. No one in his wildest imagination would have thought that someone so young, so charming and so beautiful could be taken off the face of the earth so suddenly. The security of an armour-plated Mercedes Benz with airbags all around could not prevent her death in a car accident in Paris. I tell you, none of us was expecting this!

Everyone thinks that there is more time. I'm sure Princess Diana thought there were many more years ahead. We all did. But it was not so.

That is why the whole world trembled with shock. It is not safe to assume that there is more time. The Bible warns us that because we don't know the day or the hour Christ will come, we must be ready all the time. The key word here is preparation and readiness. "...thus will I do unto thee... because I will do this unto thee...Prepare to meet thy God..." (Amos 4:12).

In Luke 12, the Bible tells the story of a man who had a successful business. He had so much that he wondered what to do with the profits. He decided to build bigger barns to store his goods. In our time this would be equivalent to opening new bank accounts. When he completed his projects, he said to himself, "Soul, thou hast much goods laid up for many years. Take thine ease, eat, drink and be merry."

God reacted immediately from Heaven and said, "...This night thy soul shall be required of thee." In other words, I want to have a discussion with you tonight. God has the right to call you up for a discussion at any time. God is showing us here that there is just a step between us and death.

There are three times in your life when people will gather to honor you. They gather when you are born and christened. Then they gather again when you are getting married. And finally, they will definitely also gather for you when you die.

Somebody might contend that he or she is too young to die. But go to the mortuary, and you will discover that even little babies die. I was once in a hospital ward with one of my assistant pastors when we happened to see the body of a little baby who had just died. Although it was a tiny baby who had just began to live, it died. That baby was not too young to die.

Dear Christian friend, do not put off your godly obligations because you think you are still young and there is more time. You never know when God will summon you to account for your life. "...thus will I do unto thee,...because I will do this unto thee...Prepare to meet thy God. O Israel" (Amos 4:12).

The Condition of Backsliding and Apostasy

24

■ IDENTIFYING SYMPTOMS OF BACKSLIDING

"And there shall be SIGNS...when ye see these things...KNOW..." (Luke 21:25-31). In the field of medicine, a symptom or sign is the outward clue of something dangerous. Often when you are searching for something that is hidden, you look out for clues to lead you. Symptoms and signs help doctors to make the right diagnosis.

A symptom is meaningless to the unlearned, but important to the learned. If a symptom is detected early it can save a life. When a doctor detects certain signs, he knows that the patient's life is in danger. But a layman may have no idea of what is going on.

When the hand of a patient shows certain signs, it is an indication of a serious disease in the liver. What has the hand got to do with the liver? They are so far apart anyway. But it may surprise you to know that a shaking and jerking hand could indicate liver failure. To the unlearned, that shaking hand is just an unusual spasm. Some may even think that it is a sign of the anointing!

The pancreas is located somewhere deep in the abdomen. How can you know whether the pancreas is working or not? The only way to know is to look out for certain symptoms or signs. As scientists search for signs to know what is going on inside the body of a man, we must also look for the signs that uncover what is happening inside the soul of a man. The early detection of some of these symptoms can save a believer from backsliding and going to hell. Knowledge of the existence of these symptoms can give you staying power for the Christian race.

There is no point in regularly attending church, knowing the Lord, and later dying as a backslider! Why should I spend all my years preaching and later become a castaway? Why do the Lord's work today, and serve the devil tomorrow?

This is a picture of what happened to the five foolish virgins (Matthew 25). They were all virgins, all ten of them, but five were foolish and five were wise. All of them had oil at a certain point in time. Later on when it really mattered some of them didn't have oil. Perhaps the year before they were all zealous and anointed with oil. But at the end of it all, some of them had dropped away

I am teaching on these symptoms and signs of backsliding, because many Christians display these symptoms. Symptoms reveal the condition. If you detect any of these symptoms in yourself, know that you may be on a dangerous path to destruction.

1. BAD COMPANY

Experience in the ministry has taught me to take note of any Christian who keeps bad company. It is a very bad symptom, with a very poor prognosis. Bad company will eventually lead you to bad places. When you see a Christian who has bad friends, it is likely he will find his way out of church one day. "Bad company ruins good morals" (1 Corinthians 15:33 Revised Standard Version).

There is a saying, "Birds of the same feather flock together." One Ghanaian proverb can be rendered: "Show me your friend, and I will show you your character." This means that we can tell the kind of person you are by just looking at the kind of friends you have.

Within every large church there are smaller groups of Christians. When you observe these groups, you will discover that they are people with the same kind of 'feather'. The friends you move with will either lead you to church or to bad places.

If you are a real believer and you want to remain in Christ, then you need to have good friends. They should be real born-again Christians, who attend a "born-again" church. They must believe the things you believe. You must go to church together. Your friends must not have anything against your going to church. If they do, they must not be your friends.

Some people do not realise that the person they marry will keep them company for the rest of their lives, and this ."marital company" will truly affect you. This is how King Solomon, who built the temple and accomplished great things for the Lord, eventually backslid. The Bible tells us that his wives turned his heart away from God. His wives were bad company for him.

You do not need to expose yourself to the circumstances of bad company. You are not more anointed than Solomon. If the Bible warns that bad company can ruin your life, you'd better believe it and save yourself.

Every wife affects her husband, and every husband has great influence over his wife. Whoever you are, your wife will influence the way you think. If your husband thinks in a certain way, in the process of time, you will eventually think in the same way. I remember a sweet old lady who had nothing against other races. However, after being married for many years to a racist, she became prejudiced herself.

If your wife does not want you to be in the ministry, you will not be in the ministry. I know this from experience. If my wife had opposed my going into the ministry, I don't think I would have been able to come this far. That is why I am very concerned about who my pastors get married to. Bad company – whether friends, brothers, husbands, or wives – will lead to backsliding. Stay clear!

2. Looking Backwards

In Genesis 19, we can study the testimony of Lot and his wife. Two angels were sent to Lot and his family in Sodom and Gomorrah. Their message was simple: "... Escape for thy life, LOOK NOT BEHIND THEE... lest thou be consumed" (Genesis 19:17). But the Bible declares that Lot's wife looked back and became a pillar of salt. Jesus also reminds us of the terrible mistake that Lot's wife made as she was escaping from Sodom and Gomorrah. She was the only member of the family who looked back at her past. We can liken this to believers who backslid because they kept looking back at the world and all it had to offer.

As born-again believers, God has delivered all of us from sin, and it is important that we do not look back.

A Christian Lady Who Looked Back

I always remember the story of a lady who stood before a Christian group to testify. She happily recounted what she had done as an unbeliever: "I used to go out with many men. They would pick me up to party with me at nightclubs and discos. I danced all night with them. It was great," she said. With great excitement in her voice, she told the Christians: "I travelled all over the world with them. We really had a good time." Then her voice dropped and she sadly said, "But I got saved, and here I am in church."

To her, salvation was rather the "bad" thing that happened to her. It was as though being saved was an unfortunate experience. This woman was looking back to the expensive cars, the chinese restaurants and the "good" times she had had as an unbeliever.

If you keep on thinking and remembering your past sinful life with nostalgia, you will turn into "a pillar of salt"! When you see a married woman who talks with excitement about her past boyfriends, then you are looking at a woman who may not be happy where she is. It is most probable that she may want to go back to her "great" guys. You will go back if you keep looking back. And you will fall if you keep looking backwards.

I am looking ahead, and I intend to go forward with God's work. As a medical doctor in full-time ministry, I could look back and consider returning to the practice of medicine. There are times when I can remember the peculiar smell of the hospital. I remember those days when I walked the wards and heard the patients call, "Dr. Mills", "Please, Dr. Mills." But I am not looking back. I am going forward, preaching, teaching and planting churches all over the world. I have no intention of going back to the full-time practice of medicine.

If there is a longing in your heart to go backwards or to look backwards, then you are manifesting a dangerous symptom of backsliding. Come before the Lord and ask Him to help you "kill" that interest in the past. Let it die!

3. Over-confidence

An over-confident person is someone who has too much trust in his abilities. It is dangerous to be over-confident as a Christian. Being too confident in your righteousness and in your own spirituality is a bad sign. "...Let him that THINKETH HE STANDETH take heed lest he fall" (1 Corinthians 10:12). If you regard yourself or your position in Christ as foolproof, you are in danger of backsliding, especially if you have had promotion in church, or have been used by God in the past.

When a Christian continues to boast about his strength, Satan hears him and decides to test him. Such a person is a potential backslider. Where you are over-confident is where you can be the weakest, because you have dropped your guard. You can also tell that a Christian is over-confident by the way he talks about the weaknesses of others. I have heard Christians criticize others as though they could never make the same mistakes. They overestimate their own ability, and look down on others. You need to be humble, otherwise one day you will find yourself in the same shoes, much to your own surprise. Staying on the right track is largely by the grace of God, and not by your own strength.

When David heard that Saul was dead, he didn't ridicule him or rejoice over his death. David could have lashed out at Saul and criticized him at that time. He could have taken the opportunity to talk about how Saul had been disobedient and stubborn. He could have discussed what led to Saul's downfall. Instead he declared, "Tell it not in Gath, publish it not in the streets of Askelon..." (2 Samuel 1:20).

Although David did not have a problem with stubbornness and disobedience, he did not venture to denounce his predecessor because of his weaknesses. We must all learn something from this example.

4. Stubbornness

The next symptom of backsliding is stubbornness. A stubborn person is prone to falling away. "The backslider in heart shall be filled with his own ways..." (Proverbs 14:14).

If you know a stubborn Christian who does not heed counsel, but will always do what he wants to do in spite of all advice, you are looking at a potential backslider. "And my people are bent to backsliding from me..." (Hosea 11:7).

Often I would counsel Christians and find at the end of the session that they are still set in their ways. They are bent on doing their own thing. "Better is a poor and a wise child than an old and foolish king, who will no more be admonished" (Ecclesiastes 4:13). Everybody needs advice. The Bible says there is safety in the multitude of counsel.

A Counselling Experience

I remember counseling a young lady not to continue in a certain unhealthy relationship.

I asked, "What makes you different from the other girls he has thrown away? He has had 17 girlfriends, and you are the 18th. The only difference between you and the others is that you are new to him. But one day you will become "old" just like the others. And he will then throw you away." Inspite of this admonition, she persisted in her ways.

Is there anybody who was mightily blessed by God although he was stubborn and rebellious? Never! Stubbornness to God, to his Word, to his pastors and to biblical counsel is a sign that backsliding is imminent.

5. CHRISTIAN SURPRISES

There is something I call "Christian surprises". "Christian surprises" are surprises that are unique to the Christian experience. These are shocks you experience in the course of your Christian walk. Unfortunately, some people get so shocked by what they see and hear in church that it actually makes them fall away.

As we grow as Christians, we will encounter these Christian surprises. Most of us are quite naïve when we become Christians. We think we have come into a perfect world. So, when the so-called born-again saints disappoint us we become so amazed. We can't believe it's true. But the Bible says we should not be amazed.

A shocked or amazed Christian can easily fall away from the faith. "...as long as ye do well, and are not afraid with any amazement" (1 Peter 3:6). The Amplified Bible puts it this way: "...and let nothing terrify you - not giving way to hysterical fears or letting anxieties unnerve you" (1 Peter 3:6 Amplified Bible).

Being in a state of shock is being in a dangerous condition. Any good doctor who sees a patient in a state of shock knows that he is dealing with someone who can easily pop off and die. Any experienced pastor who sees his members in a state of shock and surprise at what may have happened in the church also knows that he is looking at a member who can easily fall away.

One of the things that may cause Christians to fall away is disappointment in a Christian leader. Sometimes your leader can disappoint you beyond measure. Samson, David, Peter and other mighty leaders made mistakes. That could have disappointed their followers, and caused them to backslide.

The Bible tells pastors not to be greedy, pompous or lord their authority over others. It states clearly that pastors should not run after money, or women. God's ministers are supposed to do His work from their hearts. The very fact that the Bible speaks about all of these things means that Christian leaders can do them (and have done them)!

These days one of the favourite activities of the press is to write stories about fallen Men of God. Some pastors have been involved in sex, money and breakaway scandals. Christians have been surprised at such behaviour coming from the people they have loved and looked up to for many years.

Such surprising behaviour often destabilizes hitherto "stable" believers. But remember the Word of God: "... there is no new thing under the sun. Is there anything whereof it may be said, See this is new? it hath been already of old time..." (Ecclesiastes 1:9,10).

If you have all through your Christian life, put your trust in a man, then it is very likely that you will be disappointed. Fix your eyes on Jesus.

Paul said, "Follow me as I follow Christ." Which means you can only follow your Christian leader as long as he follows Christ.

I often tell my church, "The day I stop following Christ, is the day you stop following me". I remember when some great men of God in the United States fell into sin, many Christians also fell away from the faith with them. Why was this so? They had experienced a Christian surprise. But they needn't have fallen. If you fix your eyes on Christ (looking unto Jesus), you will be a stable Christian.

Christians may also become surprised when they pray, but do not get the answers they expect. A close member of the family may be terminally ill, or you may have been praying for your husband to be saved, only to see him get worse. You can easily feel surprised and shocked that God has ignored your prayers. Do not be surprised. It is not everything that you know. You are still learning, and you are still growing in the Lord.

A Personal Experience

I remember one time when I was travelling to Tamale, a town in the northern part of Ghana. I was driving with the pastors of our branches in Kumasi, Zurich and a Canadian trainee pastor. On the highway, two bicycle riders suddenly crossed my path.

I had to apply the brakes immediately in order to avoid hitting them. When I did this, my car began to skid, and before I could say "Jack Robinson", we were somersaulting in the air. The car eventually rolled to a halt some 30 metres off the road. We were now literally upside down, with the wheels of the car in the air!

When we all came out alive and well, I must admit that I was surprised - and almost angry with God. Why should God allow such a thing to happen to us? Didn't He know that we were all pastors travelling only to do more of his work?

However, a few days later the Spirit of God ministered certain things to me privately.

One thing I can tell you that He said to me was, "Instead of being angry and surprised, you should be grateful that I have allowed this to happen in order to draw your attention to something very important for your life and ministry".

You may not understand this now, but as you grow in Christ you will understand it better by and by.

Jesus Did Not Heal Everyone

When Jesus was here, He did not heal everybody. Jesus went to the pool of Bethsaida, a place that had a host of sick people. (That is the equivalent of a modern hospital.)

But he only healed one man, who had been sick for 38 years.

Why didn't he heal any of the others? Jesus said, "My Father works, and I work". Jesus meant that he was doing exactly what his Father was doing. Should we be surprised at this move of Christ? We have to learn to trust in the Sovereignty of God and not be annoyed with him.

The Disciples of Jesus

The arrest and crucifixion of Christ surprised the disciples. A week before He had sat on a donkey, and the crowds had cheered Him. They hailed and sang, "Hosanna, blessed is He that comes in the name of the Lord!"

The disciples knew that He was a great man. But a week later He was killed on the cross like a common criminal. They must have been very surprised. As we all know, these frightened, surprised and disappointed disciples deserted their Saviour and were scattered . This is the equivalent of backsliding.

Avoiding Surprise

Ever since I became a pastor, the lifestyles, habits and practices of some Christian leaders have surprised me. But I have had to teach myself not to be surprised anymore. What has been even more bewildering is the duality of some ministers. I remember one minister who spoke of committing fornication almost as if it was an everyday occurrence in his life. Yet this man was the pastor of a church. Time and time again, I have had to brace myself and decide not to be astonished or amazed by what goes on around me. Otherwise I may have left the Ministry by now!

Decide not to be surprised, astonished, dazed, bewildered, or even angry with some of the things you see in Christianity. Keep your focus on Christ and his Word.

6. To be easily offended

When you see someone who is very touchy, easily hurt and offended, you are looking at a potential backslider.

I remember one absentee church member whom we visited. We wanted to know why she was not in church anymore. She told us that once, when she came in late, the ushers wrongly seated her and later relocated her. This had happened more than once. So she became offended and decided not to come to church anymore. This person was offended by the inexperienced usher and simply left the church. Imagine that!

Some church members are irritated because the pastor does not seem to remember their names. Others are offended because the pastor did not say hello when he met them in town. Think about this for a moment; why would the pastor delibrately not say hello to his own church member? Does it make sense? Is he trying to gather people or to scatter and offend them? Could it not be that the pastor didn't recognize you, or that he genuinely did not notice you? Think about it!

If you marry a touchy person, you will always have problems. They are the ones who complain, "Why didn't you smile today? I put my toothbrush in the center, why have you moved it to the right? How come the towel is wet? Don't leave my towel on the bed. Why have you put my shoes here instead of there?" It's very difficult to live with people like that. They are not only difficult marriage partners, but also difficult church members for the pastor. They can even become offended with God Himself!

My Father Died whilst I Prayed

If I were to be easily offended, I would not have been able to continue in the ministry. Some years ago, I travelled from Ghana to start a church in Zurich.

While I was fasting and praying to establish God's work, my father died back home in Ghana. Throughout the week before he died, he had been seriously ill, but I wasn't fully informed about what was going on. Then one day after I had been praying and fasting for 5 days and nights, my father died about 11 O'clock in the morning.

One of my associate pastors called to inform me about what had happened. I was shocked and surprised. And when I put the phone down, I wept like a baby.

I had every reason to be offended with God. Wasn't I on the mission field, doing His work? I consoled myself that I would understand it better by and by and truly, I have not become disillusioned with the ministry. I am pressing on! If a Christian easily gets hurt, he is likely to backslide!

ADDITIONAL SYMPTOMS OF BACKSLIDING

1. Forgetfulness

God warned the children of Israel: "...and thou forget the Lord ...which brought thee forth..." (Deuteronomy 8:14). Christians fall away from Christ because they forget where they came from. They forget that their source is Christ. Don't ever forget that it is Christ who brought you to your position, and blessed you.

Many of us have forgotten who we used to be. We have forgotten what it was like to have a hangover in the morning. We have forgotten what it was like to have your different girlfriends 'clashing'.

We have forgotten the fear of not knowing whether you have contracted gonorrhoea or AIDS.

Let us remember where the Lord brought us from. When we bought our first church building, we were all so excited. We marched from the Korle-Bu Hospital in Accra, to our new headquarters location, amidst singing and dancing. The building was an old cinema that we rebuilt into a beautiful cathedral.

Indeed, we played before the Lord. Somebody who watched me later on video laughed and commented: "It seems that old cinema hall meant a lot to you". I replied, "You don't know where the Lord has brought me from. I have not forgotten, and I do not intend to forget."

Many churches have forgotten the vision and principles of their founders. They have forgotten the ideals and standards which their founding fathers stood for. That is why many of them are in a backslidden condition. If some founders of churches were to rise from the dead now, I believe that many of them would not join the very churches they founded. The current leaders would even reject them.

I always try to remember why I came into the ministry. Why did I leave the respected and noble practice of medicine to come into the often controversial and ridiculed job of being a pastor? My original motivation was to win souls. I keep that at the forefront of my mind and I keep pressing on to win more souls. If I forget that, I can easily slide into education, medicine, social work or even politics. Anybody who forgets can slip and slide into things he didn't intend to involve himself with.

2. Not fasting

Fasting keeps the believer from backsliding. In the Bible the word associated with fasting is affliction. In fact, the word affliction can be interchanged for fasting. "Wherefore have we fasted… wherefore have we afflicted our soul…" (Isaiah 58:3); "Be afflicted, and mourn, and weep…" (James 4:9).

According to the psalmist, one way you can afflict yourself is by fasting. "Before I was afflicted I went astray: but now have I kept thy word" (Psalm 119:67).

Fasting keeps you on track. He said that before he fasted he went astray, but when he fasted, he was able to keep God's Word and stay on track. Christians who don't fast often fall away from Christ. They gradually move away from God.

Then in Psalm 119:71, he says, "It is good for me that I have been afflicted, that I might learn thy statutes." Do you think that God is saying it is good to have sickness and disease? Affliction in that sense is not sickness. In this context God is saying that it is good for the Christian to fast.

Another word that is associated with fasting is humility. In James 4:10, the Word of God says, "Humble yourself in the sight of God and He will lift you up." When the psalmist fasted in Psalm 35:13, he said, "I humbled my soul with fasting".

During a fast, especially when you have not eaten for several days, you experience extreme weakness in your body. This kind of suffering in the flesh sobers you. It makes you humble. And if there is anything we need in this modern age of Christianity, it is humility. Remember that pride comes before a fall, and fasting will take away the pride that leads many to a fall. As a believer you need to fast, otherwise your flesh will dominate you, and lead you into fleshly sins. To be carnally minded is death.

Another reason for fasting is that there are particular problems that can only be solved through fasting. Some people have problems that are going to make them backslide. Some of these problems that cause backsliding must be solved through fasting. Jesus told his disciples after they failed to heal an epileptic, "...This kind goeth not out but by prayer and fasting" (Matthew 17:21).

Jesus meant here that not all problems are the same. Some difficult ones can be solved only through fasting. It is no wonder that christians who do not fast are weighed down by all kinds of problems.

Even winter should not prevent Christians from fasting. I have heard Christians in Europe and America complain that it is not possible to fast during the winter. It is possible. During several of my church-planting exercises, I have had to fast during the winter.

I remember once when a brother visited and realized I was fasting, he could not believe it. He asked me, "How can you fast when it is so cold?" He explained that eating helps to keep warm.

Fasting Prevents Spiritual Coldness

But this is the very reason why many African Christians who live in Europe and America are a far cry from what they used to be in their own countries.

They have stopped fasting for various reasons, and have grown spiritually cold.

Fasting is not an option. Jesus said in Matthew 6:16: "when ye fast..." He didn't say if you fast. This means He expects us to fast.

Fasting has its rewards. In Isaiah 58, God has listed some of the rewards of fasting. "Then shall thy light break forth as the morning, and thine health shall spring forth speedily... Then shalt thou call, and the Lord shall answer: thou shalt cry, and he shall say, Here I am..." (Isaiah 58:8,9).

One of the rewards of fasting is that you will stay spiritually healthy.

3. Fasting less

The next symptom of a person who is backsliding is the symptom of fasting less. Fasting is a spiritual exercise that keeps us on our toes.

The more you fast, the more spiritual energy you generate. The more you fast, the more spiritually tuned up you will be. If you used to fast regularly sometime ago, but now fast less, it is a possible sign that you are becoming 'cold'..

Fasting is not an option. The prophet Daniel was eighty years old when he fasted for three weeks. Even pregnancy should not make a Christian woman abandon her fasting life. During pregnancy, you should be able to fast to some extent, and still remain healthy. The baby may become anointed and grow even better.

Fasting less is a sign that your investment into spiritual things is gradually decreasing.

4. Anger at correction

Any believer who gets angry at correction must be watched closely. "Reprove not a scorner, lest he hate thee: rebuke a wise man, and he will love thee" (Proverbs 9:8). A wise man will be happy at correction because he will think through it and realize that he is being helped. Often the truth is painful. When Jesus told the crowd in John 8:44, "...ye are of your father the devil...," they were offended.

On one occasion, Jesus addressed Peter and said to him, "Get thee behind me, Satan." Notice that Peter was not angry at being called Satan. After this rebuke, Peter went on to become the great man of God who preached to thousands!

A friend at school told someone who was irritating him, "Satan, get thee behind me." This person was astonished, amazed and very offended at being called "Satan". His reaction was very different from Peter's!

I have never referred to anybody as Satan (although I have seen many people behave just like the devil). I wonder what would happen if I dared to correct someone by referring to him as Satan? He would probably explode in anger!

During a visit to one of my branch churches, an instrumentalist was very rude to his choir director. The pastor in charge sternly rebuked this musician. I watched this scene quietly from the side, wondering what would happen next.

Fortunately this musician did not get angry at his pastor's rebuke and is doing well up until today. I know some musicians who would have walked out at that kind of correction.

A Good father will correct you. God gave us fathers and mothers to correct and advise us. "Better is a poor and a wise child than an old and foolish king, who will no more be admonished" (Ecclesiastes 4:13). You should thank God if your parents are alive.

There are many people who do not have strong fathers to guide them. Such people often go astray. Those who do not have good parents to guide and correct them are at a disadvantage. Correction will help you stay on track, so do not be angry at correction!

5. Allowing the Cares of the World to Choke the Word

"And the cares of this world... choke the word, and it becometh unfruitful" (Mark 4:19). Jesus told the story of a sower who went out to sow (Mark 4:19). Some seeds fell on the wayside, some on stony ground, some among thorns and the rest on good ground.

Jesus compared the four types of ground to four types of hearts. In one heart, thorns choked the word. In another, the heart was like a stone, so that the Word could not enter. In another heart, the Word fell by the wayside. It was only the good heart that bore fruit. This story implies that only about a quarter of all those who hear the Word of God will eventually remain in Christ and be fruitful.

What are the cares of the world? Paying your debts, your bills, and all the responsibilities that go with family life fall under these "cares". There is nothing wrong with paying your bills or looking after your family. Indeed, if you have a wife or family, you ought to look after them. A husband's duty is to fellowship with his wife and take care of his children. These are legitimate challenges that every one in this world will have to grapple with. God warns us against becoming over burdened with these responsibilities. These cares should not dominate our lives. When they begin to dominate your life, you are in danger of backsliding. The cares of the world have begun to cause backsliding.

As a pastor, I have observed that when Christians take on new jobs, they become so engrossed in them – to the detriment of their spiritual lives. Sometimes because of such new jobs, they neither go to church nor have their quiet times any more. The cares of the world have begun to cause backsliding.

For instance, every student's "care" is to pass his examinations but God should not be excluded from your life because of your books. As a medical student I successfully combined my schoolwork with my pastoral work. For years I was a student as well as a pastor. I have never put the Word or the work of God aside because of school.

In my ministry, I have had medical students pastoring large branches of the church faithfully. It is not an impossible task. As a medical student, I often asked, "Is being a medical student a curse? Does it mean that I cannot serve God anymore? Does it mean I have to backslide?" The answer is no! Being a medical student is just another "care" of this world, which must not be allowed to choke God's Word and work.

A new baby or a pregnancy should not make you backslide. Other Christians have made it, and so can you! When our first son was born, I carried him to church when he was only seven days old. I had a preaching appointment to honour, and had to go with my wife and my newborn son. I remember how we carried our seven-day-old baby through the cold weather onto the buses, and in the streets in order to keep this preaching appointment in Geneva.

My baby didn't die. Neither will yours, if you continue to do the work of the Lord. I am sorry to say that many new mothers are backsliding Christians, because they are allowing the cares of the world to choke their Christian lives.

6. Allowing riches to choke the Word

Those who are very rich have certain problems which poorer people do not have. These problems of the rich tend to keep them away from church. "...and the deceitfulness of riches,... choke the word, and it becometh unfruitful" (Mark 4:19).

When we first purchased the Lighthouse Cathedral property, we ran into a new problem which we did not have before. We had to think of security! We hadn't thought of security before, because we had never had any property to protect.

I have noticed that as people become more successful they tend to stay away from church. When the Lord blesses you, do not make the mistake of allowing the responsibilities associated with new blessings to choke the Word.

Remember that it was God who gave you the power to acquire wealth. God, by blessing you, did not intend to keep you away from Him!

You rarely see the so-called "big-shots" at prayer meetings and crusades. They do not turn up for all night prayer meetings probably because they are tired from all the work they do, or because the time could be spent doing something "profitable".

Learn how to maintain the glow inspite of your newfound treasures. Don't allow your riches to crowd out the Lord.

7. The lust of the world

Lust for anything apart from God's Word is dangerous. It can ruin your life because you will sacrifice so many things to get what you want. "...and the lusts of other things entering in, choke the word, and it becometh unfruitful" (Mark 4:19).

There are Christians who will sacrifice anything to ride in a mercedes benz. They will steal, cheat and lie to own one. Such Believers have a strong desire to have some material possession, and they will do all they can to have it. This strong overpowering desire is what God calls lust. But lust is dangerous! It destroys.

Corruption has come into the world through lust: "...having escaped the corruption that is in the world through lust" (2 Peter 1:4). Governments are often corrupt because of officials who have strong desires to acquire certain possessions. These officials take bribes in exchange for illegal favours. They also receive gifts and handouts in exchange for signing bogus contracts which ruin the economies of entire nations.

Lust (strong desires) corrupts people. As a minister I have learnt not to have a strong desire for anything in particular. It can easily destroy your ministry. Mind you, I also have desires, but they are subject to the Word of God in me. The strongest desire in a Christian's life should be for the will of God to prevail. "...Take heed, and beware of covetousness: for a man's life consisteth not in the abundance of the things which he possesseth" (Luke 12:15).

There is nothing that is worth sacrificing your Christianity for. You will only live (or die) to regret it. If you see someone who has a very strong desire for material things, you are looking at a potential backslider. One day the devil will dangle that thing in front of you, and you may just walk out on Christ to get it.

Some Christian ladies desperately want a husband, and therefore they will break all the rules, and sacrifice every moral principle in order to get one. Others desperately want to have a child. And they will go as far as having sex with other men if their husbands are sterile.

Once when I was working in the hospital, a doctor friend explained that his work in the gynecological department had made him distrust women. He said he had seen female patients whom, when they realized their husbands were sterile, went ahead and sacrificed their marital vows in order to become pregnant.

He related how one husband had come to his house weeping for joy after his wife had had a baby. He marvelled, "This man did not know that his wife had cheated on him and had had a child by another man."

Do not let your craving for material possessions make you backslide.

8. A POOR QUALITY CONSCIENCE

A person who does not have a good conscience is a potential backslider. A good conscience is necessary to keep you on track. It is the next symptom of backsliding I want us to consider. "Holding faith, and a good conscience; which some having put away concerning faith have made shipwreck: Of whom is Hymenaeus and Alexander; whom I have delivered unto Satan, that they may learn not to blaspheme" (1 Timothy 1:19-20)

Two church members, Hymenaeus and Alexander, put away faith and a good conscience, and thus, they made shipwreck of their Christian lives. As long as we put our conscience away, we will have the capacity to do greater and greater evil until the day that we forsake God.

The conscience is the voice of that better component of a human being (whether a Christian or non-Christian). It is the conscience of a man that tries to keep him from doing evil. It is important to have a good and strong conscience (inner voice).

Protect your conscience. You can either have a strong conscience or a weak one. Paul, the great apostle, said he had a good conscience. He also revealed that he had always maintained a good conscience, even as an unbeliever.

I dare say that some unbelievers have better consciences than some Christians. When our conscience becomes hardened, it is difficult for God to speak to us. I have always tried to have a good conscience, because I know the danger of a hardened conscience. It is this conscience which pricks me everyday and keeps me from backsliding.

When your conscience is gone, that element within you that can stop the backsliding process is also gone. You are no longer touched by the anointing, by the Word of God, by the preaching, or by the Holy Ghost.

Your conscience is like the palm of your hand. Some of us have soft hands, whilst others have callous ones. Your hands will become hardened, and the softness will go away as you do hard work with your hands. In the same way, your conscience will become hardened as you continue to sin without repenting. When believers become indifferent to the promptings of God, it is a dangerous sign.

A pastor friend of mine whose entire family is saved except for one brother told me his story. He related how his mother had taken his brother to so many Full Gospel Breakfast meetings that he had become hardened.

He had heard many different testimonies from several speakers but these no longer made an impact on his life. Indeed, he knew when the speaker would make an altar call. He knew what the next item on the programme was.

Many Christians can lie and their consciences will not prick them anymore. Some of them can even invent false stories without batting an eyelid.

I have heard of pastors who say they preach best after fornicating. The difference between these pastors and you is just a gradual process of hardening. You become harder and harder as you become used to sin. Then at a point when you sin you won't be bothered anymore.

You can commit bigger or smaller sins depending on your conscience. If you have a very sensitive conscience, the sins that you can commit will be "small" ones.

But as your conscience becomes more hardened and more worn out, your ability to commit "wilder" sins grows.

Recently, I sat before a certain rich man, and I said to him, "You must be prepared to meet your God at anytime." He was with two of his wealthy friends. He replied that he was not prepared, but he really didn't care.

When you get to the stage where you don't care whether you go to heaven or hell, then you are in danger. Perhaps, when you were younger you would have cared, but now, you are so hardened that you don't care anymore.

Every Christian needs to have a sensitive conscience. Do not get used to sin. Do not get to the stage where you do not care anymore. Be sensitive to the little promptings of the inner voice, so you don't backslide!

EVEN MORE SYMPTOMS OF BACKSLIDING

1. Praying less

The next symptom of backsliding I want us to consider is praying less. Jesus said, "Pray lest you fall into temptation".

Prayer keeps us from falling away from God. Anybody you spend time talking to becomes close to you. In the same way, any Christian who spends time talking to God will become close to him. It follows that if you don't spend time praying to God, you will be far from him.

This is one of the principles that explain how people can have extra-marital affairs. Many of us forget that if you continuously communicate with somebody, he or she becomes close to you. You can unknowingly fall in love with a man or woman who is not your partner.

Spending time together with somebody makes you close, whether you intend to be close or not. So when a Christian spends less time praying, he is unknowingly moving away from God.

A Strange Woman

When you pray, God gives you strength to overcome temptations. He will strengthen you to do His will and you will not fall away. Many years ago, God knew I was going to experience a serious testing of my Christian faith so He woke me up early in the morning to pray. Tongues were flowing out of my spirit like a river and I knew something was amiss, so I prayed the more. I laid down on the floor and continued in prayer. As a young Christian I was normally doing an hour a day in prayer, but this time I prayed for over three hours. And that day I met a strange woman. The Bible tells us about a young man in Proverbs who met a strange woman. I had a similar experience. "And, behold, there met him a woman with the attire of an harlot, and subtil of heart" (Proverbs 7:10).

I had no idea what this Christian lady had in mind. But that day, I tell you my friend, God delivered me! I believe my deliverance was very much related to the prayer time I had had in the morning. I was very strong. Where did that strength come from? Jesus told His disciples to pray because they might fall into temptation. The Lord gave me strength through prayer. If you see a Christian who doesn't pray, you are looking at a Christian who will fall into one temptation after another, until he eventually backslides.

2. Not being committed

The next symptom of backsliding I want us to consider is the symptom of not being committed. Anybody who does not want to be committed to a church, will ultimately leave that church. There are countless Christians who are just visiting churches, but are not committed to any of them. These are the 'watching Christians'. They are watching out for how things will turn out by the next month. If they don't feel too happy with the pastor or his sermons, they will move to the next church.

God expects the believer to be like a tree that is planted by the rivers of water. The rivers of water are the powerful, life-changing messages that flow from the pulpit every Sunday. Every Christian must be planted in the house of the Lord. You must have somebody to relate to as your pastor. God created us in a special way so that we are like sheep, who need a shepherd. You need to belong somewhere!

I remember one friend who finally came home after sojourning in Europe for sometime. He didn't want to join this church, or that church. He was just not committed anywhere. He would go here today and there tomorrow. At a point I had to remind him that it is only the devil who goes to and fro according to the book of Job! An uncommitted Christian is a potential backslider.

3. Irregular fellowship

The next symptom is the symptom of having irregular fellowship. I think this is one of the most important symptoms. It is actually one of the most common.

Your heart is supposed to beat at regular intervals. But unfortunately, some people have an irregular heartbeat. This means that when their hearts beat correctly once or twice, it is followed by a mis-timed beat. An irregular heartbeat may be regularly irregular or irregularly irregular. A patient with an irregularly irregular heartbeat is suffering from what is called atrial fibrillation and experiences symptoms like fainting and palpitations. To prevent death such people's hearts need to be stabilized.

Unfortunately, there are many Christians who have this problem of being irregular in their spiritual walk. This irregularity is either regular or irregular. Their church attendance may be regularly (constantly) irregular. (For instance they constantly come to church once or twice a month). For some, church attendance may be irregularly irregular. For such people their church attendance may be totally unpredictable throughout the year. The pastor cannot predict when they will next be in church. Can you imagine what it would be like if you didn't know when next your heart would beat?

Television and radio sermons cannot substitute regular fellowship. You must have a specific church, which you attend regularly. Observe the irregular Christians. You will notice how they tend to backslide. But the regular feeding of your spirit will keep you from backsliding.

4. Laziness and excuses

The next symptom you must watch out for is laziness and excuses: "The slothful man saith, There is a lion without, I shall be slain in the streets" (Proverbs 22:13).

The lazy Christian is full of amazing excuses. He would say he couldn't leave his bed because of an imaginary lion in the street. Such a person will not amount to much because anyone who wants to be successful must be prepared to work hard.

When I was in Achimota school I passed with distinction at the ordinary level exams. It didn't just happen. I had to work very hard. While some of the students were playing around, I was studying very hard.

In the third year of my medical schooling I earned another distinction. In preparation for that exam, I didn't sleep in the night for six weeks. I slept in the afternoons between 2p.m. and 6p.m. Then from 6p.m. till the next day at 2p.m., I wouldn't sleep. I would go for walks, memorizing and retaining some of the course material. I remember walking up and down in the 'R' Block of the medical students' hostel, memorizing all sorts of information about worms, flies, and insects: this worm lays so many eggs per minute, that insect flies at this speed per second, it dives at this angle into the water, etc.

When other students were asleep, I was walking behind their rooms memorizing things about worms, crabs, scorpions and every other creature I had to learn about.

When you see somebody succeeding as a Christian, or doing well in any sphere, he must be working hard. "Seest thou a man diligent in his business? he shall stand before kings; he shall not stand before mean men" (Proverbs 22:29).

Laziness will not take anybody to Heaven. Seest thou a man who is slothful; he can easily go to Hell! It takes hard work to stay on track with God. Watch the lazy Christians in the church; they are prone to backsliding!

5. Coldness

Coldness is the next symptom of backsliding I want us to consider. "And because iniquity shall abound, the love of many shall wax cold" (Matthew 24:12).

You can detect coldness by first identifying "coolness" in church. Some Christians are very 'cool' in the house of the Lord. They refuse to be part of jubilant praise and worship. They don't join in shouting or clapping their hands to the Lord.

They just refuse to release themselves in the presence of the Lord. I call these people 'Christian diplomats'. To all such people I say: there is no place for diplomacy in Christianity!

If you want God to be attracted to you, then be like King David. David lost all his inhibitions when he danced before the Lord. There was no coolness about the way he danced. In fact, he danced until his clothes fell off!

The backsliding Christian has no joy in expressing himself before the Lord. To him it is a bother to lift up his hands to the Lord, or shout with the voice of triumph. It is amazing that this same "cool" Christian would lose his "coolness" when his favourite soccer team is playing. He will shout, scream and clap his hands when a goal is scored.

I have noticed that when Christians are backsliding they first become aloof, diplomatic and uninterested. They yawn, look bored and keep glancing at their watches during the service. These are manifestations of what I call "coldness" or "coolness". Watch out for them; they are sure signs of imminent backsliding.

6. Foolish questioning

Foolish questioning is another symptom of backsliding. "But foolish and unlearned questions avoid...they do gender strifes" (2 Timothy 2:23).

Someone asked, "Who made God?"

Another person said, "I'll come to church if you can tell me who Cain's wife was" (Referring to Adam and Eve's first son).

The answer to this particular question is very simple. But it is a foolish question anyway. You see, the problem is not who married Cain; the real problem is with your backsliding tendency! You now want to find some reason to doubt the authenticity of the Bible!

Others would question "Why are the pastors driving nice cars?" Again, the problem is not with the pastor's car or how much the pastors are being paid. The problem is that you are backsliding and are trying to find some fault with your church. You desperately need to find a reason to justify your actions.

These are foolish questions, a classic symptom of a backsliding Christian.

Of course, I am not against the asking of legitimate questions. But there is a difference between a genuine question and a foolish question. Watch out for those who come up with all sorts of criticisms and reviews of the church and its ministers. They often have a hidden motive.

7. Having no spiritual ambition

Another symptom of backsliding is having no spiritual ambition. As a believer if you don't go forward, you will go backwards. If you don't have in you an ambition to press forward in Christ, you will have a problem.

I have noticed that Christians who have no spiritual ambition have the tendency to grow "cold" and eventually fall away. Paul had a vision to keep pressing on: "...but this one thing I do, forgetting those things which are behind...I press toward the mark for the prize of the high calling..." (Philippians 3:13,14).

We must forget the good and the bad and press on ahead. We have all had bad and good experiences in our lifetime. But we must forget about them and press forward. Some Christians are hooked on to the past. They tell tales of the great exploits God used them to do in the past.

You cannot just be content with what happened some years ago. What about the present? What is God using you to do today? The time to minister to others is now. "For when for the time ye ought to be teachers, ye have need that one teach you again..." (Hebrews 5:12).

One thing that has kept me from falling away is my pursuit of spiritual achievements. You must have a spiritual heart, which will propel you to rise up and go ahead to minister to others.

The greatest blessing you can have is to become a blessing yourself. God promised Abraham that He would bless him so much that he would also become a blessing.

I Couldn't Preach

There was a time in my life when I couldn't preach. But I did not stay there. I knelt down before a mature Christian brother and asked him to lay hands on me so I would be able to preach. After that prayer I started preaching. I stood before little groups and began ministering to them. Maybe you also have the same problem, or you feel very shy to speak in public. Act in faith by speaking the Word with a few people, and you will be surprised at what God can do. It will keep you from backsliding.

A Christian should have the ambition to be useful in God's house. Many people do not wish to be great in God's house. On the contrary, you will be surprised at the number of believers who crave to be millionaires. They look for all the opportunities to be great in the secular world. However, when it comes to the things of God, they have no drive.

I have always wanted to be a preacher. I listened to and watched other preachers minister. I used to go home from the university to watch videos of preaching. I invested both time and money to achieve my goal. That is why I never backslid.

Pastors! Watch the sheep who have no spiritual drive.

8. Curiosity

The next symptom of backsliding to notice is the symptom of curiosity. Curiosity, they say, killed the cat. But in another sense curiosity also kills many Christians. Some Christians have been deceived by the devil into thinking that they are missing something. So they become curious and want to experiment with these forbidden areas.

Some would say, "I haven't tasted alcohol all my life. I want to know what it feels like to be drunk."

Others would say, "I have never used drugs before and I want to know what it feels like to be 'high'." You may only find out what it is like to be mad! You may acquire what we call marijuana-induced schizophrenia.

I was with my boss in a consulting room at the mental hospital one day when a mother brought in her son. This boy had been experimenting with marijuana.

The Psychiatrist took this young boy on a tour of the mental hospital. There were men in little cubicles making various strange noises. There were special places for very wild and mad men. It reminded me of the zoo.

The Psychiatrist warned this young boy that if he continued experimenting with drugs his curiosity would end him up in this "zoo"! I will never forget that tour.

It is this same kind of curiosity, which led the prodigal son out of his father's house to eat with pigs. What couldn't the prodigal son have had at home? He admitted that his own father's servants had more than enough to eat. He was just curious about what was going on out there.

You will notice men with very beautiful and charming wives, who still chase after other women. Some of these men are just curious. They think there is more to discover.

There is nothing new under the sun. There is nothing new to see. Curiosity killed the backslider!

9. Murmuring

The next symptom of backsliding is murmuring. "Do all things without murmurings and disputings" (Philippians 2:14).

Murmuring means to complain, to grumble, to mumble and to criticize. There are Christians who murmur at home, at work and in church. God is against those who murmur. He was especially displeased with the people of Israel when they murmured against him and Moses. Some complained and nagged so much that they never made it to the Promised Land.

People who murmur and complain never make it to the Promised Land. In my experience, people who murmur and complain often leave their churches and eventually backslide.

When you complain against someone, it is likely that you are angry with the person or that you don't like that person anymore. Those who complain against their governments are often angry with their government. In the same way those who murmur against the church are often angry with God and are ready to leave Him. Mark those who murmur and complain, because they are potential deserters of the ship.

10. Approval and Admiration of Evil or Wrongdoers

The next very important symptom is "approval and admiration of wrong doers". People usually become attracted to something before they go for it. In the same way, if you approve of somebody who is doing the wrong thing, then you are likely to want to do the same thing yourself. God expects the Christian to disapprove of evil. Although Saul was Jonathan's father, Jonathan acknowledged that the King, his father, was wrong in trying to kill David. David had done no wrong, but out of jealousy, Saul attempted to kill him.

Jonathan disassociated himself from what his father was doing and associated himself with the right, which was David. That is what a real Christian must do. You must not approve of what is wrong. You must be bold and say, "This is wrong, and that is right! And I stand for what is right." The Bible says: "Woe unto them that call evil good..." (Isaiah 5:20).

From experience I have noticed that if you praise evil, one day you will also commit the same evil. If someone is a rebel and you approve of the person, one day you may also be a rebel. I watch for people who do not condemn the evil going on around them. The Christian should never approve of evil. "...Wherein have we wearied him? When ye say, Every one that doeth evil is good ..." (Malachi 2:17).

Watch out for Christians who do not disapprove of evil; they are probably thinking of doing the same thing one day.

11. Poor Adaptation Reflexes

The children of Israel hung their harps upon the willows when they encountered their new circumstances. They packed up their instruments of praise because they had been carried away as captives. "...How shall we sing the Lord's song in a strange land?" (Psalm 137:4).

Christians who find it difficult to adapt to their new circumstances often backslide in their walk with God. They cannot adapt themselves to their new roles as wives, husbands, mothers, fathers and so on. They are simply unable to adapt themselves to their new jobs, new husbands, new wives, new babies and so on.

Sometimes when a Christian relocates to another city, he changes from being a strong and vibrant Christian to being cold and indifferent. He cannot adapt to his new environment. Why should you turn your back on God because of your new circumstance? Rise up in the name of Jesus! You wanted so much to have a wife, a husband and a job. Now you have it, so adapt quickly to your new circumstance, and do not backslide.

Psalm 118:14 says: "The Lord is my strength and song, and is become my salvation." Notice the relation between "my strength", "my song" and "my salvation." You cannot separate your song from your strength. Neither can you separate your strength from your salvation. They go together. You need to sing the Lord's song whatever you do and wherever you find yourself.

I once heard a "bachelor" pastor being challenged. He was told, "If you are still anointed after you marry, then you are really called of God." The message was clear. You will have a lot of adapting to do after you get married, otherwise you will backslide (1 Corinthians 7:28).

Nothing comes cheap. It was extremely difficult for me to become a doctor as well as a pastor. When you become a doctor your life changes. Your life becomes totally involved in the condition of your patients. But I had to quickly adapt to my new circumstance in order to continue with the ministry. You can't put the Lord aside just because you have travelled to a new country or to a new school.

The Christian who cannot adapt quickly to his new circumstances is likely to backslide. You must adapt in order to stay alive. Learn how to identify these things. Do not be ignorant of the devil's devices. Why fall away now that you know the Lord?

God has great plans for you, there is no doubt about it. He has plans to bless you, to prosper you and to increase you in this life. Remember, however, that such blessings are not meant to draw you away from God, but to establish your faith and confidence in Him. Do not let the new circumstances which your blessings may bring cause you to backslide. Develop staying power!

■ MY LAST ARGUMENT

This is my final argument against backsliding. You will be shown in very real terms the folly of backsliding. You will hear the testimonies of real Christians who made it to the very end. You will also hear the last statements of the backslidden and lost souls, and what they said as they approached the gates of Hell. You will see how really terrible backsliding is. In our walk with God there is a certain line that we must not cross. There is a point of no return. I have heard believers say that they will backslide, but will come back to the Lord after some time. They forget that there may be a point of no return.

We will all stand before the presence of God to account for our lives. When that time comes and you are ushered into the presence of God, what will you say? Will you be ready? Will you have done what God wanted you to do?

A Christian brother was committing fornication when he heard a loud blast. He thought it was the sound of the trumpet heralding the return of Christ. So he jumped out of the bed, but was not caught up to heaven. He was so worried, because he thought that he had been left behind at the rapture. This anxious Christian was overreacting to the honk of a big bus. A backslider lives in fear and uncertainty.

God wants to reason with you. God is a rational Being, and He wants to reason with you. "Come now, and let us reason together..." (Isaiah 1:18).

Many people think that when you deal with spiritual things you must put aside all reason and stop thinking rationally. But the Bible records that God wants us to reason with Him. If God tells you to reason, then He must be a God who thinks logically and sequentially.

ARGUMENTS FOR AND AGAINST BACKSLIDING

I am going to reason with you and argue with you about backsliding.

I will show you certain people who were happy and full of joy as they entered into the rest of God. These were Christians who served the Lord and did not fall away. On the other hand, I will show you what some dying backsliders said as they left this earth. These testimonies alone should make you decide never, never, never to backslide.

The Christians

First, I want you to notice what Bible saints had to say when they were moving from this world to the next.

1. Apostle Paul

Apostle Paul was in prison when he knew that his time of death was near. He said, "For to me... to die is gain." In other words he was happy to be dying. How many people are happy to die? If you are confident of your relationship with God you will not fear death.

2. Jacob

When the Patriarch Jacob was dying in Genesis 49:33, the Bible declares that after commanding his sons, "...He gathered up his feet into the bed, and yielded up the ghost..." What a way to go! He knew that he was going. He had time to instruct his children with confidence. After commanding his sons, he gathered his feet onto the bed and died. You see, the death of the righteous is very different from the death of the wicked. Balaam the prophet said: "...Let me die the death of the righteous..." (Numbers 23:10).

Now let's study how some ordinary people, after living a life without backsliding went on happily to be with the Lord.

3. Ignatius

Ignatius lived in 100 AD. He was the Bishop of Antioch, and a personal disciple of John the Apostle. He was sentenced to death, and as he was dying, his last words were, "I thank thee, oh God, that thou hast honoured me with thy Word, praise God!"

These were the last words of a man who was sentenced to death by burning at the stake. Some other people would have been screaming, defecating and salivating. But this man died praising God!

4. Father Polycarp

Father Polycarp, another disciple of John lived during the reign of Emperor Nero. He was also sentenced to death. He was taken to court, and there, he was given an option to either denounce Jesus or be burnt to death. Polycarp suffered much for Christ's sake. The Roman Proconsul commanded him to swear allegiance to Ceasar, saying, "Swear, and I will set thee at liberty; reproach Christ." How courageous and magnificent was Polycarp's reply!

He said, "Eighty and six years have I now served Christ, and He has never done me the least wrong. How, then, can I blaspheme my King and my Saviour?"

Further efforts to make him deny his Lord failed, and Polycarp was condemned to be burned at the stake. When the day came for him to be burned alive, those responsible for the burning wanted to nail him to the stake, but he protested: "Let me alone as I am: for He who has given me strength to endure the fire, will also enable me, without your securing me by nails, to stand without moving in the pile."

Finally he exclaimed, "Oh! Lord, Father of the Beloved Son Jesus Christ. I thank thee that thou has allotted me a place among the Martyrs."

5. Augustus Montague Toplady

Augustus Montague Toplady (1710-1778), will ever be famous as the author of one of the most evangelical hymns of the Eighteenth Century, "Rock of Ages," which was first published in 1776. During his final illness, Toplady was greatly supported by the consolations of the Gospel.

Near his last, awaking from a sleep, he said: "Oh, what delights! Who can fathom the joy of the third Heaven? The sky is clear, there is no cloud. Come, Lord Jesus, come quickly!"

He died saying, "No mortal man can live after the glories which God has manifested to my soul." And with those words he went to be with the Lord.

6. William Shakespeare

William Shakespeare (1564-1616), the world's outstanding figure in literature, of whose life, times and works a whole library of books has been written, lived near his Bible as the numerous quotations from it in his plays and dramas prove.

A Famous Man Knew the Lord

His end came when he was only 52 years old. His last will that was written in the year he died revealed his faith in God.

"I commend my soul into the hands of God my Creator, hoping and assuredly believing, through the only merits of Jesus Christ my Saviour, to be made partaker of life everlasting, and my body to the earth, whereof it is made."

7. Matthew Henry

Matthew Henry (1662-1714), was the eminent non-conformist theologian who gave the Church the devotional commentary which held a foremost place in its field. He died a week after his settlement in London as pastor of a church in Hackney, but his end was full of confidence in the Saviour's grace.

His last words were: "A life spent in the service of God, and in communion with Him, is the most comfortable life that any one can lead in this present world."

8. John Wesley

John Wesley, the founder of the great Methodist Church said, "The best of all is, God is with us." I really love these last words of this great founder.

John Wesley, of whom it has been said that eternity alone will reveal what the world owes to his mighty ministry, was active to the very end. Until the end, he was full of praise, counsel and exhortations.

The great founder died in peace. In his last moments, with what remaining strength he had, he cried out twice over, in holy triumph: "The best of all is, God is with us." The very last word Wesley was heard to articulate was: "Farewell!"

Then, without a lingering groan, the evangelist of the highways and by-ways, beloved pastor of thousands, and father of the great Methodist Church, entered into the joy of his Lord. Notice again, death to the confident Christian. It was a peaceful transition from one world to another.

9. Adoniram Judson

Adoniram Judson was a missionary to Africa. In fact, the first American missionary to Africa. He went to Burma, wrote and translated the Bible into the Burmese language. He also wrote a dictionary for them.

When he was dying he said, "No one ever left this world with brighter hopes or warmer feelings. Don't be afraid, death will not surprise me. In spite of what I say, I feel so strong in Him."

This is a man who had strength when most people are weak. Let's all pray for such staying power, that we may all prevail until the very end.

10. Charles Bridgman

Charles Bridgman died at the age of twelve. As a child he loved to read his Bible and desired spiritual knowledge. Young Charles would often rebuke his brothers if they forgot to thank God at meal times. When he became ill, he was asked whether he would rather live or die, he answered "I desire to die, that I may go to my Saviour."

The Strength of a Little Boy

As his time drew near, his last words were: "...Into thy hands I commend my soul! Now close mine eyes. Forgive me, father, mother, brother, sister and all the world! Now I am well, my pain is almost gone, my joy is at hand. Lord have mercy upon me. O Lord, receive my soul unto Thee." How many young boys of today would speak the way this young man spoke?

11. Robert Bruce

Robert Bruce, one of the most distinguished men of his time, entered the ministry and became prominent in Edinburgh. Scrupulously maintaining the established norms of the church, he exposed himself to much persecution for the truth's sake. At the time of his death, he called for the family Bible and said to his daughter: "Cast up to me the eighth chapter of Romans, and set my finger on these words, 'I am persuaded that neither death nor life...shall be able to separate me from the love of God which is in Christ Jesus my Lord."

Then Bruce said, "Is my finger on them?"

"Yes," said his daughter. Then he replied:

"Now God be with you, my children. I have just breakfasted with you, and shall sup with my Lord Jesus this night."

How exciting it must be when you know you are ready! There can be no reason to backslide when you hear these exciting testimonies.

12. And Many Others

Another dying Christian said, "How bright the room, how full of angels!"

Some other Christian said confidently, "The battle is fought. The battle is fought, and the victory is won." With those words, he went to be with the Lord.

Alexander II, full of divine faith, exclaimed: "I am sweeping through the gates, washed in the blood of the Lamb."

Someone else said, "I wish I had the power of writing to describe how pleasant it is to die."

Another one exclaimed, "Oh! That I could tell what joy I possess. I am full of rapture, the Lord shines with such power upon my soul. He is come, He is come."

One surviving believer said, "I shall soon be with Jesus. Perhaps I am too anxious!"

Another person said, "It is sweet to die." How will you be able to say, "It is sweet to die" when you have backslidden and you know judgement awaits you?

One Christian brother questioned, "Can this be death? What? It is better than living. Tell them I died happily in Jesus."

Another one said, "They sing. The angels sing. Is this dying? No, it is sweet living."

One lucky backslider, Oliver, a doctor of philosophy, had lived the life of an infidel. But shortly before his death he repented and turned to the Saviour. His final word was one of deep regret.

"Would that I could undo the mischief I have done! I was more ardent to poison men with infidel principles than any Christian is to spread the doctrines of Christ."*

The Backsliders

Now, let us consider what some backsliders and sinners said as they were dying. The pride and rebellion of these wicked people did not help matters as they approached the gates of hell and accountability. Some of these people were backslidden Christians. They died as frightened, screaming and hopelessly lost souls. The first person I want us to consider in this category is a man called Tom Paine.

1. Tom Paine

Tom Paine (1737-1809) was considered to be a literary giant. He wrote 'The Age of Reason' and lived during the revivals of John Wesley and George Whitfield. He lived a life that was against God, and drew people away from God. I believe that this is one of the people who have made Europe so anti-Christ and atheist in their way of thinking.

One person who witnessed his death said, "He is truly to be pitied."

Although he did not believe in God, at the hour of death on his bed he said, "I would give worlds, if I had them, that 'Age of Reason' had not been published. Oh! Lord help me. Oh! God, what have I done to suffer so much?" Then after that he said, "But there is no God. Yet if there is a God, what will become of me in the world after? If ever the devil had an agent, I have been that one."

When an elderly woman attending him wanted to leave the room, he said, "Stay with me. For God's sake, I cannot bear to be left alone. For it is hell to be left alone."

The very last words of Tom Paine were "My God, my God why has thou forsaken me?" And with these words he died. This is the death of the wicked. Utterly helpless and hopeless in the presence of a righteous God!

2. Voltaire

Whenever I go to Geneva, I cross over into Ferney- Voltaire, a little French village named after a noted infidel Voltaire (1694-1778). One night I drove with the pastor of my church in Geneva to look at a statue of this man.

I saw all of the tributes that were written to his name and all of the good works that he was said to have done for the community. But this man also lived and fought against Christianity. Notice what this noted French infidel said of Christ our Saviour: "Curse the wretch!" How on earth can you gather so much confidence to curse Christ and call Him a wretch? He once boasted, "In twenty years, Christianity will be no more. My single hand shall destroy the edifice it took twelve apostles to rear."

These are the people who have laid the foundations for the atheism that is so prevalent in Europe today. Shortly after his death, the very house in which he printed his foul literature became the depot of the Geneva Bible Society. The nurse who attended Voltaire said: "For all the wealth in Europe I would not see another infidel die."

The physician, Trochim, who was with Voltaire at his death said that he cried out most desperately:

"I am abandoned by God and man! I will give you half of what I am worth if you will give me six month's life. Then I shall go to hell, and you will go with me. O Christ! O Jesus Christ!"

Notice the desperation and helplessness of this blasphemer as he descended into the abyss. He himself admitted that he was on his way to hell. My dear Christian friends, let's make no mistakes about the reality of Heaven and hell.

3. Thomas Hobbes

Thomas Hobbes (1588-1674), was a noted English political philosopher whose most famous work was "Leviathan".

This cultured, clever skeptic corrupted many of the great men of his time. But what regret was his at the end of the road! What hopelessness permeated his last words: "If I had the whole world, I would give it to live one day. I am about to take a leap in the dark!"

The good news is: Christians do not take leaps into the dark! When they die they go to Heaven!

4. Thomas Cromwell

Thomas Cromwell (1540), who became Earl of Essex, was the noted English statesman who was next to the King in power and influence. He was responsible for the digging up of the bones of Thomas Becket, and their burning as those of a traitor.

Over ambitious, Cromwell lost his influence and also his head, for he was executed. Historians tell us that as he died, he said in a speech: "The Devil is ready to seduce us, and I have been seduced, but bear me witness that I die in the Catholic Faith."

Notice how people want to associate with God at the last moment. This man was insisting that he was in the faith!

5. Thomas Cork

Thomas Cork cried out in anguish as he was dying. He said, "Until this moment I thought there was neither a God nor a devil. But now I know, and I feel that there are both." He exclaimed, "I am doomed to judgment by the judgment of the Almighty."

6. Robert Green Ingersoll

Robert Green Ingersoll (1833-1899), famous American lawyer and prominent agnostic, lectured on Biblical inaccuracies and contradictions. His famed lecture "The Mistakes of Moses" led one defender of the Bible to say that he would like to hear Moses speak for five minutes on The Mistakes of Ingersoll!

When he came to the gates of hell he was frozen with terror and he said, "Oh God, if there is a God, have mercy on my soul - if I have a soul."

7. Sir Francis Gilfort

Sir Francis Gilfort, was taught early in his life about the gospel. He was a backslidden Christian. In fact, it was expected that he would become a minister, but he fell into bad company. When he was passing on to eternity, he said,

"From where is this war in my heart? What arguments do I have to assist me in matters of fact? Do I say there is no hell when I feel one in my bosom? Aye, am I certain that there is no judgment when I feel present judgment? Oh, wretch that I am. Whither shall I flee from this? That there is a God, I know, for I continually feel that of His wrath. That there is a hell, I am surely certain. Oh! That I was to lie upon the fire that never quench for a thousand years to purchase the favour of God, and to be reverted to Him again. But it is a fruitless wish. Millions and millions of years will bring me no nearer to the end of my torment. Eternity, eternity!"

As the distress of this man increased, he was asked whether he wanted some people to be invited to pray for him.

He responded "Tigers and monsters, are you devils to come to torment me? Will you give me the prospects of Heaven to make my hell more intolerable?"

Then he said, "Oh! the insufferable pangs of death." And with that he died. How frightening!

8. William Pope

William Pope, was a born-again Christian, and knew the love of God. But he backslid when his wife died, and he followed Tom Paine. Not long after he backslid, he contracted tuberculosis, which was known at that time as the "consumption".

He is said to have been the leader of a company of infidels who ridiculed everything religious. This was a classic backslider who said when he was dying, "No case is comparable to mine, I cannot revert, God will damn me forever."

One of the exercises of he and his friends was to kick the Bible about the floor, or tear it up. Friends who were present in his death-chamber spoke of it as a scene of terror.

His eyes rolled to and fro as he was dying on his bed, and he lifted up his hands as he cried out, "I have no contrition. I cannot repent. God will damn me. I know the day of grace is past ...You see one who is damned forever...Oh, Eternity! Eternity... Nothing for me but hell. Come, eternal torments... Do you not see? Do you not see him? He is coming for me. Oh! the burning flame, the hell, the pain that I feel. Eternity will explain my torment."*

And with these words, he died. These were the very last words of a backslider.

Conclusion

Dear Christian friend, what else can I say? I have shown you the real life testimonies of real people just like yourself.

If that is not enough to make you believe and stay with God, then perhaps...

I have bargained for your soul, sharing with you all that a pastor can. I have sho.5wn you why you should not backslide. I have shown you the causes of backsliding, the descriptions of backsliding, and the symptoms of backsliding. I have shown you how people who backslide behave when they approach the gates of eternity. On the other hand, I have shown you the happy farewells of Christians with staying power to the very end.

My prayer for you is that you will find Christ and stay in Christ. For on Christ the solid rock we stand. Amen!

SECTION VI

The Doctrine of Success and Prosperity

Unparalled Success 25

■ DIVINE PROVISION FOR UNPARALLED SUCCESS

Real success is the kind that does not depend on anything or anyone. It is success that does not respect the environment or adverse situations. True success is the blessing that is not affected by an economy that is up or down. It is the success that does not care whether there is unemployment or not.

Most of the time, people are affected by the adverse conditions round about them. Most of us who live in Africa can feel the frustration of unstable governments, wars and endemic poverty. The climate is sometimes hostile to the blossoming of anything successful and prosperous. Anyone who rises up high is hated and numerous insidious attempts are made to equalize the person with the masses.

There is something I call the "spirit of crabology". This is demonstrated when one puts crabs in a deep bucket. All the crabs try to come out of the bucket. As one of them begins to go up high, another one grabs unto the rising crab and pulls him down. This process continues, until in the end, not a single crab is able to come out of the bucket. Eventually, all the crabs are ready to be boiled and none of them escapes alive.

This is the picture of certain communities. Without knowing it, they keep each other down. Whereas some communities publish the hundred richest people in the nation, others harass and intimidate the hundred richest people. Political and "invisible powers", as well as all sorts of quasi-legitimate investigations are used to intimidate the successful people. They have to pay large sums of money to political parties otherwise all contracts will be cancelled.

Many of the "big time" businessmen in my country Ghana secretly support both the ruling and the opposition political parties. They want both sides to think they are with them. I have heard several business people tell me that they had identity cards, tee shirts and caps of all major political parties. The point I'm making is simple; there are environments which are hostile to progress and success. The rich fear for their wealth. That is why few foreigners invest in the country, in spite of the numerous invitations.

In such an environment, you need success that is not destroyed by the circumstances. It must be a blessing that cannot be erased by man, woman or beast.

Isaac experienced great success. The book of Genesis, chapter twenty-six describes the attempt of external circumstances to extirpate God's blessings on his life. Firstly, there was a famine in the land. A famine of those days is equivalent to a bad economy of today. The economic environment was adverse to his success. He needed the kind of success that comes from God.

THE PROSPERITY OF ISAAC

1. God blessed Isaac in spite of a harsh economic situation.

In Isaac's day, everyone was trying to get a visa to travel to Egypt. But the Lord appeared to Isaac and told him not to leave, "THERE WAS A FAMINE in the land... the Lord appeared unto him, and said... GO NOT DOWN INTO EGYPT; dwell in the land which I shall tell thee of... AND I WILL MAKE THY SEED TO MULTIPLY... and will give unto thy seed all these countries" (Genesis 26:1-4).

There are many people who want to travel out of my country in order to "make it" in other developed countries. They spend thousands of dollars trying to get a visa. If an income of less than three hundred dollars a month puts us beneath the poverty line, then most Ghanaians are economically categorized as poor. You can understand why they would want to travel elsewhere. A cleaner in Canada is paid more than some skilled workers in my country Ghana. This situation is equivalent to the famine that Isaac experienced.

The Lord blessed Isaac when he stayed in the land of famine. In spite of the economic situation, Isaac was able to prosper. He had hundred percent profit during that particular period of time. Read it for yourself and believe that success is real! "Then Isaac sowed in that land and received in the same year an hundredfold: and the Lord blessed him. And the man waxed great, and went forward, and grew until he became very great" (Genesis 26:12,13).

God can make you very great! I see God taking you forward in spite of your circumstances! No famine can keep you down anymore! Famine or no famine, you are going to make it! No matter who is in government, you are going to make it! There may be a global economic crisis, but God will give you unprecedented success!

2. People fought with Isaac over his well.

He began to have political problems with the community. The economic hardships were not the end of Isaac's challenges. He dug wells and people fought with him over the wells that he had dug, "And Isaac's servants digged in the valley, and found there a well of springing water. And the herdmen of Gerar did strive with Isaac's herdmen, saying, The water is ours" (Genesis 26:19,20).

Isaac had begun to have political problems with the community. The people in the community wanted to break down the walls of the well he had built. Is it not interesting that after a person has worked hard to build something, someone else claims the rewards? Some people always want to reap what they have not sown! "Thou art an hard man, reaping where thou hast not sown, and gathering where thou hast not strawed" (Matthew 25:24).

We Also Built a Well

Not long ago, we experienced a similar thing in our church. We built a beautiful cathedral and acquired a piece of land beside the church. We signed an agreement with the government. After a few years, a group of people arose claiming the land was theirs. After we had developed the property and spent thousands of dollars, people were now striving with us for our well.

But Isaac moved on and built another well. Lighthouse Chapel International began in a classroom. We then moved to the corridor of a school building. In spite of our circumstances, we have been blessed like Isaac. We had to leave these places and move into a cafeteria in a hospital. After two years, we were driven out of the canteen by the authorities in the hospital. We then moved to a deserted and derelict cinema hall situated next to a monstrous rubbish dump and an exploding public toilet.

Our success as a church has not depended on the circumstances surrounding us. Our church is planted deep in the heart of a depressed part of the city. In spite of this, we have prospered and become successful. People come to our church from all over the city, "And the man waxed great, and went forward, and grew until he became very great" (Genesis 26:13).

Isaac's success did not depend on that particular well. Recently, we were attacked by some traditionalists who claimed we were violating their customs by playing drums in our church on Sunday morning. Many church members were seriously injured and numerous cars were damaged.

Three days before that, at about three O'clock in the morning, an "invisible" governmental power broke down the walls surrounding our church building. We had come under political and governmental attack of the highest order. Soon after the attack, the IRS (Internal Revenue Service) descended on us to conduct a major tax investigation on our affairs. Who was behind all this intimidation and attacks? Who was trying to destroy what cannot be destroyed? Who can fight against God and win?

All the government officials I interacted with denied that they gave orders for the illegal breaking down of our walls. I smiled at each lying politician as I watched them trying to escape the blame that is theirs. Liars will not go to Heaven! It is time for politicians to know that liars will not be welcome in Heaven.

"Blessed are they that do his commandments, that they may have right to the tree of life, and may enter in through the gates into the city. For without are dogs, and sorcerers, and whoremongers, and murderers, and idolaters, and whosoever loveth and maketh a lie" (Revelations 22:14,15).

God's blessings are unparalleled. Isaac's well was taken from him on two different occasions. He lawfully built a well, but lazy and ungrateful people contended with him over it. Laziness and ingratitude are vices that cause a gloomy cloud of despondency and retrogression to settle. They lead to recurring curses of poverty.

3. Isaac continued building in spite of having been cheated.

God's success for your life will happen despite what people do and say. One minister told me, "I thought your church was 'finished' after the attack." When he paid us a visit, he was surprised that our church was larger and stronger than ever! I am happy to tell you that our church has moved from strength to strength after our attacks. I cannot begin to tell you about the divine advancement and progress we have made after our multiple and diverse persecutions.

You too can experience unbeatable success! No matter your background, family or education, God can lift you up. God is a specialist at taking you out of the dust and placing you among princes. No circumstance is too difficult for the Lord.

"He raiseth up the poor out of the dust, and lifteth the needy out of the dunghill; That he may set him with princes" (Psalm 113:7,8).

I see God setting you among princes! I see Him lifting you out of the dust of poverty! You are a winner because the God of unbeatable success is your Lord! I will now share with you how you can achieve unbeatable success through the secret of divine provision.

THE PRINCIPLES FOR DIVINE PROVISION

1. As we get to know God, he reveals himself more and more to us.

Many years ago, I met a young lady called Adelaide Baiden. I didn't know at the time that she was to become my wife. I remember once walking through the Spanish Department of the University of Ghana, and seeing her sitting on the stairs waiting for someone. She said, "Hello." I turned, but I couldn't remember her name. Later, I got to know her name. Somehow, she became a member of our fellowship and I got to know her as a member. Then I got to know her as a friend. Later as a close friend. Eventually, one day, she became my wife. That is how God relates with us.

When you become born again, you may know the Lord as someone who saves you from your sins. Then you may know Him as someone who will take you to Heaven. As I have grown in the Lord, I have gotten to know Him as someone who gives us the victory. I also know Him as someone who heals the sick and as someone who provides for my needs.

In Genesis, Chapter One, God reveals himself as Elohim, which means Creator. The word translated into God in Genesis Chapter One is the word Elohim. At another point, God reveals Himself as Jehovah, which means "I am that I am"; the one who makes promises and covenants and keeps them.

God progressively revealed himself to mankind. He showed Himself to Abraham as El'Shaddai, which means, " The Almighty God". He was trying to show another aspect of Himself to humanity. El'Shaddai - the one who is almighty and able to do all things. God was showing Abraham that although he was ninety years old, He could still make him have a child. When Abraham went to war with the five kings, God revealed himself as Adonai, which means "Master and Owner". He was the Master of the battle! When the Lord revealed Himself to Moses in the burning bush, he showed Himself as Jehovah, the one who keeps promises. Further on, God decided to reveal Himself a little more as Jehovah Rophe: "The Lord that heals".

2. Every Christian can grow in his relationship with the Lord over time.

You may have been a Christian or a pastor for a long time but you can grow in your relationship until you know God as Jehovah Rophe, the Healer. You may have walked with God for years without knowing this aspect of Him. But that is how a relationship is; it develops over time. You get to know more about a person as you continue the relationship.

When the children of Israel met with an enemy called Amalek, they fought and won a hard battle. The Lord then explained to Moses that there was another dimension to his nature. God was saying, "I am also Jehovah Nissi," the God that gives you victory. Later on, God revealed Himself even further as Jehovah M'kaddesh, which means, "The God who also sanctifies". You can see that at each stage, God is showing new dimensions ofhimself.

3. There are many aspects of Christianity that we have to experience.

In this textbook, I want you to encounter an important dimension of the Lord. I want you to find out and experience God as your provider.

4. You can experience God as a provider.

I am happy that Christ has set you free from your bondage. I am glad that your sins are washed away. But come in a little deeper and get to know another dimension of the God you serve. Maybe you have experienced God as an acquaintance or as a close friend. Now experience him as a divine provider!

This world is made up of over six billion people, all trying to provide for themselves. In every large city of the world, you will see the young and the old sweating in order to eat a little bread. It is only natural for us to rise up and provide for ourselves.

Today, I want you to know that God can also provide for you. This is called Divine Provision. It is only through divine provision that you will experience unbeatable success. God can provide food for you. God can provide cars for you. God can provide houses for you. God can supply all your needs.

I am happy that you are working. It is important that you work hard! However, there are things that your hard work cannot provide. Many people work hard, and yet cannot meet their needs. That is why you need God's divine provision.

DIVINE PROVISION FOR JACOB

Jacob was a hustler passing through town. He was travelling from place to place trying to make it in business. He had been able to get a visa and was traveling abroad. Along the journey, he rested under a tree and fell asleep.

Whilst asleep, he had a dream in which the Lord appeared to him. "And he dreamed, and behold a ladder set up on the earth, and the top of it reached to heaven: and behold the angels of God ascending and descending on it. And, behold, the Lord stood above it, and said, I am the Lord God of Abraham thy father, and the God of Isaac: the land whereon thou liest, to thee will I give it, and to thy seed; And thy seed shall be as the dust of the earth, and thou shalt spread abroad to the west, and to the east, and to the north, and to the south: and in thee and in thy seed shall all the families of the earth be blessed. And, behold, I am with thee, and will keep thee in all places whither thou goest, and will bring thee again into this land; for I will not leave thee, until I have done that which I have spoken to thee of.And Jacob awaked out of his sleep, and he said, Surely the Lord is in this place; and I knew it not. And he was afraid, and said, How dreadful is this place! this is none other but the house of God, and this is the gate of heaven. And Jacob rose up early in the morning, and took the stone that he had put for his pillows, and set it up for a pillar, and poured oil upon the top of it. And he called the name of that place Bethel: but the name of that city was called Luz at the first" (Genesis 28:12-19). When he woke up, he made a vow to God and asked for divine provision.

1. Jacob asked God for three important miracles.

a. The first thing he asked for was the miracle of divine presence. "If God will be with me…" (Genesis 28:20).

b. Then he asked for the miracle of divine protection. "...and will keep me in this way that I go…" (Genesis 28:20).

c. Finally, he asked for the miracle of divine provision. "...and will give me bread to eat, and raiment to put on…" (Genesis 28:20).

Jacob had arrived at a turning point in his life. He had come to the place where he was going to include God in all that he did. In fact, he was going to expect God to actually provide these important things for him. Jacob wanted God's involvement so much that he virtually promised to pay God a tenth of all his earnings, if the Lord agreed to help him.

Dear friend, let me tell you something. God wants to provide for you. God wants to bless you.

2. God wants to bless you the way he blessed Jacob.

He wants to provide you with bread to eat and raiment to put on. He wants to protect you and to reveal himself to you as someone who can supply all your needs.

In the third world, many educated people live below the poverty line. No matter how much they work, they can never dream of buying a car. This is where God comes in. Let there be a distinction in your mind between divine provision and human provision. Human provision is when you use your efforts and human principles to succeed. Human provision is by your own hard work.

I believe in hard work and education, but I believe just as much in God's divine provision. God is a God of miracles. We serve a miracle-working God.

I will be sharing with you principles that will cause our heavenly Father to provide for you. You will experience unbeatable success when your heavenly Father provides for you!

■ THE LAWS OF DIVINE PROVISION

If God is going to become your provider, then you must invoke divine and biblical principles that will make the Lord provide for you. God must become involved in your life so that he can become your provider.

THE LAW OF THE TITHE

"...and of all that thou shalt give me I will surely give the tenth unto thee" (Genesis 28:22). The tithe is the tenth of all your increase. It is a common fact that most Christians do not pay tithes. I am not writing this textbook because you are in my church. You are probably not a member of my church. I am writing what I am writing because you need to know the truth. I am writing for your own benefit. God is not in need of anything. He has said that the silver, gold and the cattle on a thousand hills are His. If He were in need of something, He would not ask you. "The silver is mine, and the gold is mine, saith the LORD of hosts" (Haggai 2:8).

Dear friend, we are mere human beings living a short life on this earth. No matter how much we acquire, we must leave it all behind and move on. Money must not be a god to us. What is gold? Gold is dirt. It is dug out of the ground! It is nothing! Why should it become a god to you? Let it serve you, do not serve it! I am sorry to say that most Christians are controlled by their money. Only a small percentage of Christians pay their tithes.

1. The tithe belongs to God.

One thing that every Christian must realize is that the tithe is the Lord's money. In our church we call it the "First and Best Fruits". "And all the tithe of the land, whether of the seed of the land, or of the fruit of the tree, is the Lord's: it is holy unto the Lord" (Leviticus 27:30). What does this mean? It means that ten per cent of all you earn is not yours, it is actually the Lord's money. When you put that money in the offering bowl, you have done nothing special or unusual. All you have done is to give back to God what is his!

Suppose someone asked you to keep a hundred dollars for him. When he asks for it again, would you expect him to kneel down and thank you profusely for returning his hundred dollars? Would you expect him to shower praises on you for your kindness to him? The answer is no! You have done nothing for him. You have just returned his own money to him! When you understand that the tithe is the Lord's money, it is easier for you to release it to the Lord.

2. Blessings are released into our lives when we pay our tithes.

In the book of Malachi, the Bible teaches us that when you pay your tithes, the windows of Heaven are opened over your life. Whatever these windows are, there must be some great benefit for us when they are opened. "Bring ye all the tithes into the storehouse... and prove me now herewith, saith the Lord of hosts, if I will not open you the windows of heaven, and pour you out a blessing, that there shall not be room enough to receive it" (Malachi 3:10).

3. When you pay your tithes you are showing God respect and giving him honour.

One way God receives honour from you is through your tithes. When you do not pay your tithes, you are depriving God of His respect. Blessings are released into our lives. "Honour the LORD with thy substance, and with the firstfruits of all thine increase: So shall thy barns be filled with plenty, and thy presses shall burst out with new wine" (Proverbs 3:9, 10).

4. BE A FOLLOWER OF BLESSED PEOPLE WHO PAID THEIR TITHES.

"That ye be not slothful, but followers of them who through faith and patience inherit the promises" (Hebrews 6:12). Jacob tithed. That is what invoked divine provision over his life. Be ye followers of people who experienced God's blessing and do what they did. You will be blessed as you pay your first and best fruits.

I know that some people think that paying tithes is a command of the law that must not be obeyed today. Dear friend, we are not talking about the law, we are talking about principles. The principle is that of honouring God with the first fruits of all your increase. The next law of divine provision is the law of the offering.

THE LAW OF THE OFFERING

1. DIVINE PRINCIPLE STATES THAT THE GIVERS ARE THE BLESSED ONES.

"Give, and it SHALL be given..." (Luke 6:38). Christians must learn to be generous by giving offerings to the Lord. Once again, money must not be more important to us than it really is. The Bible says that there are two types of people in the world. One group gives a lot, and the other group tends to keep rather than to give. "There is that scattereth, and yet increaseth; and there is that withholdeth more than is meet, but it tendeth to poverty" (Proverbs 11:24).

God's book, the Bible, tells us that the givers become richer and the keepers become poorer. This is a divine principle. The God who created the universe has set in place the law of giving and receiving. Our little minds cannot accept that this is real. The more you give, the richer you become; it's just a matter of time!

2. IT IS THE GIVING OF AN OFFERING TO THE LORD THAT WILL INVOKE THE LAWS OF GIVING AND RECEIVING ON YOUR BEHALF.

After giving your tithe (which is not really giving), you must now give an offering to the Lord. "Be not deceived; God is not mocked: for whatsoever a man soweth, that shall he also reap" (Galatians 6:7).

In some countries, especially in developing ones, the political and economic environment is contrary to the progress of its own citizens. If you were to go to a country like Switzerland, you would hardly ever see a foreigner rise up and own the major businesses of the nation. However in some African nations, foreigners own all the supermarkets and major shopping centres. The government has created a system where it is more profitable and easier to import the used clothing of white people than to set up a garment factory!

Our church has bought at least two former garment factories for use as church buildings. The factory owners were forced out of business by the economic decisions of the day. In some countries, whenever its own citizens rise up in great success and success, the powers that be rally to bring them down. There are nations which kill their heroes. In such nations, it is a crime to prosper. It is a crime to be successful. It is a crime to be wealthy. It is a crime to own anything. Your business may be closed down, and your property may be seized and destroyed, just because you are blessed and somebody is not happy about it!

I have sat with businessmen who are so frustrated with the political and economic realities of their nation. One man said to me, "I feel so limited and frustrated by the system. I know I could make it real big but there is so much intimidation in the country." People are afraid to be rich and wealthy even though they could be. Many are forced to take their money away from the jealous eyes of powerful politicians. This is a curse.

In the book of Deuteronomy, the Bible teaches that strangers (foreigners) would rise amongst a people and become very great. Meanwhile, the citizens of the land would wither away. "The stranger that is within thee shall get up above thee very high; and thou shalt come down very low" (Deuteronomy 28:43).

The point I am making is this. Even if you live in a difficult-to-prosper environment, God, by supernatural means, can provide for you! That is what divine provision is all about. Jacob knew that God could lift him up and establish him in this life. That is why he made an agreement with God for divine provision.

3. Offerings must be accepted at two different levels.

Whenever you give an offering in church, it must be received at two levels. First, your church receives it. Secondly, God receives it. It is important that your offering is received at both levels. The church must receive your offering and God must also receive your offering.

Remember that the church does not promise to multiply the offering back to you. The church has no such power. However, Jesus made that promise of multiplication to us. The Word of God teaches that as you cast your bread on the water, it will come back after many days. "Cast thy bread upon the waters: for thou shalt find it after many days" (Ecclesiastes 11:1).

There are some occasions where the church will not receive your money. I want to cite two examples from the Bible. First, blood money is not accepted in the house of the Lord. "And the chief priests took the silver pieces, and said, It is not lawful for to put them into the treasury, because it is the price of blood" (Matthew 27:6). Notice that when Judas attempted to return the thirty pieces of silver to the treasury of the church, it was rejected. Why was it rejected? Because it was blood money! Modern day drug money is actually blood money. It is money that is earned by the destruction and killing of many lives through cocaine and related substances. Such money is not welcome in the church.

Another Scripture tells us that money from prostitution is not accepted in the church. "Thou shalt not bring the hire of a whore, or the price of a dog, into the house of the Lord thy God for any vow: for even both these are abomination unto the Lord thy God" (Deuteronomy 23:18).

The fact that the church has received the offering does not mean that God has received the offering. As I said, the offering must be received at two different levels. If your offering is not received by the Lord, then you have wasted your money. The Word of God tells us what sort of offering is acceptable to the Lord.

FOUR CONDITIONS FOR AN ACCEPTABLE OFFERING

1. The first condition for having your offering accepted by God is that, it must not come from a wicked or sinful person.

God does not receive offerings from such people. The church may receive it because they don't know who you are or what you do. However, God does see and will not accept such an offering. "Though ye offer me burnt offerings and your meat offerings, I will not accept them...But let judgment run down...and righteousness..." (Amos 5:22,24). "I have no pleasure in you, saith the Lord of hosts, neither will I accept an offering at your hand" (Malachi 1:10).

2. The second condition is that, you must have a willing mind.

"For if there be first a willing mind, it is accepted..." (2 Corinthians 8:12). If you give grudgingly, you will not receive your blessing.

God loves a cheerful giver. Don't bother to give if you don't really want to. A businessman told me how he was invited to be the Chairman of a fundraising programme in a church. He narrated how events transpired until he was "put on the spot" during the fundraising.

He said, "I had to make a huge donation to 'save face'." This man unwillingly gave away a large amount of money to the church. He continued, "After the fundraising programme, I realized I didn't have enough money to pay the pledge." He added, "I had to sell my car to cover the donation." Shortly after settling the debt, he left the church and joined another ministry. He unwillingly gave away a huge amount of money to the church.

In such a case, who loses? The answer is everybody! The church lost a prominent member. The businessman lost his car and his blessing because he gave it up unwillingly. Always remember this: it is only accepted if it is given from a willing mind.

Pastors must not intimidate and manipulate their congregations to give what they don't want to give. Preachers can speak in a way that frightens people to give their belongings away. There are times when I try to stop people from giving certain gifts to the Lord. I do this to make sure they know what they are doing. I want them to be free and willing in their giving so that they will receive a full reward.

3. The Third Important Condition Is This: The Offering Will Be Accepted According To What You Have.

"...it is accepted ACCORDING TO THAT A MAN HATH..." (2 Corinthians 8:12). What does this mean? Everyone is supposed to give in proportion to what he has. When a person gives out of proportion to what he has, it may be unacceptable to the Lord.

For instance, if a student gives ten dollars to the Lord for a project, that offering may be acceptable to God in proportion to the student's meagre resources. But when the millionaire church member's contribution is also ten dollars, it is completely out of proportion to what he has. In proportion to what he has, the millionaire has actually not given anything.

Always remember to give according to what you have. What has God given you? How much has God put into your hands? Give according to what God has blessed you with.

4. The Fourth Important Condition For An Acceptable Offering Is This: You Must Not Give Offerings Having In Mind Things You Do Not Have

"...it is accepted...not according to that he hath not" (2 Corinthians 8:12).

If you do not have a car, and you think of it as you give, you will not give happily. If you think about the things you intend to buy, you will not be happy to give. In fact, you will start penalizing God for not having certain things. Anybody who gives an offering whilst thinking of all the things he doesn't have, is not going to be giving an acceptable offering. You need to forget about all the things you lack when it's time to build the Lord's Kingdom. Forget about your own projects and give freely to the Lord.

I once had to give substantially towards a church building project. I had my own building project to complete. That offering could have completed my project, but I still gave it. If I had thought of my own project, I would not have given to the Lord. Remember this, offerings become acceptable when they are given with a free mind, and without thinking of all the things you do not have.

May the Lord give you the spirit of revelation to grasp these powerful truths! Once you have this revelation, your offerings will always be accepted by God. You will be propelled into divine provision and unbeatable success!

THE LAW OF SEEKING THE KINGDOM

All throughout life, we try to provide for ourselves. The curse upon this planet is as real today as it has ever been. On some parts of the earth, there seem to be even more frustrations. A student goes to the university in an attempt to improve himself and provide for his future. Suddenly, a sergeant overthrows the government and closes down the university. You are forced to flee. Now, you are no longer able to continue in your pursuit of human provision.

Even in the developed world, there are many things that frustrate our ambitions to provide for ourselves. We all need divine provision. We need God. We cannot put the Lord Jesus on a side plate; He must be the main course! God cannot be a third party. He must be central to our lives and He must be a part of both our financial and social lives.

If you want God to divinely provide for you, then you must accept that there are divine laws and principles in place. These divine laws must be set to work on your behalf otherwise God will not get involved in providing for you.

I want to share with you the importance of building the kingdom of God. Matthew 6:33 admonishes you to seek first the kingdom of God and all things will be added unto you. Humanly speaking, if you seek the financial Kingdom, finances may be added to you. But that is not God's wisdom. If you want to experience divine provision, you must seek the Kingdom of God first and things will be supernaturally added to your life. That is divine provision!

Very few people actually invest in the Kingdom of God. They build their own lives and give God the pennies and the change. Listen to me dear friend! When you build God's Kingdom, it causes you to have His hand on your little kingdom. There are two main ways we can contribute to building God's Kingdom.

1. You can contribute spiritually.

Spiritually, building the Kingdom of God involves praying, fasting, preaching, counselling and witnessing.

2. Secondly, you can actually physically build the kingdom.

Physically building the kingdom of God involves using your money to construct chapels and other buildings for the glory of God. If you study this passage in the book of Haggai, you will notice that the Lord was concerned about the physical construction of his house. It is true that first of all, the church is a spiritual thing. But without the buildings, we have no where to assemble and to worship. "Go up to the mountain, and bring wood, and build the house; and I will take pleasure in it, and I will be glorified, saith the Lord."

I know of many churches that are unable to meet more than once during the week because they do not have a suitable meeting place. They do not have anywhere to worship. By the grace of God, we have our own building. On Sundays, we have five main services and several other services. After the services, we have Bible schools during the afternoons. On Tuesdays, we have a powerful teaching service. On Wednesdays, we have Bible schools. On Thursdays we have fellowship meetings. On Fridays, we have all-night meetings. On Saturdays, there are weddings and rehearsals. On Mondays, we rest, but even then, there are always some meetings going on in the church.

If we did not have a building, many of these meetings could not happen. Every church must believe God for its own building. God wants churches to have their own beautiful buildings. Buildings make you substantial. That is why God blesses people who help to build his church.

Do you want God's eyes to be on you? Then build his Kingdom. When I was a medical student, I built God's church spiritually. That is why God's grace helped me through the school. Many times when I could have gone down, God lifted me up! Once, I won a prize worth a lot of money. I was surprised that I could win such a prize! I thought, "What have I done to deserve this?" It was just the grace of God blessing me for building his Kingdom.

THE LAW OF FINANCING MISSIONS EVANGELISM AND MINISTERS

1. PAUL RECEIVED SUPPORT FROM THE PHILIPPIAN CHURCH.

One of the favourite verses of charismatic Christians is, "My God shall supply all your need according to his riches in glory by Christ Jesus" (Philippians 4:19). However, if you take the time to read the verses before this popular Scripture, you will find out that Paul had received immense support from the Philippian Christians. He was writing back and ministering a blessing of God to those who had supported him in the ministry.

You will discover that, that particular blessing was directed at the financiers of his missionary work. "Now ye Philippians know also, that in the beginning of the gospel, when I departed from Macedonia, no church communicated with me as concerning giving and receiving, but ye only" (Philippians 4:15).

2. GOD'S WORD DICTATES THE PRINCIPLE FOR ATTRACTING DIVINE PROVISION.

Do we not have thousands of Christians whose needs have not been met? Certainly! I see them everyday! But God can and wnill supply our needs if we line up with His Word. God has anointed certain men to do His work. Jesus said, whoever receives you is actually receiving me. "He that receiveth you receiveth me; and he that receiveth me receiveth him that sent me" (Matthew 10:40).

The Word of God abounds with examples of divine provision for those who finance God's servants.

Some years ago, I was in the home of a certain Christian family. I sat quietly and listened to them discuss the affairs of their priest. You see, there was a controversy in their church over a car that had been bought by the church. Some members of the church felt that the pastor should just have the use of the car. Others felt that the car should belong to the pastor. As I listened to them, I sensed that some of the people were subtly against the well-being of their pastor. To them, the important thing was the welfare of the institution. A subtle but real mindset had developed. It made the role of the pastor of secondary importance. What was important to them was the institution. These individuals were making a big mistake.

The Bible says "strike the shepherd and the sheep will scatter". The Bible doesn't say strike the building and the sheep will scatter. The Bible doesn't say strike the institution and the sheep will not attend. Our church (the institution) has been attacked with stones, sticks and even bombs. But it is still very full every Sunday morning.

As you read through the Bible, you will discover how God deals with individuals. He does not deal with groups or institutions. He is dealing with individual men and women. God is working with certain men in every nation. When you look after such men, you provoke divine provision on your life. When you care for such people, you are caring for God's precious jewels.

3. THE SHUNAMMITE WOMAN MINISTERED TO ELISHA.

Do you remember the testimony of the Shunammite woman? "And it fell on a day, that Elisha passed to Shunem, where was a great woman; and she constrained him to eat bread. And so it was, that as oft as he passed by, he turned in thither to eat bread" (2 Kings 4:8).

This was the woman who asked Elisha to come and stay in her house. She provided for him a resting place. She gave him food and shelter. This provoked a divine response. One day Elisha said to her, "...Behold, thou hast been careful for us with all this care; what is to be done for thee?" (2 Kings 4:13).

The man of God was provoked to minister a miracle of childbirth to her. It was not Elisha who gave her the child, it was God. 'And he said, About this season, according to the time of life, thou shalt embrace a son..." (2 Kings 4:16).

4. The widow fed Elijah.

Look at the testimony of Elijah. He met with a widow who was about to die from a famine. Elijah wanted to minister a miracle of supernatural supply of food to her. So he told her, "...Fear not; go and do as thou hast said: but make me thereof a little cake first, and bring it unto me, and after make for thee and for thy son" (1 Kings 17:13).

Before the blessing could come, she had to invoke the laws of divine provision by ministering to the man of God. Any time you minister personally to a man of God, you invoke the laws of divine provision. This woman would have died if she hadn't done what she did. God was merciful to her and divinely supplied what she needed. I see God supplying all your needs as you minister to the man of God in your life!

5. Ministration to the man of God opens the door to blessing.

Do you remember the testimony of Isaac? When Isaac was dying, he called his children and said, "I want to bless you." Isaac said to his firstborn son, Esau, "Make me the food I love and bring it to me. When I eat and am blessed, my soul will bless you before I die. And make me savoury meat, such as I love, and bring it to me, that I may eat; that my soul may bless thee before I die" (Genesis 27:4).

What was happening here? Why couldn't Isaac just bless his son and die? Isaac knew that if his son ministered to him, it would provoke the true blessing from a father to a son. Dear Christian friend, this principle is still true today. The Bible says that a gift maketh room for a man. Any gift you give to a man of God provokes the anointing. I try never to miss an opportunity to bless a man of God.

Under the ministry of Jesus, you will remember the woman with the alabaster box. She gave an expensive gift to Christ. Some people even criticized her for doing that. But what did Jesus say? "...Seest thou this woman? I entered into thine house, thou gavest me no water for my feet: but she hath washed my feet with her tears, and wiped them with the hairs of her head. Thou gavest me no kiss: but this woman since the time I came in hath not ceased to kiss my feet. My head with oil thou didst not anoint: but this woman hath anointed my feet with ointment. Wherefore I say unto thee, Her sins, which are many, are forgiven..." (Luke 7:44-47).

This woman received her blessing, not because she put some money in the offering, but because she ministered to the man of God himself. I encourage you to bless your pastor. Galatians 6:6 teaches us to give to them who have taught us. It is our duty to minister back to them in carnal things.

Don't be over-spiritual. Don't try to be wiser than God. Judas complained when a gift was given to Christ. He said, "This money should have been put in the offering or given to the poor." Giving directly to the man of God is a principal key to divine provision in your life.

THE LAW OF DIVINE HELP

The law of divine help is the principle that if God does not help you, no one can. This is based on the following realities.

1. There are many curses operating in the world today.

There are global and sectional curses at work. There are curses of poverty everywhere, and if God does not help us, no one will. I want to show you how much we need God's help in our lives.

"As the king of Israel was passing by upon the wall, there cried a woman unto him, saying, help, my lord, O king. And he said, If the Lord do not help thee, whence shall I help thee? out of the barnfloor, or out of the winepress? And the king said unto her, What aileth thee? And she answered, This woman said unto me, Give thy son that we may eat him today and we will eat my son tomorrow. So we boiled my son and did eat him: and I said unto her the next day, Give thy son, that we may eat him: and she hath hid her son" (2 Kings 6:26-29).

This account is one of the saddest stories in the Bible. It is about a woman who entered into a contract with her neighbour. She agreed to kill and boil her son for supper. The agreement stated that they would eat her neighbour's son after they had eaten up hers.

After she had chopped up her son and made soup out of him, her neighbour was probably overwhelmed with the horror of having to kill her son. She had seen how her friend's son had screamed and begged as he was being killed. She remembered how difficult it was to eat the child though they were all starving.

The woman who had sacrificed her son was desperate. Not only was she hungry, but she felt cheated! She had a double loss. At least, if her son were alive, they could have encouraged each other. Now he was down in her stomach! This woman saw the king walking on the wall and she shouted to him for help. The king gave an answer that every Christian should remember. He said, "If God does not help you, then how can I help you?" "And he said, If the Lord do not help thee, whence shall I help thee?" (2 Kings 6:27).

The king did not know the kind of problem this woman had. He did not even know the type of help the woman needed. He just knew this eternal principle. The principle that if God does not help, then all our efforts are in vain. What did Jesus say? He said, "...for without me ye can do nothing" (John 15:5).

2. We cannot be successful by excluding God's help and operating only by our own efforts.

In Ghana, we have tried so many forms of government. Initially, the British colonized us. At a point, we felt that the presence of the Europeans was keeping us from going forward as a nation. We clamoured for independence and eventually got it in 1957. Then we had Kwame Nkrumah, our first president, who led us for a while. After some time, we felt a change was necessary.

In 1966, there was a coup d'état and some soldiers came into power. After the soldiers had been around for a while, we went back to democracy. After we had practised democracy for a while, some soldiers took over once again. We had moved from colonization to independence to democracy to military rule and back to democracy.

After democracy, we decided to try house cleaning. We did some military house cleaning for a few months and then handed power back to a democratic government. The democratic government was allowed to work for just two years, then we had a revolution. It seemed that neither colonization, independence, democracy, military rule or even house cleaning was helping the nation. Now we had embarked upon a revolution. After the revolution went on for a while, we decided to come back to democracy.

It is a marvel how we human beings try to help ourselves, sometimes without the help of God. Our first president said, "Seek ye first the political kingdom and all other things shall be added." When the Word of God teaches us to seek the help of God first, we spoke of things contrary to God's laws. There must be a difference between seeking the Kingdom of God and seeking the political kingdom. No wonder after forty years of independence, the nation of Ghana is still not really free. You see, independence is not the same as freedom.

We are still enslaved to European nations through the loans they give us. We are actually working to pay back what we owe them. We queue at foreign embassies for visas in order to go abroad to work so we can prosper.

Is it not ironical that during the slave trade, our ancestors were shipped unwillingly to Europe and America, but now, people will drop everything for the opportunity to travel to these same destinations! Alas, our independence has not brought us the freedom and success we fought for. We owe so much, yet we continue to borrow more! Just as the Bible says, the borrower is a servant to the lender. "The rich ruleth over the poor, and the borrower is servant to the lender" (Proverbs 22:7).

White people were criticized for making inhumane castles to keep black prisoners. The ironic thing is that although we are approaching the twenty first century, black people are still using some of these castles to imprison their own brothers. Are we really free? It is sad to hear about African heads of state feeding their own black brothers to lions. We are back in the days of Daniel and the lion's den!

The point I'm trying to make is simple. If God does not help us, colonization, independence, democracy, military rule, house cleaning, revolution, or democracy cannot help us!! It is true that we must make efforts to help ourselves. I believe in education. I believe in hard work. I am a very practical person. I work for several hours every day. But none of these things can rule out the God factor. If God does not help you, no one can.

DIVINE HELP AGAINST CURSES IN THE EARTH

Inasmuch as human beings are trying to develop and help themselves, you will realize that frustrations abound everywhere. Even the superpower nations have many problems they cannot solve. Entire neighbourhoods are riddled with drug addicts, prostitution and murderous teenagers. I once heard of the citizens of peaceful Switzerland wanting to arm themselves and shoot at drug pushers in their area, in order to drive them away from their children.

Many prevailing conditions have spiritual roots, and that is why they must be dealt with spiritually. That is why you need God to break through in this life! Never ending problems are often rooted in a curse. The whole world is cursed to struggle and sweat in order to survive. It is something that will not just go away. Christians must understand that there are two major curses at work in the earth.

There is what I call "a global curse." In addition to that, there is also a sectional curse. These two curses came about at the origin of the human race. The existence of these curses makes it necessary for us to apply wisdom and spiritual strength to have victory and unbeatable success in this life.

1. The Adamic Curse

Adam was cursed to sweat and struggle in order to survive. The earth was cursed to bring forth painful thorns and thistles for Adam's children. This curse affects all people and that is why God said to Eve, "What is this that thou hast done?" And the Lord God said unto the woman, What is this that thou has done?" (Genesis 3:13a).

This curse has sentenced us all to years of very hard work in order to survive. No part of the human race is exempt from this curse. That explains why we all have to toil and labour for most of our lives. However, there is another curse originating from Noah. Please remember that just as Adam was once the only man alive on earth, Noah and his family were also the only group alive on the earth at a point in time. Whatever happened to Adam and Noah are significant for us today.

2. The Noahic Curse

Noah had three sons, from whom all the different groups of people on earth originated. Now, Noah's curse was not against all his children. It seemed to affect a particular group. It was a sectional curse that did not affect the whole human race. Noah actually blessed his other two sons. He said to Japheth,

"God shall enlarge Japheth..." (Genesis 9:27). He also blessed Shem and said, "...Blessed be the Lord God of Shem; and Canaan shall be his servant" (Genesis 9:26). But he cursed Ham's son, Canaan, and said, "...a servant of servants shall he be unto his brethren" (Genesis 9:25).

Noah and his three sons were the only people alive on the earth, at a certain point in history. One day Noah was drunk and layed down naked. One of his sons, Ham, exposed his father's nakedness whereas the two others covered him. When Noah awoke, he pronounced a curse for the dishonour that had been done him during his drunken state.

This entire human race descends from Noah's sons: Shem, Ham and Japheth. It seems as though sections of the human race were given a curse of extra frustration through the pronouncement of Father Noah. The curse was simple and it was to Ham's son Canaan. He was told, "You will be a servant to the others."

I am not interested in controversial discussions. All I am saying is that there was an Adamic curse which was global and there was also a Noahic curse which was sectional. These things are in the Bible. No part of the human race is inferior to another. Some of the differences we see in the world are due to the fact that curses are operational in certain regions. These differences are not because one group of people is inferior to another.

We must know what God has called us to be. We must understand the spiritual and historical curses and blessings that are prevailing in certain places. If God puts you in a place that is labouring under a never-ending cycle of frustration, you must understand your calling and the type of problems you will have to deal with. "...a servant of servants shall he be unto his brethren" (Genesis 9:25). Although there are exceptions to everything, a curse is a generalized word of frustration spoken against a group of people. This curse of Noah (Genesis 9:25) was a proclamation against the ability to lead and develop in a section of the human race. The absence of good leadership is obvious in many sections of the world. A servant is not a leader. A servant of servants is someone who is far from being a leader!

The failure to successfully lead nations into success and development is a reality we have to deal with everyday. Obviously, the lack of leadership has made many nations poorer than they should be. The masses of people in such nations flounder in poverty, under-development, suffering, senseless wars and corruption.

All these are signs of a lack of good leadership. People who are aware of this curse must teach on leadership and train themselves and others to become good leaders. This will help greatly to alleviate or ameliorate the effects of this curse. The absence of good leaders is one of the greatest curses that can ever befall any group of people.

Notice what the Scriptures say will happen to Israel for their disobedience. God said he would deprive them of all kinds of leaders. "For, behold, the Lord, the Lord of hosts, doth take away from Jerusalem...The mighty man, and the man of war, the judge, and the prophet, and the prudent, and the ancient, The captain of fifty, and the honourable man, and the counsellor, and the cunning artificer, and the eloquent orator. And I will give children to be their princes and babes shall rule over them..." (Isaiah 3:1-7).

A nation which murders or eliminates leaders, judges, kings, presidents, businessmen, wealthy people and spiritual leaders is truly in an unfortunate state.

Let us briefly look at the different groups of people living on earth today, and from which of the sons of Noah they originated.

a. Genealogy of Ham

Ham, the one who angered his father, had four sons: Cush, Mizraim, Phut, and Canaan. It is interesting to note who the descendants of Ham were.

Cush, the first son, was progenitor of various Ethiopian tribes that settled south of Egypt and also overran Arabia, Babylonia and India.

Mizraim, the second son of Ham was the progenitor of various Egyptian tribes. Mizraim means double. Tribes of the double Egypt (upper and lower Egypt) came from him.

Phut, the third son, was the progenitor of the Libyans and other tribes in Africa.

Canaan, the one who was cursed, was the progenitor of peoples mainly in Palestine, Arabia, Tyre, Sidon and other parts of the land promised to Abraham.

b. Genealogy of Japheth

Notice also the descendants of Japheth, the one who was promised enlargement. Japheth had seven sons: Gomer, Magog, Madai, Javan, Tubal, Meshech and Tiras. The first son Gomer was the ancient progenitor of the ancient Galatians and Phrygians from which came the natives of northern Europe and later as the Germans, French, Welsh, Irish, Britons and various other Anglo-Saxon races. These all came from the three sons of Gomer.

Magog, was the progenitor of the Scythians and Tartars whose descendants predominate in modern Russia.

Madai was the progenitor of the Medes and Persians.

Javan was the progenitor of the Greeks, Italians, Spaniards and Portuguese.

Tubal was the progenitor of the Iberians, Georgians, Capadocians, and other Asiatic and European races. Meshech was the progenitor of the Muscovite tribes which now inhabit Russia. Tiras was the progenitor of the Thracians and perhaps the Etruscans who migrated to Italy.

c. Genealogy of Shem

Notice again the sons of Shem. Remember that Shem's blessing was that his God would be blessed. He had five sons: Elam, Assur, Arphaxad, Lud, Aram.

Elam was the progenitor of the Elamite who settled near the Persian Gulf.

Assur was the progenitor of the Assyrians.

Arphaxad was the progenitor of the Arabians, Israelites, Edomites, Moabites, Ammonites, Ishmaelites, Midianites and other tribes of Asia.

Lud was the progenitor of the Lydians of Asia minor.

Aram was the progenitor of the Aramaeans later called Syrians.*

A close look at the sections of the world's population emanating from these three sons of Noah is revealing. I leave you to draw your own conclusions!

DIVINE HELP AGAINST THE CURSE OF POVERTY

Another curse you must be aware of is the curse of poverty. In order to experience unbeatable success, you must identify curses and deal with them. If you embrace a curse, it will frustrate you.

I can see curses in operation in so many places. No matter the efforts that are made, the frustrations and the sweat still remain. I also see poverty and lack, as a curse. It is important for anyone who wants to experience divine provision to see poverty as a curse.

In Deuteronomy 28, Moses listed the curses that would come upon Israel if they disobeyed the Word of God. One of the curses was poverty and lack. "Therefore shalt thou serve thine enemies which the Lord shall send against thee, in hunger, and in thirst, and in nakedness, and in want of all things..." (Deuteronomy 28:48). Why do I believe that poverty is a curse? Because the Word of God puts poverty in the category of a curse. The Word of God says that poverty is a curse.

I am aware that some people take vows of poverty. I respect them for their great sacrifice to the Lord. However, I can see clearly that when God cursed the Israelites, poverty was one of the frustrations to expect. All the curses of Deuteronomy 28 lead to poverty. But in Deuteronomy 28:48, you see it a bit more explicitly. God shall set thee up in hunger, thirst, nakedness and in want.

My pastor in the North of Ghana told me how children eat from the rubbish dump in that region. That must be a curse. We see on CNN almost everyday, the horrors of wars around the world. We see starving children and dying masses. These are not blessings.

1. Poverty leads to lack of education.

Poverty leads to lack of education. Hosea 4:6 says, "My people are destroyed for lack of knowledge..." (Hosea 4:6).

An entire nation perishes when there is lack of the knowledge of arts, science, medicine, law, etc. Poverty is a curse because it is a vicious cycle. Poverty brings about an inability to be educated. The lack of education leads to more poverty. The wealthy remain in their riches, and the poverty of the poor deepens.

2. Poverty causes poor health and disease.

Poverty causes poor health and disease. The life expectancy for rich countries is much higher than poor countries. The life expectancy for a Ghanaian is about fifty-eight years. The life expectancy for a Canadian is about seventy-six years. There is a significant difference between the figures of the peoples of these two countries. This difference is very much related to the state of wealth.

Do you remember the story of the rich man and Lazarus? Who died first? Was it not the poor man Lazarus who died first? Was Lazarus not suffering from a terrible ulcerating condition? What treatment could Lazarus afford? The only treatment Lazarus could afford was a dressing and licking of his sores by the rich man's dogs. "...Moreover the dogs came and licked his sores" (Luke 16:21). Poverty certainly leads to poor health.

3. Poverty leads to drunkenness.

Poverty is a curse because it causes people to get drunk. Many poor people drink to forget about their insurmountable problems. "Let him drink, and forget his poverty, and remember his misery no more" (Proverbs 31:7).

There are many problems without solutions. People without God cannot see the way out of their crisis. They often resort to drinking. I remember a lady I met from Uganda. She would hold a bottle in her hand and say, "Pastor, I have a lot of problems. That's why I'm drinking." The curse of poverty makes you drink.

4. Poverty leads to a lack of friends.

Another reason why poverty is a curse is because the poor man has few friends or relatives. "The poor is hated even of his own neighbour: but the rich hath many friends" (Proverbs 14:20).

One of the signs of poverty is that your relatives and friends are not interested in you. The Bible tells us that the neighbour of a poor man is very far from him.

Why is it that when Liberia was overran by anarchists, America did not seem to take much notice? However, when Iraq invaded Kuwait, the whole world took notice? I wish to suggest that the poverty of Liberia does not make it of as much concern as other places. The Bible says that even relatives are not interested in their poor brothers and sisters.

5. Poverty leads to domination by the rich.

Another reason why poverty must be a curse is that poor people are dominated and ruled by rich people. The rich nations are ruling over the poor nations. Rich Western nations continue to dominate poor African nations through monetary loans and world trade. The rich nations vary at random, the purchase prices of the items these African nations export. There is nothing that the poor nations can do except to complain in futility.

6. Poverty leads to disregard.

Poverty makes people disregard you. "There was a little city, and few men within it; and there came a great king against it, and besieged it, and built great bulwarks against it: Now there was found in it a poor wise man, and he by his wisdom delivered the city; yet no man remembered that same poor man. Then said I, Wisdom is better than strength: nevertheless the poor man's wisdom is despised, and his words are not heard" (Ecclesiastes 9:14-16).

A poor man may have much wisdom, but his wisdom is despised. I know many African Christian ministers who are very wise and anointed. They are, however, not regarded much because they come from poor backgrounds.

Even in the Church, I notice a subtle disregard of those who come from Africa. At international gatherings, many ministers from rich nations are not really interested in relating with fellow ministers from poorer countries. Although wealth and riches should not be yardstick for developing relationships, that is often the case. Many western ministers unknowingly see Africa only as a place they can add to their long list of mission fields. It enriches their résumé or curriculum vitae. The rich have no real interest in the poor. The world, and even the Church, is truly polarized into the rich and the poor.

I have been despised many times. It is a very painful experience. Truly, poverty is not a blessing from God. Do you think Japanese or Asians are loved by Westerners? The western world has been forced to relate with them because of their immense wealth. I am told that some Americans even learn to speak Japanese because it is of vital importance when doing business. I have never heard of an American or German learning to speak Twi (a prominent Ghanaian language) because it is of economic importance!

Nobody in the world is learning a Ghanaian language because it is economically important to do so. Ghanaians, on the other hand, have had to adopt a foreign language as their official language! No wonder we are not respected much by the world community.

THE TRUTH SETS US FREE

If poverty is a curse, then decide to stay away from it. The frustrations of poverty must never be yours. You can overcome every curse of poverty through the blood of Jesus. The Bible says that you shall know the truth and the truth shall make you free. "And ye shall know the truth, and the truth shall make you free" (John 8:32).

The truth of God's Word is what will liberate you from every curse and frustration. There is a law that teaches that whatsoever a man sows, that shall he reap. This is the law of reward for hard work. If you work hard, the law will be fulfilled and you will reap the blessings of success. God longs to bless his children with unbeatable success.

There is no shortcut to experiencing God's blessings. Thank God for his Word. In him is life and the life is the light of humanity. Within the Word of God, you will have direction for your life.

As you study the Word, God will give you wisdom to escape from the curse of poverty. You will escape from the global and sectional curses that are in operation in this world! Divine provision will be yours! Wisdom shall promote and establish you in unbeatable blessings! "Wisdom is the principal thing... Exalt her, and she shall promote thee: she shall bring thee to honour, when thou dost embrace her" (Proverbs 4:7,8).

People will speak about how you have unbeatable blessings. I see God giving you unbeatable success now! I see the curse of poverty breaking in your life right now! From this moment, walk out of the bondage of lack and failure! You are a child of the King! You are blessed with unbeatable success!

The Abrahamic Success Paradigm 26

■ THE SECRETS OF SUCCESS

There are many examples of people who are successful. Some of these examples are biblical characters. There are some successful people who are alive today. As Christians, we can learn from both of these groups.

Someone may ask, "Why should an unbeliever be successful since he doesn't believe in God?" Dear friend, the fact is that God has established certain principles. Anyone who abides by them will experience success. From today, I want you to know that success is not an accident.

There is a road that leads to failure, and another that leads to success. I am writing this book so that you will learn the principles that made Abraham successful. One of the things that I do in order to succeed is to observe successful people.

I once spoke with some friends who were launching out for the first time in the music industry. After listening to their music, I told them that their music was nice but that I didn't think it would sell. Then I showed them the music of some very successful singers. I sat down with them and played the music of these successful artistes. I said to my friends, "Do what these people do, and you will get to where they are!"

This is such a simple principle that it escapes most people. I have found that many people want to do complicated and difficult things. Do you want to be a successful pastor? It is difficult and yet easy. It is easy because all you have to do is to follow closely someone who has succeeded in that field. It is also difficult because it is sometimes not so easy to follow.

1. To be successful you need to understand the nature of a principle.

Principles are invisible rules that must be obeyed. Principles are not changed by circumstances. They are not altered with time. They are not even affected by your prayer and fasting. If you break a principle, the principle will break you!

The law of gravity is one such principle. If you jump off the roof of a seven-story building, you will die. You will die even if you are a Christian. You will die even if you are a diplomat or a president.

You can fast for seven days without eating or drinking water. You can pray seven hours a day for seven days. But if you break the principle and jump off a seven-story building, you will break your neck and die. You may even ask your pastor to anoint you with oil before you jump - this will not change anything.

I believe in the anointing with oil, but I also believe in the reality of a principle. It is a reality which many Christians do not want to face. They feel that because they are Christians, they don't have to study to pass exams. No matter who you are, you have to study hard if you want to pass your exams. It is a principle that applies to prayerful and non-prayerful Christians. I have watched many anointed pastors destroy their gift as they broke principles of administration and management. In fact, some of the most anointed gifts are the ones who break the principles of administration. If we do not apply the principles for success, we will not become successful.

Please understand the nature of a principle. The principle does not care who you are. It is in force and it is in place.

I often wonder when I see young pastors breaking certain principles in ministry. I have watched it happen repeatedly. A young pastor, in his zeal to establish his own ministry, would break somebody else's church, speaking evil of the senior pastor. Time and time again, this same pastor who has broken the rules, is then broken by his own mistakes. If you break somebody's house down in order to build your own, you will reap what you sow. This is the law of the Bible (Galatians 6:7).

2. If you apply the principles of success to your life early enough, you will reap good fruits.

Someone came to me once and said, "My wife is evil."

I asked, "How come?"

He said, "She has a mammy water spirit."

"Oh, I see." Their marriage was virtually broken down. I questioned him further, "Do you want to remain married?"

"Yes, but my wife and her entire family have marine spirits."

So I asked, "What are we going to do about this?"

"I need deliverance and so does she."

I said to him, "What you need is good counsel from the Word of God." As I spoke with him, I realized that he had not been faithful to his wife. He had had multiple extra-marital affairs.

"You are not being faithful to your wife," I told him. "That is what is breaking your marriage." I continued, "I am a bishop, but I don't know what you mean by marine spirits. And I don't know how you know these things. What I know is what the Word of God says and what the principles in the Bible teach us."

He still asked whether he needed deliverance. But I insisted, "You shall know the truth and the truth shall make you free. When you walk in the Word of God, it will establish you. When you keep to the principles in the Word of God they will help you have a wholesome marriage."

Dear friends, whether you are delivered from leviathan spirits or jupiter demons, if you do not keep to the principles in the Word of God your deliverance will have little effect. Happy marriages are built on the solid foundation of biblical principles!

Many of you reading this book are young enough to start applying the principles of success. If you start early, you will live to reap the fruits of a godly life. There is hope for the future. We can do well and we will succeed in our generation.

3. There is no quick way to success.

Everyone wants a quick way out! I'm sorry to inform you that there is no quick way to success. It seems to me that it is the nature of man to desire a quick fix. That is why the miracle and deliverance thing is very popular now.

People do not want to live right. They don't want to serve God. They don't want to pray everyday. They do not want to read their Bibles. They don't want to change their lives and they don't want to do what is right. People want everything to be okay now, but everything cannot be okay in a day.

Applying the principle in your life is not a formula that leads to instantaneous answers to everything. A principle is something you abide by, which in the process of time yields results. Go and ask any successful person you know whether he got there overnight. The next time you see President Mandela, ask him whether he became the leader of South Africa overnight. In Ghana, many successful people have been persecuted for their success. Some have even been to prison. It seems that there is a very long road to success and there is simply no short cut. Principles must be obeyed and they will bring you to success.

4. ONE FACET OF BEING SUCCESSFUL IS BEING PROSPEROUS.

Poverty does not help anyone. The devil has made us believe that a spiritual person is a poor person. The fact that some priests take oaths of poverty only goes to emphasize the notion that there is some virtue in abject poverty. When I read the Bible, I do not see any such doctrine. In fact, the people God walked with often turned out to be rich. It is obvious that Satan has done a good job in making us all believe that poverty is more spiritual than success.

Poor people are often frustrated people. Someone once said that he doesn't trust poor people because they don't show their true character. I have noticed that many people change when they become prosperous. What does this mean? It means there was something hidden in them, which was exposed when they became prosperous. I believe God wants you to prosper in this life.

You are of little use to God if you live on Discouragement Avenue next to Disappointment Alley. When frustration and despair are your next-door neighbors, you cannot achieve much in life. God wants to give you more money than you can use, but He wants you to love Him more than money. Money is not evil! It cannot be evil! If you love money, more than you love God you are in danger of backsliding. No one can tell me that a television is an evil thing. It is not! However, if you use television to watch evil films, then it has become an instrument of wickedness in your life.

God wants us to be successful. He wants His children to be rich and prosperous. God wants His people to build houses and to own cars. God's will for you is to have an abundance of all things. God wants you to live in a nice house and have a nice garden. What do you lose by believing this? Nothing! "BUILD YE HOUSES and dwell in them; and PLANT GARDENS and eat the fruit of them" (Jeremiah 29:5). If God told the Israelites to build houses and to plant gardens under the Old Covenant, then He is telling us to do the same. The New Covenant is a better covenant!

Some time ago, I realized that unless I speak success in a firm and confident way, it will not come into the hands of God's people. God has impressed upon me to confidently speak about riches and success because it is His will. I know that many people will still remain in poverty, but through a strong message of success many people's faith will be lifted up to receive from the Lord.

He wants you to be a millionaire, and even a billionaire. I am not saying that if someone is poor that he is out of the will of God. There will always be poor people amongst us, but it is our duty as preachers to speak the general truth of the Word of God. The general truth of God's Word is explicitly and implicitly success, riches, breakthrough, happiness, peace and success. Receive it because that is God's desire for you. "Beloved, I wish above all things that thou mayest PROSPER and be in HEALTH, even as thy soul PROSPERETH" (3 John 2).

Decide to be someone who will build a house during your lifetime. Decide to be someone who will own a car. Decide to be someone who will help other people financially. Decide today for success and riches. Decide that you will accomplish something in this life. God does not want you to borrow money; He wants you to be a giver. Don't believe the lies of the devil. I'm not saying this to you because I want money from you. I could have a lot more money practicing medicine. I am saying this because I want to help you. I am saying this because God has sent me to your life to help you climb out of darkness.

God is telling me to tell you that success is for you now! No matter who you are or where you live in this world, success can be yours by faith. I see you having a breakthrough in your financial life. I see you living long and prospering. I see you without debt. I see you with great riches. I see you getting stronger and stronger. I can see you in your house. I see you standing in the garden you have planted. I see you owning many cars. That is God's plan for you.

Oppressive Lecturers

When I was in medical school, I noticed two types of lecturers. Some lecturers were kind and taught us what we needed to know. They provided all sorts of support to help us pass our exams. On the other hand, there were some doctors who were extremely wicked to the students. They would ask unreasonable questions during examinations and fail students unnecessarily.

I have personally watched friends drop out of the medical school after repeatedly failing oppressive exams. One lecturer once told me, "To be honest with you, the standards we demand from you students are higher than they should be at the undergraduate level." Under the oppressive and wicked lectureship of certain doctors I watched two students attempt suicide. One of them succeeded. It was a great tragedy!

I always wondered why some of these lecturers were unreasonable and so mean to their students. I often asked myself, "Do these people not have their own children who will one day be medical students?"

"How do these lecturers benefit by intimidating and threatening students?" In stark contrast, there were very kind lecturers who would spend a lot of time with the students. In particular, I remember one gynecologist who spent a lot of time teaching us on the wards. When the exam time came, he was very concerned that his students passed. He helped us a great deal. As I inquired into the background of some of these lecturers, I found a general pattern. Many of the wicked lecturers were frustrated doctors. Some of them did not even own cars. Many of them were impoverished with low salaries and very poor working conditions. Their frustration was being passed on to the students. Many of the pleasant doctors were a bit more prosperous. The poverty and deprivation of highly educated lecturers was showing up in an unusual way.

Dear friend, poverty and frustration are not good things. God plans for us to succeed. He intends us to do well. What did Jesus say? He said that we should ask whatever we want that our joy should be full. When we are joyful, we are strong. What does the Word of God say? The joy of the Lord is our strength!

5. If you want to succeed, follow successful people and do what they are doing.

I study pastors that are successful. I did not have the opportunity to go to a Bible school. All I have learnt in the ministry, I learnt through observation of successful ministers. I studied the pastor of the largest church in the world. I studied anointed teachers who taught the Word. I read books written by ministers ahead of me. In my own city, Accra, I read the books of successful pastors. I am no fool! I know that God has given everyone some gift and I intend to tap what I can from them.

6. Decide to follow God's prescribed method of success.

It is time for you to succeed in life. I remember the testimony of a young man who wanted to succeed. Instead of obeying simple principles that are in the Word of God, he felt that there would be a shorter way. After deliberating on what to do, he went to see a fetish priest. The priest was going to lead him to success.

The fetish priest described what he was going to do. He was going to take a chicken and pluck off his feathers. He continued, "I will put the chicken in a room for seven days without food or water." "Then you will put your hand in a bowl and pick as many large grains of corn as can fit into your hand. You will then drop them on the floor for the chicken to eat."

Then the fetish priest explained, "When the chicken eats the grains of corn, whatever number of grains are left will be the number of years you will live after I make you successful." He continued, "You will see the chicken walk out on its own into a fire I have prepared for it outside.

This young man thought to himself, "Wow! Is that how my end will be? I will walk into the fire just like this chicken walked into the fire? Suppose the chicken leaves only three grains of corn, that means I will live only three more years."

This brother decided against using the fetish priest's method of success but to rather choose God's methods. Today he is a successful man of God. Friends, success is not an accident! It is not just good fortune. It is the ability to follow principles and secrets of the Word of God until it brings you to a place of success.

■ THE SUCCESS STORY OF FATHER ABRAHAM

The first question we have to ask ourselves is, "Was Abraham successful?" The Bible teaches us a number of important truths about him. "And Abram went up out of Egypt, he, and is wife, and all that he had, and Lot with him, into the south. And Abram was very rich in cattle, in silver, and in gold" (Genesis 13:1,2).

1. Abraham was a successful person.
2. He was married and had children.
3. He was very rich in cattle, silver and in gold. In our day, he probably would have had investments in banks, properties and in stocks.
4. Abraham was a person who knew God. The Lord spoke to him many times and answered his prayers.
5. Abraham also fought and won some battles in his lifetime.
6. Abraham died in a good old age having seen the mercies of God throughout his life.

In the New Testament, when Jesus told the story of Lazarus and the rich man, He stated that Lazarus was taken to Abraham's bosom. That meant that Abraham was still an important person even after his life. Some people are only very important in this life. In the next world, they become insignificant to society; They are banished to Hell to be punished for their sins. If Abraham were alive today, a Christian aspiring to be successful would have to ask him for an interview. You should want to ask Father Abraham, "How did you do it? What are the secrets of your success? How did you become so famous and prosperous?" You should want to ask Father Abraham, "Why did God choose you and speak to you?"

Though we are not living in the days of Father Abraham, we have in the Bible an accurate account of his life and success. By studying the Bible, we can learn some of his secrets and principles. Instead of waiting for some false prophet to tell you to bring the teeth of a lion and the tail of a tiger for success in life, join me now and let us learn the secrets of Abraham's success.

EIGHT SUCCESS PRINCIPLES OF ABRAHAM

1. The principle of obeying the Lord.

"Now the Lord had said unto Abram, Get thee out of thy country, and from thy kindred, and from thy father's house, unto a land that I will shew thee: And I will make of thee a great nation, and I will bless thee, and make thy name great; and thou shalt be a blessing: And I will bless them that bless thee, and curse him that curseth thee: and in thee shall all families of the earth be blessed" (Genesis 12:1-3).

The first time we hear of Abraham in the Bible, the Lord was giving him an instruction. God told him to leave his country and travel to a strange land. Abraham immediately obeyed the Lord. This first and great principle is something that every believer needs to accept.

a. If you obey God, it will bring blessings to your life.

God told Abraham that He would bless him and that everybody who blesses him would be blessed. God told him that he would make a great nation out of him. Notice that all of the blessings of Abraham were on the condition that he obeyed God's command. Remember that greatness is dependent on obedience to the voice of God.

There are many people in the world, and God has a blessing for everyone. However, the key that makes the blessing manifest is obedience to Him. Abraham took the decision of a lifetime. He decided to leave his family and his country and launch out in obedience to God. In our lives, we are likely to make two or three of such major decisions. These are decisions that change the course of our lives. A good example is the decision of whom to marry. If you obey God concerning marriage, your life will be relatively peaceful. If you marry the wrong person, the curses will follow you in a never-ending stream.

Many people do not obey God when they get to the crossroads of marriage. They listen to the flesh and the voice of friends. One thing that will influence your state of happiness more than anything else is your marriage. You can never escape the reality that you are married. When you come home, you meet your marriage partner. When you go out, everything you do will be related to the fact that you are married. If you obey the Lord, God will establish you with His blessing.

b. Disobedience leads to a curse.

There are many people who cry and say, "It is difficult to obey God." I want you to know that it is more difficult to disobey God. Anyone who disobeys the Lord will experience curses and frustrations in his life. Remember the testimony of Adam. God put him in a garden and told him that he could eat the fruit of every tree but that he should leave one tree alone. Adam disobeyed God and look at where we are today! Adam was cursed and the entire human race was cursed with him.

All men are now cursed to sweat and struggle in their lives in order to eat and make a living. I know of no human being on the earth that is exempt from this curse. The poor man gives several hours of hard labour and is rewarded with very little. Yet, he has to continue the hard work in order to survive. The rich man works twelve hours a day, seven days a week in order to maintain his riches. He sweats as much as the poor man but in a different way. All of us are struggling under this curse.

Women have been cursed to desire husbands, although the man will rule over their lives. I have rarely seen a woman who does not want a husband. "Unto the woman he said, I will greatly multiply thy sorrow and thy conception; in sorrow thou shalt bring forth children; and thy desire shall be to thy husband, and he shall ruler over thee" (Genesis 3:16). Even though the husband is going to dominate their lives, that is what they want!

Women have been cursed in childbirth. A woman will tell you that there is no pain like the pain of childbirth. Where did all these things come from? They came from Adam's disobedience. He disobeyed God and his life became frustrated. But we see a second Adam, Jesus Christ. For as by one man's disobedience many were made sinners, so by the obedience of one shall many be made righteous. Romans 5:19.

c. **Jesus was obedient to the Father; one act of obedience has brought so much blessing to the human race.**

A lost and dying world now has a life in Jesus Christ. God has highly exalted Jesus and given him a name above every name. Exaltation comes through obedience. If you want to be promoted in your life, begin to obey the Lord. Promotion comes through obedience to the Word of God.

2. The principle of doing God's work

Another such decision is the decision to obey God and do His work. On the 10th of March 1989, I qualified as medical doctor. After seven years of hard labour, I had arrived at a point where many people in the world would like to have been. I was now a medical doctor! Nevertheless, the Lord spoke to me to leave the medical practice and do His work full-time. I obeyed and that decision has changed my life completely. One day when standing in Jerusalem, I wondered, "How did I get to be in this place?" The Lord told me, "It is because you are following my voice that I brought you here."

You do not know the far-reaching effects of obedience to the Lord. Sometimes I stand in the church and see all the people whose lives have been changed and I wonder, "Would these people have been saved if I was a practicing doctor in a small clinic somewhere in town?" Sometimes we don't have any idea of the effects of our obedience. I think that many people will not know the effects of their disobedience to God until they get to heaven. I think some people will get to heaven and be told, "There are thirty seven thousand people who were supposed to be in heaven through your ministry! They are all in hell now, because you refused to obey my call." They will answer, "Oh I thought it was just a little teaching in Sunday school that you wanted me to do. I felt that if I didn't do it someone else would be able to do it."

That little thing that God wants you to do has a snowballing effect. It will lead to the salvation of many souls. Just do it and be blessed! Obedience is the first key to Abrahamic success.

3. The principle of obeying God fully

When you do decide to obey God, do not obey him partially. Do not add on things which God did not ask you to do.

a. **God called Abraham alone.**

God did not call Abraham with Lot; He called Abraham alone. Abraham made the mistake of taking Lot with him. This caused many problems for Abraham. You see we do not always understand the rationale behind God's instructions. God was trying to separate Abraham from his family. He was trying to set up a special line and a special person through whom he would bless all the nations of the earth.

The mistake Abraham made is the same mistake many people make when they are launching out in business or ministry. As far as ministry is concerned, God does not call a group of people. He calls a man. "And I sought for A MAN among them…" (Ezekiel 22:30). The Bible doesn't say that God sought for a group of men. God deals with us as individuals.

b. **It is important to obey what God tells you as an individual.**

Years ago in Ghana, there were no vibrant Charismatic churches however there were vibrant singing and drama ministries. I myself belonged to one of such groups, called Calvary

Road Incorporated. However, with the passage of time, God began to call some of the members of such groups into the pastoral ministry. Many of the leaders of these ministries were led to establish churches. However, some of these people made the mistake of launching out as a group into the Church world. "So Abram departed, as the Lord had spoken unto him: AND LOT WENT WITH HIM..." (Genesis 12:4).

That was a big mistake! Many people who were generally called to be successful pastors had their ministries stifled by the people they took along with them. You see, many of these people who were taken along, felt that they had equal power and equal say with the leader. Executive committees ran the singing and drama ministries, but a committee does not run a church. A church needs a strong leader supported by wise and loyal assistants.

c. God began to work with Abraham when he separated from Lot.

If you read the Bible, you will notice that there was a time when the servants of Lot quarrelled with the servants of Abraham. Lot did not tell his servants that they were privileged even to be with Abraham. He did not remind his followers that it was Abraham who was called and that he was just taken along by the grace of God.

Abraham had to settle the dispute. Abraham took the initiative to separate from Lot. When Abraham asked Lot to choose one section of the land, he took the best part and left Abraham, the real leader, with the leftovers. Sometimes when you do things as a group, the people around do not realize who the real leader is. Dear friend, it was only after Lot was separated from Abraham that God began to fulfill his initial call to Abraham.

d. Be courageous in obeying God.

Often when people are launching out in business they should really do it alone, but they go in for partnerships. I have watched many partnerships break up very painfully. If God wants you to set up a garment factory, go ahead and do it! Believe God to be able to accomplish it. Sometimes when you get yourself involved with partners who are like Lot, they forget that you are the one who had the vision. The time may come when they would even drive you out of the business you created. Just decide to obey God and to obey Him fully. If God has called you alone, go alone. He will bring people to help you. Don't be afraid! Strength is not in numbers it is in God.

4. The secret of believing God's word.

"And HE BELIEVED IN THE LORD; and he counted it to him for righteousness" (Genesis 15:6). The Bible teaches us that Abraham believed in God.

a. God was pleased with Abraham because he believed.

That is one of the prominent things about him. He was called the father of all those who believe. Because Abraham had faith in God, God was pleased with him. In the ministry of Jesus Christ, many people were healed. Jesus often told those who were healed, "Your faith has made you whole."

b. In order to experience the success that Abraham did, you need to operate in faith.

I want you to be a believer. How is it going to be possible for you to own a car? How is it going to be possible for you to own a house? How much does a car cost now? A good car costs thousands of dollars.

Many people who read this book, earn less than three hundred dollars a month. This is the whole point of faith. You must believe even when it seems impossible. What do you have to lose? Faith will bring you many blessings.

c. When you have faith in God's protective power, it pleases the Father.

You must choose to believe that God's power will destroy the power of the enemy. People talk about riches and the power of the occult. What about the power of God? As you read this book, I can show you several reasons why you may not be alive next week. There are several possibilities. Go to the mortuary and ask. You will find out that there are many reasons why you could be dead by next week.

In my short medical experience, I saw many frightening things. I remember one day, I saw a young lady who had a fever. She was just twenty-four years old. Initially, we thought she had malaria. After giving her several doses of chloroquine, we realized that the fever was still there. We soon discovered that the fever was due to leukemia (a deadly cancer of the blood). Right there I realized that not every fever was malaria and not every fever was curable. This lady was on her way to the grave, it was just a matter of time. Later, I saw a patient on the ward that had stomach discomfort. This was a successful businessman in the prime of his life. When his tummy was examined, it was discovered that his liver was as hard as a stone. He had cancer of the liver and was on his way to the grave. I remember seeing the dead body of a young man who lived with a doctor in the apartments nearby. He was driving the doctor's car when it overturned and killed himself.

When you see evil all around you can easily be frightened. But you must be able to say with David, "Yea, though I walk through the valley of the shadow of death, I will fear no evil." Choose to believe that God will keep you. "Yea, though I walk through the valley of the shadow of death, I will fear no evil: for thou art with me; thy rod and thy staff they comfort me" (Psalm 23:4).

d. God is so happy with you when you have faith in His promises.

Believe that God will give you a long life. Believe that you will live to obtain a good old age. Believe that you will live to see your children and your children's children! Believe that although a nice car costs thousands of dollars, you will have one! Expect that you will also have a nice car to give away to someone one day!

Abraham was ninety years old. He had stopped committing love with his wife. He was an old man when God told him that he was going to have a child. The possibility of Abraham having a child was nil, but he believed God. God was so happy with Abraham because he believed. "WITHOUT FAITH it is impossible to PLEASE GOD" (Hebrews 11:6).

Read through the Bible and see how people look foolish when they believe God. Do not be afraid of looking odd when you step out in faith. By faith are we saved! I promise and predict that in spite of everything, God will select you and superimpose His purpose on your life. I see God superimposing His blessings on your life in spite of contrary evidence and contradictory circumstances! God will do this because of your faith.

The more you exercise faith, the more you will prosper. The more you are blessed, the more people will speak against you. The more you prosper, the more people will hate you. Ignore their hatred, keep on and make sure that you please God with your faith. Faith was one of Abraham's key principles for a successful life.

5. THE SECRET OF FAMILY SERVICE TO GOD

One of the reasons why God chose Abraham and blessed him was because God knew that Abraham would command his entire family to serve Him. Look at Genesis 18:19 carefully and you will see that God was about to destroy Sodom and Gommorah. God thought, "Should I inform Abraham about this? Should I speak to him?"

Many people would like God to speak to them. Why did God speak to Abraham? The answer is in the Bible. "For I know him, that HE WILL COMMAND HIS CHILDREN AND HIS HOUSEHOLD after him, and they shall keep the way of the Lord, to do justice and judgment; that the Lord may bring upon Abraham that which he hath spoken of him" (Genesis 18:19).

a. Do not take the spiritual development of your children for granted.

Many people who have children do not care what happens to them spiritually. They are concerned that their children attend "good" schools and universities. In contrast, they take the spiritual development of the child for granted. I would not like to bring a child into the world that would end up in Hell. If you are going to be successful, you must concerned that your household serves the Lord. It is more important that your children serve the Lord than them having a good education. God said, "I know Abraham. He's going to bring his children to Sunday school. He's going to let them study the Bible."

Your children should attend Sunday school and learn about David, Abraham, Joshua and Jacob. They must know all the stories of Jesus Christ. They must learn about Absalom, Lucifer and Judas. Not just math and science are important! You cannot attend church and leave your children languishing at home watching evil films on television. God wants you to ensure that your entire household is serving Him. God worked with Abraham because He was confident that Abraham would make his family serve the Lord.

b. It is important to marry a Christian who will join you to serve the Lord.

If you are a young man, you must marry a Christian. Some people marry women who are not even Christians. Some men just marry a wife because she is fair and beautiful. The person is just an empty barrel. Yes, she is a fair and beautiful barrel, but she is an empty barrel. You must marry someone who has the Word and the Spirit. God said, "I know Abraham, he's going to marry a believer. He's going to bring them to church." God wants you to attend church with your spouse.

c. Use wisdom to ensure that your home has the right spiritual atmosphere.

Some Christian men allow their wives to act out of control. They come to church on their own whilst their wives stay at home. They say, "She didn't want to come, so I left her." Not so with me! My wife is under my control. I am the head of my house and I lead the way. Everything in my house is under the influence of the Holy Ghost. You've got to keep your household under control: servants, visitors and even the dogs and cats must serve the Lord.

I have some relatives who come from abroad with their live-in girlfriends. Although I have a space for guests, there is no room for such guests under my roof. I cannot allow people to come into my home and openly practice adultery. I want my whole house to follow the Lord.

Some of you women are married to non-Christians or lukewarm Christians. That means you are the automatic head of the household. You must use wisdom to ensure that spirituality prevails in your home. Your husband may concern himself with educating the children in science and math. You must make sure that they have a good spiritual education. Your husband may just watch cartoons with them, but you teach them the Bible. Cartoons cannot help a child become what he is supposed to become. Ensuring that the whole household serves the Lord was one of Abraham's secrets of success.

6. THE SECRET OF THE TITHE

"For the Lord God is a sun and shield: the Lord will give grace and glory: no good thing will he withhold from them that walk uprightly" (Psalm 84:11). "He that spared not his own Son, but delivered him up for us all, how shall he not with him also freely give us all things?" (Romans 8:32). The verses we just read tell us that God is going to freely give us everything we desire.

If God did not hold back His only son, do you think there is anything else that He will withhold from you? Satan, the master liar, has deceived the whole world that success, riches and success are evil things. He has led us to think that it is good to be poor. The Church has perpetrated this lie. I want to prove to you that the Church can sometimes make mistakes and champion the teaching of wrong doctrines.

Church Father Perpetrated a Lie: Martin Luther's Philosophy on the Jews

We all know that Martin Luther was a great man who brought about the Great Reformation. It was interesting for me to learn about some of the things he taught concerning Jews. His theories about Jews surprisingly gave support to Hitler's Third Reich during the Second World War. The Germans had fuel to emphasize what they felt about Jews. Hitler's government developed a theory that they used to exterminate six million Jews. Read this little passage below of what Martin Luther said about Jews,

"Luther who at one time wrote of the Jews, 'We are aliens and in-laws, they are blood relatives, cousins, and brothers of our Lord' - changed his views when the children of Israel did not convert to his reformed Christianity and join his assault on the Roman church. Luther said of the Jews, 'All blood kindred of Christ burn in Hell, and they are rightly served, even according to their own words they spoke to Pilate.' Moreover, 'The only Bible you have any right to,' he told the Jews, 'is that concealed beneath the sow's tail; the letters that drop from it you are free to eat and drink.' What a crude insult to the people of God!

The most vicious, hateful statements Luther ever wrote are found in his tract 'On the Jews and Their Lies.' In this work he wrote, 'Know this, Christian, you have no greater enemy than the Jew.' His tract called for the enslavement of the Jews because they were children of the devil and should never touch a Christian's hand.

Luther demanded that their synagogues be burned to the ground, their books destroyed, their homes laid waste, their cash and treasure of silver and gold be taken from them, their rabbis be forbidden to teach, and 'their tongues be cut out from their throats.' He also advised that 'young and strong Jews and Jewesses be given the flail, the ax, the hoe, the spade, the distaff, and spindle, and let them earn their bread by the sweat of their noses as is enjoined upon Adam's children. We ought to drive the lazy bones out of our system...' 'If, however,' Luther continued, "we are afraid that they might harm us personally, or our wives, children, servants, cattle, etc., then let us apply the same cleverness [expulsion] as the other nations, such as France, Spain, Bohemia, etc., and settle with them for that which they have exhorted from us, and after having divided up fairly let us drive them out of the country for all time.

"To sum up, dear princes and nobles who have Jews in your domains, if this advice of mine does not suit you, then find a better one so that you and we may all be free from this insufferable devilish burden - the Jews'."*

Is it not amazing, that Church leaders can convincingly teach things that are erroneous? Is it not surprising that the whole nation of Germany believed in this theory? Is it not amazing that such ideas can be propagated and wholly accepted by the Church?

a. Renew your thinking on prosperity to agree with God's Word.

Sometimes the Bible says one thing and Church leaders say the opposite. For example, the Bible says that Jesus became poor that we might be made rich. This is not my own idea. We are reading from the B-I-B-L-E. "For we know that the grace of our Lord Jesus Christ, that, though he was rich, yet for your sakes he became poor, that ye through his poverty might be rich" (2 Corinthians 8:9).

The Bible says I wish above all things that you will prosper and be in health (3 John 2). Many people who prosper are made to feel as though they are doing something wrong. In many societies, people think that because someone is successful and wealthy that he must be up to some kind of evil.

That fact that you are a pastor or an ordinary Christian does not mean that you have to be poor. Poverty is not from God. Poverty is one of the curses in Deuteronomy 28. To be rich is better than to be poor. The Bible says that the Lord is a sun and a shield, and no good thing will he withhold from them that walk uprightly.

Begin to approve of success from within your heart. Do not hate successful people; you can never become something that you hate. You can never approximate something that you fight against. If you hate something, you cannot have it! Years ago the Lord told me to respect certain Christian leaders in my city. He told me to bless them and warned me never to fight against them. He showed me that I would never become an important Christian leader in my city if I fought senior Christian leaders. Do not let the devil deceive you. The Bible calls Satan "...that old serpent that deceiveth the whole wide world" (Revelation 12:9). If Satan can deceive the whole wide world, he must be very good at deception. Do not let your success be taken out of your hand.

b. **The secret of the tithe is truly a secret.**

c. **In every church, there is always a small percentage of people who tithe.**

You may also have noticed, that it is only a small percentage of people who prosper. I call it a secret because it is hidden from many people. You read in Genesis 14 that Abraham paid tithes to Melchizedek. "And blessed be the most high God, which hath delivered thine enemies into thy hand. And he gave him [Melchizedek] tithes of all" (Genesis 14:20). Melchizedek was a priest of the most high God. He represented God and the Church.

d. **All successful people, who have walked with God, know that it is God who gave them what they have.**

Once David was giving an offering. He said something very important, "I'm only giving You what You first gave me." "But who am I, and what is my people, that we should be able to offer so willingly after this sort? for all things come of thee, and of thine own have we given thee" (1 Chronicles 29:14). When you realize that it is God who gives you something, you will always want to acknowledge Him.

Nebuchadenazzar the king got to a place in his life when he began to boast about what he had. God does not like people who boast about things which were given to them. God struck him down with a disease that made him think that he was an animal. For seven years, he played in the grass like an animal. When he came back to his senses, he gave glory to God.

Wherever you are in life, remember that God has made you what you are. Are you intelligent? Are you skilled? Are you beautiful? Everything is from God. "For who maketh thee to differ from another? and WHAT HAST THOU THAT THOU DIDST NOT RECEIVE? now if thou didst receive it, why dost thou glory, as if thou hadst not received it?" (1 Corinthians 4:7). When God elevates you to a position of influence and authority please remember that you are there by the grace of God. Every power has its expiry date.

Belshazzar the king was so happy in his palace that he sent for glasses from the church. "Belshazzar the king made a great feast to a thousand of his lords, and drank wine before the thousand" (Daniel 5:1). He just didn't want to drink wine. He wanted to drink wine from the holy vessels. He wanted to desecrate the Church. He ridiculed churches and pastors.

"Belshazzar, while he tasted the wine, commanded to bring the golden and silver vessels which his father Nebuchadnezzar had taken out of the temple which was in Jerusalem; that the king, and his concubines, might drink therein" (Daniel 5:2). That was a mistake! He drank wine from the vessels. "Then they brought the golden vessels that were taken out of the temple of the house of God which as at Jerusalem; and the king, and his princes, his wives, and his concubines, drank in them. They drank wine, and praised the gods of gold, and of silver, of brass, of iron, of wood, and of stone" (Daniel 5:3,4). Every position you have in this life is by the grace of God. If you don't decide to bow your knees and give glory to God, He will divinely displace and replace you.

One of the ways a successful person can give glory to God is by acknowledging the grace of God. Do you have power? Money? Husband? Wife? Cars? Position? You must remember that it is from the Lord. Abraham knew that secret. He knew that he had to acknowledge God for his success in life so he gave tithes. He gave a significant chunk of his money to the Lord. "And blessed be the most high God, which hath delivered thine enemies into thy hand. And he gave them tithes of all. And the king of Sodom said unto Abram, Give me the persons, and take the goods to thyself. And Abram said to the king of Sodom, I have lift up mine hand unto the Lord, the most high God, the possessor of heaven and earth" (Genesis 14:20-22).

e. A great blessing comes on people who pay their tithes.

I want you to notice a great blessing that came unto Abraham after he paid his tithes. God was stirred to give more blessings to Abraham. "After these things [paying his tithes] the word of the Lord came unto Abram in a vision, saying, Fear not, Abram: I am thy shield, and thy exceeding great reward... And behold, the word of the Lord came unto him, saying, This should not be thine heir; but HE THAT SHALL COME FORTH OUT OF THINE OWN BOWELS SHALL BE THINE HEIR" (Genesis 15:1,4).

This was the first time that God specifically told Abraham that he was going to have his own special child which would not be his servant's child. Abraham had everything in the world but he didn't have a child. God knows what you don't have. He knows where your need is greatest. He gave Abraham what he could not buy with money.

Abraham was a great man, he was successful and rich but he didn't have everything. He didn't have a child. He was so powerful that he had his own private army. His private army had just fought and won a war. How many people on earth today have their own private armies? Abraham had accomplishment, achievement and breakthrough but he didn't have a child. Please read your Bible and see for yourself whether what I am saying is true. In Genesis 14 Abraham paid his tithes and then in Genesis 15, in the very next few verses, God told him that he was going to have his miracle. God blesses those who pay tithes. Miracles are for those who obey the principles of God's Word.

Go into a church and find out those who have been paying tithes consistently for years. Their lives are different from those who have not been paying tithes. Come to the Lord and honor Him every month. "HONOUR THE LORD WITH THY SUBSTANCE, and with the firstfruits of all thine increase: So shall thy barns be filled with plenty, and thy presses shall burst out with new wine" (Proverbs 3:9).

God gave you the job you have. Successful people know that and respect that! The first fruit is for the Lord. Paying a tithe is not something that you must be reminded of. The fact that you are alive must remind you to pay tithes. When you give tithes to God, you become more spiritual. It makes you more committed. When your treasure is in the house of the Lord, you become interested in the church. "For where your treasure is, there will your heart be also" (Matthew 6:21).

f. It is more blessed to give than to receive.

I think that the reason why some people have difficulties in giving to the Lord is because they do not believe or understand that it is more blessed to give than to receive. If it is more blessed to give than to receive, than those who give are at an advantage compared to those who receive. If it is more blessed to give than those at the receiving end are at a disadvantage.

The so-called developing world has been receiving aid from the western powers for years. What has it done for us? Very little! The more people give to us the more we are disadvantaged. When we rise up to give, the Word of God teaches us that we are moving into a blessing. Many people grapple with this reality to their own destruction.

Some time ago, there was a terrible earthquake in Japan. Ghana made a donation of Golden Tree Chocolate to help the Japanese earthquake victims. Someone may ask, "What will these chocolates do to help the earthquake victims?" Probably not much! But it makes Ghana a giving nation. At least we gave something. Giving helps a nation to rise out of poverty into success. Learn this secret now and become a giver. Even if you have little you still have something.

g. God calculates your giving in relation to what you have in total.

God wants you to give in relation to what you have. "And there came a certain poor widow, and she threw in two mites... and [Jesus] saith unto them, Verily I say unto you, That this poor widow hath cast more in than all they which have cast into the treasury: For all they did cast in of their abundance; but she of her want did cast in ALL THAT SHE HAD, even all her living" (Mark 12:42-44).

I see you rising out of poverty, as you become a giver. I see you tithing. I see you paying your first and best fruits to the Lord. I see you entering that small percentage of people who are successful.

Listen to me, God doesn't need your money! He doesn't need our little offerings. Whether you pay your tithe or not the Church will go forward. God is just trying to help you. Abraham knew that God needed nothing from him. The Word of God says that the silver, gold and cattle belong to the Lord. If God wants to make meat stew, He will not ask you for anything.

God is the one trying to reach out to you. God wants to bless you. As you read this textbook, enter the realm of divine approval and divine promotion. I see God giving you divine promotion. I believe with all my heart that the Spirit of success and approval of God is coming upon you. Divine promotion and elevation are yours for the taking. Go forward and never go backward. God is taking you from minimum to maximum, from negative to positive. God is taking you forward. This is the principle of success - the principle of the tithe.

7. The Secret of Intercession

The Bible shows us that Abraham interceded for Sodom and Gommorah. When he began to pray for Sodom and Gommorah he was fulfilling a divine principle.

a. Most Christians are engrossed with their own problems.

Women who are married to unfaithful husbands are constantly praying for them. Many wives are consumed with the problems of their troubled marriages. They want to be prayed for and anointed over and over again. But the problem never seems to go away. Abraham had his own problems but he prayed for Sodom and Gommorah. Abraham didn't have his own child. He may have been suffering from incurable azospermia or oligospermia. The doctors had no solutions to his medical problems.

Abraham also had family problems. He had so much wealth and he didn't have anyone to inherit it. There were only servants to inherit his life's work. He had no children. Abraham now had marital problems because of a maid he had slept with. In spite of all this, Abraham found time to intercede for Sodom and Gomorrah. His prayer was so sincere and intensive that God agreed to answer his prayers. This prayer was so significant that it was recorded in the Bible. "And Abraham drew near, and said, Wilt thou also destroy the righteous with the wicked? And he said, Oh let not the Lord be angry, and I will speak yet but this once: Peradventure ten shall be found there. And he said, I will not destroy it for ten's sake" (Genesis 18:23,32).

b. Supernatural breakthroughs come when we make the problems of God's kingdom our concern.

I believe that this is one of the keys to Abrahamic success. Forget about your problems and make God's kingdom and God's problem your concern. You will begin to experience supernatural breakthroughs in your life. You will not even understand why God is blessing you. When you begin to pray for others, you have graduated into another level of Christianity. I rarely pray for myself. I know that many successful Christians rarely pray for themselves. They are always praying for and counseling other people.

Most Christians think; "When everything is okay and God has blessed me, I will start to pray for other people." But what you don't realize is that there is a divine order that must be followed. They are trying to put the cart before the horse, but the cart cannot go before the horse. Seek first the kingdom of God. After putting the kingdom of God first, you can then tackle your own kingdom. In the Lord's prayer, the first topic is 'Thy kingdom come and thy will be done'. The first prayer is not, "Bless me, give me and help me Lord."

I often counsel people who need God's help; "Get involved in the work of God. Bury yourself in God's work. Pray for other people. Let other people's problems become your concern." You will be surprised how things will take a dramatic turnaround.

c. When God sees that you want to build His house, He will be interested in building your house.

Many years ago I heard a great man of God say, "If you build a house for God, God will build a house for you." I have found this a true and reliable statement. God wants people who concern themselves with His work. Paul said about Timothy, "For I have no man likeminded, who will naturally care for your state. For all seek their own not the things which are Jesus Christ's" (Philippians 2:20).

Notice from this Scripture, an age-old problem. Everybody is thinking about himself and his problems. If you make God's kingdom your primary concern and intercede for people like Abraham did, you will attract God's supernatural blessings. As I have served the Lord these twenty years, I have made the Lord's kingdom the most important thing to me.

In 1985, when in my third year of the medical school, I took a decision for the Lord. I decided not to seek for academic laurels anymore. I had just finished the second year and had concluded that it was not worth striving for earthly crowns. I remember telling my beloved (fiancée), "From now I am not interested in gaining a distinction from this school. I don't want any prizes. All I want to do is pass." I added, "I'm going to build God's kingdom and the church."

It was from that point onwards that I began to develop into a pastor and eventually established Lighthouse Chapel International. It is interesting to note that when I took the decision not to seek great academic heights, I ended up getting distinctions and winning awards. You see, in the kingdom, the way up is the way down. In the kingdom, the way to get is to give. In the kingdom, the way to solve your problems is to solve God's problems.

Have you ever read about Job? He had more problems than any of us? Job had friends who needed spiritual help. Job decided to pray for his friends and look at what happened! "And THE LORD TURNED THE CAPTIVITY OF JOB, WHEN HE PRAYED FOR HIS FRIENDS: also the Lord gave Job twice as much as he had before" (Job 42:10). Who got the blessing when Job prayed? Who was being prayed for? The friends were being prayed for. But when God moved, it was Job's problems that were solved! Is that not amazing? Job got the blessing when he made intercession for his friends. Isn't that interesting! You pray for others and you get the blessing.

This is one of the principles of success. Husbands, wives, businesspeople, turn your attention to the things of God. In Abraham's day, God's major concern was the deplorable state of the nation Sodom and Gommorah. Abraham made that his problem and prayed earnestly about it. Because of this, God blessed Abraham above all men in his generation. This is one of the keys to a successful life on this earth. Seek first the kingdom of God! Intercede for others! Help other people! Build God's church! Build a house for God and God will build a house for you!

8. The Secret of Sacrifice

God blessed Abraham with a child. After this, Abraham faced the ultimate test. God asked him to sacrifice his son. That was a very big request from the Lord. God wanted to see whether Abraham was ready to give up everything for Him.

I believe that God wants to have you as His own without any challenge. I do not think that only Abraham was tested in this way. I believe that every Christian will have an "Isaac" that God will ask for one day. Will they be prepared to give up their Isaac? You can only give up your "Isaac" when you have nothing more to lose.

a. When you begin to walk on the road with God, He will ask you about all the "Isaac's" in your life.

He may start with music. Next, He may ask you to give up some friends. Then He may ask to give more time to Him. Perhaps I should warn you, do not let anything become too precious to you. Anything that assumes too great or important a position will attract the attention of the Lord and He may ask for it. God wants to be the only God in your life. "Little children keep yourselves from idols" (1 John 5:21).

A Vision of Gold

Many years ago, when I started out in ministry, the Lord gave me a vision. I was walking on a long and winding path. On this path were heaps of some substance. They looked like heaps of sand. As I kept walking on the path I got closer to one of the heaps and discovered that it was a heap of gold. I immediately heard the voice of God telling me, "Don't stop! Keep on walking!" Then God told me, "This is the road of ministry for you. As you walk on it, you will meet many of such heaps of gold." He said to me, "Don't stop at the gold. The gold is not important." He continued, "There are many such heaps further along. Why should you stop at one of them and settle there?" Since that time, money has in a certain way, lost its importance to me. I only see money as a tool. I see it as something I will meet along the way. It is not something I must search for and pile up.

God gave me that vision to help me to see Him as being more important than anything else is. I realized that, just following the Lord in itself would lead to a supply of all my needs. As soon something becomes too precious to you, it becomes a dangerous thing.

b. Before God can bless you in a certain way, He needs to be sure that the blessing would not take priority over Him.

The Lord did not want Abraham to replace the love of God with the love of Isaac. Dear friend, Abraham was about to become the father of many millions of children. Before God could trust him with such a blessing, He had to make sure that the blessing would never replace his love for God. Don't hold back anything from the Lord! Give it all to Him and He will make you a great and successful person in this life.

The Davidic Success Paragigm

27

■ THE SUCCESS STORY OF KING DAVID

Was King David a successful person? David was one of the most respected kings of all time. He was also a great psalmist and prophet. Above all, he was a man after God's own heart. Surely, that is a description of success. I believe that David achieved great success in his lifetime. You can read the Scriptures for yourself. "And he died in a GOOD OLD AGE, FULL OF DAYS, RICHES, and HONOUR: and Solomon his son reigned in his stead" (1 Chronicles 29:28).

1. David had a long and eventful life.
2. At the end of his life, he was rich.
3. He was respected.
4. He even had a successor; his own son, Solomon.

What an interesting description: full of age, full of riches, full of honour, and with a successor. David, however, did not get to this point easily. He suffered and struggled through many situations. Often, David came to crossroads and had to take important decisions. Many of the things he did as a young man contributed to his eventual outcome as a successful person. The holy Scriptures teach us to learn from the examples of those who have gone ahead of us. "That ye be not slothful, but followers of them who through faith and patience inherit the promises" (Hebrews 6:12).

The Bible is a practical book; it does not hide the mistakes of people, neither does it cover up the faults of mighty men. David is a person we can learn from today. In this book, I will share with you a few secrets that I believe helped David to become one of the most respected kings and prophets of all time!

THE SUCCESS KEYS OF DAVID

1. The principle of small beginnings

"And Eliab his eldest brother heard when he spake unto the men; and Eliab's anger was kindled against David, and he said, Why camest thou down hither? and with whom hast thou left those few sheep in the wilderness?..." (1 Samuel 17:28). David's brother made a derogatory remark about David's work. He spoke critically of the few sheep that David was handling.

In ministry, I have noticed that people do not want to begin in a small way. The only thing many know how to do is to "break the legs" of the pastor under whom they are working. Through deception, they draw away an entire section of the church and then use those people to start their own ministry.

A minister once approached me and sneeringly spoke of a Lighthouse church that had just a few members. I realized that this man of God did not know how to begin a church. He did not realize that the thousands of people who are attending Lighthouse Chapel today, grew out of three or four original members.

a. Do not be afraid of small beginnings; God will lift you up.

You will benefit from all the experiences you have had in your small beginnings. It was when David was looking after the few sheep that he had a fight with a bear and a lion. It is because he was used to fighting impossible situations that he was able to take on Goliath. When you have preached a thousand times to a hundred people, you will not wet your pants in fright when God lifts you up to minister to a crowd of one thousand.

I have preached so many times, that preaching is now much easier for me. I have preached in difficult atmospheres. I have ministered in hostile environments. I have preached to powerful politicians. I have ministered where people despised me. I have preached when people jeered and hooted at me. I've also ministered where they have cheered me on. There is hardly any atmosphere that I have not experienced. Many of these experiences were in small settings. This has helped me prepare for the ministry I have today.

b. Do not be in a hurry to succeed.

Why are you in a hurry to be successful? It is easier to make mistakes in front of a small crowd than a large one. Practise your business and ministry with small crowds. If you make a mistake with a hundred dollars, it will be easier for you to recover than if you make that same mistake with a hundred thousand dollars. Any businessman who is able to succeed with a small amount of money can succeed with a larger amount of money. Smallness is a necessary stage in the kingdom of God. It is a necessary stage for every business executive. It humbles you and makes you trust in God.

Jesus taught us three principles of progress:

- The principle of being faithful with small things (Luke 16:10).
- The principle of being faithful with another man's Things (Luke 16:12).
- The principle of being faithful with money (Luke 16:11).

You cannot circumvent any one of these laws. Start small and harden your forehead. Avoid people who would laugh at you and despise you. Stay with those who believe in you. Do not tell people what you are doing if they do not respect you. You can make it! God is on your side! God is with you! The Greater One is with you and in you! Do not run away from small beginnings. They are God's training ground for you. That is how King David got his education- in the school of small beginnings!

2. The Principle of Doing Menial Jobs with Joy

"And David came to Saul, and stood before him: and he loved him greatly; and he became his ARMOUR-BEARER" (1 Samuel 16:21). When studying the life of David, you soon learn that though he became king, he first performed many menial jobs. In his father's house, he was a shepherd. Whilst at the king's palace, he did the work of a musician, servant, errand boy and armour-bearer. He wasn't even a soldier! There are so many Christians who want to start out on top! But the only job that begins at the top is grave digging!

a. Do not shy away from menial jobs.

If you study the background of many great people, you will discover that they once served at the lowest levels in their professions. I have done nearly every kind of menial job in the church. I was a drummer, organist, cleaner and odd-job man. All these have helped me to be a better leader.

b. The best leader is someone who has been a follower for many years.

Because you have done menial jobs, you are more reasonable with your subordinates. You understand what they are going through and do not give impossible commands. Some leaders do not know the implications of their instructions. They just say, "Get this done!" You must understand that getting certain things done may have far-reaching implications.

3. The principle of turning away from those who despise you

"ELIAB'S ANGER WAS KINDLED AGAINST DAVID, and he said, Why camest thou down hither? and with whom hast thou left those few sheep in the wilderness? I know thy pride, and the naughtiness of thine heart; for thou art come down that thou mightest see the battle. And David said, What have I now done? Is there not a cause? And HE TURNED FROM HIM TOWARD ANOTHER" (1 Samuel 17:28-30).

This Scripture describes the persecution David faced from his brothers. Eliab, obviously intimidated by David, hurled insults at him just when he was about to fight with Goliath. The world has two types of people: those who believe in you and those who have no confidence in you.

a. Learn to turn away from people who despise you.

When I began my ministry in 1987, many people despised me. Up until today, there are groups of people who think evil of me. They speak evil about me in their homes. "That they may SHOOT IN SECRET at the perfect: suddenly do they shoot at him, and fear not. They encourage themselves in an evil matter: they commune of LAYING SNARES PRIVILY..." (Psalm 64:4,5). I can always tell when someone despises me at heart. Rejection is a spiritual thing. "Beloved, believe not every spirit, but try [test] the spirits whether they are of God..." (1 John 4:1).

b. Every leader should learn to detect the spirit of critical and hateful people.

Rejection is a spiritual thing and can be discerned spiritually. I once spoke to a doctor in the USA. I told him, "You have never believed in me. When we were medical students in Accra, you despised me." He answered, "How did you know?"

"What you are saying is true," he continued. "Somehow, in those days, I didn't like what you were doing. But now, I have come to appreciate your ministry." I had always known that this fellow despised me. Though he never said much to me, I knew it in my spirit. Just like David, I turned away from him and "flowed" with those who believed in me. No one can flourish in an environment of despisement.

In some churches, professionals are neither regarded nor respected as far as the ministry is concerned. If you are a lawyer, doctor or accountant, the ministers may consider you incapable of ministry work. I advise such people to attend a church where they can be involved in ministry without being despised. Some full-time ministers simply do not recognize the role of lay people.

In some places, poor and uneducated people are despised. It is important to turn away from an enviroment where you are despised. You can only flourish where people respect and love you.

4. The principle of choosing and staying with what you have tested

"And Saul armed David with his armour... And David said unto Saul, I CANNOT GO WITH THESE; FOR I HAVE NOT PROVED THEM. And David put them off him. And he took his staff in his hand, and chose him five smooth stones... and his sling was in his hand: and he drew near to the Philistine" (1 Samuel 17:38-40).

This was the turning point in David's ministry. He had an opportunity to have his greatest breakthrough; it was a matter of do or die!

As he went forth, he was to make one of the most important decisions of his life; to wear Saul's armour or not! He decided against wearing Saul's armour and opted for his slingshot with just five smooth stones. In this act, you see the principle of choosing what you have tested.

a. Marriage: Marry the person you know.

I marvel at the behaviour of certain Christian men. They behave normally up until the time they are about to get married. Instead of marrying someone whom they know, they go for a mysterious personality whom nobody knows. They choose a young lady who they know very little about. David refused to use Saul's armour because he hadn't tested it. How can you marry someone you hardly know?

Surely there are some nice people in the church whom you can marry! It is important to marry someone who has a good reputation in the church. There are Christians who are infected with HIV. If you make a mistake, you could end up marrying an infected person!

One of the most important decisions I took in my life was in choosing whom to marry. The lady I decided to marry was someone I had known for years. I knew her character and background. I knew a lot about her. If you really plan to win the battle against Goliath, don't use Saul's armour! That may be the prescribed and ordained method, but using that which is familiar to you will help you to be victorious!

b. Business: Stay with what you know.

In business, every field is different. I have been a sand and stone contractor and a transport business owner. I am familiar with those two areas of business. If I were to conduct business, I would not try to export pineapples. I would stay with what I know. Stay with the five smooth stones that have brought you victory in the past. If you use them in the day of your greatest challenge, you shall prosper!

c. Ministry: Choose someone whose character you can vouch for.

I know many of my church members from my secondary school days. They've also known me throughout the years. If you are a church member or a pastor, go for someone that you've known for a number of years and can trust.

5. THE PRINCIPLE OF MINISTERING TO OTHERS

"And it came to pass, when the evil spirit from God was upon Saul, that DAVID TOOK AN HARP, AND PLAYED WITH HIS HAND: SO SAUL WAS REFRESHED, and was well, and the evil spirit departed from him" (1 Samuel 16:23).

a. If you want to be successful in this life, decide to be a blessing to others.

This will unlock gates for blessings to flow into your life. The most successful people in the world have often played a vital role Maybe they were pastors who ministered to the needs of the people. Perhaps they produced something that benefited millions of people.

David took advantage of the opportunity to minister to Saul. Whenever evil spirits came to torment Saul, David refreshed him by playing the harp and singing unto the Lord. He suddenly became useful to Saul and his kingdom. Are you useful to anyone? Your value rises with your usefulness!

There are some Christians who just say, "Give me, give me, give me." When are you going to start giving something? When are you going to be a blessing to somebody? Jesus is so valuable to all of us because he saved our souls by giving his life. David's value rapidly increased after he helped Saul in his time of demonic affliction.

b. Take up your opportunity of counselling people and sharing the Word of God.

Take up the responsibility of ministering to others. I notice how people shy away from doing God's work. They feel it will be a bother. They feel it will keep them away from succeeding in their secular field.

What a mistake! They don't realize that as they help others, they become more valuable to society. The more valuable you are, the more important you will be.

6. The principle of fellowship and non-isolation

"But all Israel and Judah loved David, because HE WENT OUT AND CAME IN BEFORE THEM" (1 Samuel 18:16). Fellowship is a very important part of success. The more you interact with godly people, the more godliness will rub off on you. The more you interact with successful people, the more successful you will become. David did not isolate himself. He kept in touch and that helped him immensely.

Ministers are often tempted to isolate themselves permanently from other ministers. This is because many people who should be your brothers are often your competitors and rivals. In spite of this, it is helpful to interact and to fellowship. In fact, the Bible teaches us that this is a sign that you are a Christian. "We know that we have passed from death unto life, because WE LOVE THE BRETHREN. He that loveth not his brother abideth in death" (1 John 3:14).

If you are doing well in life, you will often be found fellowshipping. "But if we walk in the light, as he is in the light, WE HAVE FELLOWSHIP ONE WITH ANOTHER, and the blood of Jesus Christ his Son cleanseth us from all sin" (1 John 1:7). Don't stay away. Relate with people ahead of you. Befriend successful people. You will become a blessed person because you have made the right associations.

7. The principle of avoiding arrows of hatred

"And the evil spirit from the Lord was upon Saul...And Saul sought to smite David even to the wall with the javelin; but he slipped away out of Saul's presence, and he smote the javelin into the wall: and David fled, and escaped that night" (1 Samuel 19:9,10).

a. Anyone whom God has blessed will begin to have arrows of hatred and jealousy thrown at him.

You may do good and only good, but you will be hated because of your success. This is part of life. It is your duty to avoid the arrows of hatred.

Recently, our church was attacked by an armed mob of assailants. On a previous attack, my office was bombed and burnt down. These people seemed to have secret, powerful backing because anytime the police arrested them; they were promptly released with orders from "above". These arrows or bombs were being thrown at the church. All of these attacks were manifestations of hatred against the church and my ministry. On numerous occasions, these violent attacks were shown on national television.

When our problem became a national issue, many people advised me to go on television or on radio talk shows to explain our side of the problem. But I knew in my spirit that it would be a mistake to do so! Many people just wanted me to make the mistake of saying something wrong so they could criticize me.

b. When David had one spear thrown at him, he decided to run away.

Perhaps this is the reason why David lived to a good old age. When you see one arrow of Satan, you should know that there are many more out there primed to destroy you. If you sit in the same place, the next arrow will get you. There are times when it is wiser to run away than to stand and fight.

One time the Pharisees wanted to kill Jesus. When Jesus got to know of it, he withdrew himself from that area. "Then the Pharisees went out, and held a council against him, how they might destroy him. But WHEN JESUS KNEW IT, HE WITHDREW HIMSELF from thence..." (Matthew 12:14,15).

Young Christian men must know that they attract the arrows of Satan because of the gift of

God in their lives. In fact, the Bible teaches that because of the anointing on your life, young ladies will be attracted to you. "Because of the savour of thy good ointments [anointing] thy name is as OINTMENT [anointing] poured forth, therefore do THE VIRGINS LOVE THEE" (Songs of Solomon 1:3).

Young lady, because you are beautiful, many wicked and adulterous men are interested in you. Run away from those arrows immediately, otherwise, your whole life may be destroyed. The Bible teaches that precious ministers are sought for by the devil. Anyone who is a precious instrument of God will be hunted after! "For by means of a whorish woman a man is brought to a piece of bread: and THE ADULTERESS WILL HUNT FOR THE PRECIOUS LIFE" (Proverbs 6:26).

Years ago, some sisters were interested in me because of my gift. I didn't even know the danger I was in. Many sisters in Christ I ministered to were hearing wedding bells in addition to the Word of God. I would go around from house to house and room to room sharing the Word of God. Little did I know that some sisters were falling in love with me because of the anointing.

One day, the Lord instructed me to enter a relationship (unto marriage). All along I had been saying, "I will not marry for at least ten more years." But the Lord spoke to me and said, "Your life is precious. You are walking in danger that you don't even know about." He continued, "You don't know about the intricacies of a woman's heart and mind. Enter a relationship now.

This is when I discovered the Scripture in Ecclesiastes 7:26. I have never forgotten it since then. God was actually telling me to escape from spears and arrows. "And I find more bitter than death the woman, whose heart is SNARES and NETS, and her hands as BANDS: whoso pleaseth God shall escape from her; but the sinner shall be taken by her" (Ecclesiastes 7:26).

8. THE PRINCIPLE OF ADAPTING FOR PROGRESS

"And David said unto Ahimelech the priest, The king hath commanded me a business, and hath said unto me, Let no man know any thing of the business whereabout I send thee, and what I have commanded thee…Now therefore what is under thine hand? GIVE ME FIVE LOAVES OF BREAD IN MINE HAND, OR WHAT THERE IS PRESENT" (1 Samuel 21:2,3).

In the passage of Scripture above, you will realize that David acted like a poor man. In the Scripture quoted below, David pretended to be a mad man. "And David arose, and fled that day for fear of Saul, and went to Achish the king of Gath. And he changed his behaviour before them, and FEIGNED HIMSELF MAD in their hands, and scrabbled on the doors of the gate, AND LET HIS SPITTLE FALL DOWN UPON HIS BEARD" (1 Samuel 21:10,13). Was he really mad? No. He was the king's son-in-law. He was from a good family. He was certainly not out of his mind. However, for that occasion, David had to behave like a mad man in order to survive.

a. Learn to adapt in order to advance in life.

I constantly marvel at how some Christians are unable to adapt in order to make a breakthrough in life. You may have to do without a car for a season so that you can have fewer bills to pay. You may have to live in a smaller apartment so that you can save some money. Many people want to impress the outside world at all costs.

There are many that thought our church, the Lighthouse Chapel International, was non-existent for about ten years. We hardly advertised and rarely spent money on expensive outward things. There were times I would arrive unnoticed in my old Renault car. People took no notice of me. Long ago, our church could have bought ten Mercedes Benz cars of different colours for me if I wanted. But I have not seen the need for such a purchase. We have rather invested that money in church buildings and evangelistic projects. Today, people think that Lighthouse Chapel is rich.

Years ago, I compared the income of our church with the income of other churches and I noted that it was relatively lower. The leadership of the church was prepared to adapt to a lower standard of living so that the ministry could move ahead into success. When I started our church in Geneva, I lived in a students' hostel. I also lived in that hostel anytime I was in Geneva. I lived in the hostel and bathed in a common bathroom with the rest of the boarders. There were all sorts of weird looking people around the bathroom everyday.

One person once commented, "I find it amazing that you Lighthouse pastors live like schoolboys or students when you come to Europe." I just smiled. Instead of paying outrageous hotel bills, we adapted ourselves to student life and saved a lot of money. It amazes me that when someone is successful, people hate him all the more. They call him names. They say that he is proud. But they never look closely enough to see what is making that person successful. Apostle Paul said, "I adapt to all men in order that I may win some people to Christ." "To the weak became I as weak...I AM MADE ALL THINGS TO ALL MEN, that I might by all means save some" (1 Corinthians 9:22).

David adapted. Paul adapted. Why can't you adapt? Years ago, I took note of something a prominent minister did. His church was going through some hard times. The income had dropped and the membership was falling. This man of God, who had been used to a certain upper-class lifestyle, did not realize that he had to quickly adapt to the prevailing conditions. I heard that he had rented a huge mansion with several bedrooms. The rent was enormous. I thought to myself, "How will this man pay his rent?"

But that was not all. He had a perfectly functioning Toyota, but he decided to sell it and use a Mercedes Benz. I learnt that the Mercedes Benz gave him no end of problems. In the end, this man of God was left without a car and was eventually ejected from his large house. However, his crisis only deepened! This pastor began to hire taxis and could not pay the bills. Soon he owed money to several taxi drivers. Today, after having a large church in his city, he is left with about twenty people in his congregation.

Perhaps, if this man had adapted during the hard times, he would still be successful in ministry today. There is no need to impress anyone with a car or a house. It is not the car that is important, it is the one who is in it that matters!

9. THE PRINCIPLE OF BEHAVING WISELY WHEN YOU ARE BLESSED

"And David BEHAVED HIMSELF WISELY in all his ways; and the Lord was with him. Wherefore when Saul saw that he BEHAVED HIMSELF VERY WISELY, he was afraid of him. Then the princes of the Philistines went forth: and it came to pass, after they went forth, that David BEHAVED HIMSELF MORE WISELY than all the servants of Saul; so that his name was much set by" (1 Samuel 18:14,15,30).

a. At different times of your life, God will bless you and lift you up.

Many people think that problems belong to those who are poor and defeated. You will notice that David's problems did not begin until after he killed Goliath. After one breakthrough came a host of problems. But the Bible says that David behaved himself wisely. It is important to walk in wisdom when the Lord has promoted you.

Anytime I go to Takoradi, a city in Ghana, my wife points out some buildings to me; buildings which were inherited by a certain family. Although their father left them a lot of wealth and property, that family is now penniless and at the mercy of others. Although they inherited a lot of money, it did not benefit them. Perhaps they did not know how to handle their newfound riches. They misused what they inherited until they had to sell all their properties to pay their debts.

b. **The problem with many Christians is that they do not know how to behave themselves when they are blessed.**

Some young ladies backslide as soon as they get married. They forget that God gave them their husbands. They no longer attend all-night prayer meetings. They want to stay away from the church. Never forget that the Lord gave you everything you have. Learn to behave wisely everytime the Lord blesses you!

One Christian lady told me of how she backslid after her marriage. She and her husband were serious Christians who used to be at every meeting. She told me, "It is my fault. At a point during our marriage, I stopped attending prayer meetings with my husband." She told me how one night when she was lying in bed with her husband, he turned to her and asked, "Is it not time for the all-night?" She anwered, "Oh let's not bother tonight." She did that a few times until her husband backslid spiritually. Why do people fall away when they are blessed by God? Why do you have to stop going for all-night prayer meetings just because you are married? It is time to know how to behave wisely after the breakthrough comes.

Remember the testimony of the prodigal son. Many people think that it was only the younger brother who received an inheritance. Study your Bible carefully. You will see that both of them received an inheritance. Both of them were blessed equally by their father. "...A certain man had two sons: And the younger of them said to his father, Father, give me the portion of goods that falleth to me. And HE DIVIDED UNTO THEM HIS LIVING" (Luke 15:11,12).

Why is it that some people go wild after receiving a blessing? They no longer attend church, they no longer serve God, they no longer do the right things. This prodigal boy received an inheritance. He spent his money on harlots and riotous living. With experience, I have seen that many people do not prosper because they do not use the opportunities that God gives them wisely.

Some African countries are plagued with governments that enrich themselves upon arrival in office. Like vampires, they drink the blood of the nation's wealth and leave peanuts for the nation's masses. Any nation that has vampires in leadership is doomed. These governments must behave wisely, and understand that they are fortunate to be in power. "Woe to thee, O land, when THY KING IS A CHILD, and THY PRINCES EAT IN THE MORNING!" (Ecclesiastes 10:16).

c. **There are many blessings for the patient.**

This Scripture teaches that blessings abound for those that can wait to take their benefits at the right time. This is the principle of delayed rewards. If you buy that expensive car at the wrong time of your life, repairing it and buying fuel for it will be like drawing blood out of your body. It will cost you your life.

I believe in the best for myself, but I wait for the right time to enjoy the blessings that are legitimately mine. Apostle Paul said that many privileges were his to enjoy. Yet he explained, "I have used none of these things." Have we not power to eat and to drink? But I HAVE USED NONE OF THESE THINGS: neither have I written these things, that it should be done unto me: for it were better for me to die, than that any man should make my glorying void. (1 Corinthians 9:4,15).

Although Paul was blessed to have the support of the Church, he deliberately avoided using many of these privileges. A privilege will turn into a snare if you jump into it too quickly.

10. The Principle of Seeing People in the Right Way

"And he said unto his men, The Lord forbid that I should do this thing unto MY MASTER, the

Lord's anointed, to stretch forth mine hand against him, seeing he is the ANOINTED OF THE LORD. David also arose afterward, and went out of the cave, and cried after Saul, saying, MY LORD THE KING... Moreover, MY FATHER..." (1 Samuel 24:6,8,11).

a. David was always careful to honour Saul.

In this passage, David spoke about King Saul to his subordinates. What struck me about David's speech was the way he referred to the king. At one point he called him, "My lord." At another point he called him, "My king", "My master", and even "My father." He could have called him a demon-possessed man. He could have referred to him as the demoniac. We all know that Saul had a problem with evil spirits and that he was a fallen man of God. Everyone knew that the anointing had departed. Yet, David gave Saul the honour and referred to him in a spiritual and honourable way.

Some people think that titles are not important. I think that titles have a role to play, especially in a big organization. Whatever you think about titles, one of the good things they do is that they help you to see whom you are dealing with. They help you to remember at all times who you are and who you are not!

Because David constantly reminded himself that he was dealing with the anointed king, it was difficult for him to strike the Lord's anointed.

As you associate with a man of God, familiarity may make you forget whom you are with. David never forgot that Saul was his master. David never forgot that Saul was his father-in-law. David did not allow himself to forget that he was dealing with an anointed man of God. This, I believe was one of the secrets of David's success.

If David had killed Saul, it would have been because he felt justified to kill a demonized and fallen man of God. He would have thought that he was helping God to eliminate this disgraceful man. Of course, killing a raving lunatic is perceived as different from killing God's servant. However, David never allowed himself to see Saul in the wrong way.

b. David respected Saul until the end.

Notice that David's respect for Saul's office was maintained until the very end. When David heard of Saul's death, notice how he spoke of Saul. He referred to him as "the mighty". "How are the MIGHTY fallen in the midst of the battle! O Jonathan thou wast slain in thine high places" (2 Samuel 1:25).

David went on and described Saul as the beauty of Israel. "THE BEAUTY OF ISRAEL is slain upon thy high places: how are the mighty fallen! (2 Samuel 1:19). This is remarkable, considering how Saul had deteriorated in life. I believe that years later, this act of seeing King Saul in the right way saved David's life.

c. David refused to harm the Lord's anointed no matter the circumstances.

David had taught his men that kings and other anointed people are not to be murdered. The unspoken message that came through David's actions was loud and clear. Do not touch the Lord's anointed, no matter what! Years later, when David himself made a mistake and killed Uriah, he opened the door for a possible retaliatory act. Uriah the Hittite was one of the mighty men of God. You will find him listed as the last of David's mighty warriors. "These be the names of THE MIGHTY MEN whom David had...URIAH THE HITTITE: thirty and seven in all" (2 Samuel 23:8,39).

Since David had killed one of these mighty men, the other mighty men could have retaliated. They could have justified the murder of King David saying, "He's a fallen man of God." They could have said, "We know him. He's an adulterer and a murderer." But David had taught them by example, not to strike at the Lord's anointed.

d. It is important to see the Lord's anointed as they really are.

In today's world, it is important to perceive the Lord's anointed as they truly are. It is important both in private and in public to refer to your pastor in an honourable way. If you call him "Joe Diggy" when you speak about him in private that is what he will be to you. If you refer to him as "my pastor" or "my father", that is what he will be to you. You must realize that faith comes by hearing. What you hear yourself say repeatedly affects your faith.

Remember that God will often bless you through a man of God. God's method is to use men as channels and vessels of blessing.

Paul said, "Henceforth, know we no man after the flesh." In other words, I do not see people through the eyes of my flesh anymore. Wherefore henceforth know we no man after the flesh: yea, though we have known Christ after the flesh, yet now henceforth know we him no more. (2 Corinthians 5:16).

If you see a man of God as a friend, classmate or an equal, then that is what he will be to you. The most important way to relate with a person is spiritually. The reason why many wives cannot receive from their husband pastors is because they see them as marriage mates, lovers, equals and so on. Learn to keep a spiritual perspective of the people you are dealing with. It will keep you on safe ground all the time.

11. The Principle of Not Violating Fathers

"And he said unto his men, THE LORD FORBID THAT I SHOULD DO THIS THING UNTO MY MASTER, the Lord's anointed, to stretch forth mine hand against him, seeing he is the anointed of the Lord" (1 Samuel 24:6).

a. One of the secrets of success is to honour both your natural and spiritual fathers, until the very end.

One of the spirits at work in the world of ministry tries to cut off fathers from children. Surprisingly, many fathers do not flow with their children. God knows that many fathers do not live up to standard. However, he expects a certain honour to flow from children to the fathers. Just accept it! The promise is clear. If you honour your father it will be well with you and you will live long on the surface of the earth. "HONOUR THY FATHER and mother; which is the first commandment with promise; that IT MAY BE WELL WITH THEE, and THOU MAYEST LIVE LONG ON THE EARTH" (Ephesians 6:2,3).

b. Children should be careful not to retaliate, even under extreme provocation.

There are many fathers who can and do provoke their children greatly. "And, ye fathers, PROVOKE NOT your children to wrath" (Ephesians 6:4). I have been provoked many times by fathers; both natural and spiritual fathers. It has been one of my greatest commitments to honour these fathers in the midst of betrayal and direct attacks. It is not easy to honour some fathers, but I believe that it leads to God's blessing and favour.

David's father was throwing spears at him. David's father was trying to kill his son-in-law. I have had people who were supposed to be my fathers, try to destroy me in ministry. Unbelievable things occur in the ministry! I see them as great temptations of the devil.

I believe that David stood at the crossroads of his life when he had the opportunity to kill Saul. Overcoming that temptation was one of the greatest breakthroughs of his entire ministry. That is why this story is given so much prominence in the Bible. Decide not to attack a father in this life. Do not destroy your future. No matter how evil a father may seem to be, leave him to God!

12. THE PRINCIPLE OF LISTENING TO ADVICE

"And David said to Abigail, Blessed be the Lord God of Israel, which sent thee this day to meet me: And BLESSED BE THY ADVICE, and blessed be thou, which hast kept me this day from coming to shed blood, and from avenging myself with mine own hand" (1 Samuel 25:32,33).

a. Learn to be open to advice.

In this Scripture, you see David about to make a mistake. He was going to attack innocent people. Nabal had been very ungrateful to David for his services. It was the advice of Abigail that saved the day.

Once again, if King David had shed blood in his early days it could have become an embarrassment and a curse to him. This would have followed him throughout his reign as king. David said to Abigail, "Blessed be thy advice." Thank God for people who give good advice.

Be open to people's advice. Even when your enemy is speaking, take note of what he is saying. Advice is one of the cheapest ways to move ahead in life.

There are many people who advise me. I have lawyers, architects, engineers, doctors and businessmen who make a great input into my life. I am the leader, so I have to take the decision. However, I want to know what everybody thinks before I take the decision. Sometimes even children can give you good advice.

b. The one who is advising sees the issues very clearly and simply.

This is the mystery about good advice. Often, the one who is receiving the advice does not believe that things are as simple as that. Open your spirit to be able to see when good advice is coming your way.

13. THE PRINCIPLE OF ALLOWING GOD TO WORK THINGS OUT

"And David said to Abishai, DESTROY HIM NOT: for who can stretch forth his hand against the Lord's anointed, AND BE GUILTLESS?" (1 Samuel 26:9).

a. David did not get involved in the implementation of God's master plan.

David said something that I think everyone should learn from. In this passage, David reveals his inner thoughts. He said, "Even though King Saul is fighting against me, I will not kill him myself." However, David was not stupid! He knew that for the prophecies to come to pass, Saul had to die. But, he was not going to be the person to kill Saul.

"The Lord forbid that I should stretch forth mine hand against the Lord's anointed: but, I pray thee, take thou now the spear that is at his bolster, and the cruse of water, and let us go" (1 Samuel 26:11).

There was no way that David could become king as long as there was a king on the throne. David gave three options about how his dream of kingship and freedom could come to pass. "David said furthermore, As the Lord liveth, THE LORD SHALL SMITE HIM; or HIS DAY SHALL COME TO DIE; or HE SHALL DESCEND INTO BATTLE, AND PERISH" (1 Samuel 26:10).

First, he said that the Lord would strike Saul down supernaturally. The second possibility was that Saul would eventually die naturally. David said, "...his day shall come to die." The third possibility was that the king could be killed in a battle. It is interesting to note that the Lord worked out the plan for David's kingship through the third option. Saul was indeed killed in a battle. The point that I am making is that David left it to God and kept his hands clean! Everyone could see that God was doing his own thing.

b. We need to trust God for His perfect plan to materialize.

When you get involved and try to help God, you create Ishmaels who rise up to challenge your Isaacs. "And Moses said unto the people, Fear ye not, STAND STILL, AND SEE THE SALVATION OF THE LORD, which he will shew to you today: for the Egyptians whom ye have seen today, ye shall see them again no more for ever. THE LORD SHALL FIGHT FOR YOU, and ye shall hold your peace" (Exodus 14:13,14).

Pastors must know that if God wants certain people to be in their churches, there is no need to steal them from another congregation. Perhaps, the Lord will bring them to your church through one circumstance or another. Just leave it to God. Do not get involved in any unethical dealings with another pastor's church members.

If God wants you to marry that man, it will work out. Ladies, there is no need to throw yourself at a man for him to notice you. After four years of marriage, one man told his wife, "You forced yourself on me! I never even had the chance to think about it properly." Perhaps this man would have found her anyway. But because she forced herself on him, he was wondering whether he made the right decision. It is time to allow God to work things out himself. Keep your hands clean!

14. The Principle of Not Allowing Rebels into Your Life

One of the interesting events of David's life was when he put to death the man who claimed to have killed Saul in battle. "And David called one of the young men, and said, Go near, and fall upon him. And he smote him that he died. And David said unto him, Thy blood be upon thy head; for THY MOUTH HATH TESTIFIED AGAINST THEE, SAYING, I HAVE SLAIN THE LORD'S ANOINTED" (2 Samuel 1:15,16).

Another remarkable event, was when he executed the men who killed King Ishbosheth. "When one told me, saying, Behold, Saul is dead, thinking to have brought good tidings, I took hold of him, and slew him in Ziklag, who thought that I would have given him a reward for his tidings: And DAVID COMMANDED HIS YOUNG MEN, AND THEY SLEW THEM, and cut off their hands and their feet, and hanged them up over the pool in Hebron. But they took the head of Ishbosheth, and buried it..." (2 Samuel 4:10,12).

a. David eliminated rebels without delay.

Everybody knew that King Saul's existence prevented David from fulfilling his dream of becoming king. The people who claimed to have killed Saul and his son Ishbosheth thought they were doing David a great favour. I believe that one of the major secrets of David's success was to eliminate those people immediately. Once a "king killer" always a "king killer". Remember that he who criticizes others to you, will criticize you to others. David knew that these people would be dangerous to have around him. They had the ability to kill their leaders.

I have learnt that a person who is loyal to someone else is likely to be loyal to me. Years ago, a pastor joined me from another ministry. He had faithfully served another minister in London for about ten years. Due to certain circumstances, he was forced to leave London and settle in another country. That was when I met him. He made a decision to work under my ministry. The one thing that impressed me about this man was that he never spoke negatively about the church he had belonged to for the previous ten years. Although he was greatly impressed with our ministry, there was no time when a sarcastic or disloyal statement came from his mouth about his former pastor. This is a very important sign indeed; it means he is likely to behave in the same way towards a new "boss". You are not special; if a man throws his wife out of his house and you become his new mistress, do not think you will receive any better treatment.

b. Be careful of wicked, erratic, and disloyal people.

What they did to another, they will do to you one day. David prevented his own assassination by immediately eliminating traitors and rebels. A person with traitorous tendencies can practise them on any new master. Move with loyal people. Stay with the few whom you can trust. It is better to have a few loyal people than many treacherous and dangerous people around you.

15. The Principle of Being Led by the Spirit

"Therefore DAVID ENQUIRED OF THE LORD, saying, Shall I go and smite these Philistines? And the Lord said unto David, Go and smite the Philistines, and SAVE KEILAH. Then DAVID ENQUIRED OF THE LORD YET AGAIN. And the Lord answered him, and said, Arise, go down to Keilah; for I will deliver the Philistines into thine hand" (1 Samuel 23:2,4). One of the common phrases in the books of first and second Samuel is: "David enquired of the Lord".

a. The principle of David inquiring of the Lord for direction is one that is important for all of us today.

David defended the people of Keilah and delivered them from evil. When King Saul heard that David was in the city of the people of Keilah, he decided to attack. Naturally, you would have thought that the people of Keilah would protect David from Saul. David as a matter of routine inquired of the Lord. "THEN SAID DAVID, Will the men of Keilah deliver me and my men into the hand of Saul? And the Lord said, They will deliver thee up" (1 Samuel 23:12). To his surprise, the Lord told him that the people he had just saved would betray him and hand him over to Saul.

David must have been surprised when the Lord told him, "These people will be ungrateful to you. They will hand you over to Saul for your execution." Do you realize that once again, David saved his life by this act of inquiring of the Lord? That is why I call these acts, principles of success. If David had not had these principles, his life would have been cut short. If David had not developed the habit of waiting on the Lord, he would have died as a young man. David's ministry would have ended years earlier if he had not used these important principles.

b. Rely on the Holy Spirit for supernatural guidance.

There are times that the Lord has shown me things that are contrary to my understanding. The ministry is a supernatural vocation. The fact that you use your mind to take decisions does not mean that you should not listen to the Holy Spirit. I use my mind a lot, but I also rely on the supernatural guidance of the Holy Spirit. Thank God for our minds. But the Holy Spirit is leading us every day of our lives. "For as many as are led by the Spirit of God, they are the sons of God" (Romans 8:14).

If it were not necessary for God to lead us by his Spirit, he would not waste his time. Listen to the voice of the Holy Spirit and you will walk into success.

16. The Principle of Having a Pastor

"That the king said unto NATHAN THE PROPHET [his pastor], See now, I dwell in an house of cedar, but the ark of God dwelleth within curtains. And Nathan said to the king, Go, do all that is in thine heart; for the Lord is with thee. And it came to pass that night, that the word of the Lord came unto Nathan, saying, Go and tell my servant David, thus saith the Lord…" (2 Samuel 7:2-5).

a. David had a pastor. He had someone who could speak into his life spiritually.

Having a pastor is different from belonging to a church. People may belong to a church but have no shepherd over their lives. Is there anyone who can speak into your life?

There are many people in my church. I have found out that some of them want to receive counsel, whilst others do not. I do not just advise every "Tom, Dick and Harry" in the church. I speak to those who make it clear that they want that input. David consulted his pastor, Nathan, when he wanted to build a temple. Nathan gave him good advice. Pastor Nathan later brought a specific word from the Lord concerning the temple. Later, when David fell into adultery, Pastor Nathan had the confidence to minister to the king.

He knew that the king would not be offended. He knew that the king would receive it as the word of the Lord. "And the Lord sent Nathan unto David... And David's anger was greatly kindled against the man; and he said to Nathan, As the Lord liveth, the man that hath done this thing shall surely die... And Nathan said to David, THOU ART THE MAN... And DAVID SAID UNTO NATHAN, I HAVE SINNED AGAINST THE LORD. And Nathan said unto David, The Lord also hath put away thy sin; thou shalt not die" (2 Samuel 12:1,5,7,13).

I know that there are some people in my church who are living the wrong way. I have even known of people with more than one wife. But I also realize that some of these people are not open to receive the pastor's counsel. I just preach and teach generally. If they make themselves open to a direct ministration from me, I will certainly tell them what the Word of God says.

b. Be obedient to the voice of the Lord conveyed through your pastor.

Everybody needs helps but not everybody wants help! David could have reacted by arresting Nathan. He could have told Nathan that he was having bad dreams and becoming too suspicious. Jeremiah the prophet was arrested several times because of the prophetic word he gave. "Now Pashur the son of Immer the priest, who was also chief governor in the house of the Lord heard that Jeremiah prophesied these things. Then Pashur smote Jeremiah the prophet, and put him in the stocks..." (Jeremiah 20:1,2).

I once attended a government function. At this meeting, one of the government officials said the government wanted to hear the prophetic voice of the Church. When this government official said that I thought, "Does this man know what he's saying? Would the Church not be branded as an enemy or "opposition" if it speaks out against wrongdoing in the government?" It is easy to say, "We want to hear the prophetic voice of God." But do we really want it?

Even Jesus withheld certain instructions from his disciples. He said to them, "I have many things to say but you cannot bear them so I will not say them." "I have yet many things to say unto you, but ye cannot bear them now." (John 16:12). Your ability to receive certain rebukes from the Lord is seen by the way you handled the earlier word you received. David had already demonstrated that he would be obedient to the voice of the Lord. That is why his pastor was bold enough to speak to him.

17. The Principle of Being Quick to See and Admit Mistakes

It is interesting to note that God describes David as a man after his own heart. We all know that David was far from being perfect. Could it be that God was not looking for perfection?

a. Deal with your mistakes in the right way.

I believe that what makes us great in God's sight is the manner in which we deal with our mistakes. Almost every person in the Bible made mistakes. From Adam to Peter, the Bible is replete with stories of impeachable offences. Yet, God has been merciful to his children.

When Saul made a mistake, he was confronted by the pastor of his day. Notice how Saul argued with the prophet Samuel. He insisted that he had not done anything wrong.

"Wherefore then didst thou not obey the voice of the Lord, but didst fly upon the spoil, and didst evil in the sight of the Lord? And

SAUL SAID unto Samuel, YEA I HAVE OBEYED THE VOICE OF THE LORD...And Samuel said...Behold, to obey is better than sacrifice... Because thou hast rejected the word of the Lord, he hath also rejected thee from being king" (1 Samuel 15:19,20,22,23).

He argued that he had done the right thing. The evidence was there, yet he denied any wrongdoing. Compare this to David. When David was confronted by the pastor of his day (Nathan), he immediately said, "I have sinned."

b. Decide to be a David who sees and admits faults easily.

He admitted his wrongdoing, although no one could have even proved it. "Wherefore hast thou despised the commandment of the Lord, to do evil in his sight? Thou hast killed Uriah... and hast taken his wife to be thy wife... And DAVID SAID UNTO NATHAN, I HAVE SINNED AGAINST THE LORD. And Nathan said unto David, The Lord also hath put away thy sin; thou shalt not die" (2 Samuel 12:9,13).

From my experience with handling people, I know that these two types of people are found in everyday life. Remember this: Failure to admit faults is a manifestation of pride and stubbornness. God does not like proud people. The Bible says that he resists the proud!

18. The Principle of Being Merciful

"And David said, Is there yet any that is left of the house of Saul, THAT I MAY SHEW HIM KINDNESS for Jonathan's sake?" (2 Samuel 9:1). David said, "Is there anyone I can show kindness to?" God had blessed him.

a. David remembered where he had come from.

How many of us remember what God has done for us? We say that the Lord has been good to us, but do we remember the vessels through whom God blessed us? David called on an old friend's son and showed him great kindness. "Now when Mephibosheth, the son of Jonathan, the son of Saul, was come... And David said unto him, Fear not: for I WILL SURELY SHEW THEE KINDNESS FOR JONATHAN THY FATHER'S SAKE..." (2 Samuel 9:6,7).

b. Showing mercy is a key to finding favour and understanding from God.

"Let not mercy and truth forsake thee: bind them about thy neck; write them upon the table of thine heart: So shalt thou find FAVOUR and GOOD UNDERSTANDING in the sight of God and man" (Proverbs 3:3,4). If you want to receive the mercy of God in your lifetime, learn to be merciful. One of the great keys in helping us to be merciful to people is to remember what we ourselves have been through.

I once discussed with some medical student friends what their plans were for the future. One of them indicated that he would return to the medical school as a wicked lecturer. Even though he had suffered at the hands of unreasonable lecturers, he himself was intending to do worse. I always wonder why people forget what it is like to be "under".

David did not forget what it was like to be "under". He called for those below and tried to lift them up to where he was. He raised up Mephibosheth, Jonathan's son, to sit at his table. It is time to remember those who are down and below! God will bless you as you help others to come to where you are! I wrote this book because I want to share with you what God has given to me. I want you to come up to the table that the Lord has prepared for all his children.

19. Principle of Being Religious

a. David did not leave spiritual things to the prophets and pastors alone.

David was a very religious person. Although he was a king, his heart was in spiritual matters. You can see the type of person he was from the Psalms he wrote. David spoke of living in the temple of God. He thought of staying in church for long hours.

For A DAY IN THY COURTS is better than a thousand. I had rather be a doorkeeper in the house of my God, than to dwell in the tents of wickedness. (Psalm 84:10). "I WAS GLAD when they said unto me, Let us go into the house of the Lord" (Psalm 122:1).

David organized the transfer of the Ark of the Covenant to Jerusalem. It was very important to him that this was done. David wanted to build a temple. He wanted to build a church. How many politicians and people of power think about building the church? How many would say that they would like to stay in church for long periods?

b. Making God a central figure in your life is vital to success.

People with wealth and influence often fight against the church. They lift themselves up as proud and arrogant elements capable of destroying the church. Learn a lesson from David. His heart was in the church. His vision was to build God a grand temple. This is what I mean by being religious. No matter your profession, you can make God the centre of your activities. Let Jesus be the centre of your life and you will enjoy the blessings of Jehovah.

c. God rewards those who love Him.

God is not blind. He will see and reward you because you love him. Psalm 91 tells us that because you have set your love on God, he will remember you in your time of trouble. He will lift you up and establish you.

"Because HE HATH SET HIS LOVE UPON ME, therefore will I deliver him: I will set him on high, because he hath known my name. He shall call upon me, and I will answer him: I WILL BE WITH HIM IN TROUBLE; I WILL DELIVER HIM, AND HONUR HIM. With long life will I satisfy him, and shew him my salvation" (Psalm 91:14-16).

In conclusion, remember that not many people succeed in this life. It is wise to notice and to study the few that succeed. It is wise to learn from them and to tap into their secrets. Hebrews 6:12 teaches us to follow those who inherit the promises of God. David was one such person. My prayer is that you would experience success as you follow the principles that guided King David!

The Solomonic Success Paradigm 28

THE SUCCESS STORY OF KING SOLOMON

"For the Lord God is a sun and shield: the Lord will give grace and glory: no good thing will he withhold from them that walk uprightly" (Psalm 84:11). The Bible says that the Lord is a sun and a shield. This means that the same God who gives you sunshine, gives you shade. All that God is trying to tell us is that He is everything to us. Getting to know the Lord will bring us into a totally successful life.

The Lord will give grace and glory. That means that God will give you undeserved help. When the Lord gives you glory, it means you will become more beautiful. He will make you a nice and blessed person.

Success is not success unless it is total success. If you only have spiritual blessings but do not have any physical breakthroughs, then you are not really successful. If you have many physical blessings but do not have spiritual blessings, you are not enjoying true success.

The Bible says that God is a sun and a shield. That means God can be everything to us. One of the great truths of all time is that we can learn from those ahead of us. We can learn the ministry from those who are ahead in the ministry. Learn success from successful people.

THE FEATURES OF SOLOMON'S SUCCESS

One person I believe was very successful was Solomon. We need to study Solomon's secrets of success. Solomon attained the greatest wisdom ever known to mankind. He also became a world- famous leader. He was so rich that he made history. He was the richest man that ever lived. Solomon's wisdom and riches combined to make him a total success. Let us explore some of the features of Solomon's success.

1. Food

Firstly, notice what his household ate on a daily basis. "And Solomon's provision for one day was thirty measures of fine flour, and threescore measures of meal, TEN FAT OXEN and TWENTY OXEN out of the pastures, and an HUNDRED SHEEP, beside harts, and roebucks, and fallowdeer, and fatted fowl" (1 Kings 4:22).

Many of us in Ghana struggle to put meat on our plates. Yet, Solomon killed thirty oxen and a hundred sheep everyday! Remember that there were no refrigerators in those days, so they probably had to eat everything! Solomon must have had many mouths to feed.

There are many people in Ghana who, not by choice, eat their food without meat or fish. When Solomonic success enters your life, you will have enough meat for your stew. I see you having Solomonic success!

2. Safety

"For he had dominion over all the region on this side the river, from Tiphsah even to Azzah, over all the kings on this side of the river: and HE HAD PEACE ON ALL SIDES round about him" (1 Kings 4:24).

a. Under Solomon's leadership, there was peace on every side.

Not only did Solomon have enough to eat but he also had peace. That is true success! So many people want both happiness and peace. Some people live in colossal-sized mansions and have loads of money, but do not have peace. They drive in the most luxurious cars but they don't have peace. They jet-set all over the world, but they still don't have any peace. "And Judah and Israel DWELT SAFELY, EVERY MAN UNDER HIS VINE and under his fig tree, from Dan even to Beer-Sheba, all the days of Solomon" (1 Kings 4:25).

Another feature of Solomonic success was that everyone lived in security. Everyone was able to dwell under his own fig tree in security. Under Solomon's reign, there was no fear that someone would arrest and confiscate your fig tree. There was no Confiscating Assets Committee! There were no arbitrary seizures of cars and properties. The Bible says that they dwelt safely in the days of Solomon.

b. Security attracted investment during Solomon's reign.

The reason why the western world invests only "peanuts" in some countries is that they know that their investments (vines and fig trees) are not safe from arbitrary takeovers and confiscation. Little investment occurs in regions where legal agreements are not respected. Under the reign of Solomon, the rule of law was established. People built houses and established themselves securely without fear of persecution.

There are some countries where it is virtually a crime to be successful or wealthy. You are hated and intimidated just because you have planted a fig tree. This was not the case in Solomon's day. True success goes hand-in-hand with security and the rule of law. In the days of King Solomon, soldiers did not go around looting shops and harassing wealthy people. They did not strip women naked and cheat the public. The Bible says that they dwelt safely under their fig and vine trees and nobody was afraid of anything.

Look at most African countries. Who can dwell there in safety? Who can invest there and be sure of his investment? It is no wonder that the wealth of this planet gravitates towards places where people can dwell in safety under their vine trees.

c. Security entails the promotion of human liberty and the rule of law: freedom and justice.

It is interesting to note that the motto for Ghana's independence is "Freedom and Justice." But do we really have freedom and justice? Everyone knows that successful people can only flourish in a country where freedom and justice is present.

I remember many years ago when armed officers surrounded my father in his office. They had been sent to apprehend him. Can you believe that these people were arresting a civilian over a matter concerning an electricity bill? The matter was unresolved and still being debated in the courts.

Commands had come from "invisible" powers to arrest him. He was humiliated and thrown into a prison cell like a common criminal. The power that did not respect the law, had set aside legitimate court proceedings and had taken the law into its own hand. My father was humiliated and disgraced because there was no safety in the land. The courts were subject to the whims and fancies of powerful dictators who did not respect the law.

When I saw my father lying on the floor of the prison cell amongst criminals, I marvelled at the lack of safety for anyone. These same powers, which were in control of the media, continued to embarrass my father by filming him in jail and showing it twice on national television news. After that, they took a photograph of him combing his hair in the police cells and published it in the national daily newspaper.

What was his crime? Why was the government intentionally embarassing one of the nation's honourable and wealthy citizens? Is it a crime to be wealthy? Is it safe to dwell in your own country? The law meant nothing to the "invisible" powers of the day. The courts and their decisions were set aside as one would set aside a dead dog. It is no wonder that my father fell ill and died shortly after this! True success involves the peace and safety of a nation and all its citizens. When people break the law, the right thing to do is to prosecute them. However, in nations where politicians control the law, you cannot expect justice to prevail unless you are on the "right side of the fence".

Democracy is not only the vote of the majority, but also the protection of the minorities. Those of us who live in developing countries must pray that Solomonic peace and safety will one day be part of our nations. I sometimes wonder at the appeals of certain government officials for businessmen to invest in the country. If there can be an announcement one day that, "All those who have two million cedis and above should report to the nearest police station for interrogation," who will put his money into the bank? Who will invest in the country? "And Judah and Israel DWELT SAFELY, EVERY MAN UNDER HIS VINE and UNDER HIS FIG TREE..." (1 Kings 4:25).

Our church once signed a contract with a government agency. We were led to invest a lot of money into a property, thinking that the agreement was safe. However, we were awoken to the rude shock of our walls being broken down by an "invisible" power. The same invisible power was at work again. The laws were set aside and the agreements were shoved away. This is not safety and peace. Let's have Solomonic success! Solomonic success means that we will plant our fig trees and dwell under them in safety.

3. Cars

"And Solomon gathered together chariots and horsemen: and he had a thousand and four hundred chariots, and twelve thousand horsemen, whom he bestowed in the cities for chariots, and with the king at Jerusalem" (1 Kings 10:26).

a. If you want to be successful one day, applaud and encourage success.

Solomon had one thousand four hundred cars. In some countries, if you have a car, a special investigative branch may hunt you down. Nevertheless, hear me today: God wants to give you many cars! He wants you to drive to church. Do not set yourself against nice and prosperous things. If you don't have something, don't fight it! There are many people who have had to swallow their words because of things they said in their times of poverty.

Some nations have killed their leaders at various times, just for owning a house and having more than two cars. Today, those who killed others for driving nice cars are flying gliders, riding horses, driving expensive cars, walking on thick American carpets and jet-setting all over the world.

There is nothing wrong with walking on a nice carpet. But if you persecuted people years ago for their success, it becomes difficult for you to enjoy success in the day of your success. One day, you will also be successful. Solomon had many chariots. I see God blessing you with many cars!

b. The presence of one wealthy person creates wealth for many others.

One rich person creates jobs and blessings for many others. Allow people to be blessed. Allow them to go as high as they can. When a man works hard, he must be rewarded for his labour.

If his hard work and wisdom have led him to have a thousand cars, why are you so angry with him? Don't be a crab! Only crabs try to pull others down.

When I was going to get married, my father told me that I would have to work very hard to get to where he was. He told me how he had no chairs in his home when he initially married. There were only two chairs in their sitting room. Whenever there was a visitor he and my mother would play "musical chairs". Each time one came around, the other would get up and pretend to be doing something else. You see, because there were only two chairs, three people could not sit down at a time. Many people who have something today have struggled for years to acquire them.

Do not fight rich people! If Ghana is to be rich, then we cannot drive away wealth and success. We should not frighten away affluent people. We should encourage them by being a law-abiding and agreement-respecting people and government. Do you think Solomon ate thirty oxen and a hundred sheep on his own? Of course not! Many people were eating the oxen and the sheep with him. Remember that they had no refrigerators in those days. Everything had to be eaten on the same day!

You must accept the reality that some people will be excessively rich like Solomon and others will not be so rich. People are different! Some have the ability to make money against all odds. People must be allowed to be themselves!

4. Wisdom and Strategies

Let's talk about wisdom. "And God gave Solomon wisdom and understanding exceeding much, and largeness of heart, even as the sand that is on the sea shore. And Solomon's wisdom excelled the wisdom of all the children of the east country, and all the wisdom of Egypt" (1 Kings 4:29-30).

Solomon was endowed with supernatural wisdom from above. It was recorded that he was wiser than all men. In addition to all of his financial blessings, he had the wisdom of God. The Bible states that he spoke three thousand proverbs. "And he spake three thousand proverbs: and his songs were a thousand and five" (1 Kings 4:32).

5. A Good Income

Notice how much gold Solomon acquired each year. Solomon had a very good salary. His yearly income was about nineteen million, three hundred and seventy thousand US dollars. This income is more than the earnings of some of the largest gold mines in the world today! "Now the weight of gold that came to Solomon in one year was six hundred threescore and six talents of gold" (1 Kings 10:14).

6. Solomon's Decor

"And twelve lions stood there on the one side and on the other upon the six steps: there was not the like made in any kingdom. And all king Solomon's drinking vessels were of gold, and all the vessels of the house of the forest of Lebanon were of pure gold; none were of silver: it was nothing accounted of in the days of Solomon" (1 Kings 10:20,21).

The Bible records that there were twelve lions that stood on either side of his steps. Everything in Solomon's house was made out of gold. Even his plates and cups were gold. Under Solomonic success, silver was not regarded as precious; it was too common! Decide to live in a nice house. Nice things are not evil things. God will bless you with nice things as you obtain Solomonic wisdom.

7. Solomon's Pets

"For the king had at sea a navy of Tharshish with the navy of Hiram: once in three years came the navy of Tharshish, bringing gold, and silver, ivory, and APES, AND PEACOCKS" (1 Kings

10:22). Solomon did not bother to play with dogs; that was too ordinary! He had peacocks strutting all over his garden. The Bible tells us that Solomon exceeded all the kings in the earth for riches and for wisdom. The whole earth gathered at Solomon's feet to hear the wisdom that he had.

As people gathered, they brought him gifts and riches. Is it not paradoxical? A rich man was being given more gifts. When you make yourself a poor person, you drive away gifts and blessings. "So king Solomon exceeded all the kings of the earth for riches and for wisdom. And all the earth sought to Solomon, to hear his wisdom, which God had put in his heart. And they brought every man his present, vessels of silver, and vessels of gold, and garments, and armour, and spices, horses, and mules, a rate year by year " (1 Kings 10:23-25). "And the king made silver to be in Jerusalem as stones, and cedars made he to be as the sycomore trees that are in the vale, for abundance" (1 Kings 10:27).

King Solomon was so successful that he made silver to become like stones and cedars to become like sycamore trees. All of these blessings came from God. They did not come from the devil. Do not believe the lie that wealth is evil. Wealth is neutral! It can either be used for good things or bad things. I believe God can give you Solomonic success today! From now, you will never be poor anymore! From now, you will rise up in wisdom, wealth and in success!

Join me as we discover what principles Solomon used to take him to these heights of success.

FIVE SUCCESS PRINCIPLES OF SOLOMON

1. Obeying your father's instructions

It is easy to blame someone else for your situation. Human beings commonly point their fingers at the nearest scapegoat in sight. Adam said it was the woman who caused him to sin. Eve said the serpent was to blame for the problem.

Many Black people say that it is White people who are to blame for their condition. Third world countries blame Europe for colonizing them. They claim that colonization is the cause of all of Africa's problems. European countries are trying to keep away African immigrants because they feel these people are destroying their economies. I think we should begin to blame ourselves for our situations. When we take responsibility for our situations, we are better able to help ourselves; let us take responsibility for our own successes or failures. You must believe that you are the cause of your own success and failure.

Look at what other successful people did, follow them and you will be successful! If you were to work a bit harder, perhaps things would get better. If you stop blaming your relatives in the village, witches in your hometown and the curses in your family, you will progress. Perhaps if you were to adopt the strategies of Solomon, you may experience his type of success.

One of Solomon's secrets was to obey his father's instructions. King David, his father left him several important instructions as he lay dying on his bed. Solomon obeyed all of them! "Children, OBEY YOUR PARENTS in the Lord: for this is right. Honour thy father and mother; which is the first commandment with promise; That it may be well with thee, and thou mayest live long on the earth" (Ephesians 6:1-3).

If you obey your father, it will be well with you. If you do not obey your father and mother, it will not be well with you! It is as simple as that! Solomon's kingship was established because he took his father's words seriously and obeyed each instruction to the letter. Solomon would never have become what he became if he had ignored his father's instructions.

It is important to understand the principle of honouring fathers and mothers. Many church leaders have walked out into a spiritual abyss by violating these simple principles. Some ministers disappear into oblivion by dishonouring fathers that have been set in the land.

Before King David died, he called his son Solomon to his bedside and gave him some instructions. As Solomon looked upon his dying father, perhaps many thoughts ran through his mind. The man lying on the bed was someone who had made many mistakes in his life. He had committed adultery with Bathsheba and had disgraced the nation. He had murdered one of his own soldiers. David's children had been involved in the rape and murder of each other. In his latter days, David had not been able to keep his family together. It was this same ailing father, who was giving instructions to Solomon. Yet Solomon obeyed his father! Because of that obedience, Solomon prospered to the point where silver became like stones to him.

a. The first instruction that was given to Solomon was to be strong and to behave like a man.

"I go the way of all the earth: be thou strong therefore, and shew thyself a man" (1 Kings 2:2). Because I am a leader, I understand the importance of that instruction. Without strength, you cannot be a good leader. A church needs a strong leader to move it forward. Democracy and numerous committees are not helpful when you need strong leadership.

Solomon went ahead and eliminated his half-brother Adonijah, who had earlier tried to take the throne from him. The first act of strength that Solomon performed was to eliminate all possible traitors and wicked elements in his midst.

Some of you are too weak to get rid of that bad man in your life. You must get rid of that bad girl. She shouldn't be there. As long as certain people are a part of your life, you will not prosper. Temptations come through people. They do not fly in a vacuum. If you do not get rid of certain people in your life, you will have countless problems.

You need strength to obey the voice of the Lord. When God told me to be a pastor, it took a lot of strength to forge ahead into God's will. No one supported or helped me. When I started out in ministry, I found myself surrounded by people who didn't believe in me. I had to get rid of the scoffers in my life and I did just that!

I remember telling one gentleman, "From today, you are no longer part of this church." I continued, "Do not come to this church anymore. Your services are not needed!" This brother was taken aback; he wanted to stay on in the church. He wanted to continue betraying me. I knew he was disloyal to me so I decided to get rid of him. It was not an easy decision to tell a friend - go away and stay away! But it was a very necessary step for my own survival. No one can prosper if he has disloyal scorners around him. You need an environment of encouragement and peace.

b. Another instruction Solomon had from his father was to deal with Joab.

Joab was someone who had disobeyed David on several occasions. David asked Solomon to eliminate Joab. "...let not his hoar head go down to the grave in peace" (1 Kings 2:6). When the opportunity presented itself, Solomon executed Joab. David also asked Solomon to deal with Shimei. "...thou hast with thee Shimei... hold him not guiltless..." (1 Kings 2:8,9).

Shimei cursed King David when he was running away from Absalom, his son. Solomon dealt with him as well. Life is too short not to learn from your fathers. You need to believe what they are telling you. Solomon did not waste his life discovering what evil would come to him through Joab and Shimei. He just believed what his father said and executed them. You will notice that after Solomon fulfilled his father's instructions, the kingdom of Israel became established under his rule. "...And THE KINGDOM WAS ESTABLISHED in the hand of Solomon" (1 Kings 2:46). Although Solomon thought that he was just obeying his father's instructions, he was actually stabilizing the nation without even knowing it!

Obey your father's instructions, even when you don't understand them. You will unknowingly bring a blessing upon your life. A sweet spiritual blessing follows a man who honours a father. It cannot be explained logically. It is a spiritual law that has been set in place for thousands of years. Take this secret and apply it to your life. Don't fight it because you cannot! Flow with it and you will come into Solomonic success!

2. The Secret of Building the Temple of God

The next important secret in Solomon's life was the building of the temple. Many generations have come and gone, but you still hear the phrase "Solomon's temple". Solomon was the one who built a beautiful temple for Jehovah. There was no temple like the one he built. His father David could not build the temple because of the many wars he had to fight.

a. It is not possible to build anything unless you have peace and stability.

Notice the countries in the so-called developed world. Do you think that you would ever hear on the news, that the Prime Minister of Britain, Mr. Tony Blair has been overthrown in a coup d'état? Do you think that you would ever hear that a corporal has arrested Mr. Tony Blair and put him under house arrest? Do you think that you would ever hear that President George Bush has been overthrown by a sergeant and has been placed in custody? It is very unlikely.

The stability and peace that western nations enjoy is helping them to build their cities and to develop in success.

b. One of the secrets to prolonging your days on this earth is to be involved in the building of the house of God.

Some years ago, I noticed a man who was really blessed of God. The man had lived to a ripe old age and had many children and grandchildren. In his old age, he was rich and in good health. Most people at that age would be flat broke! Most of the people I know in that age group depend on their children for survival. But this man did not depend on his children at all. Some of his children even depended on him.

I asked the Lord, "Why is this man blessed?" The Lord showed me that this was a person very much involved in the building of the church. He was somebody who had spent a lot of his personal money building the church. The Spirit of God whispered to me, "The people who involve themselves in building the church, whether spiritually or physically have a special grace upon their lives."

Do you remember the centurion who needed a miracle for his servant? The people told Jesus that the man deserved a miracle because he had built them a synagogue. "And when they came to Jesus, they besought him instantly, saying, That HE WAS WORTHY for whom he should do this: For he loveth our nation, and HE HATH BUILT US A SYNAGOGUE" (Luke 7:4,5). They said, "This man is worthy because he built us a synagogue." Good things from Jesus were about to flow into this man's life because he had built a church.

Years ago, I heard a great man of God ministering at the sod-cutting ceremony of a church in my city. This man of God made a statement that I will never forget. He told the congregation, "Build God's house, and God will build a house for you." I have never forgotten those words. Build a house of stability and safety for God's people and God will make your dwelling secure.

When a church does not have a building, it is greatly limited in ministry. You will reap security for your life if you provide stability for the church. When our church used to meet in a canteen, there was no end to the harassment we suffered from the authorities. Sometimes, immediately after the service, I would receive a letter saying, "You are to meet the authorities of the Ghana Medical School on Monday morning at eight a.m. prompt." Once, we arrived at church and found out that the security officer had decided to lock the doors and keep us out of the building. We had to have our church service outside the canteen. We were at the mercy of wicked and unreasonable people.

c. **When you provide God's church with security, stability and safety, God will become your refuge.**

God will build a house for you and give you security. I have noticed that those who participate in building the temple of God are blessed. I am always grateful for the people that God gave me to help build the Lighthouse Cathedral. We would probably have disappeared into obscurity by now if we didn't have our church building. By now, we would have been hidden in a classroom somewhere.

I have watched people give their lives' savings and their entire salaries to the work of God. I have also lived to see God blessing each and every one of these people. Today, some people only give a few coins towards a church project. They don't know what they are missing. Those who have helped prolong the church's life, will have their own lives prolonged. Those who cause a church to be wealthy will reap wealth in their lives.

In Bible times, people gave up lands and properties for the building of the church and they were blessed for doing so. This is one of Solomon's keys to success. He built a house for the Lord. Glue yourself to your church and see the church building become completed. Support the project until it is fully paid for! Attach yourself and invest in the church spiritually. Help to build a larger church. God will reward you as you build his house.

The day is coming, saith the Lord, when you will no longer share a room with six other people. You will live in your own house. The day is coming, saith the Lord, when you will no longer use the toilet with fourteen strange people who you do not know. The day is coming, saith the Lord, when I will put a roof over your head and you will know no lack or want. For I the Lord will perform it. All things shall be added, because you have sought to build my kingdom.

3. The Secret of Seeking Righteousness

I want you to notice something in Solomon's prayer. "In Gibeon the Lord appeared to Solomon in a dream by night: and God said, Ask what I shall give thee... Give therefore thy servant an understanding heart to judge thy people, that I may discern between good and bad: for who is able to judge this thy so great a people?" (1 Kings 3:5,9).

a. **The Lord was impressed by Solomon's desire to seek for wisdom in order to be able to rule well.**

Solomon was having a prayer time and asked the Lord to give him an understanding heart to discern between good and bad. The Bible teaches us that his prayer pleased God.

The Bible tells us that God said, "Because you didn't ask for riches or long life, but have asked for understanding, I'm going to give you wisdom. In addition, I'm going to bless you with fantastic riches which you didn't ask for." "Behold, I have done according to thy words: lo, I have given thee a WISE AND AN UNDERSTANDING HEART... And I have also given thee that which thou hast not asked, both RICHES, AND HONOUR" (1 Kings 3:12,13). Solomon had the chance of a lifetime. He had the opportunity to ask God for anything he wanted.

Let's face it! How many of us really seek for righteousness and wisdom from God? The Bible says in Matthew 6:33, "But Seek ye first the kingdom of God, and his righteousness; and all these things shall be added unto you."

There are lay people who look at me and say, "Oh, it's okay for you to be in full-time ministry; you come from a rich family. You don't have anything to lose. Even if you don't work, your father will give you money."

I often smile and say nothing. I realize that these people do not even believe that I genuinely chose between secular riches and God's work. I know in my heart, that that was the choice I made. I decided to build God's house instead of my own life. If God has blessed me because of that, I do not apologize for the blessings of God. I give him the glory.

b. Seeking after righteousness is God's route to success.

I challenge you to seek after righteousness as Solomon did. It may not seem to be the most direct route to success and riches. But that is the route that God has set. You cannot be wiser than God. Seek first the kingdom of God and his righteousness! Decide to live a holy life. Pay the price and live for God. As you take up your cross to follow him, the angels of heaven will take note. The kingdom of heaven will acknowledge that you are on the right road. You will be rewarded with the things that all men are seeking for. They will be added to your life. You will experience success without chasing after it!

4. THE SECRET OF BUILDING YOUR OWN HOUSE

One of the secrets of success in this life is to decide to build your own house. Many people think that it is only fantastically rich people who build houses. That is not true!

a. A key to prosperity is to build yourself a house.

Solomon built a house for himself and I know that it contributed greatly to his success. I advise people who want to prosper to build houses. If you want to be a millionaire, I will say to you, "Build a house." If you already have a home, I will advise you to build another home. I have many prospective millionaires in my church. The first instruction I give them is: build a house and never stop having building projects for the rest of your life. "But Solomon WAS BUILDING HIS OWN HOUSE THIRTEEN YEARS, and he finished all his house" (1 Kings 7:1).

b. A wise person builds houses.

Solomon was a very wise man. One of the things wisdom made him do was to build his own house. A builder is a wise man. There are two types of people. Those that accumulate wealth and those that spend their wealth. Which one of these will you be? Both of these people receive an inflow of money and riches. One group accumulates this wealth wisely by building houses and investing in real estate. This group is often not outwardly impressive. The other group spends the wealth, generally having a good time. Such people impress everyone by flying all over the world, driving expensive cars and wearing designer clothing.

When all is said and done, the home builders often end up genuinely wealthy and capable of giving effortlessly to any worthy project. On the other hand, the "non-builders" who were not prepared to sacrifice to build often end up broke. Do not forget this little secret. Be like Solomon and build something for yourself. A building or property is a type of saving. It appreciates in value everyday. It represents the accumulation of all your wealth.

It took Solomon thirteen years to build his own house. Many people are in a hurry to arrive at a place of success. Solomon was a determined man. He eventually completed his own house after thirteen long years. I believe that money is not the essential element to building a house. I believe the key to building a house is wisdom. "THROUGH WISDOM IS AN HOUSE BUILDED; and by understanding it is established" (Proverbs 24:3).

Don't let the devil deceive you into thinking that you cannot build a house. Wisdom is something you can ask for from God. "IF ANY OF YOU LACK WISDOM, let him ASK OF GOD, that giveth to all men liberally, and upbraideth not; and it shall be given him" (James 1:5).

c. **There are two types of people in the world: builders and users.**

Builders erect and construct things in their lifetime. Users simply enjoy the facilities that have been created by others.

There are two types of governments: building governments and using governments. The history of Ghana has revealed that the government of Dr. Kwame Nkrumah, Ghana's first president, built many things. He built the Akosombo Dam which created the world's largest man-made lake. He built schools, universities, roads, harbours, etc. Some governments built nothing. They just use what others have built.

There are two types of pastors: "building pastors" and "user pastors." "Building pastors" build church buildings, schools, hospitals, etc. "User pastors" just preach to their congregations without building any chapels for the ministry. Archbishop Benson Idahosa was someone I admired because he built so many structures for the kingdom of God. Decide to be a builder! Being a builder makes you a more substantial person.

Instead of using all of your money to impress people with new cars, build a house! When you die your clothes and your cars may be outmoded but your buildings will not be! I remember when my father died, we assembled in Court to hear the reading of his will. The important aspects of his will related to the buildings that he had built whilst he was alive. There are people who build apartments in their stomachs. They buy all the expensive clothes from the best shops. They have so many pairs of shoes that there is no space anywhere to keep them.

I am not against nice clothes or nice cars. I have many nice things. I am trying to help you to become truly wealthy in the process of time. I want you to be an accumulator of true wealth through buildings. Let your mind mature. Become wiser about the realities of life. Life is more than eating, drinking and making merry: for you may not die tomorrow! You may live for many years and need the accumulated wealth of your better years! A wise person sacrifices to build something! What is the use of a hundred suits, a hundred dresses and a hundred pairs of shoes? I usually have one pair of shoes that I wear until they are worn out.

I have discovered that an individual either chooses to be a builder or a user in his lifetime. Because I know that buildings make a person or ministry more substantial, our church has invested in many church buildings and properties. That is one of the secrets that has moved us forward. I have decided to be someone who builds. It is not easy to build. It takes sacrifice and commitment. That is why many people do not build or own anything, although they could afford to. There are many people who earn a lot of money but don't do anything with it. A lot of money passes through their hands. One day they will ask, "What did I use all that money for?"

Solomon built both the temple and his house. Decide against being a tenant forever. Let your first project be a house or an apartment. Many people who have taken my advice on this subject have thanked me profusely after completing their buildings. Look around and you will notice that those who are wealthy and established later in life have all built houses!

I see you building a house in your lifetime! Become an accumulator of wealth! I see God lifting you from the oppression of different landlords! I see you rising from a user to a builder! Walk on, prosper and enjoy Solomonic success!

5. The Wisdom of God

The reason why many Charismatic and Pentecostal churches are not respected is because we are so spiritual that we leave our minds out of important decisions. The finances of the church are not managed by using anointing oil. They are administered by using sound financial and accounting principles. A pastor may be highly anointed with miracles but when it comes to matters of land, law, property and finances the mind and education must come into play.

Did you know that Solomon did not have as much military strength as his father David? David was a fighter and was known for winning wars. But look at Solomon. He had more peace than his father did. How did Solomon establish himself in peace and stability? He just made friends with all his neighbours and had many allies. Solomon had far more peace in his day than David his father. Wisdom was once again proving to be better than strength. "And Solomon made affinity with Pharoah king of Egypt" (1 Kings 3:1). "And the Lord gave Solomon wisdom, as he promised him: and there was peace between Hiram and Solomon; and they two made a league together" (1 Kings 5:12).

a. Solomon used the wisdom of God to rule.

In the passage below, Solomon used the wisdom of God in ruling the nation. He developed internal stability by using the wisdom of God. The use of his mind was giving him the upper hand. He was becoming more famous than even his father David. "Then the king answered and said, Give her the living child, and in no wise slay it: she is the mother therof. And all Israel heard of the judgment which the king had judged; and they feared the king: for they saw that THE WISDOM OF GOD WAS IN HIM, TO DO JUDGMENT" (1 Kings 3:27,28).

The name of the Church is often dragged through the mud. I believe in deliverance. I believe in the power of healing. I believe in miracles. But I also believe in using the wisdom of God. I believe that pastors must be well educated in order to be sound ministers of the gospel.

b. Wisdom is still the principal thing and we need to use the mind if we are to experience Solomonic success.

Parents, push your children as far as they can go in education. They will one day thank you because you helped them to develop their minds. They will experience Solomonic success because they will have used their minds just as Solomon did.

I believe very strongly in the power of the Holy Spirit. I believe in the anointing. If you were to visit any of our miracle services, you would see the power of God at work. We have a flow of the Spirit of God and we experience all kinds of manifestations. People fall under the power, people laugh in the Holy Ghost and people cry.

Many people shake and tremble under the anointing and power of the Spirit. Sometimes entire sections of the congregation are slain in the Spirit as the power of God moves like a wave through them. I speak in tongues more than I speak in English. I spend hours waiting on the Lord in prayer and fasting. However, none of these have made me send my mind away on a holiday. My mind was given to me by God and I intend to use it.

My mind needs to be alert in order for me to take important decisions that concern the administration and smooth-running of my ministry. I have heard the Holy Spirit speaking to me in my heart many times. I believe in what he tells me and I obey him. But my mind is still alert and active. I try to understand and reason out every commandment that the Lord gives me.

c. Most Christians are either so emotional or spiritual that they have no use of their minds.

Others are so logical and rational that the Spirit of God cannot move in their lives and churches. The key here is to balance the Spirit with wisdom. That is the will of God. Every Christian leader must learn to achieve a balance between the power and the wisdom. "But unto them which are called, both Jews and Greeks, CHRIST the POWER of God, and the WISDOM of God" (1 Corinthians 1:24). I have highlighted the words: Christ, Power and Wisdom. That is what I want you to get as you read this book. Christ Jesus is not only power to us. He is power and wisdom.

When you are able to effectively combine the power and the wisdom, you will begin to experience Solomonic Success. Remember, one without the other is not enough. If you are a pastor, do not rely solely on spiritual direction; remember that pastors are supposed to use their minds as well. If you use your mind, God will lift you up in ministry.

I recently noticed a church which was meeting in somebody's house in an exclusive and quiet residential neighborhood. Although I was about one hundred meters away, I could hear everything that was being said in the service. The prayer, the worship and the praise was so loud and offensive that no one on the entire street could concentrate as long as they were shouting through their microphones. Although there were just a few people there, they were using a public address system meant for large halls and hundreds of people.

I thought to myself, "Very soon this church will be shut down by the neighbours or the police."

I remembered what Jesus said, "Be wise as serpents." What is the wisdom of a serpent? The wisdom of a serpent is the ability to function without unduly attracting the enemy's attention. Snakes are everywhere. All of us would kill the next snake we see! Such is the enmity between human beings and serpents! Yet snakes flourish and are abounding all round us. How do they do this? By wisdom! I believe in that church and its pastor. But a little application of wisdom, would certainly help that church. On the other hand, there are churches which are so focused on the intellect that the Spirit of God is cut off.

Dear Christian friend, it is time for you to rise into prominence and success. Success is not reserved for unbelievers. It is your portion. Apply these principles and God will bless you!

SECTION VII

Demonology

The Attributes and Names of Satan 29

■ SPIRITUAL WARFARE: THE BATTLE AGAINST SATAN

Spiritual warfare is the art of fighting against spiritual forces on the earth.[1] These forces have captured the souls of millions. As the Bible says, the devil has deceived the whole world. We may not be able to get rid of him now, but we will definitely weaken his grip on the masses through our prayer. We know that one day he will be dealt with permanently.

"And I saw an angel come down from heaven, having the key of the bottomless pit and a great chain in his hand. And he laid hold on the dragon, that old serpent, which is the Devil, and Satan, and bound him a thousand years. And cast him into the bottomless pit, and SHUT HIM UP, and set a seal upon him, that he should DECEIVE THE NATIONS NO MORE, till the thousand years should be fulfilled: and after that he must be loosed a little season..." (Revelation 20:1-3).

"...And the devil that deceived them was cast into the lake of fire and brimstone, where the beast and the false prophet are, and shall be tormented day and night for ever and ever" (Revelation 20:10).

Let me now share with you twenty facts you should know about our battle with the demonic hordes on this earth.[2]

1. Our principal enemy is Satan and not other human beings.

He is the leader of the hordes of demonic forces on this earth. Satan is a powerful being who fell from a glorious estate.[3]

"How art thou fallen from heaven, O Lucifer, son of the morning! How art thou cut down to the ground, which didst weaken the nations! For thou hast said in thine heart, I will ascend into heaven, I will exalt my throne above the stars of God: I will sit also upon the mount of the congregation, in the sides of the north: I will ascend above the heights of the clouds; I will be like the most High. Yet thou shalt be brought down to hell, to the sides of the pit. They that see thee shall narrowly look upon thee, and consider thee, saying, Is this the man that made the earth to tremble, that did shake kingdoms; That made the world as a wilderness, and destroyed the cities thereof; that opened not the house of his prisoners? All the kings of the nations, even all of them, lie in glory, every one in his own house. "But thou art cast out of thy grave like an abominable branch, and as the raiment of those that are slain, thrust through with a sword, that go down to the stones of the pit; as a carcase trodden under feet" (Isaiah 14:12-19).

2. SATAN, AN INTELLIGENT BEING, HAS RESORTED TO THE WARFARE OF DECEPTION, TRICKS AND FANTASTIC SCHEMES.

Satan, who is our principal enemy, knows that he does not stand a chance against the might of the church.[4] "Put on the armour of God, that ye may be able to stand against the WILES of the devil" (Ephesians 6:11).

3. IN ORDER TO DEFEAT OUR ENEMY, WE MUST KNOW AS MUCH AS WE CAN ABOUT HIM.

This is one of the most important rules of war.[5] This is where secular armies engage in reconnaissance and intelligence work. Without this knowledge you will be defeated easily. Ask the US Army what happened to them in Vietnam.[6]

4. SATAN HAS A CONTAGIOUS NATURE/CHARACTER WHICH HE PASSES ON TO HIS FOLLOWERS.

A lot of information about our enemy can be gleaned by analysing the twenty names and titles of Satan. Know your enemy so that you can defeat him.[7]

5. SATAN HAS A RIGHT TO BE ON EARTH.

He told Jesus that. He showed Jesus the nations of the world and offered them to him. "And the devil said unto him, All this power will I give thee, and the glory of them: for that is delivered unto me; and to whomsoever I will I give it" (Luke 4:6).

Jesus did not tell the devil that he was lying. He knew that the devil had the power to hand over the nations of the world. He did not argue about that. If it was not so, Jesus would not have been tempted.[8]

6. THE DEVIL KNOWS THAT HE HAS A LEASE ON THE EARTH.

This lease will expire soon and the devil knows it. "And, behold, they cried out, saying, What have we to do with thee, Jesus, thou Son of God? art thou come hither to torment us BEFORE THE TIME?" (Matthew 8:29). Our enemy in spiritual warfare is the devil. Satan is aware of the expiry date on his lease.[9]

7. IT IS NOT OUR DUTY TO RID THE EARTH OF SATAN AND HIS DEMONS.

Even Jesus did not try to do that! You do not try to get a tenant out of your house before the lease expires. You know that he will fight you in court. Our duty as ministers is to weaken the grip of demonic powers over the souls on this earth. "...pulling down of strongholds" (2 Corinthians 10:4). At best our spiritual warfare can dislodge, displace or temporarily relocate demonic forces so that God's kingdom can gain ascendancy for a season.[10]

8. SATAN IS A VERY WICKED LESSEE.

A lessee is a person who holds a property by lease. Satan is the god of this world for a period. The Bible tells us that the whole world lies in Satan's wicked arms because of this. "And we know that we are of God, and THE WHOLE WORLD LIETH IN WICKEDNESS" (1 John 5:19). The property that Satan the lessee has is trembling under his evil tenancy. One day that power will be broken forever.

9. EVEN THOUGH WE CANNOT GET RID OF THE DEVIL PERMANENTLY, WE CAN ENGAGE HIM IN DIFFERENT KINDS OF WARFARE.

We can wrestle with him (Ephesians 6:12). We can cast him out of people (Mark 5:13). We can bind him (Matthew 18:18). We can pull down or weaken his strongholds (2 Corinthians 10:4).

We can fight his deception with the Word (Hebrews 4:12).[11]

10. Satan's main strategy is to capture the world into groups of "strongholds" which think in a certain way.

The devil's strategy is to make the world think in a certain way so that he can lead them into self-destruction.[12] The great philosophies of this world: humanism, atheism, communism and Marxism are manifestations of the imaginations of the devil.

It is these imaginations (trends of thinking) that lead masses of people into self-destruction "(For the weapons of our warfare are not carnal, but mighty through God to the pulling down of strong holds;) CASTING DOWN IMAGINATIONS, and every high thing that exalteth itself against the knowledge of God, and bringing into captivity every thought to the obedience of Christ" (2 Corinthians 10:4,5).[13]

11. Ministers must understand the role of the Word in spiritual warfare.

The church must destabilise and weaken strongholds on territories, nations, people and churches.

All ministers must ensure that the Word of God gains pre-eminence. As the Word of God increases, Satan loses his grip over the souls.

Read this amazing Scripture and believe in the power of the Word. "And the WORD of God INCREASED; and the number of the DISCIPLES MULTIPLIED in Jerusalem greatly..." (Acts 6:7).

As the Word of God increases, the number of Christians will multiply. That is why I write books and preach as hard as I can and as many times as possible. I know what it does to the kingdom of darkness.

12. Christian leaders must use the two-pronged weapon of prayer and the Word to defeat Satan in spiritual warfare.

The ministry of prayer and the ministry of the Word is real ministry. That is the two-edged weapon that God has given to us. The apostles practised this! They refused to be drawn away from the ministry of the Word and prayer.[14]

"Then the twelve called the multitude of the disciples unto them, and said, It is not reason that we should leave the word of God, and serve tables. But we will give ourselves continually to PRAYER, and to the MINISTRY OF THE WORD" (Acts 6:2,4).

13. The best example of spiritual warfare was Christ Jesus.

He taught and he prayed. "And in the morning, rising up a great while before day, he went out, and departed into a solitary place, and there prayed. And Simon and they that were with him followed after him. And when they had found him, they said unto him, All men seek for thee. And he said unto them, Let us go into the next towns, that I may preach there also: for therefore came I forth" (Mark 1:35-38).

If we want to have the results that Jesus had, we must use the methods that he used. And his methods were praying and teaching.[15]

14. Apart from weakening strongholds, ministers can dislodge, displace or temporarily relocate demonic forces so that God's kingdom can gain ascendancy.

In the ministry of Jesus, he relocated demons from people's bodies into swine. "And forthwith Jesus gave them leave. And the unclean spirits went out, and entered into the swine: and the herd ran violently down a steep place into the sea, (they were about two thousand;) and were choked in the sea" (Mark 5:13).

15. Anytime you defeat (weaken or dislodge) the Devil, you can expect a counter-attack.

When Jesus defeated the devil in the wilderness, the Bible says that Satan relocated for a season. The devil did not leave him forever. If you were the devil would you leave your enemy forever? No! You would retreat, regroup and attack again another day. "And when the devil had ended all the temptation, he departed from him FOR A SEASON" (Luke 4:13).

16. Prayer and fasting are weapons that weaken and dislodge demonic forces.

Jesus taught that demons could be dislodged by prayer and fasting.[16] "Howbeit this kind GOETH NOT OUT BUT BY PRAYER and fasting" (Matthew 17:21).

17. The Word of God also weakens and torments Satan.

You will notice how the demon shouted out when Jesus taught the Word. "And there was in their synagogue a man with an unclean spirit; and he cried out, Saying, LET US ALONE; what have we to do with thee, thou Jesus of Nazareth? Art thou come to destroy us? I know thee who thou art, the Holy One of God. And Jesus rebuked him, saying, Hold thy peace, and come out of him" (Mark 1:23-25).

In this story, Jesus did not pray or bind the devil. But the devil said, "Stop it! You are tormenting me! You are hurting me!" The Bible describes the Word of God as a sword. Anytime you are speaking words, you are releasing swords into the atmosphere. Every pastor must use this great sword to achieve success in ministry.[17]

18. Every minister must be careful of operating in the natural.

The Bible has warned us that we have no weapons in that realm (2 Corinthians 10:4).

Because the devil knows that we are disarmed in the natural world he tries to keep us occupied in human, secular and natural things. That is why many ministers of the Gospel today are teachers, administrators, managers, etc. Be careful not to fall into this trap.

TWENTY WAYS TO KNOW YOUR ENEMY SO YOU CAN DEFEAT HIM

In order to defeat your enemy you must know as much as you can about him. This is one of the most common rules of war. This is why secular armies engage in reconnaissance and intelligence work. Reconnaissance is the art of discovering the strengths, weaknesses, plans and location of the enemy. Without this you cannot even start your war.[18]

One of the ways by which we can know our enemy is to do a quick analysis of his names and titles. After all, a name speaks volumes about a person. Study the following twenty names or titles of Satan and you will know what you are dealing with.[19]

1. Devil

Jesus answered them, "Have not I chosen you twelve, and one of you is a DEVIL?" (John 6:70).The word "devil" comes from the Greek word diabolos. This is where the English word diabolical comes from. Diabolos reveals the essential nature of this evil being. It means to be inhumanly cruel or wicked. It also means to be outrageous or disgracefully bad.[20]

2. Satan

This comes from a Hebrew word Satan, which literally means adversary. It speaks of being diabolical or hellish. This name was first used in the book of Job. "Now there was a day when the sons of God came to present themselves before the Lord, and SATAN came also among them" (Job 1:6).

It described a very wicked being who murdered the entire household of Job and destroyed his business.[21]

Satan is the archenemy of both God and man. In this interesting passage, Satan is spoken of as a real person who seemed to have access to Heaven. He also seemed to have power to accuse the brethren and to seek their destruction.[22]

3. Accuser of the Brethren

This title explains the relentless accusations and slander that are hurled against God's servants.[23] "And I heard a loud voice saying in heaven, Now is come salvation, and strength, and the kingdom of our God, and the power of his Christ: for the ACCUSER OF OUR BRETHREN is cast down, which accused them before our God day and night" (Revelation 12:10).

4. Adversary

This name reveals the antagonistic nature of Satan as he fights against everything we do. No wonder there is such resistance, hostility and unfriendliness to the Gospel. "Be sober, be vigilant; because your ADVERSARY the devil, as a roaring lion, walketh about, seeking whom he may devour" (1 Peter 5:8).

Satan's agents, the unbelievers, are often in tune with the spirit of opposition to the church and its leaders. Many nations have laws that are hostile to the establishment of churches. Even though churches have brought so much health and educational benefits to nations, political leaders have no choice but to oppose the church.

5. Angel of the Bottomless Pit

This name reveals the final destination of Satan and his cohorts. "And they had a king over them, which is the ANGEL OF THE BOTTOMLESS PIT, whose name in the Hebrew tongue is Abaddon, but in the Greek tongue hath his name Apollyon" (Revelation 9:11).

This can explain the frantic efforts of the devil to capture every corner of this earth. We must rise up now and counteract this desperate devil at every turn.

6. Belial

Belial means worthless. "And what concord hath Christ with BELIAL? Or what part hath he that believeth with an infidel?" (2 Corinthians 6:15).

Satan is out to degrade you. Just observe someone who is under the influence of the devil. You will notice how worthless he becomes. The devil degrades young men into becoming drug addicts, school dropouts, smugglers, etc. Belial turns young ladies into prostitutes with no sense of worth.

7. Beelzebub

This means the "Lord of the flies". "But when the Pharisees heard it, they said, This fellow doth not cast out devils, but by BEELZEBUB the prince of the devils" (Matthew 12:24).

A lord of flies is obviously a supervisor of disease and death. Satan is the author of the famine, disease and death that plague millions today.[24]

8. The God of This World

"He's got the whole world in his hands." That's the song we all learnt in Sunday school, but is that really the case? If he's got the whole world in his hands, then why are there so many wars and famines everywhere? Why is there such unhappiness in the world? Why is half of the world very rich and the other half very poor?

Certainly, this would not happen under the management and leadership of Jehovah. You see, Satan is actually the god of this world. "In whom the GOD OF THIS WORLD hath blinded the minds of them which believe not, lest the light of the glorious gospel of Christ, who is the image of God, should shine unto them" (2 Corinthians 4:4).

Where Jehovah is in full control (heaven), the streets are made of gold and the people live in absolute bliss. One day when the Lord takes over the rulership of this world, there will be a different kind of earth with love, peace, and joy.

9. Murderer

This is an appropriate title for the devil. He is a murderer. He is a killer and the author of all the bloodshed in this world.

When he possesses a head of state this president may lead his nation into senseless wars which achieve nothing. "Ye are of your father the devil, and the lusts of your father ye will do. He was a MURDERER FROM THE BEGINNING, and abode not in the truth, because there is no truth in him. When he speaketh a lie, he speaketh of his own: for he is a liar, and the father of it" (John 8:44).

As the fathers, husbands and brothers of multitudes are slaughtered, the murderer is living up to his reputation.

10. Prince of devils

This title shows us the organised nature of the forces of darkness. "But when the Pharisees heard it, they said, This fellow doth not cast out devils, but by Beelzebub the PRINCE OF THE DEVILS" (Matthew 12:24).

Demons are organised into armies. They have an overall commander who is known as the prince of devils. As we move into spiritual warfare we are battling against an organized and intelligent enemy.

11. Prince of the power of the air

This reveals Satan's control over the atmosphere and airwaves in any nation. "Wherein in time past ye walked according to the course of this world, according to the PRINCE OF THE POWER OF THE AIR, the spirit that now worketh in the children of disobedience" (Ephesians 2:2).

Look closely at the radio and television waves of any nation. You will notice how Satan has dominated these fields. It is important for Christians to fight for the control of the airwaves. We must fight for the control of the arts, culture and the music of our nations. This is the domain of the prince of the power of the air and it is our duty is to dislodge him.

12. Prince of the world

This reveals Satan's rulership of the world and the systems of the world. "Hereafter I will not talk much with you: for the PRINCE OF THIS WORLD cometh, and hath nothing in me" (John 14:30). As the world develops everything becomes more and more godless.

I recently told a friend, "When I am in Europe I feel as though I am in Sodom." I said to him, "Europe is Pergamos revived!" Pergamos was the seat of Satan and the headquarters of demonic activity (Revelations 2:13).[25]

13. The old serpent

In the beginning, he was described as a serpent. "And THE SERPENT said unto the woman, Ye shall not surely die" (Genesis 3:4).

In the end, he was described as a serpent. "And the great dragon was cast out, that OLD SERPENT, called the Devil, and Satan, which deceiveth the whole world: he was cast out into the earth, and his angels were cast out with him" (Revelation 12:9).

Snakes are some of the most dangerous creatures we know about. With one stroke, they can kill a human being. Yet, snakes manage to live near human beings without being detected. This is exactly how Satan works.

He is in the church and the people don't even know it. He is nearby causing damage and yet he is unseen.

As we battle against the devil, we must be constantly aware that even though he is invisible, he is real. Anytime I walk through tall grass I am conscious of the fact that there may be dangerous snakes nearby. Every pastor must be conscious of the fact that there may be invisible demonic activity nearby.

14. The tempter

Satan is the author of temptation! He creates situations that test our resolve to obey God. "And when THE TEMPTER came to him, he said, If thou be the Son of God, command that these stones be made bread" (Matthew 4:3).

He tempted Jesus and he will tempt you and I. But God will come to your rescue. He will provide a way of escape for every temptation.

15. Unclean spirit

The word unclean is used to describe the devil many times. "When the UNCLEAN SPIRIT is gone out of a man, he walketh through dry places, seeking rest, and findeth none" (Matthew 12:43).

This is because that is what the devil is. We are fighting a being that has a contagious nature that wants to make you unclean.

The word unclean is translated from the Greek word akarthartos. It means impure, lewd, foul and unclean. It is a general term for Satan since his presence makes everything impure. Pure relationships are described as impure when unclean spirits get involved. Pure friendships become impure when the accuser points his finger at them.

16. The wicked one

The wickedness of the devil is unparalleled. "When any one heareth the word of the kingdom, and understandeth it not, then cometh the WICKED ONE, and catcheth away that which was sown in his heart. This is he which received seed by the way side" (Matthew 13:19).

Occasionally, human beings who have been greatly influenced by Satan display flashes of this hellish character. The wars of Sierra Leone, the genocide of Rwanda and Kosovo testify to the wickedness of Satan. This is the enemy we seek to dislodge and weaken. In the name of Jesus we will defeat the wicked one.

17. Lucifer

Lucifer is the name given to the angelic being that fell from grace. Lucifer is described in great detail in the book of Ezekiel.

"Thou hast been in Eden the garden of God; every precious stone was thy covering, the sardius, topaz, and the diamond, the beryl, the onyx, and the jasper, the sapphire, the emerald, and the carbuncle, and gold: the workmanship of thy tabrets and of thy pipes was prepared in thee in the day that thou wast created. Thou art the anointed cherub that covereth; and I have set thee so: thou wast upon the holy mountain of God; thou hast walked up and down in the midst of the stones of fire. Thou wast perfect in thy ways from the day that thou wast created, till iniquity was found in thee" (Ezekiel 28:13-15).

Satan's ability in the field of music (pipes and tabrets) is described in this passage. No wonder he has captivated millions through the power of unwholesome music.

You can see that he was an awesome being! The descriptions of his glory show us the kind of creature he is. "How art thou fallen from heaven, O LUCIFER, son of the morning! how art thou cut down to the ground, which didst weaken the nations! For thou hast said in thine heart, I will ascend into heaven, I will exalt my throne above the stars of God: I will sit also upon the mount of the congregation, in the sides of the north:

I will ascend above the heights of the clouds; I will be like the most High.Yet thou shalt be brought down to hell, to the sides of the pit" (Isaiah 14:12-15).

If such a being is corrupted, you can understand the kind of monster that would be unleashed.

18. Father of lies

When Saddam Hussein invaded Kuwait and declared war against the rest of the world, he frightened America by saying, "We're going to have the mother of all battles." When someone is described as a "mother" or "father", it tells us something important. "Ye are of your father the devil, and the lusts of your father ye will do. He was a murderer from the beginning, and abode not in the truth, because there is no truth in him. When he speaketh a lie, he speaketh of his own: for HE IS A LIAR, AND THE FATHER OF IT" (John 8:44)

If Satan is the father of lies then he is the parent and creator of all forms of deception. Satan's power to deceive is unparalled.

19. Abaddon

This is the angel of the abyss. "And they had a king over them, which is the angel of the bottomless PIT, whose name in the Hebrew tongue is ABADDON, but in the Greek tongue hath his name Apollyon" (Revelation 9:11).

In the book of Job this word is translated destruction. If you can't have it, destroy it! This is the very nature of the devil. Some heads of state that cannot have power any longer, delight in destroying the entire nation through war. They get this idea from their master Abaddon.

20. Principalities, powers, rulers of darkness, wicked spirits

"For we wrestle not against flesh and blood, but against principalities, against powers, against the rulers of the darkness of this world, against spiritual wickedness in high places" (Ephesians 6:12). In this Scripture, Paul groups the four main agents of Satan's outreach.

Principalities represent spirits that dominate geographical areas. It is obvious that different kinds of spirits occupy different geographical areas. . Amsterdam, for instance, has a principality of immorality. There is a saying that good boys go to Heaven and bad boys go to Amsterdam.

Powers are beings that exert control over individuals. Another name you could give to them is "spirits that influence". Wicked spirits in high places speak of wicked entities that exist in the heavenlies. It was such a being that opposed the angel who was returning to Daniel with an answer to prayer (Daniel 10:13).

Rulers of the darkness speak of the spiritual beings that control the darkness in the world. The underworld and the unbelievers are all under influence without even knowing it.[26]

The Works of Satan

30

■ THE ULTIMATE MODEL OF DEMON ACTIVITY

"And they came over unto the other side of the sea, into the country of the Gadarenes. And when he was come out of the ship, immediately there met him out of the tombs a man with an unclean spirit, Who had his dwelling among the tombs; and no man could bind him, no, not with chains: Because that he had been often bound with fetters and chains, and the chains had been plucked asunder by him, and the fetters broken in pieces: neither could any man tame him.

And always, night and day, he was in the mountains, and in the tombs, crying, and cutting himself with stones. But when he saw Jesus afar off, he ran and worshipped him, And cried with a loud voice, and said, What have I to do with thee, Jesus, thou Son of the most high God?

I adjure thee by God, that thou torment me not. For he said unto him, Come out of the man, thou unclean spirit. And he asked him, What is thy name? And he answered, saying, My name is Legion: for we are many. And he besought him much that he would not send them away out of the country. Now there was there nigh unto the mountains a great herd of swine feeding. And all the devils besought him, saying, Send us into the swine, that we may enter into them.

And forthwith Jesus gave them leave. And the unclean spirits went out, and entered into the swine: and the herd ran violently down a steep place into the sea, (they were about two thousand;) and were choked in the sea. And they that fed the swine fled, and told it in the city, and in the country. And they went out to see what it was that was done. And they come to Jesus, and see him that was possessed with the devil, and had the legion, sitting, and clothed, and in his right mind: and they were afraid. And they that saw it told them how it befell to him that was possessed with the devil, and also concerning the swine. And they began to pray him to depart out of their coasts.

And when he was come into the ship, he that had been possessed with the devil prayed him that he might be with him. Howbeit Jesus suffered him not, but saith unto him, Go home to thy friends, and tell them how great things the Lord hath done for thee, and hath had compassion on thee. And he departed, and began to publish in Decapolis how great things Jesus had done for him: and all men did marvel" (Mark 5:1-20).

THE PATHOLOGY OF DEMON ACTIVITY

You will learn many things about Satan and demons by just studying this case. The study of the mad man of Gadara is the study of the pathology of demon activity.[1] Many people wonder what pathology is all about. We often wonder why somebody will spend his time studying dead bodies. I did not understand as a medical student, how important it was for a doctor to spend time dissecting dead people.

I thought, "Once they are dead, they are dead, just leave them alone!" I came to understand that pathology is the study of the effect of various diseases on the human body. It is the study of the ultimate effect of disease. In other words, to understand what will happen if a disease is allowed to run its course, you must study pathology. Often, it is only in a dead body, that you will see the ultimate effect that diseases have.

For instance, if you dissect the dead body of a man who died from long-standing hypertension, you will notice changes in his heart, his blood vessels and his kidneys. These changes will help you to understand what hypertension is currently doing to people living with the disease. By studying the dead body, which has experienced a full-blown manifestation of a particular disease, doctors understand much more about diseases.

Similarly, by studying the mad man of Gadara, you will understand the ultimate effect of demon activity in a human being. It is a revelation of what Satan would like to do to you if he had the chance.

The story of the mad man of Gadara, is a study of the highest kind of demon infiltration. Every feature of the mad man's existence reveals a demonic trait. His condition shows different aspects of Satan's vision for you and I. If Satan had his way, you and I would end up in the same condition.

Even though most people will not become full blown "mad men of Gadara", most of us will experience to a lesser extent the same demonic trends that are demonstrated in this mad man.

The testimony of the mad man of Gadara shows us three things:

1. What demons would like to do to you if they had the chance.
2. What demons are doing to people, albeit in a gradual way.
3. The final state of a person in whom demons have had full expression.

God will reveal many things to you about the activities of demons, and how they affect you.[2]

Many think that the testimony of the mad man of Gadara is the story of a lunatic who belongs to a mental institution. They think to themselves, "Since I am not a mad man, this story does not concern me." On the contrary, this testimony concerns all of us.

Understanding the activities and intentions of your enemy are vital to winning any war. If you want to win the fight against evil spirits, you must know how and where your enemy operates. You must know what the enemy is planning against you. "Lest Satan should get an advantage of us: for we ARE NOT IGNORANT OF HIS DEVICES" (2 Corinthians 2:11).

You will be delivered from demon activity by the time you finish this book.

DARKNESS: THE HOME OF DEMONS AND DEMON ACTIVITY

The darkness of this world is the home of evil spirits. "...we wrestle...against the rulers of the DARKNESS of this world..." (Ephesians 6:12). Darkness speaks of the environment in which evil flourishes. Satan rules in the darkness of this world. Deception is a type of spiritual darkness. This is because the environment of deception is the breeding ground for evil spirits.

Satan, our defeated foe flourishes in the deepest darkness. He stands no chance when we come out into the light. This is why Satan hates the Word of God so much. Jesus is the Light that destroys Satan's influence over men. He is the Word of God. The Word of God is a light that shines in the darkness. Demon activity is greatly reduced where the Word of God is taught. "And THE LIGHT SHINETH IN DARKNESS; and the darkness comprehended it not" (John 1:5). Darkness is simply the atmosphere of deception under which Satan operates.

1. SATAN HIDES AND FIGHTS FROM A POSITION OF SECRECY, DECEPTION AND DARKNESS.

The power of Satan against the church can be likened to several wars and conflicts in the world today. When a super-power fights against an inferior army, the weaker side often knows that he does not stand a chance in open conventional warfare. This often results in guerilla warfare and terrorist activities.

For instance, the army of Israel is far more superior to the armies of the Palestinians; the Palestinians do not stand a chance against the military might of Israel. Israel is even said to be a nuclear power. Because Palestine does not stand a chance, they resort to surprise suicide attacks and terrorist activities.

Hijacking planes and killing members of the Olympic squad of the Israelis are just a few examples of the kind of warfare that the weaker army engages in.

Terrorist attacks like the one on September 11 are other examples of a weaker and smaller army fighting against a gigantic force. Similarly, the army of demons arrayed against the church, is no match for the power of God. The weapons of our warfare are mighty (2 Corinthians 10:4).

2. THE MAINSTAY OF SATAN'S OPERATIONS IS THROUGH DECEPTIVE TRICKS.

Because the devil has no chance against us, he uses what the Bible describes as "the wiles of the devil". Our greatest effort therefore must be to uncover the tricks and the traps of our illusive enemy.

Satan trembles at the mention of the name of Jesus. Demons shiver when we sing about the blood. When they see the blood, they pass over. The Word of God is a mighty sword, which slices fallen angels and evil spirits into shreds. In the realm of the spirit, we are a nuclear power fighting against an army of natives brandishing swords.

Believe it or not, one of the most successful tricks of the enemy is to make people believe that the devil does not exist.[3] This amazing lie is so successful that the devil has used it on multitudes of unsuspecting Europeans. Most European nations are plagued with hordes and hordes of demons. The neat pavements and quaint roads with perfectly arranged buildings will deceive the unspiritual into thinking that all is well. I believe that Europe is the darkest continent on this planet. It contains the most immoral, and godless communities on earth. The devil is very successful in Europe because he has convinced them that he does not exist.[4] Through this powerful deception, Sodom and Gomorrah have been recreated. The more our eyes are opened spiritually, the more the wiles of the devil will be exposed.

SATAN IS A MURDERER

The legion of demons made the mad man of Gadara cut himself with stones: "...he was in the mountains... cutting himself with stones" (Mark 5:5). Eventually, this action would have killed the mad man. This shows that the ultimate goal of Satan within the mad man's life was to kill him. Satan is called a murderer. Satan is the murderer trying to end your life if you give him a chance.[5] "Ye are of your father the devil, and the lusts of your father ye will do. HE WAS A MURDERER FROM THE BEGINNING..." (John 8:44).

It is important for every believer to understand that Satan is trying to kill him or her.[6] He would like to eliminate you from this earth. However, it is good to know that Satan cannot do whatever he wants to do. The Bible says "give no place to the devil." Unless you give a place to the devil, he cannot operate against you. Satan needs a foothold in order to proceed against you.

Every minister must be aware of this reality. "The thief cometh not, but ... TO KILL,... " (John 10:10). You must take steps to prevent the devil from having access to your life. When you stand up for the Lord, you must understand that you are a target of the enemy. The last battle of king Ahab exemplifies this fact. The enemy's instruction was very straightforward, "Fight with neither great nor small, fight only with the king." In other words, leave everyone alone and deal only with the king.

People criticize the leader as he experiences the attacks on behalf of everyone else. "But the king of Syria commanded his thirty and two captains that had rule over his chariots, saying, Fight neither with small nor great, SAVE ONLY WITH THE KING of Israel" (1 Kings 22:31). The king of Israel, who represented the leader of the armies of the Lord, knew that he was the primary target of the enemy.

The Tree in the Golf Course

Sometime ago, I was walking on a golf course and I received instruction from the Lord. I noticed a huge tree that I had passed by many times. As I looked closely at its trunk and branches, I noticed hundreds of scars on the tree. I said to Rev. Sackey, (my senior associate minister), " Have you noticed the scars on this tree? It has been hit by thousands of balls." Again, I received instruction from the Lord, "This tree is not wounded and scarred because it is a bad tree! It is not in the state that it is in because it is evil! It has suffered countless blows and shocks only because of its position in the centre of the fairway."

Many people are targets of satanic troubles because of their positions in the battle. They are good people who love the Lord. But by their positions as pastors and ministers of the gospel, they experience numerous strikes from the enemy. They are often criticized for their seemingly numerous troubles.

After twenty years of ministry, one pastor's wife said to her husband, "You at all, when will you have peace?" Do not be deceived dear friend, many of these battered warriors will be rewarded by the Lord in eternity. Close the gaps and prevent the enemy from having a foothold in your life.

The Three-Legged Table

Sometimes there are things that you must do to remove the foothold of the devil.

One day, while I was praying to the Lord about various things that were going on in my life and ministry, the Lord gave me a vision. I saw an unusual three-legged table. The Lord said to me, "The devil stands on this three-legged table to launch attacks against you." He said to me, "You have to dismantle this table by removing each of the legs." Then He showed me what each of the three legs was and asked me to remove them one by one. When I did, I noticed how the strong persistent attacks of the enemy were defused.

Sometimes, there are circumstances that Satan is delighted to have and use against you. He launches attack after attack from that position.[7] Remove the favourite launching pads of the enemy from your life and God will grant you victory over Satan's plan to kill you. Perhaps, many ministers die before their time due to stress, bad diet and a lack of exercise. These things may be Satan's launching pads. Perhaps, introducing some practical measures may stop the attacks.

If Jesus had not intervened, the mad man of Gadara would have perished in the mountains and joined the dead in the tombs. May you experience a divine intervention in your life!

ISOLATION: SATAN'S GOAL

1. Isolation is one of the fundamental demonic strategies in existence.

The mad man of Gadara was isolated in the mountains and in the tombs. "...neither abode in any house, but in the tombs" (Luke 8:27). He walked and lived in solitude, having no one to talk to. The demons that possessed him ensured that he was isolated in the tombs. It is important for Satan to isolate you if he is going to fully implement his plan against your life. The devil is described as a roaring lion, seeking someone to devour. "Be sober, be vigilant; because your adversary the devil, AS A ROARING LION, walketh about, seeking whom he may devour" (1 Peter 5:8).

All you have to do is to watch a wildlife documentary and you will understand how the devil operates. All the lion wishes for is to get an isolated antelope or a lonely deer. Even as a pastor, I have learnt not to live in isolation.

The Bible teaches that WE have the mind of Christ. The mind of Christ is not with one particular pastor or group of pastors. All of us together have the mind of Christ. That is why we need each other. "For who hath known the mind of the Lord, that he may instruct him? But WE have the mind of Christ" (1 Corinthians 2:16).

2. Anyone who isolates himself is opening himself up to deceptions and delusions.

The highest kind of deception is to think that you do not need anyone. We need one another and Satan knows that. That is why he tries to keep us from each other.

My greatest advances in the ministry have come as a result of coming near different ministers. Interaction with all of God's children has only been a blessing to me.

3. Isolation has resulted in a fragmented Church.

Unfortunately, fighting, bitterness and pride have fragmented the church into several isolated segments. The American church rarely learns from the Nigerian church. And the Nigerian church rarely learns from the church in Malawi. The white church rarely learns from the black church. And the Asian church is mostly cut off from the South American church.

As I have travelled to different continents, I have received many blessings from the different sections of the Church.

4. Isolation heightens the minister's struggle.

I have watched as ministers struggled in their lonely corners. I knew that if they were only to relate with the rest of us, their lives and ministries would be changed dramatically.

Have you noticed that the first step to backsliding of church members is staying away from fellowship?

Isolation is a primary demonic strategy that the church must fight. May the Lord unite us into one Body!

Signs of Demonic Activity

31

■ THE COMMONEST SIGN OF DEMON ACTIVITY

The mad man of Gadara was led by demons to roam through lonely mountains and graveyards. This frightening scenario made the poor man cry constantly. "And always, NIGHT and day, he was IN THE MOUNTAINS, and IN THE TOMBS, crying..." (Mark 5:5).

You can see from this that demons love to frighten their victims. Fear is a pervading sign of the presence of demons. In my opinion, the commonest sign of demon activity is fear. The pervading presence of demons is most easily noticed by the presence of fear. Most kinds of fear are of demonic origin! Through fear, Satan is able to keep most people in bondage. "And deliver them who THROUGH FEAR of death were all their lifetime SUBJECT TO BONDAGE" (Hebrews 2:15).

THE EVIL SPIRIT OF FEAR

1. Fear is actually a demon.

It is not a mood or an attitude! "For God hath not given us THE SPIRIT OF FEAR; but of power, and of love, and of a sound mind" (2 Timothy 1:7). Evil spirits constantly minister fear. That is why Jesus constantly said to people, "Fear not." When demons have their way in your life, you will be afraid. They will minister fear about every conceivable thing to you. The whole human race is subject to diverse fears. Fear of sickness, fear of death, fear of tragedy, fear of witches, fear of the night, fear of divorce and the list goes on.

When people are born again, they initially find it difficult to trust in anything good. There is a fear of the church; there is a fear of pastors; a fear of the ministry and a fear of disappointment. The ability to walk by faith is the ability to walk free of the fears that plague all of us.

The demon, which controlled the mad man of Gadara, took him into a frightening and lonely place that normal human beings would be scared to visit. This is where the devil had taken the man. You can see from this testimony that because the devil was in control, he placed the mad man in a frightening location. As long as the devil was in control, he kept the man in a place of fear.

2. When demons are in control of your life, you will be afraid of many things.

Perhaps the devil is giving you frightening pictures to scare you. That is what he did to the mad man of Gadara. Through fear, Satan keeps many people in bondage. Read it for yourself: "Forasmuch then as the children are partakers of flesh and blood, he also himself likewise took part of the same; that through death he might destroy him that had the power of death, that is,

THE DEVIL; And deliver them who THROUGH FEAR of death were all their lifetime subject to BONDAGE" (Hebrews 2:14-15). This is Satan's wish for you and me: to take us to the place of greatest fear. He wants us to live in perpetual fear. Almost all Christians harbour one fear or the other. It hounds us, influences us and guides us.

A cemetery is not a nice place to be; even in the daytime. This should tell you how wicked Satan and devils are. If the devil had a chance, he would place you in a cemetery and force you to live among the dead. It is comforting to know that the devil cannot just do what he wants with your life. If Satan had complete access to us, we would be turned into mad men dwelling in fear and isolation.

Let me ask you today: What fears are controlling you? If you are full of fear, remember that you are full of demonic influence. I cannot over-emphasize that fear is not just a thought. It is a demon. The presence of any kind of fear is a sign of demonic activity. If you are afraid to marry because of the troubled marriages around, I can understand you. However, the presence of fear is still the work of evil spirits in your life.

THE THREE EFFECTS OF THE DEMON OF FEAR

There are three effects of the demon of fear. These are spelt out in 2 Timothy 1:7. The Bible teaches that God has given us the spirit of love, the spirit of power and the spirit of a sound mind to replace the spirit of fear. Therefore, people with the spirit of fear are unable to love. They do not have power and do not have sound minds.

1. A SOUND MIND IS TAKEN AWAY BY FEAR.

When you are possessed with fear, you behave abnormally. I remember one day, I went to a harbour with a group of children to visit a ship. Unfortunately, one of the children was so scared of the ships. She screamed and screamed and refused to get out of the car. In the end, we had to leave her in the car with someone attending to her. The child was totally controlled by the fear of ships. In a sense, this child looked abnormal in relation to the other children. The others were happy and excited about the excursion but she was unhappy and paralyzed by fear.

This is what happens to us when we are controlled by fear. Fear makes us become queer and live abnormal lives. Evil spirits of fear control many women. They are unable to marry because they fear disappointment and the control that comes through marriage. Women who are not controlled by these fears marry easily. Others watch from afar and wonder how anyone could enter into such an arrangement.

Fear takes away the soundness of your mind. Fear can turn you into a mad person. Fear can drive you along a queer road and no one will understand your behaviour. When the Spirit of God is upon you, fear will leave. The frightening things we see around us cannot govern us.

I know of a couple that got married on a Saturday. Unfortunately, the bridegroom died two days after his wedding. I know a lady whose husband died a few months after they got married.

These are terrible experiences we see all around us. If we were to follow these fears, we would be immobilized and unable to function. There are tragedies of all kinds everywhere. Planes crash and cars have accidents all the time. People die everywhere and under horrible circumstances.

It was difficult for me to fly after the September 11 terrorist attack. However, I realized that if I were governed by fear, my ministry would be odd. I would be a man unable to sit on a plane. I would have to travel from West Africa to Europe by car or bicycle. Imagine that! Remember that fear is a demon and whoever follows a demon will not prosper.

Always remember that fear is a sign of the presence of demons.

2. Powerlessness is produced by fear.

When fear gets a hold of you, you become immobilized and unable to do the things God tells you to do. When I was beginning the ministry, I was afraid that it would not work. Fear takes away strength! "What about if it doesn't work? What about if she dies? What about if he gets cancer? What about if she is barren?" There are many things to fear. These fears paralyze you and make you unable to do the will of God.

Go in the opposite direction to where fear is leading you. That is how to overcome fear. Do the opposite of your fears. I know that fear is an evil spirit. I must not be controlled by evil spirits!

3. Love is destroyed by fear.

I learnt long ago that someone who fears me does not love me. "There is no fear in love; but PERFECT LOVE CASTETH OUT FEAR: because fear hath torment. He that FEARETH IS NOT MADE PERFECT IN LOVE" (1 John 4:18).

Fear destroys love. It manifests itself in suspicion and uncertainty. If my church members are suspicious of me, they do not love me. If they constantly suspect me of evil, they do not love me. Fear destroys love and that is why perfect love casts out fear.

A fearful partner always destroys the "husband and wife" relationship. Fears and insecurities in one partner can lead to a total break down of marriage. Fear leads to suspicion, accusations and counter accusations. The home is turned into a courtroom where the first accused has to constantly defend and explain every move. It is not easy to be in the accused person's box. Fear is not a replacement for love.

Fear often attacks the most beautiful and blessed people. They have everything but happiness. They are scared that they might lose what they have. This is what happened to Job! He had everything and was a super-blessed person but he was afraid. When tragedy finally struck, he confessed that he had been fearful all along. "For the thing WHICH I GREATLY FEARED is come upon me, and that which I was afraid of is come unto me" (Job 3:25).

Dear sister, you cannot make your husband love you when you are governed by insecurity! You are welcoming an evil spirit called fear into your home!

The wife of John Wesley, for instance, was someone who was blessed to have been married to one of the most committed Christian leaders of all time. However, it seemed that a spirit of fear and insecurity obsessed her. She could not stand the fact that John Wesley ministered to other women through letters. At a point, this great founder had to plead with his wife to be a friend, and not to suspect him or asperse (slander) him anymore. Notice from this excerpt, how John Wesley pleaded with his wife not to be suspicious of him.

But let me be your friend; suspect me no more; asperse me no more; provoke me no more. Do not any longer contend for mastery; for power, money or praise...Attempt no more to abridge me of the liberty that I claim by God and man.[1]

FEAR CONTROLS

This spirit of fear seeks to gain control and guide the affairs of its victim. Some people's love is so intense that it manifests as fear and self-preservation.

The spirit of fear working through John Wesley's wife tried to guide his ministry and control it. John Wesley again wrote to his wife asking her to allow him to be controlled by God and his conscience. In other words, he was demanding not to be controlled by a spirit of fear but by God. Leave me to be governed by God and my own conscience; then shall I govern you with gentle sway, and shew that I do indeed love you, even as Christ the church.[2] The end of this story is that John Wesley's marriage broke down.

Love does not break marriages but fear does. Fear is an evil spirit. The presence of fear is the commonest sign of the presence of demons.

Traditionally, fear has not been labelled as a very evil thing. It is seen more as a weakness that some are prone to. Do not be deceived dear friend; fear is one of the highest kinds of demonic attacks anyone can experience. Fear has the power to totally change the course of your life if you allow it.

A few days before I saw the first dead person raised to life in my ministry, a spirit of fear attacked me. This evil spirit tried to direct me away from the crusade I was going to preach at. I would never have seen the grace of God in that dimension if I had followed the spirit of fear. God had to speak to me in a vision to deliver me from this spirit of fear. May the power of God set you free from every evil spirit of fear!

■ DEMONS MAKE PEOPLE DO UNNATURAL THINGS

1. The demons that controlled the mad man of Gadara made him do unnatural things.

It is not natural to live in a graveyard: "...had his dwelling among the tombs..." (Mark 5:3). It is unnatural for an adult to wear no clothes: "...and ware no clothes, neither abode in any house, but in the tombs" (Luke 8:27). The testimony of the mad man of Gadara shows us that when Satan gains ultimate control of a human being, he leads him to do unnatural things.[3] Things against nature and things against God's design are often demonic in origin. It is not natural for anyone to live in the tombs of dead men. It is even scary to dwell near the dead.

However, notice that the mad man of Gadara was led to live in the cemetery itself and amongst the graves. This is an example of how Satan gets his victims to live in an unnatural way.

2. Homosexuality is a good example of an unnatural phenomenon.

It is against God's design. God created Adam and Eve (and not Adam and Steve). In spite of the numerous theories put forth by gay activists, we cannot find any of the animals created by the Lord to be homosexual in nature. I have never heard of homosexual dogs, cats, frogs, or horses. The penis was intended to be naturally inserted into the vagina and not into a rectum packed with faeces.

Homosexuality is an unnatural act and is one of the unfortunate outcomes of demonic activity. Of course, we do not condemn homosexuals. They are created by God and Christ died for all of us. Those of us who are not homosexuals may have even worse perversions in our lives, for which we need the grace of God.

Today, there are websites for people who would like to have sex with animals like dogs, snakes, horses etc. There are women who have specially trained dogs they have sex with. These are all unfortunate and unnatural perversions. The origins of this dehumanizing behaviour are demonic. Is there anything unnatural in your life? Perhaps demons are giving you these unnatural tendencies.[4]

MADNESS

Madness is not a natural behaviour. The man of Gadara was a mad man. He lived in a graveyard amongst the tombs. He was completely bonkers! Psychiatrists would have loved to have him as a case study. It was only after Jesus ministered to him that he had his mind normalized. "...the man, out of whom the devils were departed, sitting at the feet of Jesus, clothed, AND IN HIS RIGHT MIND: and they were afraid" (Luke 8:35).

There are different kinds of psychiatric disorders. The layman often thinks of all mental patients as "mad men". However, several different mental conditions exist. For example, there are anxiety disorders, chronic pain disorders, psychosexual disorders, personality disorders, etc. The more serious ones are mood disorders, which include depression, mania and schizophrenia.

In depression, there is a lowered mood varying from mild sadness to intense feelings of guilt, worthlessness and hopelessness. There is also a loss of interest generally, with reduced involvement in work and recreation. There is difficulty in thinking, including the inability to concentrate and a lack of decisiveness. In depression, there are also apparent physical complaints such as headaches, disrupted, lessened or excessive sleep and a loss of energy. There may be a change in the appetite with a decreased sexual drive. In severe depression, people are often suicidal![5]

Schizophrenia is the problem that the mad man of Gadara had.[6]

1. The highest kind of mental illness is what we call schizophrenia.

This is a serious illness, which my lecturer in medical school described as "madness". He used to say, "These people are mad."

Initially, I used to think that everybody in the mental hospital was "mad". However, with time, I understood that there were some patients who were "madder" than others. The Lord impressed on me to take a second look at the symptoms of these so-called mad men. The two cardinal symptoms are:

- Paranoid Delusions (Fears)
- Hallucinations (Accusations)

2. Paranoid Delusions

Delusions are beliefs (or fears) that are held by the individual in spite of contrary evidence. In a person suffering from these delusions, you will notice a pattern of thinking. Such people are preoccupied with the supposedly threatening behaviour exhibited by other individuals. Paranoid delusions make people afraid of things that do not exist.

"Paranoia" means "fear". Paranoid delusions are delusions in which the person is afraid of something. These people are paralyzed or motivated by terrible fears that seem so real.

This form of thought may cause some patients to adopt active counter measures such as locking doors and windows, taking up weapons and becoming enemies of genuine friends.[7]

3. Accusatory Hallucinations

The other cardinal sign of schizophrenia is auditory hallucinations (accusations). With hallucinations, the individual hears and sees unreal things. These hallucinations (accusations) are often derogatory in nature. In other words, the person hears people accusing him, insulting him and saying derogatory things about him. The accuser of the brethren is at work!

These two sets of symptoms: paranoid delusions (FEAR) and auditory derogatory hallucinations (ACCUSATIONS), mark out schizophrenia (madness) quite clearly. Simply put, fears and accusations are key weapons of the enemy.[8] Have you ever wondered why Satan is called the "accuser of the brethren"? Through the power of fear and accusations, Satan is able to convert normal people into mad men.[9] Satan also eliminates people through these two weapons. For instance, he used the weapons of fear and accusations to eliminate Christ and send Him to the cross. The reason that I brought this up is for you to see two strong techniques of the devil when he is taking control of someone's life: The techniques of delusions and accusatory hallucinations (fears and accusations)!

When Satan is given a free course, he will totally deceive. He will paralyse with fear. He will accuse, insult and criticize because that is his nature. These two weapons form the basis of the highest kind of demonic activity unleashed against human beings. Fear and accusations are the hallmarks of Satan's presence. This truth is borne out in the life of Jesus Christ.

4. Jesus Christ was the subject of the highest kind of satanic onslaught.

He suffered directly from the paranoid delusions (fears) of the Pharisees. The Pharisees feared Jesus. "And the scribes and chief priests heard it, and sought how they might destroy him: FOR THEY FEARED HIM, because all the people was astonished at his doctrine" (Mark 11:18).

They feared His ministry, His power and His authority. They were moved with fear and deception until they eliminated Him. He experienced first hand their derogatory and insulting accusations. Jesus was arrested and treated as a thief. He was insulted and accused continually until He stopped breathing on the cross. This is the highest kind of satanic attack that comes against God's messengers. Make sure you are never an agent of paranoid delusions and accusations.

The two well-known titles of Satan are "the father of lies" (John 8:44) and "the accuser of the brethren," (Revelation 12:10). He is described as "that old serpent that deceived the whole world". It is important for Christians not to imagine the nature and activity of Satan but to believe what the Bible says. The principal work of Satan is to deceive and to accuse!!!

Through accusations and criticism, Satan is able to turn the brethren against each other. He is the accuser in the midst of the brethren. He is the accuser in the midst of the church. Through the activities of the accuser, we turn against each other and destroy each other! Accusations produce guilt, confusion, hatred, pressure and erroneous counter measures and counter accusations. Accusations cause distractions and the sidetracking of a powerful army from its true purpose.

5. Delusions are the highest kind of deceptions.

A deception that a person cannot break away from, is a delusion.. The church is labouring under a variety of strong delusions. Delusions of what money is not, have led many astray. Delusions of human quest for achievement have led much of the church into deception. Unfortunately, in the world, right is paraded as wrong and wrong as right. Black is called white and white black.

Do not be an agent of accusation! When you accuse and criticize, you are employed by Satan himself. You are being used to divide the church and to bring hatred where there should be love. The greatest attack of the enemy on the church is not from without, but from within. An erroneous and zealous delusion of self-righteousness is the foundation of all accusations within the church. Remember that it was the Pharisees (zealous and error-filled religious men), who opposed and accused Christ continually. They brought Him to the cross and eliminated the holiest, the dearest and the best! Through the power of accusation, they ended the loveliest gift of God.

You have no idea what you may be destroying through your criticism and accusation. You may destroy an entire church through your accusations. Do not be an agent of delusions. The words of Christ are the words of God. No particular doctrine or teaching can replace Christ Himself. He is the way, the truth, and the life. It is in our interest to return to the words that Jesus spoke. This is the surest way to save ourselves from delusions.

Satan's Onslaught

Paranoid delusions (fear) and auditory hallucinations (accusations), are what ultimately cause madness. This is the highest kind of mental affliction of man. It is indeed the highest kind of demonic affliction. Wherever the presence of Satan is, accusations, delusions and fear will abound.[10] The mad man of Gadara who in my opinion is typical of the highest kind of demonic expression, suffered clearly from these two weapons of Satan.

A church filled with accusations and delusions will seem like a mad house. The world looks on in amazement as we fight each other and propagate erroneous doctrines about God.

May we be delivered from this madness. May the Lord set us free from delusions, fears and accusations!

■ SELF-DESTRUCTION

"...cutting himself with stones" (Mark 5:5).

Disease

The mad man of Gadara, fully under the influence of Satan, cut himself with stones. He systematically destroyed himself with stones. This is a very important manifestation of the presence of Satan: self-destruction.[11] There are many satanic and demonic diseases that are self-destructive.

Diseases like asthma are overreactions of the body to foreign bodies, which result in self-destruction. The body kills itself slowly as it tries to protect itself from these foreign bodies.

Unforgiveness

Unforgiveness is one such demonic foothold. Many do not understand that bitterness is self-destructive. By keeping the hurts and the pain, many people destroy themselves. Demons encourage us to bear grudges and to avenge all who hurt us.

God will forgive every sin we commit but He will not forgive us when we do not forgive others. Many are not aware that by maintaining a grudge, we are slowly destroying our own selves. There is nothing more self-destructive than bitterness and hurts. I have watched many self-destruct as they kept grudges and hurts.

Division

The great empires of this world have rarely been destroyed from outside. The collapse always came from within. Bitter wrangling, inner fighting and political divisions were always behind the collapse of these great empires of the world. The story of the fifth column is well known.

There was an army general who surrounded a large city with the aim of conquering it. This city was heavily fortified with a high and imposing wall and gate. The army general surrounded the city in readiness to attack.

One friend of the general came along and asked him, "Sir, how are you going to overcome the defences of this city? No one in recent history has been able to conquer this great city."

The army general smiled and said, "It's my 5th column. I'm depending on them to do the trick." The general's friend was very interested and asked, "What is this 5th column? I thought you only had four columns."

The army general replied, "I do have a 5th column."

"Oh, I see. Is it a special commando unit or are they airborne paratroopers?", the man asked. The general laughed, "No, it's none of these. My fifth column consists of my spies, agents, friends and supporters who are already within the city. You just wait. They will open those big gates from within and my armies will rush in."[12]

Destroying the Church from Within

The church cannot be destroyed by an outside force. It will only be destroyed from within. Many people think they are helping God as they accuse fathers and senior ministers of various crimes. They feel they are bringing to order the backslidden and deviant men of God. The accuser of the brethren urges them on and they are anointed from Hell to destroy the church. They generate much confusion and division within the church thinking they are doing the work of God. "They shall put you out of the synagogues: yea, the time cometh, that whosoever killeth you will think that he doeth God service" (John 16:2). "Now I beseech you, brethren, mark them which cause divisions and offences contrary to the doctrine which ye have learned; and avoid them" (Romans 16:17).

Key Strategy of Satan

Self-destruction is one of the key strategies of demonic attacks. When the spirit of Satan takes hold of a person, he will often begin to cut himself with stones. The prodigal son is a typical story of someone with a self-destructive spirit. He had everything going for him and he dwelt safely in his father's house. By one decision, he destroyed himself and his future. No external force contributed to his demise. It was all self-inflicted; he virtually cut himself with stones.

God raises up fathers and gives them sons. Sometimes the spirit of Satan possesses the sons and they go very far from their fathers. When all is said and done, the prodigal sons are all but destroyed. This is an evil that I have seen under the sun and it is common among pastors. May God save us from the spirit that makes us put a knife to our own throats!

■ ABSENCE OF CONTROL

"...and no man could bind him,..." (Mark 5:3). The fact that no one could bind the mad man of Gadara demonstrates that he had become uncontrollable. No one could bind or restrict him. This is a feature of satanic influence: uncontrollability! The prodigal son was uncontrollable. No one could advise him. He destroyed himself and his future ministry by moving out of his father's care.

There are two types of wisdom. The wisdom from above is characterized by one wonderful feature: It is easy to be entreated. "But the wisdom that is from above is first pure, then peaceable, gentle, and EASY TO BE INTREATED, full of mercy and good fruits, without partiality, and without hypocrisy" (James 3:17).

Pride, the spirit of Satan, will teach you to be unyielding and adamant. Humility and the spirit of Christ will teach you to flow and to listen to advice.

1. In God's plan, man must be under authority.

The mad man of Gadara was not under any authority. No one in the city could control him. God, however, has not designed our lives that way. We are designed to be under authority. Satan is the ultimate rebel who broke away from God's authority. Up until today, he inspires millions to break away from any kind of authority.

2. The spirit of Satan re-describes authority figures as dictators or tyrants.

This is in order to legitimize a break away from authority. Please get this message right: The mad man of Gadara symbolizes the highest expression of Satanism in a man. Ultimately, demon activity will make you rebellious![13]

The Scripture clearly states that God sets up authorities. "Every person is to be in subjection to the governing authorities. For there is no authority except from God, and those which exist are established by God" (Romans 13:1 NASB).

3. Demonic activity is often directed against three God-given authorities.

Since the devil is against God, he is also against the authorities that God sets up. Satanic rebels are against God's authority in the church, which is the pastor. Demonic activity is also against the authority in the home, which is the husband. Finally, there is demon activity against the authority of the nation, which is the government. God established all these authorities. No one is wiser than God and we must accept His Word. Like the serpent in the garden, Satan will always challenge the wisdom of God's Word.

a. The Husband's Authority

People inspired by the evil spirit of pride always challenge the legitimacy of the husband's authority in the home. Often, when a wife is influenced by demons, she will reject her husband's authority. Mostly, before people marry, the word of the husband is very important and seen as something to be obeyed and followed.

However, as time progresses and demons infiltrate, the words of the husband are despised and rejected. There is an angry reply to every instruction. There is a rejoinder to every bit of advice. I have watched as certain wives became more and more deceived through familiarity. They think they can no longer be deceived and pushed around by their husbands. Often, the reality is that demons of rebellion are at work.[14]

b. Church Authority

The same thing happens in churches. Deceived church members rise against God's servant, calling him a tyrant and a dictator but they do not know that they are totally deceived. They call for democracy and claim they will no longer tolerate nonsense. Often evil spirits of deception have taken hold of them.

One of the highest kinds of deception in the church is to fight against the pastor. Jesus said, "Judge not." While on earth, we will never see clearly enough to judge correctly. Churches are full of critical and faultfinding people. This is one of the highest kinds of demonic infiltration in the church. Show me a church filled with critical people and I will show you a church filled with demons.

The mad man of Gádara could not be controlled by anyone. In the same way, pastors, husbands or any authority figure cannot control people under demonic control.

c. Governing Authorities

Authorities within the nation must be honoured and respected. Every person is to be in subjection to the governing authorities. Romans 13:1 (New American Standard Version). When Paul wrote his letter to the Romans, Nero, one of the most evil emperors of Rome, governed Rome. Nero was known to offer up Christians to be chewed up by lions. There were times he set Christians ablaze as torches in his garden to lighten up his parties! Yet, Paul said to the Romans that God establishes every authority that exists. In other words, God established Nero.

Commonly, the people who are opposed to authority in a nation are the criminals and the dark side of society. It is in the rebellious underworld of cities that Satanic and demonic activities thrive. Prostitutes, armed robbers, thieves and criminals are just a few examples of those who stand against authority in any nation.

None could bind him, no not with chains! Is that the description of your life? None can lay hands on you? None can be a father to you? None can be a pastor to you? None can be a husband to you? None can bind you, not even with chains!

■ DEPRESSION AND SADNESS

"...he was ... in the tombs, crying,..." (Mark 5:5). Notice that the mad man of Gadara was constantly crying. He was sad, depressed and emotionally distraught.[15] This unfortunate state was caused by the legion of demons in him. It is time for you to believe that a lot of the sorrow we experience is actually caused by evil spirits. If Satan had his way, you would cry everyday! When Satan has his way in your life, sadness is what follows. Unexplained depression is most certainly the work of evil spirits.[16]

It is no surprise that anti-depressant medicines are some of the most used drugs in the world today. The greatest problems of humankind today are not bacteria or viruses but swarms of evil spirits, which invade the hearts and minds of men. It is no wonder that unexplained sadness and sleeplessness afflicts millions.

The mad man of Gadara was a man of tears and sorrows. He was in pain. He was crying constantly. This is the picture of the highest kind of demonic affliction. God is not the author of your sorrows. He is the giver of joy. God is not the one who made the mad man cry. It was a legion of demons, which made him cry. Perhaps, a legion of demons has afflicted your soul. Receive your deliverance as you read this book! May you fall into deep sleep and experience freedom from demonic attacks!

Contrary to what many think, sadness and depression are not just bad feelings. Depression is not just a bad mood. The Bible calls it the spirit of heaviness. "To appoint unto them that mourn in Zion, to give unto them beauty for ashes, the oil of joy for mourning, the garment of praise for THE SPIRIT OF HEAVINESS; that they might be called trees of righteousness, the planting of the LORD, that he might be glorified" (Isaiah 61:3).

Suicidal Tendencies

What makes people so sad that they give up on life and become suicidal? It can only be demons. These things can only be explained by the activity of evil spirits. What is the explanation to the hopelessness that grips the heart of a man with an apparently bright future? It is time for us to know the source of the problem and tackle it at its root. Do not forget that it was the legion of demons that made the mad man cry. Perhaps evil spirits are making you depressed and sorrowful. Receive your deliverance today in the name of Jesus!

■ DEMONS BRING ABOUT DISGRACE

"...and ware no clothes, neither abode in any house,..." (Luke 8:27). It was the legion of demons that made the mad man walk around naked. Walking around naked in public is one of the highest forms of disgrace.[17]

There are two types of demonic plans. There are short-term plans and long-term plans. It is important for every believer to get a revelation of the long-term plan of the enemy against your life and ministry. Recently, the Lord led me to pray about the things Satan was planning against me. You may not know it, but the enemy is planning and taking decisions about you.

Look around carefully and you will see many who were once financially blessed but are now broke. I know people who once had millions of dollars but today have little or no money. The spirit of disgrace is working against prosperous Christians to bring them to naught. If you are a businessman, it is important to pray about the wealth and establishment that God has given to you.

Many ministers were once men of renown. Today, many of these have been silenced and disgraced. This is the work of demons. Many tele-evangelists of America have been disgraced and set aside. A closer look at the American experience will reveal that there was a long-term hidden agenda behind the attacks on God's servants. Psychics have now replaced these evangelists. It was the long-term agenda of the devil to replace God's servants with fortunetellers and soothsayers.

The spirit of disgrace was actually the spirit of Satan fighting the servants of God.

DEMONS CAUSE PHYSICAL CHANGES IN HUMAN BEINGS

"...had been often bound with fetters and chains,...and NO MAN HAD STRENGTH TO TAME HIM" (Mark 5:4 ASV)

"And there were seven sons of one Sceva, a Jew, and chief of the priests, which did so. And the evil spirit answered and said, Jesus I know, and Paul I know; but who are ye? And the MAN IN WHOM THE EVIL SPIRIT WAS LEAPED ON THEM, AND OVERCAME THEM, and PREVAILED AGAINST THEM, so that they fled out of that house naked and wounded" (Acts 19:14-16).

From these two testimonies, we see that the presence of demons gave unnatural human strength. One mad man was able to beat up seven men. That is supernatural strength.[18]

1. Demons give unnatural human strength.

The mad man of Gadara was able to break chains. It is not natural to be able to break chains with your bare hands. Even the weight-lifting champions do not break chains with their bare hands.

This principle provides a very important revelation of the effect that evil spirits have on our physical lives.

2. Sickness can be caused by the presence of evil spirits in your body.

Evil spirits want to inhabit a human body so that they can affect the person physically. When you open your life to evil spirits, they can fasten themselves to your body and cause illness.[19]

I read two powerful testimonies from one of Kenneth Hagin's books, which illustrate this principle perfectly. In one of them, a twenty-three year old woman suffering from cancer of the lungs was healed when the demon was cast away. She had been brought to a meeting that Reverend Hagin was holding in a certain town, to be prayed for.

As Kenneth Hagin laid hands on her, he suddenly was enveloped in a glory cloud and he saw a little creature which looked like a monkey hanging onto a tree limb, on the outside of the woman's body. This monkey-like creature was holding on to the woman's left lung where the cancer had started.

Reverend Hagin commanded the demon to leave but it refused to go. Then Kenneth Hagin commanded it to leave in the name of the Lord Jesus Christ and it fell off the lady's body. It whimpered, and whined and shook like a beaten pup. Then Kenneth Hagin commanded it to leave the premises and he saw this creature run out of the aisle and walk out of the door. This lady was completely healed afterwards.

That same week she went to see the doctors and they told her that her lungs had been completely healed and marvelled, asking her how it happened. In the second testimony, a pastor's wife with cancer of the breast was healed as an evil spirit came out of her. The cancer had started in the lady's left breast and had spread to her lymph glands. By the time she got to the doctor, it was too late and they could not do anything for her.

Kenneth Hagin went with his wife and another pastor to pray for her. They continued praying for this lady for two days and two nights. Suddenly, the Holy Spirit told them to go and stand at the head of the bed and command the spirit of doubt and fear to leave. The moment Kenneth Hagin did that, he saw a great black bat, twice as big as a man's hand, just rise up from that dying woman's left breast and fly out of the window.

The woman instantly rose up completely healed. She praised God and danced all over the house. She was totally delivered and set free.[20] Is it not amazing how the presence of a demon can cause cancer?

3. Demons cause epilepsy

"And one of the multitude answered and said, Master, I have brought unto thee my son, which hath a dumb spirit; And wheresoever he taketh him, he teareth him: and he foameth, and gnasheth with his teeth, and pineth away: and I spake to thy disciples that they should cast him out; and they could not. He answereth him, and saith, O faithless generation, how long shall I be with you? how long shall I suffer you? bring him unto me. And they brought him unto him: and when he saw him, STRAIGHTWAY THE SPIRIT TARE HIM; AND HE FELL ON THE GROUND, AND WALLOWED FOAMING. And he asked his father, How long is it ago since this came unto him? And he said, Of a child. And ofttimes it hath cast him into the fire, and into the waters, to destroy him: but if thou canst do any thing, have compassion on us, and help us. Jesus said unto him, If thou canst believe, all things are possible to him that believeth.

And straightway the father of the child cried out, and said with tears, Lord, I believe; help thou mine unbelief. When Jesus saw that the people came running together, he rebuked the foul spirit, saying unto him, Thou dumb and deaf spirit, I charge thee, come out of him, and enter no more into him. And the spirit cried, and rent him sore, and came out of him: and he was as one dead; insomuch that many said, He is dead. But Jesus took him by the hand, and lifted him up; and he arose. And when he was come into the house, his disciples asked him privately, Why could not we cast him out? And he said unto them, This kind can come forth by nothing, but by prayer and fasting" (Mark 9:17-29).

The presence of the evil spirit made the young man experience chronic convulsions. The evil spirit made him throw himself into the fire. The presence of evil spirits causes all kinds of physical illnesses. Evil spirits can cause barrenness! Evil spirits cause cancers! Evil spirits cause heart diseases! Evil spirits cause mental illnesses![21] You should always deal with evil spirits as led by the Spirit of God.

4. Screaming and rolling

Some people do not understand why people writhe and scream when demons are going out of them. But the Scripture shows that as Philip ministered, evil spirits came out screaming.

"Then Philip went down to the city of Samaria, and preached Christ unto them. And the people with one accord gave heed unto those things which Philip spake, hearing and seeing the miracles which he did. FOR UNCLEAN SPIRITS, CRYING WITH LOUD VOICE, came out of many that were possessed with them: and many taken with palsies, and that were lame, were healed. And there was great joy in that city" (Acts 8:5-8). Screaming and rolling over, are common biblical occurrences. They are signs of evil spirits going out of human beings.[22]

There are other physical manifestations of the presence of evil spirits.

5. Some evil spirits cause an accentuation of lustful behaviour.

Some people under the influence of evil spirits, are trapped in extreme lustful and immoral behaviour. An unnatural desire and practice of sexuality leads them into all kinds of experiences.

The prophets bewailed Babylon because she had become the habitation of evil spirits. When these evil spirits inhabited Babylon what happened? She committed fornication, lived deliciously, and glorified herself.

"And he cried mightily with a strong voice, saying, Babylon the great is fallen, is fallen, and is become the habitation of devils, and the hold of every foul spirit, and a cage of every unclean and hateful bird. How much she hath glorified herself, and LIVED DELICIOUSLY, so much torment and sorrow give her: for she saith in her heart, I sit a queen, and am no widow, and shall see no sorrow. And the kings of the earth, WHO HAVE COMMITTED FORNI-CATION AND LIVED

DELICIOUSLY WITH HER, shall bewail her, and lament for her, when they shall see the smoke of her burning" (Revelation 18:2,7,9). Babylon is described as a hold for every unclean bird. It is described as a woman who has become the habitation of foul spirits.[23]

But how did these evil spirits come into her in the first place? The Bible gives us the answer. It explains that these evil spirits came because many people drank from the wine of her fornication.

Evil spirits inhabit men and women who give themselves over to fornication with multiple partners (the nations). These evil spirits inhabit the individuals and cause them to live deliciously (immorally) for a season of their lives. Often when these individuals become older and less sexually active, the evil spirits leave them for other younger candidates. Many of these individuals would never reveal the depth to which these lustful spirits have taken them. The pleasurable lifestyles of some nations are often a manifestation of demons in those countries.[24]

6. EVIL SPIRITS SOMETIMES CAUSE THE PHYSICAL APPEARANCE OF DIRT AND UNDERDEVELOPMENT.

This is characteristic of certain nations, where the people are resistant to all forms of improvement.

7. UNRELENTING WARS IN MANY NATIONS ALSO SHOW DEMON ACTIVITY.

Dear Christian friend, evil spirits do have an effect on your physical body. These effects may influence you to indulge in fleshly sins or to be violent. Evil spirits may also cause strange illnesses to fasten themselves onto a believer. The time of ignorance is past. We are no longer ignorant of the wiles of the devil.

The Nature of Demons

32

■ DEMONS WORK IN GROUPS AND TEAMS

"...Legion: for we are many" (Mark 5:9).As you can see, a band of demons afflicted the mad man of Gadara. The word "legion" means, "a band, a crowd, a host or a multitude". The mad man's condition was not caused by a single demon but by a team of evil spirits working together. The word "legion", is very revealing as it aptly describes the group nature of demonic activities. Teams of evil spirits carry out most of Satan's plans. That is why the demons answered,"...legion, for we are many."

TEN COMMON DEMONIC TEAMS

Rarely do you find demons working in isolation. There is often a complicated network of evil spirits involved in any evil situation.[1] When there is confusion in the church, you can hardly put your finger on a single cause: Is it jealousy? Is it hatred? Is it disloyalty? Is it carnality?

1. The Marriage Spoiling Team

Counselling with couples often reveals a complex array of insolvable problems. No one even knows the beginning or end of the problems. It may have begun as selfishness, continued as rudeness, anger and pride. Offences pile up and lead to bitterness and unforgiveness. The unforgiveness leads to revenge, unfaithfulness, adultery, hatred, fighting, murder and divorce. As you can see, the problems do not come in isolation. They come in groups. They come as an intricate cocktail of demonic activity. It is important to know about some of the teams of demons that commonly work together. When you understand this principle, you will know what to expect and how to deal with the enemy. "...and taketh with himself seven other spirits more wicked than himself,..." (Matthew 12:45).

2. The Stealing Team

The spirit of lying and stealing often go together. Thieves usually tell lies because they need to cover up their activities. Spirits of envy, hatred and murder often work together. The Bible teaches that Jesus Christ was crucified because of envy. "For he knew that the chief priests had delivered him FOR ENVY" (Mark 15:10).

3. The Future Spoiling Team

When a young man or woman who is full of life destroys himself through lust, drunkenness, gambling and drugs, the spirits of poverty, criminal activity and prostitution find their way into these people. This is why it is difficult to extract drug users and prostitutes from their complex array of problems.

4. The sex team

When a young person is deeply involved with multiple sexual partners, hosts of demons often flood the person. The book of Revelation declares that Babylon had become the habitation of devils because of her multiple fornications. "And he cried mightily with a strong voice, saying, Babylon the great is fallen, is fallen, and IS BECOME THE HABITATION OF DEVILS, and the hold of every foul spirit, and a cage of every unclean and hateful bird. FOR (BECAUSE) ALL NATIONS HAVE DRUNK OF THE WINE OF THE WRATH OF HER FORNICATION, and the kings of the earth have committed fornication with her, and the merchants of the earth are waxed rich through the abundance of her delicacies" (Revelation 18:2-3).

The spirits of disobedience and rebellion take root. Spirits of licentiousness, abortion and barrenness follow these. Other common members of the sex team are the spirits of HIV Aids, which work closely with the spirit of death.

5. The divorce team

Spirits of deception and divorce often move together. Most people who divorce are deceived into thinking that there is someone better than their spouse out there. This is the commonest deception in the hearts of many couples. This is why a large percentage of people who divorce remarry the same person.

6. The nation spoiling team

The problems of any country can rarely be diagnosed as emanating from a single cause. Are the problems due to a spirit of corruption, bad leadership, deception or discrimination? The spirits of poverty, sickness and death often flow together. In countries where there is a lot of poverty, there is a lot of sickness and a high mortality rate. An example of demonic teamwork is found in the book of Revelation:

"And I saw, and behold A WHITE HORSE: and he that sat on him had a bow; and a crown was given unto him: and he went forth conquering, and to conquer. And when he had opened the second seal, I heard the second beast say, Come and see. And there went out another HORSE THAT WAS RED: and power was given to him that sat thereon to take peace from the earth, and that they should kill one another: and there was given unto him a great sword. And when he had opened the third seal, I heard the third beast say, Come and see. And I beheld, and lo a BLACK HORSE; and he that sat on him had a pair of balances in his hand. And I heard a voice in the midst of the four beasts say, A measure of wheat for a penny, and three measures of barley for a penny; and see thou hurt not the oil and the wine. And I looked, and behold a PALE HORSE: and his name that sat on him was Death, and Hell followed with him. And power was given unto them over the fourth part of the earth, to kill with sword, and with hunger, and with death, and with the beasts of the earth" (Revelation 6:2-6, 8).

In this vision, four spiritual horses with four spiritual riders were seen. First, there was a white horse, then a red horse, then a black horse and finally a pale horse. Each of these horses had a different rider. The first to be introduced was the spirit of a conqueror. The second spirit was the spirit that takes peace away. And the third spirit was the spirit of famine in which three measures of barley were sold for a penny. The fourth was the spirit of death. One after another, these four spirits ravaged the earth until a quarter of the earth was killed with the sword and with hunger. You do not have to be very old to have seen this pattern. Let me give you a few examples:

a. Liberia 1990

Some years ago, Charles Taylor in Liberia, came forth conquering and to conquer. His aim was to remove President Doe from power. There was great excitement, as he seemed to be the liberator of Liberia.[2] Then came forth the second rider whose power was to take away peace. It is interesting to note that peace has never returned to Liberia since this man began his conquest. For the last ten years, there has been no electricity in that country. Various rebel groups have ravaged the countryside, taking away the peace. Famine set in. That is the third rider at work. As you watch television, you will see humanitarian groups airlifting tons and tons of food aid.

Finally, the spirit of death engulfs the region and we hear of mass graves and thousands of people losing their lives. Demons truly do work in groups.

b. Congo 1997

In The Congo, we had a similar situation. The late Kabila came forth conquering and to conquer. He marched on Kinshasa to overthrow President Mobutu. No sooner had he accomplished this feat than we heard of various rebel factions fighting within the country. It was now the turn of the second rider to take away peace. The republic became the cradle of one of the largest civil wars of Africa.

Several countries participated in this conflict and peace was taken away from the earth. We all watched CNN as the humanitarian groups airlifted tons and tons of food to dying refugees. This was the third team rider at work. The pattern is frighteningly similar. Finally, the mass graves and the death toll were announced. Indeed, all the four riders had effectively worked together again.

7. The Church Spoiling Team

In the church, the spirits of slander, backbiting, criticism, pride, self-righteousness, judgemental attitudes, disloyalty and church splits collaborate closely. They encircle churches and invade from different angles. Soon the church is embroiled in one conflict or another. It is no wonder that many churches cannot grow. Jesus taught that when an evil spirit is cast out, he recruits a larger team. A seven-member team of demons will succeed where only one failed.

"Then goeth he, and taketh with himself SEVEN OTHER SPIRITS more wicked than himself, and they enter and dwell there: and the last state of that man is worse than the first. Even so shall it be also unto this wicked generation" (Matthew 12:45).

8. The Depression Team

Spirits of broken-heartedness, disappointments, depression, suicide and death also team up quite often. This is why Paul advised the Corinthians not to be too sorrowful. He explained that the sorrow of the world leads to death. The spirits of sorrow, despair and death often work together. The mad man of Gadara shows us the ultimate desire of demons: to inhabit human beings in large groups.

9. The Quarrelling Team

A quarrelsome person is usually also proud, stubborn, cantankerous, divorce-prone and deceived. All these make up an effective team of evil spirits that work to destroy an individual.

10. The Insecurity Team

The spirits of insecurity, fear, accusations, selfishness, self-preservation and hatred also work well together. Like partners in an effective team, they often compliment each other. May your eyes be opened to see the group of evil spirits that is unleashed against your life and ministry!

It is important for every minister to have a revelation of the group of evil spirits that are working against him. Some of the problems of ministry are complicated and have several dimensions to them. Without a revelation of what is fighting you, you will find it hard to win your spiritual battle. The Bible calls Satan the "father of lies" and that "old serpent which deceiveth the whole world" (John 8:44; Revelation 12:9).

DEMONS: TERRITORIAL BY NATURE

"...he besought him much that he would NOT SEND THEM AWAY OUT OF THE COUNTRY" (Mark 5:10). This very unusual request of the demons puzzled me for many years. Why did they say, "Don't send us out of this country?" The demons could have requested a little more time to stay in the mad man. They could have asked not to be cast out in the first place. However, what seemed to concern them was their need to stay in that same country.

This teaches us an important lesson: Demons inhabit particular countries and do not want to move away. These particular demons lived in the country of the Gadarenes and wanted to stay there.

1. Principalities denote an evil influence that reigns over a territory.

One class of demons described in Ephesians is "principalities". It is not difficult to see the influence of different kinds of spirits in different areas in the world. "For we wrestle not against flesh and blood, but against PRINCIPALITIES, against powers, against the rulers of the darkness of this world, against spiritual wickedness in high places" (Ephesians 6:12).

In Matthew 12, the demons that were cast out declared, "I will return to my house." Unfortunately, demons have made certain places their homes. None of us would like to be dislodged from our usual habitat. Demons have usual habitats too.

2. There are spirits of poverty, which occupy certain parts of the world.

You can see the dirty and impoverished roads and houses in areas where these evil spirits occupy. There is often no logical reason why these nations should be the way they are. The only explanation must be evil spirits.

3. The spirit of war rests over certain parts of the world.

The beginnings of the First World War, the Second World War and the Serbian war, (which have been three of the largest conflicts to hit the world), had something to do with the Serbian region.

4. Evil spirits need places where they are comfortable.

In Matthew 12:43, demons are described as needing resting places. Demons are also shown to walk through dry places. A dry place speaks of a hostile and unwelcoming environment in which no rest can be found. These are places where demons have no rest.

I believe that Satan does not live in Africa but in Europe. Most Africans believe in God. Today in Europe, it is the Africans who fill the churches. I believe that Satan has his seat (his place of greatest victory and relaxation) in Europe. It is in Europe that deception is strongest. Most indigenous Europeans do not believe in God, in Christ or even in the existence of the devil. How comforting that must be for Satan! Europe is a place where he can call home. Your home is where you lay down to rest. Your home is where you sit down to relax and feel safe.

Do you think that Satan feels safe in Africa when meetings are organized to bind him in almost every neighbourhood? Do you think the devil can relax when people are so conscious that he is around? When songs are composed and chanted against you by thousands of people, you will not feel happy. Satan feels threatened in Africa. Read the words of a typical song sung in African churches: "In the Word of God, there is power! In the Name of Jesus, every knee shall bow!"

5. The devil is not omnipresent. He is in one place at a time.

a. In Bible times, John identified the home and seat of the devil.

He wrote a letter that revealed that Satan's home was in a city called Pergamos. "And to the angel of the church in Pergamos write; These things saith he which hath the sharp sword with two edges; I know thy works, and where thou dwellest, even WHERE SATAN'S SEAT IS: and thou holdest fast my name, and hast not denied my faith, even in those days wherein Antipas was my faithful martyr, who was slain among you, WHERE SATAN DWELLETH" (Revelation 2:12,13). As you can see, this Scripture tells us that Satan both lived and sat (was at ease) in Pergamos.

One night, I was returning home from a meeting and I put on the radio. It was midnight and there were two young men praying on the air. They were having an all-night prayer meeting in the studio. They spoke mostly in tongues and shouted their prayers to God from the bottom of their hearts. One groaned like a bear whilst the other roared like a lion throughout the night. I thought to myself, "The prince of the power of the air will not like this at all." I said to my wife, "Satan can never live in Ghana!" I knew that a programme like this could never be aired in Europe.

In the letter to the church in Pergamos we learned that Satan had his seat there. This teaches us that Satan was actually headquartered in Pergamos. There are cities that are known for immorality. If you end up in any of these places, watch out because the spirit of the city will be gunning for you.

b. Principalities love to dominate areas with their evil presence.

In Ghana for instance, there are certain harbour cities, which are well known for their immorality. Nigeria is well known to have spirits of corruption, assassination and armed robbery.

There are certain regions in Ghana that are known for their quarrelling and cantankerous nature. Evil spirits of offence drive people in these areas to quarrel all the way into their graves without ever letting up. Other sections are known for witchcraft and voodoo. Some parts of the country are known for their violence and murderous tendencies. These are works of evil spirits, which have lived in these areas for many years.

There are even sections of the road, which are inhabited by evil spirits. Spirits of accident and tragedy inhabit trees along the road. Many mysterious and inexplicable accidents have occurred at these spots. These are the works of evil spirits that dwell in certain geographical locations.

When you come into a new house, you must always sanctify it. Evil spirits dwell in various locations. For instance, a spirit of divorce may have been dwelling in a house that you have just moved into. Inexplicable quarrels may begin to occur in your marriage after you move into that apartment.

I have known of people who had happy marriages until they moved to certain countries. Thereafter their marriages deteriorated rapidly. I said to a divorcee friend, "Perhaps you wouldn't have divorced if you hadn't come to this country."

He said to me, "I agree with you 100%; this would never have happened if I had stayed in my home country." He continued. "In my country divorce is unusual but here, even pastors divorce easily."

Whenever I enter a hotel room, I pray and sanctify it before I settle in. Sometimes I lay hands on the bed and cast evil spirits out of the ceiling. No one knows what has gone on in that room before I came there. When you move into a new physical location, it is your spiritual duty to assess what kind of spiritual presence pertains.

WORSHIPPING CHRISTIANS AND DEMON ACTIVITY

"...when he saw Jesus ... he ... worshipped him" (Mark 5:6). The mad man of Gadara ran to Jesus and worshipped Him. A few minutes later, this mad man was resisting his deliverance. This is a mystery, which must be understood. It seems that it is possible for demons to invade a godly man and be compatible.[3]

I asked myself, "How can these two extreme forces be compatible? How can a man with a legion of demons worship God?" The man with a legion of demons was a worshipper of Christ Jesus. "How can a man who runs to Jesus be full of demons?"

Today, how many Christians run to worship the Lord? They come strolling into church saying in their minds, "You are lucky I came to church today!" But not so with the mad man of Gadara; he ran to Jesus! This phenomenon explains how many Christians come to church every Sunday and yet have evil spirits influencing them at home and at work.[4]

1. A Worshipper with Demons

The man in the synagogue was another worshipper who had a demon. The demon was exposed as the preaching came forth. "And there was in their synagogue a man with an unclean spirit; and he cried out, Saying, Let us alone; what have we to do with thee, thou Jesus of Nazareth? art thou come to destroy us? I know thee who thou art, the Holy One of God" (Mark 1:23-24). As you can see, churchgoers and worshippers may have evil spirits in them.

2. Satan and the Apostle

The Apostle Peter was moved by the Holy Spirit to say that Jesus was the Christ, the Son of God. Yet a few minutes later, Satan was rebuked in his life. In a surprising and stunning turn, gentle Jesus turned into a Jesus of steel and said, " Satan get thee behind me."

"And Simon Peter answered and said, Thou art the Christ, the Son of the living God. And Jesus answered and said unto him, BLESSED ART THOU, SIMON BAR-JONA: FOR FLESH AND BLOOD HATH NOT REVEALED IT UNTO THEE, but my Father which is in heaven.

Then Peter took him, and began to rebuke him, saying, Be it far from thee, Lord: this shall not be unto thee. But he turned, and SAID UNTO PETER, GET THEE BEHIND ME, SATAN: thou art an offence unto me: for thou savourest not the things that be of God, but those that be of men" (Matthew 16:16-17,22-23).

3. Samson the Judge

Samson is another example of someone who had the Spirit of God moving in him. "And the woman bare a son, and CALLED HIS NAME SAMSON: and the child grew, and the LORD blessed him. AND THE SPIRIT OF THE LORD BEGAN TO MOVE HIM..." (Judges 13:24-25).

Unfortunately, this did not stop the spirit of fornication from operating in his ministry. This phenomenon explains how some ministers seem to be very anointed and also troubled by evil spirits. Some prophets have amazing gifts and yet are subject to the influence of evil spirits.

DEMONS OPERATE FROM A SPIRITUAL DISTANCE AND NOT A PHYSICAL DISTANCE

The confusion over the apparent compatibility of the Holy Spirit and the forces of darkness can be explained by this principle. When something is physically close it does not mean that it is spiritually close by. In other words, one thousand miles of distance in the natural does not mean one thousand miles in the spirit. Something may be next door in the natural but thousands of spiritual miles away. This is why someone can be close to a spiritual person but not be affected by the anointing on his life. He is physically close but spiritually far away! Someone else may be thousands of miles away and receive a greater blessing than someone nearby.

Jesus said, "A prophet is not accepted in his own home." This means that the gifts of the prophets are unable to spiritually affect people who are nearby. The prophet's gift and anointing seems to work on people who are physically further from him. Somehow familiarity increases the spiritual distance between the anointed and the one who has to receive the anointing. "And they were offended in him. But Jesus said unto them, A prophet is not without honour, save in his own country, and in his own house" (Matthew 13:57).

I find that the anointing of the Lord flows more easily from my life into the lives of people who are further away from me physically. Many who are near in the natural are far in the spirit. This proves the theory that spiritual distance and natural distance are different things.

1. There is something like distance in the realm of the spirit.

Jesus once said to a man who came to Him, "You are not far from the Kingdom." "And when Jesus saw that he answered discreetly, he said unto him, THOU ART NOT FAR FROM THE KINGDOM OF GOD..." (Mark 12:34).

This saying proves that you can be far or near to the Kingdom. Other Scriptures speak of drawing near to God. Drawing near to God is not a physical thing. God is a spirit, and cannot be approached by any physical or natural manoeuver. Sitting next to the man of God does not make you near to him spiritually. In fact, someone sitting six thousand miles away may be closer than you sitting at his feet.

"Blessed is the man whom thou choosest, and causest to approach unto thee, that he may dwell in thy courts: we shall be satisfied with the goodness of thy house, even of thy holy temple" (Psalm 65:4). This Scripture speaks of the blessing of a man who is allowed to approach God. God chooses those He will allow to come near. Some people are nearer to God than others! We may all be physically located in New York City, but God's close friends and servants may be only five spiritual metres away from the presence of God. Whereas another Christian, also in New York City may be five thousand miles from the presence of God.

2. Spiritual distance from demonic influence depends on whether or not a person is open to such influence.

Being physically near to a shrine or a witch's house does not mean you are near to these evil things in the spirit. You are spiritually far from them unless you open yourself up to them. Give no place to the devil! The same person can be filled with the spirit of God and within a few minutes be controlled by evil spirits. This happens because within a few minutes, this same person may move very far spiritually although he is physically in the same position. This is what happened to Peter and it explains how Jesus called him "the rock" and a few minutes later called him "Satan".

The Minister Operating by Evil Powers

I remember reading a story about a minister of God switching between two spirits, from a book by Kenneth Hagin. Kenneth Hagin said that he was holding a meeting in a certain city and staying in the home of a wealthy businessman who was a member of the church where he was ministering. This man owned a shopping centre and was extremely successful in business.

The businessman asked Kenneth Hagin whether he knew a certain brother who was also a minister. Kenneth Hagin said that he knew about the man and was convinced that he was called of God and walked uprightly before God in the ministry, until he began yielding to wrong spirits. The businessman told Kenneth Hagin that their church had helped sponsor this minister in a meeting in their town and that nearly everyday, this minister would come into his office and they would talk or go out to lunch.

This businessman had an heirloom; a seven-carat diamond ring, that he had inherited from his father, which he seldom ever wore. He had wrapped it in a handkerchief in the back right corner of the chest of drawers in his bedroom.

This minister of God went into the businessman's office and told him about this heirloom given to the businessman by his father. He described in detail to the businessman where the heirloom was kept and told him that God wanted the heirloom given to him.. The businessman had naturally thought it was from God because it was supernatural knowledge, and consequently he had given the heirloom to the minister.

But this businessman had been worried about the fact that this minister of God had started cursing when someone had made him cross in his office. Moreover shortly after he had left town, two men had approached him that while the minister was in town, he had been involved in homosexuality.

He had been angry with himself for giving his heirloom to someone he thought was not even walking with God.

Reverend Hagin said in his book that the spirit of God had whispered to him that this man of God was operating in occult powers and familiar spirits when he later met him at a meeting. This minister had in the past had a marvellous healing ministry with some of his supernatural healings attested to by medical doctors. He had however yielded to the flesh and opened himself up to the devil.[5]

As you can see from this story, the man of God was operating by the Holy Spirit and then by familiar spirits.

The Strategy of Demons

33

■ DEMONIC INFLUENCE BY MEANS OF IMAGINATIONS, THOUGHT PROCESSES AND SUGGESTIONS

"Casting down IMAGINATIONS, and every ...THOUGHT ..." (2 Corinthians 10:5). Satan's entry into our lives is through the power of suggestion.[1] When Jesus was attacked by Satan in the wilderness, He had to defend Himself against clever suggestions. The suggestions of demons come in three categories; three categories of common satanic attacks.

1. Type 1 Suggestion: The suggestion to yield to fleshly desires.

"And the devil said unto him, If thou be the Son of God, command this stone that it BE MADE BREAD" (Luke 4:3). We are constantly urged by the voice of Satan to succumb to our flesh.

Jesus was hungry after forty days of fasting. The devil urged Him to follow His flesh. The voice that urges you to sleep on, to break your fast and to do immoral things is the voice of Satan. Do not be deceived; this is the first and basic entry point of demons into your life.

2. Type 2 Suggestion: The suggestion to worship and serve something other than God.

This is also a suggestion to choose the quick and easy route to your goal. "And the devil said unto him, All this power will I give thee, and the glory of them: for that is delivered unto me; and to whomsoever I will I give it. If thou therefore wilt worship me, all shall be thine" (Luke 4:6-7).

Countless Christians are urged to live for money and other earthly achievements. It is the voice of no other than Satan which urges you to spend your life, your time, your energy and your money on everything but God's work. Some people think that what I am saying is too strong. But Satan hides in the darkness and uses Christians and righteous looking people to do his work.

Remember when Peter said to Jesus, "You will not die on this terrible cross; we will do everything to prevent you from having such an unpleasant experience?" That was the first and only time Jesus rebuked him publicly. Unfortunately, decent Peter had been used by Satan to suggest the need for self-preservation. Jesus showed us that men's craving for self-preservation is of the devil. "...Then Peter took him, and began to rebuke him, saying, Be it far from thee, Lord: this shall not be unto thee. But he turned, and SAID UNTO PETER, GET THEE BEHIND ME, SATAN: thou art an offence unto me: FOR THOU SAVOUREST NOT THE THINGS THAT BE OF GOD, BUT THOSE THAT BE OF

MEN" (Matthew 16:21-23). The things that men value are often things that are not of God. God is urging you to die for Him. We must have the character of Christ; we must take up our crosses and follow Jesus to Calvary. We must embrace the plan of God and not follow the deceptions of Satan.

Die Like a Lamb or Die Like a Pig?

Christ died with the calmness of a lamb; He embraced the will of God with peace. Most Christians die for the Lord like pigs: with a lot of squealing and reluctance. We reluctantly embrace the will of God with a lot of squealing, screaming and resistance. Receive the lamb-like nature of our Saviour, Jesus Christ!

3. Type 3 Suggestion: The suggestion to misuse the gifts and blessings of God.

"And he brought him to Jerusalem, and set him on a pinnacle of the temple, and said unto him, If thou be the Son of God, cast thyself down from hence: For it is written, He shall give his angels charge over thee, to keep thee" (Luke 4:9-10). Jesus had the power to use the gift of God to protect Himself. Was He going to misuse this power at the suggestion of demons? Certainly not!

This common category of suggestion seeks to make you misuse whatever God has placed in your hand. God has given some of us spiritual gifts, callings, money, talents, education, contacts, power and influence. Most people with these gifts from God misuse them. Satan cleverly suggests that we use our God-given blessings on anything other than the will of God. This is why many blessed Christians do not support the work of God whole-heartedly but they support their own lives! This also explains why many men of God deviate from the call and misuse the gift of God. The power of suggestion seems weak and insignificant but this is the principal access route of demons.

The Pastor's Wife

I read a vision about a pastor's wife who received a type one suggestion from the devil. Jesus appeared to Kenneth Hagin and talked to him extensively on the subject of demons and demon possession. Kenneth Hagin saw in the spirit realm, a woman he recognized but did not know personally. She was a pastor's wife with a great singing ability, who was in the ministry with her husband. Kenneth Hagin saw in the spirit, what looked like a little monkey sitting on the shoulder of this pastor's wife and whispering in her ear. The demon told her she was a beautiful woman who had been robbed in life and that if she were in the world, she would have fame, fortune and popularity. The woman recognized the thought as devilish and as she rebuked the devil , the little monkey jumped off her shoulder and run off.

Jesus narrated that the demon returned repeatedly to sit on the woman's shoulder to whisper the same thing to her. Each time, she would rebuke the devil and it would leave. Kenneth Hagin saw this happen in the vision.

Jesus told Kenneth Hagin that the pastor's wife then began to think Satan's thoughts until she was obsessed with them: that she was beautiful and had been cheated in life. Kenneth Hagin saw in the spirit that the body of the pastor's wife became transparent as if it were made of glass. He saw a black dot in her head about the size of a half-dollar coin. Jesus explained to him that before, the devil oppressed this woman from outside but as she listened to the devil she became obsessed with the devil's thoughts. Eventually, she left her husband and went off with another man. She went from one man to another until at a time she had been with five different men.

As the vision continued, Kenneth Hagin saw a minister of God, at a hotel where the pastor's wife was lodging with another man. He had gone there to reconcile her back to her husband. In the vision, Kenneth Hagin found himself appearing in the hallway by this minister when he knocked on the door of a hotel room. He saw pastor's wife come to the door almost naked. She drove away the minister saying that she knew what he had come for and that she did not want to have anything to do with Jesus.

When she spoke, Kenneth Hagin saw in the spirit that big black dot in her head, move from her head down inside of her, into her heart and down into her spirit. Jesus told Kenneth Hagin that at that point, the woman had become possessed with that devil. What the devil had originally brought to this woman as a suggestion, embedded itself in her mind, and eventually possessed her heart and spirit. This illustrates how Satan used the power of suggestion until this woman was totally destroyed.[2]

Right and Wrong Thinking

This is why the Bible teaches exactly what we must think about. The mind is the battlefield for your soul. When the wrong thoughts become established in your mind, you suffer from deceptions and delusions. Satan then uses these delusions to destroy you.

It is important to constantly cast down imaginations that are contrary to the will of God. "(For the weapons of our warfare are not carnal, but mighty through God to the pulling down of strong holds)" (2 Corinthians 10:4).

You must also control the pattern of thinking in your mind. Your thoughts must pass the Philippians 4:8 test before they are allowed to stay. "Finally, brethren, whatsoever things are true, whatsoever things are honest, whatsoever things are just, whatsoever things are pure, whatsoever things are lovely, whatsoever things are of good report; if there be any virtue, and if there be any praise, think on these things" (Philippians 4:8). Thoughts are like birds, they can fly over your head. But you can prevent them from building their nests over your head.

■ DEMONS ARE PERSISTENT

"And when the devil had ended all the temptation, HE DEPARTED FROM HIM FOR A SEASON" (Luke 4:13). Satan is a very persistent being. In the temptation of Jesus, he left the Lord only for a season. Any time you are dealing with a demonic attack, you must be aware of this nature of persistence. You must counteract it with an even more persistent determination to be free.

1. Jesus was tempted in the wilderness to take a short cut to His ministry.

Satan asked Jesus to bow down and worship him so that he would give Him the whole world. It was a quick way to win the whole world, instead of having to suffer. Some years later, Satan came through Peter and opposed the idea of suffering on the cross.

"From that time forth began Jesus to shew unto his disciples, how that he must go unto Jerusalem, and suffer many things of the elders and chief priests and scribes, and be killed, and be raised again the third day. Then Peter took him, and began to rebuke him, saying, Be it far from thee, Lord: this shall not be unto thee" (Matthew 16:21-22).

Once again, Jesus had to rebuke Satan. Even later, Pontius Pilate asked Jesus, "Do you not know that I have the ability to set you free?" "Then saith Pilate unto him, Speakest thou not unto me? knowest thou not that I have power to crucify thee, and have power to release thee?" (John 19:10). This was another suggestion that Jesus could avoid the cross.

Even while Christ was on the cross, men wagged their heads and suggested that He came down from the cross to prove that He is the Son of God. "Likewise also the chief priests mocking said among themselves with the scribes, He saved others; himself he cannot save. Let Christ the King of Israel descend now from the cross, that we may see and believe. And they that were crucified with him reviled him" (Mark 15:31-32).

Satan never gave up until Jesus died. Satan will never give up until you and I are dead. You may be seventy years old but he may still try to deceive you.

2. We are dealing with a persistent enemy.

God has given us the tenacity of a mountain goat, the eye of an eagle, the heart of a lion, the endurance of a camel, the strength of a horse and the steadfastness of a shark! We are more than able to resist the onslaught of the devil.

Someone asked me when he would be free from the devil's attacks. I said to him, "Only when you are dead." He was shocked but that is the truth.

In my own life and ministry, I have watched as Satan has persisted in his attacks against my life. Satan has been relentless and unyielding in his onslaught. He shamelessly returns with the same problem after a season of respite. Sometimes he gives the problem a new look but it is the same problem repackaged and represented. Don't let the persistent nature of problems discourage you. That is the nature of the enemy we are dealing with. Rise up with the tenacity of a mountain goat, and prevail over your enemy today.

■ SNAKES AND PASTORS

Unfortunately, demons have also infiltrated the ranks of pastors and Christian leadership. There are certain spirits that greatly affect ministers. Please take note of this list of demons commonly found working among pastors and Christian leaders. It will help us all to identify and resist the enemy within our ranks.

1. Self-Promotion
2. Lust
3. Pride
4. Insecurity
5. The Fear of Man
6. Jealousy
7. Bitterness
8. Religion
9. Tradition
10. The Spirit of Discouragement
11. Depression

It is amazing how Satan creeps into our midst and works against the ministry. In the book of Job, we read how Satan came into the midst of the gathering of the sons of God. Satan has always wanted to be in the midst of the brethren to accuse, to divide and to deceive. His desire is to dwell amongst us and cause confusion. His title "accuser in the midst of the brethren", is most apt. He is able to turn the closest of friends against each other.

"Now there was a day when the sons of God came to present themselves before the LORD, and SATAN CAME ALSO AMONG THEM" (Job 1:6).

AN EXCERPT FROM "SNAKES IN THE LOBBY"

An amazing vision related by Scott MacLeod in his book, "Snakes in the Lobby" illustrates the activities of demons amongst men of God. I want to share this vision that I believe is truly revealing. It is indeed scary that our greatest enemy can infiltrate to the highest level.

"The Lobby

This is the vision: I was standing in a well-known hotel lobby, which I had literally stood in earlier that same day during a very well-known Christian music conference. In the vision the very large and open lobby was packed full, as it usually is, with men and women from all over. Many were artists, musicians or people directly involved in the business of music. The people were busy talking and going on with their business (what is commonly called "schmoozing"), each one dressed up in appropriate music attire.

Much to my astonishment and horror, I saw what looked like a massive snake lying *on the l*obby floor. I could not even begin to calculate its length, but it easily covered the full length of the room. Its fat middle was at least six feet in height and looked almost twenty feet in width. It looked totally stuffed. Amazingly, people were actually leaning up against it!

I could hardly believe what I was seeing. My first impulse was to yell and warn everyone, but I hesitated because no one else seemed to notice it--they just carried on with their business. Many people were surrounded, and some were even totally wrapped up in its monstrous coils, and yet they were still unaware. They all were in great danger. I couldn't tell if the people could not see what I was seeing, or if they had simply grown accustomed to this monster. It almost seemed welcome here.

I wondered, "Who let this thing in here? Surely the thing has to be dead for people to be standing this close to it and still be this comfortable with it."

Then it happened... IT MOVED. I couldn't believe that something that looked so heavy could actually move. But it did. It slowly poured itself in between a few groups of preoccupied people so as not to disturb anyone. It was silent, and no one saw it move. No one seemed to have a sense of danger. This was extremely confusing to me. It looked like many in this place, for some reason, had totally dropped their guard. Obviously, this seemed crazy because of what I was seeing. As I stood there, greatly perplexed by this strange scenario, I was suddenly struck with the terrifying sense that there were other snakes in the room.

I reluctantly and cautiously gazed across the room. We were surrounded! The oversized serpents were everywhere! As I continued to observe the situation, my emotions began to evolve rapidly from initial shock and terror into great frustration because no one else seemed to be aware of these snakes. Soon I was filled with a sense of compassion for the blinded victims, and finally an intense anger gripped me because these creatures had somehow infiltrated this place.

That was it. That was all I saw at first. But I knew immediately that the great snakes I had seen in this vision were the principalities and dark powers (or evil spirits) that have been controlling and manipulating much of Christian music. I knew I had seen exactly what the small group of us had just been praying about, and I told them what I had seen. It was as if a small movie screen had appeared before me and shown me these things, in color.

The vision stayed with me for about 24 hours. I was surprised that it did. I guess I had hoped that what I had seen at first was the end of it, for it was not pleasant to dwell on. But it remained very graphic and the images would not go away. After starting to get literally sick to my stomach over what I had seen, my curiosity began to grow and I began wondering what the meaning of it was. Believing there had to be a reason for this lingering scene, I finally began to ask the Lord to show me the full meaning of the vision.

He did, and this is what was revealed next:

The Big One: Self Promotion

I was taken back to the same lobby and was shown each snake in vivid detail.

The first snake that was revealed to me was the first one that I had seen earlier, it was definitely the biggest one, easily filling the full length of the large lobby with its great coils wrapped around everywhere. This grayish colored snake was so large that it took me quite some time to find its huge head. I finally spotted the head hiding in the twisted masses of the mammoth coils. It had a hollow and yet all consuming look upon its face. One word came into my mind as I studied its massive head -

HUNGER. I then observed that it had just finished devouring something, or someone. I instinctively knew it was the latter. This snake was actually feeding on the people in the lobby and still no one seemed to notice!

This serpent had the ability to slowly surround its victims with enormous coils and then swallow them whole without them even being aware of it. I knew by its immense size and its lumpy and very bloated body that it had swallowed many victims. And much to my surprise, I could see the victims were still alive inside of it. They were moving inside the creature's ever-stretched belly. I could hear them still carrying on ambitious conversations with others in the lobby.

The serpent's name was "Self-Promotion". Most of the victims did not know they had been consumed by self-promotion. But some, much to my dismay, had willingly and consciously allowed the snake to engulf them. The goal or intentions of these victims was the same as that of this bloated serpent--they all wanted to become bigger and bigger.

The Charmer: Lust

The second snake that I saw was to my left--a very beautiful-looking creature that almost made me forget the horror of the first. It was a type of chameleon, ever changing colors and appearance according to the desires of those under its power. It could look like whatever you wanted it to: male, female, young, old innocent or seductive. It was swaying back and forth, doing a hypnotic dance. I found myself drawn to it, as were many others.

Suddenly I shuddered with disgust, for I knew this hideous thing. His name was "Lust". I hadn't recognized it at first, for it was incredibly charming. There was a large group of people gathered all around it, and they were actually flirting and dancing with it and each other. Without even losing the rhythm of its cobra-like movement, Lust would strike its partners with a flash of fangs, with forked tongues that were identical to this serpent's ever flickering tongue; the people spoke deceptive flattery to one another. They were starting to realize that they could use the power for themselves. They could get what they wanted quicker by using the power of Lust. I realized that many of the victims that were now held captive in the belly of Self-Promotion had first been bitten and poisoned by "Lust".

When one is first bitten by Lust, the venom brings a real high. But not for long afterward, its victims become sick. Then often for relief, the victim goes back for another bite (for the venom is very addictive) until he or she is completely consumed with the poison. The victim in turn bites others, and the sickness spreads. I did not look at lust for long, for I knew its enticing power was great and deadly.

Two Snakes: Pride and Insecurity

The next snake I saw was, in fact, two very long snakes. They were intertwined--wrapped all around each other just like snakes do when they are mating. This, by the way is exactly what these were doing. One was red; the other was yellow. They were spinning over and over, making a very uneasy sound that pervaded the whole place. As they twisted and spun around, they appeared to be actually biting each other. All at once I understood that this writhing mass was "Pride" and "Insecurity". They were feeding off each other, and they were reproducing after their own kind.

Then I looked around the room and saw people who were turning yellow and then red. Yellow was the color of Insecurity and red was the color of Pride. People would change into these shades back and forth just like the rotating colors of the spinning serpents.

The whole lobby seemed to be aglow with these colors. The two worked well together, though they seemed to irritate one another. There was a nervous uneasiness building that made me want to scream. These two serpents made those who were affected by them (which were almost everyone, to some extent) feel miserable.

However, they didn't want to admit it, because their pride told them that they might look weak, insecure or possibly unsuccessful. So the spinning continued. Pride, Insecurity, Pride Insecurity etc.

Flesh for Scales: The Fear of Man

I was surprised that I even detected what was next. I knew it was only because the Lord was allowing me to see it--I never would have noticed it on my own. I spotted what had first appeared to be someone who had fallen down, but it was much too long to be human. It was hidden half way under the front counter and was entangled among the feet of the people.

The reason I had originally believed it was human was because it appeared to have human skin or flesh. It had what looked like a human head. Though having the color of flesh and having no scales, it was obviously still a snake. It was very low to the ground and earthly.

This one was the "Fear of Man". It didn't have to do very much, because Pride and Insecurity were doing most of its work. It just lay there moving its human-like head back and forth horizontally. Then I noticed that people all across the room were doing the very same thing, almost as if they had been entranced. They were only concerned about who was who, and how they were being perceived by others, so much so that they did not recognize the evil in their midst. This freaky creature blinded its victims from the holy fear of God and injected them with a deadly fear of man instead.

People all across the room were so busy looking at each other that they were unaware that they had become entangled by the fear of man. It would subtly wrap itself around its victims' feet until they could no longer move; they were completely paralyzed with fear. I remembered the Scripture: "The fear of man will prove to be a snare," (Proverbs 29:25).

Up High: Jealousy

I then heard a movement above me. I instinctively looked up, and there, much to my distress, I saw another serpent wrapped around the balcony, its endless tail running down the length of the escalator. This one was bright green. It looked like one of those tree snakes--very comfortable with heights. This was "Jealousy" and it was literally green with envy. It was breathing very heavily and seemed to have fire in its eyes. I could tell it was burning up inside. I didn't want it to catch me looking at it, because I was afraid it was ready to explode with fury at any moment.

Jealousy attacked the high places. It couldn't stand to be down low. Its mist-like breath released A FOG OF COMPETITION which filled the room, I could see that those who had breathed in the mist although they were chatting politely with peers, now had that same fire burning down in their eyes as did the serpent. And I knew they would attack and tear down those in the high places in order to obtain these places for themselves. Many of these people had become easy prey for Self-Promotion."[3]

It is amazing how demons hide in our midst and influence us with unbelievable delusions and deceptions. Unfortunately, many things we ministers do are influenced by the devil. The fighting, the hatred, the self-promotion are not products of the nature of God. They are characteristic of the demonic and a fallen nature.

■ DEMONS AND CHURCHES

Please take note of this list of demons commonly found working within the church. It will help you to identify and resist the enemy.

1. The Spirit of Accusation
2. Spirit of Gossip
3. Spirit of Slander
4. Spirit of Faultfinding
5. Spirit of Pride
6. Spirit of Self-Righteousness

7. Spirit of Respectability
8. Spirit of Selfish Ambition
9. Spirit of Unrighteous Judgement
10. Spirit of Jealousy
11. Spirit of the Accuser of the Brethren
12. Spirit of Intimidation
13. Spirit of Treachery
14. Spirit of Rejection
15. Spirit of Bitterness
16. Spirit of Impatience
17. Spirit of Unforgiveness
18. Spirit of Lust
19. Spirit of Hate
20. The Spirit of Division

There are many evil spirits in the church and they occupy the minds and hearts of Christians and influence their behaviour. The presence of church splits and infighting is evidence of the work of demons within the Church of Jesus Christ.

Another vision related by Rick Joyner clearly illustrates this great truth. It shows how demons use Christians to wreak havoc within the church. Self-righteous and decent looking Christians are frequently used as agents of demons.

As you read this vision, you will recognize many of the principles I have shared in earlier chapters.

- You will notice how demons operate in groups and teams.
- You will also notice how agreement with demons give them power over your life.
- You will realize that demons operate against us only through the power of deception.

Christians are deceived into thinking that their criticisms and judgements are justified. Through this deception, demons wreak havoc in churches all over the world. I have highlighted some important portions so that you do not miss them.

AN EXCERPT FROM "THE FINAL QUEST"

"The demonic army was so large that it stretched as far as I could see. It was separated into divisions, with each carrying a different banner. The foremost divisions marched under the banners of Pride, Self-righteousness, Respectability, Selfish Ambition, Unrighteous Judgement, and Jealousy. There were many more of these evil divisions beyond my scope of vision, but those in the vanguard of this terrible horde from hell seemed to be the most powerful. The leader of this army was the Accuser of the Brethren himself.

The weapons carried by this horde were also named. The swords were named Intimidation; the spears were named Treachery; and the arrows were named Accusation, Gossip, Slander and Faultfinding. Scouts and smaller companies of demons with such names as Rejection, Bitterness, Impatience, Unforgiveness and Lust were sent in advance of this army to prepare for the main attack.

These smaller companies and scouts were much fewer in number, but they were no less powerful than some of the larger divisions that followed. They were smaller only for strategic reasons. Just as John the Baptist was a single man, but was given an extraordinary anointing for baptizing the masses to prepare them for the Lord, these smaller demonic companies were given extraordinary evil powers for "baptizing the masses." A single demon of Bitterness could sow his poison into multitudes of people, even entire races or cultures. A demon of Lust would attach himself to a single performer, movie, or even advertisement, and send what appeared to be bolts of electric slime that would hit and "desensitise" great masses of people. All of this was to prepare for the great horde of evil, which followed.

This army was marching specifically against the church, but it was attacking everyone that it could. I knew that it was seeking to pre-empt a coming move of God, which was destined to sweep masses of people into the church.

The primary strategy of this army was to cause division on every possible level of relationship - churches with each other, congregations with their pastors, husbands and wives, children and parents, and even children with each other. The scouts were sent to locate the openings in churches, families or individuals that Rejection, Bitterness, Lust, etc., could exploit and make larger. Then the following divisions would pour through the openings to completely overcome their victims.

The most shocking part of this vision was that this horde was not riding on horses, but primarily on Christians! Most of them were well-dressed, respectable, and had the appearance of being refined and educated, but there also seemed to be representatives from almost every walk of life.

These people professed Christian truths in order to appease their consciences, but they lived their lives in agreement with the powers of darkness. As they agreed with those powers their assigned demons grew and more easily directed their actions.

Many of these believers were host to more than one demon, but one would obviously be in charge. The nature of the one in charge dictated which division it was marching in. Even though the divisions were all marching together, it also seemed that at the same time the entire army was on the verge of chaos. For example, the demons of hate, hated the other demons as much as they did the Christians. The demons of jealousy were all jealous of one another. The only way the leaders of this horde kept the demons from fighting each other was to keep their hatred, jealousy, etc., focused on the people they were riding. However, these people would often break out in fights with each other. I knew that this was how some of the armies that had come against Israel in the Scriptures had ended up destroying themselves. When their purpose against Israel was thwarted, their rage was uncontrollable, and they simply began fighting each other.

I noted that the demons were riding on these Christians, but were not in them as was the case with non-Christians. It was obvious that these believers had only to stop agreeing with their demons in order to get free of them. For example, if the Christian on which a demon of jealousy was riding just started to question the jealousy, that demon would weaken very fast. When this happened the weakening demon would cry out and the leader of the division would direct all of the demons around that Christian to attack him until the bitterness, etc., would build up on him again. If this did not work, the demons would begin quoting Scriptures that were perverted in such a way that would justify the bitterness, accusations, etc.

It was clear that the power of the demons was rooted almost entirely in the power of deception, but they had deceived these Christians to the point where they could use them and they would think they were being used by God. This was because banners of Self-Righteousness were being carried by almost all of the individuals so that those marching could not even see the banners that marked the true nature of these divisions.

As I looked far to the rear of this army I saw the entourage of the Accuser himself. I began to understand his strategy, and I was amazed that it was so simple. He knew that a house divided cannot stand, and this army represented an attempt to bring such division to the church that she would completely fall from grace. It was apparent that the only way he could do this was to use Christians to war against their own brethren, and that is why almost everyone in the forward divisions were Christians, or at least professing Christians. Every step that these deceived believers took in obedience to the Accuser strengthened his power over them. This made his confidence and the confidence of all of his commanders grow with the progress of the army as it marched forward. It was apparent that the power of this army depended on the agreement of these Christians with the ways of evil."[4]

Breaking Down Strongholds 34

■ THE POWER OF CHRIST AS IT CONFRONTS DEMON ACTIVITY TODAY

"Jesus Christ the same yesterday, and TODAY, and forever" (Hebrews 13:8). Jesus Christ is the same yesterday, today and forever. One of the common things that I have seen under the sun (that is on earth), is what happens when someone meets a friend he has not seen for many years. They smile, they chat, and sometimes have a drink together.

After a while, one usually says to the other, "You know, you haven't changed. Your smile is still the same. Your laughter is the same."

He continues, "You talk about the same things."

He goes on, "You still talk about the Lord. Your passion for soul- winning does not seem to have diminished. You are still preaching on buses and at crusades."

It is indeed not unusual for a man to meet his friend after many years and declare for instance, "You have not changed, and you still eat a lot."

What makes people say to one another, "You haven't changed, you are still the same?" The answer is simple. When someone does the same things he used to do, it is said that he has not changed; he is the same.

1. JESUS HEALS TODAY THROUGH HIS BODY.

How does Jesus heal today? He heals today through His body, the Church. Jesus Christ is the same. What makes Him the same yesterday, today and forever? The answer is simple. He does the same things today that He used to do years ago.[1] Years ago, He healed the sick and cast out devils. Today, He still heals the sick and casts out devils. Years ago, He visited people's homes and blessed them. Today, He still visits our homes and blesses us. He raised the dead two thousand years ago and is still raising the dead in today's world. He is the same. Accept it! Believe it today. Jesus is alive and He is stretching out His hand to minister to you now. He has not changed at all.

He loves to do the things He used to do. That is a hallmark of the ministry of Christ. I have personally seen the Lord Jesus healing the sick and casting out devils today. He has not changed. Do not let the devil deceive you. The things you read in the Bible are real and are still happening today. One of the highest kinds of deceptions is to think that the Bible is just a history book describing the miracles of a Jewish zealot who is not relevant in this modern, computerized society.

There are still mad men like the mad man of Gadara and Jesus still heals such people.[2] There are still many epileptics, who convulse and foam at the mouth. The power of Jesus still heals such people. There are still many, many women with gynaecological problems like the woman with the issue of blood. Jesus still heals such gynaecological diseases. There are many blind people in the world today. There are now schools for the blind. Christ Jesus opens blind eyes today. I have seen blind people receiving their sight in my ministry. There are many lame people in the world. Jesus is still healing such people.

Is it not amazing to note that the problems are still the same? The plagues that confronted humanity two thousand years ago are still the same. In spite of medical advances, these problems do not seem to go away. It is comforting to know that Jesus is still a healing Jesus. As you read this book, you can expect the power of Christ to confront the evil powers of Satan in your life.

He is the head and the church is the Body of Christ. No matter what the good intentions of the head are, He needs the cooperation of the hands to do His works. Your head may decide, "I am going to read this book," but it is your hands that will be used to lift the book up. Without the hands doing their part, the good intentions of the head cannot be realized. That is why the church must have healing and casting out of devils as a principal activity that goes on alongside preaching.

We are the hands and the feet of Jesus today. He is the same yesterday, today and forever. Allow Him into your life right now to heal you, to touch you and to set you free.

2. Demons are challenged by the presence of God.

"When he saw Jesus, he cried out,... I beseech thee, torment me not" (Luke 8:28). When Jesus came on the scene, the demons within the mad man were agitated. They cried out against the Lord. The presence of God is the environment which evil spirits are not comfortable with. The mad man of Gadara reacted to the presence of Jesus. The presence of God will always stir up evil spirits. That is why perfectly normal people suddenly show strange manifestations when they are in church.

In Mark 1, a perfectly normal person began screaming in the temple while Jesus was preaching. "And there was in their synagogue a man with an unclean spirit; AND HE CRIED OUT, Saying, Let us alone; what have we to do with thee, thou Jesus of Nazareth? art thou come to destroy us? I know thee who thou art, the Holy One of God. And Jesus rebuked him, saying, Hold thy peace, and come out of him. And when the unclean spirit had torn him, and cried with a loud voice, he came out of him" (Mark 1:23-26).

When you understand that the presence of God drives away evil spirits, you will constantly cultivate the presence of God in your life. You will want the presence of God at home, in your office, and at church.

Two Reasons Why the Presence of God Stirs up Evil Spirits

a. In the presence of God, the Word of God is preached and taught.

The Word of God is a sharp sword. "For the word of God is quick, and powerful, and SHARPER THAN ANY TWOEDGED SWORD,..." (Hebrews 4:12). As the Word of God comes forth, swords are thrown out in the realm of the spirit. No demon enjoys having swords thrown at him. This is why the man in the synagogue reacted to the preaching of Jesus. Jesus did not pray, He just preached. Jesus did not bind any demon; He just preached the Word of God. The Word of God is truly a sword in the spirit.

b. The Word of God is light and the light exposes the activities of demons.

"And the light shineth in darkness; and the darkness comprehended it not" (John 1:5). When the Word is preached, the light shines forth and demons are exposed. The more of the Word you have, the more the enemy is exposed. Satan can never operate effectively against you in the light. Darkness is essential for demonic activity.

INVITING THE PRESENCE OF GOD

The Bible teaches that God inhabits praises. When praise and worship goes on, the presence of God becomes very strong and the evil spirits feel the fire. "But thou art holy, O thou that INHABITEST THE PRAISES of Israel" (Psalm 22:3).

It is possible to create a church environment everywhere. You can do this by carrying your worship tapes and CDs wherever you go. You can have them in your home or in your car or in your office. Many surgeons play music while they operate. Why not play worship music while you work?

You can also carry preaching tapes with you wherever you go. Preaching and worship are the two main items for creating the right atmosphere. Wherever I go, I carry my music and my preaching tapes. From Paraguay, to Toronto, I always create my own atmosphere with preaching tapes and worship music. This environment is anti-demonic.

Many people suffer from depression because they do not know how to create the right atmosphere for their lives. Instead of having worship music, they listen to secular music from the radio. Instead of listening to preaching, they listen to political discussions and the bad news of the world.

Music and the Presence of God

Unfortunately, many Christians do not know the effect that music has on evil spirits. There are four biblical accounts, which warn us about playing with the wrong music.

1. SATAN, ONCE CALLED LUCIFER, WAS CREATED TO WORSHIP GOD.

Music was actually ingrained in him when he was formed. Lucifer was created with timbrels and pipes. Since he fell, this gift of music has been corrupted and used to fight against God.

Every Christian must be careful of secular music no matter how harmless it appears. Christian musicians must not play secular music if they want to be truly spiritual. Have you ever wondered at the kind of Christian music produced today? I have heard many spiritual people declare that they find it difficult to listen to some so-called gospel music.

"You were in Eden, the garden of God; Every precious stone was your covering: The sardius, topaz, and diamond, Beryl, onyx, and jasper, Sapphire, turquoise, and emerald with gold. THE WORKMANSHIP OF YOUR TIMBRELS AND PIPES WAS PREPARED FOR YOU ON THE DAY YOU WERE CREATED" (Ezekiel 28:13, New King James Version).

2. WHEN KING SAUL WAS TORMENTED BY AN EVIL SPIRIT, INSTRUMENTAL MUSIC WAS USED TO DRIVE AWAY THE DEMONS.

"But the Spirit of the LORD departed from Saul, and an evil spirit from the LORD troubled him. And Saul's servants said unto him, Behold now, an evil spirit from God troubleth thee. Let our Lord now command thy servants, which are before thee, to seek out a man, who is a cunning player on an harp: and it shall come to pass, when the evil spirit from God is upon thee, that he shall play with his hand, and thou shalt be well. And Saul said unto his servants, Provide me now a man that can play well, and bring him to me. Then answered one of the servants, and said, Behold, I have seen a son of Jesse the Bethlehemite, that is cunning in playing, and a mighty valiant man, and a man of war, and prudent in matters, and a comely person, and the LORD is with him.

Wherefore Saul sent messengers unto Jesse, and said, Send me David thy son, which is with the sheep. And Jesse took an ass laden with bread, and a bottle of wine, and a kid, and sent them by David his son unto Saul. And David came to Saul, and stood before him: and he loved him greatly; and he became his armourbearer. And Saul sent to Jesse, saying, Let David, I pray thee, stand before me; for he hath found favour in my sight. AND IT CAME TO PASS, WHEN THE EVIL SPIRIT FROM GOD WAS UPON SAUL, THAT DAVID TOOK AN HARP, AND PLAYED WITH HIS HAND: SO SAUL WAS REFRESHED, AND WAS WELL, AND THE EVIL SPIRIT DEPARTED FROM HIM" (1 Samuel 16:14-23).

Dear friend, if music can drive away demons, surely it is able to attract them too! Be careful about what you listen to because it may attract demons to your life. Much of the unspiritual gospel music is charged with evil spirits. People are charged with spirits of lust and violence when they listen to certain kinds of music.

"All things are lawful for me, but all things are not expedient: all things are lawful for me, but all things edify not" (1 Corinthians 10:23).

3. When Elisha needed to hear from the Spirit of God, he called for the minstrel.

As the minstrel played, the Spirit of God came upon him and he prophesied. "And Elisha said …now bring me a minstrel. And it came to pass, when the minstrel played, that the hand of the LORD came upon him. And he said, Thus saith the LORD, Make this valley full of ditches" (2 Kings 3:14-16).

Surely, this testimony must teach you something: The right music can attract the presence of God!

4. When the musicians in the temple played instruments and worshipped God, the presence of God filled the house.

"It came even to pass, AS THE TRUMPETERS AND SINGERS WERE AS ONE, to make one sound to be heard in praising and thanking the LORD; and when they lifted up their voice with the trumpets and cymbals and instruments of musick, and praised the LORD, saying, For he is good; for his mercy endureth for ever: that then THE HOUSE WAS FILLED WITH A CLOUD, EVEN THE HOUSE OF THE LORD" (2 Chronicles 5:13).

The glory cloud came in because musicians and singers were doing the right thing. Surely, we must learn from this account that the right kind of singing and the right kind of instrumental music will bring in the presence of God. Many times, I have felt the presence of God as I listened to anointed and inspired music. Music is truly a powerful medium that takes you into the presence of God.

IDENTIFYING DEMONS

"And Jesus asked him sayiing, WHAT IS THY NAME? …he said, Legion:…" (Luke 8:30). In the medical field, 80% of your work is done when you are able to identify what disease you are dealing with. The difficulty is often in being able to determine what the problem is. There are many elusive diseases, which avoid diagnoses. These are the most difficult diseases to treat. In the same way, demons and demonic activity must be identified (diagnosed), in order to be able to deal with them.[3]

Perhaps you think you are dealing with a spirit of fornication but actually you may be dealing with a spirit of death. As soon as you can pin point the problem, you are well on your way to a breakthrough.

If I were to scream, "Come here," perhaps no one in particular would come to me. However, if I were to scream, "Jack Toronto, come here", Jack Toronto would get up and come to me. In both cases, I said, "Come here." One of the commands yielded results but the other did not.

Specifically mentioning the name of the problem and dealing with it, is the key to dealing with demonic powers. That is why Jesus asked the mad man of Gadara: "What is thy name?" He needed to call out the name of the spirit to be able to cast it out. Begin to mention the names of the spirits that are harassing you. Ask God to reveal the real identity of the spirits.

Once, while I was praying, the Lord revealed the names of some demons I was dealing with. In one case, the Lord told me that the name of the problem was "death". He went on to show me that Satan was trying to kill me by using some of my pastors. We need to ask God for the Holy Spirit so that we can deal with the enemy. What is thy name? This is the most important question to ask when dealing with demons.

DISAGREEING WITH DEMONIC DECEPTIONS AND AGREEING WITH THE WORD OF GOD

"But when he saw Jesus afar off, he ran and worshipped him..." (Mark 5:6). In one lucid moment, the mad man of Gadara broke out of the control of the demons and ran to worship Jesus. Satan seeks to gain control over us. The only way he can do this is through our minds.

"And the devil said unto him…command this stone that it be made bread… Jesus answered … man shall not live by bread alone,…" (Luke 4:3-4).

"Now the serpent was more subtil than any beast of the field which the LORD God had made. And he said unto the woman, Yea, hath God said, Ye shall not eat of every tree of the garden? And the woman said unto the serpent, We may eat of the fruit of the trees of the garden: But of the fruit of the tree which is in the midst of the garden, God hath said, Ye shall not eat of it, neither shall ye touch it, lest ye die. And the serpent said unto the woman, Ye shall not surely die: For God doth know that in the day ye eat thereof, then your eyes shall be opened, and ye shall be as gods, knowing good and evil. And when the woman saw that the tree was good for food, and that it was pleasant to the eyes, and a tree to be desired to make one wise, she took of the fruit thereof, and did eat, and gave also unto her husband with her; and he did eat" (Genesis 3:1-6).

1. The Word of God fights against demonic deceptions.

Many people are held in bondage because their thinking patterns agrees with demonic deceptions. People are kept in bondage as long as their minds agree with the ideas that come from Satan. Unfortunately, the thoughts of many believers are in agreement with Satan because we do not study or believe the Word.

When a person is full of thoughts of discontentment and criticism, the demon of hatred can easily take over. Our natural thoughts for revenge, unforgiveness, depression and fear are very much in consonance with the spirit of sickness, disease and even death. This is why the Word of God is so important. It keeps us in full disagreement with the devil's suggestions.

It is very easy to agree with delusions of demons. The devil's deceptions are very similar to the truth. Many times, we are caught unawares as we drift along and agree with unbiblical suggestions. That is where steadfastness comes in.

2. Steadfastness should bring us back to the Word of God.

Steadfastness is actually derived from a navy term, which means to stay on course. It also means to come back to course after you have made a deviation. We all tend to go on excursions from time to time but the spirit of steadfastness must bring us back to the Word. Put your foot down and disagree with everything that is not biblical.

DELIVERANCE HAS A PRACTICAL SIDE

"Howbeit Jesus...saith unto him, Go...and tell them how great things the Lord hath done for thee..." (Mark 5:19). After the Lord has set you free, you need to make practical adjustments, otherwise the demons will return. You need to obey the Word of God practically.

"Then goeth he, and taketh with himself seven other spirits more wicked than himself, and they enter in and dwell there: and the last state of that man is worse than the first..." (Matthew 12:45). Notice from the Scripture that the house was empty, swept and clean. A house, which is not filled with the Word of God, will be filled with demons. I have watched as many go for deliverance sessions and yet never seem to be free. This is because we are ignoring a most basic truth from the Lord.

"And ye shall know the truth, and the truth shall make you free" (John 8:32). It is the knowledge of the truth that actually sets us free. Many pastors attempt to use the laying on of hands to accomplish what only the truth can do. However, none of us is wiser than God. We may anoint people with oil a thousand times but that cannot be substituted for the knowledge of truth.

1. Remove the footholds of the Devil.

"Neither give place to the devil" (Ephesians 4:27). Demons cannot have access to Christians unless we give them a foothold. Demons keep returning because they still have access. Often, the foothold of the devil is not removed and so the demons keep returning. What is there in your life that allows the devil to keep returning? Perhaps bad company is ruining your life. Perhaps, the alcohol you take in is opening the door to the spirit of death.

2. Without some practical steps, your deliverance from demons will never be complete.

Jesus told the mad man of Gadara to go around witnessing about what the Lord had done for him. The continued deliverance of this mad man lay in his obedience to this command. What has the Lord asked you to do? Obeying this command will keep you free from demons.

BE STRONG IN THE LORD

"Finally, my brethren, BE STRONG IN THE LORD, and in the power of his might. PUT ON THE WHOLE ARMOUR OF GOD, that ye may be able to stand against the wiles of the devil" (Ephesians 6:10-11).

When I was in boarding school, physical strength was an advantage. Form two boys would shout, "One small boy!" and we the junior ones would all have to run. However, I remember a form one boy who was bigger and stronger than the rest of us. He decided to ignore the yelling of the form two boys. They would scream, "One small boy!" but he would totally ignore them. You see, he was bigger and stronger than most of the form two boys and he could beat them up if he wanted to. As I watched this older and stronger boy, I received instruction: the stronger you are, the less trouble you will receive from certain people.

This is how I came to understand Ephesians 6:10. I realized that if I were strong in the Lord, many problems would automatically fall away. This is exactly what has happened. The stronger I became spiritually, the more distant certain problems were.

God wants us to be strong in spiritual things. Unfortunately, many are strong in other aspects of life. They are strong in their schoolwork, they are strong in politics, they are strong in sports, but they are not strong in the Lord! God's Word to us is to be strong. That means we can be strong! He did not say, "Pray for strength," neither did He say, "God will strengthen you." He said, "Be strong in the Lord." As you increase in the strength of the Lord, many of the demonic attacks in your life will lose the power they have.

PUT ON THE WHOLE ARMOUR OF GOD

"Finally, my brethren, BE STRONG IN THE LORD, and in the power of his might. PUT ON THE WHOLE ARMOUR OF GOD, that ye may be able to stand against the wiles of the devil" (Ephesians 6:10-11). Protecting yourself from the attacks of the enemy can be very complicated.

After September 11, America realized how vulnerable they were. A myriad of attacks could be launched at America from any angle.

This fact also holds true for believers and that is why we need the whole armour of God. Several attacks are planned and launched against the believer from different angles. Except we put on the whole armour, we will not be fully protected from the enemy. One prayer by a prophet does not exclude you from having to put on your armour. The armour protects you in totality and it is time for Christians to put on the whole armour. The different aspects of the armour will keep you from being invaded by demons. I had an experience years ago that served to eternally stamp this fact in my spirit.

"So use every piece of God's armour to resist the enemy whenever he attacks, and when it is all over, you will still be standing up. But to do this, you will need the strong belt of truth and the breastplate of God's approval. Wear shoes that are able to speed you on as you preach the Good News of peace with God. In every battle you will need faith as your shield to stop the fiery arrows aimed at you by Satan. And you will need the helmet of salvation and the sword of the Spirit-which is the Word of God. Pray all the time. Ask God for anything in line with the Holy Spirit's wishes. Plead with him, reminding him of your needs, and keep praying earnestly for all Christians everywhere" (Ephesians 6:13-18 TLB).

FREEDOM IN CHRIST

"Stand fast therefore in the LIBERTY WHEREWITH CHRIST HATH MADE US FREE, and be not entangled again with the yoke of bondage" (Galatians 5:1). You are free! You are free from the demons of inferiority! You are free from the demons of self-pity! You are delivered from the control of the demons of jealousy and envy!

Take authority over the spirit of depression!

You are free from the power of lust!

The power of witchcraft is broken!

Bind the demons of discouragement in your life.

You are free from anxiety!

The spirit of fear and restlessness is bound! You are free indeed!

I see you overcoming the spirit of bitterness and hatred!

You are free from the power and hold of deception!

Every stronghold of satanic intimidation is pulled down!

Amen!

MULTIPLE CHOICE QUESTIONS

Answer all options with either T (true) or F (false). All quotations are from the King James Version (KJV) of the Bible unless otherwise stated.

1. **Are the following statements true or false?**
   a. Nicodemus was a ruler of the Jews
   b. Nicodemus did not want people to see him with Jesus
   c. To be born again means you are faithful to a church
   d. Being born again is an attitude
   e. Being born again is a gradual process of change

2. **The following words correctly fit into the quotation below:**
   Jesus answered and said unto -a-, verily -b- I say unto -c-, except a man be -d- he cannot see the -e- of God. (John 3:3)
   a. Nicodemus
   b. Truly
   c. Him
   d. born again
   e. salvation

3. **The following are required if you are to be born again?**
   a. Fasting
   b. Paying tithes
   c. Being a shepherd
   d. Stopping drinking
   e. Not womanising

4. **The following statements are true:**
   a. Being a chorister means you are born again
   b. It is important to read the Bible in order to be born again
   c. Baptism is a sign to yourself and to the people around you that you are born again
   d. If you admire miracles you will one day be born again
   e. Giving to God will guarantee you a special place in Heaven

5. **Mr. Christian has been telling Mr. Mobrawa the he needs to be born again. Mr Mobrawa says he is already born again. The following are his reasons. Are the reasons true or false?**
   a. I go to church every Sunday
   b. My pastor is a personal friend and I visit him twice a week
   c. I built 5 of the 10 pillars in the church
   d. I pray 3 times a day
   e. I have been baptised and confirmed in the church

6. **Mr. Kolikoo has been married to Tsotsoo for 15 years. Tsotsoo cannot have children but Mr. Kolikoo says he will never divorce her. He will always be faithful to her. Mr. Kolikoo.**
   a. is born again
   b. will go to Heaven when he dies
   c. is an occultist
   d. is a moralist
   e. is a good Christian

7. **The following are not the same as being born again. True or False?**
   a. Confessing Jesus as your personal saviour
   b. Obeying a new set of rules
   c. Being a member of a Charismatic denomination like Lighthouse Chapel
   d. Being principled
   e. Being faithful to your spouse

8. **Are the following match-ups correct?**
   a. You must be born again
   - John 3:7
   b. The parable of the rich fool
   - Lk 16: 19-31
   c. The great commission
   - Mt 16: 15-16
   d. '...I never knew you'
   Matt 7: 23
   e. Jesus was sent by God the Father
   - John 3:2

9. **Which of the following statements are true?**
   a. A lack of understanding often leads to backsliding
   b. Christianity is a new set of rules
   c. Two other religions give the same offer as Christianity
   d. The spirit of the unsaved man is righteous and truly holy
   e. After you are saved your body is still the same; you must renew it

10. **Which of the following options correctly completes the verse below?**
    And the very God of peace sanctify you wholly; and I pray God your whole -------------- and ------------------and ------------------ be preserved blameless unto the coming of our Lord Jesus Christ (I Thess. 5:23)
    a. body, soul, spirit
    b. soul, spirit, body
    c. soul, body, spirit
    d. spirit, soul, body
    e. spirit, body, soul

11. Which of the following match-ups are correct?

a. The body is described as a house - 2 Cor 5:1
b. You are spirit, soul and body - I Thess 5:25
c. The inner man - Rom 7:22
d. The inner man - Eph 3:16
e. The soul is different from the spirit - Heb 4:14

12. According to Lk 16: 23-24

a. Jesus saves us
b. The spirit (inner) man is hidden
c. Those in Hell have eyes
d. The spirit man has a tongue
e. The soul and spirit of the unsaved man experience Hell

13. The soul can

a. be discouraged
b. be killed in Hell
c. be grieved
d. be joyful
e. remember in Hell

14. A person who is not born again is

a. deceitful
b. a sinner
c. an unregenerate person
d. an unbeliever
e. desperately wicked

15. Which of the following words correctly fit the blanks in the verse below?

The -a- is -b- above all things and -c- -d-: who can -e- it? Jer 17:9

a. spirit
b. deceitful
c. decidedly
d. wicked
e. endure

16. Which of the following match-ups is correct?

a. God's wrath is revealed against man's wickedness - Rom 1:18
b. The heart is deceitful - Jer 17:9
c. Mankind has been given over to his own desires - Rom 1:22
d. The sinfulness of man - Rom 1: 29-31
e. The unbeliever is a covenant-breaker - Rom 1:31

17. The spirit of an unsaved man is dead and desperately wicked. This statement is supported by the following Scriptures:

f. Ps 51:5
g. Rom 3:22
h. Is 64:6
i. Micah 7:2
j. Ezek 36:6

18. Which of the following options correctly fit the verses below:

-a-, if any man be in -b-, he is a new creature: old things are -d- away; behold -e- things are become new
2 Cor 5:17

a. However
b. Christ
c. creation
d. gone
e. some

19. Are the following statements true or false?

a. A man who is saved has undergone a radical transformation of the heart.
b. A man who is saved is a sinner and not worthy to approach the Lords throne
c. If we are saved we cannot be more righteous than we are today
d. If we are saved we are the righteousness of God
e. You do not need to feel righteous, to be righteous.

20. Which of the following match-ups are correct?

a. The new man is created in true righteousness and holiness - Eph 4:24
b. We are the righteousness of God in Christ - 2 Cor 5:21
c. Acknowledge the good things in you - Philemon 6
d. Put on the new man - Col 3:12
e. Righteousness is a gift - Rom 5:17

21. According to 1 Pet 2:2

As newborn -a-, -b- the sincere -c- of the -d- that ye may -e- thereby

a. children
b. desire
c. truth
d. word
e. live

22. Are the following statements true or false?

a. There is no art to find the mind's construction in the face
b. Power tends to corrupt and absolute power corrupts absolutely
c. There are 3 stages of development for a Christian
d. A spiritual baby is easily offended
e. Growth is important to bring out the true nature of the body

23. Are the following match-ups true or false?

a. The childhood stage - Eph 4: 14
b. Strong meat is for mature - Heb 5: 14
c. Ever Christian must grow up to teach the Word - Heb 5:12
d. Spiritual growth is through the Word - 1 Pet 2:2
e. The quiet time scripture - Exo 34: 1-3

24. The following are ingredients for a good quiet time

f. The early morning
g. Bible reading
h. Fasting
i. Prayer
j. Praise and worship

25. Which of the following options correctly completes the verse below?

And be not -a- to this world: but be ye -b- by the -c- of your -d- that ye may prove what is that -e-, and acceptable, and perfect will of God Rom 12:2

a. transformed
b. changed
c. renewing
d. soul
e. full

26. Your mind can be renewed by

a. Salvation
b. Deliverance
c. Receiving the Word
d. Laying on of hands
e. Joining a right church

27. Which of the following match-ups are true? Which are false?

a. The word cleanses - Jn 15:3
b. The word makes us grow - 2 Pet 2:2
c. The works of the flesh - Gal 5: 19-21
d. The word sanctifies - Eph 5:26
e. There is no good thing in the flesh - Rom 7:18

28. The following are practical ways to control the flesh. True or false?

f. Be aware of the potential evil in the flesh
g. Fast regularly
h. Do not give opportunity to the flesh
i. Flee youthful lust
j. Stand up and fight

29. Are the following statements true or false?

a. Renewing your mind does not close it to the attacks of the devil
b. Satan's most powerful tool is suggestion
c. Satan attacked Jesus through His mind
d. Thoughts are like birds that fly over your head
e. Renewing your mind closes it to the devil

30. Man is

a. A spirit, a soul and a body
b. A body, he has a spirit and lives in a soul
c. A spirit, he has a soul and lives in a body
d. A soul, he has a body and lives in the spirit
e. All of the above

31. According to 1 Thess. 5:23 what is the nature of man?

a. Man's nature is three fold
b. Man is only a spirit
c. Man does not just have a spirit but is a spirit
d. Man is not a body
e. Man is not a mind

32. The true story of Lazarus and the rich man in Luke 16:19-20, proves that

a. Man is a spirit
b. When man's body dies, his spirit lives on
c. Man is only spirit and soul
d. Man's spirit is more important than his body
e. Man's spirit never dies

33. Which of these Scriptures say that the spirit world is more important that the natural (seen) world?
a. John 4:23
b. Hebrews 1:7
c. 2 Corinthians 4:17-18
d. All of the above
e. None of the above

34. Other names for the spirit of man are
a. The soul
b. The hidden man
c. The inner man
d. The inward man
e. The outer man

35. Our spirit's characteristics include the following
a. Our spirits has senses of it's own to feel, see, hear etc
b. Our spirit depend on the body only to see, feel, hear etc
c. With our spirits (only can) we contact the spiritual realm
d. With our spirits we know God
e. When our spirits leave our bodies we die

36. When we are born again, what happens?
a. Our mind changes
b. Our spirit changes
c. Our bodies change
d. Our spirit, soul, bodies change
e. Our spirits becomes a new creation

37. What does the soul consist of?
a. Our emotions
b. Our spirits
c. Our will
d. Our minds
e. Our brains

38. The characteristics of the body include the following
a. The body is the same body it was before salvation
b. The body is natural
c. The body is not temporal but eternal
d. The body has affections that agree with those of the spirit
e. The body contacts the spiritual realm

39. Other names for the body in the Bible include
a. The flesh
b. The heart
c. The outward man
d. The earthly house
e. The Adam

40. What is the condition of the unsaved man?
a. His spirit is dead
b. He is controlled by his spirit
c. His soul is under the control of the flesh
d. He has sinned and fallen short of God's glory
e. He is not alienated from the life of God

41. When you get saved
a. Your body is not born again
b. Your spirit is not born again
c. Your soul is not born again
d. Our body, soul and spirit is born again
e. Only your spirit is born again

42. The spirit of the unsaved man is
a. Alive
b. Dead
c. Desperately wicked
d. The same as that of a saved man
e. Lost

43. The following describes the condition of unsaved man
a. He is controlled by his senses
b. His spirit is suppressed
c. His human soul has been lifted up
d. His spirit is under the control of his body
e. He is also a child of God

44. How should a believer relate to an unbeliver?
a. Be closely associated to win them
b. Do not be closely associated in any way
c. Have an unbelieving beloved and save him
d. Do not have an unbeliever as a beloved
e. Do not marry an unbeliever

45. Which of these correctly describes an unsaved man?
a. A child of the devil
b. An infidel
c. A slave to the devil
d. A sinner by nature
e. Beelzebub

46. The spirit of the saved man is
a. Righteous
b. Truly holy
c. A new creation
d. Is still sinful
e. Is still under condemnation

47. What happens when one is saved?
a. He is recreated in Christ
b. He is a creation that did not previously exist
c. He becomes a new creation gradually
d. There is an instant transformation in his spirit
e. He has not received eternal life yet

48. What are the benefits of being saved?
a. One is redeemed from the curse
b. You are no longer under condemnation
c. You are still under bondage to Satan and sin
d. The fullness of the righteousness of God is imparted on you
e. His spirit is alive to God

49. The saved man is saved from ...
a. Condemnation
b. The world to come
c. The wrath to come
d. Bondage of sin
e. Suffering

50. How should a saved person live?
a. Like a world overcomer
b. Like a fearful person
c. Soberly and righteously
d. Not in anticipation of the Lord's coming
e. Like a child of God

51. 2 Corithians 5:17 says that a saved person is
a. A new creation
b. Some old things have passed away
c. All things have become almost new
d. So many things have become new
e. All things have become new

52. What is righteousness?
a. A feeling
b. Something you work hard to attain
c. You can increase your faith in your righteousness
d. You can increase your righteousness by your faith
e. It destroys your self consciousness

53. Which of these are characteristics of righteousness
a. It is imparted on the saved
b. You cannot be more righteous than on the day you became born again
c. It makes you bold as a lion
d. Quarrels, tiredness and emotions does not change your righteousness
e. Righteousness is the same as perfection

54. How can you take advantage of your righteousness in Christ?
a. Acknowledge the good things in you to make your faith essential (effective)
b. Cast away all accusations
c. Disagree with every criticism about yourself
d. Bear fruits of righteousness
e. Be bold and courageous

55. After you are born again ...
a. Your spirit is a new born baby
b. You go through 4 basic stages of growth
c. You go through 3 basic of growth
d. You don't go through any stages of growth
e. You are complete and mature at salvation

56. The newly born-again person's stages of growth may include ...
a. The baby stage
b. The backsliding stage
c. The mature stage
d. The childhood stage
e. The sucking stage

57. Characteristics of the baby stage of growth include
a. He is very active in church work
b. He does not contribute anything to work
c. He is rather a burden
d. He is easily offended
e. He is just like an unbeliever

58. I Peter 2:2 exhorts
a. Mature believers
b. Baby believers
c. To desire the milk of the word
d. To grow by studying to show ourselves approved
e. All of the above.

59. The childhood stage has the characteristic of
a. Being tossed to and fro
b. Being unsteady and unstable
c. Wanting meat not milk
d. Being able to differentiate between false doctrines
e. Being an unstable church member

60. A mature Christian
a. Is carried by excitement, fashion and peer pressure
b. Wants meat and not milk
c. Discerns between good and evil
d. Takes responsibility and is reliable
e. Cannot teach others

61. God wants us to be
a. Always children
b. Converted to be like children
c. No more children
d. Fruitful through growth
e. Tossed to and fro

62. After you are saved
a. Your mind is changed
b. Your mind is still the same
c. Your mind needs to be renewed
d. God must renew your mind for you
e. You must develop a fresh mental attitude yourself

63. When you renew your mind
a. The realities of the new birth become apparent
b. It brings about a transformation into a Christ-like life
c. You become born again
d. You adopt a new attitude of mind
e. Your old attitude concerning giving, fasting, tribalism etc changes for good

64. The Word of God renews your mind
a. Because of its unchangeable standard
b. By dividing the soul and the spirit
c. By sanctification
d. Even when you disagree with it
e. Only when you accept what it teaches

65. Romans 12:12 says Christians should
a. Present their bodies as a living sacrifice to God
b. Be transformed to the world
c. Be transformed
d. Renew their mind
e. Do reasonable service

66. After you are born again
a. Your body is not the same
b. Your body must be brought under control
c. Your body is still the same
d. Your body has unlawful lusts which war against the spirit

67. The body must be kept under control
a. Otherwise it will humiliate you
b. Otherwise you will remain carnal
c. Because the spirit gives life to our mortal bodies to overcome weakness, tiredness, etc.
d. Through bodily exercise
e. Because we not debtors to the flesh

68. Practical ways of keeping the body under control include
a. Fasting
b. Constant Bible Study
c. Good confessions of sin
d. Speaking to the body
e. Praying

69. After you are born again
a. Your mind is still open to all kinds of thoughts
b. You must lean to think on the right things
c. Evil imaginations and thoughts must be cast down
d. The mind is open to both good and bad thoughts
e. The mind becomes a battleground.

70. Are the following statements True or False?
a. The spirit cannot be affected by physical death
b. To 'yield up the ghost' means ghosts exist
c. Judgement is a time to separate Christians from unbelievers
d. Beyond the grave there are three destinations
e. Purgatory is a place between Heaven and Hell

71. Are the following match-ups correct?
a. Man dies only once - Heb 9: 27
b. Everlasting punishment for sinners - Matt 25: 46
c. Eternal life for the righteous - Matt 25: 46
d. After death comes the judgement - Heb 9: 29
e. Sin entered the world through one man - Rom 5:12

72. Are the following statements True or False?
a. In purgatory the soul is kept for a while to be purged of sin
b. The story of Lazarus and the rich man is a parable
c. Jesus preached more about hell than any other subject
d. Sin is a family trait of all mankind
e. Children lie because mankind is born in sin

73. Which of the following options best completes the verse below? Wherefore, as by one -a- sin entered into the world, and -b- by sin; and so -c- passed upon all -d-, for all have -e-
a. man
b. death
c. life
d. mankind
e. sinned

74. The following verses show that Hell is underground (beneath us): True or False?
a. s 14: 9
b. Is 14: 15
c. Rom 5: 12
d. Rom 3: 23
e. Eph 3: 9.

75. Complete the verse below:
Enter ye in the strait -a- for -b- is the gate and -c- is the way that -d- to destruction, and -e- there be which go in there at
a. gate
b. great
c. narrow
d. goes
e. few

76. Which of the following options correctly fits the gaps?
Wherefore he saith, When he -a- on high he led -b- -c-, and gave gifts unto men. Now that he -d-, what is it but that he also descended Eph 4:8,9
a. descended
b. captive
c. captivity
d. descended
e. low

77. The following are the different departments in Hell
a. The "reception" area
b. Low Hell
c. Lower Hell
d. Lowest Hell
e. Basement Hell

78. Many of the following people who will be found in Hell
a. Kings
b. Heads of state
c. Pop stars
d. The rich
e. Great philosophers

79. The following verses show the different people to be found in Hell
a. Is 14:9
b. Is 5:14
c. Is 14: 10, 11
d. Deut 32:22
e. Rom 5:12

80. Which of the following options correctly completes the verse below?
Therefore hell hath -a- herself, and -b- her mouth -c- measure: and their glory, and their -d-, and their pomp, and he that rejoiceth shall -e- into is Is 5:14
a. enlarged
b. opened
c. with
d. number
e. ascend

81. Are the following match-ups true or false?
a. People go to the captivity of hell because they have no knowledge - Is 5: 13, 14
b. People go to hell because they are ignorant - Rom 10: 3
c. There are different levels in Hell - Deut 32: 22
d. There are different levels in Hell - Eph 4: 20
e. There are different levels in Hell - Is 14:14

82. Are the following statements true or false?
a. Many people take prayer to be some kind of religious routine they must perform.
b. Prayer implies we can talk to our heavenly father directly and receive answers.
c. God's word guarantees us a hundred percent results every time we pray
d. Jesus said we might possibly get an answer to our prayers
e. Jesus gave us three possible answers to prayer: yes, no, wait.

83. Elijah once challenged the false prophets of Baal. He said to the people '...if the Lord be God, follow Him: but if Baal, then follow him.' Where can this Scripture be found?
a. I Kings 18:21
b. I Kings 18:17
c. I Kings 18:27
d. II Kings 18:27
e. I Kings 8:27

84. God has promised to answer our prayers every time. Which of the following Scriptures gives us this assurance?
a. I Kings 8:27
b. Psalm 91:15
c. Isaiah 58:9
d. Luke 11:9
e. I John 1:7

85. The 1st step to one hundred per cent answered prayer is to:
a. Learn to trust in your pastor's prayer for you
b. Learn to pray to the father of all men
c. Learn to pray using the name of Jesus
d. Learn to pray yourself
e. Learn to use faith every time you pray.

86. As member of the Person-to-Person, soul ministry group, you met a lady who believes that it is alright to pray to the Virgin Mary. How will you set out to show her the right way to pray?

a. Teach her to learn to pray to Jesus using John 16:32, 34 or 2 Kings 1:38 instead of Mary and show her that it is not possible to pray to Mary and get an answer.

b. Using John 16:23 & 24 and Luke 1:38, teach her to learn to pray to the father and show her how wrong it is to pray to Mary.

c. Use Luke 1:28 to show her that Mary is just a 'handmaid', a mere mortal like herself and then using John 17:23,24, show her that she must pray to the Father.

d. Use Luke 1:28 to show her that Mary is just a handmaid, a mere mortal like herself and then using John 16:23,24 show her how to pray directly to Jesus

e. Use Luke 1:38 to show her that Mary is just a handmaid, a mere mortal like herself and then using John 16:23 and 24 show her how to pray to the Father using the name of Jesus.

87. Your Christian life should not depend on another person's prayers. Which of the following Scriptures can you use to assure Adjoa that she can pray for herself so long as she has received Salvation.

a. John 16:23
b. James 5:16
c. 2 Corinthians 5:21
d. John 15:7
e. 1 John 3:22

88. Are the following statements true or false?

a. You must learn to pray using the name of Jesus
b. You must pray to the Father
c. You must abide in Christ
d. You must be a fruit bearing Christian
e. You must learn to pray Lord's prayer

89. The Scripture in Acts 4:10 shows that

a. the name of Jesus can heal
b. sickness responds to the name of Jesus
c. demons respond to the name of Jesus
d. Satan will bow to the name of Jesus
e. our heavenly Father Himself responds to the name of Jesus

90. Are the following statements/match-ups true or false?

a. God's Word directs us in prayer
b. Abiding in Christ is the most important key of all to receiving any type of response from the Lord.
c. There is a link between answered prayer and bearing fruit
d. "And whatsoever we ask, we receive of him because we keep his commandments ....." - 1 John 3:21
e. "But if we walk in the light, as he is in the light, we have fellowship one with another...." - 1 John 1:17

91. How many "failure - proof" keys are there?

a. 4
b. 2
c. 3
d. 5
e. 6

92. Which of the following Scriptures emphasize on using faith every time we pray?

a. Mark 11:14
b. Hebrews 10:38
c. Hebrews 11:6
d. Romans 4:21-22
e. Hebrews 2:5

93. Under the ministry of Jesus, several people experienced personal breakthroughs. Why did they receive these miracles?

a. Because they were faithful
b. Because they had love which is the greatest of all
c. Because they knew who Jesus was and were persuaded
d. Because they were people of faith
e. None of the above

94. Who were some of the people blessed in question 12?

a. The woman with the issue of blood
b. Blind Bartimaeus
c. The sinful woman who poured alabaster box of ointment on Jesus feet.
d. The leper who returned to say thank you
e. The two blind men who came to Jesus and asked for mercy.

95. Which of the Scriptures correspond to the people mentioned in question 13?

a. Mark 5:34
b. Luke 7:50
c. Mark 10;52
d. Luke 17:9
e. Matthew 9:29

96. Are the following statements true or false?

a. Praying once and thereafter no more is one expression of faith
b. Praying over and over about the same issue, with a determination never to stop until you get an answerer is another expression of faith
c. The reason why you will get results is because you keep praying
d. Praying everyday is one of the steps to 100% answered prayer
e. The 8th and 9th steps to one hundred percent answered prayer is also referred to as failure proof keys.

97. Praying amiss means that:

a. You pray unacceptable prayers
b. You pray unsuitable prayers
c. You pray inappropriate but possible prayers
d. You pray inadmissible prayers
e. You pray unallowable but satisfactory prayer

98. There are ------------- ways you can avoid praying amiss

a. 6
b. 4
c. 5
d. 2
e. 3

99. The following are examples of illegal prayer.

a. Asking God for somebody's husband
b. An old man praying to God to make him young man
c. Asking God to give you a huge mansion when you are starting out in life
d. A pregnant woman praying that she will not experience labour pains
e. A 58 year old Pastor praying that he will not die

READ THE FOLLOWING PASSAGE AND ANSWER QUESTIONS 100-106

Ebenezer Ayimokola, a draftsman with Chubby Consult could not complete the designs and drawings needed for the new market in Ogya by the deadline given by his boss. This was because, he had to travel with some church members for his pastor's funeral. The night before reporting back to the office, he set out to pray that his boss will be struck with blindness so that he will not see the lapses in his work. Even though he had worked for only 22 months he also prayed that God should bless him with a 4 bedroom house with a pool and a Mercedes Benz E -Class before the end of the year.

When he reported the next morning in the office, his boss dismissed him. Ayimokola then entered into a 3 day prayer and fasting period, praying his wife would leave him so he could re-marry a former girl friend who was now a business tycoon so that he would not have to work hard and sweat anymore. He finally prayed that God would not let him die so that he would live to see his boss suffer for dismissing him.

100. Why did Mr. Ayimokola's prayer for his boss not work?

a. He prayed foolish prayers
b. He prayed stupid prayers
c. He prayed with all kinds of prayer
d. He prayed without faith
e. He prayed a difficult prayer

102. What prayers should Ebenezer not have prayed?

a. Foolish prayer
b. Unscriptural prayer
c. Illegal prayer
d. Difficult prayer
e. Prayer of faith

103. Praying that his wife will leave him is a prayer that he should not have prayed. Which Scripture (s) can you use to substantiate this?

a. Micah 6:8
b. Mark 10:9
c. Mark 1:9
d. Micah 8:6
e. Mark 6:8

104. Praying that his wife will divorce him is a ....prayer that he should not have prayed

a. Stupid
b. Foolish
c. An illegal
d. An unscriptural
e. Difficult

105. Which of the following Scriptures can you use to substantiate question 7?

a. Micah 6:8
b. Mark 10:9
c. Mark 1:9
d. Micah 8:6
e. Mark 6:8

106. What is wrong with Ebenezer praying that God will not let him sweat again and die?

a. Because you cannot pray that you will prosper without working hard
b. Because such prayers are illegal prayers
c. Because there is no man on earth who can escape the curse declared over Adam in Genesis 3:17
d. Because you cannot pray that you will not die
e. Because such prayers are foolish prayers

107. How many kinds of prayer is mentioned in the chapter, "How to Receive Answered Prayer?"

a. 12
b. 11
c. 8
d. 10
e. 6

108. Are the following statements true or false?

a. Prayer of consecration is the type of prayer where you offer yourself to the Lord for His perfect will to be done.
b. When you pray the prayer of consecration, God will be more likely to listen to your other prayers
c. Prayer of consecration puts all other prayer topics in their right perspective
d. Matthew 26:39 is not a Scripture that supports prayer of consecration.
e. Prayer of consecration is a prayer topic reserved for only Christians who are aspiring to become full time ministers.

109. Which of these Scriptures does not talk about praying in the spirit?

a. Jude 20
b. I Corinthians 14:2
c. Acts 2:4
d. I Corinthians 14:4
e. Acts 19:6

110. Are the following statements true or false?

a. Believing that you have already received is different from believing that you will receive it one day.
b. The prayer of faith is prayer which has a great expression of faith
c. Prayers of faith are especially effective only against sickness and disease
d. James 5:15 and Mark 11:24 are the main Scriptures for the prayer of faith.
e. Prayer of faith is used when you are praying with another person who shares the same faith.

111. Which of the following statements correspond with the attached Scripture?

a. Prayer which does not include prayer for forgiveness is insufficient: I John 1:18
b. A short but powerful prayer is well demonstrated in Mark 4:36-39 and John 11:41-42
c. There are times you need to spend many hours in prayer: Mark 11:35 and Luke 16:12
d. Jesus prayed with strong cries and so can you: Hebrews 5:7
e. Even in the midnight of your life, a prayer of thanksgiving is appropriate: I Thessalonians 5:18.

112. Jesus gave vivid examples of how persistence gives one hundred per cent answered prayer. Where can these examples be found?

a. Luke 5:20
b. Luke 11:5-8
c. Luke 8:1-8
d. Luke 1:15-18
e. Luke 18:1-8

113. The following are some of Daniel's principles of prayer:

a. Prayer is good
b. Prayer is the source of power and protection
c. Success hinders prayer
d. Prayer will lead to major healing in your life
e. Prayer will help you acquire and sustain the blessings of God

114. According to Daniel's principles of prayer

a. every nation needs holy and educated leaders
b. praying for a long time is tiring
c. the most important time to pray is in times of peace
d. for prayer to be effective, it must be sanctified
e. All of the above

115. Are the following statements True (T) or False (F)?
It is important to pray for long periods of time because

a. Jesus did
b. it is an instruction in the Word.
c. it is implied in the Word.
d. short prayers are no prayers.
e. God does not hear short prayers.

116. Are the following statements True (T) or False (F)?

a. Dan 10:6 tells us how Daniel used to pray three times a day
b. Dan 6:10 tells us how Daniel used to pray three times a day
c. Praying with a loud voice is the main physical type of prayer
d. Praying for a long time is one of Daniel's principles on prayer
e. None of the above

117. Are the following statements True (T) or False (F)?

a. Entering into your closet when praying means praying silently
b. The 4 important times to pray are morning, afternoon, evening and all the time
c. Jesus' all night prayer is found in Lk6:21
d. I Thess 5:17 says 'Pray without ceasing'
e. Jesus' dawn prayer is recorded in Mk 1:35

118. The following verses show us how often we must pray:

a. I Thess. 5:17
b. Mk 1:35
c. Mk 6:46
d. Lk 6:12
e. Gen 12:2

119. A prayer formula

a. releases an anointing for prayer
b. gives you exact words to pray
c. helps you to pray for more than 5 minutes
d. gives you guidelines for prayer.
e. teaches you the types of prayers we must pray

120. Are the following statements True (T) or False (F)?

a. The 'Timothian' prayer is found in 2 Tim 2
b. A prayer formula is something that gives power when praying
c. There are 4 types of prayers we are to offer for a person in authority
d. The 'Timothian' prayer is found in 1 Tim 2
e. The 'Timothian' prayer is found in 1 Tim 3

121. According to the Timothy prayer formula the ff types of prayers must be made for all that are in authority:

a. supplications
b. intercessions
c. authoritative prayers
d. binding and loosening
e. giving of thanks for them

122. According to the Timothian prayer formula, if you pray for those in authority you will experience

a. a hectic life
b. a quiet life
c. a godly life
d. a prayerful life
e. an honest life

123. If we do not pray for those in authority

a. war may break out
b. missionary work cannot continue
c. God will be displeased with you
d. God's intervention in the affairs of men may be hindered
e. Satan will control affairs

124. Are the following statements True (T) or False (F)?

a. 'Thou art a man, not God.................' is found in Ezek 28:4
b. 'Thou art a man, not God ....' is found in Ezek 28:2
c. The anointed Cherub was Nebuchadnezzar
d. The anointed Cherub was Satan himself
e. The king of Tyrus was not a man

125. If you pray for your boss

a. you are fulfilling the Timothian prayer
b. you will affect how he thinks about you
c. you will not become frustrated
d. you will be able to do what you like at work
e. he will understand your need to be absent from work after an all-night

126. The reason why we should pray for those in authority is

a. so that they will not make selfish decisions
b. so that a Christian can become the President
c. so that the competition will cease
d. so that there will be peace and freedom
e. All of the above

127. Are the following True (T) or False (F)?

a. 'The king's heart is in the hands of the Lord' is in Prov 20:1
b. 'The king's heart is in the hands of the Lord' is in Prov 21:1
c. There are times your life depends on what someone else thinks about you
d. Praying for our leaders will help us to live godly lives
e. You need peace and stability for the work of God to go on

128. The following are included in Ephesians prayer formula
a. Giving thanks
b. Prayer for authority
c. Prayer for miracles
d. Prayer for revelation
e. Prayer for understanding

129. The following are included in the Ephesians Prayer Formula
a. Prayer about your calling
b. Prayer for riches
c. Prayer to know the greatness of God's power
d. Prayer for divine breakthrough
e. Prayer for forgiveness

130. The following are included in the Lord's prayer formula
a. God's will be done
b. Prayer against temptation
c. Prayer for a greater anointing
d. Prayer for your enemies
e. Prayer for an annual supply of bread

131. Are the following statements True (T) or False (F)?
a. Matt 6:10 says 'Thy kingdom come...........................'
b. Matt 6:10 says 'Thy will be done on earth.........................'
c. When it comes to prayer do not depend on anybody apart from yourself
d. Matt 6:13 says 'Lead us not into temptation....'
e. Matt 6:13 says '..........deliver us from evil...........'

132. Praying for the kingdom of God to come means:
a. praying that Jesus will return soon
b. praying for church growth
c. praying that people will be saved
d. praying for your pastors
e. praying for your finances

133. "The tongue .... is an unruly evil, full of deadly poison" can be found in
a. I Peter 2:9
b. James 3:8
c. James 1:8
d. Ephesians 4:16
e. Phil. 3:3

134. "Death and life are in the power of the tongue" is found in
a. Proverbs 3:7
b. Proverbs 24:24
c. Proverbs 18:21
d. Proverbs 6:8
e. Proverbs 30:1

135. The following statements are true:
a. The tongue controls our destiny, regardless of our status as Christians or unbelievers.
b. The power of cancer, leukaemia, long life and wealth are embedded in the tongue.
c. Words created the world and brought life into being
d. Human beings also possess the same creative power God posses in their tongues.
e. " ... the tongue .... Is an unruly evil, full of deadly poison" (James 3:8) was written mainly to unbelievers.

136. The following are all poisons in the tongue
a. Lies
b. Exaggeration
c. Pride
d. Flattery
e. Confessions

137. The poison of lies
a. sears your conscience
b. makes you loos the correcting and refining influence to keep you on track
c. includes white lies
d. are tools of Satan
e. hardens your heart.

138. "..... he is a liar, and the father of it". This verse is found in
a. John 8:44
b. Proverbs 28:13
c. Revelation 21:8
d. I Timothy 4:2
e. Isaiah 32:7

139. Revelation 21:8 confirms that
a. the Bible lines up liars together with sorcerers, hinderers, and abominable people sent to hell.
b. the six things God hates includes lying
c. lying hardens your heart
d. lying is Satan's favourite tool
e. lying deceives your ownself.

140. The following statements about the poison of flattery are true.
a. Only secular leaders and politicians who fall prey to flattery hypocrites
b. Flattery is saying good things about someone
c. Flattery produces mistrust in the one flattered
d. Flattery makes the flatterer gain confidence in himself and achieves greater things
e. Flattery leads to destruction and ruin

141. **"And upon a set day .... arrayed in royal apparel, sat upon his throne, and made an oration unto them. And the people gave a shout, saying, it is the voice of God, and not of a man. And immediately the angel of the Lord smote him, because he gave not God the glory : and he was eaten of worms." This scriptural passage relates to**
a. Caesar Augustus
b. King Hezekiah
c. King Jeroboam
d. King Herod
e. Ananaias and Sapphira.

For the following questions, complete these translated flattering words, cited in chapter 12 and used as laudations for chiefs of the Ashanti tribe in Ghana.

141. **"Great warrior, you are the one who leans on a rock ..."**
a. and moves it into the sea
b. and it melts
c. and it disappears
d. and it breaks
e. and it turns into water

142. **"Great King, you are the one who steps in water ...."**
a. and creates a path in it.
b. and it turns into ice
c. and it dries up
d. and it evaporates
e. and it boils.

143. **"You are the one who goes to fetch water from the river with ... "**
a. a leaking bucket
b. a spoon
c. a net
d. a basket
e. a broken cistern

144. **"You are the one who kills ...."**
a. the bear with your bare hands
b. the lion with your bare hands
c. the tiger with your bare hands
d. the leopard with your bare hands
e. the elephant with your bare hands

145. **The following Scriptures condemn flattery:**
a. Isaiah 5:20
b. Proverbs 24:24
c. Psalm 12:2,3
d. Malachi 2:17
e. All of the above

146. **"But shun .... and vain babblings; for they will increase unto more ungodliness." (2 Tim 2:16). The missing word relates to the poison of**
a. Flattery
b. Tale bearing
c. Lying
d. Blasphemy
e. Profane language

147. **According to the Bible, the deadly poison that has the direct and immediate ability to separate best friends is**
a. Flattery
b. Tale bearing
c. Blasphemy
d. Profane language
e. Foolish talking

148. **In Proverbs 26:20 "where no wood is, there the fire goeth out..." the "wood" in this Scripture refers to**
a. Flattery
b. Tale bearing
c. Lying
d. Profane language
e. Foolish talking

149. **The biblical treatment for tale bearing stipulated in Romans 16:17 includes**
a. Rebuke them publicly
b. Pray for them to receive change of heart
c. Mark (note, identify) them
d. Restore them in humility
e. Avoid (have no fellowship) with them.

150. **The following statements are true**
a. When you speak irreverently against God it is blasphemy
b. Blasphemy does not include speaking irreverently against preaches
c. Only unbelievers can commit blasphemy against the Holy Ghost
d. Apart from blasphemy against the Holy Ghost all other sins can be forgiven
e. Blasphemy includes accusing a genuine minister of being a false prophet.

151. **In the San Francisco earthquake analogy to explain the poison of foolish talking the following are accurate details of the story. The man who escaped**
a. had been buried under the rubble for 7 days
b. said he survived because of his faith
c. said he survived because of the strong will power
d. suffered a stroke a month after and died
e. suffered a heart attack a week after and died suddenly.

152. In Hebrews 3:17 we are told that God was grieved with the people of God in the wilderness for forty years because of
a. Adultery
b. Idolatry
c. Blasphemy
d. They were involved with lying
e. They were guilty of expressing doubt.

153. Speaking maliciously untrue statements about someone is
a. Profanity
b. Blasphemy
c. Flattery
d. Slander
e. Mumuring

154. In which of the underlisted Scriptures do we find the antidote for a "backbiting tongue".
a. Proverbs 24:24
b. Proverbs 28:13
c. Proverbs 18:21
d. Proverbs 25:23
e. Proverbs 4:23

155. The following Scripture match-ups are correct
a. "Do all things without murmuring - Phil. 2:14
b. "Neither murmur ye, as some of them also murmured" - 1 Cor. 10:10
c. "let the words of my mouth ... be acceptable in thy sight, Oh Lord ..." - Psa9:14
d. "The Lord God hath given me the tongue of the learned, ..." - Isaiah 50:4
e. " ..... God gave them over to a reprobate mind ... backbiters, haters of God" .. - Romans 1:28-30

156. Duality is
a. the act of living two lives
b. the act of having two personalities
c. the act of having two nature embodied in one person
d. the act of having one life displayed in public and the other lived in private
e. all of the above

157. A dual person usually
a. has a bright public life
b. has a dark public life
c. has a bright private lifestyle
d. has a dark private lifestyle
e. None of the above is true

158. Duality encourages
a. the spirit of hypocrisy
b. the spirit of lies
c. the spirit of self-deception
d. the spirit of faith
e. the spirit of truthfulness

159. A perfect example of someone with a dual life was
a. David
b. Samson
c. Judas
d. Paul
e. Gideon

160. Duality
a. is a cursed life
b. makes people never end well
c. makes people die in disgrace
d. makes you a strongman
e. makes you lie

161. If you want to please men
a. you should please God also
b. you can never be a servant of God
c. you will never please God
d. you will be admired by God
e. None of the above is true

162. A person living a dual life
a. will do everything possible to impress his friends
b. might appear to be good, but their goodness is short-lived
c. has a temporarily good life
d. changes with the environment
e. has only one life style

163. A dual person might be loyal
a. yet slanderous
b. yet double-tongued
c. yet faithful
d. and friendly
e. but disrespectful

164. Samson was a spiritual person
a. yet carnal
b. yet brutal
c. and never made any carnal mistakes
d. and allowed the spirit to move him at certain times
e. None of the above

165. The foundation of duality is
a. deception
b. self-deception
c. lies
d. disobedience
e. foolishness

SHORT NOTE QUESTIONS

1. How important is the Word of God to us that we should develop confidence in it as a greatest book of all time.

2. In about one page briefly state what the Bible is and what is not to a new convert.

3. What do you understand by "the canon Scriptures" Give five reasons why the canon of Scripture was defined

4. Can the Bible be trusted. Why? How is the Bible superior to every other book.

5. What is Apocrypha? Why was the Apocrypha not canonised?

6. State the three languages in which the Bible was written. Briefly state following people said about the Bible:
   (i) F.F. Bruce
   (ii) HY Pickering
   (iii) John Warwick Montgomery
   (iv) Bernard Ramm

7. There are 8 major things that run through the entire Bible, what are they? Briefly explain.

8. As a Christian, what do you understand by quiet time and what things happen to you during quiet time.

9. Give examples of three great men in the Bible who had quiet time.

10. If I have to choose any thing doing first in the morning, I will choose to do my quiet time because of its powerful effect on our lifes. What are these effects/ Discuss.

11. Shallowness is a disease of charismatic Christian. This can be avoided by the power of quiet time. Give 7 symptoms of this disease in Christians

12. What tools would you need for an effective quiet time.

13. If the Bible should be interpreted, it must be interpreted correctly. How would you do this.

14. Choosing three men mentioned by Bishop in chapter 2 of this textbook, briefly discuss what these men commented of uniqueness about the Words of Jesus.

15. Enumerate the characteristics the Words of Jesus that make them so unique.

16. Explain what Jesus said to be the work of God and the key to doing the work as in John 6:29. Every decision a ministry makes is a decision between following the Holy Spirit and following the honour of men. Give 5 examples to support this statement.

17. Explain what a spiritual warfare is? Discuss (10) facts Christian must know about our battle with the demonic hordes on this earth.

18. Why must every minister be careful of operating in the natural.

19. With scriptural support each, give (10) title of Satan.

20. Explain the following Greek Words which describe Satan.
   (i) Diabolos (ii)Akerthartos.

NOTES

Chapter 1

1. Finis Jennings Dake, *Dake's Annotated Reference Bible* (Lawrence, Georgia: Dake Bible Sales, 1991), 509,510.
2. Ibid., 509,510.
3. Josh McDowell, *Evidence That Demands A Verdict, Volume 1* (San Bernadino, California: Here's Life Publishers, Inc., 1989), 38 3B 8D.
4. Ibid., 30 2C 1D.
5. Ibid., 29-30 2B 1D, 2D.
6. Ibid., 36 3B 2C.
7. Ibid., 30 3C 1D.
8. Ibid., 31 3C 2D.
9 Ibid., 31 3C 3D.
10. Ibid., 29 3A 2C.
11. Ibid., 35-36 4D.
12. Finis Jennings Dake, *Dake's Annotated Reference Bible* (Lawrence, Georgia: Dake Bible Sales, 1991), 511 Col 1,4.
13. Josh McDowell, *Evidence That Demands A Verdict, Volume 1* (San Bernadino, California: Here's Life Publishers, Inc., 1989), 35-36 4D.
14. Ibid., 33 7C 1D, 2D.
15. Ibid., 33-35 7C 3D.

Chapter 2

1. Josh McDowell, *Evidence That Demands A Verdict, Volume 1* (San Bernadino, California: Here's Life Publishers, Inc., 1989), 39 Part 1 4A 1C.
2. Ibid., 19 Part 1 4C 1D.
3. Ibid., 41, Part 1 4A 1C.
4. Ibid.,65.
5. Ibid., 16-17, Section 1 1C.
6. Ibid., 16-17, Section 1 1C and Finis Jennings Dake, *Dake's Annotated Reference Bible* (Lawrence, Georgia: Dake Bible Sales, 1991), 241, Col. 3.
7. Josh McDowell, *Evidence That Demands A Verdict, Volume 1* (San Bernadino, California: Here's Life Publishers, Inc., 1989), 18-19, Section 1 2C .
8. Ibid., 19, Section 1 3C.
9. Ibid., 19, Section 1 4C 1D.
10. Ibid., 20, Section 1 4C 2D.
11. Ibid., 21, 4C 3D.
12. Ibid., 22, Section 1 5C 1D.
13. Ibid., 23-24, 6C 3B.

Chapter 4

1. Finis Jennings Dake, *Dake's Annotated Reference Bible* (Lawrence, Georgia: Dake Bible Sales, 1991), 243.
2. Public Domain.

Chapter 13

1. Rick Joyner, *The Final Quest* (Wilkesboro, North Carolina: Morning Star Publications, 2002), 16-17.
2. Basil Miller, *John Wesley* (Bloomington, Minnesota: Bethany House Publishers, n.d.), 130-131.
3. Beverly LaHaye, *The Spirit Controlled Woman* (Eugene, Oregon: Harvest House Publishers, n.d.), 208-209.
4. John Telford, *John Wesley, Into All the World* (Belfast, Northern Ireland: Ambassador Publications, n.d.), 257-259.
5. R. Spitzer, M. Gibbon, A. Skodol and J. Williams eds, *DSM-IV®-TR Case Book, Fourth Edition* (Arlington, Virginia: American Psychiatric Publishing, Inc., n.d.), 279-281.

Chapter 14

1. John Telford, *John Wesley, Into All the World* (Belfast, Northern Ireland: Ambassador Publications, n.d.), 257-259.
2. Stephen Mansfield, *Derek Prince, A Biography* (Lake Mary, Florida: Charisma House, n.d.), 267-269.

Chapter 15

1. John Telford, *John Wesley, Into All the World* (Belfast, Northern Ireland: Ambassador Publications, n.d.), 257-259.
2. Basil Miller, *John Wesley* (Bloomington, Minnesota: Bethany House Publishers, n.d.), 130-131.

Chapter 19

1. Josh McDowell, *Evidence That Demands A Verdict, Volume 1* (San Bernadino, California: Here's Life Publishers, Inc., 1989),15 1B.
2. Phyllis McIntosh, *The Power of Faith*, Reader's Digest, October 1999.

Chapter 20

1. J. H. Armstrong, *Five Great Evangelists* (Fern, Ross-shire: Christian Focus Publications, n.d.), 113-114.

Chapter 21

1. Josh McDowell, *Evidence That Demands A Verdict, Volume 1* (San Bernadino, California: Here's Life Publishers, Inc., 1989),129-131.

2. Gordon Lindsay, Source Unknown.

Chapter 29

1. Oswald J. Chambers, *Satan 1s No Myth* (Chicago, IL: Moody Press, 1975), 7.

2. F. J. Huegel, *Successful Praying* (Minneapolis, MN: Bethany Fellowship, 1967), 62 and Watchman Nee, *The Spiritual Man* (Anaheim, CA: Living Stream Ministry, 1992), 272 - 84.
3. Elizabeth Alves, *Becoming a Prayer Warrior: A Guide to Effective and Powerful Prayer* (Ventura, CA: Regal Books, 1998), 97 - 99.
4. Ibid., 100 - 101.
5. William R. Keylor, for Microsoft ® Encarta ® Encyclopedia 2005, *Military Strategies of World War 1* (© Microsoft Corporation, 1993 - 2004).
6. Microsoft ® Encarta ® Encyclopedia 2004, *U. S. Casualties in Vietnam* (© Microsoft Corporation, 1993 - 2003).
7. Bill Subritzky, *Demons Defeated* (Tonbridge, England: Sovereign World Ltd, 1985), 18 - 20.
8. Bob Larson, *Larson's Book of Spiritual Warfare* (Nashville, TN: Thomas Nelson Publishers, 1999), 324 - 9 and Finis Jennings Dake, *Dake's Annotated Reference Bible* (Lawrence, Georgia: Dake Bible Sales, 1991), 3.
9. Ed Murphy, *The Handbook for Spiritual Warfare* (Nashville, TN: Thomas Nelson Publishers, 1996), 46 - 48.
10. Samuel Ofori Onwona, *Shadows Come to Light* (n.c.: African Christian Press, 2000), 27 - 29.
11. T. D. Jakes, *Six Pillars From Ephesians: Overcoming the Enemy* (Tulsa, OK: Albury Publishing, 2000), 65 - 71.
12. Bob Larson, *Larson's Book of Spiritual Warfare* (Nashville, TN: Thomas Nelson Publishers, 1999), 203 - 15.
13. Beth Moore, *Breaking Free from Spiritual Strongholds* (Nashville, TN: Broadman and Holman Publishers, 2000), 71 - 87 and Ed Murphy, *The Handbook for Spiritual Warfare* (Nashville, TN: Thomas Nelson Publishers, 1996), 41 - 43.
14. T. W. Hunt, *The Doctrine of Prayer* (Nashville, TN: Convention Press, 1986), 122 - 4 and B. Gordon Watt, *Effectual Fervent Prayer* (Los Angeles, CA: The Biola Book Room, 1927), 100 - 109.
15. Ed Murphy, *The Handbook for Spiritual Warfare* (Nashville, TN: Thomas Nelson Publishers, 1996), 61 - 76.
16. Ibid., 296 - 7; Edwin and Lillian Harvey, *Kneeling We Triumph* (Chicago, IL: Moody Press, 1971), 112 - 3 and Wesley L. Duewel, *Mighty Prevailing Prayer* (Grand Rapids, MI: Zondervan Publishing House, 1990), 180 - 92.
17. Edwin and Lillian Harvey, *Kneeling We Triumph* (Chicago, IL: Moody Press, 1971), 48 - 49.
18. Peter C. Wagner, *What the Bible Says about Spiritual Warfare* (Ventura, CA: Regal Books Gospel Light, 2001), 60 - 65 and Rob Finley, *Recapturing Biblical Intercession* (Memphis, Tennessee: Prayer Resources, 1982), 17 - 21.
19. Wesley L. Duewel, *Touch the World through Prayer* (Grand Rapids, MI: Zondervan Publishing House, 1986), 103 - 4; Ibid., 23 -24 and Ed Murphy, *The Handbook for Spiritual Warfare* (Nashville, TN: Thomas Nelson Publishers, 1996), 421 - 3.
20. Ibid., 405 - 7.
21. Elizabeth Alves, *Becoming a Prayer Warrior: A Guide to Effective and Powerful Prayer* (Ventura, CA: Regal Books, 1998), 99 - 100.
22. Peter C. Wagner, *What the Bible Says about Spiritual Warfare* (Ventura, CA: Regal Books Gospel Light, 2001), 55 - 59.
23. Rob Finley, *Recapturing Biblical Intercession* (Memphis, Tennessee: Prayer Resources, 1982), 19.
24. Calvin Miller, *Disarming the Darkness* (Grand Rapids, MI: Zondervan Publishing House, 1998), 91 - 156.
25. Ibid., 17 - 19.
26. Wesley L. Duewel, *Touch the World through Prayer* (Grand Rapids, MI: Zondervan Publishing House, 1986), 103 - 4.

Chapter 30

1. K. Koch, *Occult Bondage and Deliverance* (Grand Rapids, Michigan: Kregel, 1970), 57 - 58.
2. Raymond Baker Jr., *Attack from the Spirit World - A Compilation* (Wheaton, Illinois: Tyndale, 1973), 21 - 25; Merril F. Unger, *Biblical Demonology* (Wheaton, Illinois: Scripture Press, 1952), 82 - 90.
3. L. S. Chafer, *Satan* (Grand Rapids, Michigan: Zondervan, 1964), 7.
4. Micheal Green, *Believe in Satan's Downfall* (London: Hodder and Stoughton, n.d), 15 - 18; R. G. Barnhouse, *The Invisible War* (Grand Rapids: Zondervan, 1965), 156 - 7; Mark Bubeck, *The Adversary* (Chicago: Moody, 1975), 68; Warren Wiersbe, *The Strategy of Satan* (Wheaton, Illinois: Tyndale, 1979), 48 - 55.
5. Opoku Onyinah, *Overcoming Demons* (Accra, Ghana: Pentecost Press, 1995), 51.
6. Don Basham, *Deliver Us from Evil* (London: Hodder and Stoughton, 1972), 141 - 2.
7. Richard W. Dehaan ed., *Satan, Satanism and Witchcraft* (Grand Rapids, Michigan: Zondervan, 1972), 27 - 31; Victor H. Ernest, *I Talked with Spirits* (Wheaton, Illinois: Tyndale, 1970), 49 - 57, 67 - 70; Warren Wiersbe, *The Strategy of Satan* (Wheaton, Illinois: Tyndale, 1979), 37 - 50.

Chapter 31

1. J. H. Armstrong, *Five Great Evangelists,* (Fern, Ross - Shire, England: Christian Focus

Publications, 1997),113-114.

2. Ibid.,113-114.
3. John Warwick Montgomery ed., *Demon Possession* (Minneapolis, Minnesota: Bethany, 1976), 223 - 9.
4. John Warwick Montgomery ed., *Demon Possession* (Minneapolis, Minnesota: Bethany, 1976), 347 - 8; Fred Dickason, *Demon Possession and the Christian* (Chicago: Moody, 1987), 101 - 7; Grayson H. Ensign and Edward Howe, *Bothered? Bewildered? Bewitched?* (Cincinnatti: Recovery, 1984), 133 - 5; Merril F. Unger, *What Demons Can Do to Saints* (Chicago: Moody, 1977), 91 - 93, 119; Don Basham, *Deliver Us from Evil* (London: Hodder and Stoughton, 1972), 142 - 3; Roger Elwood, *Strange Things are Happening - Satanism, Witchcraft and God* (New York: Family Library, 1973), 79 - 82; Raymond Baker ed., *Attack from the Spirit World - A Compilation* (Wheaton, Illinois: Tyndale, 1973), 51 - 53; Ibid., 63 - 65; Ibid., 94; Merrill F. Unger, *Demons in the World Today* (Wheaton, Illinois: Living Books, 1971), 143 - 51.
5. R. P. Rawlins, S. R. Williams and C. K. Beck, *Mental Health-Psychiatric Nursing: A Holistic Life-Cycle Approach* (St. Louis, Missouri: Mosby-Year Book Inc., 1993), 9, 261 - 4; Nancy C. Andreason and Donald W. Black, *Introductory Textbook of Psychiatry* (Washington, DC: American Psychiatry Press Inc., 1995), 442 - 5; Eric E. Brueshke et al ed., *The World Book/Rush-Presbyterian St. Luke's Medical Center Medical Encyclopedia* (Chicago: World Book Inc., 1995), 244 - 5; Ruth Koenigsberg et al ed., *Churchill's Illustrated Medical Dictionary* (Edinburgh: Churchill Livingstone Inc., 1989), 498.
6. Nancy C. Andreason and Donald W. Black, *Introductory Textbook of Psychiatry* (Washington, DC: American Psychiatry Press Inc., 1995), 442 - 5; Eric E. Brueshke et al ed., *The World Book/Rush-Presbyterian St. Luke's Medical Center Medical Encyclopedia* (Chicago: World Book Inc., 1995), 244 - 5; Ruth Koenigsberg et al ed., *Churchill's Illustrated Medical Dictionary* (Edinburgh: Churchill Livingstone Inc., 1989), 498.
7. Eric E. Brueshke et al ed., *The World Book/Rush-Presbyterian St. Luke's Medical Center Medical Encyclopedia* (Chicago: World Book Inc., 1995),244 - 5; Ruth Koenigsberg et al ed., *Churchill's Illustrated Medical Dictionary* (Edinburgh: Churchill Livingstone Inc., 1989), 498; Nancy C. Andreason and Donald W. Black, *Introductory Textbook of Psychiatry* (Washington, DC: American Psychiatry Press Inc., 1995), 442 - 5.
8. Michael Green, *Believe in Satan's Downfall* (London: Hodder and Stoughton, n. d.), 70.
9. Ken and Nancy Curtis, *Tormented?* (Lakefield, Florida: Spiritual Warfare Ministries, Inc., 1988), 125, 128 - 9.
10. Kurt Koch, *Occult Bondage and Deliverance* (Grand Rapids, Michigan: Kregel, 1970),136 - 53.
11. Mark Bubeck, *The Adversary* (Chicago: Moody, 1975), 144 - 6.
12. Dag Heward-Mills, *Loyalty and Disloyalty* (Accra, Ghana: Parchment House, 1998), 11 - 12.
13. Kurt Koch, *Occult Bondage and Deliverance* (Grand Rapids, Michigan: Kregel, 1970), 136 - 53.
14. Fred Dickason, *Demon Possession and the Christian* (Chicago: Moody, 1987), 67 - 68; J. Dwight, *Your Adversary the Devil* (Grand Rapids, Michigan: Zondervan, 1969), 76 - 92; Fred Dickason, *Angels Elect and Evil* (Chicago: Moody, 1975), 170.
15. Opoku Onyinah, *Overcoming Demons* (Accra, Ghana: Pentecost Press, 1995), 29 - 30; Raymond Baker ed., *Attack from the Spirit World* (Wheaton, Illinois: Tyndale. 1973), 69 - 70.
16. Ken and Nancy Curtis, *Tormented?* (Lakefield, Florida: Spiritual Warfare Ministries, Inc.,1988), 124.
17. Merril F. Unger, *Biblical Demonology* (Scripture Press, 1952), 217, 218; Phillips McCandish, *The Spirit World* (Wheaton, Illinois: World Pub., Company, 1970),106 - 110.
18. Raymond Baker ed., *Attack from the Spirit World* (Wheaton, Illinois: Tyndale, 173), 55 - 58 and Walter Martin, *Exorcism: Fact or Fable* (Santa Ana, California: Vision House Publishing, 1975), 17 - 18, 21.
19. Michael Green, *Believe in Satan's Downfall* (London: Hodder and Stoughton), 72 - 73; Derek Prince, *They Shall Expel Demons* (Fort Lauderdale, Florida: Derek Prince Ministries, 1998), 192 - 202.
20. Kenneth Hagin, *The Triumphant Church* (Tulsa, Oklahoma: Faith Library Publications, 1993), 280 - 282, 284.
21. Henry A.and Mary E. Virkler, *Demonic Involvements in Human Life and Illness - Journal of Psychology and Theology 5. 2* (1977), 95 - 102; Hal Lindsay and C. C. Carlson, *Satan Is Alive and Well on Planet Earth* (Grand Rapids, Michigan: Zondervan, 1972), 56; Merril F. Unger, *Biblical Demonology* (Wheaton, Illinois: Scripture Press, 1952), 97 - 99; Merril F. Unger, *Demons in the World Today* (Wheaton, Illinois: Living Books, Tyndale, 1971), 38, 39; Fred C. Dickason, *Angels Elect and Evil* (Chicago: Moody,

1975), 174 - 5, 182, 4; Lester Sumrall, *Demonology and Deliverance* Vol. 1 (South Bend, Indiana: Sumrall Publishing, 2000), 73 - 76.
22. Derek Prince, *They Shall Expel Demons* (Fort Lauderdale, Florida: Derek Prince Ministries, 1998), 53.
23. Bill Subritzky, *Demons Defeated* (Tonbridge, England: Sovereign World Pub., 1985), 30 - 35.
24. Ibid., 20 - 21, 24 - 25.

Chapter 32

1. Derek Prince, *They Shall Expel Demons* (Fort Lauderdale, Florida: Derek Prince Ministries, 1998), 43 - 49.
2. Leonard Brehun, *Liberia: The War of Horror* (Accra, Ghana: Adwinsa Pub., 1991), 17 - 47.
3. Hal Lindsay and C. C Carlson, *Satan Is Alive and Well on Planet Earth* (Grand Rapids, Michigan: Zondervan, 1972), 159 - 62; Opoku Onyinah, *Overcoming Demons* (Accra, Ghana: Pentecost Press, 1995), 38 -42; K. A. Philpott, *Manual of Demonology and the Occult* (Grand Rapids, Michigan: Zondervan, 1976), 127, 8; Warren Wiersbe, *The Strategy of Satan* (Wheaton, Illinois: Tyndale, 1979), 117 - 125 and Derek Prince, *They Shall Expel Demons* (Fort Lauderdale, Florida: Derek Prince Ministries, 1998), 52 - 56.
4. Ken and Nancy Curtis, *Tormented?* (Lakefield, Florida: Spiritual Warfare Ministries, Inc.,1988),12-13 and Lester Sumrall, *Demonology and Deliverance vol. 1* (South Bend, Indiana: Sumrall Publishing, 2000), 83 - 92.
5. Kenneth Hagin, *He Gave Gifts Unto Men* (Tulsa, Oklahoma: Faith Library Publications, 1992), 114 - 7.

Chapter 33

1. Hal Lindsay and C. C. Carlson, *Satan Is Alive and Well on Planet Earth* (Grand Rapids, Michigan: Zondervan, 1972) , 58 - 61.
2. Kenneth Hagin, *The Triumphant Church* (Tulsa, Oklahooma: Faith Library Publications, 1993), 97 - 102.
3. Scott MacLeod, *Snakes in the Lobby* (Moravian Falls, North Carolina: MorningStar Publications, 1997), 13 - 22.
4. Rick Joyner, *The Final Quest* (Moravian Falls, North Carolina: MorningStar Publications, 2002), 16 - 19.

Chapter 34

1. John Warwick Montgomery ed., *Demon Possession* (Minneapolis, Minnesota: Bethany, 1976), 41 - 56; K. A. Philpott, *Manual of Demonology and the Occult* (Grand Rapids, Michigan: Zondervan, 1976), 66 - 71; F. J. Huegel, *That Old Serpent - The Devil* (Grand Rapids, Michigan: Zondervan, 1954), 99 - 106.
2. Josh McDowell and Don Stewart, *Handbook of Today's Religions* (Nashville, Tennesee: Thomas Nelson Pub., 1983),197, 80.
3. Derek Prince, *They Shall Expel Demons* (Fort Lauderdale, Florida: Derek Prince Ministries, 1998), 225 - 9.

BIBLIOGRAPHY

Alves, Elizabeth. *Becoming a Prayer Warrior: A Guide to Effective and Powerful Prayer*. Ventura, CA: Regal Books, 1998.

Armstrong, J. H. *Five Great Evangelists*. Fern, Ross - Shire, England: Chrisitan Focus Publications, 1997.

Baker, Raymond Jr. *Attack from the Spirit World*. Wheaton, Illinois: Tyndale, 1973.

Barnhouse, R. G. *The Invisible War*. Grand Rapids, Michigan: Zondervan, 1965.

Basham, Don. *Deliver Us from Evil*. London: Hodder and Stoughton, 1972.

Brehun, Leonard. *Liberia, the War of Horror*. Accra, Ghana: Adwinsa Pub., 1991.

Bubeck, Mark. *The Adversary*. Chicago: Moody, 1975.

Chafer, L. S. *Satan*. Grand Rapids, Michigan, Zondervan: 1964.

Chambers, Oswald. *Workmen of God*. New York: Grosset & Dunlap, 1938.

Curtis, Ken and Nancy. *Tormented?* Lakefield, Florida: Chrisitan Warfare Publications, Inc., 1988.

Dake, Finis Jennings. Dake's Annotated Reference Bible. Lawrence, Georgia: Dake Bible Sales, 1991.

Dehaan, Richard W. *Satan, Satanism and Witchcraft*. Grand Rapids, Michigan: Zondervan, 1972.

Dickason, Fred. *Angels Elect and Evil*. Chicago: Moody, 1975.

------. *Demon Possession and the Christian*. Chicago: Moody, 1987.

Duewel, Wesley L. *Mighty Prevailing Prayer*. Grand Rapids, MI: Zondervan Publishing House, 1990.

Ernest, Victor H. *I Talked with Spirits*. Wheaton, Illinois: Tyndale, 1970.

Finley, Rob. *Recapturing Biblical Intercession*. Memphis, TN: Prayer Resources, 1982.

Grayson, H. Ensign and Edward Howe. *Bothered? Bewildered? Bewitched?* Cincinnatti: Recovery, 1984.

Green, Micheal. *Believe in Satan's Downfall*. London: Hodder and Stoughton, n.d.

Hagin, Kenneth E. *He Gave Gifts to Men*. Tulsa, Oklahoma: Faith Library Publications, 1992.

------. *The Triumphant Church*. Tulsa, Oklahoma: Faith Library Publications, 1993.

Harvey, Edwin and Lillian. *Kneeling We Triumph*. Chicago, IL: Moody Press, 1971.

Heward-Mills, Dag. *Loyalty and Disloyalty*. Accra, Ghana: Parchment House, 1998.

Huegel, F. J. *Successful Praying*. Minneapolis, MN: Bethany Fellowship, 1967.

------. *That Old Serpent - The Devil*. Grand Rapids, Michigan: Zondervan, 1954.

Hunt, T. W. *The Doctrine of Prayer*. Nashville, TN: Convention Press, 1986.

Jakes, T. D. *Six Pillars From Ephesians: Overcoming the Enemy*. Tulsa, OK: Albury Publishing, 2000.

Joyner, Rick. *The Final Quest*. Moravian Hills, North Carolina: MorningStar Publications, 2002.

Keylor, William R. for Microsoft ® Encarta ® Encyclopedia 2005, *Military Strategies of World War 1* (© Microsoft Corporation, 1993-2004).

Koch, Kurt. Occult: *Bondage and Deliverance*. Grand Rapids, Michigan: Kregel, 1970.

LaHaye, Beverly. *The Spirit Controlled Woman*. Eugene, Oregon: Harvest House Publishers, ???.

Larson, Bob. *Larson's Book of Spiritual Warfare*. Nashville, TN: Thomas Nelson Publishers, 1999.

Lindsay, Hal and C. C. Carlson. *Satan Is Alive and Well on Planet Earth*. Grand Rapids, Michigan: Zondervan, 1972.

MacLeod, Scott. *Snakes in the Lobby*. Moravian Hills, North Carolina: MorningStar Publications, 1997.

Macmillan, John A. *Encounter with Demons*. Christian Publishers, 1980.

Mansfield, Stephen. *Derek Prince, A Biography*. Lake Mary, Florida: Charisma House, ???.

McDowell, Josh. *Evidence That Demands a Verdict, Volume 1*. San Bernadino, California: Here's Life Publishers, Inc., 1989.

McDowell, Josh and Don Stewart. *Handbook of Today's Religions*. Nashville, Tennesse: Thomas Nelson, 1983.

McIntosh, Phyllis. *The Power of Faith*, Reader's Digest, October 1999.

Microsoft ® Encarta ® Encyclopedia 2004, U. S. *Casualties in Vietnam*. (© Microsoft Corporation, 1993-2003).

Miller, Basil. *John Wesley*. Bloomington, MI: Bethany House Publishers, ???.

Miller, Calvin. *Disarming the Darkness*. Grand Rapids, MI: Zondervan Publishing House, 1998.

Montgomery, John Warwick. *Demon Possession*. Bethany, 1976.

Moore, Beth. *Breaking Free from Spiritual Strongholds*. Nashville, TN: Broadman and Holman Publishers, 2000.

Murphy, Ed. *The Handbook for Spiritual Warfare*. Nashville TN: Thomas Nelson Publishers, 1996.

Onwona, Samuel Ofori. *Shadows Come to Light*. n.c.: African Christian Press, 2000.

Onyinah, Opoku. *Overcoming Demons*. Accra, Ghana: Pentecost Press, 1995.

Pentecost, Dwight J. *Your Advesary the Devil*. Grand Rapids, Michigan: Zondervan, 1969.

Phillips, McCandish. *The Spirit World*. Wheaton, Illinois: World Pub. Company, 1970.

Philpott, K. *A Manual of Demonology and the Occult*. Grand Rapids, Michigan: Zondervan, 1976.

Prince, Derek. *They Shall Expel Demons*. Fort Lauderdale, Florida: Derek Prince Ministries, 1998.

Spitzer R., Gibbon M., Skodol A., Williams J. eds. *DSM-IV®-TR Case Book, Fourth Edition* Arlington, Virginia: American Psychiatric Publishing, Inc., ???.

Subritzky, Bill. *Demons Defeated*. Tonbridge, England: Sovereign World Ltd, 1985.

Sumrall, Lester. *Demonology and Deliverance*. South Bend, Indiana: Sumrall Publishing, 2000.

Telford, John. *John Wesley, Into All the World*. Belfast, Northern Ireland: Ambassador Publications, ???.

Unger, Merril F. *Biblical Demonology*. Wheaton, Illinois: Scripture Press, 1952.

------. *Demons in the World Today*. Wheaton, Illinois: Tyndale, 1971.

------. *What Demons Can Do to Saints*. Chicago: Moody, 1977.

Virkler, Henry A. and Mary E. *Demonic Involvements in Human Life and Illness*. Journal of Psychology and Theology 5. 2. 1977.

Wagner, Peter C. *Prayer Shield*. Ventura, CA: Regal Books Gospel Light, 2001.

------. *What the Bible Says about Spiritual Warfare*. Ventura, CA: Regal Books Gospel Light, 2001.

Walter, Martin. *Exorcism: Fact or Fable*. Santa Ana, Carlifornia: Vision House Pub., 1975.

Watt, Gordon B. *Effectual Fervent Prayer*. Los Angeles, CA: The Biola Book Room, 1927.

Wiersbe, Warren. *The Strategy of Satan*. Wheaton, Illinois: Tyndale, 1979.